True-Born Maroons

New World Diasporas

Florida A&M University, Tallahassee
Florida Atlantic University, Boca Raton
Florida Gulf Coast University, Ft. Myers
Florida International University, Miami
Florida State University, Tallahassee
University of Central Florida, Orlando
University of Florida, Gainesville
University of North Florida, Jacksonville
University of South Florida, Tampa
University of West Florida, Pensacola

True-Born Maroons

Kenneth M. Bilby

Foreword by Kevin Yelvington

University Press of Florida

Gainesville · Tallahassee · Tampa · Boca Raton

Pensacola · Orlando · Miami · Jacksonville · Ft. Myers

Copyright 2005 by Kenneth M. Bilby
Printed in the United States of America on acid-free paper
All rights reserved

10 09 08 07 06 05   6 5 4 3 2 1

A record of cataloging-in-publication data is available from
the Library of Congress.

ISBN 0-8130-2873-6

The University Press of Florida is the scholarly publishing
agency for the State University System of Florida, comprising
Florida A&M University, Florida Atlantic University, Florida
Gulf Coast University, Florida International University, Florida
State University, University of Central Florida, University of
Florida, University of North Florida, University of South
Florida, and University of West Florida.

University Press of Florida
15 Northwest 15th Street
Gainesville, FL 32611-2079
http://www.upf.com

To the children of Nanny and Sekesu

Contents

Figures

Foreword

To evoke the image of the maroon/*marron*/*cimarrón* in the African diaspora in the Americas today is to provoke pride and identification in these escaped slave warriors whose cunning, verve, military prowess, ritual, and practical knowledge, and their ability to endure severe privations and hardships, allowed them not only to escape slavery's inhumane cruelty but to fight to establish and maintain their autonomy in the most unfavorable of circumstances. The themes associated with the image of the maroon—heroic resistance, perseverance, an indomitability of spirit, persistence and affirmation of the African ways, a prideful and unbowed blackness—have come, under certain kinds of historical conditions, to be rendered as part of *cultural discourse* where these themes have inhabited popular cultural productions such as songs, literature, and forms of popular consciousness; they have been at the same time rendered as *discourses of culture* where the maroon-as-symbol is made to stand for the inherent potentialities of "black culture."

In the English-speaking world the Jamaican Maroons are perhaps the best known of the communities that existed throughout the Atlantic just about wherever the slave mode of production was found. The Jamaican Maroons outfought and outfoxed the local militia and colonial British troops, forcing the British overlords of this productive and valuable sugar colony to sue for peace in 1739 and 1795—with profound implications for Empiric and local politics. The various groups of Maroons living in communities in the island's rugged interior developed exclusivist, corporate senses of identity, and acted as rational, self-interested agents, sometimes, it must be said, buttressing planter and colonial governmental power by returning escaped slaves and forming strategic alliances with these groups in the pre- and post-emancipation periods. Through the years the story of the Maroons has been told by many voices, inflected by various sociopolitical positionalities. By the time of the coming of creole multicultural nationalism and the post-1962 independence era in Jamaica, the image of the Maroon as a founder of the nation, and the enshrinement of Maroon leader Nanny as a national hero(ine), tended to relegate the Maroons to Jamaica's past with present-day Maroons seen as on their way to assimilation with their particularities denied—much in the way symbols of indigenousness were appropriated in post-1910 revolutionary Mexican nationalism at the same time actual Indian communities were excluded from national life. In the present era of transformation from dominant creole nationalism to "modern blackness," as pursued by Deborah A. Thomas in *Modern Blackness: Nationalism, Globalization, and the Politics of Culture in Jamaica* (2004), the past behavior of the Maroons is either recuperated in the nationalist discourse, or reviled for what comes to be anachronistically adjudged as anti- (non-Maroon) black politics; Maroon and Afro-Jamaican ethnicity is conflated, or the Maroons take on the persona of the exotic (and primitive) Other.

And yet, as Kenneth M. Bilby shows in this impressive book, these images of the Maroons, and the uses put to these images with the emphasis on the glorious past of the Maroons, and, moreover, on the glorious Maroons of the past, all do not square with who the Maroons were and who the Maroons are now. Lost in the nationalist cacophony and the titillating drivel of the tourist guidebooks are the living men, women, and children who claim Maroon heritage, their presentations and conceptions of self, how they understand their relationships with their own ancestors as well as with other Jamaicans, Africans, and others, past and present. Theirs, as Bilby skillfully presents it, is a deeply historical view. Bilby's wide lens allows him to move beyond the recursive refractions of the discourse *on* Maroons, to the historicity *of* the Maroons. In many ways, *True-Born Maroons* is an anthropology of identity, showing how Maroon distinctiveness is (re-)produced through language, religious practices, especially the Kromanti Play rites that involve the spirits of the ancestors, through their origin stories, and their political representations made with recourse to the 1739 treaty—and thus, at another remove, Bilby is speaking to the larger concerns of the diversity of the African diaspora in the Americas, belying easy notions of pan-diaspora cultural or ethnic homogeneity.

Bilby sensitively presents the Maroons together with the rather standard archival research, yes, but utilized to quite different ends than those of the standard histories. And even more evocatively through thickly descriptive ethnography and numerous Maroon narratives assembled with care and respect by Bilby, the result of his serious, committed and continued engagement with his Windward Maroon interlocutors for nearly thirty years. The ethnography and narratives reveal the Maroons' conceptions of their place in history, their meditations on defining events, the permutations of their religious practices, and the ways they construct Africa and conceive of their relationship to it.

It is in the Maroons' narratives that we hear universal concerns with freedom and liberty, but those borne out of the Maroons' particular—and irreducible— experiences and understandings.

Kevin A. Yelvington
Series Editor

Preface

More than two and a half centuries ago, decades before the American and Haitian Revolutions, a few hundred Africans on the island of Jamaica dealt a major blow to the pride of the British empire. Forming themselves into small armies, they went on the offensive and shook that empire's premier slave colony to its very foundations, leaving West Indian sugar barons with a lesson they would never forget. News of their military successes sent shock waves across the hemisphere, striking fear into the hearts of European slaveholders everywhere.

The odds were overwhelmingly against them. They had been torn from their homelands, separated from their loved ones and friends since childhood, and brought in shackles to a distant land of unknown terrors. Pressed into the service of a brutal and dehumanizing system of agricultural production, they had fled the plantations and sought refuge in the most inaccessible parts of Jamaica's mountainous interior. In this alien wilderness, starting with little more than what they held in their heads, they had managed to create not only new societies, but also sophisticated military organizations, and had waged war on their British captors. So effective were their fighting skills that by the 1730s they had taken control of substantial portions of the island, threatening to paralyze the rapidly expanding plantation system. They were vastly outnumbered and poorly equipped, yet they repeatedly routed both the colonial militia and the imperial troops sent out against them. They suffered greatly when British forces finally succeeded in capturing and destroying one of their main settlements, but they were never defeated.

By the end of the decade, a stalemate had been reached. Fearing the destruction and eventual loss of their colony, the British resorted to what would have once been unthinkable; they entered into diplomatic relations with people defined by their own laws as "commodities" akin to livestock. In 1739, representatives of the crown concluded two separate peace treaties with these enslaved Africans who had liberated themselves, now known as Maroons (derived from Spanish *cimarrón*, originally used to refer to feral cattle in the hills of the Caribbean island of Hispaniola). These pacts recognized the Maroons' right to live as free, self-governing peoples on the territories they had won.

Today, the descendants of these warriors, many still living on these same "treaty lands," continue to think of themselves as a people apart; they distinguish themselves from other Jamaicans as "true-born Maroons" (or, in a similar spirit, as "true-blue Maroons"). This book tells the story of what it means to be a true-born Maroon. It is a story made of many stories, told from various perspectives. Here it is imparted through the spoken narratives of individuals residing in, or originating from, the four major Maroon communities that have survived to the present in different parts of the island: Moore Town, Charles Town, Scot's Hall, and Accompong. In telling this story through these various voices, this book makes available many more Jamaican Maroon versions of their own story than any other published work to date.

Based on anthropological fieldwork spanning more than two decades, the book is more than a compilation of narratives; it is also a study of "cultural memory," and the ways in which Jamaican Maroons produce, transmit, protect, and use knowledge of their past in the present. A kind of ethnography of identity, it seeks to illuminate the importance of Maroon narratives about the past in defining and reproducing collective notions of selfhood across generations, as well as their role in maintaining ethnic boundaries. It interprets the content of these stories from various perspectives, examining the cultural meanings embedded in them, and exploring their symbolic dimensions. But it does not stop at this kind of cultural analysis; it goes a step further, treating these narratives and related forms of knowledge (such as songs and esoteric verbal formulas) as authentic historical records that may be analyzed and evaluated for insights into an actual past.

The question of authenticity comes to the fore when Maroon history is discussed, debated, and theorized by non-Maroons. In thinking about their past, Maroons are increasingly drawn into the complex cultural politics of the larger Jamaican society and the wider world, where they are often obliged to confront understandings and claims that conflict with their own. Even as the epic struggles of their ancestors are enshrined in national and transnational mythologies, and representations of their past are converted by non-Maroons into profit or political symbols, the Maroons themselves must contend with a postcolonial state that has so far refused to acknowledge their claims to a separate identity, in favor of a policy of gradual assimilation. In this larger context, in which ownership of the Maroon past is highly contested and the Maroons' right to exist as a people apart may depend on their ability to demonstrate cultural distinctiveness and genuine historical consciousness, the esoteric knowledge of the past that survives in the present-day Maroon communities gains in political significance. As the stakes increase, the question of historical veracity assumes a new importance; in this political context, to dismiss the authenticity of the Maroons' knowledge of their own past is, in effect, to deny the legitimacy of their claims to a distinct ethnic identity. One result of this growing debate about their past is a heightened sensitivity among Maroons to cultural politics in the surrounding society and the world beyond. This too is an important part of what it means to be a true-born Maroon in contemporary Jamaica.

The larger story of surviving identities that runs through this book—the "master narrative" in this study of narratives—is neither entirely my construction, nor that of the Maroon narrators whose voices I recorded on tape and placed on the page. Rather, it represents the distillation of a long and convoluted exchange of views, a series of conversations between myself and many individual Maroons, both on tape and off. It is to these interlocutors—some of whom became staunch friends, as well as patient and generous teachers—that I owe the greatest thanks. To all the true-born Maroons whose words and names appear in the following pages, including those whose spirits now dwell among the "older heads" of earlier generations, I offer my profound gratitude. Listening to their stories was a life-changing experience. I must also acknowledge the Maroon leaders who have welcomed me into their communities and/or shared with me their views at various times over the years: Colonels C.L.G. Harris and Wallace Sterling of Moore Town; the late Colonel Martin-Luther Wright, and Colonels Harris Cawley, Meredie Rowe, and Sydney Peddie of Accompong; and the late Colonel Peter Latibeaudeare and present Colonel Noel Prehay of Scot's Hall.

Those scholars who steered me in the right direction while I was first exploring the possibility of anthropological fieldwork among Jamaican Maroons must not go without mention: Rex Nettleford, Mavis Campbell, and the late Barbara Kopytoff provided encouragement and helpful advice at an early stage, for which I remain grateful.

Over the following years, while the ideas behind this book slowly simmered, several other people provided assistance of various kinds. Early on, David William Cohen and Peter Seitel perused some of my raw transcriptions of Maroon narratives, offering interesting suggestions about how these might be turned into a book; although I ended up taking a rather different tack from those they suggested, their pointed comments and criticisms helped me think things through. John Westerman also read and made helpful comments on early versions of my transcriptions. Several kind souls—among them, Judith Gray, Ian Hancock, Peter Patrick, and the late George Eaton Simpson—pointed me to previously untapped archival collections (some of them privately held) that yielded valuable recordings of Jamaican Maroon oral narratives predating my own; of the latter, the field notes and recordings of Helen Roberts, Frederic Cassidy, and David DeCamp turned out to be especially useful, adding considerably to the richness and diachronic depth of the overall picture of Maroon historical consciousness offered here. The late Joseph G. Moore, who happened upon a number of Moore Town Maroons while undertaking his pioneering study of the Kumina religion in St. Thomas parish in the 1950s, generously made his own field recordings available to me, as did Laura B. Murray, who visited Moore Town in the early 1960s. Jefferson Miller, who joined me for a time in Moore Town and had the courage to come face to face with the sharp immediacy of its Maroon past in ways that few others have done, kindly contributed photographs. Kofi Agorsah extended many courtesies to me when we first stumbled upon each other deep in the Maroon forests of the Blue Mountains; it was he who introduced me to the sacred precincts of Nanny Town, where he was conducting an archaeological investigation at the time. Over the ensuing years he has continued to offer encouragement and raise important questions about the possibility of accessing the Maroon past. Ian Hancock provided much-appreciated Krio transcriptions. Igor Kopytoff gave me access to the rich ethnographic and archival materials patiently assembled by Barbara Kopytoff during her distinguished career. Wayne Cox and Sheila P. Kelley helped with photographs.

As the book neared completion, I benefited from the comments of several unusually sensitive and insightful readers. John P. Homiak, Miriam Jiménez Román, Sheila P. Kelley, Jeffrey Kerr-Ritchie, Ivor Miller, and Colin Palmer carefully scrutinized selected chapters, offering invaluable observations and suggestions. Jerome Handler, who read and reread substantial portions of the book in draft, targeted problems large and small and prodded me to rethink certain of my basic assumptions, eventually prevailing and forcing me to improve upon earlier versions. When I thought I was at last finished, Richard Price pored over the entire manuscript, zeroing in on remaining weaknesses and gently revealing that one or two difficult crossroads still lay between me and my final destination. I am fortunate indeed to have had his critical input in this project from beginning to end. His earlier dialogical experiments with Maroon keepers of the past in Suriname set a standard that no historian of plantation America can afford to ignore, and raised a challenge to hegemonic ways of inscribing history that I hope many more historians and ethnographers of Caribbean peoples will take up. Kevin Yelvington kindly helped to shepherd the manuscript to the right publisher. Historian Monica Schuler, who also read the full manuscript in its last stages (as a reviewer for the press), responded with characteristic generosity and an unerring eye for the bigger picture. Her thoughtful comments reminded me (as had a few earlier readers) that at least some practitioners of her noble profession are fully equal to the task of rewriting Caribbean history in a way that pays closer attention to the kinds of voices that speak so forcefully on the pages that follow.

Not to be forgotten are those at the University Press of Florida who have given this project their special attention, particularly John Byram and Susan Albury, whose geniality and sound advice are much appreciated.

Finally, I must acknowledge the crucial material support I received from the Organization of American States and the Smithsonian Institution at various stages of the project.

To one and all, true thanks!

A Note on the Maroon Texts

Orthography and Other Matters

Jamaica's beloved poet, Louise Bennett, has portrayed the Jamaican language as an "African transformation of English" resulting from "an act of maroon cunning" (liner notes to *"Yes M'Dear": Miss Lou Live!* [Kingston: Imani Music/Island Records, n.d.]). It is perhaps fitting, then, that the goal of capturing and standardizing Jamaican speech in writing continues to prove elusive. There is still considerable contention, in fact, over whether Jamaican Creole (which speakers most often call Patwa, or "patois") should be considered a form of English or a distinct creole language. Complicating this argument is the fact that the Jamaican language actually encompasses a speech continuum of varying forms (which linguists sometimes call a post-creole continuum), ranging from "basilectal" forms (those most different from metropolitan English) on one end to "acrolectal" forms (those closest to metropolitan English) on the other; varieties in the large middle range are referred to as "mesolectal." To accommodate this broad range of speech varieties, the linguists Frederic Cassidy and Robert Le Page (1980 [1967]: xxxvii–lxiv) devised a phonemic orthography suited to the phonology of Jamaican speech in all its complexities. Although it was designed for ease of use, this spelling system has rarely been employed by Jamaicans to write their own language. Because this orthography makes Jamaican speech look so different from English, it gives the impression (to those already schooled in English) that it would be difficult to learn; partly for this reason, there has been some resistance to adopting it.

Nonetheless, there is a venerable tradition of "dialect" writing in Jamaica (and other Anglophone Caribbean areas), especially in the composition of poetry (Brown et al 1989; Morris 1990). Whether writing poems in Patwa, or transcribing oral poetry meant to be performed aloud, "dialect" writers have generally adapted English spelling conventions to their own needs, bending the rules in their own idiosyncratic ways. Similarly, all the major published collections of Jamaican folklore and verbal arts that have appeared in recent years (e.g., Tanna 1984; Dance 1985; Watson 1991) make use of idiosyncratic English-based spellings devised by the authors on the basis of their own intuitions and understandings. In this book, I continue, with some reluctance, in this tradition.

I arrived at this compromise position only after experimenting with various alternatives, ranging from translating the texts fully into "standard English" to rendering them in the phonemic orthography mentioned above. None of these proved satisfactory for my purposes. I wanted the texts to be accessible to the broadest possible audience but also wanted to retain their immediacy—to keep them as close as possible to the actual words of the speakers. Since most of the texts tend to stay within the "mesolectal" middle range (hardly surprising, since they were told to an interlocutor whose native language was American English), it was relatively easy to render them with standard English spellings. Non-English vocabulary and certain other basilectal features are spelled in a variety of ways, with occasional annotations to aid comprehension. Annotations are also used to clarify differences between standard English and creole usage. To make the texts more accessible to non-Jamaican readers, I have chosen to use unaltered English spellings more frequently than have most Jamaican "dialect" writers. Modifications in spelling to indicate creole pronunciations are kept to a minimum, being used mainly for "flavor," to provide readers at least some idea of the sonic dimension. In fact, most of the modifications I have made are in the direction of English; thus, to take one frequently recurring example, what would be written *kyaa* in the orthography of Cassidy and Le Page here becomes *can't*.

Like most compromise solutions, this one has drawbacks. For one thing, despite my attempts to make these texts accessible to a broad audience, some of them—especially the more basilectal ones—will still present difficulties for readers unfamiliar with Jamaican speech. Even those texts that differ least from standard English may require some concentration. For instance, pronouns in basilectal Jamaican (as in many other creole languages) do not include gender distinctions, and this feature sometimes carries over into mesolectal speech. Thus, in some texts, "he" or "him" may be used by the speaker to mean "she" or "her"; sometimes both gendered and nongendered versions of the same pronoun even occur back-to-back in the same text. In such cases, I have not "corrected" the gender. While confusing at first, this feature should become less and less of a distraction as the reader adjusts to it and begins to rely more on context (as native speakers of Jamaican do) to determine to whom a pronoun refers.

The second, and perhaps more serious, drawback is that texts presented in this way may be perceived by certain readers as "broken" or disfigured English. There is a certain awkwardness in squeezing Jamaican Creole—a language that can convey thoughts with as much subtlety, beauty, and lyricism as any other—into orthographic conventions not meant for it. However, I have not been able to find a better solution for the purposes of a book such as this. At the same time, those equipped to do so will be able to "hear" and "reconvert" these texts to a more Jamaican form in reading them. In fact, virtually everything that would be needed to retranscribe them using an orthography that might better capture the nuances of Jamaican speech is still here.

Throughout the book, texts have been lightly edited to reduce the amount of repetition, remove extraneous asides and other interruptions, and so forth. My own occasional questions and responses have also been edited out, so as not to interrupt the flow.

The reader who finds an occasional text particularly laborious is encouraged to move on to easier ones. The texts need not be read in precise order to follow the thematic threads around which chapters and chapter sections are organized.

Part 1

1

Living Maroon Knowledge

Picking Sense Out of Nonsense

> di innocent an di fool could paas fi twin . . .
> wan ting set di two a dem far apawt dow
> di innocent wi hawbah dout
> check tings out
> an maybe fine out . . .
> —Linton Kwesi Johnson, "Sense outta Nansense" (1991: 50)

I arrived in Moore Town in October 1977, a young graduate student barely a year out of college. I was interested in exploring the significance of interactions between Maroons and people from outside their communities when they participated in one another's religious ceremonies; the little that had been written on the subject suggested that this might be a sphere particularly rich in symbolic expressions of ethnic identity (Hurston 1938: 70–74; Moore 1953: 65–68, 139–143; Hogg 1960). I also had ethnomusicological interests and hoped to undertake a parallel study of Maroon musical traditions. Having dutifully prepared by reading every piece of writing on contemporary Jamaican Maroons I could find, anthropological and other, I entered the field well aware of the Maroons' reputation for guardedness. Nonetheless, I was unprepared for what followed.

Within days of arriving, I had been set straight. In the most friendly and sympathetic terms, I was disabused of my misguided notions. As a non-Maroon and a white person, I was politely informed, I would never be admitted to a true Maroon "Play," for such ceremonies were closed to outsiders, for whom they posed grave dangers; nor could I hope to participate in the kinds of Maroon musical events that interested me the most, for were I to try to learn how to play the Maroon Kromanti drums, not only would I sicken and eventually die, but I would also expose any Maroon foolish enough to agree to teach me to severe spiritual sanctions. I was welcome, however, to remain and learn about the routines of daily life in the community, and about "Maroon history"—history of the kind that had long been packaged for presentation to interested outsiders, including the handful of anthropologists who had preceded me.

Rather than giving in to my initial impulse to abandon the entire project, I stayed on and decided to adjust my plans to the uncomfortable realities confronting me, and to follow whatever leads might present themselves. What else could one do? Determined not to go against the wishes of those who had graciously accepted my presence, yet wondering about the limits of knowledge acquisition for an outsider such as myself, I spent the following weeks feeling out the possibilities for respectful compromise. More quickly than I expected, I made the acquaintance of a number of practitioners of the Maroon spiritual tradition known as Kromanti and, following their cues, embarked upon the uncertain balancing act that led to the collection of texts presented here.

Through these first Kromanti contacts, I discovered that the acquisition of knowledge about their craft, even for Maroons learning their way in the tradition, was a gradual, incremental process of testing and evasion, an ongoing exercise in dodging stabs at information gathering and parrying with partial revelations. The fact that, at first, I seemed more interested in relations between Maroons and non-Maroons who might encounter one another in shared religious contexts than in Maroon ritual practice itself often irritated my initial "informants" and perhaps spurred them into a deeper engagement with the enigma with which I must have presented them. Why, after all, would one care more about how Kromanti healers and their non-Maroon patients behaved toward one another than about the historical basis and present-day efficacy of the unique spiritual power that had brought these representatives of two different Jamaican "nations" together in such ceremonies? It was clearly this power itself that really mattered. My first misdirected gropings were useful nonetheless, in that they revealed that I was not the first *obroni* (non-Maroon) who had sought such sensitive knowledge. Against the odds, I learned, a small number of non-Maroons had actually achieved the ability to work with the Kromanti power that flowed from the Maroon ancestors—though none of these, unlike myself, had come from outside Jamaica,

It was not long before I realized that my project would be transformed into something rather different from what I had imagined. The Kromanti practitioners who had decided, after careful consultation with their personal spirits, to work with me would brook no further irregularities on my part. They would do most of the talking, and only when the time was right; I would do only as much asking as they permitted. They would guide me safely through the rigorous and dangerous process of acquiring knowledge, and they, not I, would set the terms of this joint endeavor.[1] Little by little, often through hints and circuitous allusions, they dispensed fragments of knowledge that could eventually be pieced together into a larger picture—usually only after I had satisfied them that I was already part of the way there. When a number of them suddenly decided that I would become an "apprentice" and would complete the process through which a Kromanti neophyte receives the gift of a *pakit* (a Maroon personal spirit), I was given no option but to accept.

This was not ethnography quite as I had imagined it. The knowledge produced by this enterprise would be guided less by my searching questions and my active pursuit of answers through observation and listening than by the concerns and demands of the mediums and spirits who, whether I liked it or not, increasingly insinuated themselves into my consciousness, eventually placing themselves at the heart of my project. Without their willing cooperation, after all, there was little hope of learning anything of substance about the questions that had brought me to Moore Town in the first place. The field journal I kept during this period reveals very clearly my growing awareness that the process of acquiring knowledge in this setting, where secrecy and defensive posturing governed almost all exchanges of information between Maroons and outsiders, would mean relinquishing much of the control I had expected to exercise as an ethnographer. These musings to myself also give some idea of the kinds of obstacles that had to be overcome, and the special measures that had to be taken, before the narratives presented in this book—especially those felt to contain more sensitive information—could emerge.

About a month after I arrived in Moore Town, one of the friendlier residents pulled me aside for a private word of advice, setting the tone for the months ahead. I noted in my journal that "He emphasized to me over and over again that people here are going to dodge me, that many people would feel strange or bad if they saw somebody teaching me Maroon things." I had already figured out that while many "Maroon things" could not be discussed openly, some of these could nonetheless, under the proper conditions, be broached in private. "This whole issue of secrecy," I wrote in my journal a few days later, "is something which has become more and more evident in the past few weeks." Over the next few days, I frequently bemoaned the difficulties I was having in attempting to elicit information, despite the willingness of a few Kromanti specialists to sit down and talk with me: "If I'm lucky, a two or three hour interview might yield a couple of Kromanti words, and a few small points of knowledge concerning Maroon Science. Every step of the way there is interruption—to appease the spirits by blowing rum and talking, or to warn me of the dangers in proceeding recklessly while learning of Maroon things." Another entry suggests the tenor of a typical "session" with a "cooperating" Kromanti specialist at this stage in my work:

> The visit was an exhausting one; it really lasted about five hours, most of that time being spent in listening to "jokes" and "reasoning" . . . As far as direct work goes, it was amazing how little could be accomplished in that stretch of time. In order to get anywhere, I have to beat around a thousand bushes; Ba Will seems to revel in the cryptic, and it is not hard to get steered off course as he leads you into a rhetorical labyrinth. Most things must be hinted at, rather than said outright, and so the patient researcher gets snagged in a taxing guessing game.

I continued to stumble along in this fashion, gradually becoming more attuned to the protective ethos that served both to restrict "dangerous" knowledge, and to make possible its "safe" transmission over time. At the same time, in an attempt to reassert some control over my project, and in the interest of ethnographic breadth, I began to seek out a number of other Kromanti practitioners I had heard about. By enlarging my circle of "informants," I thought, and thereby avoiding reliance on only two or three specialists, I might eventually achieve a more representative picture of the social interactions and processes that interested me.

Before long, the demands of working independently, and confidentially, with several individual Kromanti specialists who lived fairly far apart had become all-consuming. They and their spirits dictated the times and places we would meet; I was expected to comply with their edicts without question (although I was able to negotiate some personal maneuvering room, within limits). My nights were now filled with private meetings and ceremonies, while the daylight hours were still devoted to observing and participating in the daily round; less and less time was available for sleep. Mine were not the only expectations upset by this mode of performing ethnography:

> It seems that my nocturnal wanderings are causing a certain amount of displeasure here on the home front. Miss Liza [in whose house I was renting a room] has been comparing my behavior to that of previous researchers here. *They* did most of *their* visiting to the Colonel [leader of the Maroons] and his family, and individuals directly recommended by them; this way, it was ensured that they dealt only with "decent" people. And they kept reasonable hours, they weren't out and about every night at midnight; they visited people at their homes in the morning or afternoon, and retired early for quiet evenings. Reports are that people ("decent people") are wondering about my shadowy late-night presence along the roads, unaccompanied and unafraid. Is that the way to go about studying history?

According to those with whom I was keeping these nocturnal appointments, this was precisely the way—and the only way—to gain exposure to a history that was inseparable from the ancestral powers that had been kept alive by Kromanti practitioners.

Nearly four months into my field trip I was finally allowed to stay through the entire night at a Kromanti ceremony, and a new path into the Maroon past opened up before me.[2] Through my direct contact with possessing spirits who had come to heal the afflictions of visiting patients (both Maroon and non-Maroon), I was introduced to Maroons who had lived and died in the past. Although hardly conducive to orderly data-gathering, these agitated late-night encounters with possessed mediums nonetheless taught me much about the Maroon past. One such confrontation that I recorded in my journal relatively late in my stay was more or less typical. I was being introduced to yet one more spirit who had never met me, and who, as always, was enraged by the "smell" of unfamiliar *obroni* "blood":

> Baba again took his protective post in front of me, while the Grandy [a Kromanti dancer, in this case a man, possessed by the spirit of a female

Maroon ancestor] went through the motions of Maroon threat. Calling for the afana [machete], she raised it up in the air and yelled at Ba Zeke and Baba to let her through to me (calling me "backra"). Ba Zeke and Baba begged for me, while she stooped down and moved from side to side, as if looking for an unguarded space through which to thrust the machete. Meanwhile, Boysie went through the motions of blowing her with rum, and offering her a drink. When she eventually cooled down somewhat, she called me out to her. I was made to stand up straight, shoulders back, while she thrust the point of the machete into my solar plexus, not quite hard enough to break the skin. Then she took my arm and made as if to slice it. She put it down for a minute, and looked me in the eye, and raised it up again, putting the sharp side to my neck. Sliding it back and forth, she applied a fair amount of pressure, and for a moment I started to get seriously worried, as the well-sharpened cold steel grazed back and forth across my jugular vein. I don't think much more pressure would have been required to make a cut.

While never losing sight of my own objectives, I had been led (at my own request) into a spiritual world in which my own priorities began to diminish in significance. Try as I might, I was unable to persuade some of my Kromanti teachers that I was in this for purely "academic" reasons—that the anticipated thesis and university degree could be the true ends of all this seeking after knowledge. They knew better. Some months earlier, Ba Uriah, one of the oldest and most respected Kromanti specialists in Moore Town, had already remonstrated with me on this point:

> Ba Uriah was cryptic today, he denied knowledge of Maroon nations, and he advised me to leave the drums alone, as they involved Science [Kromanti power], which I can't manage. They involve "calling duppies." I said I was interested in learning how to play the drums, and in learning *about* Science, but not in *using* it, in making it operate. I just wanted to know purely out of interest. I tried to explain the University's quest for knowledge. But Ba Uriah replied (very logically) that if you learn about Maroon Science, you must *use* it, it simply *has* to be used.

Within a few months, three of my Kromanti "informants" had independently presented me with ultimatums (and more were soon to follow): the time had come for me to risk the dangers of working with Maroon spirits myself. The first to press me in this direction was a fearless *fete-man* (Kromanti dancer) I shall call Ba James, who was "getting a wee bit impatient with my questions, as he contends that I will receive *all* the answers once I obtain my *pakit* [personal Maroon spirit]. My *pakit* will give me all the knowledge (of Maroons) I will ever need, so why do I waste my time on questioning him on details? Once he cleanses me with fowl blood, he insists, he will never tell me another thing about the Maroons, for it will all be revealed to me in my dreams soon thereafter." Next came Ba Will, a particularly intense Kromanti practitioner, who one night suddenly "asked me if I would like to drop with a spirit. I questioned whether it would be possible for a backra's head to turn with a Maroon spirit. 'You woulda like to bet?' he asked. He asked what kind of blood we use in my country, and then told me that I must come back the next night with a fowl—he had decided to provide me with protection for the rest of my stay here." Some weeks later, Ba John, who was as accomplished a Kromanti dancer as he was a hunter of wild hog, similarly "informed me that from now on we are not going to waste time on instruction purely from his mouth; he had decided to go through the operations that will allow me to learn directly from spirits, in my dreams. After going through all the motions, I will immediately begin to receive teaching in my dreams. I am to come to him periodically to relate these dreams, which he will 'interpret' for me. There's no postponing this. He's adamant: the time is now. In order to learn anything further in safety, I have to submit to this treatment."

So, reluctantly, and with considerable ambivalence, I became a formal "apprentice" to these (and later on, a number of other) Kromanti specialists. Under their guidance, and from my highly unusual, indeed unprecedented, subject position (being not only a non-Maroon, but also a non-Jamaican and a *bakra* [white person]), I plunged into an exploration of what it means to become a Maroon *fete-man*, a practicing Kromanti specialist.[3] I consorted with more and more of these Maroon spirit workers, living and dead, as well as the spirits they worked with, embodied both in living mediums and in dreams. To my surprise, my sleeping hours were increasingly populated with strange presences that my teachers welcomed knowingly—wispy, luminous creatures that soared through the air or slithered across the ground with amazing stealth, as well as old-time Maroon men and women who delighted in wingless flight, and who seemed to enjoy making my own body levitate while I looked on helplessly. These experiments in becoming a *pakit-man* (one who controls a personal Maroon spirit) were both exhilarating and unnerving. As I followed the instructions of my teachers and carried out the procedures they gradually revealed and explained to me, we continued at the same time to engage in lengthy conversations about "Maroon things," during which I gingerly and uneasily raised questions of my own. Sometimes these interventions on my part were tolerated, sometimes not. Over time the presence of my tape recorder became more acceptable, and I was allowed to keep it turned on much of the time.

Working in this way, late into the night and away from the crowd, certainly had its advantages. Learning privately from individual specialists spread out in several locations, who could not possibly all be in regular contact with one another, gave me the sense that I had some control over a challenging ethnographic setting, since I could (with appropriate circumspection and an insistence on maintaining the anonymity of sources) bring up and attempt to account for contradictions in the various teachings I was receiving. The reliability of "data" acquired in this setting remained a constant concern, for throughout my stay, I was presented with disquieting reminders of the suspect nature of all "facts" communicated by Maroons, as in the following typical piece of advice, offered in passing:

> Trevor told me that things in Moore Town tend to operate this way: certain of the more concerned individuals in the community will approach him after seeing the two of us chatting together, and they will want to know just what information he has been divulging. They will admonish him not to give me any "secrets." And sometimes they will go so far as to connive and reach a consensus on certain standardized falsities that shall be given to me as facts. For instance, they might all agree that I am to be told that *yarifo* [a Kromanti word that denotes "sick," "dead," or "kill"] means "fowl," and then perpetuate this fallacy as long as possible in the future.

While helping me to reduce the troubling uncertainties caused by such evasive maneuvering (something with which, as I was to find, all Kromanti specialists must themselves contend when seeking knowledge), this way of working took its toll. Moving between these various teachers and attempting to meet their sometimes conflicting demands was exhausting. My schedule was clearly becoming too full; sleep deprivation was slowing me down and contributing to emotional strain. Protecting the privacy of each of these individual Kromanti specialists while also attempting to participate in the day-to-day life of the community sometimes meant walking an emotional tightrope.

In a sense, I moved between two worlds, one nocturnal and the other diurnal, each breeding its own anxieties. Inhabiting my nights were the Kromanti practitioners (most of them elders) who, only after great hesitation, had agreed to cooperate with me in relationships that, no matter how respectful and mutually satisfying they might become, would always retain a degree of uncertainty, suspicion, and danger. (In a typical aside recorded in my field notes, one *fete-man* with whom I had become close expressed his lingering doubts about what we were doing, wondering out loud whether, as some in the community had repeatedly warned, "when I leave Moore Town, everyone can expect a *bomb* to fall sometime soon.") These nighttime meetings with secretive and wary elders alternated with days (and occasional "nights off") spent largely among my own age-mates, the "youths" of Moore Town (young men into their twenties), who had suspicions of their own. Many of this generation had been politicized by their contact with Rasta ideology, and their frequent warnings about what would befall me if I turned out to be tainted by the sins of the Babylonian oppressor added to the psychological pressure. Even as I enjoyed the companionship of these "youths"—with whom I empathized, and whose cultural and musical lives were as interesting to me as those of their elders—I was put on edge by their constant reminders that they were keeping close tabs on my movements and intentions. (At one point, a Maroon who lived near me related to me the details of a casual conversation I had had with another Maroon in a different part of Moore Town three months earlier—lending credence to the Jamaican saying, "bush have ears.") In the angst-filled waning years of Michael Manley's second term, there was considerable (and warranted) fear of covert operations and destabilization efforts supported by the U.S. government; this was as true of Moore Town—which had an active branch of the PNPYO (People's National Party Youth Organisation)—as it was of other parts of Jamaica. Not surprisingly, I was frequently accused of spying for the CIA, and my attempts at tension-relieving jokes and friendly repartee when confronted with such accusations did little to allay the suspicions of some of these younger Maroons. There was no way to separate these personally felt tensions from the larger sense of apprehension that hung in the air at the time. As poet Kwame Dawes (2002: 260) remembers, the 1970s, for many in Jamaica, "seemed like the period leading to the end times of the apocalypse."

Eventually, it was too much to handle. Gradually, I decided not to complete my training in Kromanti spirit working, realizing that I was not prepared to cross that experiential divide—not only because of what seemed to me my increasingly precarious position, but also because I had come to the conclusion that it was not my destiny, nor my honest desire, to become a full-fledged *obroni* practitioner of Kromanti. The thought of crossing over and vanishing à la Carlos Castaneda into an alternate reality on the cusp of actuality and allegory had little appeal for me. Once again to my surprise, most of my Kromanti teachers did not press me any further; rather, they gradually adjusted to a redefined relationship closer to the one I had originally envisioned. Now that I had already been introduced to the rudiments of the Kromanti tradition, and a number of their spirits had become well acquainted with me, we could continue our balancing act without any clear resolution; sooner or later things might come to a head, but for the moment we could continue talking. (I suspect that at least some of those to whom I was apprenticed knew all along that my commitment might waver during the final stage of training; perhaps they had designed these apprenticeships from the outset as yet one more kind of test.) In this resituated mode, we continued our private conversations, many of which centered on the Maroon past, until my departure from Jamaica some months later.

When I returned for a short visit a few years after this, in 1982, not only was I able to pick up where I had left off, but I also found that the pace of work was now much faster. And as I made further brief visits during the 1990s, I noticed that my conversations with these Kromanti specialists, as well as other Maroons, progressively became less fraught with distrust and apprehension. With the passing of years (and the knowledge that I had indeed completed a thesis and a university degree), my presence and my ongoing project had become less of an enigma. My explanation that I was planning eventually to write a book about what I was learning was now accepted more or less at face value. When I approached a number of Kromanti practitioners in the Moore Town area that I hadn't known before and asked if they too would contribute to this book, most of them responded favorably. In working with these new acquaintances, I found that the knowledge I had built up over the years allowed me quickly to bypass many of the defensive barriers I had faced during my first stay in Moore Town in 1977–78 (and also, to a much lesser extent, during my brief visits to the other Maroon communities of Scot's Hall, Charles Town, and Accompong during that same period).[4]

The question remains: why were my intrusions into this sacred domain of protected, highly sensitive knowledge tolerated to the extent they were? I am convinced that my youthful openness and uncertainty—my apparent humility and my readiness to relinquish control and be guided by those who, after all, were not only older than I, but also knowledgeable in ways that I could scarcely imagine—played a large part in my eventual acceptance into this closed world. Yet, at the same time, without the tenacity I showed in periodically testing the limits of what I might learn, I probably would not have gotten very far. Over time, the Kromanti specialists revealed, as part of their teachings, that both great patience and strong ambition are essential ingredients in the process of becoming a *sabiman* (a person of knowledge) in the Kromanti tradition. Taking my cues from elders who had themselves worked hard to acquire their knowledge, I pushed from time to time for new clues and further revelations; but I never pushed harder than what I came to understand was appropriate to the situation at hand. As my esoteric knowledge grew and my ability to hold my own in this intricate dance of intimation and evasion improved, I clearly earned the respect of these elders. Most importantly, after being scrutinized and tested for months, I proved myself worthy of their trust.

In deciding now to make some of this esoteric knowledge available to a larger audience in the form of a book, I face a number of difficult questions. Does publication of knowledge that has traditionally been carefully concealed constitute a violation of trust? From the outset, I was open with those who worked with me about my plans eventually to publish the results. They responded with typical indirection. Even the most guarded of the *fete-man* who cooperated with me seemed to take the position that an individual who has the wherewithal to surmount obstacles and gain sensitive knowledge has the right to dispose of it as he or she sees fit. In the end, it is his or her responsibility to use such knowledge wisely and appropriately—which means, among other things, not placing it in the hands of those foolish enough not to recognize its value, or those unworthy of trust, who might one day turn such knowledge against the one who imparted it. From the point of view of these Kromanti practitioners, the protective ethos surrounding this esoteric knowledge (which forms the subject of chapter 11) would likely suffice to keep out those undeserving of such knowledge; the sanctions imposed by watchful Maroon spirits would do the rest. If I myself were to abuse such knowledge, the risks would be my own. In any case, I was rarely told outright that I should not write about or publish what I had learned; that decision would have to be mine alone.[5] Nonetheless, as I began to think more about the shape that a book about these teachings might take, I realized that the somewhat ambiguous common understanding we had reached on this question would not do, for I wished to use these individuals' own words. With this in mind, during subsequent trips to Moore Town and other Maroon communities, while taping further conversations, I explicitly requested and received permission to publish verbatim all of the segments of taped narratives or interviews that appear in this book (including retroactive permissions for those recorded in 1977–78). I also eventually obtained permission to use the names and images of those whose words are reproduced herein—something that would have been unthinkable when this project first began to take shape in the late 1970s (since, at that time, most of these individuals were firm in their desire for total anonymity).

Even with these permissions in hand, my decision to publish these Maroon texts raises questions that are difficult, if not impossible, to resolve with any finality. The moral dilemma faced by Richard Price in thinking about whether or not to make public the once private (and highly sensitive) knowledge of Saramaka Maroon oral historians is not much different from the one confronting me here:

> There is the basic question of whether the publication of information that gains its symbolic power in part by being secret does not vitiate the very meaning of that information. Does publication of these stories, these very special symbols, fundamentally diminish their value and meaning? While a Saramaka elder always tells First-Time selectively, and carefully chooses his recipients, the publication of a book by its very nature deprives its author of control (except perhaps via the language in which it appears) over its audience. . . . Consider the name of the great Majtáu hero, Lánu, of whom it is said, "His name must never be spoken." Should it appear in this book? . . . I would want to urge outsiders (whether they are Surinamers, Dutch, Americans, or whatever) who in the course of their work or leisure come into contact with Saramakas to respect the special "unspeakable" status of this knowledge. . . . When Tebíni, for example, concluded that Lánu's name could be published, it was certainly on the assumption that it would not be spoken in Saramaka any more frequently than it is today. Very generously, he assumed that readers would share my own verbal discretion. (Price 1983: 23–24)

A mere decade after Price published these ruminations (along with a large amount of previously "secret" Saramaka information), a glossy history of Suriname intended for general consumption appeared in the Netherlands. Not only does the "unspeakable" name of Lánu figure prominently in this book's section on "Bush Negro history," but so do a number of other names of first-time Saramaka persons or spirits that should not be mentioned casually (Wíi, Ayakô, Wámba, and others)—along with substantial portions of some of the highly sensitive Saramaka texts originally made available to the public in Price's *First-Time*, here translated into Dutch (Bakker et al. 1993: 74–75). Conspicuously absent from these republished versions of Saramaka oral traditions are Price's heartfelt pleas to his readers to treat this knowledge with appropriate care and respect; like any other published information, this sacred Saramaka knowledge, as Price anticipated, is now in open circulation and beyond his or anyone else's control. And because of Price's original publication, it is certain that Saramakas, whether living in the interior of Suriname, in the capital of Paramaribo, or in Dutch cities such as Amsterdam and Rotterdam, will encounter this once-restricted knowledge (if they haven't already) in forms and contexts for which it was never intended.

Because of similar concerns, I have held off publishing much of the information in the present book some two and a half decades—permissions to do so notwithstanding. A number of considerations inform my decision to go ahead with publication at this point. As in the Saramaka case, Jamaican Maroons have become increasingly aware that much of their treasured orally transmitted knowledge of their past is at risk of being lost forever. The very controls that have traditionally prevented such knowledge from passing into the wrong hands now threaten to cut off future generations of Maroons from their ancestral heritage; preoccupied with new concerns and priorities, most younger Maroons seem unwilling to submit to the rigorous training and testing through which such knowledge is gradually accumulated. Those young Maroons who do express an interest in acquiring such knowledge complain—as younger generations of Maroons long have—that their elders mercilessly "dodge" their efforts to learn; their elders retort that the young no longer display the patience or perseverance, not to mention the respect, that demonstrates such critical knowledge can be entrusted to a new learner. The traditional Maroon caution toward the rashness of youth—the fear that the young, once possessed of such knowledge, will all too readily sell out their own people—remains strong. The Maroons may in fact have reached a crossroads; for the first time in their history, the elders may truly be prepared to go to the grave with the greater part of their secrets kept to themselves.

In recent years, the leaders of the various Maroon communities have begun to give serious thought to this quandary. Interviewed by a journalist in 1984, Colonel C.L.G. Harris of Moore Town expressed his growing concern at the rapid loss of orally transmitted knowledge in his community. "The Colonel, asked what would be the true record of the Maroons, if steps were not taken to document what was known of their past by the lettered of their group, declared that the future was not only uncertain, 'but that it bothers me very much.' For in 40 to 50 years hence, it was possible that, the legendary, indomitable courage determination and spirit of the Maroons might be lost if documentation of their past is now neglected and kept out of focus."[6] I would like to think that the present book makes a worthy contribution to the goal of recording a significant portion of this past before it is lost. In fact, it was with Colonel Harris's authorization that I carried out my work in Moore Town. Even now I marvel at the fact that the

Colonel allowed a young, still-green anthropologist such freedom of movement in his community; during our many conversations, he never once interrogated me in detail about my investigations, though he must have had qualms about the unusual manner in which I was proceeding, and no doubt from time to time had to contend with suspicious gossip about my late-night wanderings and the nature of those activities of mine that were not carried out in the open. Understanding what I had come for, he left me to find my own way. I remain grateful to him, and to his council, and I hope that this book bears out the trust they placed in me.

Some would say that any lingering doubts about the appropriateness of publishing such materials are misplaced, given the changes that have occurred since I began working in Moore Town. Whereas in 1977 the sacred Kromanti drums were almost never allowed outside of Maroon communities, and the associated music and dance, with only a few exceptions, were not performed in the presence of outsiders, over the intervening years performances by visiting groups of Maroon musicians and dancers have become quite common in Kingston and other parts of the island. A portion of the Kromanti musical repertoire is now regularly heard by non-Maroons, whether at outside heritage festivals or during the annual commemorations of the Maroon heritage in the various Maroon communities. Jamaican Maroon performing troupes have traveled to the United States and Europe several times. (The commodification of Maroon culture has advanced farthest in Accompong, where an organized performing group regularly puts on shows of "traditional Maroon music and dance" for tourists bused in from coastal resorts.) Generally speaking, Maroon oral traditions are shared much more readily with outsiders than was the case when I began my work (though this is certainly not to say that "dodging" no longer occurs). The boundaries separating sensitive from less sensitive knowledge seem to be expanding. Some Kromanti terms and meanings that were once highly restricted, for instance, are now divulged to the curious—whether non-Maroon visitors or young Maroons looking for a quick fix of "Maroon culture"—with scarcely a second thought. For better or worse, there is a clear trend toward increasing openness. Maroons themselves seem to be revising their views about how much of their "intimate culture" must remain hidden. In view of all this, the unsettling questions about publication raised above might, at least to some, appear superfluous.

In the final analysis, the pros of publication would seem to outweigh the cons (and this seems to be borne out by Price's *First-Time*, which has been received with much enthusiasm and appreciation by Saramakas themselves). Those Maroons who shared their knowledge with me have themselves given their consent (and to withhold publication any longer would be to do them a disservice). Indeed, the larger goal of this book is one with which, I believe, all the Maroons who contributed would agree. In recording a substantial portion of the Maroons' knowledge of their own past in this form, a clear picture emerges of a people whose distinctive values and way of life remain very much alive beneath the visible surface—and whose right to maintain these should be respected. The very organization of this book is intended to reflect the fundamental understandings and values underlying this demonstrably separate Maroon identity. Each chapter centers on a basic theme constitutive, in part, of this distinct Maroon identity; the particular narratives and other oral expressions that are grouped together in chapters effectively embody or illustrate these central themes.

It was through my gradual and repeated exposure to these narratives that I came to understand that my project was evolving into something considerably larger than what I had originally intended; what I was moving toward, in fact, was an ethnography of identity. My understandings of the fundamental components of this identity, discussed in chapter introductions and occasional digressions, are based not only on the narratives themselves and the elucidations provided by narrators, but also on countless other conversations, formal and informal, with Kromanti specialists and other Maroons over the years. It is my sense that even those secretive *fete-man* who steered me into apprenticeships that I failed to complete eventually came to recognize that what we were working toward was what I am now calling an ethnography of identity—understood by them as a means of validating this identity to the outside world; this helps to explain their willingness to continue cooperating after I had revised the terms of our relationships, as well as their eventually granting permission to publish their words.

In fact, from one point of view, I have little choice *but* to go ahead with publication. Not only those with whom I worked, but also the spirits they consulted, were left with the expectation that this book would eventually see the light of day. (Many of these Kromanti practitioners, I am sad to say, have since joined the ancestors, before I could present them with a copy of the finished work.) In one of my last taped conversations with a *fete-man* who contributed many of the texts in this book, it became clear that the time had come to stop gathering words and to start putting them on paper. "Me naa give you nothing more, sah, ina de book," he suddenly declared. "De people [i.e., the ancestral spirits] cry out. Dem people *cry out*, dem say, 'bwai, it is finish!'" And so it is.

Both those Maroon friends who are alive and those who have "cut loose" (quit their physical bodies) can rest assured that much of what they confided to me does not appear in this finished book. For in keeping with their teachings, I reveal here only a part of what I was privileged to learn; some I must keep for myself. And the reader will surely understand that my Maroon teachers also withheld from me, so as to keep for themselves, much of what they knew. What is published here thus represents but a fraction of the distinctive knowledge of the Maroon past that still exists in Maroon communities. To invoke an expression that is usually associated with Rastafarian dialectics but resonates equally with Maroons: "the half remains untold"—and properly so.

Then as Now: The Art of Differing

> Today, this feeling of "Maroon ethnicity" is as strong as it was during the years when they boldly resisted the British, even if aspects of their cultural distinctiveness have been lost through the passage of time and continual interaction with the larger society.
> —Beverley Hall-Alleyne (1982: 11–12)

> Today, it is not immediately obvious to people from outside Jamaica, and even to many insiders, how different the Maroons were or are from other communities.
> —Colonel C.L.G. Harris (1994: 36–37)

It is a fairly typical night in this yard about a mile from the center of Moore Town—typical except for the presence of a foreign anthropologist in the thatched bamboo dancing booth. He is not the only *obroni* here, however. Also present is a visiting *yarifo* (sick person), a middle-aged Jamaican woman from a different part of the island, along with her three children. It is two o'clock in the morning, and for much of the night both anthropologist and patient have been sequestered for their own safety in a house nearby. They had dozed off, only to be startled awake by a loud crashing noise against the wall, followed by the incomprehensible rantings of a high-pitched voice. All of a sudden, the blade of a machete had jerked through the open window next to them, blindly chopping and stabbing as another voice outside begged the wielder to show mercy to the *obroni* intruders inside. After a while, things had gotten quieter again, but it had been impossible to go back to sleep after this alarming encounter with a disembodied machete.

Another hour has gone by, and the woman is now outside, standing in a corner of the booth, where she has been left alone by the Maroon protector assigned to her. Before leaving her side, the protector had sternly warned her not to run, not even to flinch, no matter what might happen. Her back is against a wooden post. A Kromanti dancer with head wrapped in cloth—a *fete-man* whose body is temporarily inhabited by the spirit of a Maroon ancestor—races toward her with *afana* (machete) raised. Screaming out unintelligible curses, the *fete-man* frantically swings his machete, splintering the post just above the woman's head, and sending chips flying. The woman does as told, keeping her eyes to the ground and remaining motionless. The movements of the enraged *fete-man* gradually become more subdued. The choreography now seems graceful and controlled. He points the machete at her, freezing for a moment, then pulls at her clothing and threatens to cut off a piece of it. He puts the blade to her wrists and upper arms, applying just enough pressure to leave marks. He backs off, as if retreating, then suddenly spins around and throws the machete at her feet like a dagger. The tip buries itself in the ground, and the handle sways to and fro. The drama is far from over; the ailing visitor will have to endure several other trials before being granted access to the healing powers for which she has come.

Since her children, like her, possess no "Maroon blood," they too must be inducted into this dance of difference. Even the youngest boy must undergo an ordeal. The *fete-man* calls for *timbambu* (fire). His assistant, the *kwatamassa*, comes running over from a nearby cookhouse, where he has been fanning a tremendous blaze. The *kwatamassa* holds out two reddish orange embers. The possessed dancer seizes them and resumes his dance, waving them in the air and sending forth a spectacular shower of sparks. As he moves out of the lamplight into the darkness, the two embers become independent beacons creating a trailing maze of light against the black background. The body of the *fete-man* is now no more visible than the spirit possessing him. The youngest *obroni* boy faces the fire on his own. The dancer rapidly passes the embers over and around the boy's head and arms, and then holds one of the red-hot tips to the boy's skin for a brief moment. Though obviously nervous, the boy hardly moves. There are no burns.

Animating this drama are the strains of Kromanti drumming and song—a flowing, ever-changing acoustic accompaniment that is as unfamiliar to the visitors as any other aspect of the ceremony. Not only this music, but the odd, mostly unintelligible Maroon creole spoken by the possessed mediums, the mysterious (and entirely unintelligible) shouted invocations in Kromanti language, the pungent smell of herbal remedies compounded on the spot, the objects used for divination, the intricate Kromanti ritual motions and gestures that Maroons call *busubrandi*—all are new and strange to the visiting *obroni* patient. Any doubts she might have harbored about whether Maroons really are significantly different from other Jamaicans have by now disappeared.

For the Maroon participants themselves, this ceremony, called Kromanti Play, also provides abundant evidence of difference. Much like the ceremony known as Nyabinghi in the Rastafarian tradition, "where the symbolic boundaries of the sacred and definitions of insiders and outsiders are maintained at their highest level" (Homiak 1999: 97; 1985: 386), Kromanti Play constitutes the most powerful symbolic expression in Maroon life of the cosmological principle dividing inside from outside, *Yenkunkun* (Maroon) from *obroni* (non-Maroon). Concentrated within Kromanti ceremonies are many of the most potent symbols of Maroon identity and the warrior past in which it is rooted. The *afana* ("sword," i.e., machete) and *jonga* (spear), the medicinal herbs once used to close and heal the wounds of battle, the invocational music and language of the Maroon ancestors, indeed, the embodied ancestors themselves, are integral components of Kromanti Play. Whether or not visiting *obroni* happen to be present at a particular ceremony, these markers of Maroon identity point to an opposed identity, a bordering Other, even as they symbolize the collective Self; they are in part signs of difference—an essentialized difference that is dramatically enforced by the enraged spirits of ancestors whenever a visitor of a "different blood" (almost always a non-Maroon Jamaican of African descent) intrudes upon this sacred space (Bilby 1981). Maroon participants in Kromanti Play carry these complex images of opposed identities (*Yenkunkun* versus *obroni*)—this ideological residue of a past process of dual ethnogenesis (Bilby 1984b)—with them when they venture out to *obroni pre* ("*obroni* places": the outside, non-Maroon world).

Consider the artful manipulation of these symbols when we shift our view to a setting in which the Maroon actors are hidden Others in a world of strangers, rather than known persons performing familiar roles in their own territory. We are now in Port Antonio, the capital of Portland parish, and the nearest town of any size to Moore Town. Two Moore Town Maroons are making their way down William Street, a bustling side road adjoining the town square and marketplace. The narrow street is lined with restaurants and rum shops; Jamaican dancehall music comes pounding out. It is a Saturday afternoon—market day—and the town is swollen with visitors from the surrounding countryside. The throngs of pedestrians weave their way around the cars and trucks parked haphazardly along the sides. Competition for space has brought traffic to a standstill. The two Maroons walking down the street recognize another man from Moore Town in the crowd. They call him over, inviting him for a drink in a bar just ahead.

When the three enter the busy saloon, few heads turn; there is nothing about them to suggest anything out of the ordinary. They could be from any of the dozens of rural villages and districts represented among Port Antonio's swarming foot traffic on this particular day. One of the three is a *fete-man*, a Kromanti ritual specialist and healer, but the other patrons of the bar have no way of knowing this (indeed no one else in the bar even knows what a *fete-man* is). When the three Maroons receive their drinks, each tips his glass and pours a small libation on the ground before taking a sip—a gesture that is familiar to many Jamaicans, and draws no special attention in this context. They drink and chat for awhile, without incident. By the time they are on their third round, however, their conversation has become more lively; as they get more excited, they begin to occupy a larger space, and to talk more loudly. The *fete-man* raises his glass and pours another offering, this time with a dramatic flourish, while intoning the words, "bigi pripri, luku ye, na insa mi e ji unu. . . tere wi de a obroni prandes, so no mek no ogri kon naki dem nyuman ye. . . na suma fi Braka Ruba!" (old ones, look, I'm giving you some rum. . . today we're in a non-Maroon place, so don't let any evil befall these fellows. . . they are Moore Town people!). One of his drinking buddies responds, in a taut, raspy voice, "honti yu se, ba?!" (what did you say, brother?). The *fete-man* shoots back at him, "ha-ha-ha, bwai!. . . arik mi gudufa!. . . mi aksi di bigi suma dem fi waka na obroni pre wid wi, no mek no ogi kon chobl wi!" (ha-ha-ha, boy! [uttered with a menacing-sounding cackle]. . . listen to me carefully!. . . I asked the older people to walk with us in this non-Maroon place, and to keep any evil from troubling us!). The three Maroon men continue excitedly to trade comments in this private language, a Maroon creole that is normally reserved for communications between the living and the dead during Kromanti ceremonies.[7]

In walks another stranger, who has been standing just outside the entrance to the bar, paying close attention. The man looks vaguely familiar to the *fete-man*; he is sure he has seen him somewhere before. "Yenkunkun?!" (are you a Maroon?), the stranger suddenly shouts at the trio of Maroons. There is an awkward silence. The *fete-man* fixes his gaze upon the stranger, glaring at him for a long moment without blinking. Unfazed, the stranger takes another step toward him, and the crowd moves back. "Yenkunkun?!" he repeats, more insistently. "Shref-shref!" (the same as you!), shouts the *fete-man*, and they clasp hands. "Nyuman, onti yu prandes?" (Man, where is your home?) The stranger answers, "na Mashazal mi libi!" (I live in Comfort Castle).[8] "Ha-ha-ha, bwai! Na Yenkunkun pre fi turu!" (Ha-ha-ha, boy! That's a true Maroon place!)

The stranger from Comfort Castle—a branch settlement of Maroons located a few miles from Moore Town, on the other side of the Rio Grande—joins his fellow Maroons for a drink. The four now occupy center stage; all eyes are on them. The *fete-man* stands up and begins to "cut language" in a sharp, strangely emphatic tone of voice: "O Yankipong Asasi, o Kembe Kuku, o Tata Nyami, o Nyami ara! Mi bimbroni, mi bimbasi, o nangka nangka, o se din kamisho, o kamadi, o din kamadu!" Whereas some of the bystanders might have caught the meaning of a word or two of the Maroon creole spoken earlier, this new stream of invocational language, delivered even more forcefully, is totally unintelligible; unlike the old Maroon creole, the sacred Kromanti tongue has virtually no connection to English. Not to be outdone, the man from Comfort Castle comes back with a shouted Kromanti torrent of his own: "O Yankipong jo Asasi, Kembe Tutu Nyami, o wusu, o baimbaimba, o titei tei, titei tei, o bo swau, da mi fa jo wizi, amba-ee! O woondu woondu o woondu koko, da mi fa, da mi fa jo wizi, o baimba no bigi insho, o titei tei, titei titei tei, titei titei bo swau, wengkini wengkini wengkini, bobosi o wengkeni, obroni o wengkini, amba-ee!"

The *fete-man* appears to be agitated. He shifts his weight from foot to foot, looking as if he might lose balance. Suddenly he "throws" a Kromanti song:

> o kumfu nyaba-ee, yo-ee
> poor nanabeti, yo-ee
> kumfu nyaba-ee, yo-ee
> bin a nyaba-ee, yo-ee
> poor nanabeti, yo-ee

As he sings, he crosses one leg over the other and kicks backward, sending his body into a staggering pirouette—a typical Kromanti dance move—then arches his shoulders and gracefully flaps his arms, performing an abbreviated facsimile of the dance of the *opete* (vulture), the animal form preferred by his own personal spirit. "Nyuman!" he blurts out. "Kon ye!" (come here!). One by one, his Maroon companions come forward. Taking their hands and holding them up high, he spins the men around, guiding them down into a crouching position and stepping over them, thus clearing them of evil. He launches into another Kromanti song, but one of the other Moore Town men discourages him from going any further: "No, ba! Kesu, kesu!" (No, brother! Sit down, sit down!).

Energized by the display of Kromanti gestures, the man from Comfort Castle—speaking "normal" Jamaican Creole, which the watching bystanders all understand—enthusiastically tells his new acquaintances of a great spirit worker he had once known, a Kromanti dancer from his community who could pierce his body with a machete and instantly heal the wound. Unimpressed, the Moore Town *fete-man* boasts that he himself is much stronger than this and could easily outdo such common spiritual feats. Belligerently, he informs the Maroon from Comfort Castle that the man he sees before him is a true Chankofi, a Maroon from Moore Town, a man who is afraid of *no one*, a man who will stand up to *anybody*. The two begin to "chop language" again, vying with one another to see who can produce the longest and most potent Kromanti invocation. Both men know that they should refrain from such gratuitous displays of Kromanti language—that spirits should not be summoned without reason—but they keep up the barrage anyway. Before things can get out of hand, one of the other Moore Town men intercedes, shouting out, "kesu, kesu!. . . chamu chamu!" (sit down, sit down! . . . be quiet!). With these cautionary words (*chamu chamu* being kind of a code that non-Maroons are present, that care should be taken not to reveal too much), the Maroon carousers retire to the counter for another drink and settle back down into a quiet conversation. When the others leave, the *fete-man* stays behind and nurses his drink a while longer, waiting to be approached by any in the crowd whose problems might be "heavy" enough to require the unique healing powers for which Maroons are renowned. In this way (as well as by word of mouth), the *fete-man* adds to his *obroni* clientele.

In more or less random encounters such as these, Maroons routinely give visible (or audible) expression to a sense of identity that normally remains hidden from the Others with whom they daily interact—at the same time furnishing inarguable "proof" that Maroons are, despite surface appearances, substantially different from these Others. These performances of Maroon identity represent momentary unveilings of "objective" (that is to say, observable) aspects of an intimate culture—a shared body of distinctive knowledge—that lives in the minds of Maroons not only through the practice of Kromanti Play, but also, and just as importantly, through the kinds of narratives and other oral expressions presented in this book. In a sense, the knowledge transmitted through such narratives is embodied and made "real" through these ritual performances of identity, whether in the institutionalized context of Kromanti Play, or during chance encounters while traveling or living among *obroni*.

Like the private narratives of the *fete-man*, these public performances of Maroon identity are rich in symbols that bridge past and present. The role of these symbols in instilling and replenishing historical consciousness (not to mention imbuing this with an affective charge) is not to be underestimated. Paul

Connerton has given special attention to the close connection between ritual performance and "cultural memory." His "ritual action" (Connerton 1989, 44–45)—what I prefer, for present purposes, to call "ritual *inter*action" (Bilby 1979)—is a type of stylized, stereotyped, and to some extent, repetitive symbolic behavior that is not merely expressive, but also serves a mnemonic function. Such performative behavior need not be limited to temporally or spatially fixed contexts. It is, rather, a potentiality that may be activated anywhere, at any time, given the proper circumstances (Bilby 1979: 107–11; 1999b: 319–22). The ritual behavior of Maroons in such circumstances powerfully encapsulates, through symbolic means, a past that is felt to be alive in the present. Performances of distinctive music and language(s) identified with the ancestors, for instance, clearly and dramatically demonstrate this continuity between living and dead, present and past. But equally important to this equation, as Connerton argues, are bodily practices—the culturally specific postures, gestures, and movements of performers. The large repertoire of dance movements and other gestures associated with ancestral spiritual power on which a knowledgeable Maroon can draw (obvious examples being the institutionalized gestures of threat, or the "dance of the vulture" and the spinning and stepping over described above) constitute a kind of "mnemonics of the body" (Connerton 1989: 74), a repository of performative symbols through which an important portion of the Maroon community's "cultural memory" is mimetically reenacted and transmitted. Most of these Maroon bodily practices—these performative rites—are rooted in Kromanti Play. It is in that ceremonial context that they find their purest expression, when possessed Kromanti dancers, literally embodying specific ancestors, exemplify distinctive Maroon behavior. Such symbolic behavior can occur, as well, in the most mundane settings—for instance, on a bus or taxi traveling from Port Antonio, when a *fete-man* in an argument with another passenger might conspicuously engage in one variant of the Maroon behavior called "rubbing trash," suddenly pulling from his pocket a handful of crushed herbs, and performing threatening Kromanti gestures that he has repeated, and seen performed by others, countless times in the past. Such defensive maneuvering in random contexts is common in areas surrounding the Maroon communities (Bilby 1979: 106).

As Connerton (1989: 44) rightly suggests, performative rites of this kind "are not limited in their effect to the ritual occasion," for "whatever is demonstrated in rites permeates also non-ritual behaviour and mentality." As we shall see, the "knowledge" embodied in these ritual performances constitutes but a very small portion of the distinctive cultural knowledge retained by Maroons, the greater part of which is actually kept alive through verbal narratives about the past. But these performative rites—these ritual interactions—are important nonetheless; it is precisely through such sporadic displays of symbolic behavior that those whom Maroons call *obroni* are able to catch fleeting glimpses of genuine cultural difference (Bilby 1979: 73–203)—a difference that remains invisible most of the time, residing as it does in that hidden body of sacred knowledge constituted through Maroon narratives.

Against All Odds

> Many hundreds of them [escaped slaves in Jamaica] have at different times run to the Mountains . . . which I imagine they would not have done, but for the Cruelty of their Usage, because they subsist very hard and with Danger . . . if the Negro be brought in a Prisoner, he is tormented and burnt alive.
> —John Atkins (1735: 245)

There is an unavoidable tension in this book between the narrow specificity of the Jamaican Maroon story, as told by Maroons themselves, and the broader narratives of resistance and struggle that extend the significance of the Maroons' heroic history beyond the confines of time and place. As a product of culturally focused encounters with present-day Maroons, the present work speaks primarily of difference. Many, if not most, Maroons continue to view their past as not only sacred, but unique. And, for reasons discussed at length in the next chapter, they have found it increasingly necessary to stress the distinctiveness of this history in asserting a separate identity within the larger Jamaican society. Almost every Maroon narrative in this book contains the assumption, whether unspoken or stated outright, that the Maroons possess a history not shared by other Jamaicans—or, for that matter, by any other people in the world.

Yet, there is also a grand narrative here—a larger, more inclusive story that is just as true and meaningful as the private narratives of difference through which contemporary Maroons reproduce their continuing sense of singularity. It is, in a word, a narrative of survival. For the Maroon epic, whatever else it may be, is clearly a story of survival against tremendous odds.

It is in this sense that the Jamaican Maroon epic "belongs" to a larger public—the same public to whom Jamaica's most famous son, Bob Marley, spoke when naming one of his last and most compelling albums *Black Survival*.[9] The armed struggle of the Maroons to ensure individual and group survival is exceptional only in that it represents one of the more glaring of the many ways, large and small, in which enslaved Africans and their descendants managed to endure and challenge systematic, racialized oppression on a scale never before known. Ideologues and apologists for such systems have always been inconvenienced by the difficulty of reconciling the undeniable reality of such spectacular acts of resistance with their way of thinking. But today it is widely recognized that strategies for survival can take myriad forms, some much more subtle than others.[10] The military successes of the Maroons can now be seen as but one point on a continuum of strategic actions designed to counter the gradual annihilation of both spirit and body that was central to the logic of chattel slavery. This saga of endurance in the face of overwhelming odds, one might argue, belongs to the entire African diaspora—if not all of humanity.

It is this dimension of the epic Maroon past, I would argue, that transcends the historical contradictions and ideological divisions that, even today, continue to produce friction between Maroons and their fellow countrymen in Jamaica. As distasteful as certain aspects of the Maroon past might seem to those with the privilege of hindsight, it is well to remember that the actions of the historical Maroons, like those of a great many other Jamaicans, were calculated, under extreme circumstances, to ensure the survival of those they had come to identify as their own. More than two centuries later, their descendants—who have managed to maintain a distinct identity to the present—continue to be preoccupied with the question of survival. For them, there is no contradiction in the idea that they might remain in some ways apart, even while participating in larger narratives of black resistance and survival. The paradox, rather, is to be found in the notion that the continuing existence of distinct Maroon communities with histories of their own might somehow be incompatible with such larger narratives; or in the kind of thinking that sees preservation of a valued "heritage" as more important than the survival of those who have collectively preserved it. Many of today's Maroons have continued to resist such hegemonic ideas, by cherishing and privately narrating their own pasts as they see fit. And, as I hope this book shows, it is largely because of this private culture of remembrance that they remain, against all odds, among history's survivors.

2

Imagining Jamaica's Maroons

> I began to understand it was no legend that the Maroons thought of themselves as a separate, independent people—it was as though we had crossed the border of a distant, sealed-off country. . . . No longer did I question that I was in a sovereign country.
>
> —Hamilton Basso, *A Quota of Seaweed: Persons and Places in Brazil, Spain, Honduras, Jamaica, Tahiti, and Samoa (1960: 77, 81)*

Sometimes the past seems more tangible than the present. In the Blue Mountains of Jamaica, the past is written in stone. There, in a remote, uninhabited section of forest, a carved boulder bears witness to a military occupation that took place more than two and a half centuries ago. When it was uncovered in the 1960s, this slab of rock, inscribed by a British soldier, removed any doubt the authorities might have had that this was the genuine location of Nanny Town, a legendary center of Maroon power during the first decades of the eighteenth century.[1] The Maroon settlement authenticated by this stone is now, quite literally, a ghost town, its only inhabitants the spirits of Maroons long dead. The existence of such spirits in Nanny Town, however, is something only their descendants can authenticate.

It is common knowledge that communities of Maroon descendants still exist in Jamaica. But in the minds of many, both in Jamaica and elsewhere, the Maroons of the eighteenth century are more present—more vividly real—than those of today. The vast majority of writings on Jamaican Maroons dwell on the distant past. This epic past, this story of effective resistance to one of the most dehumanizing social and economic systems ever devised, continues to captivate readers and writers. Comparatively speaking, rather little has been written about what became of these people and their descendants after this system was brought down. That the "fighting Maroons" of past centuries have left clear traces in the present is the kind of detail usually relegated to a passing comment or footnote.

One might argue that the very distance of the Maroon epic from the present increases its mythic power, paradoxically making it seem more solid. The finiteness of the written record certainly comes into play here, helping to create the impression that Maroon history is a closed book. The primary sources readily available to historians are limited in number, and the better-known archival collections have been mined repeatedly by scholars. The standard eighteenth- and nineteenth-century descriptions of Jamaican Maroons continue to be recycled by

Figure 2.1. "Decem 17, 1734, This Town was took By Coll. Brook and after kept By Capt Cooke Till July 1735." Nanny Town, 1991. Photo: K. Bilby.

one writer after another attempting to reveal new insights. While there will always be room for reinterpretation of written evidence, it is difficult at times to avoid the sense that the most important "truths" about the Maroon epic are already in hand, preserved for posterity in the fixed texts of documents that can be "interrogated" in only figurative ways. Were substantial new archival sources to come to light, however, the fragile partiality of our understanding of the Maroon past would quickly be revealed.

Ironically, at a time when the significance of "Maroon heritage" is discussed and debated more than ever, those who are closest to this past, the inhabitants of present-day Maroon communities, remain largely invisible. For most of those who write and theorize about the Jamaican Maroons, these contemporary descendants are as ghostly a presence as the ancestral spirits that hover about Nanny Town.

To attribute this to some kind of willful denial of the contemporary Maroon presence by other Jamaicans would be far too simple. On the contrary, the idea of continuity with the Maroon past has great appeal in Jamaica, as it does in other parts of the Caribbean. But understandings of this continuity must be teased out of the web of contradictions that is Jamaican history. In imaginings of this history, conflicting images abound. Depending on one's outlook, Maroons may appear as heroes or traitors, freedom-loving revolutionaries or selfish manipulators, backward primitives or sophisticated survivalists. The Maroon "past" constructed out of various interests over the centuries encompasses many such contradictions. Its mythic power continues to thrive despite, or perhaps because of, these clashing ideas. It is a past that some wish to own, and others to disown.

The inhabitants of the present-day Maroon communities must thus navigate a sea of contradictions. In doing so, they bring a specific, local past of their own, adding to the complexity of Jamaica's national mythos. In some ways, this mythic terrain is a minefield. And if these Maroon descendants remain largely invisible in their own country, it is partly by choice. Their own past tells them it is best this way. Generation after generation, they have been taught to keep this past, as well as other kinds of ancestral knowledge, to themselves.

But this exclusionist ideology, born of the ancestors' collective struggle for survival, is increasingly challenged by the exigencies of history-building in a postcolonial nation-state still coming to terms with a past that often echoes painfully in the present. In the postindependence era, the historical Maroons have been turned into a powerful symbol of anticolonial resistance, as well as a fundamental component in the newly constructed history that projects a putative national identity back into the distant past. Like it or not, the living descendants of these early Maroons find themselves implicated in this process of national identity construction.[2] Their increasing visibility in the larger society throws into relief the contradictions deeply embedded in their own, as well as Jamaica's, history; at the same time it creates a new set of contradictory demands for these present-day Maroons themselves.

Who has the power to define the Maroon past? Who will interpret its significance for Jamaica or the wider world? Who possesses the "truth" about this past? Indeed, who possesses this past itself? And that most fundamental of questions: who in Jamaica is a "Maroon," and who is not? Such questions are not new, but they have become ever more salient. Seduced by the national conversation about their ancestors, and confronted with shifting political stakes, Jamaica's hidden Others, the direct descendants of the early Maroons, are gradually stepping out into plainer view. As often as not, their claims regarding the Maroon past, as well as the distinct identity they project in the present, have been greeted with doubt. Some critics have suggested that the special link with the heroic Maroons of past centuries asserted by the inhabitants of the present-day Maroon communities—the continuing Maroon presence they claim uniquely to embody—is less than authentic.

In providing a glimpse of a world largely hidden from outsiders, this book offers one possible response to such denials of authenticity.

Hidden Others: The Enigma of Identity

> Figure of savage beauty, figure of pride.
> —**Walter Adolphe Roberts**, "**The Maroon Girl**" (1955: 196)

In postcolonial societies shaped by centuries of plantation slavery, to identify with the heroic maroon is to make a clear statement of anticolonialist convictions. More broadly, it is to take a rebel stance, to challenge the injustices of the present—particularly those seen as resulting from the oppressive social and economic structures and ideologies of the past. "Rare was the Caribbean intellectual or artist of the 1960s, 1970s, or 1980s," notes Richard Price (1996b: xiii), "who failed to compare himself to a maroon." In most Caribbean territories, where maroon populations were long ago destroyed or assimilated, such acts of identification remain purely symbolic.[3] But in countries such as Jamaica, Suriname, or Colombia, where discrete populations descended from historical maroons persist to the present, the play of symbols and identities is more complex and ambiguous.

When prominent Jamaicans claim the label of "Maroon" for themselves, this gesture, for all its symbolic richness, often carries a more literal meaning. Although very few such individuals were themselves born or raised in present-day Maroon communities or can even claim close relatives who were, they most often mean to suggest actual descent from historical Maroons.[4] Marcus Garvey is perhaps the most famous twentieth-century Jamaican to have claimed Maroon descent, but many have followed in his footsteps. One of the most recent is the reggae/dancehall star Buju Banton (Mark Myrie), who did not grow up in a contemporary Maroon community, but whose press releases portray him as a Maroon.[5] Whether or not such claims to Maroon identity should be seen as "genuine" (many of them, in fact, are based on real, if distant, genealogical links to the present-day Maroon towns) is less important than what they reveal about Jamaica's social landscape. In this society the term *Maroon*, in addition to its historical referents, may denote an extant ethnic identity.

As many Jamaicans recognize, the present-day Maroon groups constitute relatively clearly bounded communities with discrete territories and histories of their own, membership in which is defined primarily by descent. In the Jamaican context, the designation "Maroon," in this more specific sense, is comparable to such labels as "Chinese," or "Indian," or "Jamaican" for that matter, in that it represents something deeper than an extension of a unidimensional historical role or condition (in this case, that of an "escaped slave" or "descendant of escaped slaves"). It implies notions of common origins in a primordial past, shared substance ("blood"), perhaps a distinctive cultural heritage, even a different language. Indeed, in areas close to the Maroon towns, people acknowledge the "ethnic" nature of these communities, sometimes characterizing their Maroon neighbors as members of a different "nation"—a term also often used by Maroons themselves (with a meaning similar to that of "tribe," or "ethnic group"). Maroons in Jamaica, then, have long represented, as they still do, an ethnic Other.

What remains ill defined, for the majority of Jamaicans, is the actual makeup—the cultural contents—of this Maroon ethnicity. As already suggested, Maroons themselves have contributed to this general lack of familiarity with their distinctive cultural heritage by adhering to an ethical system that excludes outsiders from certain areas of knowledge. But there are other, more complex, and largely historical reasons for the difficulty other Jamaicans seem to have in defining the traits that distinguish contemporary Maroons from the rest of their countrymen.

For more than two and a half centuries, since the peace of 1739, the Maroon communities have been very much part of a larger creolizing world. In the years following the treaties, as the areas surrounding their territories filled with new settlers, they were increasingly exposed to the creole culture of this larger society. Maroons also often traveled out to the coastal world of plantations and towns. By the mid-nineteenth century, a missionary presence had become firmly established in all the Maroon communities; within a few decades nearly all Maroons had been nominally converted to one variety or another of Christianity. Over time, the pressures for cultural assimilation continued to mount; by the late nineteenth century, Maroon culture, once clearly distinct, had converged to a very large extent with the broader creole culture of Jamaica (Bilby 1994a; Kopytoff 1973: 260–67). Even so, various kinds of evidence suggest that as late as the 1920s or 1930s, Maroons continued to be relatively easily distinguishable from other Jamaicans on the basis of external cultural markers. Many older Maroons at that time, for instance, still spoke as their native tongue a unique English-lexicon creole language largely unintelligible to non-Maroons (Bilby 1983; Harris 1994: 39–41). Even if they did not normally use this language in the presence of non-Maroons, it is likely that, in conversations in the Jamaican Creole ("patois") used elsewhere on the island, distinctive features remained in their speech that continued to mark them as Maroons. Within a few decades, however, even this last vestige of visible (or, rather, audible) difference had virtually disappeared.

Figure 2.2. Maroons attending Anglican church (St. Paul's Chapel), Moore Town, 1890s. Photographer unknown. National Library of Jamaica.

This is not to say that Maroons had lost all cultural distinctiveness. Rather, the balance of features that distinguished them from other Jamaicans had gradually shifted from the external to the internal; from the visible to the invisible; from the public to the private. Even as they became more and more like their neighbors on the surface, Maroons maintained among themselves a highly distinctive "intimate culture" that remained hidden from most other Jamaicans. This culture came to reside almost entirely in intangibles such as values, ethics, and consciousness of a shared past—as well as coded forms of expressive culture such as esoteric language, music, and dance—with only a smattering of material artifacts (for instance, the Maroon war horn, the *abeng*, and various kinds of drums) remaining as physical evidence of continuing difference. The "intimate culture" that remained very much alive beneath the surface carried a powerful affective charge.[6] In short, the distinctive Maroon cultural heritage, rather than fading away, had persisted almost entirely within the mind—as a form of consciousness, an ensemble of ideas. This intangible heritage, this concealed "intimate culture," continues to be imparted and reproduced in Maroon communities, through narratives such as those that make up this book, as well as through performances of other kinds.

During most of the twentieth century, then, the Maroons have existed as hidden Others, inhabiting a distinct ethnic identity, the contents of which remain largely mysterious to other Jamaicans. This fact has complex and profound implications for relations between Maroons and those they define as outsiders. Even in areas adjoining the Maroon communities, who is and is not a Maroon is

Figure 2.3. Maroon women, Accompong, early 1900s. Photographer unknown. National Library of Jamaica.

not always clear. Despite claims made in the literature that Maroons are physically distinctive, and although some non-Maroons living in the vicinity of the Maroon towns still assert that they can tell Maroons apart from others on the basis of physical appearance, Maroons are in fact no longer phenotypically distinguishable—if they ever were—from other Jamaicans of African descent.[7] Nor can they be identified by cultural markers such as distinctive dress or everyday speech. Since such external cultural diacritica no longer exist, the only way to know whether an African-Jamaican individual is a Maroon—unless that individual consciously reveals his or her Maroon identity—is to have some knowledge of the person's background: in what town he or she grew up, or to whom related. This means that when traveling or living outside their communities, individual Maroons spend the bulk of their time in an ethnically "unmarked" state; the majority of those with whom they rub shoulders in daily life remain unaware of their "Maroonness."

There are instances, however, when Maroons choose to come out of "hiding" while in the presence of outsiders. To do so requires little effort. All such an individual must do is externalize certain symbols of his or her Maroon identity, behave in ways that are understood (in areas surrounding the Maroon towns) as "Maroon"—utter bits of esoteric Kromanti language, sing unfamiliar songs,

Figure 2.4. Moore Town Maroons posing for a visiting photographer, 1908–9. Photo: Harry Johnston. Royal Geographical Society.

brandish clumps of aromatic herbs, or make mysterious motions and gestures. Such symbolic displays of "Maroonness" are sometimes used for defensive purposes, to warn away individuals behaving in a threatening or abusive manner (and since Maroons, owing to their ostensibly superior spiritual powers, tend to be regarded with respect and fear in areas neighboring their communities, such displays are usually enough to persuade offenders to back down).

At other times, Maroons externalize these normally concealed signs of distinctiveness for personal gain, to attract clients in need of healing or other spiritual help. As we saw in the last chapter, when two or more Maroons meet in outside locations and engage in such culturally marked behavior, performances of identity become yet thicker in private symbols and esoteric references, leaving little doubt in the minds of onlookers as to the depth or authenticity of the distinctive heritage being invoked. Such performances, which remain indecipherable to non-Maroons, do little to enhance outside observers' understanding of the Maroons' "intimate culture"; rather, they represent forms of boundary maintenance (Mar-

Figure 2.5. A view of Moore Town, 1908–9. Photo: Harry Johnston.
Royal Geographical Society.

tin 1973: 134–54). In this way, difference is performed without violating the
Maroon ethic of secrecy.

Maroons, thus, inhabit a peculiarly ambiguous space. Judging from the anthropological literature on ethnicity, they would appear to be exceptional, if not
unique, in the degree to which their ethnic identity is divorced from external
markers that are readily observable to the Others whose space they share. There
are few reports of ethnic minorities elsewhere in the world for whom total ethnic
anonymity is an option most of the time, as it is for Jamaican Maroons.[8]

Here, then, is an ethnic identity that, from the perspective of an outsider, is not
always easy to grasp. In the vicinity of their own communities, in parts of the

parishes of Portland, St. Thomas, St. Mary, and St. Elizabeth, their continuing presence is indisputable, if not always clearly discernible—not only because of the physical existence of the historically and geographically distinct towns they inhabit, but also because the histories of these Maroon communities are inextricably interwoven with broader local pasts. Maroons remain actors on the local stage, even if they publicly perform their special role only on occasion. The farther away one moves from the more concentrated Maroon presence in these areas, however, the more indistinct, and less veritable, this presence appears.

Maroon Pasts and Maroon Presence in Jamaica

> Those who remain in the Maroon Settlements have, we fancy, a secret pride in the name Maroon and in their history. . . . they are now, in reality, a picturesque survival of the past—picturesque from the historical point of view.
> —Anonymous (1939)[9]

> In my island, some say there are no Maroons. Well, I find that people is coming from east, west, north and south to find out about the Maroons. Well, if the Maroons are not important, why the hell [are people] coming and diving in down into the Maroons?
> —Colonel E. A. Downer, Moore Town (1960/61)[10]

More than three decades ago, Carey Robinson concluded his history, *The Fighting Maroons of Jamaica*, with the suggestion ("the truth," as he puts it) that "the strength and spirit of the Maroons are no longer the exclusive property of the mountain strongholds; they belong to all Jamaica" (Robinson 1969: 156). And who can dispute this? So long as such claims are limited to lofty abstractions such as "strength" and "spirit," the terms of debate remain unclear.[11] It is fitting that Robinson's popular history, which seldom strays from the written record, should veer, in its final pages, into the nebulous domain of myth. For a voluminous mythology surrounds the Jamaican Maroons, and its growth has been facilitated by the virtual absence of their present-day descendants and their distinctive cultural heritage from most writings about the Maroon legacy. The vagueness with which the contemporary Maroon presence is perceived by outsiders has served only to increase the mythologizing of the Maroon past.

This rich mythology includes two major strains, one primarily positive and the other primarily negative. On the positive side, the qualities cited by Robinson dominate: the "strength" and "spirit" that allowed the heroic Maroons to resist enslavement and reclaim their freedom and humanity; to preserve their cultural integrity and maintain their fidelity to the African past; to define their own identities and destinies. On the negative side are a number of ostensible weaknesses or failings: primitiveness and backwardness; isolationism; a "savage" and "cruel" temperament; and, most importantly, an apparent inability to seize, and remain faithful to, the larger ideological significance of their struggle (as evidenced by their collaboration with the white plantocracy after the treaties of 1739).

These and related themes flow through the sizable body of fictional writing that has emerged out of, and contributed to, the mythologizing of the Jamaican Maroon past. As nuanced and insightful as such literary treatments sometimes are, they rarely owe their insights to contact with living Maroons, or knowledge of what the latter think about their past. In most literature of this kind, the continuing existence of Maroon communities, though not totally without significance, is superfluous—so much so that a recent book-length study of the theme of marronage in Jamaican fiction found it unnecessary to treat "the Maroon as a sociohistorical phenomenon," and instead focused solely on "the developing persona of the maroon as a character type in creative literature" (Lalla 1996: 3). This disjuncture between Maroons viewed as actual historical agents in real space and time (both past and present) versus Maroons as tropes or symbolic personae produced by acts of literary imagination to serve ideological or artistic needs is but one manifestation of a larger tendency to detach the contemporary Maroon presence (the living, socially distinct, "ethnic" Maroons of today) from the Maroon past.[12]

This tendency is not limited to literary production by intellectuals. In less elevated forms of literature, however, it often coexists with an ambivalent acknowledgment of a significant continuing Maroon presence. As Lalla (1992: 2–3) points out, "consciousness of their distinct heritage overflows the actual Maroon communities and is upheld by other Jamaicans, who view this Maroon heritage with shared pride and who treat their saga of resistance as a national treasure."

If a distinct Maroon heritage does live on in the present-day communities, then what is it about this that is to be treasured by other Jamaicans? In representations of this heritage in the Jamaican press, images of the African past stand out; the idea of surviving "African culture" in the Maroon towns serves as a primary emblem of resistance, and of the national will to counter the oppressive ideologies inherited from a shared history of slavery and colonialism. It is widely believed that efforts by the enslavers and their colonialist successors to stamp out the African past were least successful in the Maroon enclaves. Because of this, these communities are still seen by many as repositories of an African cultural authenticity that has been lost, to a greater or lesser degree, by other Jamaicans.

"Those who have 'dared' to visit the Maroon communities as part of their work," notes one Jamaican journalist, "have been greatly impressed with the strong traditional African retentions in their everyday practices."[13] This invocation of continuing Maroon "Africanness" recurs frequently in popular writings. Encouraging Jamaicans to become tourists themselves, one local newspaper article urges them to "take a trip back into Jamaica's history and discover some of our roots," stressing that "our most authentic roots can be found in the Land of

Look Behind Maroon Country . . . the almost virgin territory of Maroon Country."[14] This imagery of "authentic roots" and "virgin territory" suggests that the Maroons live in near-pristine isolation that has allowed them, as if frozen in time, to preserve intact a pure, original "African culture." As the author of a popular book on Rastafari phrased it, "in maintaining a world unto themselves, the Maroons are protecting their essentially unaltered African culture" (Nicholas 1979: 11). For some Jamaicans, this carefully preserved heritage represents a body of cultural wealth that the Maroons hold in trust for the larger Jamaican nation. Speaking at the opening of an exhibit on Maroon heritage at the Institute of Jamaica in 1989, Dr. Paul Robertson, then Minister of Information and Culture, clearly expressed the value of these distinctive (African) Maroon "roots" for other Jamaicans. "Today," he reminded his countrymen, "we can look back on the history of the Maroons and draw inspiration from their courage, determination and ingenuity in the struggle for freedom. The cultural heritage preserved faithfully by the Maroons to this day is a valuable storehouse of a rich part of our heritage."[15]

That a "valuable storehouse" of distinctive cultural traditions has been preserved by Maroons to the present remains, for most Jamaicans, a matter of faith. Few indeed can specify the actual contents of this storehouse. Other than the *abeng* (signaling horn), and a few types of drums found exclusively or primarily in Maroon communities, there is precious little that outsiders can point to with certainty as evidence of this "faithfully preserved" heritage—not because such a distinctive heritage does not exist, but because non-Maroons rarely receive more than the most superficial glimpse of it. Nor does the idea that Maroons retain certain distinctive African-derived traditions necessarily lead to the conclusion that this makes them significantly different from other Jamaicans. As long ago as 1954, after visiting Moore Town and interviewing a number of Maroons, one journalist was able to report that "except for a tradition of African rites the Maroons are no different from the rest of the majority population of the island."[16] And in the eyes of some, at least, vaguely understood "traditions" and "rites" may not count for much.

The difficulty of pinpointing what makes Maroons culturally different from other Jamaicans has led certain writers to break faith with the idea of continuing Maroon distinctness. In the early 1960s, when the political status of the Maroon communities was thrown into question by the island's recently acquired independence, the economist and sociologist Mary Manning Carley (1963: 47) pointed out that "there is now little difference to be observed between the Maroons and other country people or 'bush' Negroes of Jamaica." She finds it necessary, however, to qualify this sweeping judgment with an afterthought: "perhaps their blood is a little purer, and their ways simpler." A decade later, historian Mavis Campbell weighed in on the same side. "The solidarity pattern among the Maroons does not add to the pluralism of Jamaica," she asserts. "They are no different in life-style and self-perception from any other law-abiding group of country folk within the island today."[17] This opinion is often echoed in journalistic representations of present-day Maroons. Some writers even take the position that "there are few true Maroons left, and those that are have dissembled [*sic*] themselves throughout Jamaica and the world."[18]

For detractors of the Maroons, the idea that today's Maroon descendants possess no significant culture of their own is a congenial one. Viewed as a people who are now distinguished only by their "simpler ways" (as Carley, cited above, would have it), the Maroons lose much of the mythic sheen of their ancestors. Thus severed from the glory of the Maroon past, these present-day descendants may be dismissed, in the words of one writer, as nothing more than "a backward, quarrelsome, grubby lot." This particular editorialist, vowing that he has had "enough of Maroon mythology or Maroon lore," maintains that "civilization has all but passed them by because of their insular way of living and pride in the history which they themselves defaced."[19]

This statement exemplifies an ideological sleight-of-hand that is common in the theorizing of the Maroon past and its relation to the present. Present-day Maroons are both denied their history and condemned for this history. Or, rather, they are dissociated from one part of their history (the heroic time of war), for having "defaced" it, and associated exclusively with another part (that less heroic part stretching from the treaties of 1739 to the present). The difficulty of this post-treaty era for interpreters of the Maroon past lies in the fact that the Maroons, in making peace with the whites, bound themselves to terms that required them to come to the aid of the colonial government in the capture of future runaway slaves and the suppression of any future slave insurrections. Many in Jamaica hold the view that, in accepting these terms, the Maroons were "denying their own past and eradicating their own history by agreeing to counteract the very means by which they had set themselves free" (Gottlieb 2000: 34). Among those who have fallen into this trap are a number of historians, professional and other, whose readiness to judge the behavior of Maroons both before and after 1739 in terms of present-day universalist, racialist, nationalist, or other ostensibly timeless categories and moralities provides some readers with validation for ideological stances toward these Maroons' descendants in the present.[20] "In chapter after chapter of [such] books," notes Zips (1999a: 75), "heroic revolutionaries [i.e., the pre-treaty Maroons] are turned into traitors to their sisters and brothers on the plantations."[21] The dilemma that this complicated history poses for interpreters of antislavery struggles is not unique to Jamaica, for groups of rebel slaves made similar treaties with European colonial powers and agreed to fight against other blacks in several other parts of the Americas as well (Price 1996a: 3–4).[22] As Eugene Genovese (1979: 51–52) found, when making a comparative study of slave revolts in the Americas, "relations between maroons and slaves after promulgation of such treaties became maddeningly ambiguous." Zips reminds us of the care that should be taken when theorizing about such complex pasts, closing his study of the Jamaican Maroons with the following caveat:

> To observers from the outside, the politics of the Maroons may appear idealist at one point and opportunistic at another, alternating between revolutionary and counterrevolutionary. In my opinion, such categories are useless. Maroons themselves have most likely devoted little thought to those kinds of questions. Instead, they have focused on devising appropriate actions in given situations to secure their status as a sovereign community with a common political and cultural experience. (Zips 1999a: 242)

"Many of today's descendants of Africans enslaved and transported in the diaspora," continues Zips, "see a link to their own history and a symbol for their future in the success of 'separatist' politics resulting from black resistance to oppression. However, the accomplishments of the Maroons during the entire colonial period also deserve recognition and respect from people who do not share the same historical experience" (242).

Such nuanced thinking, however, remains relatively rare. In the contemporary Jamaican context, the pivotal historical act of "betrayal" of which the post-treaty Maroons stand accused continues to provide a pretext for those who would deprive the inhabitants of the present-day Maroon communities of their claims to a heroic heritage. These claim for themselves (or for the "nation") an ostensibly more authentic, original Maroon identity rooted in the freedom struggles of the more distant past—an identity untainted by the post-treaty legacy of collaboration with the slavocracy, for which today's Maroon descendants continue to be held responsible. The historical blame often assigned to present-day Maroons, in fact, extends well beyond the period of slavery; as is well known in Jamaica, Maroons played a significant role in the suppression of the Morant Bay Rebellion of 1865. The fact that the leader of that uprising, Paul Bogle, has official recognition as a National Hero means that consciousness of the Maroons' history of collaboration with the colonial government has remained fresh, and perhaps even been magnified, in recent times.[23] For those who attempt to resolve the apparent contradictions of this history by imagining a clear division between the pre-treaty Maroon heroes and the post-treaty Maroon "traitors," the idea that after 1739 the Maroons forfeited all claims to their heroic past tends to go hand in hand with the belief that the residents of the present-day Maroon communities no longer possess an authentic, historically continuous culture of their own.

Contemporary Maroons have not remained entirely silent in the face of such negative characterizations. By the 1960s, the leader of the Moore Town Maroons, Colonel C.L.G. Harris, had begun regularly publishing articles on Maroon history and culture in the *Daily Gleaner* and other local newspapers. Educated at a teacher's training college in Kingston, and possessed of a special gift for language, Colonel Harris made particularly effective use of the local press to reassert his community's claims to its distinctive past. A number of his articles discussed local oral traditions that were unique to the Maroon communities, offering just enough detail to challenge the view that contemporary Maroons had lost touch with their history.

It was during this decade, in fact, that consciousness of the Maroon past became associated with new political and ideological trends. With the advent of the Black Power movement, and the emergence of a generation of intellectuals engaged in a radical reinterpretation of the role of African-Jamaicans and the African heritage in Jamaica's history, the historical Maroons became increasingly visible as icons of resistance. In 1969, when a group of these young intellectuals launched a weekly newspaper as a popular vehicle for their critique of the continuing negative reverberations of colonialism and imperialism in Jamaica, they titled it *Abeng*. The Maroon war horn known by this name, which had served as a vital means of communication during the struggles of the eighteenth century, seemed an appropriate symbol to the newspaper's founders, who derived inspiration from the earlier resistance of the Maroons. That this instrument was still used by Maroons, and was imbued with more complex and problematic meanings in areas where the contemporary Maroon presence remained strong, was largely ignored by these urban intellectuals.[24]

The question of Maroon heritage first truly came to prominence in the following decade. Visions of the Maroon past played a significant part in the active rethinking of colonialist values and ideologies that gained momentum during the Michael Manley years.[25] It was during this time that the idea of naming one of the famous Maroons of the past as a National Hero first arose. Cudjoe (or Kojo), the great leader of the Leeward Maroons during the critical period before the treaties, seemed an obvious choice. He was the best known of the historical Maroon leaders, and the one best documented in the written record. But a Windward Maroon figure, a female spiritual leader known as Nanny, held the greatest fascination for both the Jamaican public and intellectuals. Though extremely little was known about Nanny, she had long existed as a force in the popular imagination; because she embodied the great spiritual power associated with the early Maroons, her persona was surrounded by a mythic aura. The time was also ripe for official acknowledgment of growing feminist aspirations in Jamaica; the naming of a female National Hero was seen as a suitable step in this direction.

The choice of Nanny was not without complications. For one thing, this legendary figure was almost entirely absent from the written sources, and not all historians were prepared to accept that she existed other than in myth. Robinson (1969: 54), for one, left open the question of whether she "did in fact exist," pointing out that "the only real leader of the Windward Maroons who is mentioned with authenticity during the period is Quao" (who signed the Windward treaty of 1739).[26] To authenticate the historical existence of Nanny, the Jamaican government relied on research by a number of professional scholars, most notably Edward Kamau Brathwaite and Lucille Mathurin. In two publications that blended archival data with Maroon oral traditions, Brathwaite (1977) and

Mathurin (1975) helped flesh out the very vague picture of Nanny held by non-Maroon Jamaicans. Brathwaite's work in particular, explicitly designed to satisfy the need for "proof" of Nanny's actual existence, represented an impressive attempt to weigh and reconcile written and oral sources, and left little doubt that the woman known to present-day Maroons as Grandy Nanny was not only an authentic historical personage, but one who occupied a place of special importance as well: a significant force among the Windward Maroons during the time leading up to their treaty. Brathwaite's path-breaking research was unusual in the degree to which it gave credence to Maroon oral traditions about their past, and may be seen as a harbinger of the growing recognition in official discourse of a significant continuing Maroon presence.[27]

On October 10, 1977, shortly after the proclamation making her a National Hero, a monument to Nanny, paid for by the Jamaican government was officially unveiled on Bump Grave, a sacred site in Moore Town.[28] The unveiling ceremony, attended by a handful of officials from the Jamaican government, remained small and subdued.[29] By the following year, however, Moore Town was able to attract large crowds to what was to become an annual celebration of their hero. The granting of this official status to Nanny clearly had raised the profile of the contemporary Maroon towns. In Accompong, on the other side of the island, the annual celebration of Maroon heritage, with a much longer history and much better publicity, was also given a boost by this act of official recognition. From now on, at least once or twice a year, pride in the continuing Maroon presence would be felt throughout Jamaica. Particularly in Accompong, increasing media coverage and a new emphasis on cultural tourism led to an enormous growth in attendance.[30] These public celebrations of the Maroon heritage had a substantial economic impact on the various Maroon communities and certainly helped to reinforce the Maroons' own cultural identity.

There is nothing unusual about the Jamaican government's attempt to make the Maroon epic a fundamental part of the national narrative. As Charles Carnegie (2002: 137) points out, "in the making of a collective self in many Caribbean countries, maroon or runaway slaves are viewed as constituting a distinctive root that nourishes the national tree." Typically, in the process of constructing a racialized national identity, "the word *maroon* itself becomes a signifier for the idea of blackness: a noble, original, uncontaminated, defiant, New World blackness." What makes the Jamaican case different from most others, however, is that those whose "acts of rebellion have been appropriated" in the service of "present-day territorial nationalism" (69) have left living, identifiable descendants in the present who continue to act as their witnesses.

Given this continuing, living Maroon presence, it is not surprising that the elevation of the Maroon heritage in official discourse has sparked a certain amount of contention. One observer who has much experience as a cultural mediator between Maroons and other Jamaicans believes, for instance, that "Queen Nanny's elevation has taken her away from the Maroons; she is now

viewed primarily as a Jamaican and only secondarily as a Maroon, whereas previously she was purely a Maroon heroine" (Farika Birhan, cited in Gottlieb 2000:
83). At times, the sense among Maroons that the appropriation of their heritage
might be going too far has led to open confrontation. For example, when the
Jamaica National Trust Commission decided to erect a monument to the Maroon
hero Cudjoe (Kojo), the Maroons of Accompong, who claim Cudjoe as one of
their most important ancestors, were not consulted. The planners in Kingston,
perhaps wishing to stress the national significance of the Maroon epic, had decided that the monument would be built in Chapelton in Clarendon parish (in a
central location, more than forty miles to the east of the present Leeward community of Accompong), since it was from this area that Cudjoe and the nucleus of
the Leeward Maroons were thought to have escaped in 1690 (Campbell 1988:
46). When the Maroons heard on the radio what the planners were up to in the
capital, they lost no time in intervening. Colonel Martin-Luther Wright, the
leader of the Accompong Maroons at the time, remembers:

> I has to put up a strong fight. They want to put it at Chapelton, where the
> uprising first starts. [A prominent figure with the Jamaica National Heri-
> tage Trust] did want to swindle us. So I has to get up on me feet, man, and
> start to write letters, and I write it up on the radio. I get actually mad. I
> write letter to the Prime Minister. . . . I say, "no, it can't! It can't work, it
> can't work!" So those [Maroon] officers in Kingston, they get to the Prime
> Minister same time. And they phone me down here. And we went up, and
> we had three days hard negotiation. We find a way. . . . We won out.
> Because they know that Kojo's monument *must* come to Accompong. We
> had a *hard*, hard, hard verbal battle up there, man. Three days of it! . . .
> Three full days negotiation . . . They say Chapelton was where the rebellion
> starts from, so they want to make a landmark of it. I say, "no! It is in
> Accompong, *must* be in Accompong". . . . At first, they resist, but we won
> out at the end. . . . It was a hard battle. . . . We won. Must won too . . . just
> as in 1738, at the Peace Cave.[31]

Colonel Wright's passionate account of these events is as much as anything a
statement about who owns, and thus has a right to represent, the Maroon past.

Controversies over ownership of this past cannot be understood apart from
the peculiar ambiguities and contradictions that have developed around the continuing Maroon presence in Jamaica. Despite the increasing visibility of the
Maroons in public discourse, understandings of the contemporary Maroons and
their relationship to the rest of the country remain vague at best. Even as basic a
question as the current political and legal status of the Maroon communities has
yet to be resolved (Bilby 2002).

One might assume that recent Jamaican governments, given their reclamation
of the heroic Maroon past, would make it a matter of policy to cooperate with the
present-day Maroon communities in their efforts to protect their cultural integ-

Figure 2.6. Kojo monument, Accompong, 1991. Photo: K. Bilby.

Figure 2.7. Kojo monument, flanked by Accompong Maroon flag, 2002. Photo: K. Bilby.

rity and maintain some semblance of autonomy. But such is not the case. Although the present-day Maroons continue to insist that their eighteenth-century treaties remain valid, and that therefore they are entitled to special treatment under the law, no Jamaican government to date has officially recognized such claims (Zips 1996: 287); indeed, these governments have most often acted in ways that suggest the opposite. Today, as in the past, Maroons in each of the communities frequently complain about their treatment by the Jamaican state; most of these complaints center on what Maroons feel to be violations of their right to self-determination. Maroon communities on both sides of the island are embroiled in ongoing efforts to force formal recognition of their "treaty rights" and special status. Conflicts over this question are nothing new. The Maroons have been attempting to defend themselves against encroachment on their lands and a gradual whittling away of their autonomy since long before Jamaica gained political independence from Great Britain in 1962. According to anthropologist and lawyer Werner Zips (1997), "from a careful study of available sources in the Jamaican archives and the oral traditions of the Maroons one can only conclude the continuity of marginalizing policies from colonial to post-colonial times." Similarly, anthropologist Jean Besson (1997: 208) concludes that "external pressure (from the British colonial government and the post-colonial Jamaican state) to undermine the commons, and therefore maroon society and corporate identity, has continued from the post-emancipation era to the 1990s." Maroon researcher Bev Carey (1997: 614) goes so far as to assert that "the period of 1870 to [the present] has been marked by the development and existence of one overriding policy. And that policy has been, and remains to this day, the compulsory assimilation of the Maroons into the mainstream of Jamaica."

Further muddling an already clouded picture, the same Jamaican governments that have refused to recognize the Maroons' claims to a special political and legal status have nonetheless continued to acknowledge the specialness of the present-day Maroon communities in other ways. In the early 1970s, for example, even as Jamaican senator Dudley Thompson publicly declared that "there was no difference or distinction whatever in the rights and obligations as defined by the law of the land between the persons residing in the former Maroon settlements and those of any other Jamaican subject," Prime Minister Michael Manley made time in his busy schedule for meetings with visiting Maroon delegations, who continued to press for official acknowledgment of what they viewed as their special "treaty rights."[32] And every prime minister since then has remained accessible to Maroon leaders. Seldom does a year pass when government officials do not arrive from Kingston to participate formally in one or another of the annual commemorative celebrations held in the various Maroon towns.

As recently as 1997, Prime Minister P. J. Patterson made a ceremonial visit to Accompong, where he voiced his support for contemporary Maroon aspirations. Yet, a few years later, when Patterson's minister of justice, K. D. Knight, was told by a journalist that the leadership of the Accompong Maroons wished to reinstate that community's traditional right to try its own court cases, his response was, "that's not likely." Similarly, when questioned about the Maroons' insistence that their "treaty lands" could not be taxed by the Jamaican government, Arnold Bertram, the minister of local government under Patterson, "said he couldn't confirm whether there were plans to make Maroons pay taxes."[33] Clearly, the Jamaican state has shown little willingness to extend its recognition of Maroon aspirations beyond the purely symbolic. At the same time, from a Maroon perspective, the recent symbolic appropriation and glorification of the Maroon past by the state has raised the stakes dramatically.

One can only wonder why successive Jamaican governments have failed to address these ambiguities head on. Negotiating a mutually agreeable understanding with the Maroons, and writing their special status into current Jamaican law, would probably not cost the Jamaican state very much; after all, the combined acreage of the Maroon territories as presently constituted is relatively modest. Perhaps the idea of making any concessions at all is viewed as too much of an affront to the principle of national sovereignty. But by seeming to deny the validity of the Maroons' claims regarding their special legal status and their right to self-determination, while at the same time continuing to pay tribute to the "Maroon heritage" through periodic visits to present-day Maroon communities and other symbolic gestures, the Jamaican state has added to the contradictions of an already ambiguous situation. After all, how can peoples who may no longer "really" exist, in a political and legal sense, expect to exert control over a heritage that is now claimed by the larger nation into which, according to some, they have already been assimilated? If the Maroons no longer have any rights or "privileges" distinguishing them from other Jamaicans, if they no longer have legitimate claims to any kind of autonomy or separate identity, then how can it be argued that they have a right to a cultural heritage—indeed, a history—of their own?

These contradictions bring us back to a fundamental issue: ownership of a valued past. In appropriating key symbols of this past, while denying a "real" (i.e., legal) existence to the direct descendants of those who made this history— or at least refusing to give serious consideration to their current political and legal claims—the state is in effect severing the Maroons of today from their own past, which can then be claimed as the property of the nation at large. A number of writers have recognized this process for what it is—an insidious, unspoken means to an unacknowledged end: the gradual but definitive absorption of the Maroon populations into the larger Jamaican nation. The early stages of this process in the 1970s were nicely captured by the novelist Russell Banks in *The Book of Jamaica* (1980). The narrator of that book reflects on how, under Michael Manley's government, "the Maroons' treaty became a quiet, sentimentalized symbol of early resistance to slavery and colonialism. And because the government was officially in line with that resistance, was still trying to overcome the effects of those old and evil systems, it was itself actively absorbing their symbols for its own use. For this reason, Nonny [*sic*] the Warrior Mother of the Maroons had been made a national hero" (Banks 1980: 145). Banks's perceptive protagonist concludes that "the Maroons were being swallowed by the nation, hard edges, inconsistencies, contradictions and all" (Banks 1980: 145).[34]

More recently, Werner Zips (1998: 90) has commented on the ideological pressures on Maroons "to contribute to a national identity by severing their historical bonds to the Maroon lands and renouncing all claims to sovereignty"—pressures that, as he points out, are "supported by hegemonic legal and economic structures of the national state." It is easy to see how ideologically motivated representations of the post-treaty Maroons as "traitors" might be made to serve this process. The Maroons themselves, of course, have become increasingly sensitive to these contradictions. As Zips (1999a: 48) notes, "most Maroons, whose communities continue today, view the incorporation of their history into the national development as expropriation and reject this approach." While "on the one hand, they value the national recognition they deserve as forerunners of emancipation, on the other the 'nationalization' of their history is also interpreted as expropriation of their cultural singularity" (Zips 1999a: 246).

The friction caused by competing claims over the Maroon past has led to frustrations on both sides. During the 1980s, partly in defensive reaction, a number of Maroon leaders began to step up the rhetoric of self-determination; the leadership of Accompong, for instance, began to refer to that community in public statements as a "military sovereign state" (Zips 1996: 292).[35] In a publication from this period, Colonel Harris Cawley, head of the Accompong Maroons, reasserted his community's demands: "we have a right to be here; a right to be an independent people; a right to make our own laws; a right to have our own arms and regiment; a right to negotiation with any government" (Cawley n.d.: 14). As in the past, the Jamaican government avoided a direct confrontation. But when a journalist interviewed a government spokesman in 1983, the latter's dissatisfaction with the Maroons' refusal to bow to the wishes of the Jamaican state was palpable. The interviewee was Carey Robinson, author of the popular history of the Maroons quoted above, who by then was a senior official in the Jamaican Ministry of Culture. "While defending their heritage," writes the journalist, "Robinson still admits that he is exasperated by the current attitude of Maroon leaders, who have become increasingly cocky toward the government over the last few years." Robinson's comments, which are unusually candid coming from a government official, say much about the ideological lenses through which urban "defenders" of the "Maroon heritage" in postcolonial Jamaica tend to view the here-and-now Maroons and their ongoing resistance to assimilation. According to Robinson,

> the Maroons have a feeling of status . . . but it is a status that is unexamined.
> They became a mercenary force and were pitted against some of Jamaica's

national heroes, and until they come to terms with that history, they are identifying themselves as enemies of Jamaica. The North American Indians at least have a grasp of their history; the Maroons don't. There is this uncertainty in their minds about the British. Because their treaty is with Britain, they think the Queen can exert a tremendous influence on their behalf. *They don't quite get it.* (Johnson 1983: 55; italics in original)

The interviewer adds that "Robinson knows that eventually, the government will have to resolve the legal quandary." In the meantime, according to Robinson, "the towns where the Maroons live are historical sites and, as such, should be treated as national heritage property" (55). Lurking behind this statement are some of the same unresolved questions raised earlier: Who has the right to define and interpret the Maroon past? Who possesses the "truth" about this past? Indeed, to whom does this history really belong? Evidently, some in positions of power in Jamaica feel that they already have the answers: not only do Maroons have no "grasp of their history," but until they "come to terms with that history" (as understood by certain non-Maroon authorities), they are declaring themselves "enemies of Jamaica"—"enemies" whose lands (and perhaps heritage, in a broader sense) should be treated as "national property" by those who claim to have a better grasp of history than they do. So poor, apparently, is their grasp of history that the Maroons have reacted at times to perceived infringements of their rights by appealing to international bodies for help, including the current head of the European state with which their ancestors originally made their treaties.[36] The oddly dismissive tone—some would say arrogance—of statements such as the above suggests that the Maroons are not the only ones who "don't quite get it."

Similar ambiguities can be seen in popular perceptions of the present-day Maroons. Rastafarian writer and poet Farika Birhan remembers experiencing the contradictions of the Maroon past through childhood conversations with those around her: "As I grew up, I found that people either admired the Maroons for their victories against the British and their refusal to be enslaved, or spoke condescendingly of them, dwelling on the negative aspects in the treaty they signed with the British. I always noticed a hint of fear, and often a note of envy in their disapproval" (Birhan 1985: 23). Increasing media coverage of the Maroon heritage, fostered in part by the elevation of "Nanny of the Maroons" to the status of National Hero, has made many Jamaicans more conscious and proud of the continuing presence of Maroon communities in the island. But there is also much confusion about whether, and the degree to which, Maroons remain a people apart. Many Jamaicans—especially those living far from Maroon communities—seem to believe that the Maroons have already been assimilated into the larger society and that there are no longer any "real" Maroons in the island, but only "descendants" of Maroons. At the same time, many others continue to think of the present-day Maroons as "a nation within a nation," despite periodic pronouncements by Jamaican government representatives to the contrary.[37] A 1985 public opinion column from a local newspaper, titled "The Public Says," provides some idea of the extent to which Maroons continue to be seen as a people apart. As its "question of the week," the tabloid asked, "Do you think the Maroons should be left out of participating in certain national events?"[38] Although all respondents answered in the negative, taking the position that the Maroons are an important part of the national fabric and should not be omitted from such functions, both the question itself and the responses presuppose that Maroons remain separate enough from the rest of the population to make their exclusion from national events a reasonable proposition.

Also evident in the local press is a continuing tendency to mythologize the Maroon presence, sometimes in ways that touch on questions of ownership. In the minds of many, Maroon autonomy, whatever it might mean to Maroons themselves, has become a kind of mythic quality belonging to all Jamaicans. This strain of thought is neatly captured by a letter recently published in the *Gleaner*, Jamaica's main newspaper, in which the writer waxes enthusiastic about "the magic of witnessing a traditional celebration of the Maroons, our own sturdy, independent descendants of brave, runaway slaves, who still have their own state-within-a-state up in our beautiful hills."[39] The possessive intent of the wording here is clear. The Maroons, and what they stand for, "belong" to the writer of the letter, as to all Jamaicans (even if the Maroons' "state-within-a-state" also remains "their own"). This ideology, though it has a long history in Jamaica, has become increasingly common since the 1970s. Given all the media attention focused on the Maroons in recent years, it is not surprising that many Jamaicans now share the sentiments of the government cultural officer who in 1985 told a *National Geographic* reporter, "in a sense, all Jamaicans, all of us, are Maroons" (Cobb 1985: 132).

What this figurative language might mean in practical terms is not at all clear. From the perspective of the present-day Maroon communities, attempts to extend "Maroon identity" symbolically to the nation at large may appear both beneficial and threatening. Such symbolic identification may promote positive feelings toward Maroons and encourage a kind of local heritage tourism of the Maroon communities by Jamaicans themselves. At the same time, if taken too far, it may begin to look like an insidious expression of assimilationist ideology. It is not hard to imagine why Maroons might be wary of the bandying about of a label that, for them, continues to function as a very specific ethnonym.[40] After all, one might reason, if all Jamaicans can be seen as Maroons nowadays, then what claim do the residents of the various Maroon communities have to being different? And if no differences can legitimately be claimed, then what right do they have to an autonomous (or even semiautonomous) territory of their own?

The "cultural invisibility" of contemporary Maroons is an inescapable part of these peculiarly Jamaican politics of identity. As we have seen, cultural differences between Maroons and other Jamaicans, with a few exceptions, are not readily discernible to the casual observer, and it is not surprising that some, unable to see below the surface, have interpreted the Maroons' continuing resistance to assimilation as little more than a hollow expression of lingering pride in a vanished past, or, in the words of a prominent historian, "atavistic stubbornness."[41] Others have approached this question much more cautiously. Werner Zips's description of his first encounter with Accompong reads much like that of the typical short-term visitor:

> I was quite anxious to meet the descendants of the first black freedom fighters in Jamaica. Their reputation as a militant group has survived into the present. When I arrived, however, I had the impression that my hopes would be dashed. Nothing seemed to distinguish this "rebel enclave" from other Jamaican villages. (Zips 1999a: xi)

A sustained ethnographic engagement with the Accompong Maroons, however, led Zips to the conclusion that "apparent disappearance or simple lack of visibility does not necessarily indicate that cultural traditions have died off, but more likely that they are elusive to the casual observer" (Zips 1999a: 162–63). Be that as it may, the elusiveness of "Maroon culture" to outsiders continues to raise questions of cultural authenticity and identity; and what is more, these questions are no longer of purely local concern. The Maroon communities of today, after all, are emphatically not (if they ever were) the remote, isolated preserves that many imagine them to be. Not only are many Maroons, like other Jamaicans, transnationals of long standing, but the Maroon communities themselves have long been receiving adventurous visitors from other parts of the world.[42] Enchanted by the Maroon mystique, "intrepid" tourists, both Jamaican and foreign, have been making their way to the Maroon villages since the early twentieth century. By the 1930s, former Jamaican governor Sydney Olivier was already complaining of "the tourists and journalists who on their visits to Jamaica to-day conceive the Maroons and Obeah to be the chief topics of social interest in the Island" (Olivier 1933: 263).

In fact, it was during the 1930s that professional anthropologists first began to visit the Maroons, with the expectation that they, of all Jamaicans, should have preserved the most in the way of "African culture." Some of those who stayed only a short time were disappointed with what they found, including the founder of Afro-American anthropology in the United States himself, Melville Herskovits, who spent a day and a night in Accompong in 1934 (Kaplan 2002: 384–85).[43] Arriving in Accompong two years after Herskovits, Zora Neale Hurston, though she stayed somewhat longer, ended up similarly disenchanted. In a letter written to Herskovits in 1937, after finishing her Jamaican fieldwork, Hurston declared that "the Maroons are highly over rated. They are the show piece of Jamaica like a Harlem night club. In fact they are not nearly so interesting as some groups in [the parish of] St. Thomas, out from Morant Bay. I saw some marvelous stuff [among Kumina practitioners] there. There are some groups right in Kingston who do more [in the way of African-derived rituals] than the Maroons. But the government is eager to give the impression that all primitive expression has disappeared from the island except what is done by the Maroons" (Kaplan 2002: 400–401). Today, some seven decades later, most of those who come into contact with Maroons are still looking for something palpably "different."

With the emergence of Black Studies in the United States in the 1960s and 1970s, there was another brief flurry of anthropological interest in the Jamaican Maroons. The sense that whatever was left of the Maroons' distinctive culture might be on the verge of disappearance prompted some discussion of the urgent need for better ethnographic documentation of these groups (Martin 1972; Scott 1973). Although a number of high-quality anthropological studies based on long-term fieldwork in Maroon communities were undertaken during this period, the extent to which Maroons remained culturally different from other Jamaicans seemed to be difficult to determine, even for the professionals. Despite all the anthropological attention, the Maroons remained, as they do today, "some of the world's most famous but least known people" (Martin 1972: 143). Writing in the early 1970s, Richard Price (1973: 229) pointed out that "exactly how much of the [Jamaican] Maroons' distinctive cultural heritage, and which particular aspects of it remain alive below the surface is a question that only sensitive in-depth field work, carried out in the immediate future, can answer." If anthropologists remained uncertain about what made Maroons different, what were tourists and other casual visitors to think?

Over the last few decades, faced with increasingly constricted local economic opportunities and the growing problem of population loss through outmigration, many Maroons have come to view organized cultural tourism as an appealing alternative. By the 1970s, concerned observers were already anticipating the questions of authenticity that would be raised by this growing trend. One writer went so far as to lament that "today commercialized as well as real Maroons can be found in their mountain homes," pointing out that "the commercially oriented Maroon accepts Western culture enough to provide guided tours . . . to tourists, researchers, and the curious." In contrast, imagined this author, "the real Maroon disdains this means of livelihood, choosing insulation in basically African environs and having little contact with the Western world" (Nicholas 1979: 11). In any case, whether the Maroons of Accompong (the first to receive substantial numbers of tourists) were "real Maroons" or not was no easier for casual observers to tell in the 1970s than it had been for earlier visitors.

Early tour operators quickly discovered that the relative invisibility of Maroon cultural distinctiveness could disappoint visitors' expectations. In 1981, the Berlitz travel guide to Jamaica warned seekers of exotica that the Windward Maroon communities of Moore Town and Cornwall Barracks, though vaunted by some as places of special cultural significance, "look no different from any other Jamaican towns and there is no touristic reason to go there."[44] More re-

Figure 2.8. Leaflet circulated on north coast of Jamaica, late 1980s–early 1990s. Photo: K. Bilby.

cently, the Lonely Planet travel guidebook for Jamaica—to cite but one of several such passages in the current tourist literature—offered the following piece of advice to anyone contemplating a visit to Accompong: "It's hyped, but there's *nothing* unique or different about this tiny hamlet that touts itself as the capital of Maroon culture."[45] Thomas Cook's Passport guide drew more general conclusions: "Today little remains of Maroon culture."[46] But the *Rough Guide to Jamaica* came closest to replicating the problematic logic that seems so prevalent within Jamaica itself, equating apparent lack of cultural distinctiveness with absence of genuine historical consciousness. Evaluating the tourism potential of "the major remaining Maroon settlement" of Moore Town, the authors tell us that "its past is more of a draw than its present," but that Moore Town has "little apparent sense of its historical importance," leaving us to wonder who exactly it is that values (and has a right to) the past in question—a past that must be valuable since, according to the authors, it remains a "draw."[47] Increasingly aware of this problem, Maroons in some communities have begun to manufacture "cultural products" for sale to tourists, drawing partly on elements of Maroon culture once considered secret or private.[48] Another response has been to form cultural "troupes" that regularly perform music and dance genres once kept from the eyes and ears of non-Maroons. Maroons in all communities are also striving to build cultural centers and/or museums that will cater primarily to visitors—likely harbingers of further cultural commodification.[49]

One of the subtexts in this tourist literature is that the Maroons, despite everything one hears, are not really as isolated or "primitive"—not anywhere near as pristine—as they are supposed to be. More than half a century ago, after visiting Accompong, Hamilton Basso (1960: 86) was moved to comment that "I can't go along with the version of the Maroons that has got into general circulation. What the obeah situation is, I can't say. But sullen and primitive?—no, I'm afraid not." Even today, one cannot help but suspect that visitors' reactions to the lack of visible difference in present-day Maroon communities are often as much about unfulfilled romantic longings for the exotic primitive as they are about the perceived absence of cultural distinctiveness. At any rate, even with the bubble-bursting representations circulating in the tourist literature, the Maroon mystique continues to lure adventure seekers. And while some visitors are as enthralled when they leave as when they arrived, others go away disillusioned. Some, like the following journalist who braved the trek to Maroon country for an upscale travel magazine in the early 1990s, are able to take it all in stride:

> In spite of the video camera and the presence of other foreigners, I had felt intrepid about my voyage up to the two Maroon strongholds. I had set out to see the island's core, its secret self, known only to a select group of informed Jamaicans and anthropologists. Back in the United States, I mentioned my trip to Accompong to a friend who had once vacationed in Jamaica. "Ah," he said, "and did you meet the Colonel?" That's how Jamaica is. Just when you think you've reached the heart of darkness, you find a video team from Brooklyn who arrived before you. The leader of the warrior clan, you discover, has three children living in the United States and one in London.[50]

Correcting the misconceptions of visitors is not the only challenge facing Maroons as the tourist presence continues to grow. While enterprises such as cultural tourism and museums may have salutary effects, both economic and

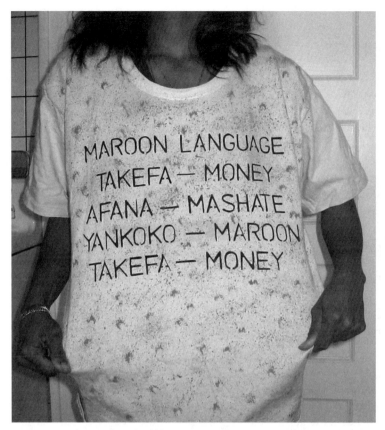

Figure 2.9. T-shirt made and sold by young Maroons in Moore Town, early 1990s.
Photo: K. Bilby.

cultural, they may bring a host of new complications as well. As once-private Maroon cultural markers and symbols are commodified and made increasingly available to a larger public, for instance, the Maroon communities may find it more difficult to maintain exclusive ownership and control of their history and their ancestral cultural heritage.[51] Even the sacred rites performed annually by Accompong Maroons for the spirits of their ancestors, according to Jean Besson (1997: 218), have "become both a tourist attraction and a symbol of Jamaica's nationhood." Emblems of "Maroon heritage" in general, whether originating among the Maroons themselves or in the imaginations of interested outsiders, are easily transformed into symbolic capital, not only by other Jamaicans who would claim these as "national" possessions, but also by those in other parts of the world who recognize the mythic power of Maroon imagery. Not only symbols, but actual cultural practices and forms of knowledge may also be appropriated, a prime example being the particular technique of smoking and spicing meat, known as "jerking," developed by the Maroons' ancestors. In the space of a few decades, this culinary technique, adopted and carried overseas by non-Maroon Jamaicans, has spread far beyond the Caribbean; dishes such as jerk pork and jerk chicken are now offered across the world as emblems of Jamaican "national cuisine," most often without acknowledgment of their Maroon origins.

The most obvious of the larger arenas in which Maroon symbolism might have special appeal is the expanding transnational ideological space that has come to be known as the Black Atlantic, some cultural manifestations of which, such as Pan-Africanism, have long displayed an awareness of the significance of the Jamaican Maroon epic.[52] As Mavis Campbell argued some three decades ago, "their heroic history is a part, not only of Jamaican history, but also of Black history and in its widest sense, a part of the history of freedom, as exemplified in the number of white scholars from the United States, United Kingdom and the Soviet Union interested in the Maroon story." On a more personal note, she observed that "when scholars from Africa as well as Afro-Americans express to me their deep interest in the Maroons, it is not merely academic curiosity; it is also an aspect of identity" (Campbell 1973: 54).[53] But Maroon imagery has traveled far and wide, and appropriations of cultural symbols once considered exclusively Maroon have occurred in surprising places. Within a decade or so of having been made a Jamaican National Hero, the Windward Maroon ancestress Nanny was being put to entirely new uses. During the 1980s, for instance, a San Francisco organization calling itself the Kerista Consciousness Church, based in the famous Haight-Ashbury district, incorporated into its pantheon of deities a "black goddess" named Sister Kerista; according to the Keristans, this deity, after which their church was named, is not only "the symbolic sister of Jesus," but also "the symbolic granddaughter of Nanny, liberator of the Maroons" (Furchgott n.d.: 20).

More recently, one of the latest in a long line of aspiring cultural brokers from abroad published a number of unusually bold claims to special knowledge of Nanny. After a speedy, ganja-soaked initiation into the mysteries of Rastafari on the north coast (the "tourist coast"), followed by a couple of brief jaunts to the Windward Maroon community of Moore Town, this newcomer to Jamaica experienced an epiphany of startling proportions, culminating in the realization that "Nanny was the first teacher of One Love on this island" (rather than, as many believe, Bob Marley). (During one of these trips to Moore Town, his wife, sharing in the enthusiasm of the moment, had been moved to exclaim, "I can just feel Nanny calling to me.") While communing with this Maroon "holy ground," the author came to feel that "the heart and soul of Nanny is weak here with the Maroons but strong and alive in Rastafari." To remedy this unfortunate situation, he would write a book about it. Better yet, he would arrange to launch it right there in Moore Town, in order to "rekindle the vision of Nanny and the Maroons, here and in the world" (Roskind 2001: 230–31). While one may wish to laugh off these well-intentioned pronouncements as the pipe dreams of a (self-defined) "ex-hippie," they point to the very real possibility of cultural appropriation of a more serious kind—whether by government planners, media-savvy Rastafarians, political activists of various stripes, cultural entrepreneurs (black or white), tourism promoters, or others.

Attempts to appropriate the glory of the Maroon epic are also found in the academic literature. In a series of recent articles in learned journals, for instance, an Islamic scholar, Sultana Afroz (1999a; 1999b), argues that the Jamaican Maroons, both during the Spanish period and after, were in fact a Muslim *ummah* (community) united by Islam in a *jihad* (holy war) against the European oppressor. Through elaborate feats of imagination that require her to ignore a mountain of evidence to the contrary, Afroz comes up with "proof" that practically every significant aspect of the Maroon cultural heritage is derived from Islam.[54] To her mind, the names of Maroon leaders such as Cudjoe, Quao, and Cuffee—though it has long been known that these are common West African "day names" (in Akan and neighboring languages) rendered in English orthography—resemble Arabic words with a variety of meanings, and therefore must be derived from Arabic. "Granny Nanny, the great Jamaican heroine," she asserts, was in reality a Muslim holy woman; "miracles and not obeah were wrought on her behalf, that 'Allah might justify His servant in the eyes both of friends and enemies.'" And this is just the beginning; the list of supposed Islamic contributions to the Maroon cultural heritage goes on. That this argument represents but one more attempt to take possession of a valued history—a history with iconic significance in a grand, mythic narrative of liberation—becomes clear when the author comes to the general conclusion that "the Islamic concept of freedom was the basis of the Maroon struggle against slavocracy." Like others who stake such claims to this glorious past, she makes the unwarranted (and arrogant) assumption that the Maroons themselves have a poor grasp of their own history. "Even present-day Maroon leaders," she tells us, "are unaware of the Islamic heritage of their forefathers" (Afroz 1999b: 168–75). She never seems to entertain the possibility that these Maroons, in failing to recognize themselves as erstwhile Muslims, might possess genuine historical consciousness, or that the non-Islamic African origins that they themselves stress might have any validity. In effect, by giving primacy to her interpretation of Maroon history, even though this conflicts with Maroon understandings, she joins other claimants to this valued history in severing the Maroons of today from their own past.

Faced with a growing interest in Maroons in Jamaica and abroad, the leaders of the Maroon communities have begun to rethink the meaning of "Maroon heritage." As the play of cultural symbols and images around their past becomes thicker, and claims to various aspects of this increasingly marketable heritage continue to multiply, questions of ownership become more pressing (cf. Handler 1991; Yelvington et al. 2002). By the mid-1990s, the Maroon colonels were ready to lend their names to a stern public statement asserting that it was time for Maroons to "exercise full control over their cultural material whether these be artifacts, music, traditions, stories, history." As reported in the local press, the Maroons were complaining that "hundreds of persons had exploited various aspects of Maroon culture for their own ends, with Maroons benefiting little from these exercises."[55] Another newspaper article from around the same time reports that "Maroons in the four native communities across the island are uniting to lobby their protest against and to put an end to the unlawful profiteering and 'rape' of their cultural and historical heritage by persons outside the community," including "foreigners aided and abetted by local influentials." Cited as beneficiaries of such "profiteering" were filmmakers and foreign researchers working on academic theses. This new language of protest, in which a reified (and gendered?) "cultural and historical heritage" could be characterized as a victim of "rape," clearly reveals that the Jamaican Maroons, or at least their leaders, were becoming sensitized to the politically charged debates about power and representation then occupying the attention of academics in the United States and Europe, as well as a growing number of intellectuals in the Caribbean.[56] But as the article unfolds, it becomes apparent that the Maroons' complaints are as much about local injustices as about exploitation by profit-seekers from abroad. "For years," the article goes on to explain, "the Maroons have been seeking full recognition of their cultural and historical significance to the country's development from the Government and all Jamaica." What "full recognition" might mean is then spelled out: "In February this year, the Maroon leaders met with Government ministers of foreign affairs, national security and the attorney general to press their demands for constitutional changes that will give them certain rights as well as seeking tangible support to put them on the road to becoming economically independent."[57]

If foreigners had not only recognized that Maroons were a "special people," but also repeatedly profited from this, then why did the Jamaican government persist in ignoring the Maroons' demands for "full recognition"? If the "Maroon heritage" surviving in the present-day communities was "real" enough to attract and materially benefit "hundreds" of outsiders, then surely the separate identity claimed by contemporary Maroons was "real" enough to be written into the Jamaican constitution. The time had come to remind the government, once again, that lip service was not enough.

Remembrance: Maroon Narratives and Maroon History

> It is a curious fact that although Jamaica is proud of its Maroons, it knows very little about them, and a still more curious fact that very often the Maroons seem to know little about themselves.
> —John Horner (1946)[58]

> The Maroon community was not a literate community but a martial one; and its proud records were compiled by others.
> —Carey Robinson (1969: 156)

Partly because there remains so little that seems "special" about the present-day Maroons on the surface, outside observers in search of difference often seize upon those few aspects of their distinctive heritage that remain tangible and obvious: most notably, their unique political organization (visible in their elected leaders and councils) and their communal lands. Yet, the symbolic power with which these tangible markers are invested depends, in large part, on a shared body of intangible ideas about the Maroon past and its relationship to the present. This close interdependence between the symbolic and material bases of Maroon identity has long been recognized by anthropologists who have carried out fieldwork in Maroon communities. After spending several weeks in Moore Town, Clarissa Scott (1968: 85), for example, was able to pin down some of the symbolic components of the distinctive Maroon identity she encountered in that community, which, as she understood, were no less important in constituting that identity than were the political and economic features that distinguished Maroons from other Jamaicans: "town meetings, the call of the abeng, the bylaws [local laws recorded on paper by the Moore Town council], Shady Tree (which served for so many generations as the informal meeting place for the village elders), the Myal Dance [i.e., Kromanti Play], the recall of the treaty, the drumming which still occasionally takes place during the night, and the myths of Maroon heroics. These enhance the cohesive feelings of cultural identity and, by so doing, support the traditional forms of political organization and land tenure." What Scott fails to stress strongly enough is that underlying this list of local symbols, and giving it meaning, is a complex, continuing history of remembrance through narrative and other forms of verbal and nonverbal re-presentation.

The Jamaican Maroon narratives presented in this book exemplify this ongoing history of remembrance. If these narratives can be characterized as forms of remembrance, however, the process of "remembering" is as much of the present as the past. For the purposes of this study, the primary significance of these narratives lies in the fact that they presently reflect, and are constitutive of, a distinct, historically continuous ethnic identity that remains today every bit as "real" as the individual Maroons who have received, refashioned, and passed on these traditions. In an important sense, then, this book, though it often dwells on the past, is concerned only secondarily with "history"; similarly, despite its focus on oral narratives, it is not directly concerned with narrative in the larger sense, or with theories of narrative. Of paramount importance here—and of greatest interest to the narrators themselves—is the content, meaning, and use of these oral statements as forms of knowledge. It is for this reason that narrative form, performative rules, aesthetic principles, and other such considerations, important as they may be to a total understanding of the texts presented in this study, are not analyzed in any depth here. Nor is the question of the "historical accuracy" of these texts given primacy (although it is a question of great concern to Maroons themselves). From the perspective taken here, oral traditions about events that may have never actually occurred are no less interesting or valuable than those that trained historians might accept as evidence of "what really happened."[59] What matters most for present purposes is the power of narrative, in what remains a largely oral culture, as a form of collective "knowing."[60] And in this ongoing narrative conversation about the past, this process of creating and transmitting knowledge, contributions from all points along the myth-history continuum may be brought to bear.

Yet, a book of and about Maroon narratives can scarcely afford to overlook the actual past ("what really happened") to which many of these narratives can be shown to refer, even if the historiographical questions these narratives raise must be treated here as secondary. To ignore the demonstrable historical veracity of many Maroon oral texts would be to do an injustice to the Maroon communities to which these narratives belong, where historical consciousness is so closely tied to sense of self.[61] Leann Martin, writing about the Maroons of Moore Town with whom she lived, makes a case for history *as* identity with which I fully agree:

> It is clear that the primary cultural tool as well as the primary ingredient in their cultural identity, is history—history with meaning in everyday life, history that not only provides explanations for current customs and conditions but also is the major source of motivation for behavior that maintains and defends the aspects of custom and situation Maroons consider essential to their identity. . . . Because of their possession and use of this past, Maroons know clearly who they are, have been, and want to be. They know who belongs and who does not, and how to act toward persons in either category (Martin 1973: 180).

The line between self and other, Martin rightly suggests, is itself defined by history; indeed, "ideas about Maroon history provide the most fundamental set of boundaries between Maroon culture and others" (67). Once this is understood, the implications of dismissing the Maroons' own historical traditions become clearer. By presuming without grounds that present-day Maroons lack genuine knowledge or understanding of their own past, those who locate Maroon history exclusively in written records "compiled by others" unilaterally declare the erasure of ethnic boundaries that remain important to Maroons themselves. Even if ownership of a valued "Maroon heritage" were not at stake, to deny out of hand the historical veracity of Maroon oral traditions would be to cast in doubt the authenticity of the ethnic identity of which these traditions are so fundamental a part.

As I carried out my initial fieldwork with Jamaican Maroons in 1977–78, these considerations were very much on my mind. Historical consciousness as such was not the focus of my research; I was primarily concerned, rather, with ritual practice, and the contexts in which Maroon ritual specialists mingled with outsiders. Yet, narratives about the past loomed large in the conversations through which my Maroon interlocutors gradually introduced me to their

Kromanti spiritual tradition. As I strengthened my relationships with these Kromanti practitioners and began to probe their specialized esoteric knowledge more deeply (as discussed in chapter 1), I gathered a large body of these historical narratives on tape, without any clear idea of what I was going to do with them.

A few years after this, as a doctoral student in anthropology at the Johns Hopkins University, I feverishly worked, between courses and heavy reading, at transcribing these taped conversations, recognizing their unique value as a kind of record of Jamaican Maroon historical thinking that had scarcely been tapped by historians. When I asked my academic advisor, Richard Price, to look at and assess a few of these texts, he responded not only with encouraging remarks, but also with a copy of the manuscript of an almost-finished book—a study of Saramaka Maroon history-making that was soon to be published as *First-Time* (1983). It is difficult to describe the sense of excitement I felt while reading this work in draft. Despite the many significant differences of time and place, the parallels between Saramaka and Jamaican Maroon visions of their pasts were nothing less than extraordinary. It was as if the Saramaka historians in Suriname, speaking through Price, were using an esoteric language—a "language" of values and emotions—to which I had already become privy in Jamaica. The contours of historical thought among these two Maroon peoples were remarkably congruent. My simultaneous exposure to Saramaka and Jamaican Maroon historical discourse provided a lasting lesson in the shaping power of collective historical experience in the construction of cultural narratives.

Price's work with Saramakas also raised important historiographical questions. Unlike most previous writers, he had treated Surinamese Maroon historical traditions (and indigenous Saramaka cultural expressions of other kinds) as authentic documents. In these oral traditions had been inscribed verifiable traces of an actual past, together with many layers of embellishment and reimagination contributed by variously positioned parties along the way to the present. That these traces represented the outcome of a radical process of selection—one that had repeatedly been conditioned by the motivations of politically interested actors—did not detract from their value as historical records that could be weighed and interpreted for insights into a past previously located exclusively in written records. The documents that had survived in Dutch colonial archives, themselves products of a process of selection, could in fact be juxtaposed with Saramaka oral narratives to create a polyphonic conversation that might enable a richer and "truer" reading of Saramaka history than would be possible relying on either source individually. In some cases, as Price demonstrated, archival documents could be used to corroborate Saramaka oral traditions, and vice versa.[62]

The Jamaican Maroon oral traditions to which I had been given access, I felt, deserved the same respectful treatment; they too ought to be investigated as possible repositories of a "real" past, one that might overlap in significant ways with the traces of the past recoverable from British writings. In pursuit of this question, I embarked on research in a number of archives in both England and Jamaica.[63] While far from exhaustive, this archival research, carried out over a number of years, greatly enriched my understandings of some of the narratives presented in this book. The more data I gathered from written records, the more I came to recognize the value of Jamaican Maroon oral narratives as historical sources that could be used—much like Saramaka historical traditions—not only to provide independent verification of certain colonial documents, but also to contest colonial biases and fill the gaps in some of these documents, and perhaps to recover portions of the Maroon past previously considered unrecoverable.

The need to redress the imbalances characterizing historical writings about the Jamaican Maroons, from which the perspectives of Maroons themselves were almost entirely absent, had become increasingly apparent to me. Each new article or book on Jamaican Maroons, it seemed, repeated the omissions of previous ones. Commenting on Mavis Campbell's *The Maroons of Jamaica 1655–1796* (1988)—an erudite and in many ways exemplary history—Nigel Bolland (1994: 211) articulates the problem succinctly: "despite the fact that she repeatedly refers to her 'fieldwork' in the different Maroon communities, not a single Maroon voice is heard in her work."[64] Having himself visited and exchanged thoughts with the descendants of the Maroons about whom Campbell writes, Bolland feels that "we should hear more of their version of the story." Few others interested in Jamaican Maroon history, however, have voiced this opinion. As we have seen, many of those who purport to value Maroon history are not prepared to accord much importance to the "version of the story" told by inhabitants of the present-day Maroon communities.[65] The result has been a series of silences in the production of Jamaican Maroon "history," some of them of the kind persuasively brought to light by Rolph Trouillot (1995) in his critical reflections on the role of power in the making of historical narratives. Yet other silences in this case resemble the omissions and "sanitation" of the past discussed by Anne Bailey (2005), whose study of African perspectives on the slave trade contrasts the apparent amnesia regarding the era of slavery in parts of both the Caribbean and Africa with the living oral "memories" of the trade she found among the Anlo Ewe of Ghana. In any case, there can be little doubt that much of what has been written about Jamaican Maroons, most based exclusively on colonial documents, is full of what Zips (1999b: 226) characterizes as "the theoretical blindspots of source-positivist thinking."

The present book presents many more Jamaican Maroon versions of their own story than any other published work to date. Told here by many voices, this story is not easily dismissed—particularly when it is supplemented with contemporary descriptions, taken from written "records compiled by others," that often appear to lend at least partial support to it. At several points in this work I include verbatim excerpts from such documents, all written from colonial perspectives. Taking a leaf out of Price's *First-Time* (as well as its sequel, *Alabi's World* [1990]), I juxtapose these archival fragments with the words of Maroon narrators. My purpose here, however, is not so much to add to the multiplicity of voices—

European colonial writers, after all, hardly need increased representation in telling the story of the Jamaican Maroons—as to co-opt these colonial documents, most of which represent observations by the Maroons' British enemies, and turn them toward new ends. Most of these passages coincided in time with the juxtaposed Maroon narratives and are roughly contemporaneous "illustrations" of phenomena or themes discussed in the Maroon texts. These fragmentary word images, framed within boxes, resemble faded (and carefully cropped) photographs; like the latter, they may evoke in the reader a sense of "being there," in a distant place and time that has much in common with the spatial and temporal world represented in the neighboring Maroon narratives, though framed rather differently from them, and reflecting a different point of view. Like the actual photographs interspersed throughout this book—indeed, like graphic illustrations in most books—these framed verbal fragments vary in the precision with which they illustrate the corresponding text. In some cases, these textual "snapshots," some of them well over two centuries old, depict specific persons or events comparable to those discussed in the juxtaposed narratives—if not actually the very same persons or events. One might argue, then, that in addition to their value as evocative illustrations, they may in some instances be read as evidence of historical veracity.

In a similar vein, throughout this book I preface certain thematically linked groups of narratives with historical commentaries of my own—brief digressions into the historicity of specific persons, places, events, or circumstances alluded to in the Maroon texts that immediately follow. Subtitled and set off from both the main introductory sections of each chapter and the Maroon narratives themselves, these contextualizing commentaries focus on relationships between particular oral traditions and aspects of the Maroon past that can be gleaned from written records. By exploring the historical veracity of selected Maroon oral narratives in these digressions, I hope to show that present-day Maroon historical discourse, despite its mythic qualities and its manipulation to suit the present, remains very much grounded in an actual past. As we shall see, some of these narratives *can* be used in conjunction with written documents to recover, or add depth to our understanding of, parts of this past. When treated with care, they may bring us closer to "what really happened" (or, more broadly, "what once was"). In this sense, at least some Maroon oral narratives may be seen as genuine, if partial and imperfect, historical records. Indeed, I would argue that in some respects these orally transmitted records hold out the promise of a richer, more nuanced, and perhaps more accurate understanding of the Maroon past than that provided by a history forced to rely exclusively on the fragmentary, highly biased, and often superficial data preserved in colonial archives—the records created by the Maroons' "literary foes" (Zips 1999b: 96).

As an attempt to grapple with the historicity of Jamaican Maroon oral traditions, this book joins a growing body of work devoted to the exploration of varying cultural constructions of the past—and, more generally, cultural representations of pastness—in different parts of the world. Much of this literature is concerned with the ways in which oral narrative, myth, social memory, and indigenous systems of historiography intersect in the history-making of peoples once assumed to be without history.[66] Whether contributing to our understanding of the role of political agency in this process (Rappaport 1990, 1994; Singer 1997), the use of historical memory and narratives about the past in the construction and maintenance of distinctive identities (White 1991; Poyer 1993), the interplay of myth, history, and power in the development of mythohistorical orientations (Hill 1988; Urton 1990), the significance of gender in the production of historical narratives (Hofmeyr 1993), or the construction of ethnic presents through performances of the past (Rodríguez 1996; Guss 2000), these explorations, and many others, continue to reveal in new ways the untenability of positivistic notions of a single, absolute historical truth that can be accessed only through the possessive magic of the written word.[67] Also contributing to this trend are a number of new histories of non-Western peoples written from self-consciously indigenist perspectives (e.g., Sioui 1989). Yet another promising avenue has been opened by scholars who have noted the existence of nondiscursive forms of social memory that encode seemingly "forgotten" histories in ritual practices and sedimented "memoryscapes"—what Rosalind Shaw (2002: 22), in her study of previously unacknowledged memories of the slave trade among the Temne of Sierra Leone, aptly characterizes as histories of "moral imagination" that are "told primarily in the language of practical memory through places and practices, images and visions, rituals and rumors." By reexamining the complex, porous relationship between conventional polarities such as myth and history, oracy and literacy, in specific cultural and historical contexts, and broadening our understandings of what may constitute historicity, this expanding literature continues to challenge the hegemonic idea that there can be any final word on the past.

The Eurocentric ideological tendency to divide humankind into two fundamental types—those with history and those ostensibly without—has been particularly acute in colonial and postcolonial settings where plantation slavery once reigned, including much of the Caribbean. Until relatively recently, academic historical writing on the English-speaking Caribbean was limited almost entirely to economic or administrative histories written by professional historians from outside the region; even the lively counter-histories that local intellectuals began to produce in the late nineteenth century were based on elitist conceptions of history, and drew primarily on metropolitan sources (Higman 1999: 46–88). In such histories, those at the bottom of the social hierarchy—the vast majority of the colonized—remained invisible. For most of the "educated" inhabitants of these societies, the proposition that the masses who had survived the trauma of transatlantic displacement and slavery could have retained and passed on any significant history among themselves—had they possessed any history to begin with—was unimaginable. Anglophone Caribbean intellectuals struggled with the region's "absence of ruins," as some still do. Lacking the time-worn architectural landmarks or great tomes used to define "civilizations" in retrospect, these ex-slave societies, or at least some among their intelligentsia, looked back and perceived a void.

The movement toward and eventual achievement of independence in the majority of Caribbean territories provided the impetus for a reevaluation of the possible sources and meanings of history—a process in which professional historians have played a rather limited role. To a large extent, the search for a usable past in the postcolonial Caribbean has been left instead to literary artists, whose primary technique for recovering a meaningful heritage has been historically informed imagination, expressed through poetry and fiction (Wilson-Tagoe 1998). (Only rarely has the region produced poet-historians, such as Kamau Brathwaite, who sometimes manage to combine the best of both worlds.) Over the last few decades, with the burgeoning of historical writing on slavery in the Americas, there has been an increasing tendency among Caribbeanist historians (following on the pioneering work of Patterson [1969: 145–283] and Brathwaite [1971: 212–39] on slave culture in Jamaica) to attempt "history from below." Yet, the difficulties of getting at this side of the story through colonial sources written almost exclusively by European observers cannot be denied. Even as historians search for ways to overcome the limitations of such archival documents, the potential of oral history for studies of slavery in the Caribbean remains largely unexplored. The methodological challenges posed by the use of oral data in this kind of work remain daunting. Indeed, as Higman (1999: 28) tells us, "professional historians have contested the view that there is much to be learned from oral history about the experience of slavery in the English-speaking Caribbean." In one of the few serious attempts by a professional historian to evaluate the usefulness of oral traditions in studies of Caribbean slave society, Michael Craton (1977: 280), writing about Jamaica, concludes that "it is now probably too late for oral testimony to be used either to add much information about formal slavery or to make an accurate judgment on whether the written sources have correctly depicted formal slavery. In the last analysis, the historian is driven back to his own traditional methods."

A rather different perspective is offered by the Jamaican historian and novelist Erna Brodber (1983: 2), who advocates "the creation of a social history of the region which sees the oral accounts of the people's past as a significant part of its data." A writer of creative fiction herself, Brodber nonetheless remains mindful of the rules of the academic historian's craft and has strong reservations about the use of unfettered creative imagination to establish "knowledge" of the past. Though in sympathy with Caribbean writers who have "found archival data inadequate for describing the responses of their forefathers," and have therefore gone "beyond events to describe feelings," she is wary of "the imposition of the writers' sentiment upon history" (4). "If not in the imagination of the creative writers," she asks, where "will we find the admissible data on the behaviour of people who left no memoirs?" (7). In attempting to answer this question, Brodber argues persuasively that oral data *do* constitute a valuable source of evidence for historians interested in the experience of slavery in places such as Jamaica. Not only songs, proverbs, and other encoded verbal forms, but also oral narratives, she contends, *can* be used to shed light on the past—even a past as distant as the era of slavery.[68] In support of her argument, she includes transcriptions of two oral accounts recorded in rural Jamaica in the 1970s, both describing events shortly before the abolition of slavery in 1834. By interpreting these in conjunction with official reports from the 1830s, she is able to show not only that these oral narratives can be used to substantiate and supplement written documents from the slavery era, but that they likely reflect in an accurate manner the "sentiments," "thoughts," and "acts" of the narrators' slave ancestors (7–10). More recently, Jean Besson (2001: 81) has collected oral histories from both Maroons and slave descendants in rural Jamaica that "reach back to the post-emancipation period and in some cases well beyond: to the slavery past, to the 'First-Time Maroons,' to the Middle Passage of the Atlantic slave trade, and to the 'shipmate' fictive kinship bond which formed the atom of African-American slave society." According to Besson, history in these Jamaican peasant communities resides not only in songs and oral narratives, but also in the land itself (Besson 2001: 87–97; see also Besson 2002: 159–93).

I suspect that there is much that can still be learned about the experience of slavery from the descendants of the enslaved in Jamaica, by carrying out the kind of research on oral culture that Brodber and Besson have begun. Even now, at the beginning of the twenty-first century, it is probably not too late to benefit from these hidden historical traces.[69] Certainly, in the case of the Maroon communities, there still exists a very significant repository of oral historical data that can be of much value in interpreting the past.[70] Many of the oral texts included in the present study likely contain valuable historical data beyond what I have recognized and chosen to discuss as such. There is no doubt, for instance, that I have not exhausted the potential of the songs, proverbs, place names, personal epithets, and bits of esoteric language that pepper these oral narratives, many of them windows on the past, as "witnesses in spite of themselves" (Bloch 1953; Price 1983: 7–8, 27–28). It is my hope that historians and others might find these oral records useful in ways that have not been addressed in this book; that they might find herein a range of data that can be further analyzed and interpreted— perhaps in ways that I have not anticipated—to get at a side of the past that remains underexposed.

To be sure, this is not an entirely straightforward task. The perils of treating oral testimony uncritically, as a simple reflection of "what really happened," are well known.[71] Despite their attempts to maintain and protect the integrity of their ancestral heritage, Jamaican Maroons, quite obviously, are not immune to the historical visions of others—especially powerful or prestigious others. Concerned about the recent "flooding" of the Saramaka Maroon system of historical knowledge with spurious information, Price (1983: 25–26) warns that "tourists, missionaries, government officials, and visiting scholars are all actively if unknowingly contributing to major revisions of First-Time knowledge." If anything, the Maroons of Jamaica are more vulnerable to such outside "interference," and have been for a long time—not only because they have always been much less isolated than Surinamese Maroons, but also because their story is better known in other parts of the world, and therefore tends to carry more personal meanings for those outsiders with whom they interact, some of whom may feel that they themselves have a strong stake in the interpretation of the history in question.

I provide an example from my own experience of how certain Maroon oral traditions have been shifting over time, in response to outside influences. When I first visited the Leeward Maroon community of Accompong in 1978, I was told by a number of elders, including Mann Rowe, who has often been portrayed as the town's leading historian, that the Maroons' original ancestors came from the "Gold Coast" in Africa. When I returned in the early 1990s, Rowe and several others now insisted that their ancestral homeland was "Nigeria." It is no coincidence that in the intervening years, during the 1980s, the Nigerian High Commission in Jamaica had become actively involved in the public management of the "Maroon heritage," regularly sending Nigerian dignitaries to the annual celebration in Accompong, and making material and symbolic contributions to the Maroons' various attempts to raise their profile in Jamaica and the wider world.[72] However, by 1999, following a ceremonial "state visit" to Accompong by West African leader Jerry Rawlings and his First Lady, Nana Konadu Agyeman Rawlings, the Maroon elders (Rowe included) were once again telling me (and others) that the earliest ancestors were from "Ghana" (the republic over which Rawlings then ruled as president)—a part of Africa that, geographically speaking, matched what they had told me in the 1970s, only now the name they used had been updated.[73] The ongoing incorporation of the Jamaican Maroons into a larger Afro-Atlantic world is reflected today not only in occasional adjustments to some of their oral traditions, to bring them into line with the expectations of others occupying this ideological space, but also in more conspicuous ways—for instance, in the contemporary "traditional" West African clothing (from Nigeria, Ghana, and elsewhere) that Maroon leaders on both sides of the island have adopted as ceremonial wear when presiding over public functions such as the annual commemorations of the Maroon heritage.

But such examples of recent changes in self-representation in response to outside influences come mostly from the public sphere; they seem to be limited almost entirely to that part of the Maroon cultural heritage that is routinely displayed for outsiders and relatively readily discussed with non-Maroons. The extent to which the more private cultural domain to which most of the narratives in this book belong has been modified as a result of outside pressures remains an open question. My impression is that many of the "deeper" Maroon oral traditions, especially those that have been passed on by Kromanti specialists, have remained relatively stable, even in the face of the recent proliferation of outside representations of the Maroon past in the mass media, to which all Maroons are increasingly exposed. A relatively high degree of stability can be seen, for instance, in the multiple retellings I recorded of certain narratives, some of which I include back-to-back in this book for comparison; when narrators whose words I had taped in 1978 retold the same story in 1982 or 1991, minor details were often added or subtracted, but the main outlines of the account usually remained the same. Certainly, those Kromanti specialists I have known over the years have been quick to reject statements about the Maroon past that contradict their own understandings; even when such statements carry the imprimatur of outsiders in positions of power or authority, the Maroons who speak in this book have generally continued to dispute them and to assert the factuality of the versions learned from their own elders.

In any case, while it is important to acknowledge the historicity of a large number of Maroon oral traditions, Jamaican Maroon claims to a separate identity, I would argue, cannot be judged on the basis of how "accurately" they understand their past (a question the epistemological complexities of which, in any case, few seekers after historical "truths" about the Maroons seem equipped to tackle).[74] Regardless of how faithfully Maroon oral narratives might recount "what really happened" in any particular case, it is clear that the Maroon oral culture represented by the texts in this book is both culturally distinctive and historically deep. As the ideational reflection and medium of a genuinely distinct, historically continuous ethnic identity, this is enough. Yet, as I have also argued, the complex question of historical veracity should not be ignored, for it has real significance for Maroons as well as non-Maroons. Like those who would uncritically embrace Maroon oral historical traditions as simple reflections of an actual past, those who assume without basis that these traditions are devoid of genuine traces of the past are on shaky ground.

Arguing that Caribbean novelists and poets were deconstructionists even before "deconstruction," Nana Wilson-Tagoe (1998: 38) points out that "the rewritings of and engagements with 'history' in the writings of West Indian authors problematize the nature of historical knowledge itself by demystifying its objectivity and making it serve the imperatives of self-definition. They are postmodernist rewritings in the sense that they re-present the past in fiction, poetry, or drama"—thereby opening the past up to the present, and preventing it from being "conclusive and teleological." "Opening up" and reclaiming the past in this way can be a liberating gesture. The difficulty of the present case, of course, is that it remains unclear exactly whose "imperative of self-definition" is to be served by this new leeway in historical interpretation. In attempting to overcome the limitations of the European colonial documents, should interpreters of the Jamaican Maroon past turn to the imaginative "deconstructions" of literary artists who write "historical fiction" (with or without the help of such written records), or to the historical discourse of the inhabitants of the present-day Maroon communities? Advocates of postmodernist experimentation will protest, rightly, that these alternative sources of historical "knowledge" need not be mutually exclusive. But until Maroon perspectives on their own past are given much greater weight by writers who imagine this past, there is a risk that, in the process of deconstruction, one kind of hegemony (that inscribed in colonial archives) may simply be replaced by others (those inscribed in the authoritative imaginings of non-Maroon writers of creative fiction).

Surely, in imagining Jamaica's Maroons, it is time to give greater consideration to how they imagine themselves. In this spirit, let us listen, in the pages that follow, to some of those Maroon descendants whose voices have so rarely been heard in written conversations about the Maroon past and its significance in the present.

Part 2

3

Leaving and Recalling Africa

Long before the first prophets of Rastafari dreamt of repatriation, the Maroons wore the badge of their ancestry with a defiant sense of pride. All through Jamaica's tortured past, those living free in the hills had kept alive the idea of Africa. After the abolition of slavery, while the missionaries and other agents of colonialism tried their best to stamp out any remaining vestiges of African culture, the Maroons continued to provide Jamaica's masses with an alternative vision. That relatively few Jamaicans ever actually visited any of the Maroon settlements mattered little; it was enough to know that in these legendary mountain strongholds, it was sons and daughters of Africa, not British colonial authorities, who proudly ruled.

For many years, popular thinking about Maroon autonomy helped perpetuate an idealized image of the post-treaty communities as bastions of unadulterated "African culture." It was widely believed that these "indomitable warriors," hidden in the imagined pristine isolation of Jamaica's most remote backlands, had preserved intact the ancestral culture that others had lost. Only recently has a postcolonial countermyth—the notion that the total assimilation of Maroons into the wider population is a fait accompli—begun to compete with this older, more romantic view. Both images remain potent in Jamaica, sometimes coexisting paradoxically within the same minds. Nevertheless, for most Jamaicans, the mythic image of Maroons as champions of "African survival" remains the dominant one. Like the distant continent of Africa itself, the Maroons have become, at least for some of their fellow countrymen, national icons of a lost identity waiting to be reclaimed.

For Maroons themselves, the idea of Africa has a somewhat different resonance than for most other Jamaicans—one that is more focused and, in some ways, more personal. For them, Africa is not only a distant land of origin, but also the ultimate source of the Kromanti spiritual powers that assured their ancestors victory in the war against the British. Maroons today maintain close spiritual ties to these ancestors and powers through an African-derived religious cosmology that continues to underpin their collective identity. Perhaps because of this continuing linkage with the spirits of their African ancestors, more traditional Maroons tend not to share the sense of loss and alienation from an African past felt by many other Jamaicans.

Perhaps for the same reason, Maroons generally show no ideological aversion to cultural forms that they recognize as being of European provenance. Observers with more than a passing knowledge of Maroons sometimes find it paradoxical that peoples so widely viewed as paragons of "African survival" should have embraced so much of the European-derived portion of Jamaica's colonial cultural heritage, ranging from British surnames to quadrille dancing. But most Maroons see no reason to feel that selective adoption of such "Europeanisms" over the generations has done anything to diminish the authenticity of their African pedigree. This lack of ideological purism has exposed Maroons to occasional criticism from more rigid exponents of Black nationalism, to which they respond with criticisms of their own.

Indeed, the antagonism expressed by many Maroon "traditionalists" toward Rastafarian ideology during the height of the Rasta cultural renaissance of the 1970s stemmed from what some Maroons saw as a fundamental lack of authenticity in certain components of the Rasta worldview. Maroon elders, some of them devout religious specialists who viewed themselves as latter-day Kromanti warriors, were quick to point out that the Maroons had *always* recognized and taken pride in their African identity. This knowledge of self had been acquired directly from their ancestors, from one generation to the next, and not from a distant Ethiopian monarch whose version of African culture, as purveyed by Bible-quoting Rastas, seemed to them very far removed from the still-living African cultural and spiritual legacy handed down directly from the "first-time" Maroons.[1]

Such ideological considerations aside, the Maroons clearly belong to the same complex creole world inhabited by other Jamaicans. As Barbara Kopytoff (1976) has shown, the distinctive ethnic identity of Jamaican Maroons developed through a historical process of creolization that drew on a variety of African pasts, producing a cultural amalgam that was new and unique. As a new people who came into being in Jamaica, the Maroons might be expected to focus in their oral traditions not on the continent from which their ancestors were stolen, but rather, on local historical events that played a crucial part in their ethnogenesis. And such is the case.

As we shall see in later chapters, among the most important local events depicted in historical narratives today are the two peace treaties made by the Maroons' ancestors and the British in 1739, which have come to serve not only as "origin myths" of a sort, but also as "sacred charters" of the Maroons' right to exist as a separate people within the Jamaican state (Kopytoff 1979). Given the primordial significance of the treaties, it is not surprising that few of the specific historical episodes or persons mentioned in Maroon oral traditions today can be placed much farther back in time than the watershed period leading up to 1739. As Kopytoff (1979: 52) states, "when Maroons today speak of the 'first time Maroons,' they mean not the first escapees from the plantations, but the people who won them the treaties, some eighty years after the Maroons had begun to collect in the interior of Jamaica"—a point also made by Werner Zips (1999a: 118).

Yet, to say that the Maroons are unaware of an earlier time in their history would be to overstate the case, as several of the narratives in this chapter and the next attest. Presented below are a variety of statements that indicate the importance of the idea of Africa for Maroons. The first section [1–10], titled "African Beginnings," is concerned with the more distant past. While certain elements of the narratives in this section, such as the theme of flying back to Africa, can be found in the folklore of people of African descent throughout the Americas (Schuler 1980: 93–96; McDaniel 1990; Walters 1997), others are known only in Jamaican Maroon communities.

The second section [11–27], "Living Links with Africa," centers on the specifically Maroon idea of Africa as a series of distinctive spiritual forces or essences that live within Maroons today, having been passed on through ethnically differentiated "tribal" lines of descent. The personal sense of direct connection with an African past that flows from this concept of "tribal" descent is rarely, if ever, discussed in the presence of non-Maroons; as an integral part of the cosmology expressed through the sacred ceremony of Kromanti Play, it is not to be divulged to outsiders. Even those who make pilgrimages to Maroon communities in the hope of reconnecting with a lost past seldom become aware of this important aspect of Maroon culture.

African Beginnings: Leaving and Returning

We begin with two texts [1–2] that indicate the specific West African origin of the founding ancestress of the Windward Maroons, Grandy Nanny; the name of her place of origin has been preserved in a Kromanti song said to have been sung originally by the great leader herself. It would appear that only a small handful of Kromanti specialists have retained knowledge of this place-name (most performances of the song in question do not include it); only a few of these specialists (independently) provided information on it, while others had heard the name but seemed unable to explicate its meaning.

The next two narratives [3–4] link the ostensibly superior spiritual powers that Maroons still possess to strategies that enabled their ancestors to smuggle the objects and knowledge of African spirituality across the ocean, even as their enslavers attempted to locate and destroy the material vehicles containing these powers. In the first case [3], the English captors begin to kill off those Africans on the slave ship who are found with suspicious materials. To protect themselves and their knowledge, the remaining ritual specialists—those who would later become Maroons in Jamaica—swallow their obeah and keep it hidden inside their bodies for the remainder of the voyage. Upon landing in Jamaica, they flee to the woods and "shit" the materials back out. Armed with these receptacles of spiritual power, they are able to keep up courage and, by communicating "telepathically" with the land from which they were torn, to attract the spirits of their African ancestors and devise the spiritual and physical weaponry that will help

Figure 3.1. Cormantin (Fort Amsterdam), Gold Coast, 1704. Many of the ancestors of the Jamaican Maroons were shipped from this slave depot on the coast of Ghana. The name of the Maroon *Kromanti* tradition is derived from this place name. Engraving reproduced in Lawrence (1964) (original source not identified). Photo courtesy of Jerome Handler.

them win their freedom. In the text after this [4], Grandy Nanny herself ensures the safe passage of her spiritual knowledge across the Atlantic by swallowing a special substance that renders her mute, so that no matter what her enslavers try, they will be unable to extract any secrets from her. When she arrives in Jamaica, she swallows the "antidote," which unlocks her speech, allowing her once again to share her secrets with those who would become the Maroons.

In both of these narratives, the Maroon ancestors are contrasted with the "Bongo" ancestors—those from whom the other African-Jamaicans (including the non-Maroon "nation" that practices the Kumina religion) are descended. According to these Maroon narrators, these other enslaved Africans failed to take certain precautions or follow certain rules, and that is why their descendants remain less spiritually powerful than Maroons today. (The Bongo ancestors, for instance, talked freely with their captors, betraying their spiritual secrets, and ate substances that reduced their power, such as salt.) Because they were more strict, the early Maroon ancestors were so powerful that some of them were even able to fly back to Africa, while others decided to stay and fight for a portion of the new land in which they found themselves.

The second group of texts in this section center on this theme of spiritually empowered flight [5–10]. Most of these narratives state (or imply) that the Maroons, unlike other Africans brought to Jamaica in slavery, remained capable of flight because they refrained from eating large amounts of salt. One of the texts [6] mentions a specific Maroon, a first-time leader named Granfa Welcome, who is remembered for having flown back to the "mother country" when his fighting days were over. The following three texts [7–9] are related to songs sung in Kromanti Play. According to some Kromanti specialists, one of these songs (included in [7]) is about the same Granfa Welcome; it preserves in Kromanti language and accompanying gestures the memory of his voyage across the ocean, borne on wings like those of a bird. The other song [referenced in 8 and 9] is one of the best known in Moore Town and the surrounding area. It speaks of a "Guinea bird"—one of the original "salt-water" Africans among the Maroons— who succeeded in breaking his earthly bonds and joining Granfa Welcome and some of the other early Maroons in their return flight to ancestral soil.[2]

As the last two texts in this section [9–10] reveal, not all of the early Maroons who wanted to return were able to do so. Like the Bongo ancestors, some of these Maroons disregarded Grandy Nanny's admonitions to avoid salt and consume only "pure" foods. In the second to last text [9], we learn of two Maroon brothers who actually leave Africa and follow the others to Jamaica of their own will, relying on their highly developed "Scientific" capacity for flight. Despite the warnings of one of the brothers, the other one eats enough salt to have a damaging effect. When the time comes to fly back to Africa, the errant brother finds himself stranded in a land he had always intended to leave. Weakened by his dietary lapses, he ends up expiring soon after his still-powerful brother completes the journey home. The final text [10], in a mixture of Kromanti language and archaic Maroon creole, references another, similar Maroon oral tradition that tells of an ancestor who, because of a lack of discipline, was unable to make the desired journey to Africa. "If only I had wings," he laments, "I would fly"— voicing a sentiment once shared by many Africans in the Americas.

[1]

> ya ye yanimi
> Grandy Nanny come-ee
> Grandy Nanny come-ee
> ya ye yanimi
> mumma come-ee
> me bring gyal, me bring bwai
> me bin a Anabo

Where him [Nanny] come from? Anabo . . . Africa. Anabo him come from, Africa—a part in Africa, on de west! (sings):

> me bin a Anabo
> me come pon Toni Riba-ee
> me bring gyal, me bring bwai
> a me come from Hanabo-ee

Anabo him come from. *Anabo!* Boy ship him there! Anabo! Sister come from
Pringfil [possibly a Jamaican rendering of "Springfield"]—Seke—come from
Pringfil [in] Africa. But Nanny come from Anabo, wha' part Science mek, nearby
de river—riches—de Golden River, Gold Coast, above Anabo Hill. Anabo Hill
him come from, Anabo him come from. (sings):

> me say me come from Nanny Town-ee
> me come from Hanabo-ee
> Anabo is direct in Africa.[3]

(Sydney McDonald, September 4, 1978)

[2]

One [sister] came from Pringfil, and one [i.e., Nanny] from Anabo. Hear Grandy
[Nanny] tune: (sings)

> me bin a Anabo-ee
> > ya ye yanimi
> me bring bwai, me bring gyal
> > ya ye yanimi
> seh me bin a Anabo-ee
> > ya ye yanimi
> me bin a Toni Riba now

(James Downer, January 25, 1991)

[3]

De people who capture we—English people—they were pirate. So after we
come pon de way, we find out dem out to kill de wisest of we. Then, we begun
to hide what we have, as storage, that was good for we, [that] we get from de
old people dem.

It was twelve different tribe of Africa. And every tribe know something different. So, when it work that them have we to come, when them reach on de ship,
dem starting fe kill de wisest one dem in de midst, all those that coulda talk and
something really happen. When we find out who left, what we have, obeah
dem could kill we for, we start to hide it. And we swallow our own. So, one tribe
swallow fe-him things, and de other tribe have it put up, hide it all about ina
dem things dem.

De Maroon swallow fe-him own. When him come in Jamaica back, him shit it
out, and mek a bag, and put it in there, and carry it with him, from ground to
ground wha' him a fight pon. And him a plant dem. And him a get dem. You no
see it? Herbs. Him get herbs. So, after him come now, him get fe-him something
and shit dem out first, and him get de first freedom fe go ina de first wood, fe
go try out him something. Him in here a wood a tan so, and him a go try out
him weapon dem, if dem good again. Him start to sing now. Well, him no know
everything then wha' him eat will affect there too, but dem had was to hide

dem. And dem was de best hider. And it all inside dem belly. So him start to sing now, back to home, by telepathic. Back to home, back to Africa, telepathic. So him a go sing now. Him say—him get him drum, and him goat, and him skin and something, and him fix up—and him start to play now. (sings, while drumming lightly with his fingers):

> me nyam penny royal, woi
> me eat penny royal-oo
> me nyam penny royal-oo
> me mumma no know, poor me-oo
>
> me eat Guinea seed, poor me-oo
> me eat Guinea seed, poor me-oo
> me eat Guinea seed, poor me-oo
> me mumma no know, poor me-oy
>
> me mumma no know, wai-oo
> me mumma no know, wai-oo
> me mumma no know, wai-oo
> me belly da grow-oy
>
> me belly da grow, poor me-oo
> me belly da grow, poor me-oo
> me belly da grow, poor me-oy
> me mumma no know-ee

And then dem spirit come. Because de thing wha' dem eat now, dem never eat it before. Dem had was to eat it because of dem escape. So dem belly feel different. So dem say dem belly a grow. And dem mumma no know, back a yard [back home, in Africa]. Yeah, dem mumma no know. When dem come out here and eat now, dem people don't know a yard back, so dem say dem eat Guinea seed, and dem mumma no know, dem eat penny royal, dem no know, and dem belly a grow. You understand.

Well, a right de so dem head turn [well, it was right there that they were possessed by the spirit]. And dem something, well, dem start shit dem out back, and get dem, and build wha' dem a build, and build one little ball with dem, and do another one, carry dem all a dem pocket, and mek one pocket. So dem no fight with nothing more than de pocket . . .

Well, de Bongo dem now, when dem tek dem drum now and start to play, when dem play (he sings, and drums lightly with fingers),

> gill wut a guma, quatty wut a lard
> gill wut a guma, quatty wut a lard
> me seh Jak-oo, Jak-oo, quatty wut a lard
> me seh gyal him walk-oo, quatty wut a lard
> Jak-oh, Jak-oh, quatty wut a lard
> gill wut a guma, quatty wut a lard . . .

Dem spirit can't come. De things dem wha' dem have, wha' fix build spirit, like this thing now that you knot to hold up . . . it well feel up, and spirit disinfleck [is deflected] and all dem thing. And nothing can't come out of it again. Dem magnet spoil. Dem couldn't do it when dem come here. It spoil pon de way coming, enemy spoil it.

(David Gray, February 19, 1978)

[4]

When dem coming ina de ship, I heard, dem never know where dem going, for dem never know Jamaica. Right? Dem only know say dem carrying dem to a island, but where de island is, dem don't know. You understand. So, Grandy Nanny now, Grandy Nanny sight de play. Grandy Nanny sight de play, and when dem deh ask him question, she never answer. When dem deh ask him question, she dumb herself.[4] Well, little do dem know. . . . Dem never notice say when dem reach pon de spot, him have another something to swallow that she can talk. You get that? When she coming, she dumb herself. But she have something with her, that when she reach where she going, she have a different things now to swallow to mek she talk.

She never want dem [the whites] to get de full experience or de knowledge. Is a reason why she dumb herself. Boy, dem question her too much. And she don't want dem to know him secret. You get that? So therefore she dumb herself, that she can't talk. And when she come pon de spot now, where she want to go, she swallow something and have to talk to dem now. Because she reach where him want to go.

Well, de Bongo dem talk all de time.[5] De Bongo dem talk all de time, till dem reach. But dem [the whites] couldn't get a word from Nanny. So that's why Nanny tek way himself from de Bongo dem. Him say de Bongo dem sell demself. That's why Maroon get to a different spot from Bongo. Bongo get to a spot, and Maroon get to a spot. That's wha' divide dem.

(Adolphus Whyte, June 15, 1978)

[5]

Some of de Maroon dem go way back a Africa, you know. When dem come to this country first, dem never eat salt. Dem eat no salt at all. And dem was strict. And de government couldn't manage dem. And some of dem fly away go back a Africa.

(William Shackleford, September 21, 1978)

[6]

That now [referring to the term *Chankofi*, here meaning Maroon] is a different nation of people. That one now no eat salt. That nation now, wha' no eat salt, can fly, and dem fly go back a Africa. One wha' fly way go back, name Granfa Welcome—fly go up, go a Africa. Because Africa a de mother country, you know. All Maroon come from Africa, you know. De foreparents dem come from Africa.

(Uriah McLean, September 19, 1978)

[7]

De two [Maroons and Bongo people], all two men correspond with one another. But is only one different thing with Bongo and Maroon. Bongo can't fly.[6] Never fly. But Maroon fly. It funny? Bongo never fly. But Maroon fly. One of de man that Nanny carry come here with him, when de man come a Jamaica and finding out de set up a Jamaica, him say him naa tan.

Him say, "me pikibo, me naa tan a that country here with unu, you know." Maroon man a say, "me pikibo, me naa tan a that country here with you, you know. Me deh go a me prandes back" [my child, I'm not going to stay in this country with you, you know. I'm going back home].

Because Nanny dem going fight war, and him say him no ina de war, him deh go home back.

Nanny say, "all right, massa, if you waan go, go."

Him say, "tomorrow morning, when debekri [dawn], tomorrow morning debekin [dawn], if you no see me, me gone. But ina evening, when you see one little dew rain fall, me reach in country" [when you see a bit of rain in the evening, you will know that I've arrived back in Africa].

When him going fly, de morning, de Maroon man do him hand so (flaps his arms like wings, in demonstration). Him say: (sings)
poi . . . a numa derenke ma du mi-ee[7]
a numa derenke du mi
a numa derenke ma du mi-ee
a numa renkwa du mi

o fambusu famba
o fambusu famba
numa renkwa dumi-ee
Him do so! (flaps his arms like wings, in demonstration, and then claps his hands once)—chock back a him country [all the way back to his country].

(Richard Barnes, May 25, 1978)

[8]

poor me Guinea massa
'ca me a Guinea massa
bwai, me come from de Guinea Coast-ee

oy-oo, me a Guinea massa-oo
poor me Guinea bud-oo
Guinea bud, me come from Guinea world-ee

ee, ee-de-ee
Guinea bud-oo
Guinea bud, me gone home-ee

Guinea bud-oo, me come from Guinea Coast-oo
me Guinea bud-oo, Guinea bud-oo
him gone home-oo

(James Downer, January 25, 1991)[8]

[9]

Two brother. And de two of dem fly from Africa come a Moore Town, under Science. And when dem land in Moore Town de brother give de other brother a command.

Him say, "now, you no fe eat no salt, because if you eat salt, and when we ready fe go back a Africa, you no going can go, because you no going can fly. A wha' de other brother deh tell de other brother. But de other brother now, everywhere him go now, anything wha' anybody give him, him eat. So him eat plenty salt. And it work out now, one of de day come now when de two of dem fe fly back to Africa. De two of dem get up de morning and prime themself and lift up dem hand (intoning the Kromanti words): "wenu wenu wenu wenu wenu, o wenu koko, o wenu wenu wenu, o wenu koko, o fambusu o fam tere."

De one singing de tune over here, him hand a him two wing. A wing him deh wing dem (flaps his arms up and down like the wings of a bird). When him say, "o wenu wenu," de hand say, "o wenu wenu, o wenu koko."[9] Him fly like from here so to me house there. Him drop.

De other brother di-de [was there]. "O wenu wenu, o wenu koko, o wenu wenu, o wenu koko." Him can't fly, him can't fly.

Well, all right.

De other brother turn back and say, "all right, man. Me already tell you say you no fe eat too much salt because you no going can go home back. And you wouldn't believe wha' me say. So you know wha' happen? Me a give you one little white dog, and anytime me land home today, as me land a me country de white dog will spin round three time and dead. Anytime you see de white dog spin round and dead, that mean say me reach."

And same as de boy come back, de boy mek fe-him capers, and away back to Africa. And same as me learn say him land home—"so ram," de little dog just spin round three time and just dead a de brother foot. And same as de dog dead a de brother foot, de brother dead follow de dog immediately. Heart fever kill de brother right away too with de dog, because him eat too much. Him couldn't fly, him heavy, him eat too much salt.[10]

(Hardie Stanford, March 5, 1978)

[10]

"O tíbibi an tíbibi, o tíbibi an tíbibi": one big Country [i.e., an important Kromanti expression]. Ai, de man say, "o pínya dáaku-ee" [a Maroon Kromanti expression representing the cry of a hawk]. Him say, if him min got [wings]: "ef mi min gat prába, mi da flei [if I had wings, I would fly]. Andu!" He! "Ef mi min gat wing mi a frei, bwai." Him come back, him say [speaking a Kromanti incantation], "o frei, da mi fa, da mi fa, da mi fa jo wízi. O Yénkunkun, o Yénkunkun shref-shrelf."

(Richard Barnes, February 2, 1991)

Living Links with Africa: Tribes within the Maroon Nation

As the texts below indicate, Maroons in the eastern communities, unlike most Jamaicans, can point to a number of specific, named African "nations" (which they most often call "tribes" or "races"), from which they claim descent. The Maroon concept of "tribal" descent, however, is rather vague, and is limited today almost entirely to older people who have been exposed to the traditional Maroon religion practiced in the context of Kromanti Play.

Those Maroons who retain a substantial knowledge of Kromanti Play believe that every Maroon, whether aware of it or not, is descended predominantly from one of the several ancestral "tribes" or "nations" whose names are remembered today. People who continue to speak of such tribes readily admit that because of a long and ongoing history of intermarriage, no Maroon today can actually claim pure descent from a single group. Despite such admissions, however, some individuals still claim to "be," for instance, Ibo, Mandinga, or Dokose. It is as though a single spiritual essence associated with a specific tribe could be passed on and somehow come to dominate in an individual's personal makeup, overshadowing the contributions of all ancestors belonging to other tribes.

Today the concept of Maroon "tribes" has very little, if any, impact on everyday social life. Notions of tribal descent and affiliation exist purely at the level of ideation. There appears to be no discernible relationship between these named tribes and actual social structure or forms of domestic organization in any of the present-day Maroon communities. Furthermore, even within a single, relatively homogeneous Maroon community such as Moore Town, where multiple ties of kinship and marriage connect virtually the entire population, understandings of the concept of tribal affiliation may vary considerably. Yet, the conviction that such "tribal" lines of descent do exist is widely shared within Windward Maroon communities. And though this Maroon concept of tribal affiliation may seem vague and insubstantial, it remains at the core of a complex and more or less coherent system of interconnected beliefs about the nature of the spiritual world within which the original Katawud (Maroon) people and their descendants continue to interact—the world accessed through Kromanti Play.

Implicit in the cosmology of the Maroon Kromanti religion, and linked to the concept of ancestral "tribes," is an elaborate mythology of descent. At the foundation of this mythos is the idea that there are *four* original Maroon tribes that go back to the formative period of Maroon society. There is little agreement, however, on which tribes these are. In fact, whether or not the tribes can actually be named with any consistency seems less important than the belief that there are four of them. Those that are named most often would seem to be Papa (also pronounced Prapa, or Prapra), Mandinga, Ibo, and Mongala (also pronounced Mongola, or Mangola). Other names, however, such as Dokose, Timbambu, or Nago, sometimes appear among the primary four instead of the more common names. Though many Maroon Kromanti specialists acknowledge that a number of other African peoples contributed to early Maroon society, the original four are seen as the most important.

Each of these four main tribes is said to have originally been headed by one of four early Maroon leaders who fought during the time of war under the founding ancestress, Grandy Nanny. Although there is considerable variation on this point as well, the four "heads" most often named, in Moore Town at least, are Swiplomento, Welcome, Okonoko, and Puss (all of whom are males). (As we shall later see, some Maroons state that there were actually five tribes and leaders at the beginning, but that one later "died out," after its leader betrayed Nanny.) Some also maintain that there were four "seconds" (lower-ranking officers) who served under the four "top leaders"; these lesser leaders are sometimes called the "four [head] Kofis," or the "four [head] Kwakus."

All Windward Maroons today are said to be Grandy Nanny's *yoyo*—her "children," or descendants. By virtue of birth into the Maroon community, they inherit membership in her tribe, the Kromanti tribe, which overarches the entire Maroon "nation." At the same time, it is sometimes said that every "pure" (*puropuro*) Maroon also descends from one of the founding male heads of the four main tribes and therefore belongs to one of these subtribes as well, all subsumed under the all-embracing Kromanti tribe. While membership in the Kromanti tribe is shared by all Maroons, it is thought that only a portion can claim to be, for instance, Ibo (with all Ibos theoretically being descended through male links from the same Ibo founding leader); and this Ibo segment is believed to be distinct from other such segments composed of Papa, Mandinga, or Mongala descendants.[11]

Part of what lends this mythology of descent its force in the present is the belief that African tribal names and paths of descent are closely linked with a number of the "English" family names adopted by Maroons in past centuries. That is, membership in each of the four main African tribes described above is said to correspond, in an imperfect way, to an English family name believed to have passed through the same primary lines of descent.[12] As a result, these family names have come to be viewed, much like the African-derived "nation" names, as labels of "tribes" or "races" of people related through common descent. (When

Maroons speak of "the Harris tribe" or "the Ellis race," this is generally what is meant.) Once again, there is little agreement as to which English names specifically match which African tribes. But three family names, in particular, are cited more often than others in discussions of correspondences between English names and the four main African tribes: the names Harris, Osbourne, and Ellis. (The name said to correspond to the fourth tribe is usually one of a large number of other common surnames in Windward Maroon communities, such as Bernard, Whyte, or Gray).[13]

The idea that members of the same tribe possess in common a kind of "spiritual essence" is implicit in the frequent statements made by Maroons about attributes believed to be shared by all those belonging to a given tribe. Some of these "inherited" tribal traits are seen as having practical consequences. It is believed, for instance, that members of some tribes should refrain from eating certain things, or else they will become ill (as suggested in some of the passages below). Members of other tribes are prohibited from drinking out of certain types of containers, or from cooking over certain kinds of fires. One hears yet other general statements about the different tribes. It is sometimes said, for example, that whenever a particular type of fog enshrouds the Johncrow Mountains, one can be sure that a member of the "Whyte tribe" will soon die. When members of certain other tribes die, it is said, heavy rains will always follow. Today, however, these beliefs appear to be shared by only a relatively small portion of the Maroon population (though one that is scattered across a wide area).[14]

Only in Kromanti ceremonies do all of these notions crystallize into a more coherent cosmological structure, and only there do they attain any real practical significance. Indeed, it is often in the context of Kromanti Play that Maroons first discover their tribal affiliations. One's tribe may be revealed, for instance, when a sympathetic reaction to the songs and drumming of a particular tribal category leads to the possession of a person by an ancestral spirit from that tribe. (It is said, for example, that when an Ibo song is played, people belonging to the Ibo tribe are more likely than others to become possessed, and several "Ibo people" may be possessed simultaneously.) Or, to take another example, a patient may learn his tribal affiliation only after the spirit possessing a *fete-man* decides that successful treatment requires a special "weed" (herb) selected to correspond to that person's tribe. In many cases, there will be little chance of recovery if a treatment does not include such a properly matched herbal remedy.

A still closer look at the Maroon Kromanti religion reveals that the concept of tribal affiliation is but one expression of a larger cosmological principle expressed through the recurring, almost mystical, number *four*. Even if there is little consensus regarding individual components (such as specific names of founding ancestors and tribes) or the precise correspondences held to exist between them, their abstract cosmological framework, consisting of several parallel sets of four elements, remains relatively neat and stable. Taken together, the various parts form a fairly coherent whole: as we have seen, all Maroons are said to be descended from *four* founding leaders (sometimes named as Swiplomento, Welcome, Okonoko, and Puss) and their *four* tribes (usually said to be Papa, Ibo, Mandinga, and Mongala). Each of these four tribes corresponds to one of the *four* cardinal points (east, west, north, south). It is also generally agreed that there are *four* primary categories of "heavier" (more spiritually powerful) songs, drumming styles, and dance movements in Kromanti Play (usually named as Papa, Ibo, Mandinga, and Mongala); these match the four main tribes and can be used to invoke the spirits of ancestors belonging to them. Finally, there are *four* primary herbs named after the four main tribes (Papa Weed, Mandinga Weed, and Ibo Weed are most commonly mentioned), and each of these contains a type of spiritual power specially suited to descendants of its corresponding tribe.[15]

This system of ideas around the theme of tribal descent has grown vague with time. Today at least, exactly who belongs (or belonged while alive) to what tribe, and what larger significance this may have, is far from clear. Not surprisingly, claims regarding tribal affiliation are open to negotiation. In fact, such questions are unlikely even to arise outside of the context of Kromanti ceremonies.

As the importance of Kromanti Play in daily life has waned over the last few decades, so has interest in such matters. Nonetheless, even today among Windward Maroon "traditionalists," this concept of direct spiritual linkage with ancestral African "nations" (through ostensibly unbroken lines of descent) at once helps define what it is to be Maroon and distinguishes Maroons from other Jamaicans. This cultural ideology belongs to that totally private, internalized dimension of Maroon identity that has never been shared with more than a handful of non-Maroons (among them a few probing and persistent ethnographers).

The last text [27], from Accompong, acknowledges that ethnic diversity among the early Maroons at times presented challenges to the quest for political unity. The narrator summarizes a well-known oral tradition symbolically embodied in the community's sacred Kindah Tree. This oral tradition continues to explain to present-day Leeward Maroons how their ancestors on this side of the island, under the leadership of Kojo, were able, despite internal ethnic divisions, to use ritual means to create a sense of themselves as "one family" acting together in the struggle against their British enemies.

Though long hidden from most outsiders, the mythologies of tribal descent that remain alive within the Maroon communities can hardly be said to have had no effect on relations between Maroons and others. At the very least, they have helped to ground Maroons' own sense of their distinctness in a primordial cosmology that goes much deeper than any politics of the moment. How much longer they will continue to do so, however, remains to be seen.

[11]

Hear me now, what I want to tell you. They all come here as slave. You have Guinea man, you have de Mandinga man, you have de Wusu man, and you have Prapa man. They *all* are from Africa. But they are from different-different district, different-different tribes that come down here.

(Johnny Minott, June 4, 1978)

[12]

The Maroons, they have got various tribes of them. And they talk Koromanti—you see?—one of the tribes of Africa. We talk Koromanti. And some Ashanti. Some talk Ashanti, some talk Ibo, some talk Dokose. Those are different tribes of the Maroons.

(J. T. Harris, 1960/61)[16]

[13]

You have Papa. You have Mandinga. You have Dokose. Tribe by tribe.

(Noel Lewis, February 4, 1991)

[14]

Remember, a no one tribe of Maroon, you know. A four tribe. Four tribe. But all of dem correspond to one. Every bit correspond to one.

(Charles Bernard, December 18, 1982)

[15]

Jankofi a tribe. Dokose a tribe. You have east, west, north, south. And you can't call south "east." And you can't call east "north." Everybody got fi-dem name. East, west, north, south.

(Hardie Stanford, February 1, 1991)

[16]

East, west, north south. A four pole. Four pole. A me ina de four pole. Me can't go a five. A four tribe.

(Hardie Stanford, February 7, 1991)

[17]

> ee—, Baimba ma Mankwaba
> Obronikwashi-oo, Kwashibroni
> Obronikwashi-oo, Baimba
> sinting de da ring-oo
> so dem seh

The tune is speaking of four different names, or four different sides. So it means that the four different sides is coming from the tradition of the four different generals, from top points coming down. [The four different names are]: Baimba, Mankwaba, Obronikwashi, Kwashiobroni.

You have four generals, having four tribes, and there are the four names there now that the man [who originally sang the song] is talking or singing about. That means the man is calling upon both sides [i.e., both the "lower" and "higher" generals] for assistance. [The highest four generals, who ranked above those named in this song, were]: Mento, Okonoko, Welcome, Puss.

(Johnny Minott, September 10, 1978)

[18]

What me know—you have Harris, Osbourne, Ellis, and then you have Minott. Then you have bystander ina it—waitamigls [white-a-middles] like Bernards, Whytes, and all those. You have Mento tribe, you have Okonoko, you have Welcome, and Puss. So those are de four leaders' tribe there so, with Nanny. Well, coming down you have mixeded tribe now. You have all like de Whyte, you have Bernards, and such like. And you have Downers and all those. Those are mixeded tribes.

(Johnny Minott, August 20, 1978)

[19]

Mento race a de Harris dem. Now in Moore Town, you may find twenty [true] Harris there today. But all [the others named Harris] do not come from de tribes of Mento. [Harris] a Mento tribe. And then you have Welcome, which is de Osbourne. [The Osbournes come] from that tribe. Then you have Okro now— you have Okonoko. Those are de Ellis.

Those are de three race leave in Moore Town [today].

Those are de four top man's tribe, when they talk about these four. These four things that dem talk, is four tune also. They are also four tune. You have Kromanti, Ibo, Mandinga, and Papa. Four of dem. That's four tribe. That's four tribe. You have tribes coming down. De songs made according to different-different tribe coming down. I mek a song, have a song made fe me. When my son come up, him can mek a song too. And that song belonging to him for his part.

We have Mento. Mento coming from de Kromanti side. Then you have de Mongola, coming from de Ellis side. Then you have a Papa, coming from de Osbourne side. And then you have de Ibo, coming from de other side. And otherwise you have whole heap of Maroon tune, and you can't place de tune according to find de race.

(Johnny Minott, February 6, 1991)

[20]

Now, [in the music of Kromanti Play] you have Mandinga, you have Prapa, you have Ibo, and you have Mongala—a that name you call Kromanti. De four of dem come off of de one: Ibo, Mandinga, Prapa, and Mongola.

(George Osbourne, October 3, 1978)

[21]

If de drum playing there now, every nation of Maroon have a Country [song], no? Every nation of Maroon have a Country. And if dem playing de drum, it playing there now, and de song wha' dem throw pertaining to your Country, you head turn. You know? If you a Timbambu, and dem throw Timbambu song, any song wha' Timbambu use, it just turn you. And you start dancing. If you is a Chankofi, and dem start to play, you head turn. So everybody have they own tribe of thing, you know?

Chankofi big. De highest dem a Chankofi.[17] You have as much tribe of nation of people, but you only have four of de head Kofi dem. But any nation of Maroon people have dem own tribe. Those four Kofi a de head of de Maroon.

Suppose you come from Timbambu, or you come from Dokose, or you come from that, or you come from this—you see, you have you own nation of people.

(Margaret Harris, June 1, 1978)

[22]

De nation, de tribe—when you going call a tribe, you call, talk fe-him Country [language]. Four tribe. Every man to dem own Country. Every man have dem own Country fe call dem. So when you going go call those people, you have fe call ina fe-dem different Country.

(Hardie Stanford, July 5, 1978)

[23]

[sings the words]:
      Me seh me a mini mini mai osei
Me come from many tribe. (sings):
      Me a mini mini mai osei
Four: Ibo, Mangola, Nago, Maroon. Four tribes. (sings):
      we a mini mini mai osei
      we a mini mini mai osei
      some a we a chanko bya min-oo
      some a chanko bya da, and some a chanko be
      a dedi wenkini
      mi seh o mini mini mai osei

me ha mini mini mai osei
chanko bya min-ee

(Sydney McDonald, September 14, 1978)

[24]

Him [an elder] tell me say [there are] many tribe—like you have a tree, you
know. De tree got leave, and it got all different branch pon it. Right? But it come
from de one tree. You understand? Him tell me all different tribe. Every one of
dem got dem own bush. You got Ibo. You got Chankofi. You got Mandinga.
You got plenty of dem. You got Ibo. Mangala. You got Ibo. You got Timbambu.
You got Dokose. You got whole heap of dem. Mongala, dem know dem weed.
And de Ibo know dem weed. De Timbambu know him weed. De Dokose know
him weed. And all dem know dem different weed, and how to differentiate it,
how to match it up.

(Adolphus Whyte, December 18, 1982)

[25]

Mandinga weed—Mandinga use that. Is a weed. Well, those type of weed now,
you use them pon de person according to him tribe. Because a that tribe, that
kind of weed that person use, with de fete-man. You use that weed now, if anything go wrong with him. Like you got a snake weed, or you got all some weed
wha' you tek it cure that type of people. Some people don't eat goat, for instance, don't eat goat meat. And is against them. Well, that type of weed, you
don't work it pon that person. You say you no eat this, you eat that. So there is
a tribe of people that use a certain thing. You got some people don't eat calalu.
Some eat calalu. And the type of calalu too, you don't eat that type. You eat
that type. So you use the weed according to the person, wha' de person use,
you use it pon him.

   Some tribe of de Maroon no use goat at all. We are a people that is what we
would call "allergic." It's like a natural-born thing, individually. It works with individually. It's not a general thing, in the Maroon set-up. You got some people in
de Maroon, you see, don't eat beef. You got individual [prohibitions] in the
tribe.

(Caleb Anderson, February 3, 1991)

[26]

You have all different tribe of people. You have some wha' no drink out of bamboo, wha' no drink nothing out of bamboo, like how you da cut a bamboo now,
a bamboo joint, and throw water ina it. Dem no drink out of it. You had some
wha' no drink out of nothing but gourdie, paki. Right? You had some wha' you
couldn't throw a drink of rum. Like how you come on ya now, you throw a drink

of rum ina one glass and give him. Him no want it ina it. So you have all different type of nation of people [within the Maroon nation].

(Uriah McLean, September 19, 1978)

[27]

When the Spanish freed their slaves, and asked them to help them to fight the British, after the defeat of the Spanish, these slaves, these freed negroes, who get freed now, they come to the hills. But what they did, they formed themselves into their tribes that they belong to, from Africa. Therefore you have different tribes within the community.

Now, for survival, they could not [have stayed divided] in their [different] groups, they could not have survived very long. So it was under that mango tree that Kojo calls all leaders of all tribes to sit under that mango tree. And under that mango tree now they form a pact, that we are one family, we are kin, so let us join together and put our resources together, and fight the British. Because we are from one place, we are the same people, we are kin, and we are free. So therefore let us put everything together and fight the British here, and see if we can win. Hence the tree was known as "Kindah": "we are a family."[18]

(Melville Curry, November 14, 1999)

Figure 3.2. Kindah Tree, Accompong, 1991. Photo: K. Bilby.

4

Captivity and Marronage

These Maroons seem ever hovering around the horizon of Jamaican history, keeping the Whites in a temper of hostility and the Slaves in a simmering feeling that their bondage was artificial, as the Negro was evidently quite able to sustain himself in joyous freedom if only the White man's greed would allow it.
—A. Caldecott (1898: 35)

More than a hundred and forty years after emancipation was proclaimed, as Jamaica prepared to enter the final quarter of the twentieth century, a haunting question exploded from jukeboxes and sound systems across the island. "Do you remember the days of slavery?" asked the singer Winston Rodney, better known as Burning Spear.

With Rastafarian consciousness newly ascendant, the time had come for the nation to face the brutality of its past head on. Burning Spear's call to remembrance was one of many politically charged reggae anthems that provided a soundtrack for the turbulent 1970s, but few artists matched the conviction and clarity of Rodney as he recounted the punishments and indignities endured by earlier generations. Alternating with the insistent question of the chorus, Rodney reminded Jamaica's masses of how "they beat us . . . and they work us so hard . . . and they use us . . . till they refuse us." Countering those of his countrymen who would just as soon consign so traumatic a history to oblivion, the singer left his listeners with a fading plea to "try and remember, please remember."[1]

The Maroons, for their part, needed no help recalling the ordeal of slavery. Their very identity was predicated on a history of resistance to enslavement. Indeed, it was through their liberation struggles that they had actually emerged as a people; much of their distinctive culture, including the ethnic label they proudly bore, served as a constant reminder of the long and successful war their ancestors had waged against their British captors. Though hostilities between them and the slaveholding plantocracy had officially ceased with the peace treaties of 1739, the Maroons could not forget the torments that had driven the founding ancestors to run away from the plantations in the first place; nor did they lose sight of the cruelties that continued to be inflicted on those less fortunate ones who remained in bondage up until emancipation. Though living as free people, the Maroons knew all too well what it was to live under the yoke of slavery.

If stories depicting the harshness and inhumanity of life on the slave plantations still arouse visceral reactions in Maroons today, it is because they remain aware that there was a time when their own ancestors, like those of other Jamaicans, were bound to this life and its immense suffering. While the shared historical experience of plantation bondage gives Maroons the ability to empathize with their countrymen whenever the horrors of slavery are recalled, this capacity for empathy, as they see it, is not reciprocal. In their view, those whom Maroons know as *obroni* (outsiders) can neither fully appreciate the special tribulations the Maroon ancestors lived through, nor share in the glory of their final triumph over those who enslaved them.

In this sense, Maroons may be said to possess a kind of dual historical consciousness. As both the offspring and the antithesis of plantation slavery, they are simultaneously of, and not of, the sociocultural world that emerged from this peculiar form of economic production. The narratives that follow reflect this duality. While some represent slavery in a nonspecific way that might apply equally to the ancestors of all Jamaicans of African descent, the majority focus on more specifically Maroon themes. Open acts of defiance, conspiracy, rebellion, flight from slavery, treks through the wilderness, new dominions carved out of the forest—these are the stuff of Maroon oral traditions tied to the era when slavery reigned in Jamaica.

Given the pride Maroons feel in their own unique past, it should come as no surprise that a minority of the texts that follow—those in the first section of this chapter—dwell on the abuses suffered by plantation slaves. Yet, even these woeful accounts of bondage and suffering say something special to Maroons; implicit in each such narrative is a poignant image of difference. After all, had the Maroon ancestors not escaped and fought to remain free, they would have ended up sharing the dismal fate of those who remained behind. The fact that they did fight, ultimately forcing their former colonial masters to acknowledge their freedom, sets them apart. This pivotal historical circumstance is at the heart of all the other differences believed by Maroons to separate them from other Jamaicans, a primordial "social fact" that runs as a subtext through every one of the narratives in this chapter.

Captivity

> Open the little slave book
> Run come take a look
> At our history
> Our culture
> —Burning Spear, "Queen of the Mountain" (1986)[2]

The stories that present-day Maroons recite about slavery vary considerably. Some stress the drudgery, punishments, and other indignities of daily life on slave plantations [e.g., 1–4], ranging from backbreaking labor, sometimes under pouring rain, to time on the treadmill making sugar; others recount the more extreme acts of inhumanity—the most brutal atrocities—perpetrated from time to time against those singled out for particularly harsh treatment [5–6] (a prime example being burial while still alive). According to the narrators, these are the circumstances that made life unbearable, and impelled the first-time Maroon ancestors to take flight, establish new communities, and maintain their freedom through military struggle. As already suggested, narratives such as these serve as markers of difference; they remind their tellers of the more overt forms of resistance that distinguished the first-time Maroons from the people who remained enslaved on the plantations and continued to endure these indignities.

This is not to say that Maroons do not acknowledge the attempts of those who stayed behind to better their condition. Certain of their oral traditions speak clearly on this question. There is, for instance, a well-known Maroon song [7–10], in which a disgruntled slave requests permission of a driver to go and talk to the overseer, so that he can complain and seek amelioration. He has worked for seven long years, he reminds the driver, and he is not a "boy." This and similar oral traditions acknowledge that those who remained plantation slaves did not always passively accept their fate, even if the majority did not resort to violent resistance. Indeed, as some of the Maroons' own oral accounts suggest, their first-time ancestors were not the only ones who chose to flee from slavery. But, as Maroons today see it, when faced with the severe hardships that permanent marronage meant (including the possibility of recapture, torture, and death), their ancestors were the only ones who held out to the end and fought resolutely to maintain their freedom. From a Maroon perspective, this different history is ultimately what sets Maroons apart from other Jamaicans of African descent. In the words of one of the Maroons who speak below, "de Maroon fight, but de niega man run."

Although many Maroon oral traditions center on hostilities between Maroons and slaves (see chapter 9 for several examples), others display empathy with those who remained enslaved and their descendants. A number of narratives sympathetically recount the abolition of slavery in Jamaica in 1834 (with full emancipation occurring in 1838); one example is included here [11]. Although Maroons are usually careful to point out that they won their freedom roughly a century before other Jamaicans were granted theirs, they have long shown their solidarity with the freedmen and their descendants by celebrating and commemorating Emancipation along with them. Narratives such as the one below, with its emphasis on the role played by the English queen in the freeing of the enslaved, represent for Maroons today both an appreciation of freedom as a universal good, and the understanding that the conditions under which they and other Jamaicans achieved freedom were fundamentally different.

The final text in this section [12] relates a memory of an incident personally experienced by the narrator, Ruth Lindsay (who was born in 1901), early in the twentieth century. It is included here because it demonstrates particularly clearly how different layers of Maroon history may be collapsed and interwoven with personal memories that continue to summon up deep emotions in the present.

This Maroon elder recalls how, in her younger days, while she was on her way to the coastal town of Port Antonio, she happened upon a group of indentured Indian laborers assigned to Windsor Estate, just to the north of Moore Town.[3] As she watched, a woman who badly needed to urinate broke away from the work gang and came running over in her direction to get away from the *busha* (white supervisor). But the white man noticed her absence. Catching her in the act of relieving herself, the *busha* began to flog the Indian woman with a bull pizzle whip, ignoring her cries for mercy.[4] More than half a century later, with obvious feeling, the Maroon narrator remembers how the scene brought tears to her eyes, not only because of her compassion for this woman, but also because she was able to imagine right then and there the humiliations her own ancestors would have suffered at the hands of the whites if the Maroons hadn't fought for their freedom—the same kind she had just seen the "mad *bakra*" (fierce white man) inflict on this "slave Coolie" (indentured Indian worker).

[1]

Ina de slave day now, de government wha' ruling catch de people dem, de same people. A two people now back then: de Maroon fight, but de niega man run, and dem catch de niega man now. When dem catch de negro dem—de other side a wha' we call "negro"—dem catch dem, and dem tek a yebeke—a goat call so, "yebeke"—dem tie yabeke, dem do it on de slave head. And de other word is "opete"—it mean johncrow—come down and nyam off that live goat, kill de goat, nyam de dead goat off of de live man head. Him have fe tan there. Dem tie up him hand. Dem tie up him foot. And a johncrow come there and nyam off that dead goat off a de live man. A slave, man, a slave. De slave master, de slave master [did it]. Because it was a slave, and perhaps some of dem don't want to work. You see? Slave meaning that you compell to work. So dem tie that goat now, and opete now come here and nyam off that goat off of that man there.

　　Slave . . . it hurt me. Because, see it here now. Right now, we are into a state of life where actually, [if] you want shad, you can't get, you want herring, you can't get, you want sugar, you can't get it. It coming back to de *same* stage. So whether de mama or tata, me want fe talk, me have fe talk, because it true. Because me feel it. Slave is just slave. And when a man disadvantage a man, him just disadvantage de man. And when you disadvantage a man, me *vex* with you.

(Richard Barnes, September 12, 1978)

[2]

Me granny tell me, him say dem tek dem, de live man dem, when dem no want work—according to how de poor man now a slave, dem work till dem tired— but dem slavemaster, dem wicked man, order de boy. Suppose him no want work. Him say dem catch de live man. De slavemaster order de worker man dem fe catch de slave man, carry him go up pon stick, tie him pon any tree, and kill goat. When dem kill de goat, dem tek de goat, and tie pon de live man. And de goat must tan till de opete nyam him off—that mean to say, when johncrow nyam him off. And a fe-me family now, me sorry. And when night come, de family dem wha' in there got a piece of that—suppose a fe-you family—when dem give him de food, dem hide piece of de food, and broke it, hide. A when everybody gone to bed. That person tek piece of de food, and go loose de man hand, and give him de piece of food, and wash off de something off of him hand, and tie him back. A so him have fe do with de man so till when de something rotten off of him. Well, a so de slave run.[5]

(Richard Barnes, February 4, 1991)

[3]

Me a give you one of de song wha' de slave dem dance [in] de slavery dem was passing through. Well, Maroon sing too, you know? Same way. (sings)
    so te, so te-oo, so te de day a judgment
    so te-oo, so te, so te de day a judgment
    That a before slavery abolish, you know? That a when de slave dem a dance to mill, fe mek tread, and fe mash tread fe mek sugar. Dem have fe sing that, say dem a dance de treadmill so till de day of judgment [until the day of judgment].[6]

(Abraham Goodwin, April 15, 1978)

[4]

When de slave dem wet now, when dem working in de rain and wet, dem have fe mek up big fire, tek off dem clothes and jump round de fire to dry dem clothes. Dem sing this song: (sings)
    fire, fire, fire, fire
    fire da bun-oo, fire rákita
    fire da bun-oo, fire rákita
    fai-oo, fai-oo
    fire da bun-oo, fire rákita

(Abraham Goodwin, April 15, 1978)

Horrors Escaped: "Massa, Me No Dead Yet!"

If there is a single orally transmitted "memory" among Jamaican Maroons that represents more clearly than any other the grotesque cruelty that characterized slavery on coastal plantations, it is probably the following story of calculated premature burial.

Figure 4.1. "An Interior View of a Jamaica House of Correction," c. 1837. Engraving produced by abolitionists on the eve of final emancipation. National Library of Jamaica.

The narrative that follows, told by a Maroon man who learned the story from his grandmother, represents a variant of an oral tradition that appears to have once been widely known in Jamaica. In fact, it may be traceable in part to an actual event, or series of events, that took place in the late eighteenth century.

By the early 1800s, a very similar example of extreme cruelty had already been recorded and encapsulated in a popular slave song, as shown by a contemporary published account authored by a British observer, John Stewart.[7] As an example of the excesses of certain slavemasters, Stewart (1808: 161) mentions a particular owner "who, when his negroes became useless by age or disease, ordered them to be precipitated into the cavern of a rock! This man was an incredible monster of inhumanity, and was so notorious throughout the island, that there is still a general song among the negroes relative to him, the burthen of which is a poor negro, while he is dragging to this horrible fate, exclaiming, 'Massa me no dead yet!'"

A decade or so later, in 1818, Matthew Gregory Lewis heard what was apparently a variant of the same slave song, associated with a similarly heinous act of cruelty committed by a slavemaster in the parish of Westmoreland.[8] Writes Lewis,

> It was his constant practice, whenever a sick negro was pronounced incurable, to order the poor wretch to be carried to a solitary vale upon his estate, called the Gulley, where he was thrown down, and abandoned to his fate; which fate was generally to be half devoured by the john-crows, be-

fore death had put an end to his sufferings. By this proceeding the avaricious owner avoided the expence of maintaining the slave during his last illness; and in order that he might be as little a loser as possible, he always enjoined the negro bearers of the dying man to strip him naked before leaving the Gulley, and not to forget to bring back his frock and the board on which he had been carried down. (Lewis 1834: 204)

Lewis recorded the song in his journal as follows:

"Take him to the Gulley! Take him to the Gulley!
But bringee back the frock and board."—
"Oh! massa, massa! me no deadee yet!"—
"Take him to the Gulley! Take him to the Gulley!"
"Carry him along." (Lewis 1834: 203)

Much more recently, in the early 1930s, H. P. Jacobs (1972: 11) recorded yet another variant of the same oral tradition, related by one Samuel Burke. This man's grandmother, who was born in 1818, had told how "once a slave was being carried to burial in his coffin. He was not really dead, and cried out: 'Massa, me no dead yet!' The master answered: 'Carry him go 'long!'"

The Maroon narrative below includes, in near-verbatim form, each of the major elements of these earlier recorded versions: the slave's desperate plea ("me no dead yet!"); the master's unfeeling response ("carry him go 'long"); and the additional demand by the master, adding insult to injury, to "carry back me board." That this Maroon version agrees so closely with these others would seem to indicate that this oral tradition was once more widespread than Jacobs realized.[9]

Though not exclusive to Maroons, this tradition has a special meaning for them. Their version differs from the others in that the victim is buried alive not because of age or infirmity, but as a punishment for willfully *refusing* to work. For the Maroon narrator below, the atrocious punishment meted out to this recalcitrant slave not only represents the offense to the human spirit that plantation slavery was, but also gives proof of the courage of his own Maroon ancestors, who were undeterred by the enormous risks entailed by open resistance to enslavement, including the threat of such horrifying punishments.

[5]

Me granny tell about de slave. She say that when de slave going on, there was a man. De man no dead. But de slavemaster order de other man dem [to bury this man]. Because de man won't work, no work suit him. And dem mek de man box. And dem tek de live man, and put ina de box. And de slavemaster order dem fe go bury de man.

De man *bawl* out ina de box: "me no dead yet-oy! Me no dead yet!"

De slavemaster say, "carry him go 'long! Carry him go 'long! And go bury him. And carry back me board."

And dem carry de live man, go bury, and carry back de slavemaster board come give him. So de slavemaster got him board fe tie dem down pon, and get man, de same slave, and dig de hole, and bury de *live* man. And when dem bury dem done, dem carry back de board come give him.

(Richard Barnes, February 4, 1991)

[6]

When dem ready fe ill treat dem, dem carry de slave, de woman dem, tie dem pon stick, tie de woman dem pon tree, and *beat* de woman there. And dem *beat* de woman there now, and *beat* de woman there until, when dem dead pon de tree, dem left dem there. Opete go there, go nyam dem. Johncrow nyam dem.

(Richard Barnes, February 4, 1991)

[7]

> driver, gi me leave fe talk to busha
> driver, gi me leave fe talk to busha
> driver, gi me leave fe talk to busha-oo
> long coat, no bwai ya-ee
>
> whole a seven year me work fe white man
> whole a seven year me work fe busha-ee
> whole a seven year me work fe busha-oo
> long coat, no bwai ya-ee[10]

(Leonard Whyte, August 17, 1978)

[8]

> driver, gi we leave, mek we talk to unu-ee
> come driver, gi we leave, mek we talk to unu-ee
> driver, gi we leave, we a talk to unu
> but long boot, we seh we no bwai-ee

(James Downer, September 18, 1978)

[9]

> whole a seven year me deh wait pon busha-oo
> whole a seven year me da work fe busha-ee
> whole a seven year me da work fe busha-oo
> long boot, a no bwai-ee

> driver, gi we leave fe talk to massa-ee
> bad driver, gi me leave fe talk to busha-ee
> bad driver, gi me leave fe talk to busha-oo
> long boot, a no bwai-ee

(Hardie Stanford, February 1, 1991)

[10]

> driver, gi me leave fe talk to busha-ee
> seven long years me da work

Well, that [song] come off of de time when dem did have slavery, you know?

One time dem did have a slavery. Dem have a certain amount of people wherein dem have dem in slave. You did have a man at Millbank, wherein him capture de people dem that is around de area, and after him capture dem now him have dem under punishment . . . kill some. That man was de name of Bernard. So he capture some people there. So now, dem did under de punishment of that man Bernard, under de punishment so till one of de time, one of de brave one really hear about how dem coulda get free.

Dem call that man now "bakra"—same Old Bernard, dem call him "bakra." So then him [the brave slave] throw de song now. Him say, "driver, gi me leave fe talk to bakra." Him want fe push, but him go now before now to talk to de bakra now and beg him fe release dem from de punishment wha' dem under.

All dem small-size one wha' no look manly dem, him [the bakra named Bernard] have men there that castrate dem. Because that one now no look bulky. Those now wha' look boldly, now, dem no castrate that one now. So like you da have a pig or so and you see him not looking as bulky, like him could turn a bran [boar], you castrate him and turn him ina barrow.

(Uriah McLean, June 23, 1978)

[11]

One morning Missus Queen write a letter to de slavemaster, tell him say him must let go all de donkey dem [i.e., slaves] wha' him got. Because de hour come now fe him let go dem.

De slavemaster say, "wha' you say?"

De letter say him must let go all de donkey dem—"you got dem too long." All right.

And de slavemaster say to de people dem, "unu go home a unu yard! Go home a unu yard. Unu, Missus Queen give unu free."

De people dem sit down. Dem no go.

Him say, "unu no hear wha' me say? Unu go home a unu yard, Missus Queen give unu free."

Dem stay sit down back, and fraid de man.

Well, de man catch some of dem, and *fling* dem out of him yard, and shut de
gate.

"Me say, unu go home a unu yard! Missis Queen give unu free."

Well now, when dem come out, and go along, go along, dem see de
slavemaster naa speak. Him go round. Dem go round a de road, and dem look,
turn de curve, and see say de master, de slavemaster, no call dem back. Dem begin to dance. (sings)

> dis is de year of Jubilee
> dis is de year of Jubilee
> tenk God, Miss Queen gi me free
> dis is de year of Jubilee

Then dem go back again, dem seh: (sings)

> no more, no more
> no more flogging
> no more
> no more half a hoe
> no more

And a de last one dem deh sing now: (sings)

> no more flogging
> no more
> no more half a hoe
> no more
> Missis Queen gi we free
> dis is de year of Jubilee
> dis is de year of Jubilee[11]

And dem *gone* a dem yard.

(Richard Barnes, February 4, 1991)

[12]

Bakra come rent Windsor property, plant banana and cocoa, cut trench. Bakra.
Dem carry Coolie. Slave Coolie. Dem mek barracks. All dem house wha' you see
out a de road there, a min barracks, a Windsor. Sometime a night-time you pass
there, you hear Coolie—ina night-time—you hear Coolie, "krok-krok-krok-krok-
krok," e grate off coconut.

One day I was going to Port Antoni. That time [in the early part of the twentieth century] we no min got vehicle, you know, we have fe walk. And I see one
of de busha lead de slave dem now fe get ina there fe go to work. And a Coolie
woman run off. Me going, and dem coming. And when me come right off of
one apple tree now—me can put you hand pon it—de Coolie was so want-pee,
de Coolie run [the Indian woman felt the need to urinate so badly that she ran
off]. Want pee-pee. Him run now fe go a de place fe go to, before de bakra, de
busha, come. And when de woman come run, as him come right where me
coming now, him just go dive right there so, you see, sah? And to me, mek me

tell you, a *pain* to me. Water come a me eye. And when de busha come and see de Coolie woman butu [squat down] so so fe go pee, him draw him cow-cod [his whip, made from the pizzle of a bull]. Him got him whip, hell of a cow-cod whip, a him hand. (She imitates the sound of the whip being wielded by the white man): "W-w-was-s-h! W-w-was-s-h!" De Coolie have fe jump so, catch up, hold up so, run. (Imitating an "Indian accent"): "Lawd, busha! Busha!"

When me go, me say, "Lawd, Massa God, help dem deh Coolie fe mek fe-dem slave up" [Lord God, help those Indians get their slavery over with]. Because me just *imagine* wha' dem [whites] woulda do de Maroon if dem no min fight fe dem freedom: wha' me see de mad *bakra* dem do de *Coolie* dem!

(Ruth Lindsay, February 1, 1991)

Marronage

> On the northside of the eastern end of the Blue Mountain range . . . lies the Maroon settlement of Moore Town. Every ridge of this portion of the range is alive with legends of the Maroon wars . . .
> —Charles Ward (1893: 77)

> If only the stones of the Stony River could speak, we would learn volumes.
> —Bev Carey (1997: 374)

As we have seen, the Maroons' beginnings are sometimes traced back to the African continent. But for most of those who speak in this book, the critical, defining moment in their history occurs when one or more of their captive ancestors decides not to work, vowing to fight instead. The first text below [13] begins with a theme common in Maroon (and other Afro-American) narratives—the deceitful means (in this case, false promises of wealth, also mentioned in [16]) used to trick the African ancestors and make possible their capture—but ends with the pledge of a portion of those stranded in Jamaica to fight until they attain victory over their enslavers and force them to send them back to their land of origin. The next text [14] similarly starts with a reference to the shared "Guinea Coast" origins of the enslaved, but concludes with the assertion that the ancestors of the Maroons distinguished themselves at the very outset by refusing to work, choosing combat instead.

An oral tradition associated with a well-known Maroon song [15] tells of an encounter between a complaining slave—a member of "Nanny's tribe" who is on the verge of running away—and a white overseer. The slave defiantly tells the overseer that he has been working from dawn to dusk, and it is time to go home to his family. But the white man orders him to keep at his task, reminding him that he is a slave. The future Maroon responds with a song addressed to his "brothers" working on a hill nearby. His song belittles the white man and lets the others know that he will soon be "robbing" the slave master of his "time" and setting off for "home" (a coded reference to his impending flight into the interior).

Other narratives [16–19] recapitulate the beginnings of new societies and military organizations—the initial banding together of diverse individuals into groups capable of concerted action. Ethnic heterogeneity had to be managed, a structure of command formulated, tasks assigned, and planning counsels held [16]. An autonomous territory had to be staked out and claimed in the interior [17]. Food crops had to be planted [18]. Relations had to be maintained with slaves on the coastal plantations, on whom Maroon groups relied for material assistance and crucial intelligence, and from whom they recruited new members [18–19].

Much like Saramaka Maroons in Suriname (Price 1983) or Aluku Maroons in French Guiana (Bilby 1994b: 155–56), whose historical narratives record details of specific stops and settlements in their ancestors' flight from coast to interior, Jamaican Maroons keep alive memories of their first days by roaming in their minds over the specific terrain in which the movements of the founding ancestors are inscribed [20–30]. This ancestral geography of flight is studded with place-names that have special meaning for Maroons—Grasset, Flat Grass, Cotton Tree, Lookout, Aja Pass, Sweat Hill, Kill Dead, Thatch Rock, Old Abraham, Barry Hill, Watch Hill, Back River, Besi Water, Kamanti, Bubby Tick Bottom, Bitter Water, Stone Wall—names that bear witness to the great treks of the first-time Windward Maroons through forests and over mountains on their way to the sanctuary they finally found deep in the interior at Nanny Town.

This sacred site is called Stony River, after the body of water that runs just below it. Few places elicit the awe that Maroons clearly feel when speaking of Stony River (Toni Ribba). The river itself is the most important of the inland creeks and streams that helped their ancestors find their bearings as they escaped into the wilderness. (As one narrator states [26], Grandy Nanny and her followers, like other Maroons, were people who "follow river." See also the section on "Staying to the River" in chapter 5.) As the strategically located stronghold from which Nanny launched her war against the whites, Stony River (in the more specific sense of Nanny Town) is viewed today as the place in which the spiritual power of this great founding ancestress is most concentrated.

The trek to Stony River [27–30] during the early eighteenth century is seen by Maroons as one of the high points of their ancestral flight to freedom. They commemorate it in song [27]. Their accounts of the journey are filled with stories of the miracles that unfolded as the ancestors came closer to their providential destination. The two final narratives in this section [29–30] center on one such story. Two "brothers" have fled slavery. One has reached Stony River (Nanny Town), and the other is on his way. The one who is still on the run reaches a particularly difficult spot on the Back River (a tributary of the Rio Grande that leads to the Stony River). The raging waters caused by heavy rains have made it impossible to cross. He calls upon God and his ancestors, and, with the help of his *jege* (oracle bundle), like Moses parting the Red Sea, he changes the course of the river, opening a pathway to the other side. Though still miles apart, the two Maroons are able to communicate by using the "Science" of their *jege*s, and one guides the other to the safety of Nanny Town. There, under orders from Nanny, the two begin to construct a rectangular "stone wall," marking out a space in which the resolve of her future soldiers will be tested for the battles that lie ahead. Soon they are joined by other escapees, who help them complete the wall.

The rather unremarkable-looking structure that Maroons today know as Stone Wall is one of the very few manifestations of human occupation to have survived on the surface at the Nanny Town site, which was abandoned more than two and a half centuries ago, following a prolonged siege by British colonial troops. Though only a handful of present-day Maroons have actually seen this assemblage of stones, many know of it and its sacred qualities. It is sometimes spoken of as "Nanny's house," and is regarded by them with a reverence that is difficult for most non-Maroons to fathom.[12] Unlike the handful of *obroni* who have managed to visit this remote site over the last century, Nanny's children know that concentrated within the four walls of this unprepossessing stone edifice is a living vestige of the spiritual Science that led her and the other first-time ancestors, after many years of flight and struggle, to their final victory.

[13]

Dem [the whites] go way, go a Africa, go tell de African dem say dem find out a piece of land, [that] de sea have end. And nothing deh pon de tree dem but money. So dem must come go with dem, go pick off money. So dem even got de sing say, "bakra come ya, him seh go pick money, money deh pon de tree." Dem got de sing. And when him come now, dem carry dem axe and pick and dem thing—and dem no know—ina de ship. And when dem board out de ship now, dem give dem, say dem must go fall tree. And dem turn back. De African dem *can't* go again, because dem can't cross sea fe come a dem land. Then dem left dem ina wood. Well, some say dem will work. Some say dem naa work. Dem a fight. Because dem *must* have fe go back a dem land. Some say dem can't—dem n'e go back. Dem will work. Well, dem turn slave. Dem tek dem fe slave. And then de other balance of dem will fight fe victory, *must* fight fe dem send back.

(Ruth Lindsay, February 1, 1991)

[14]

De whole of dem come here as slave. De whole of dem come here as slave. Dem come from Guinea Coast. Spaniard carry dem come here. And after de Englishman come to fight de Spaniard for to take de country, after de Englishman tek de country, you know, a body of dem say, "well, boy, me naa work no more a slaving, you know." Well, some say dem will work. And some say, "me naa work." So that's how de fight start. That's where it start. When generally de fight going on, you have others run way, de slave, leave and come and join dem too, you know. Yeah, man, during de war. That's where it start. Because they did not want to work again anymore as slave under de Englishman.

(Johnny Minott, February 6, 1991)

[15]

    John, Kwako, Buke, me da go me ways-ee
    little bit a wiza, bwai, we waan go home
    John, Kwako, Buke, sun hot-oo
    wish we ha sun raise-oo, dasha, me da go home-ee
    John, Kwako, Buke, me say sun raise-oo
    sun dung a hill, dasha, me waan go home-ee
    John, Kwako, Buke, sun dung-oh
    sun raise a hill-oo, me waan go home-ee
    John, Kwako, Buke, sun hot-oo
    sun hot dung a hill-oo, look ya, bwai-ee
    John, Kwako, Buke, come we go home-oo
    come we go home a yard-oo
    niega mout-ee
    John, Kwako, Buke, sun raise-oo
    sun a dung a hill-oo
    me rob de dasha fe me time-ee[13]

Is a man what working with a busha man. Sun raise a morning, go to work seven o'clock.

When sun have fe go down a hill, [he] say, "bakra, time fe me go home." Bakra man say, "time no come yet, because a slavery you ina."[14]

[He] throw him tune to him family, brother dem [named John, Kwako, and Buke] up pon hill a work. Him say: (sings)

    John, Kwako, Buke, me de go home-oo
    likkle bit a busha bwai
    me waan go home, yaw?

Him say: lili busha boy, him want fe left fe go a him prandes go look fe-him obwato dem [little boss, boy, (I) want to leave to go home and see (my) children]. (Sings)

    John, Kwako, Buke, sun dung-oo
    likkle bit a bakra bwai, me waan go home-ee

Him say, sake of de little bakra man, him can't go. Because that time dem ina slave. So dem have fe tan there. Is a Maroon man throw de tune. He was a slave. He was in there. That time him a try fe go away. Dem a cut out. Because Nanny tribe no work, you know. Nanny's tribe no work.

(Sydney McDonald, September 14, 1978)

[16]

Remember, you know, when de boat land, outside St. Thomas parish, dem land
at different points. And when we land there, we find suma there which part we
can tuajina with [we found people there with whom we could talk in private].

[One man] say, "well, you, now, is man. Me naa work, you know."

Him [the other man] say, "boy, if you not really satisfy fe work, I won't be
working."

Him say, "well, all right, I going to back you."

Him say, "all right, I will tek you as my captain, me second."

So him call up church man, and say, "war a field now, brother."

Those time was bakra tek de people from Africa to come to Jamaica fe come
build Jamaica. After they went, they start coming up. They come at Breastwork.
After leave from there, they come along to Golden Vale.

After dem come to Golden Vale, then Nanny say, "now, listen me. Mek me
tell unu something. A nuff of we come a Jamaica."

You have Kongo come a Jamaica. Nago. I mean, is a mixed multitude of
people. Because de people want to leave dem country and come to Jamaica, because dem say money is in Jamaica, when they were coming in slave. This is
what they say they were leaving into from abroad. But when dem come in Jamaica, it was slave dem into.

De slavemaster have they wagon. Dem have to draw de wagon with all dem
thing, and they have de slavemaster back of dem driving. All right.

Nanny say, "look here. Kojo, me naa work, you know."

Captain say, "if you is de root, and you say you naa work, what you believe
can done?"

And him say, "well, mek we go fight for it."

Him say, "well, we no have no soldier."

Him say, "yes, we have soldier."

Well, dem call out, and de old lady start—de boiling house was at Golden
Vale—and him start battle up himself, back up himself, back up himself, back up
himself. And him find so many thousand soldier.

But she was under Science, from de Almighty—not [from] a man on this
earth. And when dem catch up now pon mountain, and when de bakra come in,
and de old lady wheel . . . (sings)

    wheel him-oo, wheel him, buddy

    oo, wheel him-oo, go wheel him, buddy-oo

    ladies all

    me handsome fe go ride bínasal

And o tonbaig [she turned back], come, and dem say, "well, war out fe
start."

And him say, "well, then, mek we go see howfa sonti tan" [let's go and see
how things stand].

And dem start work pon Golden Vale, going in, work going in, dig road. Dem
a prepare place fe de war. But muster ground [ceremonial meeting place, otherwise known as *Asafo Ground*] up pon hill there so was ready set.

Well, apart from everything wha' Nanny feel fe himself, him say, "bobo siyumande" [a Maroon Kromanti phrase].

O [she] couldn't fight de battle unless him send fe him brother, and sister, Fanti Rose.

Him come a tuakwantan [she came to the crossroads], him throw him tune, boy. (sings)

> a me an you, charmin-ee
> a me an you, charmin-oo, fare you well-ee
> hand de da rope, me dasha-ee
> braggin done-ee

When him turn around, him say: (sings)

> ee——
> run come beg fe me gyal, dasha
> me naa go home wid dem-ee

Well, dem a hold talk. Well, I never get de details of de thing, when dem go a Besi Water—over Back River corner there, Besi Water. When dem went there, something was talk.

(Sydney McDonald, September 14, 1978)

[17]

My Grandy Nanny is from Africa, Gold Coast. Her husband, Granfara Jo, landed in the island before her, and also Captain Kojo, Granfa Kwako, Granfa Witi-Oprako, Mami Jetu, Mami Dendentu, and Mami Grace.

When she come down in de island, she said to her brother Captain Kojo, "biamba shanti kotankoril, jang gusung greng" [Kromanti language].

Granfa Kojo answer back to her, say, "jang gusung greng, kusun kwaman ki mbebwa."

That simply mean that she want a place like a house to lodge in, and to have her private business done as a woman, then.

And Captain Kojo said to Grandy Nanny that she must go to his husband Granfara Jo, [and] Granfara Kwako, and Granfa Witi-Oprako. And they go together, an dem have fe go and live in de Ashanti.[15] They live in de Ashanti for a time, and after living in de Ashanti for a time, Grandy Nanny rebelled against de English government, that she won't able to work. She and her subject dem won't be able to work in slavery. She rebel, she have a rebellion started. And after de rebellion, martial law.

(Abraham Goodwin, April 15, 1978)

[18]

Those people now, those Maroons, dem would travel from Portland, and from Clarendon, and straight across to Accompong, and to other Maroon settlement. Is so dem used to do it. Well, after dem leave, when dem break away from de slavemasters then, at first dem used to have other slaves that dem get in contact with one another, and those will steal from de plantation, and all dem kind of things. And any set-up that dem a vote there, dem would tell de Maroons, until dem go deeper now down ina de woods. And dem start to cultivate dem food crops, fe keep dem. So whenever time de Englishmen dem now should attack dem village, dem would run from that place and go to another place. But dem always be on dem guard. De abeng that you hear dem blow there now, dem have it from those times. And dem have men now on hideout, like say, de village then is down at de flat, down a de hill foot there. . . . whenever time a slave get de chance, him run away and join Kojo and de other people.

(Thomas Rowe, January 7, 1991)

[19]

Kojo get a few men, as how him go and steal dem, him tek way de slave man, him tek way de slave. Slave deh right around, you know, there was slave right around. Everybody, every district in Jamaica have slave, de whole country was slave people. And therefore, Kojo and fe-him men dem go to where de slave was, a night, and him thief away de people dem until him get a few men with him, and start to mek dem provide, and dem plan.

(Geretius McKenzie, January 9, 1991)

[20]

You know where it start? A Port Antoni, at Grasset backyard. Grasset backyard, a Port Antoni, down a Port Antoni there. Hear what I'm telling you. Dem [the whites] trail dem [Nanny's people] from Grasset backyard, go right round, right round, right round and catch Stony River. They trail dem [from Port Antonio]. So she work from there, go right round, Flat Grass, Manchioneal, is right through that hill there, a there dem trail dem through, you know.

(Adolphus Whyte, June 7, 1978)

[21]

Nanny land, come from St. Thomas, and work St. Thomas a Lookout there—one place in there, dem call Lookout. Round down so. Nuff of de Maroon dem live there now, you know, there a Hayfield. You see? So dem cut so. Dem have fe follow him. So when dem follow him, and wha' him want—dem woulda give him Port Morant—him seh him no want there, because it near de sea. So him tek it from Hayfield, cut ina de wood, come down.

(Ruth Lindsay, January 30, 1991)

Figure 4.2. In the Blue Mountain wilderness, on the way to Nanny Town, 1991.
Photo: K. Bilby.

[22]

She [Grandy Nanny] work from Port Antonio, and go right round, go east Portland, and go St. Thomas line. She never go in St. Thomas. [She reached] a part
in St. Thomas, and she turn right back, follow de hill, all de time, follow de hill,
follow de bush, go through de bush, go through de bush, till dem come a Lookout. She build a camp there. When she leave from Lookout, she follow de bush.
Well, she reach Barry Hill. She mek another camp. And when she leave Barry Hill
now, she go a Watch Hill. My grandpa wife told me that.

   Well, when dem start from Watch Hill, all those hill dem go through, you
know. Watch Hill is one of de mainest town, away from Stony River. Watch Hill
was Grandy Nanny town. When sun is well hot, you know, Watch Hill burn
down, you know, without anybody put fire there. You ever hear about that?

   Well, when dem leave, [at] Old Abraham dem was station, de day dem mek
dem camp. Yes, Grandy Nanny mek his camp at Old Abraham. Is a *high* hill.
Well, him going to live up on that hill. It facing Stony River. At de time dem
fighting, Grandy Nanny, after dem leave everywhere, a there dem live, you
know. A where dem station. Well, after Grandy Nanny leave from there now,
him never return back. Him never return back.

(Adolphus Whyte, June 15, 1978)

[23]

When de soldier down pon dem, dem leave to Stony River, and build a tent, and dem call de place Old Abraham. Dem can see around dem. Well, after dem leave from Old Abraham now, dem go down to Stony River, where dem sign de treaty. A there dem end up everything.

(Adolphus Whyte, December 18, 1982)

[24]

Him [Nanny] started from Morant Bay. And him come through Baying Hill, that hill there we call Bean Hill. And him drop out a [Cornwall] Barracks. There so dem call Thatch Rock. After him left Thatch Rock now, him go a Moore Town. After him left Moore Town now, him go a Watch Hill. Listen me carefully. After him gone Watch Hill, him turn so. Him go a Maroon Town now, we call Toni Ribba [Stony River]. A de end that deh so.

(Richard Barnes, December 18, 1982)

[25]

Dem left and dem go a Stony River, a one place dem call Old Abraham. And dem build dem tent there. And dem still trail dem, right down into de yard wha' dem mek, de Stone Wall.

(Adolphus Whyte, February 3, 1991)

[26]

White man say, "you fe work." Grandy Nanny say, "me not working!" And she tek de river, follow river! She follow river.

(Charles Bernard, September 12, 1978)

[27]

> ya ye yanimi
> you go a Toni Riba
> ya ye yanimi
> you bring gyal, you bring bwai
> ya ye yanimi
> go a Toni Riba

That was de tune that they were playing when dem a march ina de town [of Stony River]. Dem marching going ina de town—Maroon. Because dem and de white nation dem deh fight. And it a come through from all about, and go in there and find him position.

(Uriah McLean, June 23, 1978)

Figure 4.3. Stony River, near Nanny Town, 1991. Photo: K. Bilby.

[28]

They had a river there that dem call Stony River. De white, like you there now—de English that came from all different nationality, but they join together—they were in their different nationality and heard about Nanny, and heard about how Nanny find herself so wise. Wiser than dem knew. And they would like either to destroy Nanny, to obtain her wiseness, or to have him along with dem.

(Robert Dennis, May 17, 1978)

[29]

Two brother. Dem left John Thomas go a Stony River.[16] Dem walk Back River mouth. [They] come from Hayfield, come down. Dem man who ride dem walk dem foot—Science.[17]

When him near [to Nanny's camp], tata pass de bundle [the elder consulted his jege], him turn him something so-so, him turn him something so-so, look pon him something, look pon him something so, him do so, say, "aha, ha. Look here. Something no tan good."

[This was] right a Back River mouth. Him tek him seke [jege] out of him pocket—a de same jege.[18] Him tek out de something out of him pocket and him do so, him say, "o Yankipong Asasi, o Krembe Tutu, Nyami" [invoking the Supreme Being in Maroon Kromanti language].

And him do so (points down to the ground) [saying]: "Asasi, no insho. Insho cut pon!" [Land, no water. Waters part!]

Water draw, left de big file ina de middle there so [the river waters parted, leaving a large, open path in the middle (for him to walk through)]. [He] talk to him foot, and him seh, "Go! Tell de old lady say war deh pon [we]" [tell Nanny that war is upon us].

That time, dem a fight battle, against bakra. Him go up where dem call Aja Pass. Him stop. Him turn him eye, look east. Him turn him eye, him turn him eye, him turn round and him look. Him say, "aha . . ." (sings)

> o simpo wai ako ma byada-ee
> o simpo wai ako ma byada-ee
> diamba-oo, taki
> bobo taki-oo, him chat-ee

De other [brother] did check yonder, you know. De other brother did check yonder. (sings)

> Besi-oo, brindo-oo
> wiamba Besi-oo, we no know
> wiamba nikya nikya Besi-oo
> because we a jimigwak-oo
> we a man-ee

Wha' me say to you now?

Him talk to de brother. Him brother tan there a Back River. One brother stop out here, and one gone pon hill, a place we call Aja Pass. A nuff mile, man, nuff mile, man [from Back River mouth to Aja Pass], but dem can talk dem language. You know, like how you and me deh ya now, we move with one another, then me talk me language, and you jege answer. Because if you got you jege ina you pocket, any time you talk any word here so, him jege start a dance.

Tek him out. Him ina you pocket, ina you pocket a you side. Tek him out, look pon him so-so-so, say, "Sheke! Honti?" [Jege! What?]

Turn him over so, him something, and listen.

Him say, "aha . . . oy!" Him say, "oy! Brother deh pon battle field."

Brother deh pon battle field, because him a come.

When de old lady [Grandy Nanny] deh a wood, you know, [at] that camp, a only soldier dem have.

Well, dem go up. De old lady send call de man. So when dem go up a Kamanti, you have one place dem call Bubby Tick Bottom. [He] tek out him something, turn so, him say, "well, bakra a come. Yes, mek we go, go set something to am, a Bitter Water!"

You hear dem sing that same tune there: (sings)

> Bitter Water come down, me can't cross-ee
> de Bitter Water muddy-oo, how me fe go home-ee?
> Bitter Water come down-oo, me can't cross-oo
> maka [thorn] tear off me gown tail, you ting hard

Dem deh language, you know—those are big people that we tek learning from. Your head grow with those people.

(Sydney McDonald, September 4, 1978)

Figure 4.4. Stone Wall ("Nanny House"), Nanny Town. Photo taken shortly after overgrowth was cleared for an archaeological expedition, 1991. Photo: K. Bilby.

[30]

A man run from Golden Vale ina de forest. And when him come from Golden Vale, him run across a river dem call name Back River. And when him run cross Back River—it bite me, man![19]—when him run cross Back River, that time him a run from de same martial law fight. And when him come, him run a Back River. And Back River run out ina Rio Grande. And when him run there, him Science [i.e., his jege] drop out of him pocket, and drop ina Back River so, "wap!" It turn de river same place! Up to now, de river turn. It turn way, like how me and you ina house here, it turn way from you, ina de wood there, and tek fe-him own path a world. And de man go over. And when de man go over, de man stand up, and him look pon it. Him look pon it. Him stand up. Him say, "o jet knot, jet knot, jet get cut, an náatid náatid náati yebrém get go dong go wáka" [a Kromanti incantation].

And him gone.

Him run to a place dem call name Stone Wall. Stone Wall. And when him drop a Stone Wall, him stop there. And him sleep there, sleep till de morning. When him get up de morning, him see a next friend come off of de slave type. Dem build a stone wall, wha' dem start pon, build a stone wall, round and round. Not a earthly thing catch ina it.

One tree left a de stone wall. One tree deh a that doorway there.[20] And when him di-de [was there], de tree di-de [was there]. A that mek [that's why] we know him, you know. Him get a pint of red rum and put there.

And night, there so, you see nuff people come in, a run go a him same wall.
They build de stone wall that nobody can't go through, except de one doorway.
No room no deh fe nobody go through, except de one doorway.
(Henry Shepherd, February 19, 1991)

The Parting of the Ways: Two Sisters and Their Children

From then my whole body would quicken
at the birth of everyone of my people's children.
—Lorna Goodison, "Nanny" (1984: 127)

In the beginning there had been two sisters—Nanny and Sekesu. Nanny
fled slavery. Sekesu remained a slave. Some said this was the difference between the sisters.
     It was believed that all island children were descended from one or the
other. All island people were first cousins.
—Michelle Cliff (1984: 18)[21]

No Maroon oral tradition more clearly illustrates the historical basis of the ideological boundary separating Maroons from other Jamaicans than that of the
"two sister pikni" (two sisters' children). As I have argued elsewhere (Bilby
1984b), the story of Nanny and the variously named sister with whom she parted
ways is best understood as a mythic account of dual ethnogenesis.[22] Even as it
helps explain to Maroons and their neighbors the high degree of cultural overlap
between them, this myth recapitulates the historical process through which those
who remained enslaved on the coastal plantations and those who escaped to the
mountains developed separate identities.

     This process must have begun almost as soon as the first viable settlements
sprang up beyond the plantation zone. As Maroons built new societies in the
forest, their still-forming creole culture began to diverge from that of their plan-
tation-bound "cousins." As a result, a distinct Maroon variant of Jamaican culture gradually emerged; some aspects (as this book demonstrates) have survived
"under the surface" to the present. This process of divergence was later reinforced by the treaties of 1739, which imposed clear legal distinctions between
Maroons and slaves (Bilby 1994a: 79–83).

     The story of the "two sister pikni" neatly encapsulates this long and complex
history: the "disagreement" that caused the split between Nanny and her sister
represents the historical schism that created two peoples from what might otherwise have remained one.[23] After the two sisters parted, Nanny's descendants are
said to have multiplied in the interior of the island to become the Maroons, while
those of her sister populated the other areas and became the people known to
Maroons today (as stated in a number of the texts below) as *niega* or Bongo.
Though represented in mythic terms as the Maroons' "first cousins," these other
Jamaicans of African descent are also classified by Maroons as "Strangers," or

obroni; as such, they belong to the same larger category of outsiders to which *bakra* (whites) belong.

Enmeshed within the story of the two sisters are a number of images of difference. According to most versions, the Maroons (like their "mother," Nanny) refused to work as slaves, while other Jamaicans of African descent (like Nanny's sister) ultimately accepted their lot. The Maroons (like Nanny) fought for their freedom, while other Jamaicans (like her sister) did not. The Maroons received the "right teaching," and so benefited from better spiritual training than other Jamaicans. The Maroons maintained the spiritual power they brought with them from Africa by ingesting only wild plants and animals, while other Jamaicans lost theirs by eating the salted foods given them by the whites; as a result, Maroons are "strong," while other Jamaicans, in comparison, are "weak." Maroon healers still rely exclusively on herbs for healing and other kinds of spiritual work, while other Jamaicans use artificial oils and powders.[24] These and other images of difference have been primordialized by their association with this dual origin myth. They have become for Maroons an immutable part of the natural order.

The same natural order, however, also contains a built-in potential for temporary co-identification. For the long-separated "cousins" have maintained a marked family resemblance; Maroon culture shares many objective traits with Jamaican culture more generally, owing to common African origins, as well as creole roots that go back to the early plantation experience. These cultural similarities may be invoked, alongside the mythic tie of kinship embedded in the story of the two sisters, in those contexts in which Maroons and their neighbors wish to decrease social distance and foster feelings of camaraderie and mutual trust. "After all," a Maroon might say to a wary visitor to his community, "we are two sister pikni, we come from the same place, and to treat each other like enemies is foolishness."

One of the most interesting things about the "two sister pikni" myth is the way it has been extended in the relatively recent past to encompass another culturally distinct group of Jamaicans—those who practice the religion known as Kumina and identify themselves as members of the "Bongo nation." Centered in St. Thomas parish, not far from Moore Town, the Kumina religion (also known locally as the African Dance) parallels the Maroons' Kromanti religion in many respects. Although the African-derived ritual languages and musical styles of the two traditions remain clearly distinct and are traceable in large part to different parts of the continent (Kumina showing a predominant Kongo influence [Bilby and Fu-Kiau 1983: 65–97; Carter 1996], and Maroon Kromanti a stronger Akan influence [Dalby 1971]), there is much overlap between the religious concepts and practices of Maroons and Kumina people at a more general level. That the two groups have maintained religions more visibly African than those practiced by most other Jamaicans is itself a factor encouraging co-identification.

As Monica Schuler (1980) has shown, Kumina did not have its origins in slave religion but, rather, grew from practices introduced by post-emancipation contract laborers who arrived in Jamaica between 1841 and 1865, many from the Kongo region and neighboring areas. Over the years, as Maroons and Kumina practitioners interacted with increasing frequency, the story of the two sisters was adjusted and made to accommodate these newly arrived Africans, though their ancestors, in fact, had never been slaves on Jamaican plantations. Today, many Maroons, unaware of this fact, consider Kumina people to be the most direct descendants of Nanny's sister; they, like Maroons, have held on to a distinctive, community-based African-derived religion. Reinterpreted and "updated" in this way, the story of Nanny and her "Bongo sister" continues to provide members of both groups with a symbolic means of reaffirming their shared "Africanness." Whenever Maroons find themselves at Kumina ceremonies, whether as casual visitors or as invited guests, the theme of the two sisters is likely to be broached.

The narratives below are arranged along a sort of rough continuum, beginning with those [31–40] that stress the earlier period of slavery and identify Nanny's sister with the general Afro-Jamaican population, and gradually shading into those [41–48] that focus more specifically on the relationship between Maroons and Kumina practitioners (who are referred to, and refer to themselves, as Bongo people or Africans). The last few texts [50–52], grouped separately under the heading of "Bongo Voices," consist of statements by Kumina devotees themselves and are included here for comparison. While some of these reveal a distinctive perspective—one that is perhaps less flattering to Maroons—they also complement the Maroon narratives, showing that the myth of the two sisters, stripped down to its essentials, has become the joint property of Maroons and the Bongo people of St. Thomas. This complementarity now forms part of the everyday ethnic landscape within which Windward Maroons operate when traveling to neighboring communities, particularly in St. Thomas.[25]

In Kumina, Maroons have found common spiritual ground as well as a special "Other"—an Other whose views of Maroons in many ways complement and reinforce the way they see themselves.

I. Maroon (Kromanti) Voices

[31]

Every niega and every Maroon is two first cousin, two sisters' child. One fight fe freedom, and one run way. So is only two sisters' child. Every niega, every Maroon, is two first cousin. So a fool man going fool mek we deh fight one another [so it's only because men are going to be fools that we fight one another].

(Hardie Stanford, November 6, 1977)

[32]

Two sister: Fanti Rose and Shanti Rose.[26] One is Maroon, and one is African. One of dem wear a heavy coat [skirt], and the other one is a slim woman. One is African and one is Maroon. The African never fight, but we fight. They [the Africans] was stand-off.

(Sydney McDonald, June 26, 1978)

[33]

A min a two sister, you know. Same place dem come from, you know. But a only when dem come down here so, through Nanny say him naa work, [they ended up splitting up].

(Dungu Johnson, July 18, 1978)

[34]

There were two leaders of those type of tribe of people. And those were two sisters—de elder one, and you call dem leaders. They were two sisters, and de one was Grandy Nanny, and de other was him sister too. There were two sisters. One was Fanti Rose and one was Shanti Rose—de Maroon call him "Grandy Nanny," because of certain type of honor.

Now, in de days when dem come here, dem *all* was slave and dem *all* work here. But when de English man come and tek de island, and de Spaniard flee, according to de slavery, dem say, "well, here is ammunition. Fight for de country, for it is yours." Nuff of de Spaniards flee too—[to] Cuba, some [to] British Honduras and such like—[those] who coulda run way. But who couldn't run have fe stay.

Good.

Well, de two sisters met and they was arguing. And one say, well, him a fight. And one say him naa fight.

And I will tell you now as far as this—one say, "o biamba Shanti, o biamba Shanti, o kotoku, o biamba so brindíng." And him stop there so. And one say, "o biamba Ashanti, o biamba Ashanti, kotoku, o biamba so brindíng, seh o Shanti kotoku, seh konkondebá!" One says, him naa fight, for him don't like de shed of blood. One say him don't like de shed of blood, so him naa fight, him better fe turn slave. De other side say him will fight, right? And him going fight till de battle rotten. Well, a that side becomes de Maroon side. For him did fight and becomes victory.

That's how de split come. Now, after dem fight, and I becomes freedom and you becomes slavery, there are certain different type of rules now exist ina my freedom state [than] what exist ina your state, though we all are from de same place. That's how de *bars* mek now between both of us.

(Johnny Minott, June 4, 1978)

[35]

One sister say him naa fight, for him no like de bloodshed. Well, de other one say him will fight. That's how de separation come now. You find you get de Maroon different from [those] you da call de "outside niega."

(Johnny Minott, August 20, 1978)

[36]

Some come from Sierra Leone, and some come from de Ashanti, come down here. But all come in one, start a group, you know. That mean, they were not divided. When they come down here, there were no difference, for they were all slaves. For they come here under the arms of the Spaniard, not the English.

When Nanny come down here, it was not Nanny alone, it was she and him sister—two heads of a generation. So when the English come in and start, the Spaniard say to the slaves, "here is the country. Is yours. Fight fe it." Because dem couldn't fight anymore, so dem have fe run now.

Well, Nanny met with him sister and says, "well, now, let us fight."

Well, I have a section of people on my side, you have a section on your side.

Well, she [the sister on the other side] say she naa go in de fight, for she side never love de bloodshed. Well, Nanny say she would fight. That's how de split come between de Maroons and [those] who you hear dem say [are] "niega." Because one fight and get de freedom, and de other didn't. But that don't mean that de other side never got good tactics neither. The other side *did* got good tactics, too.

(Johnny Minott, September 10, 1978)

[37]

One day when they ready to fight, Nanny sister say to him, "biamba Shanti, o biamba Shanti a kotoku, o biamba seh brinding."

Well, Nanny say, "o biamba Shanti, o biamba Ashanti o kotoku, o biamba seh brinding, so Ashanti o kotoku, seh kunkundeva."

One says they don't like the bloodshed, so they won't fight. And the other says, they will fight till the battle rotten. That was Nanny's words. And we all know the battle never rotten yet.[27]

(Johnny Minott, September 10, 1978)

[38]

A Nanny and Sarah—Grandy Nanny and Sarah Opinya. Dem call him [Nanny's sister] Opinya. A big name dem deh, you know! We call dem [Sarah Opinya's children] "niega." Nanny now a fe Maroon. And Sarah a fe de Stranger.

(William Harris, September 11, 1978)

[39]

Two sister.

Well, one fly away back abroad. Me no remember that sister name—Grandy Grace? Him fly go a Bemandora.[28] Bemandora she fly go. She fly. She no tek no ship or nothing, him just clap herself and just lift up in de air, fly back.

And de other sister say him naa go, him a fight. Him leave de other sister here. Nanny. And Nanny fight. Him fight, and him fight, and him fight. Him have fe live ina bush, him and him follower dem, men and woman. Him no fight fe de Maroon alone, him fight fe Jamaica, inside of Jamaica.

Because de other sister was fighting one side, and Nanny fighting fe we de Maroon. Him [Nanny's sister] fight fe de country people dem, which a de slave. And dem was beating fe-dem foreparents. So she couldn't stand it, she fly way.

And Nanny fight and get freedom. So de freedom is not fe we alone. Because if fe-dem woman didn't gone way, she woulda fight fe dem, but him couldn't stand de fighting, so she flew away. And Nanny still remain and fight, till dem get freedom. So all those wha' did a slave, dem come over to she. Dem beat dem and so, you know?—dem foreparents—flog dem. So she left dem, couldn't stand it. But Nanny stand to de war, and to de fight.

When she [Nanny's sister] going away now, she [Nanny] sing: (sings)

    me a ribba janga [crayfish]
        kelembe[29]
    me name riechel
        kelembe
    me live under stone
        kelembe
    me name riechel
        kelembe

She sing. This one, Nanny now, a sing, saying de two of dem come, and him gone and leave him one.

Dem [those who remained slaves on the plantations] was helping Nanny. Dem was on Nanny side. Both of dem. But when dem tired fe fight, dem leave Nanny *one* stand up to it. Dem tired. I don't know where dem go, but dem leave. Nanny one stand up now, Nanny *one*. Every battle, Nanny one stand up.

Nanny tek one side fe himself. Him tek him own side. And dem [the other side] leave him, can't fight no more. And dem leave, left Nanny one fe fight. And him one fight till him win de battle.

De rest wha' outside, after Nanny get freedom, every bit of dem get free. Nanny one a fight. And him fight till him win de victory.

(Elizabeth Brown, November 8, 1977)

[40]

You have two sister, Grandy Nanny and Grandy Nellie. When they came, one choose de sea beach, and one choose de river. Grandy Nanny choose de river, and Grandy Nellie choose de sea beach. White man say, "you fe work." Grandy Nanny say, "me not working!" And she tek de river, follow river. She follow river.

(Charles Bernard, September 12, 1978)

[41]

My grandmother told me that de African and de Maroon is two sister. And him say [one] go St. Thomas, and one stay in Moore Town.

(William Watson, June 25, 1978)

[42]

De Bongo and de Maroon must be from de same place in Africa. I mean, there were two sisters land in Jamaica, as slaves—de Bongo mother and de Maroon mother, right? Just as simple as that. De Bongo mother say she prefer to be slave than to stand de hardship. Because Nanny call her, and both of dem sit down and discuss matters, to fight against slavery. But after a couple of days, or reach a month, she say, well, she prefer to work as slave than to stand de hardship. Right? So Nanny go it alone. That was de only division.

(Charles Aarons, June 26, 1978)

[43]

Bongo [people] don't strong as Maroon. You know why de Bongo don't strong as Maroon? Maroon people scatter a wood. Dem name Katawud, you know— "Scatterwood." Because when Grandy Nanny was fighting, [it was] Grandy Nanny and Grandy Sekesu—two sister, you know. Bakra dem did want de Maroons dem were to become slave. And Grandy Nanny say fe-him people dem, him *cannot* mek dem turn slave. So him tek fe-him portion of people, and scatter a wood with dem, into a place name Stony River—scatter a wood with fe-him set of people. And de other sister wha' name Sekesu tek fe-him set of people and cling to St. Thomas. And then him go now, go raise up Bongo pikni dem. So we call those people now "Bongo." So dem call Maroon people now "Scatterwood."

(Margaret Harris, June 1, 1978)

[44]

Two sister pikni—Maroon, African. That's why I tell you say dem near. So de drum that play, if you know it de right way, you can play from one to de other. But is two different drum. De Maroon people use a taller drum, and they drum are very tricky. And they use things that you call "wedge." And they play it in a different form from de African.

(Nehemiah Johnson, July 24, 1978)

[45]

De tambu drum there now—is only two sisters' child.[30] One play Bongo drum, one play Maroon drum. A only two sister pikni. So de Maroon man dance off of de Bongo drum, and de Bongo man himself, him dance off of de Maroon drum. Because both of dem work with spirit.

(Hardie Stanford, November 6, 1977)

[46]

De Bongo and de Maroon is one combined thing, you know, is one thing. Is brother and sister. Yes. De Bongo drum and de Maroon is brother and sister. De same sing wha' we play in de Maroon as Country, is de same sing de Bongo play round there too, but only in a different tongue.

Is two sister of dem, you know, two sister of de Maroon, who trod with de Maroon. And one back down. And one fight for de end, one fight to de end. Grandy [Nanny] fight. Good. And de other sister, him name Grandy Sukeso. Him cut. A him go to de west. Sukeso go to de west. So him cut out of it. So that's why you find it coming that Maroon now call one of dem now "niega." Well, a just so it work.

De Maroon and who we call de Bongo a de same one African. That's right.

(Emmanuel Palmer, September 13, 1978)

[47]

Who we call "African"—de Bongo—get dem freedom first of August. Is what drum dem play, though?—de short drum, and dem sit down pon it.[31] A there dem get dem freedom from, first of August. First day of August a de Bongo get dem freedom, because dem don't fight fe nothing, you know, dem don't fight fe a *thing*. So Maroon against them. Like how you hate a man, then.

If a Maroon man a come here mek him [Kromanti] Play, no matter how de Bongo man a talk, him *can't* come a de Maroon Play. And if him come a de Maroon Play, from de moment de spirit change de Maroon man, him will damage him!—same like how him woulda damage you [as a white man] or damage anyone. Yes, because de two of dem can't agree.

A two sister, two sister couldn't agree. De first sister say: "me mama get me!" And from de moment him say "me mama get me," dem shoot him. A Bongo race. That mean say him born from him mother, and him shouldn't call that word. You *father* supposed to *get* you, but you mother *bring* you. You mother birth you, then. Because, a you mother feel all those pain, you know. But you father only *get* you with you mother. You mother bring you, feel that pain and carry come here in this world, to show people. But you father no feel no pain, so you father only *get* you with you mother. So you have to call pon de father, say, "me father get me," or "me tata get me," then.

If you say "me mama get me," you can't catch something. Mother is a weak side. Mother weak. So bakra shoot him.

A two sister. That woman, before de fighting, have some children. Those children wha' him have we da call now "African." Fanti Rose and Shanti Rose [are the two sisters' names].

(James Downer, June 25, 1978)

[48]

You see, [the] African—those people in St. Thomas, such as Arcadia, Soho, Pear Tree River, Leith Hall, Danvers Pen, and Whitehall, and around Seaforth, and back to Golden Grove and Dalvey—they sit down on they kyas [one of the two drums used in the Kumina religion] and dem [play], "pú-dum, pú-dum, pú-dum, pú-dum, pú-dum . . ." And they sing they song a different way from how we sing our song.

Our old custom of our old foreparents say we are all one family, we and de African is all one family. We is tie-up. Same [people] from de two sisters—Granny Nanny, and Granny Sekobu.

There were two sisters came here. Granny Nanny came and he link with his tribes. De other sister fell with de outsider—what we calls a "Stranger." And she dwelt there. And after she dwelt there, she find herself, by moving around, having children. We call dem "African"—"Bongo." Dem short. By moving around dem get a different language, and different movement, different teaching. But de right teaching is de Maroon teaching, because you can find it in de history.

Two sisters—is two different tribes. De two of dem came from Africa, came here, you know. I told you that dem fly. And when dem came to Jamaica, one flew to de English, which is de white. And one flew to we de Maroon, which is Nanny. Nanny came here, Nanny fought a hard fight fe we.

(Robert Dennis, May 17, 1978)

[49]

Remember, I tell you a two sister. Don't get away from that. Fanti and Shanti Rose.

(James Downer, January 25, 1991)

II. Bongo (Kumina) Voices

[50]

Me hear dem talk so, say dem a two sister pikni, de African and de Maroons. My older people, dem say Maroon and de Africans are family, they are related. My older people say that.

(Eric Minott, July 19, 1978)

[51]

A two sister child, you know. Well, one was Grandy Nanny, that's the Maroon. And de other one is Mother Ibo, a African woman. Two sister child. So, Maroon is fe Grandy Nanny, and we [Bongo people] are Mother Ibo grandchild.

We was warned. We was warned not to eat salt. But, you know, some can't bear hungry. Anything him got, him eat. But Maroon never eat, in de slavery time dem never eat, they feed on green bush.

(Rolland Bailey, July 28, 1978)

[52]

That's why they [the English] give dem [Maroons] freedom to live, and all those things. Because dem tell dem [to] feed dem [the slaves] on pepper and salt fe cut down dem wings, that they don't fly—yes, feed dem on pepper and salt— de African nation.

My grandmother told me that it was *two woman* come to Golden Vale in slavery days, from Africa. Thirty thousand on de first shipment!—to Jamaica, out a property, Golden Vale. Yeah. And when one sister says to him, "you will work?," she says, "oh, no." And de sister say to her, "if you deh work, work, and you will be called a 'niega.'" And she fly away. And that's why we have been called de name of a "niega," because dem is a slavemaster for that.

They all was an African, from Ethiopian. And she refuse from work fe Britannia—one of de sister. She ask her [the other sister] if she deh work, and she say yes. Him say, "you are a niega." And she flap her hand and fly away.

(Arthur McNaughton, June 5, 1978)

Fleeing with Children

For eighteenth-century Jamaican Maroons, as for all human groups, children represented the bridge to future generations. Quite obviously, social reproduction in these nascent societies depended upon biological reproduction. As precious and desired as children must have been to those trying to construct new lives in the wilderness, they also posed special problems. Infants, in particular, could be a liability to communities living under constant threat of attack. For the Maroons' guerrilla ancestors, survival was predicated on stealth and agility, and both of these were seriously compromised by the presence of small children and other dependents.

The several narratives making up the first part of this section [53–59] share a central theme, which I have elsewhere labeled "the abandoned child" (Bilby 1995). In this group of texts, a Maroon woman running from colonial troops is forced to abandon, or even kill, her crying child in order to save herself from capture and certain death. Faced with one of the most wrenching decisions imaginable—she must choose between the child she has borne and nurtured and her own survival—she opts for the latter. (In some cases, as in the stories about the children named Keto and Shedo, the mother is happily able to retrieve the abandoned child at a later point.)

Filled with pathos, these "abandoned child" stories not only exemplify the sufferings and sacrifices of the ancestors, but also invest images of a trying past with a strong emotional charge. Beyond this, they contain an implicit ethical statement about the paramount importance of ensuring personal and social survival at all costs, at the same time underscoring the need to act swiftly and decisively—as unfortunate Maroon mothers were once forced to do—in the face of the cruel dilemmas that this imperative may sometimes pose.

The second group of narratives [60–66] consists of variations on the more general theme of "fleeing with children," the major difference being that in these latter stories, whether because the child is still in utero, or because the mother and child have already been cornered or caught, abandonment is no longer an option. These narratives, in contrast to those in the previous group, end in victory for the Maroon woman, who manages to escape to safety with her child. In one story, she does this by sliding down a slope so treacherously steep that the pursuing soldier is forced to give up the chase. In another, it is the spiritually empowered fetus she is carrying that takes defensive action, shattering the sword with which her captor has threatened to cut open the mother's womb, and causing the man to drop dead. While these narratives, like the "abandoned child" stories, summon up images of a past full of tribulations, they are actually closer in tenor to the expressions of defiance and indomitability that form the subject of chapter 10.

The final narrative in this section [66], concerning the origin of a particular place-name, gives further evidence that not only mothers and infants, but also even the unborn, were among the victims of the war with the whites. According to the narrator, the name "Cut Hill" records a British attack that occurred in that location, when the invaders gave vent to their fury by slicing open a number of pregnant Maroon women with their swords, letting the unborn fetuses drop to one side, and their mothers to the other. Calamities such as this, as well as abandonment or loss of infants and small children during flight from enemy troops, eventually led the Windward Maroons to devise a military solution: as stated in the opening narrative of this section, they decided to place vulnerable women and children in a hidden settlement, called Woman Town, some distance from their main towns. This refuge for women and children is discussed in more detail in chapter 5.

Maroons are hardly alone in the passion with which they recall a sometimes painful past. All of Jamaica can look back with horror on the abomination of slavery. But it appears that only Maroons sing old songs and recite first-time narratives lamenting the innocent victims of a time when a mother might at any moment find herself fleeing through the forest with a burden that, though as precious as life itself, could in an instant call forth death and destruction.[32]

I. The Abandoned Child

[53]

Dem walk in de bush, dem couldn't walk pon road. Because dem a hide from bakra. When de woman have him baby on him back, if de baby say, "naan!"— when me say "naan," that mean say, if him *cry*, if him *bawl*—then him put him down.

When de woman a carry him baby fe go a Stony River, and de baby bawl, him put him down [and left it there]. That mean say, him naa carry him. So therefore a that mek dem put dem [the women] a Uman Tong [Woman Town]

(James Downer, October 3, 1978)

[54]

When dem left St. Thomas come around, dem go through that bush there. And when dem go through de bush there, that bush name Millbank. And when dem go through Millbank, and coming along, coming along, over and over, till a certain time, they stop. And when dem stop, dem have one little pikni—a little baby. Well, they were sleeping, you know? Nanny have de pikni, a little pikni, but de pikni can't walk, you know? De pikni can't walk. So when she were coming, dem stop. So de soldier dem were coming on. So dem get up and run a de night. Dem *run!* So de night tek dem. Dem go to sleep. Soldier were coming *down* on dem. Right. When they were coming, de crew a come down. Dem start to run. Dem start fe run. Because, you know, when a man a sleep and somebody a come pon you, you have fe run. That's right. So when dem run off, dem dodge now—hide dem hide off de soldier dem. When dem hide dem off, ina de night, when day da light, when dem cannot see nothing, you hear a sound—de pikni begin to cry. Pikni say: (sings)

po po po po po popopo Keto-ee

De pikni a bawl. But a fe-dem Spanish, a fe-dem word go that way. So when de pikni a cry, pikni say: (sings)

po po po o Popo Keto

Nanny hear Popo Keto voice. And Nanny answer, Nanny say: (sings) o po po po o Popo Keto

    ee—a wi ar-oo

    Popo Keto-ee

You know that tune? When dem a play de drum, you know, when dem a play de *drum*. (sings)

    ee—a wi ar-oo

    Popo Keto-ee

Well, after him answer, when Nanny say, "Popo Keto, a wi ar-ee," de pikni come down. Well, this word now mean to say, dem run left him, but a *all* of dem ina de worries.[33] That's right. Dem left de pikni, dem left Popo Keto. So after dem left de pikni there now, de pikni wake up ina de morning and a bawl. So dem answer him and get him in. That's right.

(Richard Barnes, May 25, 1978)

[55]

Him have a little pikni. And when dem coming through de wood, obroni come down pon dem, obroni come down pon Nanny. Dem coming with a force. And him pikni begin mek noise, like how that pikni a go on there now (referring to his granddaughter's child in the same room, who is crying at the moment). De pikni min a mek noise.

    Him drop de pikni.

    Nanny say, "ba, da pikibo tei mi fútu. So mek wi lego in. Tumára mi mei jet wan néda wan" [brother, that child is tying my feet. So let's let her go. Maybe tomorrow I will get another one].

    Nanny tek him, stuff ina one hole. De soldier dem come and pass de pikin, dem no see him at all. But while him stuff ina de hole, him [Nanny] darken de soldier dem eye. Because dat deh woman dem call Nanny a nothing but ina de spirit world. A no fool-fool somebody. Dem can fly when dem want fly.

    All right.

    So when Nanny come a [Cornwall] Barracks, just below Barry Hill—down where we call Barracks [today]—one level di-de. Nanny stop there ina de night hours. After him stop there, de pikni bawl, call de mother. Right there so now, Nanny find [the child].

    De pikni bawl. De pikni say: (sings)

    po po po

    Popo Keto

    o Popo Keto-oo

(Richard Barnes, February 4, 1991)

[56]

    me hamba-ee, o si one da-ee

    Shedo, poor me bwai Nana Shedo

me ha one daku man deh

You have *one* pikni, one gal pikni: *daku*. Fe-me old time people no call it "pikni' like how we call him, you know. [Rather, they would use the word] *dakuma*.³⁴ *Dakuma*. (sings)

o—, no si one da-ee
baimba-ee, no si one da-ee
Shedo, poor me o bwai, Nana Shedo
me ha one one o baku, a me all on deh
Shedo, you no sumin da-ee

[A Kromanti invocation]: Biámba, biámba, biámba Shanti kotoku, o kunkwándebá.

Bigi, bigi, bigi. Me hand cut. Me foot cut. Printing, a me one. Bigi. Biamba. Bigi. Dead suma. (sings)

me ha one dako, no si one dako man deh
dede-oo, o si one da-ee
no si one da-ee
Shedo, poor me bwai, Nana Shedo
one daku, me no ha one deh³⁵

De word mean, you have one pikibo. You no have nobody else, *one* pikibo. You see one da ye—dakuma—one no-more pikibo. One pikibo. Only and only one pikni, lost a wudu, deh a wudu, deh a wudu bere. Forest. Deep wood.³⁶

(Sydney McDonald, September 4, 1978)

[57]

seh me a byaku yau
o Shedo, a si one da-ee
o poor Nana Shedo
no si one dako ya-ee

That mean say, "a me one. A me one."

Me naa give you de whole of it, though. Because, we as Maroon, we say, "bush got ears." And when you get ina bush, a somebody di-de.

"Me a byaku yau"—that mean say, "me no have nobody." When me say "byaku yau," [it] mean me no have nobody.

De man name Shedo. I give you *half* of it! A *man*. Him say: (sings)

Shedo, o si one da-ee
seh hamba-ee, o si one da-ee
o Shedo, poor Nana Shedo
o mi a byaku yau-ee

That mean say a me *one* left. All of unu gone and left me one. Me werewu a mande pon me now. Me a call you fe come help me. When me say "werewu a mande," me mean to say, "see me sick deh pon me here"—me werewu a mande. That mean say de sick deh pon me. See me sick deh, deh pon me now. (sings) o Shedo, o si one da-ee

That mean say, you ask him if him no see me. (sings)

    hamba-ee

When me say "hamba," me mean if you no see me. (sings):

    o Shedo, seh me a poor Nana Shedo

    si me a byaku yau-ee

"O si one da"—that mean say, if you no see me, how me a punish, if you no see me, me a suffer. That mean say, me no have nothing.

Him deh way out in de bush. Him a walk out ina de deep part of bush.

Me [the lost child] say: (sings)

    hamba-ee . . .

A you [the child's mother, listening in the distance] going answer me [the child] now.

(James Downer, October 26, 1978)

[58]

Shedo mek Kromanti drum. Him lost ina wood. Him lost ina wood, and him find him piece of elastic, and cut cabbage skin, head it. And play him way out.[37]

(Charles Aarons, January 30, 1991)

[59]

So, me a tell you about de woman now. A de woman me a go tell you about, but me naa go so far.

De woman got de pikni a him lap. (sprays some rum, and begins a Kromanti oration)

O jo si mi! (sprays some more rum.) Kwádjampúni! (sprays some more rum) Go si kon tel, bwai! O tíkya kófi, tikyándi. O wérewu nánti, o wérewu jéfri. O jéfri jéfri. Mi a píkibo píkibo. Go si kon tel Gadamaiti. Wa mi kyaan du, mi kyaan du, an we mi kyan du, Gadamaiti wi du wid mi.

So me a tell you about de woman. De woman got de pikni. And de woman run. Him run, him run, him run, him run, him run, him run, him run. Him run so-till. Him got de pikni, you know. Him naa left it. *One* little pikni him got. And when him run, me say, him go to one place dem call Ants Nest Bump.

When him go a Ants Nest Bump, him stand up.

That a Maroon something you gone down ina, you know. A Maroon you gone down ina.[38]

And him catch to de Ants Nest Bump. And him stand up.

De pikni say, "nyeh! . . . nyeh!" (mimicking sound of baby crying).

And him look pon de pikni. And him run. A war him a run from, you know, fe save him life. And when him look pon de pikni, go fe go, de pikni bawl again.

And him hold de pikni by de two foot, and *tear* him in two! (laughs loudly, without humor, but with a sardonic tone) Tear him in two—hold de two foot—

hold dat deh foot deh, and hold dis ya foot, and tear de pikni right in two, and drop him there.

Him gone, left him, a run from war, you know, from dead.

And when him gone, him run, him run—him no know where him a go—him run, him run, him run so till him go to one place where dem call name Dunrobin. Dunrobin. And when him run there, him no know where fe come out. And him ina de wood, ina de forest, where nobody no know nothing about him.

(Henry Shepherd, February 19, 1991)[39]

II. Cornered with Child

[60]

We call him [a particular woman] Three Finger, you know. But him tie de baby here so (points to his back) all de while. That's why dem catch him. Because when him a run, that time de little baby on him a bawl. So, we got one place ina de wood there wha' him go down now, we call Three Finger Woman Tumble.

(Dungu Johnson, July 18, 1978)

[61]

There is a place [near] Moore Town now, a precipice. Dem call de place Owere Tumble. Is a precipice, dem call it Owere Tumble. Me no know if dem ever tell you about it in Moore Town, for me no know if de younger one dem know, but dem call de place Owere Tumble.

A woman have her baby in her hand so. That time dem deh catch dem fe mek slave. English man grab after her, with de baby in her hand, and she go right down pon her bottom. And she say, "hókro fi gomina máso! Hókro fi gomina máso!"[40] And when de white man look, when de English man look, him see her over de other side of de precipice there with de baby ina her hand same way. And all him coulda do is stand up and peep over de precipice. If him go down there him neck could broke. Him couldn't go down there.

(William Shackleford, September 21, 1978)

[62]

De spring di-de [is there] now. Dem call it Three Finger. You see? And up to now, de place di-de, with de rock. Is at de time when Nanny a hunt ina de wood. Because him can't tan [stay] out a outside there, him have fe ina wood. So, dem mek after him. But one of de woman did have stomach [i.e., was pregnant]. So him couldn't mek no run. So de only thing him coulda do, when him see dem coming now, him sit down pon him bottom, and roll down. Him sit down pon him bottom straight, and shove down. And so dem a mek after him,

him roll now, bare rock. And him run right down to Mattie River, one river dem call Mattie River where Rio Grande meet up. Right down to de Mattie River, go right down ina Rio Grande.

(Ruth Lindsay, January 30, 1991)

[63]

We have a place ina Cunu Cunu bush there. If you see that place, and you learn de history of wha' happen to that place, boy, it woulda surprise to you. We have a spring course, a hell of a long spring course. Straight down. And dem say a woman name Three Finger got him baby. And me learn say, when bakra mek after de woman, me hear say de woman just catch him pikni, and put a him shoulder so, and just go a de precipice edge, and just draw pon him bati, draw pon him bati, draw pon him bati, him never stop, draw pon him bati, him never stop, draw pon him bati, till him go right down ina de spring course pon de level. And him get way from bakra. Him name Three Finger Lagunanan.[41] Three Finger Lagunanan. A three finger dem say him got.

(Hardie Stanford, February 1, 1991)

[64]

When those war, Kongo Mother have *big belly*, you know. When those war, Kongo Mother have big belly.[42]

That time dem deh look fe all de Maroon dem now to catch dem to mek *slave*. Listen good wha' me a say, that you can retain it back. And, that time, a wood dem live, dem live a wood. And de white people dem, de white man dem now, dem hunt dem down like dog and something fe catch dem fe mek slave, when they did run a wood and hide.

And Kongo Mother, him got him big belly. And when him go way, she down a one spring, was hiding. You ever hear that? She down a one spring, and when she saw de soldier was coming, she run down de spring with de helluva belly! Right? And de soldier run down and grab her, run down and catch her. And when de soldier catch her, she got *big* belly before him. And de soldier carry her, and lean pon a stick like this, lean de woman pon a stick, and draw out him sword.

And him say to de pikni wha' deh a de woman belly, him say, "if you tell me you a wha', me no going kill you mother, but if you no tell me a wha', me going kill de two of unu."

Me say—listen good—me say, when him lean de woman pon de stick, him tek out de sword now fe *kill* de pikni [and the] woman.

And him say to de baby inside of de woman belly, him say, "if you tell me you a wha', you mother will save, and you will save."

Wha' de baby min say to him? Dem tell you wha' de baby say to de soldier?

Well, de boy ina de woman belly say, "me a man."

And him couldn't kill de woman, you know. De sword wha' him got, it break up—dat deh piece wha' him got ina him hand—drop out of him hand.

This tree [that the soldier leaned the woman against] is a dangerous tree, wha' him never know that him shouldn't lean de woman pon. Him lucky him never kill himself! But de poor woman never know. And him lean de woman pon de tree, same as him catch de woman, just rest down pon de tree. And same as him brace de woman, him brace de woman pon de direct tree wha' de woman fe go pon.

And him tek out de sword and him say, "boy . . ." Him say, "you a woman or you a man? I going kill you mother if you don't tell me."

De boy say, "me a man."

Sword mash up ina him hand to fart!

(Adolphus Whyte, June 15, 1978)

[65]

[An English] soldier lean de mother pon a tree. And that soldier now going kill de mother, you know, going to split de mother belly.

And him ask de baby in de mother belly, "you is what?"

Him say, "I'm a man."

Right?

And de soldier have to leave.

Well, de tree wha' him leaning pon is what we call a feril tree [type of Jamaican tree fern]—a feril tree, that him brace de mother pon. Him going kill de mother. Is a feril tree. De spring name Jack Mandora.[43] De spring where you going see him stand up ina de spring, de spring name Jack Mandora. And him lean him pon de tree, and talk to de baby, and de baby talk to him. Right?

Now, a hide dem was hiding, you know, when de soldier find out. She was hiding. Dem was hiding from de soldier. When dem find de woman with de big belly, when dem going to destroy de baby, when de baby call to de soldier, a hide dem was hiding. And de soldier search and find dem. And when dem find dem, after de baby talk to de soldier done, de baby tell de soldier that it will never be another soldier in this world again. And de soldier die. Directly him die. Right?

Well, dem [the other Maroons] took de mother. I don't remember de place where dem carry de mother to. But dem carry de mother. But de mother never die.

(Adolphus Whyte, December 18, 1982)

[66]

Dem call de place Cut Hill.[44] So de reason wha' mek dem call it Cut Hill, there were woman with dem baby, coming up. And dem [the white soldiers] just went, tek dem sword, and jam it so ina dem, and do it so. Baby drop one side, and de pikibo [young woman, the mother] drop one side. So dem give de place name—Cut Hill—through de soldier dem kill de woman with de baby. That's why dem call it Cut Hill.

(Richard Barnes, February 4, 1991)

5

Living by One's Wits

I never heard of any Party, whether of Militia, or Regulars, that could
stand against the ambushes of those People.
—Lieutenant Philip Thicknesse (1788: 106)

Even as we leave behind a century defined by images of unprecedented violence
and destruction, it is difficult to imagine the extreme conditions under which
Jamaican Maroons lived, labored, and fought more than 250 years ago. Nanny's
yoyo, however, experience no difficulty in summoning up this past. When visual-
izing the world from which their ancestors emerged as a people, Maroons today—at least those brought up in the ways of the "older heads"—feel no need to
indulge in conscious acts of imagination. Rather, they remain ever mindful of
what oral accounts—narratives very much like those that follow—have taught
them about the tribulations endured by the first-time Yenkunkun. Conditions
seem to have been as daunting in Jamaica as elsewhere in the Americas. As Richard Price (1996: 5) points out, "the maroon viewpoint, as we know it from a few
precious accounts, suggests . . . that the harsh natural environments of early
communities at first presented terrifying obstacles, and that it was only with a
great deal of suffering, and by bringing to bear the full range of their collective
cultural experience and creativity" that maroons adapted to their new environments and survived.[1]

Most Maroons know something of the risks and challenges facing those who
first fled into a largely unfamiliar wilderness. They know of the survival foods on
which the ancestors had to depend during lean times—wild plant and animal
products such as *cacoon*, *thatch-head*, and *busu soup* that are still eaten on occasion and remain important symbols of Maroon identity.[2] They know that the
foreparents harnessed the spiritual and medicinal potential residing in local plant
life, over time developing a unique pharmacopoeia that continues to be the envy
of other Jamaicans. They know that even under the best of circumstances, survival in the deep forest (*wudu bere*), then as now, presented formidable challenges and required special knowledge.

Rarely did the early Maroons find themselves operating under the best of
circumstances. As Werner Zips (1999b: 219) says, "generations of Jamaican
Maroons lived on the cutting edge of extinction." During the watershed period
leading up to the treaties, the hardships they faced were greatly magnified by the
escalating presence of a powerful enemy—in terms of sheer military might, the

most powerful in the world—an enemy that wanted nothing more than their total annihilation. Building a new life in the wilderness was exacting enough; doing so while under siege was something that only the hardiest spirits could bear. As Maroons today tell it, there was no middle road, only extinction or war. The sense of peoplehood that Maroons affirm throughout these pages was forged in the fires of this military imperative.

Not only did the ancestors endure, but they also gave more than they got. Vastly outnumbered and outgunned, they repeatedly vanquished the British forces sent out against them, as often as not taking the offensive in battle. Maroons today continue to credit the ultimate victory of the first-time people in their war for survival to the ingenious methods and strategies, both offensive and defensive, that they devised. These live on in narratives such as those presented below. Techniques of evasion; military drilling in the Kromanti fashion; surprise attack; stealth in both war and the daily round; disguise and ambush; sequestration of the vulnerable; dexterity in hunting and combat—these are among the examples of the ancestral "wit" that Maroons today still claim as their heritage.

The term *witty* is heard frequently among those trained in the powers of Kromanti. When Maroons use this word to describe one of their own, they mean to convey a deadly serious quality. To be witty is not only to be clever (in the sense of cunning and ingenious), but also to be resourceful, strong in body and mind, and, above all, spiritually powerful. As one of the narrators below, a female elder from Moore Town, says about the cacoon plant that Maroons value so highly as a survival food, "when you cut it and hold it in you mouth, you drink that water, and you feel strong, and you *witty*, and have strength" [8]. By the same token, when present-day Maroons "drink" of the knowledge of how their foreparents lived by their wits, they claim for themselves and their posterity a share of this ancient wisdom and courage.

Survival in the Forest

> The most important thing that the Maroons have that is separate is their primitive medicine. THAT IS IMPORTANT.
> —Zora Neale Hurston, 1937 (Kaplan 2002: 401)

Visitors to the annual commemorative festivities held in the different Maroon communities sometimes wonder what it means when they see that some of the participants are draped in greenery—a sprig inserted into a hatband or the folds of a head-tie; a leafy vine tied around the shoulders or the waist; or even an entire branch of some bushy plant sported as a sash across the chest. These are worn as emblems of the wilderness that provided the Maroon ancestors with a refuge of last resort. They also signify the spiritual power that all plant life contains. Behind each such bodily adornment lies a body of "memories" concerning the ability of the first-time Maroons, especially in times of emergency, to live off the

Figure 5.1. Moore Town Maroon woman sporting wild plants as a badge of Maroon identity at the annual Maroon celebration, Moore Town, October 10, 1978. Photo: Jefferson Miller.

raw products of the forest. Oral traditions of this kind also reveal that the ancestors' knowledge of local flora and fauna made possible certain strategies of evasion. Some of the narratives below [4–5], for instance, stress that during British military campaigns against them, the ancestors were forced to eat only uncooked food—that is, survival foods growing in the wild that required little or no preparation—since smoke would have given away their location; only when the forest was covered in mist or fog could they afford the luxury of a fire.

Maroons are generally recognized today as the Jamaicans who know the forest best. They are still widely thought of as "bush people." Many Maroons bristle at the negative side of this image, the connotations of "backwardness" and "primitiveness" that are often attached. But the positive side remains strong, both among Maroons themselves and among other Jamaicans. Maroons continue to be viewed, and to view themselves, as the seminal "bush doctors" of Jamaica, the very best of the island's indigenous herbalists. As Cohen (1973: 168) notes, "the belief in the superiority of Maroon herbal treatment is still widely held today."[3] "This special power which [Maroons] associate with the herbs," he adds, "extends and gives identity to their existence as a people. Herbs are related to the very idea of 'Maroonness'" (172). Like the other forms of knowledge that helped the ancestors to survive in the forest, the Maroons' deep spiritual connection with, and practical understanding of, herbs (or "weeds," as they call all wild plants), are closely intertwined with notions of what it means to be a Maroon today.[4]

[1]

Dem live in de bush. Nanny, and all de follower dem with him, live in there. Dem have baby ina de bush. When him get freedom, come out, a big man—big man and big woman.

   Dem couldn't come out fe buy nothing. Dem eat all bush something—leaf, thatch-head—a something grow ina bush, a wood. Dem cut it and eat de heart of it, fe food. Before dem get freedom, a wha' dem have fe live pon.

(Elizabeth Brown, November 8, 1977)

[2]

When him [Nanny] fighting against de bakra, him run away in de wood, from de slavery. In de wood, him have eating thatch-head [heart of palm], cacoon [the edible bean of a type of leafy vine], all those thing.

(James Downer, 1978)

[3]

De Maroon man, now, those are drastic man. Those Maroon man nyam stick, trash [wild plants] a wood, go a wood pick weed, feed pon weed two, three day. [They] nyam weed, put a indi [belly], nyam stick trash, drink weed, drink wild trash water. [They] go a insho [water, in this case meaning "river"], when insho come down, put him indi [ear] a insho there, listen wha' insho a say.[5]

(Sydney McDonald, September 14, 1978)

[4]

Maroon people scatter a wood. Dem name Katawud, you know— "scatterwood." Because when Grandy Nanny was fighting—Grandy Nanny and Grandy Sekesu, two sister, you know—bakra dem did want de Maroons dem

---

[A band of Windward Maroons] had along while lived on the wild produce of the woods alone where they died very fast in their Marches, and within three days killed four of their men who were so weak with hunger that they could not keep pace with the rest. (testimony of "an Ebo named Cupid belonging to Samuel Taylor having found means to make his Escape from the Rebells," January 31, 1734, PRO/CO 137/21, 207)

—— ✦ ——

We followed the partys track, which led us to the foot of a high hill, on the top of which we heard a Dog bark, and which we made to in an hours time. After we heard some Negroes talking together whom we Suspected to be Rebells, and it accordingly proved to be some of them drying of wild Game. We sent a Detachment of 12 Shots to get round them, but the Rebells discovering them Escaped. ("The Journal of William Lamport and Thomas Williams," entry of March 2, 1734; PRO/CO 137/55, 165–66)

were to become slave. And Grandy Nanny say fe-him people dem, him cannot mek dem turn slave. So him tek fe-him portion of people, and scatter a wood with dem, into a place name Stony River. . . . So dem call Maroon people now "scatterwood" . . . because dem go to wood and dem eat leaves, eat all dem leaves and everything. Dem no eat nothing wha' cook with fire. For dem couldn't mek up fire fe cook anything, for de bakra woulda find dem. So dem use hand a ground, cook all de while, you know? And when de fog go out pon de field, dem mek fire, until de fog go way. Now dem cook way de makoka [a type of grub-like worm] and eat dem. So de bakra couldn't manage dem.
(Margaret Harris, June 1, 1978)

[5]

Him [Grandy Nanny] couldn't mek fire. Him couldn't mek fire. Him plant him pumpkin. Everything, dem have fe eat it raw. Dem can't mek fire. De pumpkin bear de same day. Dem eat it, because [they] hungry. Dem eat raw food. Dem mad [i.e., fierce]. When dem people come out, dem mad. You think you can eat it with dem? No. Dem will win. Dem got strength. When you see dem, dem wild as deer. De only thing dem do—hog in there. A wild hog. [They] no tend to goat. Wild hog. Wild hog. De Maroon people no use goat. All now, Maroon n'e eat goat. Dem use hog. A wild hog dem use.
(Ruth Lindsay, February 1, 1991)

[6]

De real old-time Maroon no eat salt, through dem no min a come buy from bakra. Because dem no know how fe spend de money fe come buy, because dem no know wha' bakra fe do with dem deh. So dem eat dem *fresh* food. Fresh food. When me say "fresh food," you understand what I mean?—no salt at all. So dem eat fresh food. That mean say dem never dead. Dem a eat fresh

---

[In addition to several types of stored food such as corn, flour, peas, cassava, etc., we also found in their huts] wild yams, China Roots, Thatch Cabbage, Mountain Cabbage which they got About the Mountain, they had no Plantation nor was there any Ground plantable within 2 miles. (Journal of a British officer, entry of September 24, 1732, PRO/CO 137/20, 114)

---

food, eat fresh food. Because when dem go bust dem cacoon, dem put it, dem soak it, dem eat it. Dem eat dem thatch-head. Dem just free from bakra.

(James Downer, October 3, 1978)

[7]

Down ina de wood there, him [bakra] *cannot* find dem. Him *can't* find dem. Because dem naa wash clothes. Because dem no wear clothes. A bush dem ina. And dem naa cook. Dem eat de wild thatch, thatch-head. Any time dem go, dem cut de thatch-head, and peel it, and eat de food. Cabbage skin. Thatch-head different from cabbage, you know, cabbage skin. Dem eat every bit. When dem done, dem cut de cacoon, drink water, or de wild pine.[6] Dem gone. Dem *hot* more. Dem gone, ina fighting. So dem [the whites] couldn't manage dem. Dem couldn't manage dem. Dem [the Maroons] woulda *kill* de whole nation of dem.

(Ruth Lindsay, January 30, 1991)

[8]

We use herb. And we use bush, as calalu [edible greens], and wild meat. Yes, for our body. And we drink de bush, de stick that call cacoon. When you cut it and hold it in you mouth, you drink that water, and you feel strong, and you witty, and have strength. And then, we fight and sing our song, de old [songs], and blow our war horn, that lead us on to strength. When our war horn blow, we have strength.

(Mother "F," 1952)[7]

[9]

(Holding up a bottle of Maroon medicine): This is our compound of our own Grandy Nanny weed. You fix up this medicine now, set it, and boil it, fe all complaint of human being. All beast also. We fix up this one fe give everybody who

Figure 5.2. Moore Town Maroon herbal healer George Bernard, Cornwall Barracks, Portland, 1978. Photo: K. Bilby.

sick, all complaint, don't care what it is. This one good fe any complaint that you have, human being. We call this now Grandy Nanny business. This medicine now is Grandy Nanny medicine [from] our tribe—from Grandy Nanny to Grandy Sekesu, whole of dem, with dem tribe. And then now we learn that, mek we fix up this. This medicine go to a lots of people, over a thousand. And dem get dem benefit. This is our weed. We just call dem Grandy Nanny weed.

(Holding up an individual plant): Well, this one invokes business, all like spirit and all such. Dem love de rose. So we keep all these thing, and call these thing Yenkunkun weed. And this is Grandy Nanny and Grandy Sekesu [weed].

Well, me say ["cutting" Kromanti language]: "mámbráwa, o seh o mámbráwa du mi. O seh o pikibo na mi din kámadú. Seh ámba fikándu, seh ámba díla, ámba jan méso, seh o píndáku-ee! O seh o wédu wédu, o seh o wíni kóko, o seh o méte, o seh o méte. O seh o bábasí o wéngkini, o dábra. O seh o fámbusu, o seh o fámba. Seh púopuo kéto, o seh o púopuo ála, púopuo puo kéto, kófi ala, seh lágu laas a údu-oo, seh o móko bram-ee."[8]

So, we keep up this as our plan. Well, when we have de drum, and we sweet music, we dance. But when we don't have de drum and we sweet music and all such, we no bother with de dance, we only tek we trash, and when we tek we trash, we rub dem up.[9] We rub we trash for a purpose, and anoint anybody that sick. And before nine days, you must hearty.

(George Bernard, October, 1978)

[10]

Anabo [a type of tree that produces medicinal leaves and beans] a trash [spiritually potent plant], you know, in fighting. We direct know say we come here with dem something. Maroon come here with dem something. And, is a runaway slave. Runaway slave, dat mean Katawud. We wouldn't say "scatterwood," we woulda say "Katawud."

(James Downer, January 25, 1991)

Staying to the River

The importance of rivers—as escape routes as well as sources of food and water—is a theme shared by Maroon peoples in various parts of the Americas. The use of dogs to hunt down escaped slaves was a strategy favored by slave owners throughout plantation America.[10] According to Zips (1999: 99), "it was nearly impossible to trick the bloodhounds, no matter how ingeniously one's body scent had been camouflaged by particular plants." Many maroons who found themselves being tracked in this way waded and swam up rivers to mask their scent from the hounds. Oral traditions regarding this stratagem are common among Jamaican Maroons, especially in the eastern communities, where they are associated with a sacred song that forms an integral part of Kromanti ceremonies (Bilby 1994a: 78–79). It is likely that this song is hundreds of years old; distinct variants of it are found in all three Windward Maroon communities, which descended from a single Maroon group and separated in the eighteenth century.[11]

[11]

> o jo fara liba [follow river], o jo a de
> o jo fara liba, o jo a de
> o wiri ankoma, o jo a de
> o jo fara liba, o jo a de

(William Shackleford, September 21, 1978)

[12]

> ee, jo fara de, jo fara ribba
> ee, jo fara ribba, o jo méte méte
> jo suma méte, jo fa ribba
>
> ee, jo fara de, ee fara de
> ee, jo fara de
> yo méte méte
> yo fa ribba
> jo fa ribba-ee
> jo méte méte
> jo suma-ee

Him have fe dodge from de people dem. So through him have fe dodge, him have fe follow river. Yeah, him have fe dodge. That's wha' him say: (sings)

> ee, jo fara ribba, yo méte méte
> jo fara ribba-ee
> o jo fa ribba
> yo méte méte

De man say him have fe follow river, hide from de people dem. A de tune him throw. De man say him have fe follow de river. Same like how you woulda hide. Suppose you deh come now, and you a catch up. You have fe walk ina middle and come down there. So de man say him fe follow river, fe hide from de soldier dem, because de war too hot. So him have fe tek way himself from dem and follow river. A wha' de man say.

You know who dem say talk so? A Kojo word that. Kojo. Kojo say him have fe hide from de white man, because him coward. Him have fe follow river. Kojo. Him come with Nanny too. Him say him have fe hide from de white man because him no got gun, him no got sword, him no got machete. Nanny can stand to it, but him can't stand it, so him have fe hide from dem. So therefore him have fe follow river.

(Richard Barnes, September 12, 1978)

[13]

When Nanny tek de hills, dem come after Nanny. But Nanny choose de river. And when they go a certain part, fe catch Nanny, dem couldn't pass. Then everyone go to de water, drop ina de water. Dem tek de Newfoundland dog fe hunt down Nanny, and everyone go to de water. Dem drop ina de water, you know. And there was a hill—I don't know if I shoulda tell you that—but when they go to that water, everyone drop ina that water. That time Nanny is already up on de hill. And when him drop ina that water now—dem go round de hill, but there is no pass fe dem—that time Nanny already up there.

(Charles Bernard, December 18, 1982)

[14]

jo fa riva, jo a de
jo fa riva, jo a de
kwizan kwama, jo a de

jo fa riva, jo a de
jo fa riva, jo a de
kwaman kwama, jo a de

(Abraham Goodwin, April 15, 1978)[12]

[15]

De Englishman dem come out with some dog, dem big all about so: And Nanny say, "haste to de river!" And after you cross de river, nothing no wrong again. No dog. No dog bark. Any dog enter de river, you going find dem drown. You going find dem drown, and dead.

(Noel Lewis, February 2, 1991)

[16]

When de Maroons were puzzling de British, that was another so glorious feat of de Maroons. De English, they went to Cuba to import bloodhound to catch de Maroons. But it was useless. They wouldn't have any success. Because immediately de dogs entered de woods, some way or de other, Maroon realize that that was what happen. Then dem no walk on de land anymore. (laughs under his breath) You understand. They walk in de water, follow up de Stony River, walk in de water. And therefore, de dogs couldn't tek dem scent. De dogs couldn't tek dem scent at all. A man know say, well, from de moment him ina de river, it give de dog a hard time. If you cross de river and go over, de dog will cross de river and go over and pick up back de trail. But as long as you no go over—you no go across de river—him can't find you. Straight up de river.

(Charles Aarons, January 30, 1991)

> Every barrack . . . *was furnished with a pack of dogs, provided by the church-wardens of the respective parishes*; it being foreseen that these animals would prove extremely serviceable, not only in guarding *against surprises in the night*, but in tracking the enemy. (Edwards 1796: xi; *italics in original*)

Figure 5.3. "A Spanish Chasseur of the Island of Cuba." Specially trained dogs were imported from Cuba to hunt down escaped slaves in Jamaica at various points in time. From Dallas (1803).

[17]

come go da river
o jo a de
come go da river
o jo a de
oo dede bi ankama
jo a de

(Charles Town Maroons, November 12, 1977)[13]

Preparing for War

Each of the Windward Maroon towns has a special, sacred spot known as the Safo (or Asafo) Ground (sometimes also called the "muster ground"). This is the place where public Kromanti ceremonies are traditionally held. It is here that the linkage between the Kromanti religion and Maroon military practices of past centuries is most apparent.

Like many other elements of the Maroon cultural heritage, the name of this sacred space is derived from the Akan-speaking peoples of West Africa. In the Asante-Twi and Fanti languages of what is today Ghana, *asàfo* refers to a type of warriors' association that continues to play a prominent role in daily life (Christaller 1933: 419). (The related term *asáfoo* is the plural form for *osáni* "warrior" [Redden and Owusu 1963: 217].)[14]

Today the Kromanti religion retains much from its warrior past. Among the wonders associated with Kromanti spiritual power is the ability to induce bodily invulnerability and, when this fails, to heal injuries almost instantly. Maroons claim that the greatest Kromanti specialists can eat glass bottles, dance on fire, deflect bullets and knives, and miraculously close up gaping wounds (see chapters 6 and 9 for more on ideas about Kromanti power). It is widely recognized by Maroons today that these spiritual abilities were critical to their ancestors' victories during the time of war, and they are still among the most valued skills accessed through Kromanti ceremonies (Bilby 1981: 66–67).

Oral traditions such as those presented below state that military training during the war took place at the Asafo Ground. It was here that Kromanti experts drilled the troops, testing the spiritual powers used to protect them from the blows of swords and other weapons. Moore Town Kromanti specialists recall that those whose protection was insufficient—those who sustained wounds in training—were rushed to the healing waters of a nearby place known as Sanda (an area that remains popular as a swimming spot today). Only those who passed this test were deemed ready for war; the others, though their wounds could be instantly healed at Sanda, would have to wait until another day to fight.

[18]

When dem a train de Maroon soldier dem fe go fight against bakra, dem train dem right out where de clinic di-de [the present Moore Town clinic, which is located next to the site of the old Asafo Ground (also known as Asafo House)]. And when dem a train dem, dem pick certain amount of man, and a clever man dem too. A wise man too dem pick. And dem got dem afana. And when dem come, dem call you now. Dem got one *sipple* one there, and him come, him look pon you, him call you, him spin you round ina ring there, him tek up him machete, him do so pon you, "wup!" And machete just do so, chisel [glance] off.

Him say, "all right, boy, you fit fe bakra."

Him shub you one side. And if a twelve man fe go fight bakra today, him call de twelve man.

And one of de time him may see—when he pick up de machete and do pon one of de man so, "wup!"—all him gut come out of him. Him just put everything [the guts that have come out] a him shoulder. And him do so, "wup," [go to] Sanda. And same as him go a Sanda, him just tek it, dash dem ina Sanda water. And by de [time the] two of dem rise and come out, de man a hearty, strong man. Every scar pon him well up.

Him say, "all right, you tan one side. You can't go a bakra today, boy. If you go a bakra, bakra will catch you, do you in."

Dem go over back again [to the Asafo Ground], dem see one other one. Dem tek him so, "bap," and dem do so, "wam!" pon him, him gut belly come out. Dem do so, bring him again a Sanda. Dem dive under Sanda bottom, but when him come out again, everything pon him well.

Then him come again, him call one other one, him chop him so, "wam!" De machete *chisel* [glance] off of him.

Him say, "all right, boy, you well trim, you can go fight bakra today."

So a right out there dem train all dem soldier. And *all* wha' damage happen to dem soldier a Sanda, dem go there, go cleanse all wha' deh pon any one of fe-dem man wha' dem chop. Dem go there, go well de cut, up a Sanda.

So a out there *all* Maroon train, fe mek dem can go fight bakra.

Some a dem [those that passed the test]—those trim. Those under mission, those under Science. Under fe-dem own Maroon [Science]. Dem understand so, go fight against bakra, that all when bakra going fling a shot pon dem, that shot going just come off. But anyone wha' you see de machete cut, that mean say if him go a war, bakra going kill him. But de one wha' you chop with de machete, and de machete just chisel [glance] off so, that mean say, if bakra lick him *one thousand* time with gun, it can't give him a blow pon him skin [here meaning the entire body]. All de gunshot going chisel [glance] off. But de one wha' dem chop, or strike, and blood come, him can't go a war. Dem carry him go a Sanda go better him there.

So that mean say, those wha' you see now get de blow, those are well train—fit. Me have fe call dem Science man dem, or fete-man dem. So dem prem dem

---

The Chief Employment of these Captains [Maroon under-officers appointed by the Chief Commander] was to Exercise their respective men in the Use of the Lance, & small arms after the manner of the Negroes on the Coast of Guinea, To Conduct the Bold & active in Robbing the Planta. of Slaves, Arms, Ammunition &ct. (eighteenth-century British manuscript cited in Kopytoff 1973: 75)

body, like how Nanny min prem him body when dem min deh shot him, and when him catch all de ball dem.

So a out there [at the Asafo Ground] dem trim de whole of dem.

(Hardie Stanford, January 31, 1978)

[19]

We have now what we call "Safo House." And when dem go now, dem go to dem Safo House, and they have a captain just trim dem like soldier, you know. And when dem go now, dem mek dem plan, and dem fix dem business, how dem fe operate. We call de captain Captain Phillip.[15] When him going train de soldier now, you have like a muster ground, like dem old Safo House. Dem come out now, and training de soldiers. And every man do your portion of work. De man who is de fastest man, him get a certain portion of training to him fastness. De one wha' slow, him get a portion of training to de slowness. And every [man] got a portion of work. You see? And when those men train now, is to meet de English soldier. Well, all right. So when dem train now, dem know de day when de English going attack dem. And dem tell dem what dem fe do. Every man got you portion of work. And as de soldier dem come pon dem, every man go to dem work.

For instant now, those days, you know, it is bow and arrow. De bow and arrow man climb a tree. And him practice dem, de man wha' going climb de tree. When him use de bow and arrow, him can't miss, because him practice that. You have man wha' practice fe run. Right? And when him run, you can't catch him, because him run and dodge. De other one now, him going come to you face to face, and you catch him. You say you conquer him. And you say now, "show me de pass fe go up Blue Mountain." And him say yes. And him carry you through de narrow track. That a where him know say de bow and arrow man deh. That bow and arrow man climb that tree. And him deh there now, and watch you. And him carry you to where de bow and arrow man deh. Him know directly where him deh, you know. And him carry you same place. And meanwhile you going with him now, him dodge you, slip you and dodge you. And as quick as him dodge you, de bow and arrow man down pon you with de bow and arrow. You know? And him kill off every man, left one. Him kill off every soldier. And then you hear dem tell you about de one [that was left alive]. (laughs) Well, dem capture de one. Dem capture de one. That a one part of de history.

(Charles Bernard, December 18, 1982)

[20]

You see where de clinic out deh? A out a de big muster ground. Dem go tek de whole of dem . . . de chief of quarters. De chief of quarters.

(To me): No frighten of me. (He picks up a machete.) No frighten because me draw this sword. *Don't* frighten of me. Me naa hurt you.

Dem afana sharp to fart.

No frighten of me. A me and you deh ya. Me only a show a illustration. So as me swing it [the machete] so, you don't frighten, man. Me naa hurt you, man. (Swings the machete toward me.)

[They] send this upon you, "wup!" And de somebody wha' dem chop, dem *gut* come out of dem. Because him no fix fe de war.

[They would then shout to the soldier who was not sufficiently prepared]: "Go up Sanda!"

When dem do so, you no fit.

[They] train de thirty, forty soldier fe go fight. And so, "wup!": "you gut come out." And so, "wup!": "you blood run." "Wup!": "[go to] Sanda."

That was one of de Maroon fighting spot. So a de most of Maroon victory deh, up a de Sanda deh.[16]

(Hardie Stanford, February 7, 1991)

Fighting Fire with Fire

Maroons on both sides of the island, like their British foes, used fire as a highly effective weapon. But in contrast to British troops, whose scorched-earth tactics required them to drive their enemies out of their villages by brute force before burning everything to the ground, the Maroons combined the strategic use of fire with a masterful command of the element of surprise. Attacking in the middle of the night or early morning, when the sleeping troops were at their most vulnerable, and with such stealth that even sentries were caught unawares, the Maroons were able to minimize their own casualties while dealing devastating blows to the more numerous and better-armed British forces. The skillful use of flaming projectiles, allowing Maroons to launch their surprise attacks from a distance, contributed to the enemy's confusion and gave the Maroons a further edge.

These narratives about defeating the British with fire have an important symbolic value for Maroons today, exemplifying the military ingenuity that enabled their ancestors successfully to defend their freedom against terrible odds. This body of traditions is of additional interest in that it appears to be linked to an important historical episode: the siege of Nanny Town during the 1730s. Richard Hart heard a version of this oral tradition in Moore Town more than fifty years ago that concerned "the fighting at Nanny Town" (Hart 1985: 84).[17] In the narrative by Major John Crawford below, recorded in 1958, an explicit connection is also made with a British attempt to occupy Nanny Town. This linkage with the campaign against Nanny Town is less clear in most of the more recent accounts I was given (although clearly stated by Colonel Harris of Moore Town in his narrative below).

In any case, the denouement, and the central theme contained within it, remain the same: the lone British survivor of the Maroon raid is forced to write on a leaf (or a piece of bark, or sheath of a palm bough) a defiant challenge, dictated by his Maroon captors and posted where British reinforcements will be sure to find it, to send "thousands" or "millions" more soldiers. According to Maroon narrators, it was this psychological maneuver, along with the brilliant display of military acumen preceding it, that led directly to what Maroons today consider victory in the war against the British. Realizing the futility of their position, the latter were forced to admit defeat and ask the Maroons for a treaty of peace.[18] When Maroons today boast that their ancestors "subdued" the British, they do so with this background in mind.[19]

Even if the events recounted in these Maroon narratives cannot be precisely matched to any described in archival records, they serve to reveal the great difference between Maroon perspectives on their ancestral war of liberation and those of their British enemies, whose contemporaneous written reports display a distinct tendency to downplay Maroon accomplishments. Werner Zips (1999b: 212) is not far from the truth when he asserts that "every achievement and victory of Maroons became reinterpreted as weakness, stubbornness or defeat in the colonial reports." That both views, eighteenth-century British and twentieth-century Maroon, contain elements of truth, just as both are partial, cannot be doubted. For our purposes, however, what matters most is that those elements of truth preserved by Maroons over the generations remain a living and integral part of who they are as a people today.

[21]

Maroon want fe destroy dem [the whites], and Maroon going destroy dem too. A de same thatch house dem min got too, like de Maroon, when dem and de Maroon deh fight. And when de Maroon see wha' happening, dem take de stick, chop it and split it, and, me say, when dem catch it pon de lighter, it blaze more than candle. And that time bakra man deh a dem place, feel so sweet and happy. When Maroon go to work, dem create one point though, and put fire pon de top. Is a little piece of stick, and dem carve de point part down ya so, and dem put de fire pon top of this now. Dem tek it now, and dem light it, and hold it a dem hand, and dem fling it, and it drop ina de trash, stand up ina de trash! And dem fling about six or seven. That time, when de big bakra man dem in there, one may do so. . . . (cups his ear with his hand as if listening).

   The other one say, "no, man, is bird eating cherry, man, and cherry dropping on the hut, man."

   Dem hear one other: "chap!"

   Call to de bakra man again. Bakra man say, "no, man, a bird a eat cherry."

   And when hours fall, dem all burn down, burn down, and kill dem in there. And *one* save. And when de fire cease—a Science a work, you know—dem go and dem tek out de one wha' there, and dem write pon paper give him, say:

"when you go tell bakra, say fe send five more million bakra come back." So dem left one fe tell de tales. And dem got that one fe send back to bakra now [with the message] fe send five million more bakra come mek Maroon and bakra fight again. Because Maroon going kill dem out.

(Hardie Stanford, July 5, 1978)

[22]

It was a time when de soldiers mek up dem camp, that de Maroon mek what you call de "poison butas."

Now, I wonder if you understand. There is a wood inside de woodland. As green as it may be, [when] you strike a match, it lights. It blows.

Well, you ever see a buta? Well, a buta is a thing like a bow and arrow, a thing that you draw. They use that now—placing de buta here, placing de wood here, sticking like a wire inside de wood. And you stay a distance, and you draw it back, and it drop a de camp top. And de wire stick in there, and that wood stay ablaze . . . blazing. In those days now, de camp, is not de zinc, what they used to use [to make roofs]. They use de thatch.

Well, all de soldier dem camp there ina that big hut, and dem have dem powder and dem gun. Because those days gun never use with cartridge, like how you just slip in a cartridge and fire gun. Dem use powder, and you hear dem call it de "ramrod." At those days dem call gun "mascot" (i.e., musket). It was not like our days now. We call it "guns," they call it "mascot." Big heavy something. Big heavy something to carry.

Well, at those days, that was de last points of de war, and when de huts catch fire, de soldiers have to leave. Well, dem leaving dem gun now, for fire is on dem. Well, de Maroons come down now, and bawl dem at de doorway. And as fast as men come out, dem kill. As fast as dem come out, dem kill. For you can't run with no gun, you know. You a run fe life! Well, de last one come out. There was no more. Dem never kill that one, dem hold onto him. And dem say now, "write." And those days dem write on a cabbage skin [the sheath of a bough of an *Areca* or related species of palm]. And him wrote on there, him wrote.

This is what him wrote: "telling Missus Queen that Maroon has kill all his soldiers, and are there to kill ten thousand more."

And that's how de war cease. De Maroon could not read at those days. Neither could they write. But de Englishman write. After him finish writing, dem kill him. Dem kill him. Well, dem carry that now, go stick it up, that de white man—wha' you da call de officials—could see. That's what cease de type of war.

(Johnny Minott, June 4, 1978)

[23]

After de English took Jamaica, those slaves took their refuge into de bushes. And de English hunt dem, till after a certain period, Captain Stoddart and Lieutenant Sadler said in England dem must give dem eight hundred soldiers, and they will come to Jamaica and bring de Maroons to settlement. When they came, they were led up by a spy into Nanny Town. And they found de huts of de Maroons on a mountain top. So de soldiers really wouldn't pitch their tent, fe settle down in those huts. And at midnight the Maroons throw torch on de huts. In de morning, when they woke, they find one soldier in a valley that was alive. His leg was broken. And they took a thing they call kanda [the large lower sheath of a palm bough]—cabbage skin, a palm skin thing. And they cut his hand, and catch de blood, and took a little piece of stick and use as a pen. And they wrote down what happen. Soldier wrote. And they stick up that in de road, at a place they call Corn Husk, that lead through Golden Vale over Watch Hill into Nanny Town. And when de soldier that was going up with de mess saw it, they took it to Port Antonio. Because they saw what happen. And they get de Maroons a certain date fix fe settlement.

(Major John Crawford, December 8, 1958)[20]

[24]

Maroon burn down bakra house dem. When dem used to fight, dem split de wood—dem call de something dem "kaja" [a type of inflammable wood, also pronounced "kandia"] . . . stick deh a wood. It come like kerosene oil, it blow fire. And dem sit down a day-time, sit down a day-time, and dem cut dem out, cut dem out good and sharpen dem. That time de bakra got him good place there. So dem go back a de bakra man house, pawn [grasp] de trash dem [and throw them onto the thatch roof], "jau!" That deh one stand up. De other one, "jau!" It stand up. That time de bakra man inside now feel so happy, say him have some bird cutting some berry, throwing on de house. That time Maroon deh back there with dem fire deh pon dem little stick, de trash dem. Every fling

---

This present Morning a great number of Rebellious Negro's, he believes about Two hundred Shott atack't him in his Quarters Shooting one of the Centry's dead, and the other dangerously wounded thro the face, rushing into the Piazza, the Soldiers, being all in Bed, got ready as fast as possible, & Fought the Rebells for three Hours, but the Rebells setting Fire to all the Houses, the said [sergeant named] Portis, & all the Soldiers retired, and came down, leaving the Rebells in Possession of the Plantation. (deposition of Sergeant William Portis, St. Elizabeth, June 14, 1735, PRO/CO 137/21, 228)

dem fling, it stand up. Every fling dem fling, it stand up, till when dem surround de housetop with fire. Dem travel, tek way demself now go a wood. And when hours fall, de whole building burn down, burn down. And dem able fe go capture de bakra.

In de midst of war, you can imagine wha' happen when war time, you know. When enemy deh fight against enemy, you must know wha' happen. Dem kill few of dem, and send back one, say him fe go tell bakra, say fe send so much more come. Dem kill one and tek blood, and tek blood and write it, tell bakra say fe send so much more soldier come. That a wha' Maroon send go back, go challenge bakra: "send how much more soldier come." Because if dem send five more thousand soldier, is a certain thing say Maroon going capture dem.

Older head sit down and teach you things wha' you never know. And since me come now, me start to do a thing again now, more experience now come to me [via dreams and visions]. But old people tell you a lots.

(Hardie Stanford, February 27, 1982)

[25]

[The huts of the British soldiers] were made of thatch, and so on. So they decided to burn down the place, with the soldiers in it. Because that would be such a terrible blow to the enemy. And so they got this wood, kandia.

We have a tree. It was plentiful up there, up at Nanny Town. It is a special type of wood. Because it blazes, whether green or dry. You strike your match and you light it. Just as if—almost like you dip it in gasoline or so. I'm exaggerating a little bit, but then, that's the character of the wood. It blazes. Kandia. That's what they call that wood.

And so what they did, they split them. They split them into lengths of about a yard or so, and lit them, when the soldiers, the British men, were sleeping—were gone to bed, thinking that all was well. And then they threw them. They lit them and threw them on the thatch, and burnt down the entire place. You can imagine the type of fear that pervaded the entire atmosphere of these soldiers who had first thought that they had conquered, and so all would be well.

Well now, somebody went up close to one of the huts. And he heard two soldiers. They lay side by side there.

And one of them said—when the flaming rods struck the roof—one of them said, "Jake, what's that?"

The other one—he wanted so much to sleep—he said, he answered, right away, answered, as if he was such an authority on the thing—he said, "oh, it's only parrots cutting berries."

You know? (laughs).

So the other one was lulled to sleep. And so it was that a little after that now they realized that something was amiss. And the entire Nanny Town was burnt down.

(Colonel C.L.G. Harris, January 31, 1991)

Hitting the Plantations

Maroons in the Americas varied in the degree of their connection to the world of the plantations from which they had fled (Price 1996a: 12–13). Even within Jamaica, Maroon groups appear to have differed from one another in this respect. While the written historical record shows that in the western part of the island Kojo tended to avoid confrontations, apparently favoring a policy of non-interference, the Windward Maroons under Nanny behaved more aggressively toward the coastal society. As European settlement continued to expand in this part of the island, the Maroons stepped up their raids on coastal plantations. It is clear that these frequent raids were launched for several reasons. In some cases, the Maroons wished to augment their numbers by freeing or abducting slaves from the plantations. Female slaves were especially sought, since the Maroon communities suffered from a severe shortage of women during the early years. Sabotage and revenge against slavemasters, overseers, or other personnel were also motives for hitting the plantations (as in the final narrative in this section [30], involving an attempt to poison an estate's drinking water). But judging by oral accounts like those below, hunger was more often the driving force. As the following narratives show, when driven to the brink of starvation by British military campaigns, the Maroons did not have to depend solely on the wild foods of the forest for survival; they could also retaliate by striking coastal estates, in the process acquiring some of the food sources—such as cattle—that they desperately needed.[21]

[26]

They generally go out sometimes and rob the plantations, you know, so as to get food, and material, and clothing, and such like. And you have plenty of tactics-man who change themself to these forms of animal and go down [to the plantation]. Sometimes the man will out there with a gun and he see a goat pass by. But really, is not a goat, is a man. So it may be that type of way or position why plenty [of Maroons] don't eat the goat again.

(Johnny Minott, September 10, 1978)

[27]

Dem raid de plantation many time, man. De Maroon dem go down and raid de plantation, raid slavemaster plantation and get food.

(Johnny Minott, February 6, 1991)

[28]

That time now, him [one of Nanny's soldiers] go a London [name given in recent times to a section of the Maroon territory located between Seaman's Valley and

> By night, they seized the favourable opportunity that darkness gave them, of stealing into the settlements, where they set fire to cane fields and out-houses, killed all the cattle they could find, and carried the slaves into captivity. (Edwards 1796: viii)

the center of Moore Town]. That a Wild Cane cross [a crossing point on the Wild Cane River], deh so man turn, have fe mek him something deh so so. Him talk word to de old lady [Nanny]. Him talk word, talk word, talk word, talk word, talk word, talk word.

Him say [to the other Maroons], "me a go send two of you [to] obroni [the territory of the whites, i.e., the coastal plantation area], come see wha' happen. Hungry naa tek soldier now, you know. Bakra got cow."

And him [Nanny] say, "go! See howfa sonti tan [Go! See how things are]."

Dem a go kill bakra cow, you know, but bakra can't hurt dem, because bakra can't hold dem. Because when him do so [try to catch a Maroon], a insho [to the water, i.e., the river]. If him see a man a come [i.e., someone who might announce his presence], him say to man, "me a go catch something." Him run a wood gone—[camouflaged as a] big bundle, bush. Because you hear dem say, Maroon people [are] Katawud [i.e., "scatter wood people"].

(Sydney McDonald, September 4, 1978)

[29]

That was where they get food sometimes, go down there go catch cow and so. Golden Vale. An estate was there. So at night they go down and get livestock. They had cows there, and probably other animals, you know? Domestic animal. Because that is where de Maroons go down, when they short of meat, when

> A Body of the Rebells consisting of about 80 or 90 came down & took possession of a plantation & two penns or cattle pastures. . . . Thus the Enemy were left in possession of great plenty of cattle & other provisions. ("The Relation of John Smith planter residing in the Parish of St. George in the Island of Jamaica," 1733, PRO/CO 137/21, 8)

dem run out of meat. Go down there, and by night, go kill cow. You understand. Anything dem hunt, dem eat.

(Charles Aarons, January 30, 1991)

[30]

Me big grand-uncle, him says, Nanny send one of his brother with Science, deadly Science and deadly poison, down to de English plantation. You understand. One of de Science going to go into de drinking water. And one of de Science going put down outside de tank, scatter it outside de tank, a tank that government build, and got water ina. Drinking water. And a down there dem go. And same as him get in, fe go put it in de water, somebody hold him. Somebody hold him.

And when de somebody hold him, him say to de somebody, say, "hold me!"

And hear him answer, say, "mi ma fring!" [an old phrase, the precise meaning of which is unclear]

"Hold me!"

Him answer, say, "mi ma fring!"

Him say, "wait! How ma fring fi come hold me?"

Him say, "fring mek me see."

And de somebody open him hand [forced by the Maroon man's spiritual power to let go], him get way out of him hand. You see? Him get way out of him hand. And all when dem run him, de man say him remember say, Nanny say, all wha' dem going go do, any difficult dem get ina, try haste to de water, to de river, where de water deh, whether it be spring or river, and try leap over. And after him leap over, dem all right. And a there him run to. You see? Him run to there. That's a keynote.[22]

(Noel Lewis, February 4, 1991)

Camouflage

One of the most remarkable guerrilla techniques devised by Jamaican Maroons is the form of camouflage they call *ambush*. (Among Maroons this term has a special sense. They use it to refer both to the act of camouflage and to the materials used in camouflage, rather than in the more general standard English sense of "unexpected attack.") While all the present-day Maroon communities possess oral traditions regarding such camouflage and reenact versions of it during their annual festivals, it is in the Windward community of Moore Town that the tradition has been retained in its most elaborate form. In this community, the dressing of an individual with *ambush* remains a solemn rite with a powerful spiritual dimension. As the suit of cacoon vines is prepared and carefully wrapped around the person, sacred Kromanti songs and incantations may be performed, along with libations of white rum to the ancestors. In contrast to the other communi-

Figure 5.4. Ceremonial *ambush*, Seaman's Valley, Portland (*first view*), 1978. Photo: Jefferson Miller.

Figure 5.5. Ceremonial *ambush* (*second view,* computer-enhanced to make the camouflaged warrior with *jonga* stand out).

Figure 5.6. Scot's Hall Maroons sing to a man in ceremonial *ambush*, Scot's Hall, St. Mary, 1993. Photo: K. Bilby.

ties, Moore Town Maroons insist that true ambush—the only kind deserving of the name—must cover every inch of the warrior's body, from head to toe. Not even the eyes should be visible. Any weapons borne by the individual, such as the Maroon lance called *jonga*, should also be thoroughly concealed under a dense blanket of cacoon leaves. The fabrication of this intricate disguise is an art requiring considerable skill, passed down across the generations from the time of war.

It is clear that this method of camouflage, though rarely featured in British accounts from the time, played an important part in the military successes of the eighteenth-century Maroons. It is not surprising that it is only fleetingly mentioned in written historical sources; after all, as Maroons today point out, it was a Maroon "state secret," and the British colonial forces were not entirely aware of the extent of its use, nor did they fully understand its military potential.

Today its significance is primarily symbolic (although Maroons are quick to point out that, if necessary, it could be put to effective use again in the future). Indeed, there may be no better way to visually represent the skill of "dodging" that remains a central feature of Maroon cultural ideology than with this sacred suit of foliage.

[31]

Dem use weed, and ambush. A man come here now, and him cut a cocoa leaf, like Kojo now, brave like you. Him cut. Then another one tek a cocoa-tree [cacao tree, *Theobroma cacao*], and put it pon Kojo back, right here so. And it deh pon Kojo back, big cocoa-tree. And Kojo sit down here so. Kojo deh pon a route, like Seaman's Valley bridge, that is a gate. When you [i.e., the bakra soldier] come where him deh, and you start dead, is only big cocoa-tree you start dead from. Or a banana tree that ripe: you come there to pick it to eat, and you start dead from de banana. De banana just start to lance you with knife and kill you. That is a weed that grow on de banana, and him sit down a de banana road, him foot face stay so when you a step through. Ambush. And dem place de ambush. And him deh there with dem machete fe work out, like sword. And dem work dem, and dem tek it, and when you come and you pick off one banana and you eat, dem just do so, "buk," throw you. And de other white man look—him a Englishman—and him see one Englishman drop, "buf!" De whole of dem get up and start fight now: Opong, Kojokwako [and the other Maroon warriors].

(David Gray, February 19, 1978)

[32]

Some of dem tek bush, cacoon, and ambush up demself, and stand up. Dem got dem sword ina dem hand, you know, and dem stand up. And when any of dem come near dem, dem tek dem osunudaja and kill dem. Dem call dem machete "osunudaja." Dem kill dem. A afana, but dem call it "osunudaja"—a stick like sword. A it dem tek kill de white man dem. So white people couldn't manage Maroon people, you know.

(Margaret Harris, June 1, 1978)

[33]

Dem [the Maroon fighters] no stay a ground. Dem up pon de tree. A tree dem stand. Dem ina de tree wood there sit down. Dem come down a night. But ina de day time, dem up there now. Dem say "bráye": dem braye demself [wrap themselves] with de cacoon [vine]. Braye.[23] And wrap. Dem tek it mek boot. Dem tek it mek hand. De only thing deh ya you can see a de eye. A de eye of yoyo [literally, the eye of Nanny's descendant, used here generically to mean

---

The Maroons received us [at Charles Town] as if they were much pleased with our visit; the women danced, and the men went through their war exercise for us. . . . their military manoeuvres seemed to consist entirely of ambuscade; taking aim at their enemy from behind trees, leaping up, and rolling about, to avoid being wounded themselves. Altogether it was so savage and frightful, that I could not help feeling a little panic, by merely looking at them. (Journal of Lady Maria Nugent, entry of March 18, 1802 [Wright (1966: 75)])

The Negroes [i.e., Maroons], some of whom, had been in our rear, all the preceeding day, and others before us, had placed themselves, from top to bottom, on a very steep mountain, thickly covered with trees and bushes. . . . The wild Negroes at the same time, firing and calling out, *Becara* [i.e., bakra, white men] run away— *Becara* run away, it is probable too, that we should have followed, but fortunately, there were some large masses of the mountain which had caved down, & which lay in the middle of the stream, just under the foot of the ambush, and we took shelter behind them, but though we could hear the Negroes and even converse with them, not one was to be seen!! (from an eyewitness account of an unsuccessful mission against the Windward Maroons in the 1730s, by British officer Philip Thicknesse [1788: 99–102])

"Maroon"]. But you can't see *nothing*, you know. A de tree you see. And dem over here a look pon you. So any time you gone now, you pass underneath dem deh so, and you no see dem. Dem come down a night, and tek de bomb and thing, and go up back pon de tree. And as you [white people, i.e., the British soldiers] coulda crowd come deh, so-so-so, bomb dem, as you gone, dem drop it pon you. Dem kill that deh crowd. And you no see dem. You look, you can't find where it come from. But dem kill de crowd. That crowd dead. And dem gone. As de crowd dead now, dem go down tek up all de bullet, de gun and something, and de powder, and thing wha' dem got, and go up back ina de tree go sit down, till when, a day time, another batch come in. Dem look fe you. As dem watch you, see say a batch in there, you naa realize dem deh go up there.

A bomb. Dem kill you. So dem [the whites] don't know how fe catch dem, dem don't know where dem deh. You see. Dem no know where fe catch none of dem. Because dem no got de thought fe know say a up pon de tree dem deh. Because bare [nothing but] bush dem see there.

(Ruth Lindsay, January 30, 1991)

[34]

The Maroon was Scientifically worked-up. Some of them, they will stand up in the way here, you pass and don't see them. And they look like a green tree, like ambushes. [They] begin ambush. And they look like a tree. And you'll pass. When the soldier, the English soldier, pass by, you wouldn't know it's them. And they can catch you at the back. Because you passed me, and you didn't know it's me, and when you turn around, then I could catch you at the back. So they couldn't manage really fight them down, because they couldn't understand. So the English soldier couldn't get at them. They passed them on the way, but they couldn't know it's them.

(Caleb Anderson, February 3, 1991)

These Maroons would secrete themselves in trees, and arrest the whites as they passed along; they would pretend to guide them, when they would beat and abuse them as the whites did their slaves. . . . (Nancy Prince [1853: 59], relating an oral tradition she encountered while traveling in Jamaica in 1841)

After a long *trumpet parle*, they [the Maroons] agreed to send one of their Captains, in exchange, for one of ours, in order to settle *preliminaries*, and this being agreed; to our utmost astonishment! we saw in an instant, an acre of under wood cut down, and that acre covered with Negroes! every man having cut down a bush at one blow in the twinkling of an eye! (British officer Philip Thickness describing Windward Maroon fighters cutting off their *ambush* camouflage during peace negotiations, instantly revealing their previously hidden presence; from his eyewitness account of the making of the treaty with Nanny's people in 1739 [Thicknesse 1788: 117–18])

[35]

When they kill de British soldiers, they get guns from dem. You understand. Whatever ammunition those soldiers travel with, they take dem. They have they jonga, and they have they ambush, which was de greatest of all. It was de greatest of all, de ambush. Because when they wrap in that bush, de English coming, but you couldn't see dem fe identify that is human being. That's a sweet lot of bush. And they [the English] passing through. And they lost they lives. They [the Maroons] must receive that knowledge [of ambush] from God.

(Charles Aarons, January 30, 1991)

[The Maroons'] appearance, decorated with their well-known "war paint," covered with bushes and twigs of the Lignum vitae, struck terror into the hearts of the rebels at Portland and St. Thomas in the East. Where they lay down, nothing was discernable of their bodies,—nothing but the living bush that covered them. In this way they march without observation, and in this way, they spring like tigers upon their prey, who, seeing nothing but a forrest [sic] of bush, imigine [sic] themselves secure. (a journalist's description of the Maroons' use of *ambush* during the suppression of the Morant Bay rebellion of 1865; from "The Maroons," *The Gleaner and Cordova's Advertising Sheet*, October 19, 1865)

When the Maroons desire to do honor to expected guests, a certain number of them await the party two or three miles from their settlement and escort them into their "town," as the cluster of huts is termed. On such occasions, the Maroons cover themselves with trails of moss, ferns or branches of trees, wound round their bodies and heads till they look like so many May day Jacks-in-the-green. This, in Maroon parlance, is their "Civez," and its use is obvious, for when on the warpath it renders them almost indistinguishable when they are creeping through the bush. (Blake 1898: 564–65)

A Haven for Women

Women and children were critical to the long-term survival of the Jamaican Maroons. Successful biological and social reproduction could not be taken for granted among groups living under siege (a situation further complicated by chronic shortages of female members among the pre-treaty Maroons). Particularly among the Windward Maroons led by Nanny—whose aggressive tactics ensured frequent retaliation by British troops—the strategic problems posed by women, children, and dependents became acute. Infants and young children, though they represented the hope of future generations, could be serious liabilities for communities whose survival depended on stealth, speed, and physical endurance. Women with children greatly hindered the movements of Maroon groups on the retreat, sometimes with fatal results. As the "abandoned child" narratives presented in chapter 4 show, mothers (or the groups to which they belonged) were sometimes forced, while being pursued by colonial troops, to sacrifice their children for their own survival. Present-day Windward Maroons cite this conundrum as the catalyst that led to the founding of a separate settlement known as Woman Town, not far from present-day Moore Town, where women and their children could be safely sequestered whenever hostilities appeared to be escalating.[24] Though Woman Town has been abandoned for centuries, people in Moore Town today remain well aware of its location. Hidden high up on the slopes of a nearby mountain, this haven for women was much less accessible than the main Maroon settlements in the Blue Mountains, which typically were located at somewhat lower elevations, sometimes in deep valleys, along or near the rivers that provided residents with a reliable supply of fresh water and much of their keep.

Interestingly enough, according to the last narrative in this section [40], it was Grandy Nanny herself who devised this defensive strategy and ordered the founding of a separate settlement where women and children would be safe. As the narrator, Ruth Lindsay, asserts, Nanny was "the head," and no man was ever in a higher position than her. Rather than pointing to the weak position of women in this military society, then, oral traditions about this hideout for women might be taken as a confirmation of the crucial role played by mothers and their children in the struggle for survival—an importance that is further symbolized by the person of Nanny herself. She was not only the commander of male soldiers, but also the "mother" of her people, and the architect of this separate town for women.[25]

[36]

What me hear about Woman Town, me hear it was there dem took de woman generally when dem a fight de war. Woman Town.

(Johnny Minott, February 6, 1991)

Figure 5.7. Joe Hill, with Moore Town in foreground. The site of Woman Town is hidden on its back slopes. 1991. Photo: K. Bilby.

[37]

When it come pon certain time so, when dem fight dem so, a that time dem got one place there wha' min call Uman Tong (Woman Town). [They] put all woman there! All woman tan a that place there. No woman no pass out of that place there. Dem call it Uman Tong.

(James Downer, 1978)

[38]

Dem have a place wha' dem call *Big Ginger*. All woman stay there so. Big Ginger. All woman stay there so. That mean dem call that place *Uman Tong*! That mean say Uman Tong deh right back of de hill there, when you pass Sanda go over. That mean to say now, dem put *all* woman a that place. So dem call it Uman Tong. No man no di-de [were there]. That a *bare* woman [only women] there.[26] That's right. So dem walk pon de hill there, and dem mek dem hut.

(James Downer, October 3, 1978)

[39]

Maroons always a tricky people. There is a place up in de Johncrow Mountains there called Woman Town. Well, they leave de woman dem there, and go out. In case of any war, or any attack, dem woman safe at home. We call it Woman [Town], on account of that. We call it Woman Town. Right up in Johncrow Mountain there, Joe Hill section, but further up. If you go there, you will find ar- tifacts, if a even broken bottles, broken plates, and so on. You realize that people were living there. Is a kind of hideout, you know.

(Charles Aarons, January 30, 1991)

[40]

[Woman Town] a up there so. (She points to Joe Hill, across the valley from her house.) A there when him [Nanny] a live here [in the Moore Town area], a draw him trash fe mek house. De man dem down here [in the valley]. But every time when dem gone, gone look go, him [Nanny] got him gun, you know. A him a de leader. Him come like de colonel. Nanny. A him boss dem. A no man boss Moore Town, you know. A woman. A Nanny boss Moore Town, you know. Moore Town belongs to *Nanny*, it no belongs to no man. But de man dem fol- low him. What order him give, a wha' dem have fe tek it. So him [Nanny] put de woman dem up so, say dem can't fight war. Dem call there "Woman Town." You see? And him put de man dem pon road fe fight. But a she a de head. And a no man a head of Nanny. No man no head of him. A *she* just like de colonel— Nanny. That woman, him is a brave woman, fe Portland. Nanny say a woman fe live up there [in Woman Town].

(Ruth Lindsay, January 30, 1991)

Finding and Preparing Thatch: The Importance of Stealth

> Nanny did not bundle thatch for you alone.
> —Moore Town Maroon figure of speech, used to criticize selfishness

Next to the problem of food and potable water was that of shelter. Especially during the 1730s, when British raids several times displaced Windward Maroon communities in the Blue Mountains, maintaining adequate housing was a con- stant concern. Here, in one of the rainiest parts of Jamaica, life without a sturdy

Figure 5.8. Leopold Shelton, a Moore Town Maroon, demonstrating how to bundle thatch for easy transport, Nanny Town, 1991. Photo: K. Bilby.

cover over one's head would be miserable. Nanny's people had adapted well to this rain forest environment, and possessed a thatching technology perfectly suited to their needs. When on the run, however, this technology posed serious challenges. Although the thatching methods used by the Maroons were compatible with their need for mobility—emergency shelters could be built and thatched relatively quickly—the preparation of thatch involved noise levels that were unacceptable to communities in hiding. As a number of the narrators below note, the palm fronds used for thatching are stiff, and make loud crackling, rustling noises when cut, folded, and bundled for transport. Pursuing colonial troops might at any time be alerted to the presence of Maroons by these sounds. Indeed, British military reports from the period show that the noise made by thatch preparation did at times lead the Maroons' enemies to their hiding places.

According to Maroons today, Nanny's solution was to centralize thatch production in a single strategic location. Rising high above present-day Moore Town, Barry Hill was surrounded by abundant stands of the palm varieties used for thatching. With a clear view in several directions, it also served as a lookout; sentries who formed part of a network of abeng blowers could be kept apprised of the movements of colonial troops. After the devastating attacks on Nanny Town, while the Maroons were recovering from their losses, it was here that all thatching materials were brought to be bundled and tied up, so that they could be transported easily and stealthily to settlements hidden in the valleys below (Harris n.d.: 75).

We began our march as usuall taking our Rout Northwesterly till 8
a Clock, then Westerly, and about 10 came upon their track, we
followed the same very brisk, and about two in the afternoon came
up with their hutts, where they had lyen the Night before. They
now grew more weary in Cutting Thatch, and marched harder than
before. ("The Journal of William Lamport and Thomas Williams,"
entry of February 26, 1734; PRO/CO 137/55, 165–66)

Among Moore Town Maroons, the memory of Nanny's central role in devis-
ing this strategy is preserved in a common figure of speech: "Nanny did not
bundle thatch for you alone." As Carey (1997: 447) notes, this expression has
long been used by Maroons in that community to convey "criticism of selfish
actions when one should make decisions which considered the welfare of the
whole community."

[41]

Ina Moore Town dem got one place dem call Barry Hill. A there dem bari trash
[bundle up palm fronds].[27] A there dem bari trash, round there. Dem walk
through wood, because dem couldn't walk pon road. Bakra woulda see dem.
Dem have fe hide from bakra. Dem naa come where dem catch dem.
(James Downer, 1978)

[42]

In fighting de war a Stony River, those man bari trash. That is de reason why
dem call [that place] Barry Hill.
(James Downer, October 3, 1978)

We Begun our March and Continued the pursuit as yesterday, and
about 10 aClock found we had got into the midst of the Rebells,
hearing them cutting Thatch all round us, and immediately came
to their hutts in which were Severall of the Rebells, who on our
firing on them, and pushing forwards, run up a high hill firing
some shotts at us. ("The Journal of William Lamport and Thomas
Williams," entry of February 25, 1734; PRO/CO 137/21, 211)

[43]

They used to bari trash there [at Barry Hill]. In those days, it was de thatch
houses de Maroons live into. And then de man go and cut de thatch in de
woods, and carry it there a Barry Hill. And then dem bari it. It mean dem bundle
dem.

(Charles Aarons, January 30, 1991)

[44]

Dem cut de trash from Woman Town. That time Maroon and bakra deh fight.
Dem cut de trash from Woman Town, from way up ina here so, and draw dem
[the palm fronds]. Dem draw dem, dem draw dem through de wood, dem *draw*
dem through de interior part, till dem come out a de place name Barry Hill, ina
de district here, come bari. Dem come mek dem house. Because dem say if dem
back a de wood there deh bari de trash dem, by de breaking of de trash dem,
bakra may hear dem. So bakra may come there, come capture dem. So dem
bring de trash down from there. They go a Barry Hill. And when you do dem
[the palm fronds] so now, you carry as much of dem—all thirty bone [fronds, referring specifically to the hard center "rib"]. If a thirty bone, you can plat
[weave, or plait] and carry that kind of way.

De trash bone dem kris [stiff] too. Dem kris too. So before dem sit down
there, dem move dem from there to Barry Hill. When dem go a Barry Hill, dem
say bakra no going hear dem. So a de reason mek dem call there "Barry Hill,"
because a there de Maroon carry dem trash go bari when dem and bakra a
fight.

(Hardie Stanford, February 27, 1982)

[45]

Is there dem bari thatch fe carry go a Stone Wall. That's why dem call up there
Barry Hill. A up there dem bari de thatch. Dem bari it: that mean dem twist it,
twist de thatch. Is so de English don't find dem. Because is through de wood,
you know, through wood.

(Johnny Minott, February 6, 1991)

[46]

Nanny and bakra start to fight. And we have one place up so dem call Krakasa
Hill.[28] Krakasa Hill, way up ina de hills there. As much long-thatch up there wha'
can build house fe de whole Jamaica. And Nanny and his colleagues dem want a
house. And dem cut de trash from way to hell up ina de mountain there, and
draw dem, draw dem, draw dem through de wood, draw dem through de
wood, draw dem through de wood come a one place up there dem call Barry

─── ✺ ───

> We began our March as usuall and at 7 in the morning came to a Small Spring of Water, Here we halted for 2 hours to refresh our Selves, then proceeded on our March, and about Noon came to a place where the Rebells had cutt abundance of Thatch and we very soon after lost their Track having Scattered and covered it as they went along, but about three in the afternoon found it again and pursued the same till 5, and lay by this Night. ("The Journal of William Lamport and Thomas Williams," entry of February 27, 1734, PRO/CO 137/21, 211)

Hill, where me born and grow. And dem come there, come bari de trash dem, fi mek dem house. Because, dem say if dem tan up a de wood there fe bari de trash dem, bakra will hear when de trash dem a bari, "krei, krei, krei, krei, krei." Some of dem leaf, dem kris [stiff]. So bakra will hear when dem broke. So bakra will come in there pon dem. But dem *draw* it from ina de wood there, go out a Barry Hill now. When dem deh a Barry Hill now, dem can see. Dem can look round, right round dem.

(Hardie Stanford, February 1, 1991)

[47]

Nanny go up ina de wood, go cut thatch, fe carry come a Moore Town here, come mek house. But according to enemy, when Nanny a pass through there ina de wood fe come here come mek him house, him no walk a day time. Him walk a night. And him no trust fe bari de trash down there [in the valley], and dem might hear him. So him draw it. And it never done till when him come up a de hill a Barry Hill here. And him tan there, bari de trash dem fe carry dem come down here [lower down in Moore Town]. A that dem call de Barry Hill there.

(Ruth Lindsay, January 30, 1991)

Military Prowess and Ingenuity: A Miscellany

The resourcefulness and military genius of first-time Maroons is further reflected in a wide range of narratives centering on a variety of themes, represented in the selections below. Here we glimpse a few of the additional strategies that present-day Maroons recall in discussing the triumphs of their ancestors: walking backwards to create footprints that would confuse enemy trackers[29] [48–49]; posting abeng-blowing sentinels on a series of mountaintops so that Maroon settlements miles apart could be instantly alerted to enemy movements [50]; luring English

Figure 5.9. View from Barry Hill, Moore Town, looking toward Cornwall Barracks, 1991. Photo: K. Bilby.

soldiers to precipices from which there was no escape, or into narrow passage-ways to be trapped and attacked with boulders, logs, or salvos of arrows and bullets [51–53; 57–59]; inventing the "tinderbox" (a dependable means of start-ing fires in one of the wettest places on earth)[30] [54]; and using goats to test water for poisoning by the enemy, but also the eventual banning of these same goats from Nanny's domain because their cries threatened to betray the locations of Maroon settlements[31] [55–56]. These are among the variations on the theme of survival that continue to find life through the words of Maroon oral historians.

[48]

Nanny walk backway, all de time, walk backway. If him going to de east, him turn him back to de east. Him gone backway. Ai. Him futu [foot] turn that way. But him walk backway. When you think say him gone that way, him coming backway. You are tracking, say him gone so. Him no gone so, him gone that way. That's right. So him walk backways. Him show dem all de time. You come, you see him futu [here meaning footprints] dem turn back, up right there so. But him no gone so. Him gone backway. When you see him gone a Port Antonio now, him turn him foot to Portland [in the opposite direction]. When you say him gone a Lookout now, that time there, him gone backway, him gone a Cut Hill [another name for Watch Hill, in the opposite direction].

(Richard Barnes, December 18, 1982)

> [Nanny's people] were so much afraid of being discovered that they
> filled up or smoothed their tracks when they went over sand or Soft
> Earth. (testimony of "an Ebo Named Cupid belonging to Samuel
> Taylor having found means to make his Escape from the Rebells,"
> January 31, 1734, PRO/CO 137/21, 207)

[49]

Dem say him [Kojo] walk from Chapelton backway through de Cockpit so-till
him reach a Accompong. You know? A through de Cockpit. Miles, you know!
Miles. And dem say a backway him walk till him reach here, him come rest here.
(Magdalene Reid, January 9, 1991)

[50]

There was a trail there that leads into Nanny Town, at Golden Vale. A when they
up at Watch Hill. When de Maroons up at Watch Hill. And when de British soldiers coming on that trail, at Golden Vale, then they saw dem, and blow de
abeng. De Maroons have sentinels on Watch Hill, and have sentinels on
Abrahams. You understand. So when de abeng blow at Watch Hill, those at
Abrahams got de sound. And then Abrahams blow and notify Stone Wall. Because Abrahams is on this side of de river, in going up. Abrahams is on de left-
hand side of de river. You have de Stony River, and then you have de Stone Wall
on de right. No distance, just de width of de river. Just de width of de river between the foot of Abraham and Stone Wall. And de Stone Wall now, that was
where de Maroons work de Science. Four corners square. It's still there. It's still
there. And they did live around, you know? They dwelling around de surrounding, but that place specially made for a purpose. So after those out a Watch Hill

> After two or three days march from Hobby's [plantation], towards
> the sun setting, we came to a spot, on which the impression of
> human feet, of *all ages*, were very thick upon the sands, as well as
> dogs, & c. We were certain therefore, that the object of our search
> was near. (from an account of a military expedition against the
> Windward Maroons in the 1730s, by British officer Philip Thick-
> nesse [1788: 94])

[A captured Maroon abeng-man belonging to Nanny's group] assured us . . . that we should fail, if we attempted to possess ourselves of their town by force; it was so situated, he said, that no BODY of men, or scarce an individual could approach it, that they would not have five or six hours notice, by their detached watchmen, or out centinels. (Thicknesse 1788: 114–15)

They were seldom surprised. They communicated with one another by means of horns; and when these could scarcely be heard by other people, they distinguished the orders that the sounds conveyed. It is very remarkable, that the Maroons had a particular call upon the horn for each individual, by which he was summoned from a distance, as easily as he would have been spoken to by name, had he been near. (Dallas 1803a: 89)

The sound of their wild war horns as they rush without warning and without apparent discipline to the plains strikes terror into the hearts of every one that hears it. (letter from Colonel Alexander Fyfe, commander of Maroon troops during the Morant Bay Rebellion, to Governor Eyre, October 31, 1865; cited in Lumsden [2001: 479])

---

spy de enemy, dem blow de abeng, and those at Abrahams hear. And Abrahams blow on those down Stone Wall. So they couldn't tek no unexpected [attack]. De Maroons always alert.

(Charles Aarons, January 30, 1991)

[51]

There's a fall near Stone Wall called Chacha River Fall.[32] It is so difficult. It is so dangerous. And I understand that at one time, when de English soldiers trailing de Maroon, all of dem run down that precipice. There's a waterfall, but it is so dangerous. You fly drop over it. And they say they [the Maroons] run dem down. When dem [the English soldiers] circle around now, believing that Maroon supposed to dead, dem no see nobody—[but] Grandy [Nanny was there].

Figure 5.10. George Harris, official abeng blower of the Moore Town Maroons for most of the late twentieth century, Moore Town, 1977. Photo: K. Bilby.

Figure 5.11. Abeng blower, Scot's Hall, 1993. Photo: K. Bilby.

In the morning very Early going to march being the Distance of 3 miles from the Said Towne We heard the Wild Negros following us and come up to us blowing their Horns and Immediately fired on us We stood to Our Arms and fought them and drove them off at the Same time I had not above 40 men as Stood by me We still marched on and in less than a Quarter of a Mile they pursued us again Our Hindermost people Seeing them come on So fast that they threw themselves into the River called the back River Grandy with wch. severall of them were drowned: Capt Swartons Cobenah, Quashy, and a White man named Wm. Hill and severall more but unknown as yet the River being very high. (Journal of Henry Shuttleworth, commander of a party sent against the Maroons of Nanny Town, entry of August 4, 1734; BM/Add MSS, 32,689, f. 467–68)

(laughs) They fight with de jonga. They fight with they jonga [and forced the English soldiers over the precipice].

(Charles Aarons, January 30, 1991)

Military Prowess and Ingenuity: Rolling Boulders and Logs

The two texts below [52–53] appear to be related to a military strategy used by Maroons on several occasions and documented in a number of British military reports: the rolling of large boulders down steep and narrow passageways into which attacking British soldiers had been lured.[33] This technique was used both to cause injury and to create confusion among the enemy.[34] In the oral accounts below, the stones or boulders are replaced with a "stick" or log.[35]

[52]

When dem stand pon de Watch Hill, and see de *bare* regiment of soldier dem coming towards dem, dem stay pon de high hill, and dem see dem like out so. And Granfara Parro have a stick. And when dem put [it] down, dem watch dem till dem come near dem. And when dem come, him throw de stick, and Grandy Nanny say, *"fall down!!"* And every *one* of dem fall down a ground—de soldier dem. And dem went in and kill half-part, long lot of dem. [It was] a special stick. Because dem reach round there, it in him hand, him had to change it, and Grandy say, "fall down!" And every one of dem fall down. Dem enemy dem fall down. And dem go in, and dem kill some of dem.

(Margaret Harris, June 1, 1978)

⁂

Our Party became Masters of the Towns [of Nanny's people] or rather the ground[,] the Negros having Set fire to All the houses & left behind only a few Potts & Crockery Ware, the place they flew to for refuge was a Top of Carrion Crow Hill where a body of 52 Men pursued under the Command of a Lieutenant who were defeated by a Stratagem the Rebels had taken in pileing up a Vast heap of Stones against which they Set up Props till our Party come near, So soon as which, the Hill being Excessive Steep, they pull'd away and the Stones run down with great Violence on them, the rebels Seeing the Confusion this had put them into followed the Stones Close & distroy'd Several of the Party & took 3 Alive; this is the best Inteligence I can as yet come at. (letter of J. Draper, Titchfield, June 25, 1733, PRO/CO 137/20)

[53]

Grandy Nanny flee to Stony River, with fe-him troop—him and him two brother, Granfara Parro, and Granfara Jinsandi. And when dem deh pon de mountain there now, and him see de people dem [the white soldiers] coming after dem now, Granfara Jinsandi have a stick. And him throw down de stick. And him say, "fall down." And every one of dem fall down a ground. And dem get in, and dem kill dem. You see? Granfara Jinsandi. When him see dem coming towards dem, him throw down de stick, and him say, "fall down!"—use de words, say "fall down"—and all of dem fall down a ground now. And then dem [the Maroons] get to capture dem [the white soldiers].

(Margaret Harris, February 4, 1991)

[54]

A when me [i.e., my Maroon ancestors] a run, until dem fire done. Grandy Nanny chip a stick, peel off piece of it and give him soldier dem.

Him say, "strike it pon unu finger nail."

And every one that strike it pon dem finger nail get fire. A out of it dem invent tinderbox—fe-his own soldier, Nanny.

(Emmanuel Salvin, August 13, 1978)

[55]

De thing wha' mek Maroon no eat goat, you know, a goat dem did have a lead de troop—Maroon soldier—a goat did a lead it. The other enemy, now, used to poison de water fe kill out de Maroon. And anywhere a de water where de goat

The rebellious Negroes did not See us that was before till we got within forty or fifty Yards of the Guard house that was on the Pitch of the Hill, as Soon as they discover'd us they immediately muster'd all hands & arm'd themselves with Guns, Stones, Lances, & other weapons They had Several great Stones, tyed up in Withs & the Ends of the Withs made fast to the posts of the Guard House. They Seeing that we Still advanced ply'd us very warmly with rowling of great Stones & throwing Small ones, they cutt the Withs & the Stones roll'd down the Hill very thick they fir'd Several Shotts at us but We being under them they Shott over our heads, we avoided most of the Stones by keeping in the Path that was Crook'd just in that place, finding that they still continued reso-lute & that we had 30 or 40 Yards to go up that was almost perpen-dicular. I order'd the men that was behind to keep a continual fire at the Negroes in the Guard House whilst we got up in the Smoak, as soon as we got Close to the Guard House We found there could not above two go a breast in the town. (Journal of a British officer, entry of September 22, 1732, PRO/CO 137/20, 112)

stop and drink now, all de Maroon drink [because if the goat didn't die after drinking the water, then they knew they could safely drink it]. So that come like a it dem worship, you see. A it lead fe-dem Maroon troop. So dem wouldn't eat goat. Any one of de water wha' de goat drink, all de Maroon drink. A de ramgoat wha' guide dem from de poison. So that's why dem no eat goat. And during time past, if Maroon really eat goat, him mash up, him sore [i.e., he would be afflicted with spiritually caused ailments]. Because him shouldn't eat it. (Mansel Sutherland, August 5, 1978)

[56]

Nanny let go sabreke [goat, in Maroon Kromanti language], give bakra, because him got split hoof. Because him bawl, call war pon him. So him let go. (sings)
>   me n'e govern me life-oo, fe sake a love-oo
>   me n'e govern me life-oo, fe sake a love-oo
>   me n'e govern me life-oo, fe sake a love-oo
>   oo, handsome no done a world-oo
>   a hundred a we de ya

Nanny have some goats. Everybody come in at five, you know, goat come in at five, come back in de village. And him know say bakra a go overcome him through de goat dem a come in. Him shift him deal. Him say him naa run him life fe sake of sabreke. That's why him no want no goat. Because dem mek noise, mek bakra catch dem! Dem carry news.

(Sydney McDonald, September 9, 1978)

Military Prowess and Ingenuity: Trapping the English at the Peace Cave

The following three texts [57–59], all from Accompong, exemplify the close connection between local geography and historical knowledge in Maroon communities. All three narratives concern the same event: the last major battle between the Leeward Maroons and British troops before the conclusion of the treaty with Kojo in 1739. It is general knowledge in Accompong that this occurred at the site known today as "Peace Cave" or "Ambush Cave."

Although contemporary archival descriptions of this final military victory over the British have not as yet been brought to light, a number of other writers have made reference to the oral tradition narrated below. Archibald Cooper, for instance, learned during his fieldwork in the 1930s that "about a mile and a half from the village is a cave which is either called "Ambush Cave" or "Peace Cave." As Ambush Cave it represents the chief spot where the British forces, if they came from the east, were waylaid."[36] And in 1943, Richard Hart heard a more complete account that agrees in most details with those below. According to Hart's informants,

> the Maroons prepared an ambush for a body of soldiers advancing to attack them. In their advance the soldiers had to pass across the mouth of this cave [i.e., the Peace Cave] where there was a large flat stone. The Maroons placed a scout within the cave where he could hear the echo of the footsteps as the soldiers trod on the stone. When the echoes ceased the scout knew that the last man had entered the trap and emerged from the cave to sound the signal for the attack on his "aketty" [horn]. Entirely surrounded, all the soldiers were killed (Hart 1985: 96).[37]

The Peace Cave, or Ambush Cave, is one of the few sacred landmarks in Accompong to have withstood the repeated assaults of Christian missionaries and their Maroon converts on the traditional religion of Accompong, and to have survived to the present. As Cooper noted more than sixty years ago, "it is quite a sacred spot, and is considered a favorite hangout for the "Old People," that is the ghosts of the war-time Maroons. In the rear of the cave is hidden a bottle of rum for the use of the spirits when they visit there."[38] More recently, Jean Besson (2000: 122) was told that "a rum-bottle, annually replenished, is placed for Cudjoe's spirit inside the Cave." A half-empty bottle of rum, left as an offering to the "Old People," still lies in the Peace Cave today.

Present-day Maroons keep alive the traditions associated with the Peace Cave during the celebrations on January 6, when they visit it on the way to Old Town

Figure 5.12. Peace Cave, on the way to Old Town, Accompong, 1991. Photo: K. Bilby.

and perform rites from which non-Maroons are excluded. Through these annual observances the sacred site helps to keep each new generation mindful of the unmatched fighting skills of the ancestors. Like the Moore Town accounts of flaming arrows or spears used to sow confusion and flush *bakra* soldiers from their camps, the story of the strategically placed noisemaking stone (or "springboard") that allowed Accompong warriors to determine when all of the enemy soldiers had filed past a certain point in the narrow pass and to count them as well, captures in a single, potent image the military genius of the "Old People." Likewise, the sparing of only one or two British soldiers so that they could return and convey to their superiors the news of their defeat, along with the Maroons' challenge to send more soldiers—a thematic element shared with the Moore Town narratives—strengthens the Maroons' conviction that it was *their* ancestors, not the British, who won the war.[39]

[57]

Kojo wouldn't meet dem [the British soldiers] there, because he didn't want dem to know where him lives. Is just a mile from down there, Old Town there, across to de Peace Cave.

So this ambush now is when de soldiers dem dressed in green bush. So "ambush" means. It was first called "ambush."

Those [Maroon] soldiers wasn't in de Peace Cave. Is only *one*, only de bugleman [i.e., the abeng blower], that one, was in de Peace Cave. Dem set a trapboard, go into a little trap, that every time, every soldiers, every foot that step pon it, that board mek uproar, "pókop pok." So dem coulda stay there and know how many [British] soldiers. It was a board. It's a board, set on a little something like a spring, that when dem step, it go down so, and when dem step off it, it come back up. Another one come and step, it go, and go back so. That was it.

So there was two bugle-man, one inside de Peace Cave, [and then] another one—[one] in de east there, and another one down de west there. So this bugle-man now that Kojo give his words—that if de enemy dem come that way, that if de man pass, wait till when all of dem pass and come in here—then him sound de abeng. When all passes through, him will blow de abeng.

And dem call fire—mean dem put on dem guns—and kill sixty of dem one day. Dem kill sixty soldiers. That was de last of dem. [And that's why] Sir Edward Trelawny, de Governor Edward, say send a message to de king to send troops immediately, otherwise it won't be a Jamaica [anymore], according to certain reports. And then him send troops.

De king said, "oh, my God, I can't allow plenty some sovereign people losing they life and lands."

And a so him sent out two esquires, Colonel John Guthrie Ellis and Lieutenant Francis Sadler, to negotiate and make a final conclusion of peace and friendship amongst us in de name of God, forever and ever, amen. So a peace treaty sign.

(Mann Rowe, January 7, 1991)

[58]

I learn that one night—I think dem say it was a woman was passing through, from Portland, fe go down to St. James, and tell dem that de redcoat dem expect to attack. Now, a myal she dance, and draw dem up.[40] And when she tell Kojo about it, Kojo call up him people dem, and dem set an ambush. For those time, a hundred Maroon out there so, and you don't know, because you don't see no difference beside de bush. That time now dem dress up demself ina de green bush. You can't know. So, right in front of de Peace Cave now, is there de track was. And it is there until now. Dem have a stone set right ina de path. And dem set it in a form of way that anytime you step up on it and you step off, it slam. Right. And dem set a man inside de cave. And I believe it was around three hundred of dem, of de redcoat, de morning. And after dem count dem, de man inside of de cave, him count how much time de stone slam. And after when de last one pass through now, him give dem de signal. Him blow de abeng. And de Maroon ina de ambush. Dem just come down and pen dem up. And dem slaughter dem. Dem slaughter de English soldiers dem, and left one. And why dem leave that one, is fe carry back de news to England. And after when him carry back de news to England now, then dem send out these two men, Francis Sadler and John Guthrie. Is those men now come out and shook hands with Kojo, and offer de peace term.

(Thomas Rowe, January 7, 1991)

[59]

De Maroons live here. Kojo came and live here with his brother. So de English was trying to penetrate this village, you see, to get Kojo. Because he was de strong man. So they were always desirous of getting Kojo. And they knew he was here. Well, de English camp down at Appleton there [where there is presently a large sugar and rum-producing estate], in de plains there. And then they plan to invade Accompong, say they plan to invade Accompong tomorrow.

So tonight de spirits of de dead dance with an old lady. We call that process "myalism." [I don't remember that old lady's name], regrettable that those things were not [written], but orally, it pass from one generation to de other. So de spirit of de dead dance with an old lady, and reveal to de old lady that de English was about to invade Accompong, or Amferi Town[41] then.

And Kojo have de abeng blown, and call de people together, and told dem what de message [was]. Well, Kojo know that it was only one track to Accompong. And it's on de eastern section. So Kojo knew a cave at de side of de track. And Kojo know de cave as a hollow. From this end, you could see de cave, that de cave was a hollow, but coming from de east, you couldn't see it. So Kojo put seven of his men in de cave, with dem muskets loaded. And he puts de man that blows de abeng inside.

Well, in de trap, they put a flat stone, that any soldier step on it, it would rock and mek a noise. So he told de men in de cave to check de footsteps. Well, in ambush, he put de greater regiment to de advancing soldiers, all hidden away among trees and rocks, and even cover demself, camouflage, cover demself with leaves of de tree. So when de men in de cave, de soldiers were coming then. So when de men in de cave didn't hear de stone mek any rock, they presume that they would be on de cave. So de man in de cave, de man with de abeng, came out and sound de abeng. And de soldiers that were in de cave block this entrance. And those that were ambush came out and block that entrance. So, by so doing, they trap de English in de middle. They could neither go backward nor forward.

And Kojo give de command: "shoot!"

And every soldier that carries a gun fell dead. Yeah. They didn't kill two generals, they save dem.

Kojo told dem, "go back to Parliament, and tell your officers to send more men come."

But . . . (laughs) . . . they didn't respond.

Well, they kill every soldier carries a gun. Well, twenty-five Maroons got wounded. But none got killed. Because Maroons were expert gunners. They were good at throwing swords, they were good at using knives. And they were great warriors, because they learned it from Africa, you know, learned de skill of war in Africa. So as a boy, Kojo was well versed in guerrilla warfare. Yeah. So that was how de hostility came to an end.

De treaty was signed de following year, 1739, right below de Peace Cave, just chains below de Peace Cave. 1739.

(Colonel Martin-Luther Wright, January 8, 1991)

Figure 5.13. Maroon hog hunter Joel Osborne with his hunting dogs and *jonga*, Hayfield, St. Thomas, 1991. Photo: K. Bilby.

Hunting the Wild Hog

Jerk pork is now a fixture of nouvelle Caribbean cuisine. In this savory Jamaican recipe (along with its recent spinoffs, jerk chicken and jerk fish, as well as a slew of bottled jerk sauces now sold in supermarkets around the world), the advancing tide of culinary globalization intersects with the deepest currents of Jamaican Maroon history.[42] So rapidly have Jamaican-style jerk dishes spread to other parts of the Caribbean—not to mention northern cities such as New York, Toronto, and London—that it is easy to forget that jerk pork was once an almost exclusively Jamaican Maroon food. When I began my fieldwork in Moore Town in 1977, I was told that jerk pork could be found in only one or two places in Jamaica outside of Maroon communities—at Boston Bay, and in Port Antonio (at a single spot across from the marketplace), both located in Portland parish, not far from three of the main Maroon communities.[43] Even this, I was cautioned, was not "real" jerk pork. Only Maroons knew how to prepare the genuine item, for only Maroons knew how to hunt the wild hog, as their ancestors had for centuries.[44] Nothing less than the succulent red meat of a wild pig, which all its life had fed on roots and berries, could do justice to the Maroon recipe. And only Maroons knew the exact details of this method of preparation that had served the first-time people as a survival technique during the seventeenth and eighteenth centuries.[45]

Like the lance known as *jonga*—a Maroon weapon that retains utilitarian value only in the context of hunting—the pursuit of the wild hog has become a potent symbol of Maroon identity. The hunt, where it is still practiced, is accompanied by ritual gestures and offerings to ancestral and forest spirits, and is suffused with notions of Maroon pride and independence.[46] Nanny herself is said to have had special power over the wild pigs on her territory, and could call them to her when she wanted them; like the forest itself, these animals belonged to her.[47]

While this hunting tradition apparently faded away among the Accompong Maroons decades ago (people there claim that wild pigs have long been extinct in the Cockpit Country), it is alive and well in the deep wilderness of the Blue Mountains, where Moore Town Maroons are blessed with a still-substantial population of wild hogs. For young Maroons in Moore Town, the stereotype of the "hog man"—the tough-as-nails old-time Maroon hunter who was largely ignorant of "modern" town life, but remained master of the bush—is an ambivalent one, viewed as often as not with mocking condescension. Their elders, however, continue to relive the excitement of the chase through vivid accounts such as those that follow.[48] And when the occasional hunter returns to Moore Town with his catch, already jerked and redolent of a proud past, both young and old are happy to partake.

[60]

(As he speaks, the narrator sharpens the blade of the lance he is holding.) We use this this way in de old time as a jonga. De old-time people call it "osunudaja." We use this to kill wild hog, and we travel with it to de bush, all de time, this way. And we attempt this way fe kill a wild hog. De wild hog is a *very* dangerous thing. And so we have to have this now, as a defense.

De old-time people used to have it this way, as gun, fe defend demself, fe fight against white people, from Grandy Nanny days. Dem have to have it this way, and de right way to kill wild hog. We use it all different kind of ways in old-time days. We have it at de Maroon area, as a defense. We have to have it as a gun, this way, to prove that de Maroon is a *very* dangerous people. Therefore Maroon carry all different kind of fame, this way.

Sometime when we go in de bush, we have fe move all different kind of way. We have fe attempt with dog. And serious dog too. And we have fe hold dem [the dogs] this way, put on direct fe kill de hog. Sometime we have fe spin, pass, and come round all different kind of way, and come back to de same movement where we is. And wild hog is a *very* dangerous thing. Therefore we have to got osunudaja this kind of way, all de while, ina de bush, to kill dem.

(Leonard Whyte, October, 1978)

[61]

The last day I and my friend go to hunting, and we come across a large white boar. And I have a dog name Pekori.

And after seeing de hog, I said "catch him! Climb catch him. Catch him, me dog! Run up to him, pass, hold him! Hold him! Anywhere you go, haul! Haul! No let him go! See him so, mek we do so! Tek him again! Anywhere him go! Hold him! Hold him, I say."

And dem back him out. And dem back him up round de rock.

I say [to my hunting partner], "shoot him."

Yeah. And I jump off a highest cliff, and swing down on a stick. And I draw out my jonga, and hit him in his side. And my friend cut his throat.

And then we mek up we large fire, and we caban [barbecue frame] over it, and we start eat.[49]

Well, [we] roast de hog like how we want it to roast now, jerk and such like, and tie it into one intete [hamper, large basket].

(Anonymous Moore Town Maroon, 1952)[50]

[62]

You have wild hog up ina de wood there. Well, all dem wild hog wha' ina wood a fe-Nanny. A fe-him dem. And when it come pon certain time of year, Nanny call dem "Bess." So him call de wild hog dem, "Bess." And certain time of year, you hear de spirit a call: "come, Bess! Come, Bess! Come, Bess!" Dem a call up de hog dem. Some of de hog dem, you get in, you go sit down, and you can't go near dem. Dem kill off all you dog dem.

We have a thing wha' we make. We tek machete, de wear-out machete, and we cut it, and nail it pon stick, and tek we file and grind it. We call it "osunudaja." A so we call it, "osunudaja."

As me hit de riverside, me got a bush wha' me tek, work pon dem [his hunting dogs], mek dem go before me. And sometime a dog will bawl ina de wood, about a mile from me. But if me up on de hill, me hear de sound. But if me under de hill, de sound going come over, me no going hear de sound. So me still a walk a go along. And sometime you see a hog a run, a come there so so.

Sometime you get ina bush, and you have nuff men, when dem get ina bush, dem carry needle, carry needle and thread, [to be used] anytime a boar a cut a dog. Sometime when him catch him so and cut him so, all of him gut, him inside, come out. And man catch him up, and tek time, and put in back him belly, and sew up de place—especially you good dog—tek de needle and thread and bore him flesh, and sew up it, and tek him, put him ina crocus bag [burlap sack], hang a him back here, and him come home a him yard, come put it down, and keep on bathe it, and dress it till it well.

[Once you've killed a hog], you cut off a little piece of de liver, you cut a little piece of de meat, and you have some man call de name of some of dem old-time people dem, and tie de dog dem, no mek de dog no trouble it, and put it down there, and say that a fe-dem.

De hog a fe-Nanny. All of dem a fe-Nanny. Because when it come on to December time, and a man a get ina wild wood, you have fe understand youself in going in there, or you will lost. Spirit will fool you, and carry you way. So you have fe got protection pon you [in the form of "weeds"] fe disguise dem away from you. Yes.

Now, you kill de hog now. You mek fire, cut up wood, mek fire now. You lift de hog now, and you put pon it, singe him. You scrape him off. When you done now, you split him, and tek out de inside. Then suppose a four of unu. A four foot him got. A four quarter. You get a quarter, me get a quarter, de other man get a quarter, and de other man get a quarter. Well now, we clean up de head now, and de four foot, if we want now, put pot pon fire. And we boil. And we drink de soup, and eat dat amount of meat. And you come home.

(Noel Lewis, February 4, 1991)

[63]

We go out hunting. We started from home here one morning, before day.

You would have fe go a hill careful, go sit down till daylight. For you know, when dem first-time Maroon deh hunt, nobody no fe see dem before dem go way. . . .

De hog dem ina Missa Griffith old ground. And as dem tek up pon de flat a de top, de two dog go find de hog dem ina Griffith old ground. And as dem bark after dem, dem say, "w-w-w-w hou hou hou hou hou hou hou!" "Pam!" De hogs dem *travel* now deh come, fe come go way a backwood. And as dem run up pon de flat where Missa Cross is, and me brother Uriah, fe-me brother Uriah *lift* him gun off of him shoulder. And him *lick*, him shoot a "boom!" De boar run, and de shoat coming to me. But I under a rock, and him run on de rock, a top. When him mount pon de rock, a top, when I look up I see de bran [boar] pon de rock, a top. And him stand as high as dat rock be. Him stand pon de rock, and *fly* off like a bird, quite down ina de gully bottom, so "wap!" now going to where me brother Esau him deh now.[51]

I bend down, I say, "watch out! A de hog!"

And when I look, de leader a come same place where de hog deh, but him couldn't fly. Him turn back, and come down, and come run cross me round, and going after de hog. Now de hog going up fe go way a backwood. When him almost catch up to me brother, him smell him. And him stop. But him no contented! Him can't stop. For de dog deh behind him deh come, and him smell a dead before. So him turn sideway now. At this time, me brother see him, when him come up. And him turn sideway, and go against a rock, and stand up.

So me brother hanging with him gun now fe when him come out of de rock, but him said, "no. After him left round where him go there, him going down ina that gully bottom there. Me no going catch him."

So him tek time, and move. And when him look, him see de bare mouth of de hog hang against de rock.

Him say, "well, I can't allow you fe fly way from there."

And him put hand pon de hog mouth. "Pou!" . . . "prim!" . . . a ground.

Not a sign him no hear.

Him say, "boy, a wha' happen?!"

So him go down. Him start fe go down go see what happen. When him go down, de hog get up. But at this time, him shoot de mouth, cut off de tongue, broke de bottom jawbone. A de hog get up and rush after him! But him didn't know that him so badly shoot, [so] him run back. And de hog jump round, and tek pon de road. For is only de mouth humbug. But de lip tear, hang down, dat when him fe run, him foot catch ina it. Him can't go quick. And him tek pon de road now, deh go way a big wood, deh go way a deep wood now. And de two of de dog, dem run him. And dem down pon him. Down pon him. And dem deh follow him with de blood.

Well, till I come up from down a de gully, and come up where I hear de alarm, I only see blood drip a de road, and I following de blood. And we go about a half-mile from there before dem coulda put him pass, stop there. Well, de two dog run down pon him so much that him turn himself ina one big broad-leaf [a tree, *Terminalia latifolia*] root, and put up himself in there, and left out de head. But de head out there when me brother dem run down pon him now, and find that him is so badly shoot.

Him say, "well, if I had known that you shoot so bad, I woulda thump him with de gun bottom. I wouldn't run when him rush after me!"

Well, I run in. Well, when I run in with fe-me loaded gun, me brother say, "see him there? Him cotch [stuck] up in there so."

Me say, "but then, it best fe hit him again."

Him say, "but . . ."

Me say, "cho, man! Hit him again!"

And I put hand pon him. "Ton-n-n-n!," ina de bati [buttocks]. Right ina de bati, say "w-w-wouz!" And him sink, roll back. And we throw down gun. And we mount him with we hand. We lay hold of him, and we wring him. Oh, God! *One* boar. One boar, sah! De three of we now turn him over, and we wipe de neck with knives now, me brother, mount him. And we haul him out of de hole where him put himself ina, and pitch him pon bank, got him dead.

Now, those other two men, dem tie him, and sling him carry come down a road a de old camp, and come after we now, coming after we. When dem come and come find we, with de boar, ai, massa!

We say, "ha-ha-ha-ha! Happy time, boy! Happy time."

Well, we tie de boar, and me and de other fellow sling him. And me brother

Esau, him carry de three gun. And we push out, and when we come where dem kill de other one, we lay dem down there, and then we catch up we fire, mek up fire, and we clean dem up same place. Now, de two hog was so big and good that we no even bother fe follow de shoat. Him left. Him left ina de bush there.

All right. Well, we clean dem up de Saturday, and come out.

(Emmanuel Rowe, June 5, 1959)[52]

6

Prominent Presences

Memorable Persons, Places, and Deeds

Sometimes I think that historians, although they don't mean to, perhaps want to put us in an historical time and they don't allow us to say "but it is alive today." This oratory is here today and we can still hear these things. We know the words today. Historians perhaps want us to say, well it used to be like that. Yes, it used to be like that, but it still is, and it will be for the future, and I believe this.
—Francis Boots/Ateronhiatakon (1989: 39)

Aunty Roachy seh, "A so! But black people never got nobody fi write fi-dem hero deservin deeds eena book, so from generation to generation dem write it dung eena dem rememberance. An my granmodder tell me seh fi-her granmodder tell her seh dat a fi-her granmodder did tell her seh a so!"
—Louise Bennett, "Hero Nanny" (1993 [1975]: 16)

During the early 1980s, a Jamaican government agency dedicated to the promotion of literacy, the Jamal Foundation, issued an educational pamphlet titled *The Maroons—Who Are They?* Although the question posed in the title is in the present tense, the booklet itself dwells almost entirely on the distant past, ending with the Second Maroon War and the deportation of the Trelawny Town Maroons to Nova Scotia and then to Sierra Leone some two hundred years ago.

Only on the second to last page of this publication do present-day Maroons make an appearance. There the reader learns that "Maroon towns now look like any other town in the Jamaican countryside," and that "the people look no different from other Jamaicans in small, farming communities" (Hernandez 1983: 26). If some older Maroons have maintained "old customs" and still "sing the old songs, and tell the old stories," many younger Maroons, we are told, have stopped practicing these "older customs." As a result, Maroons today "behave like other Jamaicans who are not Maroons and they are gradually becoming a part of life in Jamaica" (28).

With such short shrift given to Maroon life in the present, one might well conclude that the answer to the question posed on the pamphlet's cover is that Maroons are a people who once *were*, but no longer really *are*.

Who the Maroons are today certainly has much to do with the deeds of past generations, and the traces these have left in contemporary Maroon expressive culture. In a very real sense, those who continue to identify themselves as Katawud people *are* the stories they tell and the songs they sing. These stories and songs belong to an experiential universe that differs sharply from that constructed by outside chroniclers, for whom only the handful of Maroons mentioned in colonial documents of two or three hundred years ago have any "real" existence. Although this private Maroon universe intersects in increasingly complicated ways with conventional historiography based on the written word, it remains largely independent of it.

What distinguishes this Maroon universe most dramatically from the world of outside writers is that it is firmly grounded in local historical experience. Contemporary Maroon narratives wander over a specific, historically defined social terrain that has been continuously inhabited by Maroons since at least the eighteenth century, and within which the narrators spend their daily lives.[1] This local social geography lends these songs and stories a special immediacy. It is precisely because of the ways in which these specific ancestors and places, and the events they call to mind, are remembered today that they remain connected to a local present.

The narratives and songs that follow were selected to convey this sense of immediacy. We begin with a variety of accounts about Grandy Nanny, the eighteenth-century spiritual leader revered by Maroons today as a founding ancestress [1–22], then move on to the famous story of Nanny's "magical pot"—the specially prepared cauldron she used to lure unsuspecting British soldiers to their doom [23–25]. Following this is a section devoted to the controversial Maroon oral tradition that represents Nanny as a catcher of bullets; the authenticity of this tradition has been contested by some non-Maroons, but it nonetheless remains a core tradition within Maroon communities [26–41]. Next comes a selection of statements about various first-time Maroon ancestors whose names, passed down over the generations, continue to resonate in the present [42–59]. Many of these names are unknown outside of Maroon areas. Rounding out the chapter are a number of oral traditions about first-time ancestors who are remembered in a less favorable light—the despised traitors who "sold out" the Maroons to the enemy, compounding the odds the ancestors had to overcome to survive [60–68].

Grandy Nanny: Queen and Mother

> Such an intricate network of myth and legend [is woven around Nanny] that it is impossible to get at the real facts about her. This has been made more complicated by the recent romantic panegyrics on her purporting to be "history."
> —Mavis Campbell (1988: 50–51)

> Nanny now exists more in legend than fact . . .
> —Barbara Bush (1990: 70)

Outsiders believed that she was someone that the Maroons had created to confound them, a "tall tale" nurtured by the colonial government.
—Bev Carey (1997: 447)

Nanny dead and gone
Nanny dead and gone
And she no lef no will
And she no lef no will
But she lef' property
Ah fe the whole a wi [it belongs to all of us]
But the bigga busha [overseer, boss]
He take it wey from wi
Chorus: Glory to God, Glory to God
     Ah fi the whole a wi
—Sistren Theatre Collective [song performed at "A Tea Meeting Tribute" held by The Organization of Women for Progress and the Women Resource and Outreach Centre in commemoration of International Women's Day, Kingston, March 3, 1990 (lyrics taken from program)]

So mek wi soun de abeng
fi Nanny
—Jean "Binta" Breeze, "Nanny" (1995: 261)

Up until the mid-1970s, Nanny remained for most Jamaicans—or rather, those few with some knowledge of Maroons—a mere "legend." So scanty and ambiguous was the written documentation on this eighteenth-century Maroon leader that some historians were not prepared to concede that she ever actually existed.[2] Mavis Campbell (1988: 283) points out that while conducting archival and field research in Jamaica during the mid-1970s, she was constantly asked whether, given the paucity and fragmentary nature of the evidence, "Nanny's being made a national hero could be justified." A major change came in 1975–76, when government-sponsored research by poet-historian Edward Kamau Brathwaite authenticated Nanny's existence and persuaded the Jamaican authorities to declare her a Jamaican National Hero (Higman 1999: 211–12).[3] Today, few Jamaicans would question the flesh-and-blood reality of this national symbol of triumph over slavery, who now bears the venerable title "The Rt. Excellent Nanny" and shares the media spotlight with other officially sanctioned Jamaican heroes such as Sam Sharpe, Paul Bogle, George William Gordon, and Marcus Garvey.

Nanny has indeed come a long way in the last few decades. A recent publication on the national heroes of Jamaica treats her as if her life story were known in considerable detail. Not only does it specify her supposed life span (1680–1750), but it also states that she was "a small, wiry woman with piercing eyes" (though no contemporary observer described her this way) and lists a number of her ostensible personal attributes: "uncompromising personal integrity"; "a total dedication to the needs of the people in the community"; "love for all the people"; and "a willingness to allow her town leaders to develop their own

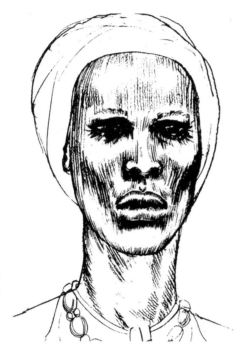

Figure 6.1. "Portrait" of Nanny used in Jamaican government publications, late 1970s. Produced by the Agency for Public Information.

Figure 6.2. "Portrait" of Nanny widely circulated in Jamaica during the 1980s. Artist unknown.

ideas" (Johnson 2001: 1–2). No wonder many today feel that—as a recent newspaper article confidently declares—"the story of Nanny is one of the most faithfully preserved in the rich body of black Caribbean culture."[4]

For Maroons themselves, Grandy Nanny has *always* been vitally and unquestionably real. The passage of countless generations since her corporeal existence came to an end has not diminished her presence. Like the possessing ancestors

Figure 6.3. "Portrait" of Nanny, on cloth (silk screen), 2000. Artist: Fitzroyal Pulinski. Photo: K. Bilby.

Figure 6.4. "Portrait" of Nanny, from house mural in Accompong, 1991. Photo: K. Bilby.

Figure 6.5. "Portrait" of Nanny, mural, Accompong, 2002. Photo: K. Bilby.

Figure 6.6. "Portrait" of Nanny, mural, Accompong, 2002. Photo: K. Bilby.

Figure 6.7. "Portrait" of Nanny by Jamaican "intuitive" artist Evadney Cruickshank, c. 2003. Courtesy of Wayne Cox. Photo: K. Bilby.

Figure 6.8. Patriotic "Nanny of the Maroons" banner sold in shops in Jamaica, 2004. Photo: K. Bilby.

who come to visit and counsel their living descendants at Kromanti dances, narratives and songs such as those below temporarily collapse generational time. Through such verbal representations, the narrators experience a personal and highly focused sense of direct linkage with their ancestral queen. At times their words even join in counterpoint with those of the founding "mother" herself, who speaks through formulaic quotes, sometimes in the Kromanti tongue.

The images are vivid: in the early days, the most powerful Maroon leaders come together and transfer their collective knowledge and wisdom to the young Grandy Nanny, including their own individual *pakits*—a type of spirit form still used by Maroon specialists today—and then make her their queen. She hides her followers in her mountain stronghold above Stony River, and begins to propagate the generations to come ("bring a Toni River, me bring gyal, me bring bwai"). She addresses her adopted "children" with the word *yoyo*, a term that is specifically *hers*. (The word is repeatedly characterized as "Grandy Nanny statement," or what "Grandy call dem"—"[her] 'yoyo' dem"—and as something [she] "claims *all* [Maroons] to be"). She exhorts them with words such as "a pikibo na mi fútu, an mi pikibo a mi din kámadi" (my children are before me [literally, at my feet], and my children are behind me). And while wielding a *jege*—a standard tool of Nanny's trade, used by every Moore Town *fete-man* or *fete-woman* since—mediums of her spirit in later years can be heard to utter her signature phrase (a Kromanti incantation that will appear again, with slight variations, in the following pages): "o Shanti, Shanti kotoku, o kunkwandeba!"[5]

Nanny's presence has remained so vivid in Maroon narratives partly because of the numerous and palpable ways in which her spirit has continued to reside among the living.[6] Over the generations, "Grandy," as her name is often affectionately abbreviated, has continued to "return" and to "visit" her "children" in a variety of institutionalized contexts. Like other Maroon ancestors, for example, she has reappeared among the living from time to time through reincarnation.

In the Windward Maroon communities, reincarnation follows a general pattern that is widespread in West African societies. According to Maroon belief, a child *must* be given at least one of the names of the deceased person who has chosen to be reborn in his or her body; if this is not done, the reincarnating spirit will depart and the child will waste away and die.[7] It is rare today for an ancestral spirit as ancient as Nanny's to manifest itself through reincarnation, although it is known to have been more common in the recent past. Nonetheless, the general practice of naming children after returning spirits, which is still often followed in Moore Town, has generated chains of names and spiritual links that cut across generations; among those whose names have been transmitted in this manner is Grandy Nanny herself, as well as a number of prominent mediums for her spirit who also chose, after their own deaths, to reincarnate in members of later generations. Although one cannot be certain, it is probable that this practice is partly responsible for the frequency of *Nanny* (as well as a number of other recurring names) as a personal name for women in Moore Town well into the nineteenth century.[8]

An even more immediate tie to Nanny is maintained through occasional possession by her spirit in the context of Kromanti Play. As suggested in the final narrative passage below [22], possessions by the greatest ancestor of them all have in recent years tended to be brief, random, and relatively rare. Grandy Nanny tends to come for only a few minutes at a time, to dance and "pleasure herself." Not so long ago, however, Nanny had a number of favored mediums in Moore Town through whom she appeared on a regular basis to dispense advice and spiritual aid to her *yoyo*. One of the last of these was Nanny Ellis, the nineteenth-century *fete-woman* mentioned in the second to last text below [21], who is well remembered in the Moore Town area today as a great dancer and healer. That the spirit of her exalted namesake chose to pass on to her one of her own personal *pakit*s (part of the process of becoming a regular medium for an ancestral spirit) lent this eminent member of "the Ellis tribe" near-divine status.[9]

When Nanny Ellis died, her mediumship (along with Grandy Nanny's *pakit*) was passed on to another *fete-woman* named Emily Ellis, better known as Gallie Ellis (the great-grandaunt of the former Colonel of Moore Town, C.L.G. Harris, and the grandaunt of Ruth Lindsay, the narrator of the passage about Nanny Ellis below). Gallie Ellis (affectionately referred to as Auntie Gallie) served as Grandy Nanny's regular mouthpiece until her death some time in the first half of the twentieth century (probably before 1940). Since her death, no one has yet emerged in Moore Town to take her place as Nanny's recognized medium (although Auntie Gallie's own spirit has made its presence felt in other ways—for example, by reincarnating in the body of a current Moore Town resident). At least two of the Moore Town Maroons whose narratives appear in this book can remember exchanging words with Grandy Nanny during their youth, one while playing the very Kromanti drums that helped summon Nanny's spirit into Gallie Ellis's head on such occasions, the other while dancing at this medium's side.

Grandy Nanny's ongoing "return" through spirit possession has meant that not only some of her original, "first-time" utterances, but also later words of hers spoken through the mouths of more recent mediums, have become lodged in oral traditions that have come down to the present. One example, which we will meet again in chapter 10, is remembered in connection with an attempt by the British colonial government, despite the Maroons' objections, to run a road through a sacred site in Moore Town. On the day that the government surveyor arrived, the same Gallie Ellis mentioned above began to show the first signs of possession, presumably with the spirit of Grandy Nanny. When Gallie's sister attempted to restrain her and prevent her from dancing, telling her to sit down and calm herself, Grandy Nanny appeared in the head of another dancer, this time a male medium, and angrily rebuked the offending sister with the following words: "u sisa kon fi fete obroni fi Braka Ruba. U te en se fi go sjroom. Arete, arete. Tere tere yu wi a fi yarifo suma!" (your sister [i.e., Gallie Ellis] has come to fight the whites

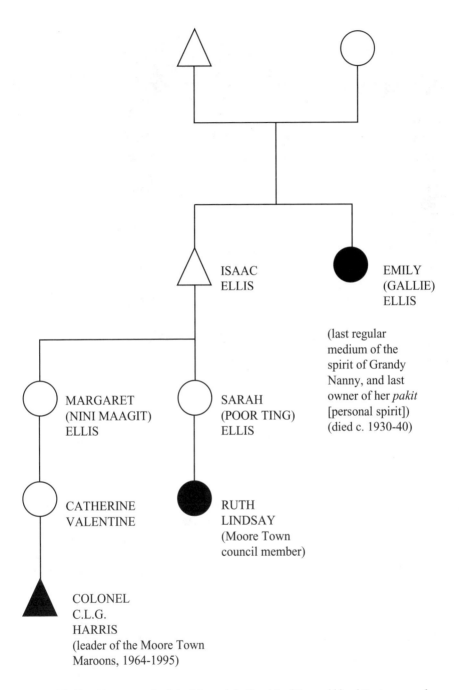

Figure 6.9. How Nanny remains linked through both spiritual ties and blood ties to some of her "children" in Moore Town. Diagram shows family links between two prominent Moore Town Maroons (and contributors to this book), Colonel C.L.G. Harris and Ruth Lindsay, and Gallie Ellis, the last regular medium (to date) for the spirit of Grandy Nanny in Kromanti Play.

Figure 6.10. Plaque on monument to Nanny, Bump Grave, Moore Town. 1991. (Plaque put in place in 1977.) Photo: K. Bilby.

for Black River [i.e., New Nanny Town/Moore Town]. Yet you tell her to go sit down. All right, all right. Today you will have to kill someone!) These words of Nanny are etched into the minds of leading Moore Town elders, for whom they continue to resonate as if spoken yesterday.

From a contemporary Maroon perspective, the immediacy of this founding ancestress in the lives of her descendants gives Maroons a very special claim to authority whenever the question of Nanny's portrayal as a National Hero arises. One of the more recent controversies resulting from differences of interpretation occurred in 1994 when an imaginary depiction of Nanny, drawn by an artist who apparently never bothered to consult the Maroons, began to circulate on the new Jamaican five hundred dollar bill. Colonel Harris of Moore Town was quick to respond with a letter to the main Jamaican newspaper, the *Daily Gleaner*. After politely thanking those responsible for immortalizing Nanny's image on the nation's currency, the Maroon chief registered the following rather strongly worded complaint:

A pall of sadness settles on our sensibilities at the realization that it is now almost a total impossibility for Jamaicans ever to visualise the invincible Chieftainess as she in fact appeared! Grandy Nanny did not wrap her head in that manner. She tied it. And the tying was consummated in a giant butterfly-knot at the back of the head. Evidence of this knot would be visible even from a full, frontal view.[10]

Many older Maroons would say that Colonel Harris is on very firm ground in his assertion; when returning to possess the living at Kromanti Play, Maroon ancestors always have their heads tied in very specific ways, reflecting, it is felt, their preferences when they were alive.[11] Moreover, methods of tying are gender specific; while mediums possessed by female spirits wear an elaborate knot with loose ends at the back of the head, much like what Colonel Harris describes, those possessed by male spirits do not. Since cross-sex possession is not unusual at Kromanti Play, the presence or absence of such a large "butterfly-knot" at the back of a medium's head-tie (*sagl*) communicates important information about the identity (including gender) of the spirit possessing an individual at any given moment (Bilby and Steady 1981: 463–64). When Grandy Nanny used to come and spend long hours visiting with her *yoyo* at Kromanti ceremonies earlier this century, her medium's head would be tied with just such a knot. Indeed, some older Moore Town women tied their heads in this way in daily life well into the twentieth century.

Such details may have little significance in the eyes of government bureaucrats in Kingston, but from a Maroon point of view they furnish inarguable proof of the Maroons' superior grasp of the facts about this illustrious ancestor who, after all, has always been one of their own.

[1]

Nanny was out there as de *queen* of de Maroons, or of de people who fight de cause of de Africans. Because those days they was not name "Maroon." So you call dem de "African" then. So Nanny was out there, fighting de battle as de slaves' queen.

(Johnny Minott, June 4, 1978)

Figure 6.11. Jamaican "Nanny" (as the country's $500 bill is now popularly known).

Figure 6.12. One of Grandy Nanny's descendants wearing woman's head wrap tied in the traditional Maroon manner, Moore Town, 1908–9. Photo: Harry Johnston. Royal Geographical Society.

[2]

> Grandy Nanny come-oo
>   ya yo yanimi
> you come from Toni Ruba
>   ya yo yanimi
> you bring gyal, you bring bwai
>   ya yo yanimi
> Grandy Nanny come-oo
>   ya yo yanimi
> you bring gyal, you bring bwai
>   ya yo yanimi
> come from Baka Ruba
>   ya yo yanimi
> you come from Toni Ruba
>   ya yo yanimi

(George Bernard, October, 1978)

As she [Mother Searchwell, an almost 90-year-old Maroon] spoke of the Legendary "Nanny," warrior chieftainess of the earlier Maroons, who knew things which without doubt were the practice of ancient Africa, the dignity became more pronounced for the Moore Town Maroons claim descent from this warrior queen, who from her mountain stronghold at the source of the Stony River in the Blue Mountains directed the warfare. (Ulrich D. Simmonds, "Land of 'Go and Come Back,'" *Daily Gleaner*, July 22, 1954)

[3]

Dem put Grandy, *trim* Grandy, as a queen, put up there! That four man wha' min a fight de war, dem trim Grandy and put out dem toe fe dem queen. Truly, truly. Dem put him out there, and show him. Is a woman fe de bakra–de bakra got a woman sitting fe dem. Dem [the Maroons] have a woman who stand fe dem too, as de Maroon. But dem never name "Maroon" before dem min fight de war done. After de war fight, dem [took the name] "Maroon" now. But dem name what? *Katawud!*—or runaway slave.

(James Downer, June 25, 1978)

[4]

     Grandy Nanny-oo, weh dem deh?
       Grandy Nanny-oo, ya ye
    Grandy Nanny-oo, grow pon hill-oo
       Grandy Nanny-oo, ya ye
    Grandy Nanny-oo, weh dem deh?
       Grandy Nanny-oo, ya ye
    Grandy Nanny-oo, de voice call-oo
       Grandy Nanny-oo, ya ye
    Grandy Nanny-oo, jo fa river
       Grandy Nanny-oo, ya ye
    Grandy Nanny-oo, weh dem de?
       Grandy Nanny-oo, ya ye

(Scot's Hall Maroons, March 28, 1978)[12]

[5]

Those big men [the early Maroons], when dem coming on de ship [from Africa] now, those people are Scientist, you know. Dem have wha' we call "pakit." We call it "pakit." And all de old men dem now trim Nanny. That time Nanny a young girl. And dem give Nanny every bit of what dem have. Everyone prime Nanny. When me say "prime"—you know how Maroon dealing. Dem prime Nanny. And dem give Nanny everything wha' dem have. That time Nanny a young girl, Nanny no even know. And when dem give Nanny all de training, after dem do that now, dem give Nanny all de training, and mek him know what him going face.

And after dem fix up Nanny now, when Nanny come, after a time now, de white men, or de government, tek all de seafront become slave[holding areas]. Dem fe work. And Nanny say no, him no decide fe work as slave. And Nanny tek up fe-him troops, and a flee way. But at that time, she was already trim. She was already trim fe dat, you know? She was already trim fe dat.

(Charles Bernard, December 18, 1982)

[6]

Me know say Nanny fight. By himself, Nanny fight. Because him was de fighter. De man dem only put him, groom him up, and put him, and dem deh behind. And him was a warranted woman. Nanny a de head, fe fight.

(Ruth Lindsay, February 1, 1991)

[7]

Grandy Nanny was the queen of the Maroons. All the tribes of the Maroons, they made Grandy Nanny a queen. They crown her a queen. Scientifically, they wawatu her. In other words, they crowned her. "Wawatu" is to honor. We honored her. Wawatu. We honored her—you see?—and make her a queen, a queen fe Maroon. So I will impart some of my Science to her, you will part some, all these Science people part their influence and their knowledge to her. So she's full of wisdom. So she becomes the queen, like the queen of England now. She becomes the queen.

(Caleb Anderson, February 3, 1991)

[8]

It's like the queen [of England] going to go to a place. They have people who will groom [her], tell her what to say—they make up a speech for her, and she don't go on her own.

Well, Nanny now, when Nanny going to go out now, the fete-man them come around, and they will pass knowledge and sense to her. And she'll go out and perform great miracles, great works. Yeah. Great works she can do. Any type of thing she can do. Yeah, because she's well groomed, and you cannot hurt her. She died a natural death, because there is nobody can hurt her.

She was then a maiden—a young girl, sixteen, eighteen—when they make her a queen. But she was tall—good fe see too. She looked that way.

And they say, "well, you will be the one fit for a queen."

So they anointed her queen, with the Science—we call it "Science bath." That is [a] kind of spiritual type of thing—when we say we going to give you pakit. In other words, [an individual *fete-man's*] days on earth is going to be ended then. So he could turn over his pakit—that is what him work with—turn it over to you. And then you will succeed him in that part of Science.

Now, some people use a snake [pakit], for instance. When they're going to do Science, a snake come to them. They use a snake to do a thing. So eventually they could turn it over to the other bloke.

Grandy Nanny use all, because everybody give her their pakit when they go now, fe perform alone. So she's strong. You understand what I mean?

If I am going out now, and you give me an advice, and you give me an advice, and you give me an advice, and you give me an advice, I've got them all. So when people ask me anything, I could use your advice, I could use mine, I could use the other man, I could use the other man.

(Caleb Anderson, February 3, 1991)

[9]

When he [Grandy Nanny] come here, he have seven brother. Him have seven brother. But de seven brother a seven business-man [Kromanti practitioners, otherwise known as *fete-man*]. Right. And de seven brother go, and dem tek up everything [all their knowledge], and give it to her, to de one sister, say, "you is travel on, and we'll travel back of you. But you must deh before."

(Adolphus Whyte, February 3, 1991)

[10]

Grandy Nanny never got no man [husband] there. A him brother dem. A seven brother him got. And de seven of dem deh with him. De seven of dem a seven obeah man. Learn that. De seven of dem a seven obeah man. And when dem come a Grasset backyard, when de white people dem deh fool round dem, dem tek everything [all their powers] off of dem, put pon dem sister.

(Adolphus Whyte, February 3, 1991)

[11]

God mek that woman [Grandy Nanny] as a true-born Yenkunkun pikibo, from Yenkunkun prandes, to be what you call a hero, to defend his nation, and to defend his yoyo—tribes and yoyo. When you say "yoyo," [it means] de smaller one coming up—either "pikibo" or "yoyo"—de younger one.

(Robert Dennis, June 28, 1978)

[12]

Grandy [Nanny] say, if is one of his yoyo, him must stand fe tell de congregation—de majority—of de people what going on. When me say "yoyo," you
know what me mean? [It] can [mean] baby. That mean say, a "yoyo" Grandy
call dem [her followers], you know—yoyo. Coming down now, I would say
"pikibo," or "obwato." "Obwato" mean little pikni—pikibo.

(James Downer, October 26, 1978)

[13]

We [Maroons] is Grandy Nanny yoyo, him children dem, him race of family
dem, Grandy Nanny family dem. Him say him "yoyo" dem, call we him yoyo—
mean to say him family dem.

(Margaret Harris, February 4, 1991)

[14]

We wha' left [in the present], we call weself "yoyo." That yoyo deh now—
Grandy Nanny statement now say, "a pikibo . . ." A him yoyo him a talk now,
you know. Him say: "a pikibo na mi fútu, an mi pikibo a mi din kámadi."[13]
Grandy Nanny yoyo a we today. You see? There is another word fe de yoyo. We
now a pikibo. When me say "pikibo," that mean to say we [Maroons of today]
come like him grandchildren dem.

(Noel Lewis, February 4, 1991)

[15]

Him [Grandy Nanny] claims all [Maroons] to be de same yoyo. See if you understand. Him claims de whole of dem, say a fe-him yoyo dem. You understand
wha' I mean? When [they were fighting] de war, anytime him do him hand so
(demonstrates with a gesture, stretching his arms straight out in front of him,
with the palms of his hands facing down), all of dem call him "mother." A so me
hear. So, a so him do. When [they were fighting] de war, and when dem a cease
it, when him want dem fe stop, all when de drum a play, and anytime him do
so, do him hand so, dem stop play. You understand. Sometime him put him
hand pon de drum so. And dem stop. All of dem, every bit of dem, decide fe
stay and hear wha' him got fe say.[14] Because all de power, a him got it. So every
bit of dem come underneath, in one unity, underneath fe-him supervision.
Whatsoever wha' him say, a so it go. Nobody naa go over it, de way how him
got de power.

I hear say all of dem [early Maroon leaders] did powerful. So me hear. Dem
[the whites] crown a queen. So when dem crown de queen, all de Maroons say

dem want a queen of fe-dem tribe too. So all of dem now tek *all* fe-dem Science, and give to Nanny one, and say dem crown him as queen. See if you get de knowledge. So dem crown him as queen.

(Noel Lewis, February 4, 1991)

[16]

Grandy [Nanny] was set there as the queen.

She stand as de representing queen, because she fought de battle. She was out there by these four tactics men. [They] place him out there as de queen, to fight their battle. And she get all de fame. Grandy was de queen of de Maroon. She was de one wha' mek de peace.

(Johnny Minott, February 6, 1991)

[17]

When Nanny come here, him come for a purpose. Him come to seek him pikibo right—Jamaica people right. But dem turn it ina war. De government no like nobody fe wise like demself. You understand? But Nanny come now to defend him people. Nanny come to Jamaica now to defend him people. Him find something wrong, because de government no want to free his people. De government start to fight him now.

Dem [the government] say, "wha' you come here for, man? Me want you fe turn slave, man."

Him want him fe turn slave.

Nanny say, "no, man. Free me people dem, man."

Government say, "no, me n'e *free* dem, because if me free dem . . ."

(before finishing the statement, he pauses to cut Kromanti language): Da mi fa, da mi fa jo wízi, o titéi tei titéi!

Nanny say, "*no, man*. Me people dem fe free." Nanny say, "da mi fra, da mi fa jo wízi, o titéi tei." Him say, a him own people dem him come fe shield. A wha' him mean. Him say, "me going shield me people dem. Da mi fa, da mi fa jo wízi, o titéi tei titéi"—him say a him blood, a him own people dem wha' him fe shield. Like how you come here now, me know you, anywhere me stay, me know you. Him say, "me come fe *shield* me people dem. So free dem!"

De white man say, "no, me n'e free dem, a *me slave!*" Him say, "a me slave dem. If me free dem, me no going get me cane fe cut, me no going get me ground fe dig. Me no going get nothing."

Nanny say, "no man, free dem." Nanny say, "wha' you hold dem up so long for?"

De white man say, "*if me free dem*, me have fe go tek me two hand, go work."

That mean to say, dat deh word now say: "o fámbusu fámba, o kápa wéru, o titéi tei, titéi tei tei tei, bo swao." That mean say him fe tek him hand now fe go chop de grass himself, and white man no want that.

White man want you, fe hold you fe work fe dem. You get me? White man want you fe hold you now fe work fe dem. So anytime him free me, him cane going left, or him factory have fe put aside. So, while him hold de people, de people dem *damn* must have fe work.

Nanny say, "no, man." Nanny say, "what a cause you fe hold dem up?"

Him say to Nanny say, "white man no mek fe punish, white man no fe punish. White man mek fe have a body of people fe work fe dem."

Nanny say, "no, man, that no right."

(Richard Barnes, September 6, 1978)

[18]

    ingia mayongo
    behave o yo
    ingi mengo
    behave o yong'e
    nenge, Nanny call fa

    embia mayongo
    behave o yo
    embi yongo
    behave o yongo
    nenge, Nanny call fa

    embia mayongo
    behave o yo
    engi mengo
    behave o yongo
    nenge, Nanny call fa[15]

(Johnny Chambers, January 11, 1978)

[19]

A Nanny me a tell you about, you know. (sings)
    dala yard, dala yard
    de gyal dem gone
    dem lef me fe mourn
    an tan a yard
Nanny gone, but Nanny left him yoyo dem here, fe mourn and tan [stay] ya. Nanny dead. Nanny dead, because de world belonging to God Almighty.

De last sing wha' Nanny sing—and anytime me tell you de last sing wha' Nanny sing now, me naa give you no more—Nanny say, de last of him condition: "dodge him-oo, yu krach i go, yu krach i come, Kromanti no got no ending." That mean to say Maroon language, Maroon condition, no got no ending, till God Almighty come.

(Noel Lewis, February 2, 1991)

[20]

> Fanti man you kremeni
> a many man en kremeni
> Tata Nyami come
> Fanti man you kremeni
> you many man en kremeni
> me kumfu nyaba-ee

When me tell you about Fanti—"o Shanti, Shanti, bwantu Fanti o Shanti, Shanti kotoku, o kunkwandeba"—a Fanti Rose [i.e., Grandy Nanny's] tune me a throw give you. That's Fanti Rose tune me a give you. (sings)

> Fanti man you kremeni
> you bigi man you kremeni
> you kumfu nyaba-ee

(Sydney McDonald, September 14, 1978)

[21]

[On a Maroon woman from Moore Town named Nanny Ellis, who lived during the later nineteenth century]: You know why dem call him so, say a de Nanny? After de death of [Grandy] Nanny now, when Nanny dead now and bury and dem live here, a him [Grandy Nanny] dance pon [routinely possessed] her. So dem call him Nanny. You see? And when him drop ina ring [became possessed at Kromanti Play], man can't stand against him. Nanny. Nanny. From him born, dem just only call him de Nanny. A Nanny dem call him. Nanny Ellis.

(Ruth Lindsay, January 30, 1991)

[22]

> ya ye yanimi
> Grandy Nanny come-oo
> bring a Toni River-ee
> bring gyal, me bring bwai
> bring gyal, you bring bwai
> Grandy Nanny come-oo
> Grandy Nanny come-oo
> bring a Toni River-ee
> bring gyal, you bring bwai

Now, Grandy Nanny—when you hear we call that woman there now [to a

Kromanti Play], you have fe start [to be careful]. Anyway, him n'e dance pon [i.e., regularly possess] nobody now. No way.

We see him dance pon people ina de long everlasting past. But when him do come [in recent times], him no do no business [serious spiritual work]. Him just come and pleasure himself. Him just come there—we deh a printing [we are on the drums]—him just walk come here, come see wha' we deh do, and him gone. Him n'e stand up pon nobody and do no business.[16]

(Hardie Stanford, September 10, 1978)

Nanny's Pot

> Even Maroons with little or no knowledge of their history can become rather articulate when it comes to recounting the great deeds of "Granny Nanny."
> —Mavis Campbell (1988: 51)

The legend of Nanny's pot is one of the best-known Maroon oral traditions outside of Maroon communities. One can only speculate as to why this particular tradition should have become so well known among the larger Jamaican population. For Maroons themselves, it is but one—and not necessarily one of the more important—of a large body of stories about their founding ancestress passed down from their foreparents.

According to Maroon narrators, Nanny's pot contained a powerful brew that boiled continuously, even though no fire ever burned beneath it. Curious British soldiers who peered into the pot would fall in and meet their doom.

This tradition is sometimes rationalized by historians who conjecture that Nanny's pot is actually nothing more than a metaphorical allusion to a dangerous section of river—a turbulent, frothy pool lying at the bottom of a treacherous precipice at the confluence of the Macungo and Stony Rivers near Nanny Town, where pursuing British soldiers once plunged to their deaths (Robinson 1969: 53; Campbell 1988: 51). Jamaican Maroons today, however, reject such metaphorical interpretations; they insist that what they are talking about is an actual pot and not part of a river. Interestingly enough, the Aluku Maroons of French Guiana and Suriname (and other Guianese Maroons) have similar oral traditions about special pots once used for making war obeah, which boiled and frothed, they say, without any fire underneath.[17] Like the themes of miracle food and bullet catching (see chapter 7, and further on in this chapter), also shared by Maroons in the Guianas, the story of Nanny's pot suggests that more careful research into West African systems of spiritual protection and healing, particularly those associated with war, could shed much light on the specific cultural origins and meanings of certain Maroon oral traditions (Bilby 1995). Narratives such as these, apparently heavily influenced by African cultural ideas and practices, indicate that it is wiser not to stray too far from Maroons' own interpretations when trying to make sense of their oral traditions.

Whatever its origins, this story succeeds eminently in conveying the spiritual giftedness that, according to many, remains a fundamental and unique part of what it is to be a Maroon.

[23]

Him [Grandy Nanny] have a pot. It boil up, it boil up, boil up, boil up. And she sit down there. She naa pay dem [the British soldiers] no mind. And everyone that come and see de pot is a stone dead man. You get that? And she naa pay nobody no mind. All dem wha' deh drop dead, she naa pay nobody no mind.

(Adolphus Whyte, June 7, 1978)

[24]

After dem leave from Old Abraham now, dem go down to Stony River, where dem sign de treaty. A there dem end up everything. And when de [British] soldier come, is a place like this little mouth [edge of an area], you know. And de pot deh, right a de mouth there, and everyone [who] behold de pot is a dead man.

(Adolphus Whyte, December 18, 1982)

[25]

They [Nanny's fighters] have Science where they could put a pot to boil up without any fire underneath it now. And while they [the British soldiers] passing, and look in the pot, he becomes dead. Because it's amazing to see a pot with water just boiling up, without any fire underneath it. So, they take it as a advantage to look at it. And by going in and looking at it, they drop.

(Caleb Anderson, February 3, 1991)

Catching Bullets

Nanny proved such a successful leader in frequent battles that a fantastic legend surrounds her memory to this day. To her is attributed the supernatural power of attracting the bullets of the white soldiers to her posterior where they were caught and rendered harmless.
—Richard Hart (1950: 54)

From Maroon Nanny teck her body
Bounce bullet back pon man. . . .
Jamaica oman teck her time
Dah mount an meck de grade.
—Louise Bennett, "Jamaica Oman" (1982: 22)

Before the 1970s, when she was enshrined as a National Hero and speculation about the "facts" of her life began in earnest, there was little concept of Nanny as a flesh-and-blood individual, except within Maroon communities. For most Jamaicans, the Nanny of "legend" and Nanny the person were indistinguishable. The central image associated with this shadowy figure—an image that, because it was so striking, was probably largely responsible for the legend's staying power—was that of Nanny as a catcher of bullets (or, in some variants, "cannonballs"). The image was in some ways a disturbing one; in most retellings of the legend, by Maroons as well as by outsiders, the method used by Nanny to trap and neutralize the deadly projectiles of the enemy violated widely held notions of both "rationality" and propriety.[18] Even today, the idea that this National Hero used her buttocks (or, according to others, her vagina) in such a way appears to some as not just ludicrous, but also shocking and offensive.

Notwithstanding the offense that this oral tradition causes to some, a number of feminist writers have embraced it and reinterpreted it in their own terms. In her fictionalization of Nanny, the Jamaican novelist Michelle Cliff (1984: 19), for example, envisions the unique skill for which this Maroon leader is best remembered as her greatest military asset, one that she jealously guards for herself: "She teaches [her troops] to become bulletproof. To catch a bullet in their left hand and fire it back at their attackers. Only she can catch a bullet between her buttocks— that is a secret she keeps for herself." For Honor Ford-Smith (1987: 4) of the Kingston-based theater collective Sistren, "the tale about [Nanny] bouncing bullets off her bottom might describe something which literally took place. On the other hand, the tale is offering a greater truth—one which states that the female body brings forth life. In so doing women can turn back death."

Others reject this aspect of the oral tradition entirely, impugning its authenticity. The most vocal of these is Edward Kamau Brathwaite (1994: 120–24, 126), who goes so far as to suggest that the tradition (or at least the part of it involving buttocks) was invented by a British colonial police officer and author, Inspector Herbert Thomas, perhaps during an expedition to Nanny Town in 1890, and then adopted by Maroons who came in contact with him or his book about the expedition, or with other individuals familiar with his writings; by this means, it is supposed to have found its way into their oral history. Brathwaite (1977: 33–34) had earlier surmised that "half-heard, half-understood stories about Nanny" conveyed by the likes of Thomas were interpreted by non-Maroons as "facts," rather than the "symbols" Maroons understood them to be, and that these "facts" were then "debased into the fabrication that has reached us." Eventually this "fabrication," according to this argument, was also accepted by the Maroons themselves. "This story," says Brathwaite, "has been repeated—uncritically repeated—by nearly every if not every writer since Thomas—INC[LU-DING] MAROON LEADERS AND WRITERS THEMSELVES INVOKING ORAL TRADITION" (Brathwaite 1994: 121; caps in original).[19] Brathwaite goes on to argue that this "distortion" reflects the need of colonial historians and ideologues to represent Nanny as something less than "real"—to "buttockicize" her, reducing her to a part-person rather than a whole—and to deflect attention from the real achievements of the Maroons, making successful marronage seem "miraculous" and "inexplicable." It is, he concludes, a way of "shutting up" and "shutting down" Nanny. This interpretation has since been accepted by a number of other writers, such as Werner Zips (1998: 204) and Karla Gottlieb (2000: 51–53). Taking cues from an earlier work by Brathwaite (1977), Gottlieb argues that in the original version of the oral tradition, Nanny used only her hands to catch bullets, but that in more recent times the story "has taken a vulgar twist because of British colonialists who were being derisive about her, claiming that she caught bullets with her buttocks." In this view, the larger theme of bullet catching might be seen as authentic, but versions that bring the buttocks (or other "objectionable" body parts) into play could only have resulted from "burlesque interference" produced by ideologically motivated outsiders (51–53).

Among those who assert the authenticity and ancientness of this oral tradition of Grandy Nanny's using her private parts to catch bullets is the self-identified Maroon author Bev Carey. "The Maroons' oral history," she says, "record[s] that she went down to the Breastworks which was located on Golden Vale Property and there demonstrated to amazed soldiers her tremendous skills as a 'metaphysical scientist' by ordering them to fire their muskets at her. The ancient Maroons say that she caught them in her anus without being hurt and propelled them back at the troops."[20] Anticipating the response of those who believe that an older, more authentic version of the oral tradition must have had Nanny using her hands rather than a more controversial part of her body to carry out this amazing feat, she adds that "educated twentieth century Maroon descendants found the story of Nanny's catching of musket balls embarrassing and appeared to modify that account to indicate that Nanny stooped down and caught the musket balls with her hands placed between her knees" (Carey 1997: 351).[21]

Virtually every Maroon with whom I have discussed this "controversy" is in agreement with Carey on this point.[22] Those of Nanny's descendants who are generally credited with being the most knowledgeable about their history scoff at the suggestion that this oral tradition centering on Nanny's ability to catch bullets using her buttocks might represent a fabrication that agents of British colonialism prevailed upon their elders to accept. They have good reason. The oldest of those whose narratives appear in this book were in their late eighties and early nineties in the late 1970s. They first heard accounts of this particular historical feat from elders in the 1890s, when they were children; indeed, some of them likely heard allusions to it from the mouths of mediums possessed by the spirit of Grandy Nanny herself. The notion that a lone British police official—a mistrusted *bobosi awengkini* [policeman][23]—visiting their area for a short time in 1890 could have introduced such a major modification into a core oral tradition such as this (whether directly or through a book he published in the same year) seems far-fetched. The idea that an "obscenity" dreamed up by a foreign visitor/

writer and with no clear ideological appeal for Maroons could have rapidly penetrated their oral culture, spread to all the other Maroon communities, and become virtually universally accepted stretches credulity to the breaking point. Why, after all, would Maroons agree to "buttockicize" their founding ancestress and culture hero?

Much more likely is the possibility that the key elements of this oral tradition have been handed down over many generations and are based on religious and spiritual concepts that have their origins in Africa—an idea earlier suggested by Kopytoff (1973: 97) and Craton (1982: 81), among others. Although the question of African origins has yet to be investigated carefully, there exists compelling evidence from another part of the Caribbean. (Brathwaite [1994: 121] appears to reject an African origin, at least for the part of the story involving Nanny's buttocks, citing lack of evidence.) Hundreds of miles from Jamaica, in the interior rainforest of French Guiana and Suriname, the Aluku (also known as Boni) Maroons tell that their own founding ancestor, Tata Boni—like Grandy Nanny, renowned for his expertise in the Kumanti (Kromanti) powers brought from Africa—defeated Dutch soldiers during the eighteenth century by catching and flinging back their bullets (Bilby 1995: 174–75). The existence of a cognate tradition among Maroons in the Guianas proves virtually beyond a doubt that Jamaican and Guianese concepts of bullet catching stem from common African roots.[24] According to the Aluku oral historians I interviewed while conducting fieldwork in the Lawa River area in the 1980s and 1990s, Tata Boni was able to catch bullets not only with his hands, but with bodily orifices as well. The same oral tradition was also encountered by the anthropologist Shelby Givens (1984: 40) when he worked among the Aluku in the 1970s. According to Givens, "it is said that one of Boni's *obias* (amulet/spirit) protected him against gunfire. By one legendary account, he caught the enemy bullets with his mouth and then removed them from his anus while proceeding to kill his attackers." Boni, thus, like Nanny, is depicted by his descendants as having returned bullets to the enemy from his anus, with fatal results. Is he also to be seen as a victim of "buttockicization" by colonial thinkers? Or should we instead accept the Aluku interpretation, which attributes this remarkable ability to his mastery of African-derived techniques of warfare?

Brathwaite and those who have taken up his position do have a point. The biases inherent in colonial historiography have long been producing distortions, and some make their way into the accounts of subject peoples. The story of Nanny catching bullets with her posterior may well, as they suggest, have an appeal for outsiders different than for Maroons, and may even, when reinterpreted by non-Maroons, serve to reinforce colonial distortions. But to conclude on this basis that the Maroons' own version of this oral tradition is inauthentic and historically shallow—especially when there is good evidence to the contrary—risks creating new distortions and, much like those who stand accused of "buttockicizing" Nanny, imposing a version of history from without. That a scholar such as Brathwaite—one of the most acclaimed, and certainly most insightful, writers on Afro-Caribbean history and culture, and an ardent campaigner for the serious study of oral history in the region—should end up in such an unlikely position says much about the complexity of theorizing Maroon history in societies such as Jamaica, where contestation by living Maroons is still possible.

The reason this story of Nanny using her buttocks to neutralize bullets is so widely told and retains such force in Maroon communities, I would suggest, is that it contains fundamental cultural and ethical truths. As I have argued elsewhere (Bilby 1995: 174–77), this oral tradition is polysemic: even as it taps deep cultural currents through its allusions to the ancestral forces preserved in the Kromanti tradition, it powerfully embodies the self-concept of Maroons as ever indomitable. Nothing better conveys the spiritual efficacy of Kromanti discipline than the story of Grandy Nanny catching and throwing back bullets, just as nothing better evokes the Maroon spirit of resistance than the image of this spiritual leader and "queen" taunting frightened British troops and daring them to shoot, while presenting her backside in a gesture of contempt still widely used in the Caribbean.[25] The spirit of defiance represented in Nanny's unforgettable gesture (often reenacted mimetically in the telling) is still transmitted to young Maroons as an ethical principle that runs through the narratives of their elders.[26]

If this image reduces Nanny to a caricature, a mere "part-person," in the minds of outsiders, it does nothing of the sort for her descendants. For them, it is but one—though a particularly vivid one—of a larger set of narratives (several appearing in this book) that depict Nanny performing a variety of deeds in a range of settings. Grandy Nanny, her *yoyo* will tell you, is as "real" and as "whole" a person in the spirit today as she was when she lived among them "in the flesh" more than two centuries ago.

[26]

Nannie say, I will show you some tricks. Then it was set. So white soldiers who have been sent with arms ready to fire. After fire 57 volleys, turn herself and catch balls, hold them in her hand. Peace made that day. True story. On record. Never seen nothing happen like that. Signed blood treaty that day in May 1738. Captain Accompong, Captain Cudjo and Nannie.

(Anonymous Accompong Maroon, 1921)[27]

[27]

The chief entertained us with an account of how his people conquered the British, through the magic of their queen, whom they called Nanna. She had caught in her hands[28] the bullets the British had fired, while inciting to wondrous deeds of valor her own men, so that the British were repulsed with fearful losses and the result had been the signing of the blood treaty.

(Helen Roberts, paraphrasing an oral tradition related to her by Colonel H. A. Rowe, chief of the Accompong Maroons, in early 1921)[29]

[28]

Nanny would go out on the open and squat down with her buttocks pointed towards the enemy. The resulting barrage of bullets would be attracted to her vagina, and would travel harmelessly [sic] through her body & out of her mouth into her waiting hands. Before these bullets were used they were washed in rum and weeds to take off any charm that the British might have put on them. Then the bullets were fired, and because of their treatment [were] infallible: they never missed their mark.

(Archibald Cooper, summarizing oral traditions related to him by various Accompong Maroons in 1939)[30]

[29]

That's de ancestor. That's our ancestor. She takes her posterior and catch ball during de rebellion. Grandy Nanny.

(C. U. Walters, 1950)[31]

[30]

Grandy Nanny *tek* him bati and catch ball. And when soldier *shoot* him, when soldier *shoot* him so, him tek out [the bullets] and show him, say, "see ball here, see ball here." Him show him it. And dem couldn't shoot him. Dem *shoot*, and dem couldn't shoot him. And bakra say, well, all right, dem fe mek peace with him.

(James Downer, 1978)

[31]

Grandy Nanny [was] a powerful woman. Him *guide* fe-him people dem. Because [she] tek him bottom and catch ball—something like gunshot. And when him catch de gunshot dem done, him turn round, him say [to the white soldiers], "unu finish?"

Dem say, "hm . . ."

Him say, "see unu ball dem here."

Him tek de ball, him show dem every ball wha' dem fire after him. None of dem couldn't hurt her.

(Margaret Harris, June 1, 1978)

[32]

Nanny was de head into that midst of fight. And Nanny stand all de bullet. Dem fire de bullet, and him set him bottom, and him reach it. And him catch it. And Nanny was still standing strong to fight de war. And when dem find out, dem didn't have nothing to do with Nanny. Dem draw back. And dem come together, and dem mek peace.

(Johnny Chambers, January 6, 1991)

[33]

Nanny was a good fighter. When dem send de balls on him, him turn him bati and catch it, catch de gunshot. You understand. So now, [the whites] don't have nothing to do with him again. You see de meaning. For from de man shot out a you, and you tek you bottom and catch it there—not even you hand, just you bati you turn and catch it—wha' you have fe do with him? Nothing fe do with him again. You can't do him nothing, man. (laughs) So as far as that now, dem say, boy, dem can't manage that fight here. You see. Dem can't manage that fight here. That a de greatest ina history, you know. De greatest that. Is a Science, man. Him great. That a de greatest ina history, man, ina de history of de Maroon. And a gunshot dem a fire, you know. And you know, dem deh time, a long gun, you know. And you know de long gun, how dem powerful. A long distant shot. And a that dem give Nanny, ina him bati, man. And Nanny stand it, man. Nothing can't do him. And him deh woulda kill dem off. You see wha' me mean. That is de history of de Maroon. All wha' you hear man a go say, trust dat deh history of de Maroon.

(Johnny Chambers, January 5, 1991)

[34]

[It was] when they were really marching, those people. She [Nanny] go in front, and order dem [the whites] to fire. And dem could fire till dem all having *no* cartridge left. And when de last one fire, she able to gather all those [bullets] fast, and give to dem, de nation that was fighting against her.

(Uriah McLean, June 23, 1978)

[35]

Grandy Nanny, now, fought with de Maroon people. De first word him use in his battle is de word, "fámbusu, o famséri." And when him say so now, all de bullet wha' fire pon him, him catch dem ina him hand. And him pass dem through him rum, and they becomes cold.

(David Phillips, July 17, 1978)

[36]

When dem [Nanny's people] go up, dem smoke and stop. And dem was coming up. Dem have dem gun and all dem weeds dem. Dem [the whites] shoot it at him [Nanny]. And him show dem [their bullets], him say, "see it here." Him tek it and push ina fe-him gun, and when him shoot, thousand of white men dead.

(Emmanuel Salvin, August 13, 1978)

[37]

Him say yes, him [Nanny] agree fe dem [she and the English] mek up [when she decided to accept the peace proposals]. But him [the British officer] must count de soldiers dem, say how many soldiers him have, and put dem out in a row. And him going face dem—dat deh little Nanny, you know. A no de *man* dem [it wasn't the *men*]. [Rather, it was] Nanny. And Nanny going fight dem. A no de man dem. A *Nanny* going fight dem. And him double him frock [dress], lap [bunched up between her legs] him frock, and say dem must fire a him. And *all* de soldier fire a him. And him tek up every one of de ball dem, put ina him paki [calabash bowl]. And when him done, him shake him frock.[32]

Him say, "you done?"
Dem say, "yes."
Him say, "count dem."
And him count it. And Nanny [still] living. Dem *frighten*!

(Ruth Lindsay, January 30, 1991)

[38]

When de white man fight after Nanny, to every bullet wha' de white man do so, "wup!" pon Nanny, Nanny just do so (gets up and stoops over, acting out the motion of Nanny aiming her buttocks at the British soldiers), and tek every damn ball, with wha' him have—catch every *damn* one of de white man ball dem. Him catch every *damn* one.

So when we learn about Nanny, those are noble fight.

(Hardie Stanford, February 1, 1991)

[39]

That's a woman! And dem fix de woman [Nanny] ina man [i.e., they ritually prepared her as they would a male soldier]. And dem carry him over on de place wha' dem call name Pumpkin Hill, a one peak. And when him go up there, you got a bigger flat more than wha' you a see here so, flat. There so dem go, through that deh area flat.

De woman say, "we a go fight battle!"
A de woman dem fix. Woman dem fix. Me a go tell you de name of de

woman [in a while]. When dem fix de woman, de woman go up there. Dem put de woman there. And dem yeri [saw (literally, "heard") the sails of] a ship blow. And when dem see de ship blow, dem see a *hells* of soldier come up, a come up de hill. You can't walk so, you can't walk so, you can't walk so, you can't walk so. A hill. You ever go through a de hills nuh? If you walk so, man will kill you. If you walk so, man will kill you, anywhere you walk. But dem deh Maroon soldier deh pon de top. And when him go up there, him look, him see soldier come up bad, man!

Me a tell you now: that a wha' dem call de Grandy Nanny. Dem call him Grandy Nanny, but a woman.

And when him [the British soldier] come up, when him come up under de hill there, when him go up pon de peak—remember, you know, dem no got no gun, de Maroon people never got no gun [at that particular time]—and when him come up, and him [Nanny] say, "where you a go?," him [the British soldier] say him come fe kill out de Maroon dem.

Him [Nanny] say, "you want kill de Maroon?"

Him say, "yes."

"All right, boy. [To the other Maroons]: Him say him want kill de Maroon too."

And him [Nanny] go pon de machete—but dem call it *afana*. And wha' lance wha' dem got, dem call it *jonga*. And de woman stand up pon de hill there.

And de woman say, "since you come fe shoot Maroon, shoot me!"

And [she] "wap!" dem [hit them a heavy blow] with him jonga, you know. And dem fire gun, you know.

Him say, "shoot me! Shoot me a me laas [ass]—see ya so—shoot me a me laas!"[33]

Him turn him bati, and him catch [the bullets].

Him say, "shoot me!"

Him say dem fe shoot him a him raas.

Him say, "shoot me a me laas!"

And dem shoot him, you know!

That time me and you no mek a world, no world no mek fe me and you. But a history.

And when dem start a *shoot*, you know, soldier dem a *shoot* him! And so perhaps you shoot him, him do so. (Gestures as if taking a bullet from between his buttocks, and throwing it aside.) Him throw you ball there. You can't shoot him more than so. And him lick dem, him lick dem, him lick dem with him machete.

And de last soldier wha' left, de *last* one wha' left, him catch him, and him tek way every gun. All dem deh wha' him a lick, him a tek way de gun dem from dem. You see? Like you dead, me tek way you gun, put it pon de hill. Everything put pon de hill.

So de last one wha' left now—that one now must be de captain, or de captain son—him catch him.

Him [the white soldier] say to him [Nanny], say, "do [please], Ma, no kill me!"

Him [Nanny] say, "no, me naa kill you. You know wha' you do? Go back to you boss where you come from, and tell him say him must send ten thousand more."

(Henry Shepherd, February 19, 1991)

[40]

When de soldier, de Captain Stoddart, attack Nanny, him try a firearms—wha' we de Maroon call "otúa" [gun, in Kromanti language]. And Nanny stretch his bottom and catch de bullet, and tek it from him bottom, and fling it back on de gunman. (While narrating, he reenacts the scene he is describing with gestures, playing the role of Nanny taking the captured bullets from between her buttocks.)

And Nanny say, "mi máami sáli rénden túa mi nan du! (long pause) Jet, jet, jet not loose, tei am, no tei am. O máliko, o máliko salám" [ritual incantation].

They run out! And when Nanny fling back de ball pon de gunman, they catch their fraid.

Nanny started to use afana. Him use afana.

Him say, "afana bíba."

(long pause, while he rubs some plants together in his hands, and then puts them in his pants pocket)

Nanny sung this sing. (sings):

    o yani-oo
    o yani-oy
    o yani-oo
    o yani-oy
    o andi Kofi
    in kii konson kwaimba
    o andi-oo
    mayan done-ee

(long pause)

It a mek me skin hot like fart. Mek me skin hot! Me skin hot, man.[34]

(Noel Lewis, February 2, 1991)

[41]

Mek me tell you. Mek me tándabósokom.[35] Mek me stand up. (He stands up.) Mek me stand up, show you something.

When de soldier dem come down pon Nanny so, when dem do so, "bam!," when dem go shoot-shoot, till when de gun done, dem lean pon it so, "boom!" Dem do so in de bing [rear end] so.

[Nanny said]: "O jéekum!"

Watch me now!

(He begins now to mime the actions of Nanny as he narrates the story, stooping down and presenting his rear end to the British soldiers.)

Dem do so in de bing.

[Nanny said]: "O jéekum!"

"Bam!"

Him turn him bati. A him bati him mean. Him turn him bing so, him bing.

"Pou!"

Him bottom. Dem [the Maroon fighters] catch every shot in him [Nanny's] bing, catch every shot.

"Bong!" pon Nanny.

Nanny do so.

"O jéeku!"

"Bam!"

"O jéeku!"

Every shot go ina Nanny bottom. Dem [the Maroons fighting with her] tek him bottom mek gun now. Him no bother with gun. Tek him bottom.

"Boom!" pon Nanny.

Him turn him bottom.

"Boom!" pon him bottom so.

But *every* shot go ina him bottom, Nanny bottom. Nanny tek him bottom mek gun.[36] And every shot dem shot, him use that word: "o jéekum!"—"kill it, kill de shot."[37] De shot can't do him nothing. Dem da shoot him from now till judgment morning, dem can't do him nothing. And not a man out of dem give Nanny no shot. Every "bam!," him turn him bottom: "o jéekum!" Every shot go ina him bati ya so, him bottom. Every shot. A Nanny bottom him tek catch every ball.

Shww! (blows some rum).

(Addresses the spirit of Nanny): All right, Nanny. Me shouldn't tell da nyuman da sónti, but o so i go. You see da no lie me a tell. Him waan fe know wha' min deh happen, time of old, and unu fight de war an sinting. A dat min deh happen deh. Him waan fe know time of old wha' min deh happen. So me have fe tell him de past times, wha' you have e gwan wid.[38] (Sprays some more rum on himself from his mouth)

(Richard Barnes, February 4, 1991)

Other First-Time Ancestors

There is an interesting discrepancy between the first-time ancestors remembered by present-day Maroons and those whose names commonly appear in the representations of non-Maroon historians and other outsiders. To be sure, there is some overlap between the two. For instance, both the Maroons themselves and those outsiders who have written about them give great importance to Kojo (Cudjoe), who is probably the best documented of the early Maroon leaders in the written records kept by Europeans. Nanny, in contrast, receives scant mention in colonial documents, and it was only in the 1970s, when she was named a National Hero, that her name began to appear regularly in print.

Virtually none of the other early leaders whose names often appear in the accounts of Europeans (and, therefore, other outsiders) plays a significant part in Maroon oral traditions. With the exception of Kojo's "brother" Accompong—the founder of the present-day Leeward Maroon town named after him, whose spirit was for many generations at the center of the traditional religion of that community (Kopytoff 1987)—the various leaders listed in the two treaties of 1739 seem to have all but disappeared from contemporary Maroon narratives about the past. Johnny, Cuffee, and Quaco, listed in the Leeward treaty along with Accompong as "captains" under Cudjoe, seem to have left few if any traces (at least under those names) in present-day Accompong oral traditions. It is true that leaders and other spokesmen for the Accompong Maroons sometimes mention Johnny, Cuffee, and Quaco in public orations, but this probably stems from the fact that this community is still in possession of a paper copy of the treaty upon which those names were inscribed by the British co-signatories. Other than Accompong himself, who as the "Town Master" remained a vivid spiritual presence among the Leeward Maroons well into the twentieth century, the "captains" under Cudjoe mentioned by name in the treaty seem to have significance for present-day Accompong Maroons only in the context of the sacred document in which their names were preserved.

Likewise, in the Windward communities, none of which have retained an original copy of their treaty, all but one of the names of the Maroon leaders mentioned in that document appear to be absent from older oral traditions. (The one possible exception is Apong, who may be the same person as the warrior known as Opong, featured in several narratives in this book, most notably those on "Refusing the Peace" discussed in chapter 8.)[39] In the Windward treaty, the main Maroon leader and co-signatory is Quao, and the "captains" under him are named as Thomboy, Apong, Blackwall, and Clash. It appears that even Quao, despite the crucial role he played in concluding the treaty, is virtually never mentioned (at least under that name) in present-day Windward Maroon oral traditions—although, once again, Windward leaders who have read about Maroon history (some of whom have seen the text of the 1739 treaty in books or other printed sources) do sometimes pay homage to Quao and his "captains" on formal occasions at which visiting dignitaries are present. The ancestral leader universally remembered by Windward Maroons today as the individual who authorized their treaty with the British is not Quao, but rather, Nanny (whose name does not appear in the treaty). Few if any of those Windward Maroons who are unfamiliar with written accounts of the treaty have even heard of Quao.[40] Nonetheless, in the eyes of many outsiders, the latter remains, after Nanny, the most important Windward Maroon figure of the eighteenth century.

Many of the first-time Maroons mentioned in present-day narratives have a real existence only for the Maroons who have maintained these oral traditions, most of whom are Kromanti practitioners (although, as we shall see, the existence of at least some of these legendary figures can be independently corroborated with the help of written sources). Although these historical Maroons are not widely known today, even in the particular Maroon communities with which their stories are associated, knowledge of them continues to be passed on among a select few, and in this sense they remain a part of the "intimate culture" of the Maroons.

Presented below is a sampling of texts [42–59] about a few important first-time Maroon ancestors who seldom, if ever, make appearances in written sources. Some of these individuals are remembered primarily because of their association with songs or Kromanti proverbs, such as Kwako (Quaco) of the Windward Maroons, who learned direct from the source to respect the fact that "the snake has no breasts, but still she raises her children" [42]. Others are remembered partly because they occupy key positions within the structure of Kromanti cosmology; among the latter are the four "top generals," Granfa Swifomento (or Swiplomento, also known as Do-an-Consider), Granfa Welcome, Granfa Okonoko (or Okronokro), and Granfa Puss [43–55], as well as other first-time heroes such as Granfa Parro and Granfa Okobisani. We also learn in some of the statements that follow [56–58] that Grandy Nanny was not the only woman with leadership qualities among the first-time Maroons. Mama Juba, for instance, is said to have been, like her "cousin" Nanny, a dangerous "soldier." And just as today, there were numerous women in the early days who excelled, alongside Grandy Nanny, as Kromanti specialists—great *fete-uman* such as Grandy Wanika and Grandy Dokose.

Through such verbal representations we also begin to learn of particular attributes of these individuals. Granfa Swiplomento is said to have been Nanny's "private secretary" as well as her "man" or "husband"; he is also remembered for having risen to a top leadership position, after persuading his people to continue the fight when some, out of desperation, were ready to surrender (see chapter 7). In addition to being a great warrior, he was a "watchman," a guide, and an intelligence gatherer—one who warned Nanny and her people of approaching dangers. We learn as well that he also had an "English name," Rose Harris. Another early leader, Granfa Puss, is said to have been Nanny's "son" (by another man, not Swiplomento). (According to some narrators, Nanny actually had a number of children, including a daughter named after herself, and a son named Kojo.)

Knowledge about these individuals, since it is highly sensitive, is often transmitted in fragments (as in the texts below). Nonetheless, these first-time Maroons remain a powerful presence among the living. For one thing, some of them make frequent "cameo" appearances in narratives that do not center on them. (The attentive reader will quickly recognize that some of these names occur in other chapters of this book.) Furthermore, like deceased Maroons of more recent generations, these older ancestors sometimes visit their descendants to participate in Kromanti ceremonies. As James Downer emphasizes in one of his statements [52], first-time Maroons such as the four "generals," who were born in Africa, are very particular when they take possession of living mediums. The smallest details of behavior, things that are taken for granted by present-day Maroons, may suddenly be thrown into question when the oldest generations of Katawud people come to share the physical space of their descendants. Downer provides a dramatic example, pointing out that when a first-time ancestor such as Granfa Swifomento or Granfa Okonoko takes possession of a Kromanti dancer, the latter will immediately try to kick off his or her shoes, since these are entirely alien to what these ancestors knew when they were alive.

Not only through ritual performance of this kind, but also through narratives about such behavior, the first-time people continue to assert their presence in the world of the living.

[42]

De snake say, "o sirio man de, o sirio man dead-oo."

De man lick after de snake with him stick, him say, "o nangka nangka, o nangka nangka bishó."

Him say, "snake, you no have no bubby [female breast]."

De snake say, "o sirio man dead-oh"—him say him no have no bubby, but him raise him pikni dem.

That a old time man, man. That man dead and gone. A one of dem Kwako, either Li [Little] Kwako or Big Kwako, but a one of dem old time man.

(William Shackleford, September 21, 1978)

[43]

You have four man [leading the early Maroons]. You have Granfa Swifomento. You have Granfa Welcome. You have Granfa Okonoko. You have Granfa Puss. Four man.

(James Downer, October 3, 1978)

[44]

[It was] *four* man, and Grandy [Nanny] swelf [self]. You have Granfa Swipomento, Granfa Welcome, Granfa Okonoko, Granfa Puss. You have Grandy's private secretary. You have Grandy husband. And him son.

(James Downer, 1978)

[45]

De Maroon man have a tune sing for all generals—all those five men—or those four, de four men—you have tune wha' sing for de four. But that mean, whenever time de Maroon man going sing those four tune, it mean that is something serious.

(Before naming the four generals he blows some rum, and cuts some Kromanti language): Kwába kwa kwé! Okonoko, yampóni yantáni.

Swiplomento, Okonoko, Welcome, Puss [are the four generals]. Bosco come out, because Bosco become a traitor. So that's de four of dem.

These four sings don't sing for any petty matters, and not jokes. It must be seriousness that you hear these sings sing. They are not sing for simple doings, nor simple action. They sing for special occasions, or in times of help.

(Johnny Minott, June 4, 1978)

[46]

It was four of dem. You have one dem call Granfa Siplomento, [and] Okronokro, Welcome, and Puss. Four of dem. You have Siplomento, you have Okonoko, you have Welcome, and then you have Puss. Four top men. Well, he [Puss] was de head when they start to fight. But evidently when de fight goes hard, de head change to somebody else.

(Johnny Minott, February 6, 1991)

[47]

Mento was Grandy's [i.e., Nanny's] private secretary. That mean him was Grandy's man. Puss was Grandy's son, but he was not Mento's child. At the starting point of the fighting, Puss was the head, you know. But when it come down that the voice call to Mento, he become the head.

(Johnny Minott, September 10, 1978)

[48]

Do-an-Consider [a.k.a, Mento, or Swiplomento] was de man who, when they have fought for twenty and nine years, [became leader].

(Johnny Minott, June 4, 1978)

[49]

You would heard de Maroon man sing a tune, "falla river, wa jo fa river."[41] Is that man tune—Swiplomento. His [English] name was Rose Harris.

(Johnny Minott, June 4, 1978)

[50]

Mento [was] Grandy's private secretary—[that] mean him was Grandy man.
Him was Grandy man. Dem have children, three children. Well, one of de chil-
dren was name after Nanny's name—you know, Grandy Nanny. Him name
Nanny. That was de daughter. [The other two were]: Ampong and Kojo.
(Johnny Minott, February 6, 1991)

[51]

Me hear plenty man was talking—Maroon man too—about Kojo, Nanny, has
fight so much battle. Me say, "which one of de Nanny?" For me know,
Nanny—which is Grandy [Nanny's] daughter—have never fought no battle.
[Grandy] Nanny fought battle. Dem mother has fought battle, but de daughter
have never fought no battle. De daughter was in Kojo's and Accompong days.
(Johnny Minott, June 4, 1978)

[52]

Granfa Parro come from Africa. Granfa Welcome come from Africa. Granfa
Swiplomento, him come from Africa. Dem come from Africa. Granfa Puss come
from Africa. A four man. Granfa Okonoko come from Africa.

　　Granfa Swifomento, Granfa Okonoko—that mean say, from de moment dem
deh man a go come here and ride a man [i.e., possess a medium], dem no know
this (points to his shoes). Dem no know it, none at all. That mean say dem
wouldn't dance ina it [shoes] none at all. Because dem no know it. A man come
down off of dem [i.e., even an ancestor of a later generation] wouldn't dance on
it too. Because dem fraid it. From de moment him come pon de man, and him
look pon it and say, well, something deh pon him foot like that, him a go flick it
off! Him never used to it.
(James Downer, May 31, 1978)

[53]

De fight fix up with woman and man. It's a mixed multitude. You got Granfa
Parro, one of de head of de fighter. You got Grandy Sukasi. You got Granfa Welcome. And then you have de world champion, which is Grandy Nanny. And
[when we] fight any damn battle, we *can't* lose.

　　Me hear [of] Granfara Parro, Granfa Welcome. Granfa Okro.

　　Granfa Swiplomento was one of de smartest man with Grandy Nanny. Him a
Nanny second—de hero Nanny. Him a de second fighter with Nanny. [He] see
all de danger with you. And clear de danger. See all de danger with *you* [i.e.,
white people]. Him clear Nanny. Meanwhile, Nanny out there a fight, you know.
(sings)

mind how you walk-oo
danger di-de-oo
boman pel-oo
mind how you walk
danger maka [literally, dangerous thorn] di-de [is there]

So meanwhile, Nanny out there a fight. Some of de time when Nanny deh
fight, him no see danger. So de same man [Swiplomento] talk to him: (sings)

boman pel-oo
mind how you walk-ee
we da boman pel-oo
mind how we walk
danger maka di-de

Him mean say unu [you whites] deh pon we. So him must damn be careful!

So those man come like expert, with Nanny. Nanny a boss, though. But in
everything, you have one under boy. And de under boy ride same way like you.

But, you know, sometime when you deh fight, you no see de danger. Because fight you e fight. But de expert man sit down now, and him gather all
wha' deh happen. Because nothing no e pass wha' him no see. But Nanny ina
battle deh fight. "Mind how you walk"—him say, but be careful!

(Hardie Stanford, February 7, 1991)

[54]

Swifolomento. Now, that man is a fighter. Him fight with Maroon, and him fight
with Nanny. De man say him swipple. Nobody can't do him nothing. And nobody can't do him pikibo dem nothing. Him say, "nóbá cháan du mi píkin de
nótn" [nobody can do anything to my children].

That mean say him good at everything. So you can't shoot him, you can't
kill him, you can't chop him. Even him pikibo, him children, him pikni dem, you
can't do dem nothing. You can't hold him, you can't shoot him, you can't do
him nothing. You have fe just left him to himself. Any damn thing wha' him
want fe do, it must done, this man Swiplomento. Him swipple fe true.

Swiplomento a watchman. This man now is a watchman, Swiplomente [alter-
native pronunciation]. Anywhere de bigger body of Maroon deh, and want fe
know anything, dem go to him. And him woulda direct dem, and tell you where
de things happen, or if de somebody krému nánti anywhere—meaning de
somebody dead—and you want find him. So dem can't do without him, him is a
guide fe de Maroon. Him swipple.

Dem go to him, say, "Mary dead, we no know where him deh, we can't find
him." Him say, "ba! Unu so wókris [worthless, in old Maroon creole]. Cho! Unu
no have no use." A cuss him deh quarrel with you now. "Unu no have no use,
ba. Cho! Give me de insa [rum, in Kromanti language]!" Dem give him de insa.
Him blow. Him say, "go a da pre [place, in old Maroon creole] de"—whether
Marshall's Hall, or Moore Town. Him say, "go a big siton [stone]. You see Mary

lie down there." When you go there, you will see if a opete [vulture, in Kromanti language] deh pon him, you will find him.

So, him a one of de Maroon guide. And him tell with him strength, with him tricks. De word "swipple" [tricky—literally, slippery] mean to say, you can't do none of me family nothing. Because me see before you even start.

(Richard Barnes, February 4, 1991)

[55]

Swifiomento, he was something else. He was brilliant. He was a left-hander. And he used the left hand. And he was such a skilled thrower of the spear, the jonga, that—though all jonga-men in those days were so skillful—yet he was like the dean of the jonga throwers. He never missed. Never missed. Swiporomente [alternative pronunciation]. He was the chief of the throwers. As I said, he was a left-hander. And he was a perfect thrower.

(Colonel C.L.G. Harris, January 31, 1991)

Leaders Written Out of History: Welcome and Swiplomento

At least two of the male ancestral leaders whose names recur in the above narratives—Welcome and Swiplomento (also known as Swifomento, Sipliomento, Swifiomento, Swifolomento, or by a number of other pronunciations)—can, I believe, be matched with names and persons mentioned in eighteenth-century archival sources.

The case of Granfa Welcome seems particularly clear. In a letter of May 3, 1767, the governor's secretary writes the following to Charles Swigle, the superintendent at Moore Town:

> Capt. Sambos Badge by the Govrs. Order I have return'd to him again, and have rebuked Clash for presuming to take it from him Capt. Welcome's Badge I have kept for the present—and Welcome, who was the Bearer of your Letter,—You have the Govrs. Authority to give him the Commission and Rank of Lieutenant (Jacobs 1949: 107).[42]

In this letter, written nearly two decades after the Windward treaty of 1739, we learn that the last of the captains mentioned in that treaty, Clash (elsewhere in the letter referred to as "Captain Clash"), is still alive and living outside of Moore Town near Bath. The letter would seem to suggest that Clash's fellow officer, "Captain Welcome," had recently died (his badge being "kept for the present" by the writer of the letter). The other "Welcome" mentioned in the letter appears to have been another Maroon, possibly Captain Welcome's son, who carried the letter to the governor, and was given the "commission and rank of lieutenant," but not Captain Welcome's badge—at least not at that time (Jacobs 1949: 80).

The Captain Welcome referred to in this letter, a contemporary of Captain Clash, appears to have been, like the latter, a fighter during the days before the treaty.[43] Why he should figure so prominently in Maroon narratives today (as one of the original "four man"), while several of the other leaders mentioned in the treaty, including Clash, appear to have been forgotten in Moore Town, remains a mystery.[44]

The case of Swiplomento is more ambiguous than that of Welcome, but in several respects even more interesting. After Grandy Nanny, Granfa Swiplomento (whose name, as we have seen, varies considerably) is without question the early Maroon leader most frequently mentioned in present-day narratives from Moore Town. It is he (sometimes called by the shortened version of his name, Mento) who is most often portrayed as the one who received the message from God that encouraged the Maroons not to give up, assuring them victory if they would keep up the fight but a short while longer (see chapter 7). In some versions, it is only after he hears "the voice" (of God) that he becomes the "head" of all the other male leaders. In other accounts he is identified as Grandy Nanny's "man," her "husband," and/or her "private secretary."[45] Virtually always, he is represented as the top-ranking of "the four man"—the four main ancestral "generals" said to have led the troops under Grandy Nanny during the time of war. In some accounts, one of the other four (such as Granfa Puss) starts out as the "head," but later loses the position to Granfa Swiplomento.

The archives twice mention an early Maroon leader named Scipio who fought under Nanny. In one document from 1733, a captured Maroon named Seyrus/ Sarra, under torture, reveals plans for defending one of the main towns from an expected attack. Before being captured, this escaped slave had spent time in Nanny Town, and had apparently been entrusted with the following information:

> that they [the Maroons] had determined on hearing the Partys coming to Ambush them in the Rivers Course, that a gang of 100 was to lay on Carion Crow Hill, & 100 More Hobbys [plantation] Way, that a Drum was to be placed on the Ridge over the Town to View the Partys & the women in the town to burn the houses in case the Party should be too strong, if not the three Gangs to surround them on the beat of Drum, all under the Command of Scipio ("Copy of the confession made by Seyrus a negro belonging to Mr. Geo. Taylor," 1733, PRO: CO 137/20, 179).

This passage, written approximately 6 years before the treaty with Nanny's people was concluded, makes it clear that a commander named Scipio was one of the highest-ranking leaders at that time. Basing himself on the same document, Richard Hart (1985: 116) deduces that "Scipio . . . had been placed in over- all command of the warriors who had ambushed the expedition against the windward Maroons in August 1733." Also citing this document, Mavis Campbell (1988: 74) similarly concludes that "apparently Scipio was in charge of the most strategic town with the greatest ascent." Bev Carey (1997: 249) interprets the same document in a similar way.

The other mention of Scipio is found in the testimony of a slave who had apparently been living in the mountains among the Maroons against his will, but had managed to "escape" back to the coastal plantation zone. This man testified in January 1734 that

> Adou [another Maroon leader] keeps still to windward (Viz. about Edwards, John Brooks's and Hobbeys [plantations] with a great party and amongst them Mr Orgills Scipio Cesar and Adubal also Nanny and her Husband who is a greater man than Adou but never went in their Battles (testimony of "an Ebo named Cupid belonging to Samuel Taylor having found means to make his Escape from the Rebells," January 31, 1734, PRO: CO 137/21, 207).

Though this passage remains somewhat unclear, it contains a number of intriguing details. As in several of the oral narratives above, mention is made of four or five important men who are closely associated with Nanny (in this case, Adou, Nanny's [unnamed] "husband," Adubal, Scipio, and Cesar [or, perhaps, a single person named Scipio-Cesar]). As in the oral accounts, Nanny has a "husband" who occupies an important position (being seen as "greater" than at least one of the others, Adou); while it is implied that Scipio and Nanny's "husband" are different persons, we cannot be certain.

In any case, this passage, which corroborates the close connection between Scipio and Nanny, complements the previous archival fragment, which shows Scipio to have been in command of three separate "gangs" (each with its own subcommander, according to another section of the same document, making four commanders in all—perhaps the "four generals" often cited by Maroon Kromanti specialists today). On the basis of these combined sources, then, we can at least say with some confidence that Scipio was, if not Nanny's "husband," her confidant and one of the very highest-ranking headmen with her.

Given the degree of overlap between these archival sources and the oral narratives—as well as the phonological correspondences[46]—it seems safe to conclude that the early Maroon leader called Swiplomento by present-day Maroon Kromanti specialists is at least in part the same person known to eighteenth-century British military intelligence gatherers as Scipio.[47]

Although only a handful of specialists have preserved the knowledge of Swiplomento's role in the ancestors' war of independence, this early leader's name—and along with it, something of his defiant spirit—has nonetheless survived in the vocabularies of many other Maroons. For there exists in the Moore Town area today, even among those with no knowledge of the Kromanti tradition, a well-known challenge sometimes uttered to a person who is behaving impudently or aggressively: "you a Swiplomento, you can come!" (i.e., since you're a Swiplomento, come on [and see if you can handle me]!).

[56]

> Mama Juba
> surobeng
> cut in de middle

Mama Juba now is a woman near to Grandy Nanny, a cousin. She was a sol-
dier, like me and you. But she was very dangerous, almost [as much as] Grandy
Nanny. What make her so very dangerous, she was Grandy Nanny second. And
seeing that she is Grandy Nanny second, that was her name, Mama Juba.
Grandy Nanny teach her all about everything. And Grandy Nanny was great. So
therefore Mama Juba was very dangerous. She know a lot of things about
Grandy Nanny business. Because Grandy Nanny never hide [from] de woman.
Mama Juba sing this song, him say: (sings)

> River Grande come dung
> me can't cross deh

Okobisani was another brother of Mama Juba, another cousin of Nanny, a
ex-fighter. Him know a whole heap of things to de Maroon, and him was a Maroon too. Him fight in all de war wha' Grandy Nanny fight with obroni, him and
Mama Juba. Ina those days, Grandy Nanny ambush himself, him and Mama
Juba, and that other cousin.

(Leonard Whyte, September 6, 1978)

[57]

Those women dem a fete-woman dem. Grandy Dokose, Grandy Wanika, and
Mami Sali. Dem deh woman deh a fete-woman dem. A fete-woman and a fete-
man just only dance according to de drum. A man sick, dem put de drum on
there, and him play and him sing and dance, and they pick de Maroon bush.

(Noel Lewis, February 4, 1991)

[58]

You have Papa. You have Mandinga. You have Dokose. Tribe by tribe. You have
Grandy Dokose. You have Grandy Wanika. You have Mami Sali. A three high
Maroon woman wha' nearly next door to Nanny.

(Noel Lewis, February 4, 1991)

[59]

(Kromanti oration to invoke ancestors while preparing an herbal mixture in an
enameled basin): Granfa Jinsan, Granfa Elisan, Grandy Wanika, every bit a unu.
Seh o síyumándi, o síyumándi kojo, bo báimba nába dínkwin, seh Okobisani!
Seh dóko sherí, im seh wendáandu kofi, im seh simpánti máti máti, im seh o ján
pan tíla. Im seh o foul fut neba kil im pikni, im seh konjo siid neva laas. Yu mash,

yu chap, yu kyaan brok im wing. Im seh yu finga tink, yu kyaan kot it chruo weh. So fi put evriting gud, yu ha fi kot kata ina tu.[48] (sings)

> seh Mama Juba
>> súrobeng
> cut ina miggle
>> súrobeng

> Mama Juba
>> súrobeng
> cut ina miggle
>> súrobeng

(Leonard Whyte, October, 1978)

Maroon (and Other) Traitors

As Bev Carey (1997: 205) points out, "the Maroons would find that there were traitors among them, persons who, when the going got tough, would return to Busha to give him information detrimental to the security and welfare of the Maroons." In the same vein, Werner Zips (1999: 66) reminds us that "there were instances of treachery when runaways left the Maroons after finding themselves unable to adapt to that society. If they were captured while attempting to live in town without being recognized and subjected to torture to force them to reveal the locations of the Maroon settlements and other secrets, their "confessions" endangered the existence of the insurrectionists."

Evidence of such betrayal is plentiful in both the written record and Maroon oral traditions. According to Daniel Schafer (1973: 110), "field reports to the Governor refer repeatedly to slave men and women who escaped the Maroon camps and later returned with government forces to guide surprise attacks." Schafer also found, as have I, that "legends of such betrayal are remarkably alive among today's Maroons and are recounted with great scorn and bitterness" (110). The following set of texts [60–68] features individual Maroons—or one-time friends of Maroons—whose names live on in infamy because of their treachery. Through narratives like these, first-time traitors such as Joe Hill Kwaku, Granfa Bosco, Granfa Puss, or the white collaborator Dunbar signal the constant possibility of betrayal. The actions of such characters show that trust is a double-edged sword; the same time-tested trust that forms the basis of Maroon solidarity represents a potential weakness, which can be exploited by enemies to penetrate Maroon defenses. The subtext of these narratives is clear enough: the temptation to "sell out" Maroon secrets remains very much alive in the present, and Maroons must remain constantly vigilant against such acts of betrayal.[49]

[60]

Unu [referring to some young Maroons, who are on the side, listening to a conversation with a visiting linguist] know too much something quick. That's wha' mek Missy Be Kwashi min tek de whole *damn* lot of Maroon go fling way. Dem know something too much. That mek Missy Be Kwashi catch we all, say bakra say fe come, [so] give it. Dem pay Missy Be hundred pound.[50] Mm-hm.

Maroon business have fe carry dodge-him-oo pensa go dead. (sings)

dodge him-oo pensa

dodge him-oo, you dodge me-ee

dodge him-oo pensa

but when dodge him-oo, me kumfu-ee

Me n'e give you no more of me Katawud business.

(John Harris, December 7, 1958)[51]

[61]

One of de man [out of the five original Maroon leaders] come out of de lot. One of de man come out of de lot. One man couldn't bear it. Him never fly, never go back to Africa. Him couldn't stay in de bush no more, and out of de five [leaders], de four man look pon him and say, well then, him a go tell [their whereabouts to the whites] now.

(James Downer, May 31, 1978)

[62]

Now, at that [early] stage, Bosco was there, mek him fight. But Bosco betray [the Maroons], becomes a traitor. And Bosco get dead. Right? So it only leave four [Maroon leaders].

(Johnny Minott, June 4, 1978)

[63]

It was five man [leading the Maroons] then, because you have Joe Hill Kwaku, you know. That man, Joe Hill Kwaku, when dem min fighting, him say him can't

He [a captured Maroon giving information to the British while under torture] says he came from the Negroe Town 4 weeks agoe to see what [British military] Partys were fitting out [and] that the Rebels told him of their design in robbing Sparks & Hobby's Plantations . . . [and] that afterwards if he found the Partys in Titchfield Town [i.e., Port Antonio] not too strong, on his return to them they would come & take it. ("Confession made by Seyrus a negro belonging to Mr. Geo. Taylor," 1733, PRO/CO 137/20, 179)

The wife of the chief Obra [*sic*] man promises to shew the town and great cave where they send their women and children to, when any party comes upon them etc. (extract from Colonel Campbell's letter on the examination of some "rebellious negroes lately taken"; Calendar of State Papers, vol. 38, 1731, #25iii, p. 24)

---

fight no more, therefore him a go up, go give himself up to bakra. And dem feel to demself say him a go tell bakra which part dem deh ina de wood. And therefore, him dead pon de pass. Him never have no talking.

(James Downer, June 25, 1978)

[64]

Well, in de times of fighting, Bosco were there with dem. That meaning it becomes five men [who were leading the Maroons]. When Bosco time, it was five of dem.

Well, Bosco go on and go on and go on, and dem fight and dem fight and fight till Bosco says to his colleagues, "I am going to see how de war is proceeding."

But at de same time, Bosco only went to betray dem, to give de Maroon away.

Him says to de Englishman now, "I will go and show you where de Maroons lie."

But, incidentally, he was de first man died. And de reason why him never reach [and] lead de English to de Maroon—fire. It was fire come down.

He ask dem [the whites] to let him be free. That mean him not going to be any slave any more, he will be free, and he will show dem definitely where [the Maroons were hiding].

Dem [the Maroons] tell him say him fe check back about five days time, mek dem know wha' a go on.

[So he said to the English], "I can show you where de hiding place is, where de rebels are, if you will free me."

Traitor.

Him die for it. And there was something there that he never know exist.

(Johnny Minott, June 4, 1978)

[65]

Bosco was a traitor. Him was de traitor. Him was de one who leave de rest at Stone Wall and say him a go out go see how de war going on. But when him go out, him tell de Englishman say if dem will save him life, him will carry dem go show him where de Maroon is. So him was leading de troop of soldiers, to go where de Maroon is. But fire come down and burn him up. Him a de first man die. That's Bosco.

(Johnny Minott, February 6, 1991)

[66]

Granfa Puss is a hard man fe deal with.[52]

You know what Puss do? Puss climb on a tree. When de dog deh after de cat so, "r-r-r-am!" (sound of growling), after de cat deh so, "br-r-r-r!" pon a tree. You know wha' de puss say. (laughs) When de puss go up pon de tree top so, him turn down.

De puss seh, "law-w-w-d . . ." (loud laugh) . . . (in a gruff voice): "law-w-w-d! O wóondu wóondu, me better than you."

So this Granfa Puss, no man catch him. No man shoot him. He's a part of de Maroon, Granfa Puss. No man catch him. No man shoot him. A trickify man.

Sometime dem people want fe go thief [from the plantations]. Well, Granfa Puss, him pick some bush give you, and rub you up, rub you up.

Him say (in a gruff voice), "ba, wen yu go da da pre, tek da sonti ye, rob yu díindi so, rob yu díindi, rob yu díindi"[53]—rub him face.

Him say, "go a de man pre. Go there, go do, then tónbaig. Tek anything you want. De man can't see you at all."

You go ina de man house. De man ina him house. You walk, tek anything you want, and you come out. Like puss, [you] got one something a you foot bottom, we call it "pad." And you woulda walk ina de house, six, seven some-body di-de [are there], and you tek out *anything* wha' you want tek out, and come out. You tek anything you want, and you come out, and *nobody* see you. *Nobody* can't shoot you. Nobody know say a de somebody come in there.

So this man, dem use him now fe find where de white man soldier dem deh. A fe-him job that, Granfa Puss, fe find where dem locate. Anywhere dem locate, that man tell dem where fe go find dem. Granfa Puss. Anything dem [the whites] kesu [sit down, in old Maroon creole] and talk together, Granfa Puss tell Maroon wha' dem say. Same like how you radio woulda tell you wha' happen a foreign. You see? Granfa Puss tell dem *every* secret.

[A recently escaped slave who had become a Maroon and then been captured by whites near Port Antonio] said that if he was pardoned he would "carry them to a place where the rebells were, consisting of fifty shot and a great number of women and children." (British archival document dated February 27, 1735, cited by Carey [1997: 290])

> Aseeba, belonging about six years ago to Mr. Garbrand's estate, came from the rebels of her own accord, and guided colonel D'warris to the town, which he took. . . . recommended for her freedom by the late colonel D'warris. (Journals of the House of Assembly of Jamaica, volume 3, May 1, 1739, p. 490)

> Venus, belonging to Mr. Lamport, in Clarendon, deserted from Accompong's town, acquainted Colonel Blake that most of the rebels being gone out a hunting or robbing, it was a good opportunity to take the town, and led a party faithfully to the town. . . . recommended for her freedom by Colonel Blake. (Journals of the House of Assembly of Jamaica, volume 3, May 1, 1739, p. 490)

Him seh, "ba! You know honti done?" [do you know what was done?] Him say, "Nanny, you know honti? Obroni deh a you prandes, you know [Nanny, you know what? The whites have penetrated your home, you know]. Obroni got one thousand men coming! Look out, Nanny! Me no business with dem, me only a de guide. Look out! Look out Cut Hill [i.e., Watch Hill]. Look out Cut Hill. Look out there a Cut Hill, dem coming, you know."

And Nanny get ready. Nanny got all of dem soldier.

After a time, when dem go on, go on, go on, [a British soldier] go to him [Granfa Puss], and tell him say him will give dem any money fe tell him Nanny secret, or how fe overthrow Nanny.

It nearly happen, but it no happen.

So, [for] a time him was doing good with her, fighting with Nanny a good time. But one other time come now, him want to be head. And Nanny no agree.

So him say, "well, me going to show you something, because me swipple."

And him go way—same like how you also woulda do—go way and tell Nanny enemy—that mean de white man dem—which part fe walk, and how fe capture Nanny. And Nanny know [what Puss did]. So after Nanny know, Nanny send him soldier dem pon him, fe shoot him. But him tek way himself.

So Nanny say, "ba, o titéi tei, titéi tei, bo swáo. Me and you, me no business with you again! No come to me. Me and you not working again. Opéte bíu sáka!"[54]

And Nanny *cuss* him off.

So, him turn a traitor.

(Richard Barnes, February 4, 1991)

Maroon Traitors: A *Bakra* Friend Turned Enemy

The intriguing song that follows ("wonder wha' dem do wid Dunbar") and the associated texts bear a complex relationship with both the orally inscribed past and the narrative present. As in all the narratives in this section, the themes of trust and betrayal are central, but here they are given a new twist. In this case, the traitor is not a Maroon, but a white man who has been captured, and is being held by the Maroons so that they can use him to learn some of the "secrets" of the whites. The white man, Dunbar, agrees to act as a spy for the Maroons, and eventually gains their trust. After living among them for a time, he is entrusted with some of the Maroons' secrets as well. However, when some Maroon warriors are killed during an engagement with British soldiers, Dunbar is held responsible; suspected of being a double spy, he is accused of having revealed to the whites the secret of the Maroons' "ambush" (camouflage techniques). Though he has become a close "friend," the Maroons fear that his real aim is to "kill out" the Maroons by divulging their military secrets to the enemy. When Dunbar tells them that he is going to leave them for a time, the Maroons take action. A Maroon named Kwashibroni (Kwashi for short), who has had a close association with Dunbar (both of them being practitioners of "Science" or obeah), is the one who takes the latter's life.

With the traitor out of the way, the Maroons reprise the events in a mocking song. "I wonder what they've done with Dunbar?" ask the whites waiting on the coast for the latest batch of secrets he has promised to bring them upon his return from the forest. "The penny has killed the shilling," answer the Maroons sarcastically (i.e., a man assumed to be of lower status [a black Maroon] has toppled one supposed to be worth more [a white Englishman])—"the Maroon soldier Kwashibroni has killed Dunbar."[55]

But there is of course more to it than this. The narrator, James Downer, bridges past and present by using the story preserved in this song as a warning to the current listener (the present author, who at that moment is capturing the performance on tape). Like Dunbar, the ethnographer has come to live among the Maroons and learn their "secrets"; like him, he has come to be accepted (at least by the narrator) as a friend—indeed, as a "brother." Should he ever entertain thoughts of betrayal, he should remember the fate of the white traitor, Dunbar.

Archival documents from the eighteenth century do show that at least two whites who were captured by Windward Maroons lived for a time among them and cooperated with them. Slender though the evidence is, the details related in these documents, both dating from 1733, bear an uncanny resemblance to certain elements of this Maroon oral tradition. In one document, a suspected spy for the Maroons apprehended in Port Antonio (variously named as Cyrus, Seyrus, Sarra, or Ned) testifies under torture that a keg of gunpowder was recently transported secretly to one of the Maroon settlements:

He says that the way they got Powder is, they have with them 2 white boys, one named Jno. Done or Dun, who belonged to blind Ffletcher of Passage Fort, the other Charles (his other name he knows not) that these 2 boys writes Passes in Coll. Nedham's name and one Quashee goes to Kingstown with it to one Jacob a Jew in Church Street, that he went once last month & brought with him two larg horns full, that they have now he believes 200 horns full, but very little Shott, tho' Guns & Launces enugh. ("Copy of the confession made by Seyrus a negro belonging to Mr. Geo. Taylor," 1733, PRO: CO 137/20, 179).

In later testimony, the same Maroon prisoner corrects himself, stating that the Maroon who went to Kingston to arrange for supplies of gunpowder was not Quashee, but another man named Cuffee, adding that

it was Quashee and Cudjo who were the Spys at Port Antonio . . . and that Quashee and Cudjo . . . were mostly entertain'd while at Port Antonio by Col. Needham's Negroes (1733, PRO: CO 137/20, 179).

Is there a relationship between the "facts" preserved in this written record, now more than 260 years old, and those contained in the oral narratives below? Much like Kwashi (Kwashibroni) and Dunbar in James Downer's oral account, Quashee and Dun, in these archival fragments, seem to be closely connected. Dun, a white "boy" living among the Maroons, forges passes in Col. Nedham's name, providing the Maroons with what they need to obtain gunpowder; Quashee, who is part of the same gunpowder-smuggling team, is a Maroon spy who spends much time in Port Antonio with slaves owned by the same Col. Nedham in whose name Dun writes counterfeit passes. The similarity of the names that have come down to us in these independent texts (Quashee/Kwashi and Dun/Dunbar) is remarkable.[56] It is tempting to conclude that the Quashee and Dun of the archives are the same persons as the Kwashi and Dunbar who appear in this Windward Maroon oral tradition. But the evidence on both sides is so sparse that we may never know with certainty. What we do know, in any case, is that the events described in the oral accounts are, at the very least, entirely plausible—a conclusion that can only be strengthened by the striking parallels offered by archival records such as these.

[67]

Dunbar was a Maroon soldier, you know. And him no Maroon, but Maroon hold him like how you deh ya now, and *me* tek you in. Well, me can see with dem two eye, majority up a Moore Town tek you in. And *me* tek you in. Me tek you in like you is my brother, like two of we come from a mother, then.
    All right.
    "Maroon soldier kill off Dunbar. Penny-penny kill shilling, wonder-ee. Say wonder wha' dem do wid Dunbar."

Maroon soldier dem kill Dunbar.

Dunbar, him no Maroon. Him a soldier—not fe Maroon. Me say, Dunbar a soldier, but a no fe Maroon. Dunbar a soldier, but Dunbar come fe kill de Maroon. Dem hold him close, you know, dem have him close, like how me and you a good friend. But Dunbar a no Maroon. (sings)

> penny-penny him kill shilling, seh wonder-ee
> but Maroon soldier kill Dunbar, wonder-ee
> everyday we kill shilling-oo, wonder-ee
> Maroon soldier kill Dunbar, poor me-ee

That mean say Dunbar now a fe unu [i.e., was one of you whites]. But Maroon hold him close.

When de Maroon have him now, Maroon say, "bakra a go talk." Him say, "no go talk."

That mean say, if *you* talk, dem kill you. So now, a de tune.

When Dunbar a turn way, Maroon see say him a go way from dem fe go tell *you* [the whites] say a so Maroon turn backra bush. You know wha' dem call backra?[57] When you see dem [the berries of the backra plant] burst so, dem turn ink. Dem bear seed pon dem.

Maroon turn backra [bush], turn dem bush deh, and stand up a bush corner, stand up ina bush corner. That mean say bakra [white people] no know dem. Bakra no know say dem turn dem thing deh.

So a Dunbar now *tell* bakra say a wha' Maroon turn.

Listen wha' me a say.

Him [the Maroon] a wrap ina de bush, ina de cacoon trash. Him turn de backra bush, turn *backra* [bush].

Him tell dem [the whites] say, "whenever you go and see backra [bush], a Maroon turn dem deh something, you know."

So dem [the whites] get fe shoot some of dem [Maroons].

Dunbar tell dem so, because him min know Maroon secret, like how me and you a talk here now. Dem [Maroons] capture him and hold him fe tell him some of de secret from de bakra. When dem hold him there now, dem tell him some of de secret [of the Maroons].

Him say, "all right. A so."

De bakra tell him say now, if him, Dunbar, get de secret of de Maroon, dem would get fe come in back and capture him, capture de Maroon dem. Because dem no know de secret fe catch de Maroon dem.

All right.

After Dunbar come up there now, dem [Maroons] hold him. Dem got Dunbar, you know. And dem and Dunbar deh so till Dunbar say him a go way from dem.

But a man like you, you know—Dunbar. A no Maroon.

After dem and Dunbar talk done, Dunbar mek bakra know say a so dem turn backra bush.

De half never been told.

A that mek Maroon kill him, because after him go and tell dem say a so Maroon do, him come back to Maroon now. (sings)

> penny-penny kill shilling-oo, wonder-ee
> wonder wha' dem do, Kwashi, wonder-ee
> Kwashibroni kill Dunbar, wonder-oo
> wonder wha' dem do wid Dunbar, poor me one-ee

That mean to say, Dunbar a man who come in to de Maroon. That mean say Maroon would capture him same like how Maroon capture Three Finger Jack.

Kwashibroni a Maroon man. You never hear me talk a Country say, "Kwashibroni so tani"?

(James Downer, September 24, 1978)

[68]

> seh wonder-oo
> wonder wha' we do wid Dunbar, wonder-ee
> me seh Maroon soldier kill Dunbar, seh wonder-ee
> penny-penny you kill shilling-oo, seh wonder-ee

Kwashibroni kill Dunbar. Kwashibroni now, Kwashi now, a Maroon man. And Dunbar a Stranger [i.e., a non-Maroon]. But Dunbar want now fe come fight against Maroon, fe get Maroon Science. Because Dunbar a man who is a obeah man. Obeah man. Same like how you da come here now and me give you me Science there now. Same way. A so Dunbar min stay, like you. So Dunbar min stay. That mean say Dunbar a go *fight* against Maroon now fe get dem Science. So Maroon now say *no!* Him can't fight against dem. So Kwashi now—hear wha' me a say good, you know—Kwashi now say, "mm-mm." Dunbar couldn't come fight against him fe get himself. *Him*, Kwashi, will fight and get de Science. That mean say, when me say "Science," me mean de Maroon *gift*. That's right. So now, a right there so Maroon turn de soldier dem pon him, and kill him off. So when you hear dem say, "Maroon soldier *kill off* Dunbar," [it is] because dem min a come, come fight against Maroon fe *tek* Maroon, *capture* Maroon. See what I mean. So, Kwashi now kill off Dunbar. So a it there now [so that's it there now]: dem ask him wha' dem do with Dunbar. That mean say a bakra ask dem say wha' dem do with Dunbar? So a Maroon tell dem say dem kill Dunbar—yarifo him.

(James Downer, October 3, 1978)

Tellers

Some of Those Whose Words Appear in This Book

Charles Aarons (Moore Town Maroons),
Moore Town, 1993. Photo: K. Bilby.

Caleb Anderson
(Moore Town Ma-
roons), Comfort
Castle, 1991.
Photo: K. Bilby.

Richard Barnes (Moore Town Maroons), Comfort Castle, 1982. Photo: K. Bilby.

Elizabeth Brown with her great grandson (Moore Town Maroons), Moore Town, 1978. Photo: Jefferson Miller.

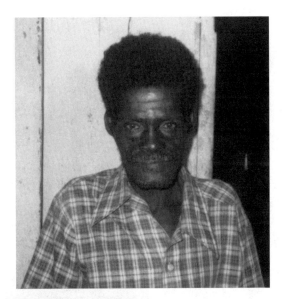

Johnny Chambers (Accompong Maroons), Accompong, 1991. Photo: K. Bilby.

Richard Deans (Moore Town Maroons), Moore Town, 1978. Photo: K. Bilby.

Robert Dennis (Moore Town Maroons), Moore Town, 1978. Photo: K. Bilby.

James Downer (Moore Town Maroons), Bath, St. Thomas, 1982. Photo: K. Bilby.

Abraham Goodwin (Scot's Hall Maroons), Scot's Hall, 1978. Photo: K. Bilby.

David Gray (Moore Town Maroons), Comfort Castle, 1978. Photo: Jefferson Miller.

Colonel C.L.G. Harris (Moore Town Maroons), Moore Town, 1991. Photo: K. Bilby.

Margaret Harris (Moore Town Maroons), Kent, 1991. Photo: K. Bilby.

Noel Lewis (Moore
Town Maroons),
Comfort Castle, 1991.
Photo: K. Bilby.

Ruth Lindsay (Moore
Town Maroons),
Moore Town, 1991.
Photo: K. Bilby.

Sydney McDonald (Moore Town Maroons), at Smithsonian Festival of American Folklife, Washington, D.C., 1989. Photo: K. Bilby.

Geretius McKenzie (Accompong Maroons), Accompong, 1991. Photo: K. Bilby.

Johnny Minott (Moore Town Maroons), Brownsfield, 1991. Photo: K. Bilby.

George Osbourne (Moore Town Maroons), Kent, 1982. Photo: K. Bilby.

Emmanuel Palmer (Moore Town Maroons), Moore Town, 1993. Photo: K. Bilby.

Magdalene Reid (Accompong Maroons), Accompong, 1991. Photo: K. Bilby.

Alfred Rowe
(Accompong
Maroons),
Accompong,
1991. Photo:
K. Bilby.

Thomas Rowe
(Accompong Maroons),
Accompong, 1991.
Photo: K. Bilby.

Henry Shepherd (Moore Town Maroons), Stony Hill, Portland, 1982. Photo: K. Bilby.

Hardie Stanford (Moore Town Maroons), Moore Town, 1991. Photo: K. Bilby.

George Sterling (Moore Town Maroons), Moore Town, 1978. Photo: Jefferson Miller.

William Watson (Moore Town Maroons), Seaman's Valley, 1978. Photo: K. Bilby.

Adolphus Whyte (Moore Town Maroons), Comfort Castle, 1982. Photo: K. Bilby.

Colonel Martin-Luther Wright (Accompong Maroons), Accompong, 1978. Photo: K. Bilby.

7

The Chosen People

Underlying most of the narratives in this book is the conviction that Maroons are a special people. For generations, those who tell such narratives have taught their children that no other Jamaicans share the glorious history that is theirs—that in seizing their freedom from the British nearly a century before slavery was abolished in Jamaica, the Maroons stood alone. According to Maroons today, the special knowledge, skills, and spiritual powers that brought the early fighters victory were bequeathed only to their descendants, and remain their exclusive property.

The historian Mavis Campbell (1988: 260) has written that present-day Maroons hold "a perception of themselves that borders on 'the chosen.'" This feeling that they have been singled out for divine favor, she concludes, is grounded in "the abstract notion of [their] history exemplified by their Treaties and lands, sacrosanct to them and inalienable." If anything, Campbell's phrasing—"borders on 'the chosen'"—fails to state the Maroon position boldly enough. In the minds of more traditional Maroons, there is no room for doubt; they *are* the chosen.[1] (Indeed, for Maroons brought up to feel this way, it requires no great leap of imagination to see parallels between themselves and the ancient Israelites, as does the narrator of the final text in this chapter.)[2] However, rather than stemming, as Campbell suggests, from some purely "abstract notion" of history (of which she sees the sacred treaties and communal land holdings as the most salient concrete expressions), the Maroons' belief that they are "a chosen people" actually has its basis, at least in the Windward communities, in a specific oral tradition believed to go back to the first days. In this mythic story, the founding ancestors are portrayed, in quite literal terms, as God's elect.

All but the first and last narratives presented in this chapter revolve around this saga of divine intercession during the time of war. Although certain details, and even some of the central characters, vary from one account to the next, the basic elements remain the same. These can be summarized as follows.

At a particularly trying moment in their war with the whites, one of the original four or five top leaders (usually named as either Granfa Mento or Grandy Nanny) hears a mysterious "voice" issuing from an unknown source. (In some accounts, this occurs during a dream or vision.) The voice urges the Maroons, who are suffering from a severe food shortage, to keep up the fight, assuring them that if they hold out only a little longer, they will win the war. The leaders assemble, and each is asked in turn whether he is responsible for this anonymous pronouncement. When it is determined that the voice came from none of those present, the *jege* (a Maroon instrument of divination) is consulted. Queried about other possible human sources, such as Maroon allies, dead ancestors, or enemy decoys, the *jege* lies still. When asked, finally, if the voice was that of Yankipong, the Supreme Being, it leaps into the air and gyrates wildly about, signaling affirmation. This revelation casts the Maroons' struggle in a new light; before this, they had put their confidence solely in the knowledge and powers of their ancestors. Secure in the new knowledge that "God deh a we side" (God is on our side), the Maroons renew their commitment to fight to the end. Shortly after this, the leader who first received the message from God finds a single pumpkin seed and is instructed by the same divine voice to plant it immediately. A matter of hours after the seed is placed in the ground, an entire crop of mature pumpkins springs forth, providing enough nourishment to sustain the Maroons until they emerge victorious.[3]

This sacred myth underpins the more general belief, long instilled in Maroons by their elders, that the various qualities and powers that distinguish them from other Jamaicans, though passed on through human blood lines, derive ultimately from Yankipong (as the Supreme God is known in the esoteric Kromanti language). Only because the early Maroons were handpicked by Yankipong to serve as conduits of His divine power were they able to overcome what to ordinary mortals would have seemed a hopeless situation. Only because God was on their side were they able, despite the enormous hardships facing them, to persevere when others might have relented.

[1]

Maroon is de people who God have blessed to do certain miracles that they feel should spread round and round, throughout de whole globe, or throughout de whole constituency, in other words. Remember, you should heard about when de Maroon fight and fight and fight so till when dem go right at Stony River. Right. Is there they had signed de last treaty, which is their pledge.

(Robert Dennis, May 17, 1978)

[2]

When they have fought for twenty and nine years, all dem sit down, like tonight, and tomorrow they are going to give up, for they have fought, and they fought under a whole heap of tactics, and still yet de Englishman is down on dem. Me mean dem kill Englishman too, but, you know, de Englishman is down on dem—clothes tearing off, food going out. And dem decide now to return back [to slavery].

(Johnny Minott, June 4, 1978)

[3]

Dem run to one place dem call name Pumpkin Hill. When dem go a Pumpkin Hill, him [Nanny] sit down. And him tan there.

Him say, "me hear somebody call me, you know"—ina him sleep, de night, you know, ina de night—him say, "me hear somebody call me, you know."

Him say, "a you call me?" [was it you who called me?]—like me woulda talk to you now, me say, "a you call me?"

Hear that friend say, "no, man."

Me say, "a no you call me?" [it wasn't you who called me?]

Him say, "no, man."

Me say, "me see something come to me."

Him say, "wha' come to you?"

Me say, "me see a man come to me. Him say we fe fight *one* day more."

A Nanny come, you know.

"Him say we fe fight *one* day more. Hear me now. I want gain de battle."

And him say, "all right."

(Henry Shepherd, February 19, 1991)

[4]

They had fought for twenty-nine years. De war last fe more than hundred years, but I am telling you about Nanny's war. For twenty-nine years. And all generals meet, and they sung a song.

They say, "well, we have fought for so long, and mek so many tactics, and so much invention, but de English get in here now, just achieve we go back now to being slave."

And they have made several inventions. They take all like thatch-heads, cacoon, and all those [various survival foods]. That's de Maroon inventions of ancient, during de days of war.

At de time, one man may sleep like up my shop, one man sleep down there, one man sleep up there, one man sleep there. Dem don't all sleep one place. For their tactic was that if de English capture one, de other three must carry on. But at that time they decide, like tomorrow, to get out.

That night there was a voice call to Mento. At those days he was not Mento, he was "Do-an-Consider."[4] And when de voice call to him, and when he realize, him call, mek him signal—you know how de Maroon have dem signal with war—and him mek him signal.[5] And all four generals meet.

And I would say to you, say, "if you call me?"

And you say, "no."

"You call me?"

You say, "no."

You say, "you call me?"

You say, "no."

You say, "how then me hear a voice call?"

So dem is proving now to demself, you know, whether it did be de enemy is near, or what it may be. But it was de voice of de true and living God who call.

This voice call to him, say, "Mento, Mento, fight one year more."

One year more. And de war has come to cease before de one year.

Now, listen me now. To prove demself towards that, wherein this voice is coming from, dem have dem jeges, ina those days. And when de four of dem meet and [found that] nobody call him, there was a seership to see if there were enemy near, or not. But there were no sign of enemies near.

So, at those days, in all de affairs, they were not calling upon de true and living God. They were only fighting upon de existence of knowings. Knowings. But at that time now dem call upon God, and dem jege start to jump, and it stop and drop a ground. So dem find that God is on dem side.

(Johnny Minott, June 4, 1978)

[5]

After they fight fe twenty-nine years, de English was still upon dem. And most of de tactics dem do, still de English break out pon dem. They decide now to go on back and surrender now—otherwise, go back go turn slave then. But at that time, these four man do not sleep one place, that in case if de English catch one, de other three should carry on. Grandy [Nanny] was set there as the queen. At that very night, there was a call. They hear a voice call, to Mento. He do not know where de voice call to him. So he call all de other three men—because dem know it was war—to find out if it was really de English is near.

And when dem meet, they ask each other, "did you call me?"

You ask that one, him say no, ask that one, him say no, ask that one, him say no.

Him say, "well, boy, I hear a voice. But I don't know where this voice come from."

Well, dem put down dem jege, and talk. Jege stay still. Well, that mean dem don't get no answer.

Dem say, "well, boy, I don't know wha' fe do, boy."

So one man say, "well, boy, mek we call pon God."

You know? And when dem call pon God, de jege answer. Then they could says, "boy, God deh a we side."

Because de voice said to him, "Mento, Mento, fight one year more." And that year was de victory for Maroon winning de English battle. (ends the narrative by blowing a mouthful of rum across his shoulders)

(Johnny Minott, February 6, 1991)

[6]

    o taki bio mi manda
    o manda manda manda

o debren kri da mi manda
o manda manda manda manda
ee, Kwajo manda-oo
seh mankwaba man tide

Well, hear me now. That sing sing direct to de Almighty. That is a prayer tune. Now, mek I give you a instance how that tune comes, and I will tell you how that tune is a prayer tune.

Is when de Maroon fight, fight, fight for so long, and all fails. All tactics fails. And de generals meet like tonight, and dem sit down and say, "well, boy, tomorrow we going to give up, for we can't fight any more longer."

And dem never sleep one place. One sleep there, one sleep there. Four different places still. But dem a go surrender tomorrow. And de voice call to one tonight. Hear Mento say dem fe fight one year more.

That tune mek as a prayer for success.

(Johnny Minott, August 20, 1978)

[7]

When de four of dem [the four original Maroon chiefs] a sleep—one sleep like out there so, one sleep there so, one sleep there—when de voice call to him, him say, "Mento, Mento!" Him say, "fight one more year."

Him never know which [one] call him, call, him believe say a bakra. Him jump up! When me say "jump up," me mean say *wake*, rather than sleep.

Him call, him say, "a who call me, man?"

Dem [the other chiefs] say, "me no know a who."

"Who call me, man?" Him say, "who call me?"

Dem say, "no."

Him say, "boy, bakra deh pon we."

That mean say, *enemy*!

Him tek out him jege—him *jege*. That's right, him tek it out and him look pon it. And when him look pon it so, him *talk word*! . . . talk to de jege so!

Him call pon man, him jege tan there.

Him call pon Yankipong Asasi, jege come up, go up ina de air, come down back, go up in de air, come down back, go up in de air, come back.

Him say, "well, all right. Yankipong Asasi deh a we side."

That mean say, from de moment him look, say it a Yankipong Asasi, him fight, and capture bakra. A there so de fight come from, a there so him capture bakra.

(James Downer, October 3, 1978)

[8]

When de four man deh a bush, and dem hear de voice call to him, dem hear de voice say, "Mento, Mento!" Him say, "fight one more year." Him look. Him no see nobody. Him call to de other one.

Him say, "ba, a you call me?"
Him say, "no."
Him say, "ba, you call me?"
Him say, "no."
Him say, "ba, a you call me?"
Him say, "no."
Him say, "mm . . . boy, bakra deh pon we." Him say, "well all right . . ."

Him *put* him something, him jege, in de something so. When him put him jege ina de something so, so, so, him call pon man so. When him call pon man so, him jege tan there. Him *call* pon man so, him jege tan there! *Call* pon Yankipong Asasi so. Call pon Yankipong Asasi so. Him call pon Yankipong Asasi so, so till jege *come* go up ina de air so, so, come go up ina de air so, so so, go down go back so.

Dem say, "wha' happen?"

Him say, "boy, God deh a we side. And we just find out. Him a fight, and Him a kill nation. Him a kill nation!"

So, a so. Dem fight. Dem fight, dem da kill nation.

So me ascendants is from Africa! Grandy come here with him Science to *fight*, against bakra. And him *fight* it fe true! And him get it, and him gain victory. Him gain victory.

We are fighting, and we are a fighter. We are a fighter. We are one and two, we naa fail. And we a fight. And we naa stop fight until we hear de voice say "fight no more."

(James Downer, 1978)

[9]

[Granfa Swifomento] never a de head. But a him de voice call to. A him de voice call to, and say, "Mento, Mento, me say fight one more year." That's right. [That's why he became] de head.

(James Downer, January 25, 1991)

[10]

Wha' de reason mek Granfa Swifomento get de head: because a him de voice min call to—de voice wha' call to him, when dem was fighting! Because dem cunny, and dem come from Africa with dem Science, and dem no know that there is a God. Dem no check pon a God above. Dem know say dem sabi, dem swipple. So when de voice call to dem, dem say, "me no check pon that there is a God."[6] That mean to say, dem no min check pon Him from long time. Dem only min a fight because dem *sabi*, dem *swipple*. Dem min swipple, and dem know demself.

(James Downer, June 25, 1978)

[11]

When de voice call to Swifomento, Okonoko min a de head. That is Grandy's [i.e., Nanny's] husband. When de whole of dem sit down there now, and when de voice call to him, it say, "Mento, Mento, fight one more year!"

And him jump up pon him foot, him call to de other man out there, him say, "a you call me?"

Him say, "no."

Him call de other one, him say, "you call me?"

Him say, "no."

Him call de other one, him say, "a you call me?"

Him say, "no."

Everybody start cry now. And when him pick up him jege, him look pon it, him call pon man, see if a enemy deh near him. When him call pon man, see if de enemy deh near him, de jege no rock. Him call pon God Almighty, de jege go up in de air, come down back. So when de jege come down back, him say, "God on we side, so we can fight!" And from de moment dem start fight, bakra couldn't bear it.

(James Downer, June 25, 1978)

[12]

Bakra *fight* against him [Nanny], very hard, fight against him *very hard*! Fight him very hard! And Grandy plant pumpkin, and by twelve o'clock him pick it and him feed soldier. And soldier eat.

(James Downer, 1978)

[13]

De first miracle with Nanny, away from fight white and get victory, is to plant de pumpkin. That is a miracle work. Plant de pumpkin de same day, reap de pumpkin de same day. That is a marvelous work.

(Hardie Stanford, February 1, 1991)

[14]

De pumpkin seed was plant de morning, and bear all full by twelve o'clock and feed soldier, up a one hill dem call Pumpkin Hill there.

(Johnny Minott, August 20, 1978)

[15]

He [Grandy Nanny] planted a pumpkin. De same day he plant it, he able to pick it and to feed his soldiers dem, like Granfa Parro, Granfara Winkudandu, and all dem Kofi dem, all dem people there—*his* people dem—de *same* day. That's wha' mek dem call de hill up there so now Pumpkin Hill, or otherwise, Watch Hill.

(Uriah McLean, June 23, 1978)

[16]

Him [Grandy Nanny] tek up him people dem and him go to a hill up there dem call name Watch Hill—in front of Stony River—up a Watch Hill. And that hill up there, they call that hill Pumpkin Hill. And that brother named Granfara Parro plant a pumpkin de same day, and dem get de pumpkin fe dem dinner de evening. Can you beat that? Plant de pumpkin de same day, and dem get de pumpkin fe dem dinner de same evening.

(Margaret Harris, June 1, 1978)

[17]

Dem go to a hill dem call Pumpkin Hill. Well, him [Nanny] could stay there now and see when de troop coming after dem. So dem plant a pumpkin there that day. And de same day dem plant de pumpkin, de pumpkin bear, and dem get de pumpkin fe dem dinner that night.

(Margaret Harris, February 4, 1991)

[18]

Bakra nearly gain Maroon through shortage of food. When Nanny and all his high ranks dem go to dead, dem hear a sound say, "fight fe few more years." But although dem hear de voice, food leave dem. Dem hear a voice say, "fight fe few more years." But food fail dem.

When dem wake out of that sleep, dem shake each other, [and each asked the other] if dem hear de sound. Dis ya one say, "no." De other one say, "no." Dem have a thing dem call "jege." A dem Science that. And dem tek it, and dem put ina one plate. And when dem put ina de plate, dem call for Granfa Welcome. De jege lie down still.

"Granfa Parro . . .?"
De jege lie down still.
"Grandy Sukasi . . .?"
De jege lie down still.
"Grandy Ayinting . . .?"
De jege was lie down still.
Dem say, "God Almighty then?"
When dem say "God Almighty," de jege start to *mash up* de plate, mash up de plate, mash up de plate. Dem have fe catch dem yoyo hold.[7]

Now, when dem a call pon dem name there, dem did believe say a anyone of de man dem. But when dem throw de jege, and when de jege never move, and when dem call pon God Almighty, and when de jege start to move, well, Maroon—Nanny, then—find out say God ina dem midst. And through God, mek Nanny then fight and gain victory, ina de war wha' Nanny fight. And until now, Nanny represent himself to be de first hero in de world, to that.

A man did have *one* pumpkin seed in his pocket, one of de followers of Nanny. One of Nanny fighter, one of de hero, have a pumpkin seed in his pocket. And him took out de pumpkin seed, because foodstuff short. And him plant it this morning. And by de evening de pumpkin bear full, and dem have food fe sustain dem fe fight and gain victory over bakra. [They received the message to plant the seed] from God Almighty. A wha' de jege tell dem. God Almighty: Yankipong Asasi, O Kembu Tutu, O Tata Nyami.

(Hardie Stanford, January 17, 1978)

[19]

When Maroon and bakra enter war, is only a nit [seed] mek bakra never capture Maroon. Is only a nit mek bakra never capture Maroon through de shortage of food. After a man hungry, you can't fight. But on de journey going to deliver demself to bakra, dem hear a voice say, "fight fe few more years." And everyone ask de question, "who talk?" And out of de amount, every one say a no dem talk. And dem go to a fair place. And de whole of dem tek out dem jege out of dem pocket.

This one say, "Grandy, a you talk?"

Him say, "no."

Him say, "Granfa, a you talk?"

Him say, "no."

And dem ask demself de question.

And when dem tek out de jege dem and put pon de place there now, dem say, "God Almighty, a you talk?"

All de jege dem ina de place there now, all of de jege dem *mad*, mad, mad. And de voice come back.

One of dem have *one* pumpkin seed.

And de voice say, "plant de pumpkin seed immediately."

And immediately him plant de pumpkin seed, and by a evening, de pumpkin bear, and sustain dem with food ina de hills, till dem capture bakra.

(Hardie Stanford, February 27, 1982)

[20]

When de bakra and Maroon fight go to a mention, and when dem realize, *all* de Maroon food done. *All* Nanny food done. Nanny no got nothing now fe keep up now, fe feed fe-him soldier dem now, fe fight bakra. And de whole of dem move now, say, "well, boy, we ina de wood there, we hungry, so de only thing we have fe go do now, we have fe go deliver weself to bakra."

And when dem travel a go, dem hear one voice say, "fight fe few more years."

And dem ask dem one another, "Grandy Dis, Grandy Dat, a you talk? Granfa Dis, Granfara, a you talk?"

De whole of dem say no, a no none of dem talk. And those man got dem jege. (sings)

> Dandy Raial, behave-ee
> Dandy Raial, seh hard behave
> mek poor los im jege

All those man got dem instrument with dem. And de whole of dem come to one clean place now. Clean place. Dem no use plate. Dem use bowl. A bowl dem got deh fight with. And de *whole* of dem tek out dem jege now—*whole* of dem, you know—put ina de basin.

And dem call, "Grandy Dis, a you talk?"

De jege dem lie down.

"Granfara Dat, a you talk?"

De jege dem lie down.

And dem call all de soldier dem wha' deh fight, fe find out if a dem talk anything. And de jege lie down ina de bowl same way. And when dem talk, talk, talk, dem say, "God Almighty, a you talk?"

All de jege dem ina de bowl tearing mad! Tearing mad. Everybody have fe catch out fe-dem, catch fe-dem, catch fe-dem, catch fe-dem, catch fe-dem, and tek it out of de bowl.

And one of dem min got *one* pumpkin seed. And dem just dig a hole, said time, and plant de one pumpkin seed. And by de time evening fe come, de pumpkin bear. Dem eat dem dinner out there. And dem got food fe serve dem till dem fight and gain victory.

One pumpkin seed. So that is a noble work. Is a miracle. Miracle.

Granfara Welcome, Granfara Parro, Grandy Sukasi, and Grandy Nanny, Grandy Ayinting. Dem hear de sound. De whole of dem hear de sound, say, "fight fe few more years." De whole of dem min hear de sound. But where de sound come from dem never know. Dem believe say a any one of dem ina de company use de same words, "fight fe few more years."

Well, a when dem put jege now, mek jege fe go tell de truth, when dem call pon de whole of dem name now, de jege ina de bowl lie down same way. And dem say, "God Almighty, a you talk?" And de jege dem tearing mad. And de whole of dem tek out fe-dem [jege] one-one-one-one, shove a dem pocket.

And one min got *one* naked pumpkin seed. And him just dig de doti [earth] so, and put it on. By a evening, pumpkin bear till it coulda sustain de world with food.

(Hardie Stanford, January 31, 1991)

Figure 7.1. Maroon woman sowing seeds, Scot's Hall, 1978. Photo: K. Bilby.

[21]

A there [at Watch Hill] him get de news, when dem tired now, say him must fight again. And him plant de pumpkin.

Him say him dream. De man come to him, say, "get up, and fight a three day more."

Him min want give up now, dem get tired. Where dem sit down now, rest, a sleep, Nanny just lay down. Him just hear somebody, like a voice, say to him, say, "get up and stand up, fe fight three days more."

And same time, him no say nothing. Him sit down again, like in here. De person call to him.

So him tell dem say, "wake. Me get a news, say we fe fight three day more."

And him tek him jege wha' him got, and him throw it a ground.

Him say, "[was it] Yankipong Asasi—God above—call to me fe fight three day [and then] we will win, we will get up?"

Same time, him see de jege stand up, jump up so, jump up. And dem get up. And dem go parry. And is after fight de three day, dem [the whites] call fe peace. Bakra couldn't manage dem.

After him dream, dem get up again fe fight. Dem get up now fe start de fight again. In de three day, de government call to him fe peace, bakra.

Him find de pumpkin seed on de ground. And him dig de ground and plant it. And by de [same] day, de pumpkin grow and bear, that dem get de pumpkin, because dem hungry. And dem get de pumpkin eat. Dem call there Watch Hill [or] Pumpkin Hill. A there de pumpkin bear and grow. When him sit down there, him plant de pumpkin. De pumpkin bear de *same* day. De same day dem get fe eat.

You can do that? [i.e., make a pumpkin seed bear fruit the same day you plant it]

Dem [the whites] couldn't manage dem.

(Ruth Lindsay, January 30, 1991)

[22]

We are de skin of de island. De skin of de island.[8] We, de Maroons, we are Israelites. And we are Africans. We are warlike and peaceful people. It was de English people dem proclaim war on us, and Kojo retaliated back to dem. And we fought, and gain victory. So is God's Kojo and Lady Queen Nanny that give us our freedom. And God, I must say, was with us—we, de only nations that flog de English at war.

(Mann Rowe, January 7, 1991)

Chosen People: Reprise

> Members [of the Jamaica National Heritage Trust] could not overcome the perception that recorded history had to be seen in a ruin of mortar and stone, they could not see in the terrain, the ambience and aura of the area, the story of the Maroons.
> —Bev Carey (1997: 352)

Each time a resident of the Maroon community of Moore Town travels by road to the outside world—as many routinely do—he or she is presented with a conspicuous reminder of the collective blessing bestowed upon the ancestors. A few miles north of Moore Town, on the way to the coastal town of Port Antonio and points beyond, the road winds through an area called Rivers View, named for the stunning vista that stretches out to one side. Here one peers out at the gateway to the mountain wilderness that once provided the Maroons' ancestors with an impenetrable refuge. The Grand Ridge of the Blue Mountains, some of its peaks soaring to more than 7,000 feet, forms a magnificent backdrop. A few hundred yards below the roadway, the Rio Grande, Jamaica's largest river, cuts through a verdant flood plain, branching off into a tributary called the Back Rio Grande. Known to Maroons as Back River (or Baka Ribba), this hallowed body of water

Figure 7.2. Rio Grande seen from Rivers View, Portland, 1991. Watch Hill in center and Back River in front of it, forking to the right. Photo: K. Bilby.

quickly takes cover behind a curtain of foothills, rising through miles of uninhabited rainforest all the way to the hidden site of Stony River, or Nanny Town—the capital of the Windward Maroons when they ruled this part of the island during the early eighteenth century. Dominating the patch of low hills hemmed in by the river's two arms is an odd-looking, nearly bald peak. Looming like a giant sentry over the natural route to the interior afforded by the Rio Grande, the barren hilltop instantly draws attention to itself. Known as Watch Hill, this landmark is remembered in contemporary oral traditions as the primary lookout from which Maroon sentinels once spied the movements of enemy troops. Unseen from the road is a back ridge, which slants down to a slightly lower summit known to Maroons as Pumpkin Hill. On these very slopes, many Maroons will tell you, grew the miraculous harvest of pumpkins that saved their ancestors when they were on the brink of disaster. As one of the most prominent features of the Rio Grande Valley, the Watch Hill/Pumpkin Hill formation serves as a daily reminder to "the chosen" of their special place in history.[9]

Like most representations of social reality, the oral tradition presented above admits of several interpretations. Elsewhere, I have tried to show how the "miracle food" (or "instant pumpkins") story of the Windward Maroons embodies not only the themes of social regeneration and continuity (Bilby and Steady 1981: 458–59), but also the values of resourcefulness and endurance (Bilby 1995)—themes and values that have loomed large in this book and will continue to appear in yet other guises in the pages to come.[10]

But the key theme overarching and uniting the various pieces of the larger story told above is that of "the chosen people." Even those Maroons who do not know the first part of this oral tradition (the more esoteric segment concerning the "voice" and the divination revealing that it belonged to God) are likely to be familiar with the connected story of the blessed seed and the instant crop of pumpkins that sustained the ancestors through their darkest hour. Coming as a gift from God, this miracle offered definitive proof to those who had earlier heard "the voice" that they had indeed been singled out for divine blessing. Today, among their descendants, the memory of this proof of Yankipong's blessing stands as firm as the topographic monument in which it has been inscribed.

Built into this "memory" is an unspoken presumption of "otherness"; the idea of "the chosen," like the concept of ethnic identity itself, depends upon the existence of a contrasting category (in this case, those whom we might call "the *un*chosen"). Whether explicitly stated or not, this fundamental distinction between "the chosen" and "the unchosen"—between Maroons (Katawud) and others (*obroni*)—lies behind virtually every representation of what it is that makes Maroons special in the narratives that make up the rest of this book.

8

Underwritten with Blood

The main terms of the treaty were discussed and agreed upon and, with due ceremonies, concluded. It was drawn up in English, and is reputed to have been executed in the Coromanti fashion by the mingling of the blood of the signatories . . . Some historians doubt the mode of execution, but the descendants of the Maroons are emphatic on the point.
—**Richard Hart (1950: 70, 79)**

Too many of the old Africans suffered and died for the treaty, they say, to let someone today get away with treating it like a scrap of paper. That's why the Maroons call it the "Blood Treaty," that and because it was signed in blood by the Maroons and the Englishmen as well.
—**Russell Banks (1980: 261)**

Refusing the Peace

The idea of entering into diplomatic relations with people they had once held as slaves—in their eyes, no more than "wild Negroes" and "savages"—must have been a very distasteful one for the British rulers of Jamaica (Zips 1998: 98). The fact that the British continued to press for a peace settlement with the Maroons over a number of years during the 1730s, despite several setbacks along the way, clearly indicates that the Maroons, who by then were de facto rulers of portions of the island, had put them in an untenable position. For the colonial government, there was simply no acceptable alternative to what would have once been unthinkable: negotiating with their former slaves for a cessation of hostilities. As Richard Hart (1950: 70) argues, "it was a tremendous blow to the prestige of the British 'Raj' to have to make a treaty with the few hundred rebels who had successfully resisted many times their number of well armed regular soldiers, militia, volunteers, mercenaries and 'blackshot.' This was a bitter pill to swallow."

For at least some of the Maroons, the idea of making peace with those who had caused them tremendous suffering—those powerful and relentless foes who still held thousands in bondage on coastal plantations, and who had done everything in their power to extinguish the more fortunate ones who had broken their bonds and opted for freedom in the interior—was equally distasteful.

The written record shows that prior to the treaty of 1739, beginning in the mid-1730s, the colonial government made a number of overtures to the Windward Maroons, all of which were rebuffed.[1] The first British envoys to carry proposals of peace to Nanny's people were either killed, or threatened and sent away (Campbell 1988: 102–3, 122–23). All indications are that the Windward Maroons, despite being under tremendous pressure during this period (especially after their main settlement, Nanny Town, had been destroyed by the British), remained fiercely defiant in the face of such conciliatory gestures. It was only after learning that Kojo's group in the Cockpit Country had already come to terms with the British that Nanny's people in the Blue Mountains showed any receptivity to the idea of peace.[2] Knowing that Kojo had pledged to aid the whites should any of the other Maroon groups remain hostile to the colonial government, the last holdouts under Nanny were forced to recognize that peace could no longer be refused; the fact that their British enemies would now likely receive support from Kojo's warriors, who possessed bush fighting skills similar to their own, had suddenly and dramatically tipped the scales against them.

Nanny's descendants in Moore Town and the surrounding area still assert that the first-time Maroons accepted peace with the whites only reluctantly. Nanny herself, they say, at first vehemently rejected the proposed treaty, vowing to fight the *bakra* enemy to the death [1]; only gradually did she change her position, finally placing the survival of her people above her hatred of the whites, and choosing a path that might allow future generations of her *yoyo* to prosper in peace.

Not all of Nanny's fighters, however, could let go of past grudges and abide by her decision. This continuing refusal to accept peace with the whites is one of the most common themes in Windward Maroon oral traditions about the making of their treaty. Below are several examples of narratives expressing this idea [2–21]. This theme of resistance to the death is most often embodied in a single warrior—in some cases named as Ojedu, in others, Opong, Kwaku, or Welcome—who remains absolute in his opposition to the peace. So bitter is his hatred that he leaves his people forever, rather than joining them in making peace with the whites. In some versions, he plunges into a blue hole or a river pool and becomes a fish; in others, he vanishes into a particular cave near the Stony River, where his protesting spirit lingers to this day, making loud rumbling noises whenever a white person comes too near; in yet others, he flies away back to Africa, never to return (thus reprising a theme of flight to the motherland found in several other Maroon oral traditions).

This uncompromising warrior is also associated with another oral tradition relating to the last days before the treaty (usually under the name Opong) [12–14]. According to this story, it was Opong who perfectly personified the Maroons' unshakeable defiance by hurling an immortal insult at the British enemy in the heat of combat; observing that the white soldiers had run out of ammunition, he had shouted out that they could borrow bullets from him. He had thus humiliated those who, though they always came to the battle much better armed than their opponents, were unable to defeat these guerrilla warriors. Today this incident is most often recalled through an elliptical reference—the common expression, "governor borrow bullet from Opong," or "bakra borrow bullet from Opong."

Other narratives [15–21] suggest that even after the treaty, some of Nanny's soldiers who had agreed to the peace eventually experienced a change of heart and attempted to back out. Among this faction, the unyielding defiance and old hatred of the British remained alive and became a source of internal conflict.[3] One such dissenter, according to the final group of texts in this section, was Granfa Puss (also known as Kwashkwaku).[4] One of the original four (or five) leaders under Nanny, Puss was unable to contain his hostility toward the whites with whom Nanny had sworn a sacred oath of friendship; he ended up leaving her group forever. But first, in a grand gesture of protest, he "sealed" (buried) his "Science" (spiritual paraphernalia) at a strategic location in Moore Town. He then renounced his *pakit* (personal spirit guide) and "threw" his *jege* (power object) at Nanny—the spiritual leader upon whom he had originally bestowed a portion of its power. Compounding the injury, he then seized and burned the Maroon "title"—meaning either the Windward Maroons' own paper copy of the peace treaty itself, or perhaps their copy of the official land grant in the vicinity of Moore Town obtained from the colonial government in 1740 by "Nanny and the people now residing with her."[5] Because of this irreparable breach with Grandy Nanny, Granfa Puss's entire "tribe" disappeared, and his descendants are no longer found among the Moore Town Maroons.

British documents relating to the treaties of 1739 tend to give the impression that, in coming to terms with the colonial rulers of the island, the Maroons were "submitting" themselves to a greater authority.[6] But many Maroons today do not see it that way. As their foreparents frequently reminded them, the Maroons were the victors in this conflict, and they negotiated peace as equals. They were, and remain, indomitable. Among Maroons who remember these stories about ancestors more defiant than the indomitable Nanny herself, the concept of "submission" is a foreign one.

[1]

Grandy [Nanny] *say* him will fight till de battle (/bakl/) rotten.[7] So Grandy talk, you know. [And] him say him will fight till de bottle (/bakl/) rotten—*bakl*. Grandy no call *this* no different way (points to a glass bottle sitting nearby)— "bakl."[8] Ina fe-him Maroon talking, him say "bakl." And it [a glass bottle] can't rotten. Him say, "o biámba Shanti, seh o Shanti o kotoku, so o brindíng, seh o shanti kotoku, so o kunkundeba, o biámba Shanti, seh o Shanti o kotoku, seh o brindíng, seh o Shanti o kotoku, seh o kunkundeba!"

(James Downer, September 18, 1978)

I was very inquisitive to know in what manner the poor *laird* [who had earlier arrived among Nanny's people with a proposal for peace] was put to death, but all I could obtain, upon that subject, was, that he had pleaded his own cause, and the Negroes too, so well (for he was a man of sense, and learning) that *Quoha* told me, he had put bracelets upon his wrists, and determined to have sent him down to Governor Trelawney, with offers of submission upon the same terms, the *laird* had assured him, *Cudjoe* had accepted; but said *Quoha*, when I consulted our *Obea woman*, she opposed the measure, and said, *him bring becara* [white man] *for take the town, so cut him head off.* But God knows what the poor laird suffered, previous to that kind operation. (Thicknesse 1788: 120–21)

---

[2]

You have de brother [of Nanny] wha' go through de rock [into a cave]. That a river fort. That is de rock me want tell you [about]. Him go through that rock. Nobody see him from that time till now. [That happened] when Grandy come to bakra, come fe come sign de peace treaty.

(Sydney McDonald, September 4, 1978)

[3]

[When a British officer approached Nanny to negotiate peace], she say yes. Well, Opong say no. One of de brother say no. Him don't agree. Him must kill every one of dem. Every one of de white that come there must be a dead man, for dem trail dem too far. You know? Dem follow dem up too far. So then him out fe kill dem. And de sister say no, him mustn't hurt dem. De sister say no, him don't want to hurt dem. Him mustn't hurt dem.

(Adolphus Whyte, February 3, 1991)

[4]

Opong fly way, say Grandy Nanny fe kill dem [the whites who came to make peace]. Grandy Nanny say no, him no agree fe kill dem. Him must mek dem sign de pledge. And Opong fly way. Opong never witness it. Opong fly way.

(Adolphus Whyte, February 3, 1991)

[5]

Opong rough. If you hear him say him deh go out there so, you can't stop him. A so him gone. You understand. But de other brother dem no so. They will hear wha' de sister say. But anything you hear Opong talk, a wha' Opong mean. So when you hear him say, "Opong, o kúmfu dája-ee," that mean to say you damn well dead. You dead to shit.

Him say him blood a fe-him. Him blood a no fe-you. Him blood a fe-him. Wha' him mean a wha' him talk.

(Adolphus Whyte, February 3, 1991)

[6]

[When a British officer asked Nanny and her brothers to make peace] de brother wha' dem call Opong—that is de smallest brother, de last brother fe her—him say him no agree. Dem no fe mek no peace. Him fe kill de officer. For dem trail dem too far, right round Grassett backyard a Port Antonio, go right round back of that hill there, come round, rest St. Thomas, and come down there a hill here, and go every way. And reach clear a Stony River. De brother say him trail dem too far, so therefore, none no fe tell de tales.

Opong say no. And meanwhile, dem deh talk, Opong fly gone to hell about him ways. When dem write down de [treaty] and fix it up, not one of dem see Opong until today. Opong go back a Africa. Yes, him deh a Africa. Yeah, Opong fly way gone a Africa. Those people no eat nothing wha' salt put on, you know, and all dem thing there. Dem no use salt. Dem use green, and all wha' green. Dem no eat no meat. No, dem no eat dem thing there. Dem eat de green, like wha' we da call calalu. All wha' green, dem use. You understand. So him fly gone about him ways. Out of de seven [brothers], de balance left there. And dem sign de treaty.

(Adolphus Whyte, June 7, 1978)

One of the rebels call'd to us & told us in his Country Language (as we were inform'd by some of our negroes who understood him) that he would come in [if] we would not kill him, We encouraged him by one of our Negroes to come in & that he or any of them should have their Liberty [,] he continued talking to the Negro till he got Sight of him, at which time he Shot him through the body, & [the man who translated the offer of "liberty"] died in a Short time after. ("A Journal of the proceedings of the Parties Commanded by Edward Creswell & Ebenezer Lambe kept by Ebenezer Lambe," entry of March 10, 1732; PRO/CO 137/54, 166)

[7]

Captain Jedu never enter when de treaty a sign. Him hide back a one corner, sit down. And him sit down. And when dem call him, him say him blood a him blood. Him blood wha' him got, a fe-him already. Him no need fe go drink it again. So then, if him mek any other decision from that time, I don't get de teaching. A Old Jedu, man. A Old Jedu.

(Noel Lewis, February 4, 1991)

[8]

[After Nanny agreed to make peace with the whites], de baddest man, wha' dem call Ojedu, say, "mm-*mm!*"

Ojedu say, mm-mm, him no agree neither: "Ba, me no agree fe white man suck me blood."

Him say him no agree with white man at *all*, fe suck him blood.

All right. But him no call it so. Him say "cut bujufwa." So dem call de blood. "Cut bujufra, cut bujufra." A de blood dem mean.

Ojedu say him no agree at all fe cut him bujufra with white man.[9] Him no agree.

Ojedu say, "Ba, me naa agree fe anybody cut fe-me blood fe white man." Him no agree with all wha' done.

Him fold him arms, him no business, and him go back down and get ina one cavity, one big hole—a one of fe-Nanny soldier, you know—one of de big hole, everlasting trench. And that, de greatest man, him go ina that hole and dead. That's right. And when me and de white man go there now, you hear that man—de spirit, then—about like from here to out de road and up a de level here so.[10] And you da hear de place beating [making a noise], "bim bim bim bim bim bim bim bim bim," anytime de white man dem come. You see like when a truck stop? A so it go, de sound coming. It go: "bim bim bim bim bim bim bim bim." And it will be there beating so till.

Well, a that man, Ojedu, a him down a de hole there. Because, him say him rather fe dead more than fe sign treaty. Him kill himself, stay till him dead.

(Richard Barnes, May 25, 1978)

[9]

Ojedu dead ina de wood there. Ojedu fight, fight fe Nanny. Ojedu fight.

Ojedu say, "me fight with de white man, and me fight dem fe so many year . . ."

But Nanny say him fight till him tired. White man say him fe mek peace.

Granfa Ojedu say, "me n'e mek no peace with white man, no peace me n'e mek with white man before him cut bujufra!"

Nanny send him fe cut bujufra, say him fe cut him blood. When him say "cut bujufra," a him blood him mean.

I met with a party of the Wild Negroes the 5th of this month, one of them was so ingenious, as to tell me that some small partys were determined to kill me if they mett me, that my business was well known, But that they were determined never to believe a Baccara [white person]. The Negro that Spoke to me seemed to bear great authority. . . . he advised me to make haste back with a caution not to come out again after them, for if I should, I should certainly be killed. (letter of February 6, 1734 from Bevill Granville to Governor John Ayscough, describing his peace mission to the Windward Maroons; PRO/CO 137/21, 208)

Him [Ojedu] say, "me n'e cut no bujufra with white man, because me punish too much! White man mek me have fe go through rain, me have fe go through sun, me have fe hide from white man. Me n'e cut no bujufra!"

[That] mean to say, him n'e cut him blood. Nanny say white man punish dem too much, [but] white man say mek we mek peace.

Ojedu say, "me n'e mek no peace with dem. Because me blood a fe-me, me n'e cut no bujufra!"

And Nanny say, "all right, me fight till me tired, and me want fe rest now, me want fe-me people dem [to be able to rest]."

Ojedu say, "no, me no agree! Me rather tan in here, kremu nanti [I would rather stay in here and die]"[11]—stay that time till him dead, you know, a wha' him mean—"me n'e mek no peace with white man!"

Well, Nanny want rest.

Nanny drink de white man blood, and de white man drink fe-Nanny blood. And dem mek de peace, which stop dem from fight.

But, Ojedu say, "me no ina it! Me rather tan a de wood here and dead!"

And Ojedu tan a de wood and dead.

And till today Ojedu no mek no peace with white man. Him dead ina de wood, Nanny House.

You have a big *cavity*, meaning a big hole. Ojedu go ina de hole, one big hole ina Nanny House, and go in there and lie down till him dead. And when you go there now, it's one square chain of level, and him go below de level and dead there. Anytime you go to de level and it is a white man come there, you hear de whole place [make a rumbling noise]: "bim, bim, bimbimbimbimbimbimbimbim." A so dem do it, you know. De whole place, all like when you see a truck rest and him naa shut off, "bimbimbimbimbimbimbim," a beat. Ojedu tek him rest there.

And till today, Ojedu say, "me no agree with de white man dem, because wha' white man talk, a no wha' him mean!" A wha' Ojedu say: "wha' white man talk, a no wha' him mean!"

Because dem deh man a no fool-fool [simple or foolish person], you know.

Well, Nanny mek de peace with white man. And, as a truth, wha' Ojedu say—wha' white man talk, until today, a no wha' him mean at all, whether you want to believe me or no.

(Richard Barnes, September 6, 1978)

[10]

Granfara Jedu. There is a falling [waterfall] there, a one place so, where water a come off of de rock. Granfara Jedu up underneath there.

So when de blood mixed up with de white rum, with Captain Stoddart and Nanny, Kojo, Kwaashi, Johnny, Apong, [then] Jedu say—a de same Granfara Jedu me a tell you bout, a him back of de fall there—him say, Ojedu say, "me blood a me blood. Me naa drink it."

And me going talk ina de Maroon language mek you know now. Him say, "o síka, o síka o síka mankwába, o dángkwa a mi fren!"

All de while, him never agree. Him never agree. All fe-him intention is to fight de war, so him no agree fe mek no peace. But seeing as Nanny, being a famous fighter, [her wishes prevailed over his].

When Jedu min under de cotton tree, him have a gun side of him. But him have a afana ina him hand so, and a look pon it so, and de flame of it and such like, you know? Him come a dem. When dem mix de blood, Jedu say him naa drink none.

Dem mix up, cut white man blood and black man blood, throw ina white rum, and mix dem up. Cut man, cut man, man, and lean all there so, blood a run off, drop ina vessel. Everybody cut blood, drop ina vessel. Open white rum, throw it pon it. Well, a no dem ya rum wha' we call "overproof." We now call de white rum an "overproof." But dem call it "white seal." Mix up with big something, a white rum and blood.

Everybody tek you cup, cup like this. Everybody drink. (And while drinking, they spoke the words): "Peace and surety."

Well, Granfara Jedu, well, him say him naa do that. Because, him say, "o síka, o síka mankwába, o dángkwa a mi freng" [a Maroon Kromanti phrase]. That mean to say him say him blood a him blood. Him naa drink him blood. Because him got it already. And him naa give it away. So that's how de treaty sign.

(Noel Lewis, February 2, 1991)

The rebellious Negroes on the Top of the Hill hallowed to us to Come up for they was ready for us, & told us three times we Came for to fight 'em & run away like a parcel of white liver'd Sons of bitches. (Journal of a British officer, entry of September 22, 1732; PRO/CO 137/20, 112)

On this hill they immediatly laid two ambushes, as soon as they had so done, they fired two Shotts more, and blowed their horns, then called to us to Come up, but that we not attempting / as it was not adviseable / that way they told us, they would dine with us very soon, they would Barbacue us, and used us with abundance of other threatning and abusive Language, We then informed them of the Encouragement offered for their Comeing in [to make peace], but to this they gave no Ear for they still Continued their abusive Language in the same manner as before. ("The Journal of William Lamport and Thomas Williams," entry of February 25, 1734, PRO/CO 137/ 21, 211)

[11]

Nanny says de only peace that he can made is Captain Stoddart have to cut demself, and catch de blood, and him cut fe-him and dem, and catch de blood, and put into a vessel, and they mix up dem together with white rum, and share it, and everybody tek a drink of it.

But there [was] one man out of de game sit down at a corner, name Ojedu. Ojedu say him naa drink it, because him blood a him blood.

Andu píkin ándu! Magróni magróni magróni matída. [a Kromanti incantation] (long pause)

So then, we have Baka River, and we have Blaka River.[12] Soft river run deep. A no everything good fe eat good fe talk.[13] Dodge-him-oo pensa ina de game, until today.[14] Andu píkin ándu. (blows some rum, and asks for a cigarette)

Ojedu say, "ko wak kom . . . ko wak kom-oy! . . . ko wak kom."

Him turn roaring bull.

Ojedu say, "rain-oo..." (sings)

    rain-oo
    rain-oo, Dandy
    Dandy Man, you a do you time
    me Dandy
    rain-oo
    rain-oo, Dandy
    Dandy Man, a you a do you time
    congo-worm a go nyam you[15]

Nanny sing de last sing. Nanny say—and him dance it—him say: (sings)

    me win-oo
    me win-oo
    me win lion and tiger[16]
    me win-oo
    me win-oo
    me win lion and tiger

They [the few remaining soldiers who didn't desert their officers during an ambush] See ye Wild Negros Advance within two Muskett lengths of their Comander & ye rest of ye people with him ye Wild Negroes Some Said Dam 'em no Shoot Backaras [white men] take 'em Alive Lieut. Strutten Spy'd a conveneant rock where he carried Lieut. Thos. Swanton too with ye small Body that Stood by him there remained all night ye Wild Negros call'd out you Backaras what make you come too day you rong Sambo [a "party negro" helping the whites] no here till to morrow. (letter from J. Draper, September 4, 1733, PRO/CO 137/20, 187)

O tandabasokom, o kánshika sa man fríngi! Me naa tell you no more. (blows some rum) Ey! Ey! (laughs to himself) Mi siyumandi. Mi siyumandi Kojo [more Kromanti incantations]. (blows some more rum)

(Addresses spirits partially in old Maroon creole, attempting to placate them for talking about such things with an outsider): Bigi piipl, mi ting yu si. Bot wach ya, bigi piipl. Yu wáshi wan klii fi di big sumadi. Yu gat mánaz fi bígi príprí. Bígi príprí símpatáiz wid yu. O kimáiki. Mi a drink sangána.

Him no say nothing more, man. Jedu sit down a one place.

(Noel Lewis, February 2, 1991)

[12]

There was some exchange of bullet between Opong and de British governor.

(Charles Aarons, January 30, 1991)

[13]

"Governor borrow bullet from Opong": de *one* bullet wha' dem [the British] tek from Opong capture fe-dem war, a cause de treaty fe sign—because of de one bullet wha' him [the bakra] borrow from de old man wha' Nanny left give him. De word say: "governor borrow bullet from Opong."

Opong a one little old man live ina one little old tatu [hut] where nobody come, like [he] no count.

(Noel Lewis, February 2, 1991)

[14]

Now, Opong was a man that nobody ever respect or count. You know? Him was a low-down man. So when de bakra dem fighting dem war now, Opong sit down one side and mek him little bullet dem—mek him little bullet dem, and

---

⁕

[Captain Williams and Lambe] came thither this Morning about eight or nine aClock, I asked them how they came to let the Wild Negroes drive them out of the Towns, They told me they kept possession as long as they had any Ammunition left. . . . They inform'd me that the wild Negroes Surrounded them and fir'd very briskly upon them, the Wild Negroes call'd to our People and ask'd them if they wanted any Powder or balls, if they did, they would let them have some. (letter from J. Draper to Titchfield, June 27, 1733, PRO/ CO 137/20, 150)

---

save dem up. So when de bakra dem fire, fire out all of fe-dem bullet now, dem say [they] no have no bullet. But as Opong was so funny, and stay bad, nobody no did count Opong fe go borrow nothing from Opong. But one of dem seh mek dem go, go see if Opong can help dem. And dem go, and go and borrow de bullet from Opong. And Opong give dem de bullet, and coulda able fe fight dem war, through Opong bullet.

Yes, him borrow de bullet from Opong. We have one little phrase here now. You say: "[I never knew] how you did great. Me never even know say you coulda borrow bullet." Because nobody couldn't go borrow nothing from Opong. You understand? [If] anybody a talk foolishness, you say, "you go borrow bullet from Opong."

Nobody never count him. But de bakra dem have to count him, when fe-dem bullet done, say dem a go borrow it from him—borrow de bullet from Opong, fe fight dem war, because dem war done, dem bullet done. Dem go borrow de bullet from Opong.

Opong was a Maroon man, you know.

(Margaret Harris, February 4, 1991)

[15]

On de day when Nanny sign de treaty, Mento, as de tactics-man, throw his thing—de Maroon say his "pakit"—upon Nanny. And him tek way, for nobody know where him min go to. And nobody know where him last go to.

(Johnny Minott, June 4, 1978)

[16]

[There was a] tactics-man, when Nanny was making the peace, who throw his pakit pon Nanny, and him follow the river, and nobody no know where him end up to. That was the time when Nanny making the peace. As I tell you already, none of those generals never witness the peace. So that man who throws his tactics pakit pon Nanny, he follow the river. Nobody no know where him come out to, nobody no know where him end up, nobody no know where him die neither.

(Johnny Minott, September 10, 1978)

[17]

Right a Back River mouth that peace mek. And de one wha' dem call Granfa Puss tek out him pakit and throw pon Grandy Nanny, and him turn fish, and him swim up and down ina river. That mean him never witness that peace. That peace, him never witness it at all.

Granfa Puss seal him something a Safo House, and *burn* Maroon title, and turn a Guava Piece. Nobody no see him, up to today. So dat deh race deh *dead*.

(James Downer, 1978)

[18]

You have one [of Nanny's fighters] turn a big fish. A when him deh a one blue hole [deep place in a river]. Nobody know whether him come out, or wherever him go. Two never left Stony River. Nobody no know if him come out there or where him gone to. That a down Back River there. A down there Grandy [Nanny] mek de peace there—I mean Grandy mek his covenant, right down Back River there.

(Johnny Minott, August 20, 1978)

[19]

I want to tell you as far as I learn from my older heads. When Grandy [Nanny] mek de peace, none of these four men [the four original leaders] never witness it. None of dem. And *no* Maroon can't tell where any of these four men die. (Long pause.) And what I am telling you here, me a tell you solemnly. No man can tell where any of these four men—otherwise me woulda call dem Kwaku, de Maroon way, de Maroon call these four "Kwaku"—Kwaku, Kofi, de same thing—nobody know where none of dem die.

After de peace mek, all de races were at Moore Town. One side, de Puss side, de Puss race, then, dem seal dem jege a Asafo House, and burn de title, until no Maroon know where dem end up to. At that time, de peace mek long time.

I mean, de things wha' dem use to mek dem tactics—you may call it their magic, or whatsoever you may feel—dem bury it there, man. And dem gone. Dem burn de title—de document dem get in war, de paper.

But it were de whole race leave Moore Town. De whole race. Whole family. Kwashkwaku race. That a de same Puss race.

(Johnny Minott, February 6, 1991)

[20]

None of these four general, as I tell you, do not witness peace, do not see de peace, because they did not want it. All four did not want it. You know, de day of peace, Mento throw him jege pon Grandy [Nanny] and follow river. Nobody no know where him end to. [Granfa] Welcome turn one big hog-nose wha' ina dem river. Nobody know where him went. [He] turn one fish, one hog-nose [type of mullet]. Yes. And de other two man left at Stone Wall. Nobody know what happen to dem. No Maroon can't tell. If any Maroon tell that, say, that man dead here so, or that one dead so, dem a tell lie. Dem don't know. Whether dem ben go back to Africa, or where dem end out to, nobody know.

(Johnny Minott, February 6, 1991)

[21]

Kwaku did not agree to the signing of de treaty. His intention was that they should—according to him—that they should never stop till they kill out all de English soldiers in de country. So he never agree with de peace treaty.

So him walk backway, from Stony River, to go and listen, where de treaty was sign, listen what happen. But him never turn him face to witness it.

And then, after that, him run way ina de Millbank wood. If you go in de Millbank area, up there you call Kwaku (Quaco) River. That is de reason why they give it that name. Him run to there, and throw himself into a blue hole [deep place in a river]. And, I mean, people follow him, you know? But from de moment him throw himself in de blue hole, dem no see nobody again. De only thing they witness in de river was a big, huge fish. But they didn't find any human body. So they call it Kwaku River, up in Millbank, passing Millbank going to St. Thomas.

Kwaku. That is one of Nanny brother.

(Charles Aarons, January 30, 1991)

Peace, Perfect Peace

> It is a known fact that unilateral abrogation of treaties is a distasteful thing to the majority of peoples throughout the world and the treaty between the Government and the Maroons is regarded by the latter as unique and inviolable since it entailed the mixing of blood of the signatories on both sides. It can be stated categorically that *the treaty is not abolished.*
> —Colonel C.L.G. Harris, 1977 (Harris n.d.: 60)

Written treaties are, among other things, tangible objects. One can run one's fingers over the paper fibers on which a treaty's text is fixed, ponder the wording, and take the time to read between the lines. Even when the legality of such a document is in question, its materiality is not. Whether made in good faith or bad, whether amended, superseded, abrogated, nullified, violated, or simply for-gotten, written treaties retain a certain aura of authority; at the very least, they bear witness to past events, corroborating that the particular acts of diplomacy of which they are no more than artifacts actually did take place.

The two treaties concluded by Maroon leaders and envoys of the British crown in 1739 have long formed a leitmotif in writings about Jamaican Ma-roons. Travel writers, historians, and ethnographers have repeatedly latched onto these historic documents, finding in them a kind of ultimate explanation of the Maroon condition. And it is easy to see why. The Maroon treaties are, after all, indisputably, physically "real." They constitute our most tangible evidence of what might be regarded as a defining moment in Maroon history.

Equally importantly, they are relatively accessible. The complete texts of both documents have been reproduced in multiple sources, and generations of schol-ars have written about their significance. Moreover, the treaties loom as large in Maroon oral tradition as they do in the written literature. And unlike most other symbols of Maroon identity, they are readily discussed—up to a point, at least—with outsiders. Forming the legal basis of the relationship between Maroons and succeeding Jamaican governments since 1739, they have long been part of the island's public political culture and therefore exempt from the veil of secrecy that has traditionally shrouded other aspects of Maroon history.[17]

Few Maroons would take issue with the ongoing tendency of historians and social scientists to privilege the treaties in their analyses; Maroons too consider the events of 1739 to be of paramount importance. But Maroon understandings of their treaties differ fundamentally from those of non-Maroons. As Werner Zips (1999b: 231) has noted, recent Jamaican governments have tended to rep-resent these documents in a derogatory way, as "colonial treaties." Whereas most outsiders, including government officials, view the treaties in rather literal terms as legal and political documents whose interest is primarily historical, Maroons regard them, as Barbara Kopytoff (1979) has shown, as "sacred charters" that carry as much weight today as they did when first agreed upon more than two centuries ago. From a government point of view, the degree to which they remain valid—if this question is to be given any serious consideration at all—is a matter for legal experts and can be resolved only on the basis of clause-by-clause dissec-tion. But in the eyes of Maroons, such questions are largely immaterial, for the treaties are much more than the sums of their parts. Much more important than the specific provisions spelled out on paper is the *spirit* in which the original agreements were made (Bilby 1997). Not only did this entail reconciliation and cooperation between former enemies, but also and more importantly, from a Maroon perspective, it gave formal recognition to the Maroons' fundamental right to self-determination.

Maroons today are unanimous in asserting that their treaties were conse-crated with blood oaths. While contemporary written documents lend no sup-port to this Maroon oral tradition, it is safe to conclude that the Jamaican Maroons, like their counterparts in the Guianas, did in fact employ African-derived forms of oath taking—including blood oaths—to conclude their treaties.[18] So central is the idea of a blood oath to Maroon understandings of their treaties that to question the historicity of this oral tradition would be, for Maroons, not only to reduce a sacred pact to a mere "scrap of paper," but also to "rewrite" history. That the British colonial archives are silent on this matter says much about the one-sidedness of the written record traditionally available to historians.

The Maroons' private knowledge of their sacred treaties is not limited to the details of the exchange of blood between the ancestors and their British adversaries. As several of the following texts show, the treaties are remembered and "made real" for each generation through a variety of esoteric stories and allusions to local persons and places. Both Leeward and Windward Maroon narrators, for instance, cite specific locations where treaty negotiations are said to have taken place [e.g., 26, 28, 29, 33–36]; these places still vibrate with ancestral power. Windward Maroons assert that blood was the ink used to sign the original treaty [32, 40, 42, 46], and that the writing implement was not any ordinary quill, but the feather of a particular bird inhabited by a powerful spirit—one of the *pakits*, or personal spirits, used by Grandy Nanny herself [40, 44–46]. And they repeat formulaic Kromanti phrases associated with these events, said to have been uttered originally by those who experienced them "in the flesh."

Above all, these narratives demonstrate that for Maroons the treaties of 1739 are a living reality, and not the dead documents of a bygone era that some in Jamaica make them out to be. The possessors of this living Maroon knowledge are certain that enlightened legal scholars—those equipped to interpret not only the letter but also the spirit of the law—will one day prove them right.

I. The Leeward Treaty (Kojo's Peace)

[22]

At the peace treaty the white officer when remaining fifty soldiers. Made peace by sticking his arm and the arm of the Maroon officer, caught the blood into a silver cup which was made into punch with wine and drunken by both party. This was done the Maroon's said that this would be only for a time. The whites asked what more they wanted. The maroons said, "We want a treaty, a document for ever." Later it was given in a book with . . . agreement and authority.

(Colonel H. A. Rowe, July 13, 1937)[19]

[23]

Dem mek peace. And dem say, "we must cut each other blood and suck it." So de white cut his blood—his hand—and de black suck it. And de black cut fe-him

Figure 8.1. Mann Rowe displaying the Accompong Maroons' original copy of the Leeward Maroon treaty of 1739 (Kojo's Treaty), Accompong, 1991. Photo: K. Bilby.

hand, and de white suck it. And we mek a peace forever and ever amen. So we own this piece of land, up into Accompong Town.

(Johnny Chambers, January 6, 1991)

[24]

Sir Edward Trelawny was de then governor of Jamaica. And he sent a message to de king, to send troops immediately, or otherwise it won't be a Jamaica to send reports [to anymore]. King George, de sovereign monarch of Great Britain, sent out two esquires called Colonel John Guthrie Ellis and Francis Sadler Ellis to negotiate, and mek a final conclusion of peace and friendship in de name of God, forever and ever, amen.

Is a blood treaty. Because de English—Francis Sadler Ellis and John Guthrie Ellis—dem inject they veins and caught de blood, and drank it in de needle.

So our treaty is stronger than [others]. De late emperor Kaiser William of Germany style a treaty to be a scrap of paper. Our treaty is a solid, sound, and religious treaty signed in de name of God, forever and ever, amen.

(Mann Rowe, January 7, 1991)

[25]

We fought [for] our freedom. We defeat de English in de warfare. And dem
have to come to us on a peace term, for we are de victor.

Well, we as Maroons, we don't pay taxes fe our lands. Everything is free. And
de treaty told us that we have rights to every benefit, as much as de other
people who bought their lands and paying taxes. And when we say "paying
taxes," we pay taxes too. But we don't pay land tax.

But until now, we do not have de right amount of privilege. And you can see
that de Jamaica government, if dem could wipe us out, dem would do that. But
without de Maroons, de history of Jamaica don't value anything.

Dem fail to handle us as dem should. Because dem know that our powers
and our rights to de country is more than theirs. Because we are two hundred
and fifty-one years now on our own. So that means, if dem could wipe us out,
dem would do it.

[When the treaty was made], as a token of peace, dem use de said white
rum. Dem have a thing dem call de calabash, or otherwise gourdy. A it those
people dem used to use. So dem both now cut dem hands, and drain de blood
ina de calabash, and throw white rum pon it, and mix it up. And de both of dem
drink it. So dem say, from that time now, coming on, is just one link between de
Maroons and de white men dem. Yes. And dem bound us to a certain amount
of lands. And we don't pay no taxes fe those lands. So we live as we like.

(Thomas Rowe, January 7, 1991)

[26]

De treaty mek a Peace Cave. De governor give Maroon a treaty. De white man
cut fe-him blood, and give it to put ina rum, and give it to Kojo. And Kojo cut
fe-him too. And de two of dem drink, drink de blood from each other. That is a
blood treaty, sah. Can't broke. Dem drink, dem tek de one another blood, and
dem throw ina one tumbler, and dem drink de blood. That's a "blood treaty,"
dem call it. Blood treaty can't mash.[20]

(Geretius McKenzie, January 9, 1991)

II. The Windward Treaty (Nanny's Peace)

[27]

There was a treaty that was signed between the Maroons and the Europeans, or
the English people. It was around 1738, the time of George the First, I think. Because, you know, the Maroons were always fighting for their rights, and for their
freedom. They did not like to be overruled. Well, finding that they were giving
so much trouble, they were granted certain privileges. And therefore a treaty
was signed with the imperial government, that they are to remain as free

Figure 8.2. "Old Cudjoe Making Peace," 1739. From Dallas (1803).

people. And owing to that, there were certain discretions, and certain privileges that were granted to them, through that treaty, which is resting up until today.

(Colonel Ernest Downer, 1952)[21]

[28]

Bakra say, "me can't manage de Maroon people dem, therefore we a mek peace."

De peace mek a Back River mouth. That mean say, if you get a drink of water from Back River, you all right.[22] That mean say, a right there so dem mek peace with bakra. Right there a Back River mouth, dem mek peace.

All right. Bakra say Maroon no fe fight against dem, and dem no fe fight against Maroon. But if any nation come in fe fight dem, Maroon fe back dem.

But dem a drift now [from the terms of the treaty]. Dem drifting!

(James Downer, October 3, 1978)

[29]

I learn that de peace did made right out at Back River—right at Golden Vale, come that way, Corn Husk, come that way. Two Back River we have. If you go out back round Fruitful Vale, you will find Back River. Both of dem come from de same. One come this way, one come that way.

De peace made there, it was a blood covenant peace. De white man drink de Maroon blood, and de Maroon drink de white man blood. It was a blood covenant. That was Grandy [Nanny's] treaty. It was a blood covenant. Kojo and de rest sign treaty, but Grandy made blood covenant. Is not fe-her alone blood they do it. De rest of soldiers, or Maroon with him, is dem cut dem blood, that de white man can drink. And de white man cut his, and drink. You know, you drink my blood, I drink yours. Is that made that kind of blood covenant.

(Johnny Minott, February 6, 1991)

[30]

After dem fight now, and dem couldn't capture dem, dem [the whites] have fe call fe a peace treaty. Over barracks there, it was there that de peace treaty mek between de white and de black, never to rebel against each other as long as grass groweth. So those are de treaty dem that you get a glimpse of, and other men also.

(Uriah McLean, June 23, 1978)

[31]

I want to tell you something. Mek me give you a instance about de treaty. Nanny never sign no treaty. Nanny made blood covenant. De Maroon man cut his blood, and de white man cut his blood, and dem both drinks each other blood. De white man drinks de Maroon man blood, and de Maroon man drinks de white man blood. That was Nanny's type of rules.

(Johnny Minott, August 20, 1978)

[32]

Well, it want to come to a close now. De white soldier find that dem couldn't manage Nanny. De white soldier britallion [battalion] find that dem couldn't manage Nanny. That's right. And they come and dem write a petition. Dem tek ink and dem write.

Dem [the Maroons] have a fighting ground up top where dem can't pass there. And dem send a man there de night, de white soldier, and put de right to Nanny, say him want to mek peace.

Well, Nanny tek fe-him blood and write. Him no got pen, but him cut him hand, him blood, and dip him hand in there and write.

Nanny write ina him blood now, and him say, "all right, I don't know if me soldier dem agree, but me agree. But de only way me will agree to you [is] if you will set me people dem free."

Because, they were fighting fe land. From Morant Bay, a land dem fighting for—for freedom fe land.

Well, Nanny say, "all right, me agree fe mek peace."

But dem fe set him children free, so him can mek him pikibo dem go a dem prandes, or dem property, then, and catch dem janga [crayfish], shoot dem pigeon, and catch dem wild pig, and free demself—all like that. Him will agree.

De white man say, yes, him will give dem de authority.

Nanny say then, "if you agree fe give me pikibo de authority fe go a de crown land and tek what dem want to get, and free dem to go through and through, then me agree too."

Nanny and de other people dem, friend dem, they get together, and de next day dem go up to de draw, because dem no fraid. Everybody put down fighting tool now, and dem talk together now. Dem going to mek peace now, dem say.

Nanny cut fe-him blood, put ina wha' dem call "obwasu"—one big paki [calabash] bowl so. Obwasu. Dem tek de paki, and fe-him people dem, fe-him side of blood people cut de blood, throw ina de obwasu. And de white man cut fe-dem blood and dem throw ina de obwasu. That's right. And dem drink little. De white man drink first, and Nanny drink after.

And dem mek peace there so, for *all time*.

Well, up to now, white man no come to dem word. We get de freedom all de same, but you know say white people all de time deh dodge. Me got one word ina Kromanti—me say, "o dodge him-oo, kumfu du mi." White man deh dodge you all de time. "Dodge him-oo, kumfu du mi"—mean to say, de man a dodge from you. A so fe-we Maroon man word say: "oo dodge him-oo, kumfu du mi."[23] That word mean to say, me deh hide from you. Maroon word that.

So, true, de white man now, today, dem still deh dodge from [us]. Wha' dem tell you yesterday, a no wha' white man mean today. White man da come and tell you [things], and taming you, and tell you all kind of thing, and tame you, *all* kind of thing. But when dem come see that black people mean fe tek root, then *all* dem motive [is] fe turn on soldier pon you fe kill you—fe kill black people.

But black people come from Africa, and they are *very* smart people. *Yes*. Very smart people.

(Richard Barnes, May 25, 1978)

[33]

Fe-we foreparents, we was a slave, you know. And dem have to *fight*. Dem have to fight white people fe get freedom, you know. Yeah, dem have to fight. Dem have fe fight fe get freedom, otherwise *we* woulda be a slave right now. So is that dem fight for, fe do away with de slavery business, to let *we* free. You get that?

All right. Well, dem have to sign treaty, you know—those two part, de white and de black, have to sign treaty. Well, I go where de treaty sign. And I know where it sign, ina de town [of Stony River]. Two place dem sign it. One a down along river. You have fe cross ina de water, about like ten yard under de place. And dem go under there and sign de treaty under there. You have fe cross through de water. When you go there now, you have to got light, when you go ina that hole, to see that treaty wha' sign [i.e., to clearly see the place where the treaty was made]. But de other one you see plain.

(Adolphus Whyte, June 7, 1978)

[34]

Dem cut bujufra, cut bujufra right there so, and sign dem treaty.[24] And me can go carry you right now to de two place, show you say, a here so dem cut bujufra. One place, one first level, dem cut bujufra. And dem go to de second level, and sign de treaty. Government sign de treaty. That a before you go ina de Nanny House. That's right. Two level.

(Addresses Nanny's spirit in an approximation of the old Maroon creole, while pouring a libation): Obroni de a mi prandes, an na yong man. Im waan fi nuo húfa bot, hou yu fait di war an al laik dat. So, yu no fi békes. Bot na hónti mi si, mi de tak. No békes.[25]

Sometime him [Grandy Nanny] no want you fe talk where him hiding place [is]. So sometime you have fe talk to dem [the ancestors] too. Because me see, and me know. You no see dem, but when you deh talk about Maroon, dem come. Dem listen. De bigger old people dem come. A breeze dem, but dem a listen. De breeze is a wind, but de wind blow to and fro.

De first level where dem mek de peace—"báimba, o báimba ye yedéng, o fréi, ámba-ee!"—de first level dem mek de peace, dem call that place Obáimbáimbá. De other place, dem call it Báimba Yedéng. Out there, dem call it Báimba Yedéng, de second one, Báimba Yedéng.

De first place a one big stick wood so, down by one little level, first level, call it Obáimbáimbá. Stony River. And den you walk, and de other place name Báimba Yédeng. Báimba Yedéng.

(Richard Barnes, February 4, 1991)

[35]

White people dem want de Maroon, de Kyatawud dem, fe turn slave. Right? And she [Nanny] say, she prefer *dead* [than] fe know that fe-him people dem turn slave. Dem must be free! Dem no fe ina no bondage. You understand that? So a that dem deh fight for.

Dem [the whites] want dem fe turn slave, and she say, "my people is to free!"

All right.

And when dem [the British soldiers] dead and left de officer one, she sit down there and deh look up a de Stone Wall. Me naa tell you no lie. And every damn one [of the British soldiers] dead lie down there. She naa even turn back [to] look, because him know say every one wha' see de pot going dead. Him know anyone wha' look ina de pot, that one is a dead man. And she naa pay dem no mind.

And de [white] officer call to her, call to her, and him say, "Nanny, turn round, I want to speak to you."

She say to de officer, "speak as much. I'm hearing you. I don't deaf."

De officer say, "I want you to turn round and let we meet face to face."

De seven brother was there. One name Charlie. Charlie say to him sister, him say, "turn round and talk to de man."

And Grandy Nanny wheel round—that was de biggest brother, Charlie—and when him turn round, him say, "and what is your request?"

De officer say to her, "why I want to see your face, is a reason."

She say, "what is de reason?"

De officer say to her, "you are too pretty, and you are too good looking to dead and go to hell, so I am asking you, if you are so kind enough, please, to mek we mek peace."

Anyone ever tell you so?

De other brother dem say, whilst de officer deh fe peace, de sister must mek peace. De sister call him.

And Grandy Nanny say to him, "what you want me to do? What you request? What is your request?"

Him say, "I want fe mek peace."

Me see de two treaty [that they made], man. One down a de river, down where you going cross.

Everything wha' happen, it write pon de stone. A no lie me a tell, it write pon de stone.

(Adolphus Whyte, June 7, 1978)

[36]

De treaty [was] signed among de Maroon and de English government. They sign de treaty at Charles Town, with milk, coffee, and rum. And all draw their blood. De English government draw their blood, and de Maroon draw their blood, and dem empty it out into a white basin. They mix it, and each party drink together. And after that, de basin was washed out ina Stony River.

(Abraham Goodwin, April 15, 1978)

[37]

Nanny say to de white man say, "now, me fight unu till me tired now. Unu can't conquer me. Unu offer now fe mek peace. Me agree now fe mek peace."

A peace dem deh mek now. A land dem min deh fight for, you know, from Morant Bay. Dem start off from Morant Bay.

Nanny say to de white man say, "if unu no agree fe me pikibo dem catch bird, kill wild hog, kill pigeon, plant wha' dem want plant, and feed demself, ina de crown land, me n'e mek no peace with unu."

White man say him agree.

Nanny say, "if you agree, then mek we cut bujufra then."

So him call up him people dem.

White man say, "all right. Me going mek peace with you, Nanny. Get you obwasu, carry come."

Nanny carry him paki come.

Him say, "well, now, cut bujufra now."

That's right. Nanny deh talk now.

Nanny cut him blood and him drop ina de paki.

Nanny say, "cut bujufra too."

White man cut fe-him blood and throw it ina de paki. Dem mix it up.

Him say, "well, all right, me going mek peace now. So this peace wha' we going mek now, if you no agree fe me pikibo dem fe go through de wood, fe free demself, catch dem bird and catch dem hog and plant wha' dem want plant a de wood, me n'e mek no peace."

White man say, "me agree."

Dem cut bujufra now. Nanny drink de white man blood, and de white man drink fe-Nanny blood.

And dem mek de peace, which stop dem from fight.

(Richard Barnes, September 6, 1978)

[38]

Today I am very happy to be a Maroon. Some people really believe that Maroons are things of the past. But today, I can assure that I am a true-born Maroon. And I am alive. And I am happy to tell this story of the tradition of Maroons, how we came about to be Maroons, under the leadership of Nanny, Kojo, Kweku, and Siformento, and other leaders, and the brothers of Nanny, who fought strenuously in these hills around, and has been victorious in conquering those British, and British slave masters.

It was miraculous to know how it happens. But it did happen in truth. Nanny Scientifically works her way out. And de British has got to subdue, by asking for a peace treaty to be sign betwixt de Maroons and de British government. And it was so done, with de signing of both British blood and Maroon blood. It was also mix with rum, and was dranken by each parties, as a oath that there should be no war again with de Maroons and de British government. And because of that, I am happy to be a Maroon today, as a freedom fighter.

And it was so happy that a few years after Maroon got their freedom, then de government find it possible to give freedom to de rest of slaves de first day of August in that year. So, today we are happy that Jamaica is a free country, beginning from de Maroons, who fought strenuously for freedom for their race.

(George Sterling, October, 1978)

[39]

De soldier stand up over a spring, a little spring. And him call to Nanny, say him want to talk to Nanny, him must turn round. And Nanny turn round.

And him say to Nanny, "you are too good looking fe dead and go to hell."

And Nanny call up de other rest of brother dem—that time Opong gone— say dem must let dem mek peace.

And when dem going to mek de peace now, Nanny say, "de peace is this"— him say, "my seed not to cross de sea, to go in foreign."

You understand that?

And de soldier say to him, "well, we going sign de treaty, that we will never fight again. De white and de black will never fight again."

And dem sign de treaty with that. So, that's why you see plenty [Maroon] people [who] go to sea, dem can't live. De right true Maroon, you know. De right Maroon [who] go to foreign can't live—must dead.

Dem sign de treaty that dem not to go there. Nanny sign de treaty, that dem must not cross de sea. You understand that? And de officer sign that him will never fight against black again.

Is a oath him tek. That is a oath that dem tek against de sea. That same seed not to left de island and go over to de white man country.

Súku dátidáti, da mi fri.[26]

That is a secret—state secret.

(Adolphus Whyte, December 18, 1982)

[40]

De government call to him fe peace—bakra . . . And Nanny say yes, him agree. But still yet, him no trust dem. So dem have fe cut dem hand—cut, run dem blood. And him cut fe-him blood, and dem drink it.

A no pen him tek mek peace treaty. A johncrow wing. Johncrow feather. Him tek de feather, tek de blood, dip de blood—dip fe-de white one blood, and fe-him blood—and write de peace treaty.

And now dem drink it. And dem drink it fe death. Fe *death*! Dem not to war again, bakra and Maroon.

(Ruth Lindsay, January 30, 1991)

[41]

Well, I going give you my knowledge.

After they [the English] really couldn't manage de Maroon, they put up a notice, and call de Maroon soldier dem, call Nanny.

They say, "well, all right, we can't manage you, we will just surrender."

Dem surrender now, and said, "well, all right, come down, Maroon, now. Mek we mek a treaty."

So, a blood they tek. A blood. And they comes in, the war man, with Nanny, de soldier, fe-our Maroon soldier.

And they say, "well, all right, there is a treaty. There will be no more war again against we. And there's no tribes, and there's no quarrel, there's no fuss. So we going mek a treaty now."

And the Englishman stick his hand like that, and blood drain down in de glass. And Nanny then stick her hand, and blood drain down. When blood drain down now, they drink it. Both of dem drink de blood.

And what they give now to de Maroon for compensation, the land allotted to them, and all the agreement, is there in London now.

So they drink the blood, and they becomes one. And they sign the treaty, knot in a position with each other. And there's the ending of it.

(Caleb Anderson, February 3, 1991)

[42]

Dem stretch out dem hand. And Nanny cut de white man hand, cut de white man hand. (stretches out his arm, showing how it was done) Yes, [she] cut de white man hand. And him cut de other brother hand, put in there. And she cut her hand, put in there. (he holds up a cup, showing how the blood of all parties was drained into a vessel) And dem tek de blood, and mek de treaty.

A dem blood. Is not ink. Is blood dem tek and sign this treaty.

(Adolphus Whyte, February 3, 1991)

[43]

De white man dem say to Nanny, "mek we mek peace."

Him call him.

Nanny say no, him naa mek no peace unless—ándu fikándu!—Nanny say—(blows some rum)—to dem, "nyuman! Me can't mek peace. Seven year, dasha, me have me pikibo dem, have me pikibo dem up and down de world, up and down de world. And so me n'e mek no peace. We have fe cut bujufra first." Nanny say to de white man dem, "we have fe cut bujufra first, before we mek any peace. You agree?"

De white man dem say yes.

And dem go to work.

One man in there say, "no! If me head fe cut, me naa mek peace with de obroni."

All right.

And Nanny beg him, Nanny beg him.

And him say, "no, ba, mi n'e mek no peace with white man. Dem punish me too much."

All right.

After dem go to peace, Nanny tek—(pauses to blow some rum)—one obwesu, wha' we call paki. And him get de paki, and dem cut de paki. And when dem cut de paki, dem scrape it out.

(pauses to address the spirits in the old Maroon creole): "Pikibo, obroni a mi prandes. A no mi want im. Obroni want im."[27]

Him scrape de paki. And every *one* of dem cut, all de [Maroon] men dem cut—we call that word, "cut bujufra"—throw ina de paki. All de soldier dem.

And white man cut fe-him bujufra so, throw ina de paki.

And dem mix it up.

(Richard Barnes, February 4, 1991)

[44]

De treaty wha' Nanny sign, if you walk ina de whole entire area, from Four Feet fe catch Ampong Town, is only thirty man can tell you wha' dem tek sign de treaty: [the feather of the] jabin crow [Jamaican crow, *Corvus jamaicensis*]. Jabin crow. De jabin crow is a bird ina de spy wha' Nanny got. No bird on earth can see far so.

(Noel Lewis, February 2, 1991)

[45]

> okrema maso, okrema minfo
> okrema maso, okrema minfo
> okrema-oo, okrema kofi-oo
> okrema-ee

That is a chickenhawk, a bird. That is a Science, that is a okrema [chickenhawk, in Kromanti language] pakit, a bird. When him up there, him talk, ina de air, and him turn sideway.

[They] call [to] him, say: (sings)

> okrema-ee, yo-ee
> okrema-ee
> oo, okrema kofi-oo
> oo, okrema-ee

Dem get one of de feather, a chickenhawk feather, and tek sign de treaty. A de feather dem tek sign de treaty.

It was a spirit. But dem call him and him come, and give him wha' him want.

Figure 8.3. Colonel C.L.G. Harris posing in his home, under engraving of "Old Cudjoe Making Peace," Moore Town, 1991. Photo: K. Bilby.

De man name Kojo.[28] When him go up, go sign de peace treaty with Nanny up a hill there, him [the spirit of his pakit, or personal spirit] come and ride him [possessed him].

Time come now fe go sign with bakra. Bakra call peace treaty. [They] come now, ready fe peace treaty. That time him throw de sing fe get de bird, and him [the chickenhawk] must come down. Because him got it [as his pakit]. [It] come down, and him get it. Him right wing feather. Him get him right wing feather.

That man was a man. A fe-him pakit that.

Him get it, and him sign de paper. And him give him it [the feather] back [to the bird].

And him say, "go, let go. [Go] a Bitter Water."

And from him turn so, him no come back. That bird no come back, that one no come back.

Like you pikni pikni tek you, put step. You know wha' me mean? Me have fe use pikni, because fe-me pikni pikni a go tek me footstep.

[His grandchild is going to say]: "Well, daddy deh gone, him left something give me. Okrema, help me."

And when him call him daddy pakit, it come to him.

But is to rule it. Because meanwhile, those thing is coming up, old people a dress [move] back. Dem a go down, you know. Because dem old people get ripe. Dem only a tell you, de young, say, "boy, so-so-so-so-so happen, such-and-such a time."

Like today, Monday, de treaty was sign.

(Sydney McDonald, September 4, 1978)

[46]

When Maroon and bakra min deh go sign treaty fe mek we abandon de fool-fool war, a *blood* and feather.

"A dangka na mi blood! A dangka na mi blood." [a Kromanti expression]

A blood and feather.

Dem tek de feather, and cut it like pen—no dem ya pen [of today], before-time [pens]. Dem ya pen no got no nib now. But before-time pen got de nib.

Dem cut de feather, pick de feather like nib, and write ina de blood: "Maroon and bakra. All right. We fight war fe so much in year. So, we come to a peace treaty now, wha' done."

And a blood. And it can't be abolish. A *blood*!

"A dangka na mi fren."

Maroon sign de treaty with bakra: "bakra, Maroon, de time has come. We kill out that fighting war, and both of us are friend."

And dem tek de feather, and dip ina de blood, and write [with] a pakit feather. A Nanny pakit. Because Nanny and bakra sign de treaty.

And [they] write ina de blood: "bakra, you and Maroon fight fe so much in years. And we come to a treaty sign now."

So, a *blood* sign de treaty.

So as long as life last, me [as a Maroon] and you [as a white man] have fe friend, man. We can't be enemy again, Ken.

(Hardie Stanford, February 7, 1991)

9

Maroons and the "Other Side of People"

For Jamaica's most famous warriors, the Maroons, combat has always been as much a spiritual undertaking as a physical one. Those who have written about Maroons, mostly historians, are not entirely unacquainted with this dimension of Maroon warfare. Several primary sources make mention of the "magic" used by eighteenth-century Maroon soldiers, as well as insurgent slaves and obeah practitioners on the plantations, to steel themselves against the formidable weaponry deployed by the colonial slavocracy (Schuler 1970: 382–84; Craton 1982: 131). But the only way one can begin to grasp the full importance of this spiritual background is to listen to the descendants and spiritual heirs of these first-time fighters, the Kromanti specialists of today; some speak on these matters in the passages that follow.

Kromanti Play remains a metaphysical battlefield. The *fete-man* is a spiritual warrior—literally, a "fight-man" who puts his life on the line every time he dances Kromanti. Virtually every serious Kromanti Play, every dance held to confront a crisis, entails a deadly contest between the spirits under his control and those manipulated by another spirit worker.[1] Such struggles between spiritual opponents produce no truces, only winners and losers. Kromanti Play—the sanctified space where Maroons "put drum a ring" and call upon their ancestors—is the ultimate proving ground, the stage upon which Maroon spiritual superiority is publicly tested again and again.[2] Even in more private workings, the *fete-man* and his spirits routinely go up against hostile forces—enemy duppies that must be subdued and finally vanquished, lest they return to exact vengeance. For the *fete-man*, almost every attempt at healing is an act of spiritual warfare.[3]

As in the past, a great many of the spiritual battles fought by Maroons today implicate actors and forces from outside. Many of the clients received by Kromanti specialists (or solicited by them in outside locations) are *obroni* (non-Maroons), and almost all of these belong to the more specific category Maroons call *niega* (non-Maroons of African descent). Invariably, when taking on such a case, the Maroon *fete-man* finds himself engaged in a duel with a *kumfu joni* (a *niega* obeah man). For all its dangers, many *fete-man* relish this archetypal contest of power; it is an epic game of risk, a test of courage, that is part of the very definition of what it is to be a *fete-man*. The Maroon spirit worker who emerges triumphant from this drama boosts his credentials as a "true" Maroon and achieves an enhanced sense of personal power. In a sense, he has fulfilled, once more, his destiny as a *fete-man*.

The Kromanti warriors of today see their metaphysical craft as directly continuous with the physical warfare of past centuries. The tools, techniques, and varieties of spiritual power are the same. The herbs applied by possessed *fete-man* today are, they claim, no different from those used to close the wounds and mend the broken bones of Maroon soldiers more than two centuries ago. Kromanti specialists from past generations remain accessible to the living, from time to time visiting Kromanti Play and borrowing the bodies of mediums to dance and speak; even the fighters of old themselves—the original Maroon soldiers who fought under Nanny and Kojo—still possess mediums on occasion. Just as the line between spiritual and physical warfare is tenuous and elastic (present-day *fete-man* assert, for instance, that Kromanti power can still be used to induce invulnerability to bullets in the event of a return to the days of war), the temporal gulf separating today's Kromanti practitioners from their first-time counterparts is regularly collapsed through ritual performance and narratives about the exploits of those who went before.

This intersection of physical and metaphysical, past and present, is fundamental to the *fete-man*'s (and, by extension, other Maroons') concepts of self and other. The very idea of a separate Katawud "nation," it must be remembered, emerged in opposition to what Maroons call "the other side of people"—those who remained enslaved until emancipation, and their descendants. For the *fete-man*, this primordial division is most powerfully and poignantly captured in the image of the Maroon Kromanti specialist engaged in a life-or-death struggle with a non-Maroon obeah man.

In many narratives, particularly those relating to the period between the signing of the treaty in 1739 and general emancipation in 1834, this contest of power revolves around a Maroon tracker in pursuit of an escaped slave, whom he intends to apprehend and return to the whites. This most sensitive of themes has an entirely different ideological significance for Maroons than for other Jamaicans. For the latter, it generally represents betrayal; for the former, it contains more complex meanings and messages, having to do primarily with spiritual power and ethnic identity (some of these are discussed below). In Maroon narratives, these fleeing slaves are not helpless prey. On the contrary, they are formidable opponents, ethnic Others with whom the Maroon tracker must match wits and courage. Although the Maroon protagonist almost always comes out the winner, this is often achieved at considerable cost, and only after the Maroon has found a way to overcome his foe's own protective power. On rare occasions, the Maroon tracker, by making mistakes, forfeits his life, and his opponent emerges the victor.

These narratives pitting Maroon bounty hunters against renegade slaves are, as much as anything, statements about Maroon spiritual superiority. In virtually all of them, the fleeing slave is himself a powerful obeah man, a highly developed spiritual being, and it is only because of this that his eventual defeat has significance and continues to resonate emotionally among Maroon listeners today. Indeed, these texts are but part of a larger body of narratives, including some that tell of contests between Maroon *fete-man* and non-Maroon opponents (such as Paul Bogle) after the abolition of slavery. In the minds of the narrators, most of whom are *fete-man* themselves, such historical contests of power shade into personal memories of their own experiences challenging and defeating *kumfu joni* (outside obeah men) and their spirit surrogates in the present day.

The narratives gathered in this chapter span a considerable stretch of time, but all involve contests between Maroon men of power and non-Maroon antagonists. (In a few instances, the challenge to which the Maroon *fete-man* must respond has no explicit "spiritual" component, but the cleverness that allows him to prevail is taken as a sign of his spiritual power.) Some of the non-Maroon combatants are Africans (identified, for instance, as Mandinga, Kongo, or "Guinea-man"), themselves trained in ancestral "Science tactics" similar to those of the Kromanti tradition (though seen as inferior to them). Others, such as Paul Bogle (who was Jamaican born, and a Baptist deacon), represent a different era and kind of spiritual power. Constant through time, however, is the fundamental opposition between Maroon and *obroni*, and the basic premise of Maroon spiritual (and thus, military) superiority.

Science Tactics: Maroons versus "The Other Side of People"

> The general animosity between the Maroons and the slaves, resulting from the office of the former in apprehending the latter . . . had been invariably maintained from the time of their treaty . . .
> —Dallas (1803a: 126)

> Bogle a mi uncle
> an Nanny rule mi head
> —Jean "Binta" Breeze, "Maroon Song" (1997: 20)

When the *fete-man* today speaks of the life-or-death duels between his Maroon predecessors and the escaped slaves they pursued, there are no apologies or justifications. These narratives belong to a discursive world that remains largely detached from the political ideologies and humanitarian preoccupations of the present age. There is no attempt here to prettify a harsh scenario.[4] In the many contests that took place between Maroon trackers and their opponents from "the other side of people"—at least as these have come down to the present through Maroon oral traditions—the object was first and foremost to defeat a dangerous enemy. Maroons considered themselves (and to a large extent still do) a people apart; all others, categorized as *obroni*, were potential enemies. Maroon bounty hunters, to judge by these accounts, felt no remorse for capturing and returning the people of the "other side," their estranged "cousins" who had remained in slavery.[5] The Maroons had adapted, in their own militaristic manner, to a world that was remarkable for its cruelty and brutality.[6]

Figure 9.1. Spirit worker from one "side": Maroon *fete-man*, 1982. Photo: K. Bilby.

At the same time, these narratives do contain suggestions of subtler ways of viewing the human dimensions of this troubled and troubling history. The combatants in these accounts are generally represented as near equals (although in one narrative [14] the slave being pursued is likened to a "wild pig"); a certain respect for the *fete-man*'s non-Maroon opponent is often implied, if not expressed outright.[7] Indeed, in some cases, the Maroon's antagonist is portrayed as a former friend, suggesting that amicable relations could exist across the line separating post-treaty Maroons from slaves.[8] One basis for such relations might have been overlapping African-derived religious concepts and practices. This is suggested in these texts by the frequent identification of the fleeing slave with a particular African "nation" such as Mandinga or Nago—peoples represented to some extent within the Maroons' own ethnic makeup and still referenced, as we have seen, in their ideology of "tribal" descent.

In narratives such as these, and in more general conversations about spiritual power, present-day Kromanti practitioners tend to imagine ritual specialists, both Maroon and non-Maroon, as belonging to a kind of spiritual network. Those who work with unseen forces constitute a sort of fraternity of seekers after spiritual power. All spirit workers, whatever their "nation," are life-long learners who strive to increase their knowledge through contact with like-minded indi-

Figure 9.2. Spirit worker from the other "side": non-Maroon *obeah man* (*kumfu joni*), 1982. Photo: K. Bilby.

viduals, both living and dead. The general notion of Maroon spiritual supremacy does not preclude the possibility of "linking" with non-Maroon "wise men," including *kumfu joni* (obeah men) from "the other side of people," who may have useful knowledge of their own to share. In fact, exchanges of esoteric knowledge between Maroon and non-Maroon spirit workers remain common in the present. In rare cases, a *fete-man* may even bestow a Maroon *pakit* (personal spirit) on a trusted *obroni* practitioner of "Science." Indeed, despite their frequent deprecation of outside obeah men, and their great reluctance to share Kromanti knowledge with outsiders, most Maroon Kromanti specialists maintain friendships with a number of non-Maroon spirit workers in areas surrounding their communities. These they view as both colleagues and potential enemies, against whom they may one day have to do spiritual battle, should the two of them, or the powers they control, come into conflict. In the minds of the Maroon Kromanti practitioners who speak below, this present is fully continuous with the past that is recorded in the stories of spiritual duels with outsiders—including those between Maroons and fleeing slaves—that have been handed down to them.

Soldiers Turned Trackers: Maroon Bounty Hunters

Opening the narratives in this chapter are a few general statements and song texts about the role of Maroons in the apprehension of escaped slaves following the treaties of 1739. The song that appears in some of these opening texts [2–4] is still sung by Windward Maroons as a jawbone song. The militant lyrics tell of the Maroons being armed by the whites with "guns and powder" and preparing to "walk pon" (walk on, or over) their slave opponents. After this are a few general comments on the slave obeah men against whom Maroon trackers once tested their skills [5–6].

[1]

The Maroon used to capture the negroes, the other type of negroes, to hand over to de police—to hand over to de Englishman. And they help dem to capture de slaves.

　　When they [the whites] couldn't overthrow [the Maroons], couldn't capture the Maroons, then they asked the Maroon to join with dem to fight against the other side of people. And they did so.

(Caleb Anderson, February 3, 1991)

[2]

　　　　we na Maroon-oo, we honor Maroon soldier
　　　　　　ee—, walk pon dem-ee
　　　　we honor Maroon-oo, bakra come an gi we gun an powder
　　　　　　ee—, walk pon dem-ee
　　　　me seh walk pon dem, galang-oo, we a walk on a slave deed, bwai
　　　　　　ee—, walk pon dem
　　　　walk pon dem galang-oo, mek we falla Maroon rule-ee
　　　　　　ee—, walk pon dem-ee
　　　　we honor Maroon-oo, we honor Maroon soldier
　　　　　　ee—, walk pon dem-ee

(James Downer, William Watson, and Richard Deans, October 2, 1978)

[3]

　　　　seh walk pon dem
　　　　talk fe dem-oo
　　　　walk fe dem
　　　　oo talk fe dem

walk pon dem head-oo
well gi me gun and powder-ee
seh walk fe dem-oo
me a Maroon soldier-ee
ee-de—, walk pon dem-ee
gi me gun and powder
but walk with dem
but talk with dem
but walk pon dem
but laugh with dem-oo
ee-de—, walk with dem-oo

Me going go tell you de meaning now of that tune. Him say, "walk pon dem *head*. But walk pon dem *foot*." Him say, "me a Maroon soldier." Him say, "give me gun and powder fe go walk and talk fire fe dem"—fe niega. Him say, "give me gun and powder fe go walk and talk so."

(Leonard Whyte, August 17, 1978)

[4]

me da Maroon-oo
becau governor gi me gun an powder
    ee-de—, me a Maroon-ee
me a Maroon-oo
me a Maroon soldier
    ee-de—, me a Maroon-oo
we wi walk pon dem, galang, dasha
we walk corner side
    ee-de—, walk pon dem-ee

That time you know wha' man min a do? Man a try man with obeah, [to see] if man bad. Two of dem know obeah. *Those* [Maroon trackers] put something pon bóbosi awéngkini [non-Maroons]—and fántan du koro do bi, kembe wasa kominyadu [a Kromanti phrase, uttered without interpretation]. And Minott a *lion*, you know! Minott a lion—Ellis, Minott [Maroon "tribes" associated with English-derived family names]. They say, "kill to raas, man!"

(Sydney McDonald, September 4, 1978)

[5]

Dem [the slaves on the plantations] got good tactics, man, for after the war [between the English and Nanny's people] had settled, you have plenty of these slaves that run away. And generally the Maroons were the persons who they really tek to capture these men back to de slavemasters. And they meet plenty [runaway slaves] with great tacklings. They were not so easy to catch.

(Johnny Minott, September 10, 1978)

[6]

De Nago man dem wha' Maroon catch give bakra—or who dem no get fe
catch—a dem man come out, work out there so [in the coastal communities surrounding the Maroon territories]. Because obeah man *different*. Obeah man different from de man who deal with fallen angel. You get that? Obeah man shoot
that tree there fe you now, "bo!"—a morning you dead. And if you a Maroon
man, if you a good Maroon man, and you a fight against de obeah man, and
you know say you can't fight against him, no go against him, because him will
kill you fe true.

(James Downer, September 27, 1978)

Foiling Slave Obeah

The following narratives about Isaac Ellis and Briscoe [7–8] belong to a larger
body of stories embodying the themes of trust and betrayal, discussed in more
depth in chapter 11. But they also, just as effectively, exemplify the theme of
spiritual dueling that is such an important part of the *fete-man*'s discourse. Ellis
and Briscoe (about whom we will hear more, later in this chapter) are Maroon
soldiers who have gone out with a larger party in pursuit of a Mandinga man
wanted by the colonial authorities. They know that capturing the Mandinga man
will be a major challenge. He is a powerful spirit worker who, like Maroon
Kromanti specialists, is able to heal himself instantly whenever his skin is penetrated by bullets. Because of his spiritual protection, he has been able to elude
previous Maroon trackers. But Isaac Ellis knows the secret of his power (an
object "planted" under a particular tree)—only because the two of them were
once close friends; in an unguarded moment, the Mandinga man had revealed it
to him. Not wanting to go after his former friend himself, Isaac Ellis tells Briscoe
exactly what to do, and what he needs to load his gun with, to neutralize their
opponent's spiritual protection. He must aim for the man's one vulnerable spot,
the sole of his foot. (In some versions of the story, Briscoe is the one with this
knowledge, and it is he who betrays the Mandinga man to Isaac Ellis.) Only then
are Briscoe and Ellis able to bring their powerful adversary down.

Next is the story of another Mandinga (or Mandingo) man, an escaped slave
named Charles Robinson who has been hiding out in the forest a few miles from
Moore Town [9–10]. (In some versions, he is portrayed as a "Nago" man.) The
Maroons have been unable to capture Robinson, for he too has powerful protection. Whenever they get within range of his hut, he quickly grabs and manipu-
lates a spiritually empowered plant (or "tree") at his doorway that makes him
invisible. Frustrated by the man's vanishing act, the Maroons hold a Kromanti
Play to consult with the spirits of their ancestors. During this ceremony, the secret
of the man's power of invisibility is revealed. The next time the Maroon trackers
go out after the Mandinga man, they creep silently on their bellies up to his
doorway and change the position of the magical plant, "turning" and squeezing

it so as to render it ineffective. This time, when they yell at Robinson to come out, his usual trick fails, and the Maroons take him alive. Tying him up, both spiritually and literally, they deliver him to the whites.

In yet other stories—including one summarized below [11]—a Mandinga man fleeing from Maroons is defeated when the latter counteract his powerful and spiritually protective song by "crossing" (negating) it with one of their own. (The Maroons then "catch" the Mandinga man's song and its power for themselves, incorporating it into the repertoire of Kromanti Play, of which it is still a part.)

[7]

Round town you have Briscoe and you have Isaac Ellis. Isaac Ellis a war general, and Briscoe [too]. Briscoe have dog. Joseph Briscoe. Briscoe and Isaac is a two friend, two good friend. Dem two man catch Three Finger Jack, yes. Isaac Ellis know de secret, but Isaac Ellis never want to let out de secret fe mek dem know say a him, Isaac Ellis, a do de business. So him tell it to Briscoe—de secret of de Mandinga man.

You have a Mandinga man, him have a *tree*, and him mek him Science in de tree root, a de root of de tree.

So when bakra call Maroon fe go a him country, de tune say: (sings)
me a Maroon-oo, me a Maroon soldier
     ee-de-ee, me a Maroon-oo
seh me a Maroon-oo, bakra gi we gun and powder
     ee-de-ee, seh we a Maroon-oo
we a Maroon-oo, but we a walk corner still, bwai

That mean to say now, a dem word this: dem a walk pon de road, but dem naa walk straight to de road. Dem a walk cornerside fe go find de niega dem, fe catch de niega dem. But a Science man dem, though. A Science man dem.

So when dem go, they have de first batch of Maroon *meet* de man. And when dem meet de man, dem bawl him, and dem shoot him. De gut come out. Dem call out fe him, fe him run, mek dem shoot him. Because de Maroon know say a de tree where him got de Science. So dem bawl him fe him run. Dem can't shoot him by de tree.

But Issac Ellis min know a there de Science deh. A there him got fe-him Science—de Mandinga man. A Mandinga man.

So when him come, him see man. De first batch of Maroon meet him. Because dem never have no knowledge of him Science. And dem bawl him, and dem shoot him! Him gut come out, him put it in back. Him catch it and put it in back! Him mend it, him put it in back. De second batch come, and shoot him! It come out same place. Him put it in back ina him.

So Isaac Ellis a come ina de third batch, him and Briscoe. And when dem a come, Isaac Ellis tell Briscoe wha' fe tek load de gun, de something him have fe tek load de gun.

And Isaac Ellis tell him say, "when you bawl him, hold off, and same as you see him foot bottom, shoot him on him foot bottom. Shoot him there."

Because Isaac Ellis did have all de tactics of de Science. De Mandinga man a him friend. De Mandinga man and Isaac Ellis a two good friend, like how me and you deh now, we a friend.

Mandinga man no min a Maroon, but him *have* Science. Him have a nanabo tree, and a right there him plant him Science. That mean, when him bawl him, when Briscoe bawl de Mandinga man, de Mandinga man know direct say de first batch of Maroon, de second batch, and de third batch dem shoot him. And de last batch, him know say dem can't shoot him.

When Briscoe look on him, Briscoe *bawl* him, and him run off. And same as him run off, him foot bottom ease up, and Briscoe *shoot* with de gun, on him foot bottom, and him never have on no shoes. Same when him shoot him, him couldn't stop. Him hold de tree, de Mandinga man hold de tree, him say: (sings)

    oo nanabo, anabwa kwajo
    oo nanabo, anabwa kwajo
    yo se janta hipan bufa anabwa-ee[9]

That mean say de tree catch fire! De tree catch fire from de root. From down here so, right up to de head.

And him dead. De man dead. Because him shoot him. Because de man find de secret of him. A him foot bottom.

Isaac Ellis and de Mandinga man is a two good friend. Isaac Ellis is a Maroon and Briscoe is a Maroon. So Isaac Ellis never want fe shoot him [the Mandinga man], because a him friend. But Isaac Ellis tell Briscoe, mek Briscoe get de fame.

A him friend. But wha' de reason why Isaac Ellis tell him: dem sign with de bakra, say any man come in fe fight against dem, Maroon must back dem. Because bakra never check pon nobody away from Maroon ina Science.

(James Downer, June 25, 1978)

[8]

Well, that tune—it was martial law, and it was a Mandinga man tune that. It was under the leadership of Isaac Ellis and Briscoe. And when they reach Manchioneal, them meet *that* Mandinga man there. The troops [that] them lead was in four batches. Well, the first batch shoot him so till, but nothing couldn't do him. That mean they couldn't kill him. The second batch shoot him, they couldn't kill him either. The third batch shoot him, till him belly cut. And him catch it and charm it, and it mend. Well, the last batch now coming. So when the last batch coming now, Briscoe tell Isaac Ellis what say him fe tek ina him wad load the gun. So same as them see him now, and him run off, you know, when that man run off, Isaac Ellis shoot him ina him foot bottom. And him throw [out] him hand, and him catch pon a snake-wood [type of greenheart tree, *Colubrina ferruginosa*], and him throw that tune:

    ananabo, ananabo yedeng
    ananabo, ananabo yedeng
    yo se jancha simpan bofre seh ananabo

That meaning, it was his partner tactics really that [he] tek and conquer him. So that was de tune dem sing. If it was not his own tactics them take, they wouldn't able to kill him.

Briscoe and de man was a friend, you hear, man? They were friends, so Briscoe know [the secret of his Science].

(Johnny Minott, September 10, 1978)

[9]

I hear about one man, he was named Charles Robinson. That was his name. But, anyway, de Maroon man in de other side call him "de Mandinga man." He was a man [that] have his little hut, after him run way from slaves [i.e., slavery], and when de Maroon went out to catch him, they see him. They see him. But soon as they bawl him, he have a weed plant at his hut door, and him just turn it on de stump same place, and none of dem don't see him again. So dem have fe leave him that day, or that month. Well, de Maroon go back and find out that was what happening, and they start what you call "ambushing." When I say ambushing—we, de crowd, coming now. And probably two man, or three man start out six o'clock, and we start out, say, eight, that they reach in time before us. So when him realize—him was in de hut, and dem know [it] was de weed— so by de time dem bawl him and him jump out to turn de weed, de Maroon man turn de weed already. That's how dem get fe catch him.

(Johnny Minott, September 10, 1978)

[10]

De Maroon man deh a Moore Town. De Mandinga man live a Kent. Dem want catch him fe go give bakra, because bakra want him. Bakra tell Maroon fe catch him. Him want Maroon fe catch him, because bakra no min hold de two side, but only de Maroon and dem[self].[10] Only de two of dem carry de island—de two stiffest. De *two stiffest!* So if dem [non-Maroon Jamaicans] come, come say dem spoil, say Maroon no worth nothing, no listen to dem!

Dem go play drum a Moore Town, go catch Mandinga man! Dem plant de trash before him out door!

Him got him hut a him ground—de Mandinga man, a Kent, up ina de bush. Him plant it, [put] down a niega trash before him, a him hut.

And [the Maroons] *play* drum a Moore Town. Dem couldn't find him!

De Mandinga man a slave, but him get afar from dem. But him never fight, him never do no fighting. Him plant de trash right ina him hut doorway, him plant it.

And man *dance* fe find de Mandinga man. As fast as dem find him, dem couldn't find him. And man *dance* a Moore Town, say "wha' happen?"—so till him [a possessed medium] say, well then, a de trash him [the Mandinga man] turn. When dem *bawl* him, him turn de trash. So when you hear dem sing (he sings),

>Mandingo man-ee, ee—
>Ibo man-ee[11]

A so dem mean. That a de trash dem catch and wring it raatid [in an extremely angry or annoyed manner]!

When de Maroon see him plant de trash, and dem see trash deh a him hut, dem play drum. That time when dem play, Maroon man go there. And when dem out a gate, dem see smoke ina him hut! That mean say him mek fire, fe go cook. And de Maroon man a creep pon him belly, *creep* pon him belly, *creep* pon him belly, come to where de trash deh. That time de Mandingo man ina him hut. Him never know say Maroon man a come there.

Him creep pon him belly, him come there so, "wap!," him *bawl* [shouted out at] de Mandingo man! So when him jump out so, "wap!" so, him hold it. Maroon man hold de trash. (sings)

>seh Mandingo man-ee, ee—
>Ibo man . . .

That time him wring de trash, you know, wring-wring de trash to raas, catch him, tie him, bring him to de bakra to raas! A *me* a tell you so, you know, whether you want believe me, yes or no. Hold him raas! *TIE* him!!

De Maroon man catch de song from de Mandinga man, because when him wring de trash there now, him know say Mandinga man a that kind of man. So him sing tune say: (sings)

>Mandingo man-ee, ee—
>Ibo . . .

When him a knot something, you know. Because a knot dem min knot him fe catch him, you know. Because fe-him knot him mek, him catch him, because dem min smart.

A little bit of man dem, little bit of man dem [the Mandinga people]. A no big man dem.

(James Downer, September 14, 1978)

[11]

>abete kuma, kuma kuma lad-ee
>ha du mi-aa, ha du mi ara-ee[12]

That tune is directly a Mandingo man's tune, you know, a Mandingo tune. One time when they used to go catch a man, it was a Mandingo man's tune that. The Maroons went to catch him too.

And, you know, after [they] bombard him, he throw his tune to get out [of] the hand, you know, to get away from them: "so gwangkoma, obeti kuma, kuma kuma lad-ee."

Well, the Maroon say, "o du mi-aa, o du mi ara-ee."

So the Maroon get catch him. You understand, the Maroon cross the tune.[13]

(Johnny Minott, September 10, 1978)

Formidable Opponents: Lost Battles and Close Calls

In some stories, as in the next set of narratives [12–16], it is the Maroons' slave opponent who prevails. In what is essentially a cautionary tale, an experienced Maroon bounty hunter has been teaching his young apprentice (usually said to be his nephew) how to capture escaped slaves. Each time they go out together and successfully bring in a slave, the uncle shares with his young apprentice a portion of his earnings. Eventually, the young man's mother (in some versions, his father) complains that her son is now a full-grown man and deserves more money for the work he is doing. The next time they go out, the uncle tells his nephew that since he is now a big man, he can handle himself. When the younger man finds himself cornered by their opponent—a particularly powerful and dangerous "Guinea man"—he cries out to his uncle for help. Refusing to come to his rescue, the uncle shouts out, "big man, big money!" (an elliptical way of saying, "since you claim to be a big enough man now to deserve full pay, prove it!"). Lacking the fully developed spiritual knowledge and skills of his uncle, the young man is no match for the powerful Guinea man, who kills him and gets away. While cautioning listeners about the rashness and foolhardiness of youth, the story also serves to remind them that one must never underestimate one's foe, just as one must never overestimate one's own abilities.

Presented next is an isolated instance [17] of a common story element found in the various Maroon communities: the powerful obeah man who cannot be killed, for as soon as his head is severed, it jumps back onto his neck and reattaches itself. In this case, the obeah of the fleeing slave, a powerful "Bongo man," is defeated when the Maroon ancestors, consulted during a Kromanti Play, reveal that the severed head will not be able to rejoin the body if dirt is thrown upon it the moment it is cut off.

The importance of cunning in confrontations between Maroons and their slave adversaries is represented in the last text in this section [18]. Here, it is the Maroon protagonist who is cast as the prey. A young Maroon man (a "boy") is preparing a meal out in the woods by himself. He is surprised by a much larger man, an escaped slave who pounces on him, intending to kill him and take his food. Pinning him down with one hand, the man pulls his folding knife from his pocket and opens it with his teeth. Thinking fast, the Maroon "boy" grabs the knife and closes it over the man's fingers. While the two are locked in a death struggle—the slave trying to strangle the Maroon with one hand, the Maroon bearing down on the knife, threatening to cut the fingers off of the other—the Maroon uses his free hand to pull a piece of cord out of the other man's pocket. Before he knows it, the slave aggressor is tied up and helpless. The triumphant Maroon "boy" turns his foe over to the whites. Much as in anansi stories told throughout the African diaspora, the smaller and weaker protagonist prevails by relying on his agility and wits.

[12]

There was a man who used to go out with his nephew. And later on, the father of this young man complained to his brother that he wasn't giving the young man enough money. And this man got vexed. And so the next time, when they went out, this young man was hard pressed. He was so skilled. But on this occasion it was so hard for him.

Well, the uncle should have come in now, to help him.

So he called to him. He said, "onki-oo!"

That means he is calling for the uncle to come and help him.

Then the uncle stood up out there.

His answer was, "bigi moni-oo!"

You see. What a wicked man.

The man called again, the young man called again, "honki-oo!"

He replied, "bigi moni-oo."

Because they wanted more money, so he alone should go on, and be overwhelmed.

"Bigi moni."

(Colonel C.L.G. Harris, January 31, 1991)

[13]

Every day dem go fe catch Guinea man. Every day de uncle carry him fe go catch Guinea man. De two of dem go fe catch Guinea man. And when dem catch Guinea man come, him give him one pound. De uncle give him nephew—de boy fe call him "uncle"—give him one pound fe catch Guinea man.

When him go, de mother, from de brother—that a de brother sister—say to him say, "me son, you a big man. One pound can't do dem something there."

De uncle say, "a-oah? A so? Well, all right."

De uncle hear.

De uncle say, "well, all right, boy, we a go catch Guinea man today, you know."

So when him go way, him send him nephew before him.

Him say, "see Guinea man there, go catch him. Big man!! Because you a big man, so any time you a big man you can work fe big money. Big man a big money."

So when him [the nephew] go round de corner there, when him look, him see Guinea man. Him bawl Guinea man so! A bawl him bawl Guinea man. That time de uncle deh lost—de uncle deh like down a Windsor, and him deh like up here. Him bawl Guinea man! Him shout out, shout out! And Guinea man come down pon him fe true.

Him turn, look, him bawl, him say, "onku! onku [uncle]!"

And from when him say, "onku," him no see onku.

Guinea man come down pon him.

Onku say, "big man, big money."

De Guinea man kill him, because him never know de tactics of it. Him mother tell him say him a big man, say him can work fe pound, because him a big man—big man now. So everyday him brother a carry him go fe go catch Guinea man, and a pound dem a go give him.

Him a catch de Guinea man fe give bakra.

"Bigi man, bigi money!! When you see Guinea man there, catch Guinea man. See him out there, catch him nuh! Catch Guinea man!"

(James Downer, September 14, 1978)

[14]

Those men wha' [my grandmother] used to tell me about—two man did a go a wudu bere [deep in the forest], go hunt Guinea man—one Nago man and one Kongo man obwato [boy]. Two pikni, two different nation. Dem go a wood, go hunting. So now, this little man wha' deh a wudu bere, wha' dem search for, [he] a come like wild hog, fe-dem hog.

Two nation—one a Kongo, and one a Maroon. De Maroon boy and de Kongo boy hunting together. One a Maroon man pikibo, and one a Kongo man pikibo.

Well, after o [he] go a wudu bere, o [he] find say Guinea man deh a wudu [in the forest]. Him walk wudu, him walk wudu, him walk wudu, him walk wudu, him walk wudu, him walk wudu, him walk wudu till de [Kongo] boy asleep.

Now, him mumma say, after him deh go wudu bere so long with Maroon man, him should know hofa [how] kill Guinea man. But de Maroon man sipple more than de Kongo man.

[They] go, go, go, go, go, go, go a wudu bere. In dem going, going, going, going, going, dem find bigi something more than all wha' dem used to find. And when boy jump go so, jump come down, when o [he] drop, go on battle-field—like how you had a house there now, you have fe go run around it four, five time—a de battlefield that, where dem a go tek kill de Guinea man. After dem go round and round him, dem a go stop, mek a sudden stop, and Guinea man a go come down pon him, and him a go kill him. De Guinea man look see [Kongo] boy out there, man, and when him, Guinea man, come down pon him so, come down pon him so, Maroon man shift himself.

Guinea man come down pon de Kongo man, and him lash him! And de boy drop. Boy come to yonder, a yonder country, yarifo.[14]

O let go, o tonbaig go, come a him prandes [he let go, he turned and went back, and came back to his home].

Him [the Maroon man] call him [the Kongo man's] mama, him say, "woh!, o yarifo, o come to yonder [oh! he's dead, he died]."

When de Maroon man come out and tell de Kongo boy pikibo [child's] mama, him mama throw one Country: (sings)

    han me de boman tiday

han me de boman tiday
Dogin-oo, me han fire-ee
Dogin back a bun-ee
han me de boman tiday
me kapen bun i han fire
han me de boman tiday
poor man Dogin-ee
han me de poor man tiday

A de Maroon man name that: Dogin. My grandfather—me mother father, when him throw de tune, him tell me say, when de boy get dead, when him [the Maroon man] come out and tell him [the Kongo man's] mumma, him mumma say to him say, "Dogin, wha' you say?" Him say: (sings)

han me de boman
han me de boman

A bigi man, you know! That mek dem no call him hog a wood. Guinea man. Wild something! Guinea man. Cross [fierce tempered] man. [He] live a wudu [in the forest].

Yes, him [the Kongo man] a hunt de Guinea man, [but] de Guinea man kill him. Maroon come out there, see say [Kongo] man yarifo.

Him min tonbaig [had turned back], come out back come, come tell him parents dem say Guinea man kill de boy. And de woman throw de tune.

Wha' mek de Guinea man kill de other one—a hog hunter. And him [the Kongo boy's] tata [father] a titei-man [Kromanti practitioner]. So when him a go a wudu bere, him tata put on something pon de boy, that Guinea man can't kill him. So when o tonbaig fe go a wudu bere now, o find out to himself say, him tata give him something, but de boy no get nothing fe go fight Guinea man, because de boy mama a fete [was fighting, quarreling].[15]

Kongo man, him say o so, o sabi, o so, o sabi [he knew things].

Well, de Maroon man say, "me n'e go show him hofa [how] something tan. Whilst him say him sabi, mek him go siyubobo siyumandi."[16]

De Kongo man say him sabi something.

And de Maroon man say, "well, whilst him say him sabi something, me n'e go show him nothing wha' fe-me tata show me. Mek we go a wudu bere, because we a two hunter man. Better man will tell."

So him mek Guinea man yarifo [kill] de boy. De Guinea man gone, gone a wudu bere. Him no kill him [the Maroon man], because him yarifo de boy. A enemy that [Guinea man].

Now, Guinea man come like dem wild pig up a Moore Town there, wild pig ina de woodland. Dem catch you, dem will kill you! Like all dem bear, and all dem something. Old-time people call dem "Guinea man." Strong elephant dem. Dem was a slave.

This is knowledge just like a book. Well, that is knowledge you getting from de older head, to show de light ina de world, that who to come, you can tell dem what pass [happen].

(Sydney McDonald, September 14, 1978)

[15]

De man used to go, and him catch slave.

A slave dem used to catch, you know. Slave. Dem catch slave. And when dem catch de slave, carry back to slavemasters, or de government, de white man dem, dem pay dem fe it.

But this man, him know him tricks, wha' him can tek and catch de slaves. But de young boy never know. Him [the older man] was him uncle, de boy uncle. And when him uncle come and give him money, de mother start to quarrel, say him shoulda get more, because him a man.

A boy, and him a catch man so.

After him [the mother] start quarrel, de day when dem go fe go catch now, him uncle tell him say fe walk over there so, because—"boy, you a big man, so you a go catch man."

So when him go over there, him meet one man.

When him meet de man, him a call to him uncle, say, "onku-oy! See one bigi man!"

De uncle say, "bigi man, bigi money."

De man kill him.

Him uncle say to him back, say, "bigi man, bigi money."

So that slave kill him. Him never know de tricks. A de uncle who knows de tricks.

So de mother was foolish.

(Johnny Minott, February 6, 1991)

[16]

Me hear about a Guinea man. You hear about that? Guinea man.

Him come like how me and you here, and you woulda want mek me do you business, because me a work with you. And meanwhile de woman, de fellow mumma, tell him say de money wha' de [other] man a pay him, it too small. So him must mek him pay more.

So him say, "yes?"

Him say, "yes."

So [the other] man say, "all right."

De boy go and say him mumma say him fe pay him bigger money, because him a work fe nothing. You see.

And [the other] man say, "since you can't work fe nothing, you can work fe money." Him say, "me a go show you." Him say, see if him a man—if him can't work fe nothing—"so see Guinea man there. Catch de Guinea man."

So when him catch Guinea man, when de boy go up to de Guinea man, de Guinea man *strike* him!

And him deh, and him say, "Onku! . . ."

De man say to him say—me no know de man name—de man say to him say, "yu mama se yu sa wóko fi bíga móni. So, yu si bíga man de nou. Kil in."[17]

So him uncle shift [himself]. A Science-man him work with, you know. And him shift himself, and mek de boy go tek de dead. Because him say him mumma say him a work fe bigger money. But him can't work like him. So him left de man there.

That man, Guinea man, a bad man, you know! Him lance him, kill him.

So when de boy call out fe him uncle, him say, "honku"—that time him a call him fe arrest [the Guinea man]—de man say to him, say, "yu múma se yu sa wóko fi bíga takifa [money]. So now, si bíga takifa de nou. Yu se yu sa kil im. So yu no si im kil yu de nou?"[18]

So Guinea man kill him there now.

"Bigi man, bigi moni."

Me naa give you no more [information about this story].

(Henry Shepherd, February 19, 1991)

[17]

When de white fight de war with de Maroon, they couldn't capture de Maroon, but dem capture de African. But after de war were fighting, a Bongo man live ina de wood wha' dem couldn't manage. Dem man couldn't manage him, neither Maroon or Bongo couldn't manage him. And de bigger authority dem send some Maroon man ina de wood—pay dem and send dem in there to capture that Bongo man. And dem have to put drum a ring, right ina Moore Town, you know—Maroon.

But that Bongo man, him no have no help, a only *him one* left ina de world—I mean, as strong man, who know de fight. And dem send two Maroon man fe him. And dem fight him a whole day, and dem couldn't manage him, you know.

And dem throw de drum a ring a Moore Town, and dem say, "well, cut off him head and bring him head come."

And every [man] tek dem knife, dem machete, and do so, "wam!" and tek off de neck. De neck jump on back pon de body.

Dem capture him. But you know how dem capture him?

Well, there was two Maroon against him one as Bongo, fighting him. And when dem cut off him head and see de head a fly on back, dem no know wha' to do.

And dem throw drum a ring a Moore Town, and man spirit tell dem say, "throw dirt! [Throw] de dirt deh pon de head, and it can't go on back."

And dem throw on de dirt! Same as dem cut off de head, dem throw dirt pon it, and him [the head] start to run. De head just walk off and start to sing this tune here: (sings)

    me all an all-oo, wha' me going go do

    all an all-oo, me tun dog-oo

Him walk to fart, and no man see that head again till today. No mek nobody tell you say dem see it. Nobody no see it until today. De head walk away and left de body—de head wha' cut off. A de head a sing that, a go way.

(Emmanuel Salvin, August 13, 1978)

[18]

A boy live in de wood. This boy now, in de wood, him a cook roast plantain, jerk meat. A little boy, but a Maroon boy.

A big man now go ina de wood. So when de man get ina de wood, him see him.

Same as him see him, him [the bigger man] say, "debre kom out a tere [death has come out today]!"

De boy see him, say, "a me debe kill [I am the one who kills]!"

[The bigger man] say, "debre kom out a tere."

And de boy say, "a me debe kill."

Him lift up de boy—is a big man—him lift up de boy, him drop him a ground. That mean say him [the "boy"] a go tie him [the other man] up fe come give bakra—that a de man. But de man wha' a go tie *him*, a no Maroon man. Is a niega man [a non-Maroon African]. But him lift up de boy and throw him a ground. Him [the "boy"] a go tie him, go give bakra.

When him [the bigger man] say, "debre kom out a tere," that mean say him a go kill de boy. That mean say dead come out betwixt him and de boy. Dead betwixt him and de boy!

So de boy mek him know say, a *him* debre kill—"a *me* debre kill."

So him lift up de boy now, him throw a ground. Him shove him hand ina him pocket, tek out him knife—him shut knife [pen knife]—fe open de knife, fe cut de boy throat. A kill him a go kill de boy.

Because him say, "debre come out deh today." Like how you a go on with a quarrel and de man say, "hell betwixt me and you!"—him say, "debe kom out a tere."

De boy say, "a me debe kill."

Him shove him hand ina him pocket and tek out him knife. And him do so, tek him teeth and open de knife. And same as him open de knife, de boy shut de knife pon him hand, *hold* de knife.

And him hold de boy throat.

De boy say, "let go me throat!"

Him say, "let go me hand!"

That mean say, him hold it and a squeeze de knife ina de hand.

And him got him hand a de boy throat (he makes choking noises). That mean say him a choke de boy.

And de boy hold him—*hold* him, you know. De boy shove him hand ina him pocket, him tek out de trash-cord. And de boy *tie* him, him two hand so (puts his hands together as if they are tied), same like you see me put it here—tie so—and *tie* him! *Tie* him!

Because when him come go see de boy, him want fe tek way de boy food wha' de boy have, and kill de boy for it.

But de boy *tie* him, carry come give bakra. De boy *hold* de hand with de knife ina de same way so till him tie him done. When him tie him done, him see say him can't get way. Him tek him, march him, carry him come out, come give bakra.

(James Downer, October 4, 1978)

Three Finger Jack

Probably the most famous escaped slave apprehended by Maroons—certainly the best-known outside of Maroon communities—is the larger-than-life eighteenth-century figure known as Three Finger Jack.[19] Jack Mansong, as he was also known, is remembered as a giant of a man who lived with his wife in a series of caves in the hills of St. Thomas parish. At the beginning of the 1780s, he gained notoriety by carrying out a string of daring robberies along the Windward road east of Kingston. For a period of nearly two years, he terrorized the eastern part of the island, and his exploits became a topic of daily conversation in the capital. His name was derived from the fact that he had lost two of his fingers in a duel with a Scot's Hall Maroon named Quashee (also known by an English name,

Figure 9.3. Commemorative marker in honor of Three Finger Jack, placed by the Jamaica National Heritage Trust Commission on the Kingston–St. Thomas road. Photo taken in 1995. Photo: K. Bilby.

James [or in some accounts, John] Reeder). According to various written sources, it was this same Quashee who, along with a party of Windward Maroons, finally succeeded in killing him in 1781. These sources stress the important role played by spiritual power in this contest (Cundall 1930: 9–10; Williams 1934: 113–24; Black 1966: 114–19; Eyre 1973: 12–14). Three Finger Jack was rumored to be invincible because of the particularly powerful amulet acquired from a renowned obeah man he had sought out in the forest after escaping from his plantation. His Maroon opponents, Quashee and Sam, were confident that their obeah was superior, and they were proven right when they returned to Morant Bay with Jack's head in a pail of rum. Black (1966: 110) cites a "Jamaican folk-song" commemorating this epic encounter between competing obeahs:

> Beat big drum—wave fine flag;
> Bring good news to Kingston Town, O!
> No fear Jack's Obi-bag—
> Quashee knock him down, O!

For a time during the early nineteenth century, Three Finger Jack, romantically reimagined as a kind of African Robin Hood, became the toast of England. Plays, novels, and poems were written about him and some of these became important vehicles of antislavery sentiment as the abolitionist movement gained momentum.[20]

In Windward Maroon oral tradition, Three Finger Jack is remembered primarily through his association with a place known as Three Finger Woman Tumble, located on the Cunu Cunu Pass, part of an old trail through the Blue Mountains that Maroons used to take when traveling on foot from Moore Town to St. Thomas parish and Kingston [19–23]. It was here, according to this oral tradition, that Jack's wife escaped from the Maroons, sliding down a steep, slippery rock slope with her baby on her back, never to be found again. (This oral tradition is clearly related to another one, discussed in chapter 4, about an eighteenth-century Maroon woman escaping with her child from pursuing British soldiers in exactly the same way, and in the same place.) In the Maroon oral tradition, as in the written accounts, Three Finger Jack himself is not so fortunate; his spiritual protection, powerful though it is, cannot save him, and his Maroon opponents finally corner and kill him.

[19]

Three Finger Jack. Him no got more than three finger pon one hand. And up to today, de place where him live, me can carry you go show you it too. A ina Cunu Cunu Wood. Dem call it Three Finger. That is de reason why de road can't go through fe come out a St. Thomas.

(Noel Lewis, February 2, 1991)

[20]

You have Three Finger Jack, and him wife. And him thief. Him *thief!* And bakra send fe Maroon, tell him say fe catch Three Finger Jack. Him live ina cave. Him cave down there, and him wife. Dem bawl Three Finger Jack. Him wife tek de pikni pon him back and run through from Kingston to St. Thomas. And when him come, him run through St. Thomas, and him come straight down. (sings)
    jam break har
    go a wood, break i
(James Downer, October 26, 1978)

[21]

Dem got one [place] dem call Three Finger Jack, a Woman Tumble—that a ina Cunu Cunu Wood. And when Three Finger Jack run fe save him life from de war, you know, him jam this hand pon one rock. De rock long like from here fe go down a road. Not even a grass deh pon it. Nothing no deh fe hold so. And when him go down and drop, and when him drop so "brap" down a de bottom of de river, him grand-pikni a him back, Jack say: (sings)
    jam bréka
(laughs) Good God a heaven! (claps his hands) Him say: (sings)
    jam bréka
    go a wood, bréka
    jam bréka
    go a wood-ee

———— ❦ ————

We have the pleasure to inform the public, of the death of that daring freebooter Three-fingered Jack.—He was surprised on Saturday last, by a Maroon Negro named John Reeder, and six others, near the summit of Mount Libanus, being alone and armed with two muskets and a cutlass.—The party came upon him so suddenly, that he had only time to seize the cutlass, with which he desperately defended himself, refusing all submission, till having received three bullets in his body and covered with wounds, he threw himself about forty feet down a precipice, and was followed by Reeder, who soon overpowered him, and severed his head and arm from the body which were brought to this town on Thursday last.—Reeder and another Maroon were wounded in the conflict.—The intrepidity of Reeder in particular, and the behaviour of his associates in general justly entitle them to the reward offered by the public. (*Royal Gazette* [Kingston], February 3, 1781; cited in Williams [1934: 117–18])

Jack turn. And from Jack turn, nobody no hear nothing yet. Him *gone* a bush. Nobody no hear nothing of him yet.

(Henry Shepherd, February 19, 1991)

[22]

Hear me now.

You have a man. I don't know if you hear about that man. Him was de name of Three Finger Jack. De Maroons went out plenty of times to catch that man and dem never catch him. For him live in a cave and him use a ladder. When him go down in there, him pull him ladder. You can't go down there. Is a rope ladder. You understand. Him use a ladder, go down like this. So when him reach down and pull him ladder, you can't go down. And him can't come out unless him have him ladder. You can't come in—you see what I mean—for if you come, you will come down, but you will drop, and probably kill youself, or break up somewhere, or anything like that.

Good.

Well, de Maroon man go out several days fe that man and never catch him.

But as dem turn back, dem catch him. Because, when de man going down on de ladder, men was going down on de ladder too, so de ladder couldn't pull. And dem catch him.

And de woman down there, wha' him have, run way from there, and him run to a place wha' dem call Three Finger Woman Tumble, up ina de Cuna Cuna Wood there. Dem never catch him either. Dem never catch de woman, because de woman go over that gully. Me forgot wha' de woman name, but dem call her "Three Finger Woman Tumble"—de place dem call "Three Finger Woman Tumble," that him come down. And by [the time that they] go round, dem never see her.

But dem catch de man.

(Johnny Minott, June 4, 1978)

I saw the Obi of the famous negro robber, *Three-fingered* Jack. . . . the Maroons who slew him brought it to me. His Obi consisted of the end of a goat's horn, filled with a compound of grave dirt, ashes, the blood of a black cat, and human fat; all mixed into a kind of paste. A black cat's foot, a dried toad, a pig's tail, a slip of parchment of kid's skin, with characters marked in blood on it, were also in his *Obian* bag. These, with a keen sabre, and two guns, like *Robinson Crusoe*, were all his Obi. . . . By his magic he was not only the dread of the negroes, but there were many white people, who believed he was possessed of some supernatural power. (Dr. Benjamin Moseley, *Treatise on Sugar*, London, 1799 [cited in Cundall 1930: 9])

[23]

Well, Three Finger Jack live at Three Mile, in town [here meaning near, but not in, Kingston]. And him was thief. [He robbed] store, and all dem way. And him have him woman down in de cave.

So, bakra send fe Maroon fe come and catch Three Finger Jack.

Three Finger Jack, now, a only three finger him have.

So, him have a ladder wha' him walk pon and go down de hole. When Maroon go and see Three Finger Jack, him bawl him.

Him have swiri [spiritual power, obtained by swearing a pact with a spirit]. Because him is a swiri-man [a spirit worker]. Him was a Science-man, a swiri-man, a Nago [here used generically, to mean an African].[21]

So him down in de hole.

And when Maroon bawl him, de woman tek him baby, him pikni, and put pon him back, and go round through St. Thomas.

You ever hear about [a place named] Three Finger Woman Tumble? So when him going right through St. Thomas, coming in de wood, [at] Three Finger Woman Tumble, you have de bottom side, and coming from top side, in de wood, dem call [it] Brokfas Spring, a come off of de rock.

That mean, when you reach so, you want water fe drink—anybody at all— you going stop there so, and you have you something fe eat. You a go stop there so and you a go eat and drink water. And you gone again.

So when de woman going through St. Thomas, and him come, same as him go round de rock, him *jam* [got cut or pierced]. De woman put him finger, as him lick de baby pon him back, and him put it there, him say: (sings)

 jam break har
go a wood, break har
go a wood-ee, Maroon break i
 jam break har
go a wood, break i
Maroon break i

And him go ina de rock. Nobody see him again—de woman. She throw that sing. A put him put him hand pon de rock. De rock swipple, swipple rock. Him a go down, de baby deh pon him back.

Him say (sings)
 jam break har
A no Maroon woman.

When him a say, "jam break har," now, it mean say a jam him jam [she just cut] fe-him hand from de place, and going down. So him going down back way.

Him husband name Three Finger Jack. Him min deh Eleven Mile, a town. Nobody see de woman again. Him slip off of de rock and go right down.

Dem catch Three Finger Jack, Maroon catch Three Finger Jack.

(James Downer, June 25, 1978)

The Tragedy of Paul Bogle

The rest of the narratives in this chapter [24–44] concern confrontations between Maroons and non-Maroons after the abolition of slavery in 1834. The primordial division between the "two sister pikni"—the children of Grandy Nanny (the Maroons) and those of Grandy Sekesu (other Jamaicans of African descent)—was not effaced by this change of legal status for the majority of Jamaicans. Though all were now free, the Maroons continued to view their black Jamaican "cousins," like all other *obroni*, with aloofness and distrust. When Paul Bogle's rebellion erupted in Morant Bay in 1865, the Windward Maroons decided, after carefully weighing their options, to side with the colonial government. For the first time in more than a quarter of a century, spiritually primed Maroon *feteman* went out in pursuit of adversaries from "the other side of people," some of whom, as in former times, wielded their own spiritual weaponry.[22]

Following a Maroon song about the events of 1865 [24] is the first text relating to Bogle's war [25]. This text recounts an incident said to have occurred at the very outset of the rebellion. A non-Maroon *kumfu joni*, or obeah man, named Bryce, who is living in the Moore Town area, has learned that the Maroons are planning to take action against Bogle and his supporters. A Bogle sympathizer himself, Bryce takes his gun and hides in a tree on the Cornwall Barracks road, knowing that the Maroon troops will have to pass by there on their way to Morant Bay. He knows that he will probably not survive the encounter, but vows to kill at least one of the Maroons as they march past. However, the Maroons' superior spiritual protection causes his shot to miss its mark. The Maroons respond with a volley that kills Bryce. Though not strong enough to save him, Bryce's obeah is still so powerful that when he expires it causes three days of darkness, forcing the Maroons to delay their march to St. Thomas.[23]

The most renowned of the spiritually powerful rivals mentioned in Maroon narratives about the 1865 rebellion is Paul Bogle himself. Bogle is still seen by the

Figure 9.4. Mural depicting Paul Bogle's rebellion, Morant Bay, St. Thomas, 1995. Photo: K. Bilby.

descendants of those who captured him as a skilled "Scientist"—though one who showed poor judgment in launching an armed revolt that was bound to fail. Many Maroons feel that Bogle's rebellion against the particularly oppressive regime of Governor Eyre, though justified, was not sufficiently thought out, and came at an inopportune time; it was, they say, doomed from the start, and it is hardly surprising that their ancestors refused to sacrifice themselves to such an ill-conceived plan.[24] Many would agree with the narrator below [26, 28] who suggests that Bogle did not inform the Maroons of his plans early enough, and did not give proper consideration to their treaty obligations and the oath with which they had bound themselves to the whites; if he had taken the time to devise a better plan and to persuade them that it was truly in their interest, according to this argument, the Maroons might then have joined with him in the rebellion.

As it turned out, the tensions simmering in St. Thomas boiled over before any kind of mutual understanding could be reached, and Bogle found himself up against the superior power of the Maroons. According to the narratives about these events that follow [27–30], it was the veteran Moore Town fighter Joseph Briscoe who finally brought him down—though not without a struggle. The resistance offered by Bogle, however, was of a spiritual, rather than physical, nature. In one account [27], Bogle evades his pursuers by disguising himself as a woman—not just by donning women's clothing, but by using spiritual power to trick the eyes and ears of his opponents. This ruse works only for a time, for the Kromanti power of the Maroon pursuers allows them to see through it. In another account [30], Bogle actually does receive spiritual assistance from at least some Maroon sympathizers, who agree to show him how to use Kromanti power to protect himself from bullets. He is cautioned, however, that this protection will remain effective only so long as he observes a prohibition against eating the quintessential *bakra* food, sugarcane. Eventually, Bogle succumbs to hunger and violates the prohibition, cutting and sucking on a piece of sugarcane while on the run.[25] Soon after this he is shot and captured (significantly, he was apprehended in a cane field, according to both oral and written accounts).

As with the narratives that pit Maroon trackers against escaped slaves in the pre-emancipation era, those relating to Bogle's war depict the Maroons' opponents as worthy adversaries. Rather than defenseless victims, Bogle's supporters are formidable guerrilla fighters who occasionally inflict serious damage on Maroon troops. One prominent oral tradition [31–35] records a particularly poignant Maroon casualty. A Maroon living in Hayfield, St. Thomas—an abeng blower usually named as Thomas Minott—sets off to alert the Maroons in Moore Town to the outbreak in Morant Bay. A veteran fighter who had lost a leg in battle, Minott must make the long journey through the mountains on crutches. On the way, he is ambushed by one of Bogle's sharpshooters hidden in a tree, and is hit in the eye. But the bullet does not stop him. Although blinded in one eye and suffering from a terrible head wound, he heroically continues sounding his abeng. By relying on the Kromanti herbal knowledge and spiritual power of his ancestors, he overcomes his devastating injury long enough to reach Moore Town and make sure that the Maroons there have received the message. As usual, there is an explanation for the initial failure of what should have been infallible Kromanti spiritual protection. Finding himself caught in the middle of an ambush, Minott had made the mistake of calling upon his mother and her ancestors ("mi mama!") rather than his father and the ancestors on that side ("mi tata!"), thus temporarily weakening his defenses.

[24]

> wonder wha' me do
> mek Bogle raise war-ee
> dis ya Bogle, you gone and raise war-ee
> dis ya Bogle, Paul Bogle, raise war
> dis ya Bogle, Paul Bogle, raise war pon we
> ee—de—
> ee—de—
> come ride de binasal-ee

(Sydney McDonald, September 4, 1978)

[25]

Maroon a go a Hayfield, a go a St. Thomas. When dem a go a St. Thomas fe catch Paul Bogle, when dem a walk through [Cornwall] Barracks, dem have a man up there, dem call him Bryce.

So Bryce say to him mother say, "Maroon a go pass here. Maroon a go pass."

And out of de lot, him going kill one of de Maroon.

Bryce living in Barracks, at Belrose Spring. You have a mango tree on de top side, same as you'll have de grade going down, tek de level. Is right there so dem call Belrose Spring. You see a water run cross over de road before you reach a Cotton Tree.

So Bryce *climb* de mango tree, and Bryce hear de Maroon a come, hear Maroon a come, hear de abeng a blow, de akrekre. So when Bryce climb de mango tree, same as Maroon dem come under de mango tree, Bryce got him gun. Him load him gun now. Bryce let go de shot, it go "bu-boom!" A shoot him shoot, let go de shot! And when him let go de shot, so "wap!," ina de crowd of de Maroon so . . . smoke . . . *smoke!* Maroon no see a who. But Bryce deh pon mango tree now. Maroon no see a who, with de smoke.

Maroon stand up, *all* Maroon stand up. When de smoke *wear* off, that smoke wear off of dem, dem *look* up ina de tree so, dem see Bryce up there. Dem *turn*, line up de something so, "boom!," shoot Bryce. Bryce *drop* a ground before dem.

Three day darkness. Three day.

So you can see Bryce was a clever man. Bryce supposed to clever.

Three day darkness. Maroon couldn't pass. Because when dem shoot, dem kill him, you know.

A fight dem a go fight, you know, a war dem a go fight. So Bryce tell fe-him mumma say out of de lot of Maroon him going kill one. And him climb de mango tree fe mek Maroon no see him. And same as dem come on there, so "wap!," him shoot de gun, and it go "wap!" It no kill *one* out of de lot. Him no shoot *one*. And remember say a nuff people, and if him shoot ina de middle, one must dead. But after that, a none no dead. And Bryce dead.

Three day darkness.

Bryce is a niega. So Bryce do him kumfu joni—that mean to say, him a work obeah. That's right.

Maroon pass and go a St. Thomas. That time dem got martial law. So Maroon go there now. Bakra now call dem now fe help dem fight. So that's where dem a walk, fe go a St. Thomas, fe go through de wood. So a that mek Bryce say him a go kill one, if even de tiniest Maroon in de batch, but him going kill *one*.

And most Maroon clever.

Good.

(James Downer, September 27, 1978)

[26]

When Bogle mek him rebellion, Bogle was depending solely upon de Maroon to back his affairs. But he have never told de Maroon.[26] Because Bogle's rebellion was that Grandy [Nanny] should have not allow any white man to live on de island.[27] That was Bogle's rebellion, you know. That's what Bogle start with. But, at de same time, it was down written that whatsoever occur on de island, anything that happen, de Maroon must help de English. And if anything happen to de Maroon, de English must help de Maroon. So de Maroon couldn't *otherwise* more than help de government in de Bogle's rebellion. For it was a treaty sign. You see, it was a treaty sign, so you couldn't otherwise. That was de thing. But probably if Bogle did *tell* de Maroon that it was their cause, probably dem coulda broke dem rules of treaty and helped him.

(Johnny Minott, June 4, 1978)

Maroons versus "The Other Side of People": Captain Briscoe in Bogle's War

The next two texts [27–28] mention a Moore Town Maroon named Briscoe, whose name we have already encountered in a number of other narratives (sometimes identified more specifically as Joseph Briscoe).[28] The existence of a nineteenth-century Maroon officer named Joseph Briscoe, who led military detachments during the suppression of the Morant Bay rebellion, is corroborated in written reports by contemporary observers. The missionary Henry Bleby, for

[Paul Bogle's] whereabouts was suspected, and a party, under the veteran Captain Briscoe (Maroon), proceeded to Spring Garden, and formed a cordon round a certain unfrequented district. A boy, a mere child in years, say between 10 and 14, was ordered to advance centrally to a certain spot indicated, and if the rebel chief was there the boy was to sound a horn for his immediate capture. Boldly the little fellow advanced, the cordon of Maroons drawing closer to the centre as he advanced. True enough, Paul was there in the thicket reading his Hymn-book. He coolly looked up and asked the boy who he was; "I am a Maroon," was the answer. "And what do you want here?" demanded Paul. "We are come to take you." "No you won't," said the rebel springing at him; but the boy was quick, for immediately sounding his horn as he broke away from the rebel chief, his warlike race rushed to the rescue with every rifle levelled at the notorious Paul. He surrendered in a sullen manner, muttering, "I will surrender to your people; but I never would have to any other." He was then securely bound and brought in to meet the doom that was so justly awarded him. ("The Rebellion in Jamaica," report from unidentified 1865 newspaper clipping in West India Reference Library, National Library of Jamaica, located by Barbara Kopytoff)

instance, reporting on the carnage that followed the outbreak, writes of "Briscoe, one of these ruffianly Maroons, who was identified with many acts of wanton cruelty and murder, and called himself Captain Briscoe." At a later point, this author again brings up "the before-mentioned ruffianly Maroon, who was intrusted with some petty command, and suffered to assume the title of Captain Briscoe," and goes on to accuse him and the Maroons under his command of several acts of brutality against a number of peasants in St. Thomas parish toward whom they harbored personal grudges (Bleby 1868: 70–75).[29] That this same Maroon officer was in the party that captured Bogle is confirmed by Heuman (1994: 132), who cites an archival document in which "a Maroon captain, Joseph Briscoe, recalled Bogle's reaction when arrested."[30]

Despite the obviously inaccurate statement in one of the texts below [27] that "Paul Bogle is not a Jamaican, is a foreigner," both narratives give descriptions of the main *Maroon* character, Joseph Briscoe, that match those in contemporary written sources.[31] For example, "Briscoe him was de top man . . . in Moore Town who lead out de soldiers . . . to help in this martial law." And: "Isaac Ellis and Joseph Briscoe, a those man catch Paul Bogle."[32] Both narratives also agree with written sources that state Bogle was caught by Maroons in, or near, a cane field (e.g., Black 1965: 200).

[27]

Is Maroon go to catch Paul Bogle. Maroon go fe catch Paul Bogle.

When Paul Bogle deh a St. Thomas, Paul Bogle a fight fe human right of privilege. Him a fight down St. Thomas, a fight!

You will hear a song say: (sings)

>wam chiri wam
>me kill Bogle
>wam chiri wam
>Morant Bay[33]

That mean say when Maroon go, every man go fe catch Paul Bogle. Dem couldn't catch him because Paul Bogle have [on] a broad hat [while] walking, put on a frock [dress] like woman. Paul Bogle sit down pon bridge, like him a woman, have on him frock, got on him broad hat. Dem wouldn't know say a Paul Bogle.[34]

Paul Bogle is not a Jamaican, is a foreigner. But him come fe fight fe human right of privilege. But him couldn't manage it because government look and see say him a fight dem too much, so dem call Maroon fe come catch him.

Isaac Ellis and Joseph Briscoe, a those man catch Paul Bogle. Dem light de cane-piece [a field with sugar cane growing in it] a fire, because Paul Bogle a travel down, and dem see Paul Bogle a come down. And Maroon know demself, and know say a Paul Bogle.

That mean say him put on a frock [a woman's dress]. Him a change from dem, change himself, fe know if Maroon know demself fe true! Because Paul Bogle know himself. That mean say, him have Science. Him have Science, *have* it!

(James Downer, June 25, 1978)

[28]

After de generation coming down, coming right down, coming down, coming down, coming down, it was a time when you have what Maroon call "martial law." At those days, whenever de riot raise up on de English in this country, de Maroon would have to help. Because that was how de treaty sign. If anybody come to fight de English, de Maroon have to help. If anybody to fight de Maroon, de English have to help.

So, at those days, Briscoe him was de top man. And him second was Isaac Ellis. They were de two top men in Moore Town who lead out de soldiers or de army go out to help in this martial law. They do very good work. They go out, and they fight, and they captured de enemies too. But at de same time, dem do whole heap of killing too.

Well, at those days, it was de same slavery people who mek these riots in Jamaica. It wasn't definitely nothing from abroad or thing like that. Like you da have all dem Bogle war and all those. You know, dem call it "martial law."

De Maroon did really sign that treaty, or that blood covenant, with de En-

⸙

We have been informed, on good authority, that the Maroons have refused to accept the 400 l. which his Excellency the Governor had offered for the capture of the blood-thirsty miscreant, Paul Bogle. The Maroon, Captain Downer, by whom Bogle was "tripped up" and held fast till the others came up and secured the prisoner, was among the guests of the city on Monday last. He is quite a youth. (from "The Maroons," *The Gleaner and Cordova's Advertising Sheet,* October 19, 1865)

glish. If anyone rise against de English, de Maroon would have to help. If anyone rise against de Maroon, de English have to help. That was de covenant. So they couldn't really change it, to help somebody else to fight against de English, unless if it was their self—if it were their self want to fight. But they really couldn't change it, to go and fight with somebody else against de English, because that mean now they would [be] breaking de treaty, de covenant.

When Bogle start his fight there, de governor of this country at those days call to de Maroons fe help. They will have to.

They captured him when him was going, and when de war start, they capture him. In a cane field they catch Bogle. It was a cane field.

(Johnny Minott, February 6, 1991)

[29]

They [the Maroons] run against Paul Bogle and William George Gordon, from Pinnacle up to St. Thomas.[35] There you have a propaganda that he [Bogle] is going to keep church service. After de abolishment of slavery, he will take up all de slave for his own self. De English government never agree about that.

De English government led him away to de Maroon to capture him, and de Maroon did capture him. De Maroon run him from up a Pinnacle over in Portland to Seaman's Valley, up to St. Thomas.

He run into his church for rescue, but him never know. My Grandy min have some of his troop inside de church there, waiting for Paul Bogle. Him [Bogle] never know that dem have so much there waiting.

I going tell you a secret now. It's hard, but I have to do it, since I'm giving it to you, then. Dem have a black puss inside de church—my great-grandmother. One of de Maroon hold his tail, and two hold his head. And they have a piece of black velvet—I shouldn't give you that [knowledge]—rubbing de puss, and rubbing and rubbing de puss, till de whole church catch in fire.[36] And is there where they able to capture Paul Bogle and William George Gordon.

They [Bogle and his men] run from there, and dem run into de church, think they were running fe rescue. And after dem ina de church, dem meet up with fire. Dem jump through de window. And after jump through de window of de church, dem jump outside. There de Maroons were able to catch him and capture him, and have him hang on a cashew tree.

(Abraham Goodwin, April 15, 1978)

[30]

Paul Bogle. When de Maroon min capture him, dem shoot Paul Bogle a him back. When dem capture him so, a shoot dem shoot him.

De Maroon dem got a rule. And when dem going to fight de morning, dem say to Paul Bogle say him no fe eat no white cane, no cane at all, no cane, no cane.

And while dem were going to fight de battle a morning, him tek out him pen knife. And one white cane deh a de pass, and him cut de cane. And him taste it. Him eat one little piece.

And de Maroon man dem begin to throw mouth: "nyuman! Na hónti yu du? Hónti yu du?! Ba, túre dei ye, al a wi opóng jwéko kúmfu dáda."[37]

Because him broke de rule. And when dem soldier dem down pon him, de other one run. And then, Paul Bogle there couldn't do nothing.

A him broke de rule, because dem tell him say him no fe eat nothing, no bakra cane, white cane.

All him can do, when him see one door, then him grab de door so, put a him back. And they go round so, and dem shoot him, Paul Bogle, through de board, a him neck, kill him. So a so Paul Bogle done. A so him dead. . . .

"Andu! Fikandu!" [a Kromanti expression]

Him throw him mouth, you know, him throw him sing. A Bogle himself, after dem shoot him, him sing de tune, say: "poor Bogle, poor Bogle, him hand a him head-oo, Bogle, you gone home, poor Bogle." And then him drop. Bogle sing de tune, man. (sings)

> Bogle-oo
> poor Bogle-oo
> Bogle, gyal, you ina ring-oo
> Poor Bogle say him gone.

Him say, "Bogle, you gone, man. Bogle, you ina ring, but you gone. Poor Bogle. You ina ring. You hand a you head today."

When dem say him hand a him head today, it mean to say, him deh cringe. Him deh cringe. Him get de shot, but him hand a him head, and [him] deh bawl. (sings)

> Bogle-oo
> poor Bogle-oo
> poor Bogle tide [today]
> Bogle-oo, you gone home-oo
> Bogle tide
> Bogle-oo
> you hand a you head-oo

(Richard Barnes, February 4, 1991)

Maroons versus "The Other Side of People":
The Abeng-Blower Who Wouldn't Quit

For Maroons today, the following narratives [31–35] about a Maroon soldier whose eye was shot out during Bogle's war demonstrate the great bravery of their ancestors. Some eighteenth- and nineteenth-century British writers criticize the Maroons for their avoidance of open combat—the implication being that the guerrilla tactics they employed were cowardly. John Stewart (1808: 294), for example, asserts that "the Maroons, however successful they were in their surprises, skirmishes, and ambuscades, were certainly, as before remarked, deficient in one of the first qualities of a soldier, courage." Other British writers recognized the great courage shown by Maroon warriors. Dallas (1803a: 251–52), for instance, was much impressed by the valor of the Maroon commander Captain Johnson during the Second Maroon War in 1795. "Far from screening himself during the engagement," writes Dallas, "he was loud in giving his orders . . . Being wounded with a ball, he immediately cut it out with his knife, and continued exerting himself to the utmost to obtain the victory." In Dallas's description, Johnson behaves much like the Maroon whose eye is shot out in a number of the narratives below, continuing to carry out his mission though suffering from a grave injury.

The story also serves as a reminder of the herbal knowledge and healing powers of the ancestors, since the protagonist knows how to take measures that temporarily lessen the impact of the medical emergency and is able, with the help of other Maroons who apply herbs, to recover from this devastating injury, even though he never fully regains his sight.

Interestingly enough, depositions taken from Maroons who participated in the suppression of Bogle's rebellion do make mention of a Maroon whose eye was shot out by Bogle's men, though they name this man as James Harris (Carey 1997: 598–99), rather than Thomas Minott (the name given in some of the narratives below) or Ellis (in one narrative).[38]

[31]

When running off Hayfield, come along short cut a Hayfield fe go down a Bath, one mango tree deh right a de short cut. And dem go up there, go lay wait fe him with de gun, wait fe dem. De rebels dem wha' a fight a St. Thomas [were lying in wait for the Maroons]. And when de Maroon passing, one of dem, him hear a tree broke. And when de tree broke, one [of the Maroons] hold up him eye so. Him get a bullet a him eye. One of de Maroon man. As him hear de "krep" now, him look pon de tree fe see is who. De gun catch him ina him eye. So then de rest now put dem abeng a dem mouth, dem horn, and blow.

(Ruth Lindsay, January 30, 1991)

[32]

Dem [Bogle's men] shoot him eye. When dem shoot de Maroon man a him eye, him catch one something so [i.e., some herbs], and cork up de eye, and shut de eye. And de same man, de [Maroon] soldier, fight de war till de war dead, and win de war. When a evening, dem no conquer him, but dem shoot him. After dem shoot him, dem tek de weed and cork de eye. And him never drop until a evening, when dem knock off. But Paul Bogle dead on de ground.

   Sake of Paul Bogle, dem shoot Ellis ina him eye. And de other Maroon come in, and tek dem weed, tek dem weed, and cork de eye. And him able fe fight de war so till, a evening, him knock off. Well, him lose de eye, but him no min dead on de spot. Him dead one other time. But after that, dem dress de eye till de eye well too. Him get shot ina him eye fe true.

(Richard Barnes, February 4, 1991)

[33]

[Thomas Minott] was a one-foot man. When de war [with Bogle] start, him was de man who left Hayfield and come a Moore Town, and mek de Maroon know that de war start there and it going reach. So that mean de Maroon can prepare. You understand? He didn't come a Moore Town and walk and tell everybody. He just come, and when him come up a Barry Hill there, him tek his horn and him . . . (imitates the blowing of the abeng)—you know what me talking. And every Maroon know what he says.

(Johnny Minott, February 6, 1991)

[34]

Dem ever tell you about—in catching Paul Bogle—de man who min a blow de akrekre? That man name Thomas Minott. Now, that man wha' dem call Thomas Minott was a wonderful man. De man was carrying message coming from St. Thomas, come tell de Moore Town people dem. Is a martial law, when dem a fight fe come kill Paul Bogle. Bogle. And when him tek de abeng and a blow, de niega fire de gun and shoot him ina him eye. [He] fire gun—gun!—shoot him ina him eye. But he's a one-foot man [i.e., he had only one leg]. Therefore him tek this hand [the one that he wasn't using to support himself with a crutch] and hold him eye. One-foot man! That mean say him have one foot. But him name Thomas Minott. So, him lose him eye, through de man shoot him and lick out de eye. Him tek him hand and hold it, and tek de trash and put it over it—de trash—and a blow de abeng, and a walk from St. Thomas here to Moore Town. Is de martial law.

   That man now [Thomas Minott] dem call "Uncle." Him was a messenger. Messenger! And him tek de message to de Maroon dem. That's why abeng blow. Him carry message say de people dem down pon dem.

(James Downer, January 25, 1991)

[35]

That was in de martial law, that was de man who was blowing de abeng. I heard that they went to St. Thomas in this martial law. And they were cooking. You know, dem stop and cook. And after they were cooking, they [Bogle's men] start to a fire shot all about. And de jump him jump out of de kitchen [the moment the Maroon man jumped out of the kitchen], dem ball catch him, tek him a him eye. And when de ball tek him a him eye catch him, him say, "mi mama!" And that cause him eye fe blind.

Well, de Maroon tek weed and draw out back de bullet, but de eye still blind. De eye blind. Because him call pon de weak side [i.e., the mother's side] (blows some rum).

But it was different from today, because him still have to blow [the abeng]. Though him eye was blind, him still have to have him blowing. Today some of dem woulda say, "boy, me can't bother with it, because me eye blind." But in those days, it was not like that.

[If he had called out "mi tata!" instead], de bullet wouldn't affect him.

(Johnny Minott, February 6, 1991)

The Maroons Meet Their Match: The Story of Bangula

The remaining narratives [36–44] in this chapter all concern competitive encounters between Maroon *fete-man* and non-Maroon opponents in the more recent past (mostly in the late nineteenth century). These take place in varying contexts. In the first group of texts [36–39], two Maroon Kromanti specialists from Moore Town are skeptical of the growing reputation of an obeah man in St. Thomas parish named Bangula—a member of the "Bongo nation" who works within the Kumina tradition. They decide to pay Bangula a surprise visit, so that they can "test" his powers. As they approach his house, while they are still too far away to be seen by him, Bangula treats them to a song. "Two Maroon men have come here," he sings out, "to see what Bangula is made out of!" Just as a good Maroon *fete-man* would have done, Bangula has "seen" and anticipated their every move. Impressed by this demonstration of power, the two Maroon challengers avoid a direct confrontation and turn back to Moore Town, carrying Bangula's song with them (where it is still sung in Kromanti Play).[39]

[36]

One man min name Bangula. Bangula was a Bongo man. And this man now, Bangula, every man hear about him, and dem want fe drop him. So, Maroon man dem hear about Bangula [too].

(David Gray, February 19, 1978)

[37]

Two man hear about Bangula, and dem want fe go find out what type man Bangula was. Because dem know say where smart concern, nobody shouldn't better than dem. And dem hear about this man dem call Bangula. And de two of dem just say, well, all right, dem have fe go have a chat, and mek dem and Bangula talk.

And when Bangula deh a him yard, de same two man deh come.

Bangula throw him sing to de two man, mek de two man know say dem deh come here today fe come test Bangula, and find out what kind of man Bangula is. (sings)

> two man a come ye fe come see wha' Bangula mek outa-ee
> two man a come ye fe come see wha' Bangula mek outa

A so it go. A two man deh come test Bangula. Because everybody say Bangula a sipple-man [clever spiritual worker]. And de two man say nobody shouldn't wise more than de two man. So dem deh come test Bangula.

(Hardie Stanford, January 31, 1978)

[38]

Bangula is a peculiar man, you know, tricky man. Tricky man! That's why dem call him Bangula.

So, him have a [Maroon] friend. Bangula tricky, you know. And de friend tricky too. De two of dem a two trick man. But Bangula tricky more than de other friend.

So when Bangula come now, Bangula say to him, de friend, him say, "okrúwa nanti!" [a fragment of Maroon Kromanti language, spoken by Bangula to show that, even though he is from a different "nation," he knows some Kromanti]

Him [Maroon] friend say to him, "Kromanti Kofi-oo."

De other one [another Maroon man] say, "me deh go see wha' Bangula mek out of."

Bangula was a Bongo man. But de two Maroon man feel say Bangula no know nothing. But dem never know what Bangula know. Bangula know more than dem. So dem couldn't exercise Bangula.

And de time dem leave dem room coming, Bangula see dem [saw them spiritually, not physically]. So when dem come, Bangula ina de house, sit up. Bangula say: (sings)

> two Maloon man kon ye[40]
> two Maloon man kon ye
> kon see wha' Bangula mek outa
> mek outa
> Bangula mek outa

That time Bangula shut up ina him room there [where his view of the approaching Maroon men was blocked], deh knot him thread. (sings)

    mek outa
    woy!
    mek outa
    woy!
    mek outa
    mek outa
    Bangula mek outa

So Bangula tie dem up! Dem was coming like nothing to Bangula. So Bangula was a Bongo fe true.

But, you see Bongo? Bongo know Science bad, you know. A no easy people dem, you know! A somebody dem wha' me deal with, you know. Dem high. Dem know good Science fe true, Bongo. Don't joke with dem.

(Adolphus Whyte, June 15, 1978)

[39]

De Maroon come from Portland, go to St. Thomas, go to de Bongo man now. De Bongo man live at St. Thomas.

So de Maroon man say, "well, boy! Me hear say one Bongo man deh a St. Thomas, and him *warm*!"

Him say, "mek we go there, go see wha' him mek out of."

But de Kongo man, de same Bongo man, know say a wha' dem come after. Because dem want fe find wha' him mek out of, if him have any use at all. So de Bongo man say now to him other friend: (sings)

    eh—
    two Maroon man come ya las night
    two Maroon man come ya las night
    fe see wha' Bangula mek outa

De other man say: (sings)

    eh—
    eh—, mam
    eh—, mam
    wha' dem Bangula mek outa

Him say mek dem come. When dem come, dem will find out something.

Anyhow, de Bongo man and de Maroon man go to war. De Maroon man mek him plan. De Bongo man see all wha' de Maroon man out for. De Maroon man aim fe defeat de Bongo man. But de Bongo man know him Science *same like* de Maroon, because it only a *little* different—only a little different between de two of dem.

(Richard Barnes, September 12, 1978)

Enemy Ghosts and Ghostly Enemies in a New Jamaica

Continuing the theme of encounters between Maroon and non-Maroon adversaries in post-emancipation Jamaica, the next narrative [40] tells of a Moore Town Maroon *fete-man* named Elick Downer. This story clearly illustrates how the old tradition of warfare between Maroons and slaves survived after emancipation, the physical battles of the past giving way to purely metaphysical confrontations. Instead of clashing in actual combat as their predecessors once had, Maroon *fete-man* and their opponents now left the fighting entirely to the duppies, or spirits, they controlled. In this particular narrative (one of several I heard about this nineteenth-century *fete-man*), Elick Downer goes to an outside district to work for a client. A local obeah man approaches him and brazenly challenges him, scoffing at the Maroons' reputation as great spirit workers. Downer accepts the challenge, and they order two drinks of rum. When Downer steps outside to prepare himself for the contest, the obeah man switches their drinks. Returning to the rum shop, Downer picks up his glass. But rather than drinking from it, he drops it to the ground and begins to unleash a torrent of invocational Kromanti language. The obeah man is overwhelmed when he "sees" a huge number of duppies assemble around his Maroon opponent, summoned by these mysterious utterances. Realizing that the two or three duppies he himself controls are no match for this army of Maroon spirits, the obeah man backs off and admits defeat.

The same theme of inferior non-Maroon obeah is evident in the next narrative [41], which centers on a powerful *fete-man*, Chaal (Charles) Watson, and his notorious *kumfu joni* rival, Bryce, who once lived in the Maroon settlement of Cornwall Barracks near Moore Town (a different individual, I was told, from the Bryce who appears in narratives about Bogle's war). Chaal Watson was married to Bryce's sister (one of many examples of intermarriage between Maroon men and non-Maroon women during the nineteenth century). In this story, Chaal Watson's wife conspires with her brother to "tie" (or "knot") her husband—to use a kind of "love obeah" to keep him bound to her. Following Bryce's instructions, she steals a pair of her husband's underwear and gives it to her brother. Bryce works on the article of clothing with obeah, and then gives it to a johncrow (vulture), which flies away with it. The obeah makes Chaal Watson sick. Sensing that the cause is spiritual, he calls a Kromanti ceremony, during which the ancestors reveal what has happened. Commanded by the superior power of Maroon Kromanti, the johncrow comes to the site of the ceremony and flies overhead with the underwear in its beak. While everyone watches, the johncrow drops the underwear to the ground, and Chaal Watson reclaims this personal article, allowing him to neutralize the obeah with which his wife tried to tie him. Angered by this, the wife goes back to her brother and asks him to afflict her husband with a more powerful kind of obeah. This he does by magically inserting a broken glass bottle into his brother-in-law's stomach. Using Maroon herbs and his superior power, Chaal Watson is able to extract the bottle without sustaining any injuries.

This oral tradition would appear to reflect, among other things, the increasing contact between Maroons and other Jamaicans during the second half of the nineteenth century, a time when many non-Maroons were moving into areas bordering the Maroon communities. The next narrative [42], focusing on yet another confrontation between spirit workers, suggests that Kromanti Play began to play a more prominent role in the maintenance of ethnic boundaries during this period. A *kumfu joni* named David Gray, who lives in the village of Windsor near Moore Town, is curious about Kromanti Play. He knows that non-Maroons such as himself are not welcome at Kromanti dances; but he is a powerful obeah man—such is his power that he can make his obeah dolls move on their own as if they were alive—and he feels entitled to attend Maroon ceremonies as an equal. Gray tells Thomas Minott, a Maroon *fete-man* with whom he is acquainted, that he is going to attend a Kromanti Play, no matter what anyone says. Minott humors Gray, ignoring this implied challenge to the idea of Maroon spiritual supremacy, and tells him that he ought to come to the Kromanti ceremony that will be held in the neighboring Maroon community of Brownsfield that very night. The moment the *kumfu joni* arrives in Brownsfield, he blacks out. When he regains consciousness the next morning, he is somewhere deep in the forest, totally lost, and cannot remember how he got there. As an obeah man, he realizes what happened: Thomas Minott and his Maroon colleagues used a Maroon spirit to overpower his consciousness, take over his body, and lead him into the forest. The next time the obeah man meets up with Minott, he shakes his hand and congratulates him, saying, "yes, you are a Maroon man."

In the later nineteenth century, as the non-Maroon presence increased in areas surrounding the Maroon communities, growing numbers of Maroons were also traveling out to other parts of the island. Some of these travelers took advantage of the Maroons' reputation as superior herbalists, making a living by preparing and selling medicines outside their own communities. The same Joseph Briscoe discussed above, remembered for his many face-offs with non-Maroon adversaries, including Paul Bogle, was one such traveling Maroon bush doctor. When his fighting days were over, the illustrious Briscoe redirected his energies to healing. His new vocation took him to distant parts of the island, far from any of the Maroon communities, where he would "boil medicine" for the other Jamaicans, those who had been emancipated only a few decades earlier.

The last two texts in this section [43–44] describe a harrowing encounter between Briscoe and two treacherous *niega* clients during one such journey. In this story and others like it, the old theme of matching wits and challenging opponents is updated to a new, peacetime context. Briscoe has gone to a distant parish to sell his medicines. Since he is far from home, one of his patients provides accommodations for the night. He is shown to a room of his own and given sheets and a pillow. When Briscoe lies down, he is unable to sleep; his restlessness is a sign from his spirit that there is danger at hand. Before long, a small child comes to him and confides that the man and woman at whose house he is staying—the child's parents—are outside digging a grave, where they plan to bury him after killing him. The scheming couple has concluded that Briscoe must be carrying a great deal of money, as a Maroon healer who has been seeing many clients in the area. It should be easy to murder him and take his money, since he is far from home and no one is likely to come looking for him. Briscoe quickly devises a defensive strategy. He takes the pillow and bedclothes and bunches them up, simulating the shape of a man lying on the bed with his head covered by the top sheet. He then goes outside and waits for his hosts to return. Standing outdoors on the other side of the bedroom wall, he positions his head inches from where it would have been had he been asleep inside. When his would-be murderers come back, he pretends to be snoring inside, using ventriloquism to project his voice. They dim the lamp, and the treacherous host steals into Briscoe's bedroom with a machete. The moment he starts chopping the bedclothes, Briscoe stops snoring, and the man, believing him dead, shouts out triumphantly, "Briscoe, I have you today, boy!" When they hear a voice from the other side of the wall saying, "you lie, it's your sheet and pillow," the aggressors flee in terror. The Maroon *fete-man*, though no longer armed by *bakra* with "gun and powder," has once again outmaneuvered the *obroni* enemy.

[40]

You ever hear of a Maroon man dem call Elick Downer? I going give you a illustration off of that man.

Elick Downer go a Manchioneal. When him go a Manchioneal, a Cholan,[41] him go there fe go do business [to work Science]. And when him go there him meet one kumfu joni man—obeah man. Him go there fe go do business, him meet one obeah man, beat him fe true.

So when him go now get ina de shop, de obeah man see him.

Him [the obeah man] say (in a slurred, threatening voice), "every day unu come ya, say man Mawoon man.[42] Mawoon man fart."

So him talk, ina him head [with a nasal tone]. That a de obeah man.

Him say, every day dem come here, every day dem come say dem a Maroon man. Maroon man fart. As man blow de breeze ina dem, dem go, dem can't come back.

A de obeah man a tell Elick Downer so. That a when him go a Cholan. Him a obeah man! Him can see! [that Elick Downer was a Maroon Science-man].

Him say, "everyday unu come here say unu a Maroon man. Maroon man fart. As man blow de breeze, you tan a home, you can't come back. Well, all right, me a go see if you a Maroon man."

Him call fe two drink of rum. Because dem deh time two drink of rum a fe thruppence, so quattie [another small unit of money] fe one drink and quattie fe de other one. That's right.

Good.

Elick Downer get fe-him drink, him tek fe-him. Elick Downer look pon him. Elick Downer look pon de drink, because him know say [he himself was a] Maroon man.

So Elick Downer say, "hm, boy! You kaka hot up before fart!"[43]

So him a say. A so Maroon man talk dem something.

All right.

Him say, "all right."

Him look around.

Him say, "boy!"

A one young man ina de shop too, a Cholan.

Him say, "go up a de three-eye man [coconut tree] there so, get me one three-eye man [coconut], but no mek him touch asasi [the earth]."

That mean say him have fe carry it off of de tree without it drop a ground.

De boy carry come give him, him carry come give him, "so wap!"

Him say, "ha ha, boy! Mind youself. Mind you rosebud. When you want lesson from me, mind you rosebud, you know. A me a tell you so. Mind you rosebud, man."

And when Elick Downer come, and him come so, "wap!," Elick Downer do so, "wap!," so-so-so, prim [prepare] himself with this, do so-so, "wap" so, throw something.

Dat deh time, when him gone up there, de other man swap fe-him glass, swap de glass. A try him a try see if a man Maroon fe true. When Elick Downer gone look about de coconut, same as him turn out, him left him drink ina de shop, and de man just tek him fingers and put it there.

And Downer just come back and do so-so ina it "so wap!" And Downer stop.

Listen wha' me a say good, you know.

Elick Downer him no drink it! Him just drop [it] pon ground and stand up so. And him *talk* Country, him *talk* Country, and him talk Kromanti, and him talk Kromanti, and him talk Kromanti, and him talk Kromanti.

And when him talk Kromanti so, de obeah man spot him.

Him say, "no talk no more. You a Maroon man, you a Maroon man to fart. You a Maroon man, you a Maroon man. You have duppy [ghosts]!"

Because Maroon have duppy.

When him talk Kromanti, too much duppy come out there. Him see too much duppy. De obeah man see too much duppy.

When him spot dem, him say, "no talk no more Kromanti. You a Maroon man, because Maroon man have duppy, Maroon man have duppy."

(James Downer, September 27, 1978)

[41]

You have a man a Moore Town dem call old Chaal Watson. Chaal Watson live a Old Schoolhouse Bump. Old Chaal Watson have a wife from [Cornwall] Barracks. Him wife have a brother. Him brother name Bryce.

Bryce is a man wha' have a cow-tail and a gourdy [gourd or calabash container], cow-tail and a gourdy. That mean to say, him is a obeah man. And when him catch him cow-tail and him gourdy, and when him go a crossroad, and any time him sweep de crossroad, sweep de crossroad three time and put ina de gourdy, and you hear him say, "if a you, Ken. . . ."

Hear him say: (sings)

    kon Johnny fe me, kon Johnny fe me, kon Johnny fe me
    in zek . . . in zeke ke ke, in zek . . .

. . . then you dead.

Him sweep de gourd, him sweep de gourd, with de cow-tail, a say [it is] fe you. If you name so—if you name John or whatsoever, or if you name Ken now—him say: (sings)

    kon Kenny fe me, kon Kenny fe me, kon Kenny fe me, in zek

Him sweep it, put it in there.

Him say, "in zek ke ke ke ke, in zek."

Him sweep it, put it in there. That mean say him a obeah man. Him plans [come] from niega side. But him a obeah man. That mean say him will kill you nine day time. That's right.

All right, him sweep it, put it in there fe you. That time you dead.

Old Chaal, him married to him sister—him *sister*. Him sister tek Old Chaal underpant, or brief, then. Him carry go give brother. Brother trim it, give johncrow, opete! Him got it in de air a fly with it.

Old Chaal yarifo [sick] now. Him yarifo now.

Old Chaal a *sabi-man*. Him sipple, though! When me say "sipple," me mean say, wha' him no know, him no mek. Maroon man.

Old Chaal a come "so wap!" so, mek him knot so, sit down there, mek him knot so, sit down there, say, "we a go mek Play, *mek Play*, Kromanti Play."

And when de man dem dance, him tell him say, a so johncrow got him underpant up there a fly with it in de air.

Him say two woman a go sing jawbone out there, certain time of day, sing jawbone.

And when johncrow come out there so, him min hear dem so. Him turn back a corner there so.

De two woman shake, yanga demself [did a swaying dance]. That mean say dem a dance jawbone. [They] say: (sings)

    john johncrow, Mama Singila
    seh warra me done-oo
    me seh john johncrow, Mama Singila
    seh hasty love-ee

John crow fret, say, "he he he he he he he he he."

Him drop dem pant give him. Chaal tek it—*tek* it!

Old Chaal better. Old Chaal better.

De wife say, "all right, you good. So since you so good, me going show you gooder man more than you."

Him go back to him brother, tell him brother, "put glass bottle ina Old Chaal belly."

[He] put glass bottle ina Old Chaal belly, put it in there, put it ina him belly.

Old Chaal tek it out! Old Chaal tek it out, Old Chaal Watson, tek it out, with him work, him Science. Him fix him something, same like how you a come here now, and me is a Maroon man now. Him come here now, him go back ina him belly. That mean say him *can't* eat.

When him go there, him chat, him go a wood, him pick him trash, pick him trash, nyam him trash, *nyam* him trash, nyam it—that mean squeeze it ina him mouth, you know.

Him work out de glass bottle down there, "wap!" Glass bottle come out. Glass bottle come out of him belly to fart.

(James Downer, October 26, 1978)

[42]

Thomas Minott, him a Maroon man. So one time him go a Windsor and him meet a man. But that man now a kumfu joni man.

Him [the other man] say, "Thomas, every night unu a play Kromanti a Brownsfield. One of de night me a come, mek me see wha' unu a do."

Thomas Minott him say, "yes, you fe come. Because we a go play tonight. So you can come."

Him say, "yes."

That man now, him name David Gray. Him have two baby wha' him work with.[44] But dem can talk, because dem have power. So dem can move demself.

So, all right.

De night when him a go a Brownsfield now fe go a de Kromanti Play, when de drum a play, dem a go cross [Rio] Grande, round there.

Because every Maroon town have a river run right through, you know.

So dem have a place wha' dem call name Tan Foot Level, or in other words, Cambron. So dem a walk through it. A there him a walk through now fe come on de Kromanti Play. And dem a play de Kromanti drum ina de night so, play Kromanti drum in Brownsfield there, *play* Kromanti drum up a Brownsfield there.

David Gray say, "boy, me a go a Brownsfield tonight, you know."

But Thomas Minott is a Maroon man.

When dem deh a Brownsfield a play de night there, David Gray a come a Brownsfield a de Play fe true. And when him realize, him find himself a wudu bere—that mean a far wood. Him find himself—when daylight, de morning, when sun raise—him find himself one place dem call name Daley. A daylight, and de Play him a come. Him no know de road fe come there. Daylight.

Thomas Minott turn him there, turn him so as him fe go a wood. And him go a wood fe true.

De other day when him meet Thomas Minott, him shake him hand.

Him say, "yes, you a Maroon man."

A ghost lead him there, to wudu bere. Maroon man do that.

So, a kumfu joni man can't high as a Maroon man, him can't good like a Maroon man.

Thomas Minott a *man* who just run ina kitchen there now and shove up two fire-stick ina him fireside so, business come to wha' him want.

(James Downer, October 4, 1978)

[43]

Briscoe go down country.

And when dem ina first-time days, you know, Briscoe is a man who boil medicine and go to people. *Medicine.*

All right.

And when Briscoe go down there, Briscoe get ina house. Briscoe ina de house.

De man dem tek up dem machete. Dem going sharpen dem machete. But Briscoe never know say de man dem a go kill him. Joseph Briscoe me a talk, man. Him never know say dem a go kill him—de niega dem. Him never know say dem a go kill him.

That a way down a St. Catherine. Briscoe boil medicine. A Maroon man, you know. Him boil medicine, go down there fe give dem niega—Maroon woulda say "niega" then.

So him ina de house.

Dem a sharpen de machete, sharpen de machete. De woman and him husband sharpen de machete fe Briscoe. Because dem believe say Briscoe got money.

So when Briscoe ina de house, Briscoe want sleep. So dem spread bed and give Briscoe. Dem time dem use lantern. So when Briscoe lie down, Briscoe a go sleep now. So when Briscoe go fe go sleep—mm-mm, him couldn't sleep. Him get up back. Him *jija* [felt restless]. Him jija. De meaning of "jija"—that meaning to say, after him lie down there, it come like say him can't sleep. Like him woulda get up and have fe sit down fe de whole night.

All right.

After Briscoe lie down—mm-mm. Briscoe couldn't lie down. Briscoe have fe stand up back!

When Briscoe get up back, one little pikni ina de house, him say to him say, "look here now, sah." Him say, "no sleep, you know. Because wha' you think happen now?" Him say, "Mama and Puppa gone a coffee walk [a grove of coffee trees] and dig grave fe bury you, because dem a go kill you."

Briscoe *get up*! When Briscoe get up so, Briscoe tek de sheet and him tek de pillow, and Briscoe mek de sheet pon de bed like somebody, and put de pillow fe lie down. Him tek de sheet, and him cover de bed. Him mek de shape of somebody. Briscoe mek him good, put him pon him bed lie down.

Briscoe come out of de house! Briscoe a go show dem say him a Maroon man. Briscoe come out of de house. De same place which part de head turn, where de somebody lie down, Briscoe go up there [outside, next to the wall of the house]. And Briscoe a start draw snore. Briscoe start snore. A same place where him put him head, you know, but him di-de [was there]. Him no asleep, him outside, him outside. But which part him turn de head of de something, up a de head, Briscoe di-de. A snore him a draw.

And when dem come from coffee walk, dem walk now fe come ina de house. Same as dem come ina de house, when dem come ina de house, machete *well sharp*, you know. Because a chop dem a chop up Briscoe, because dem see Briscoe asleep now. And when dem come ina de house, "so wap!," dem out de lamp now, dem put de house in de dark. De house dark now.

Dem pick up de machete and do so, "*WAP!*," ina de sheet. One side of de sheet go so, and one go so. That time de house dark, you know.

Him say, "Briscoe, Briscoe, I got you today, boy!" Him say, "Briscoe, Briscoe, I got you today, boy."

Briscoe out a road there. Briscoe say, "a no me, a sheet and pillow."

Truly! [to me]: Look pon me.

Briscoe say, "a no me, [but a] sheet and pillow!"

And when dem hear him a talk so, a run dem a run now. Dem a run now! And Briscoe tek way himself. Briscoe escape.

Dem escape too!

(James Downer, September 24, 1978)

[44]

Briscoe deh a St. Ann's [parish]. I don't know de direct part in St. Ann's, but it was St. Ann's. Him go round, him was giving medicine and thing like that, and dem plan fe kill him. In those days, I mean, Jamaica never so civilized then. And those days, you go out and people find that if you have money, dem will kill you, ina night time, bury you ina coffee walk. And you a stranger go there, nobody no know you, and dem say nobody naa look fe you.

So Briscoe go there, and after Briscoe di-de [was there], dem want fe kill Briscoe now.

Dem gone a one coffee walk and dig de grave before dem kill de person, you know. A so dem do it.

So when dem gone dig de grave, one little pikni come and say to Briscoe, say (in a whisper), "you asleep?"

Him say, "no."

Him say, "mumma and puppa go and gone dig grave a coffee walk fe bury you. Dem a come back come kill you."

So Briscoe get up and come out, and fix up de sheet and pillow—put de pillow, and cover it up with de sheet, and go outside of de house, and rest him head pon de same place where him did lie down, and him a draw [snore]. But him naa sleep. But outside of de house him deh.

And de man come in, ina de dark, and when him chop de sheet, "wap!"—
him chop!—Briscoe stop snore. Briscoe stop snore, like him dead.

And de man say, "all right, Briscoe. Briscoe, me have you today, boy!"

And Briscoe out a door, and say (laughing), "you lie, man! A you sheet and
pillow."

So Briscoe a run from de man dem, and de man dem a run now, say Briscoe a
go kill dem, because him a Maroon. Dem fraid him, you know! And through
dem no kill him there now, dem say, "boy, Briscoe a go kill we!" So dem a run.
And Briscoe a run say dem a go kill him, and dem man (dissolves into laughter) a
run from Briscoe.

(Johnny Minott, February 6, 1991)

Maroons versus "The Other Side of People" Revisited

Do Maroons today have opponents in Jamaica analogous to those who populate
their narratives about the past? For the practicing *fete-man*, this question is not
merely rhetorical. It is a question of life and death, and his survival depends on
answering it correctly. For many other Maroons—perhaps the vast majority—
the thrust of this question is easily translated into broader metaphors. The primordial breach between Nanny's children and those of her sister has yet to be
completely healed. At times it seems that this history weighs heavily indeed. In an
era when nationalism fosters robust myths, old hostilities find fertile ground.
Phrasing things with diplomacy, Olive Lewin (2000: 154) notes the continuing
existence of "gaps in understanding and lack of warmth between the Maroons
and certain Jamaicans, even today, over two hundred years after the signing of
the treaties. It is still felt, in some quarters, that the Maroons were responsible for
the British capture of Three-Fingered Jack, the arrest and hanging of Paul Bogle,
who is now a national hero, and the massacre of scores of his followers in Morant
Bay Square and other parts of St. Thomas in 1865." Along the same lines, Mavis
Campbell (1988: 162) remarks that "the Maroons' collaboration in quelling this
uprising is not easily forgotten by the wider Jamaican society. On occasion, it
makes for feelings of hostility toward the Maroons to this day." Indeed, as Maroon chronicler Bev Carey (1997: 646) complains, "every October since 1975 the
Maroons have been castigated for the failure of Bogle's rebellion and his subsequent execution."

It is not just that the awful aftermath of the Morant Bay uprising (close to 500
persons hastily executed) belongs to the relatively recent past, and thus remains
comparatively fresh in the collective memory. In the backward-looking search for
ways to frame the present, bitter recriminations over the contradictions of the
Maroon past begin, rather than end, at 1865. For every upbeat call to remembrance in the local press, every salute to Jamaica's original freedom fighters, there
is an aggrieved voice reminding the celebrants that these same Maroons became

Figure 9.5. Jamaican National Hero Paul Bogle on the country's recently retired $2 bill.

slave catchers. A recent example from the *Daily Gleaner* is typical. In response to an article in which the Maroons are portrayed positively, one letter writer protests that "these Maroons did an excellent job of ensuring that slavery continued on its murderous path by suppressing slave revolts left, right, and centre in addition to capturing our brothers and handing them over to their slave owner bosses."[45] Another recent example comes from the *Jamaica Observer*, where a letter under the heading "Support the Maroons" was met with the following outburst by a reader who used the "talk back" feature on the newspaper's web site to post a response:

> Yes! Let's remember how they sold us out to the British when they got their freedom!! Let's remember how they captured our foreparents trying to escape from slavery and handed them back to massa. Yes. Let us remember them and their history. Let's not ever forget it!!![46]

Yet another recent letter to the same newspaper asserts that

> the Maroons, as a group, have been aligned with the forces of oppression since 1739 when they signed a treaty which guaranteed them only 1500 acres of rocky slopes and institutionalised betrayal of their brother-Africans. They were exemplary in the slaughter of their own brothers in 1831 and 1865. There is no more dubious imagery of emancipation than the one in which Maroons are cast as heroes. Talk about mental slavery![47]

It is perhaps no accident that the first writer to do literary justice to the tragic dimensions of this lingering past is an outside observer from another part of the Caribbean, Maryse Condé. Looking on from a distance, yet able to sense parallels with her own native Guadeloupe, Condé perceives with particular clarity the mythic pull of the historical contradictions embedded in Jamaica's social landscape. In her novella, *Nanna-ya* (1999 [1985]), Condé embodies the still-prob-

Figure 9.6. Monument to Tacky, Port Maria, St. Mary, 2002. Photo: K. Bilby.

lematic relationship between the Maroons and "the other side of people" in two central characters and their troubled marriage.[48] Grace, a descendant of the Moore Town Maroons, is joined in wedlock with George, a descendant of plantation slaves. While Grace is known to be directly descended from Nanny, George views himself as a descendant of Tacky, the famous leader of a major slave rebellion in 1760, who was killed by Maroon trackers in an encounter much like those recounted in the Maroon narratives making up much of this chapter.[49] It is not long before these mythologized genealogies begin to haunt their marriage:

> The very day after his wedding night, [George] started looking for reasons to resent his wife. She was fragile, shy, quiet. Then his hatred found a precise object. Wasn't she a descendant of the maroons? After the agreement signed with the English, wasn't it a maroon that had aimed at Tacky with his long contraband gun and killed him with a shot to the head? Tacky, his hero, possibly his ancestor! (Condé 1999: 88)

George's goal in life becomes the writing of a history of Tacky; his real motive is to discredit the Maroons, the people responsible for Tacky's demise, who have improperly been enshrined as heroes. Not only would his history "be an homage to a martyr, but at the same time it would illustrate the sad story of the maroons, those freedom fighters paradoxically turned watchdogs for the English whenever someone else's freedom was at stake." George imagines the centerpiece of his

Figure 9.7. Monument to Tacky (close up), 2002. Photo: K. Bilby.

book to be "the relationship between the maroons and the slave population living in the plains"—much as he imagines his own marriage. "Oh, how much he wanted to destroy the myth that had formed around [the Maroons]" (Condé 1999: 88–89). The book project turns into an obsession that drags on for years and threatens to destroy what is left of his marriage. Only after his manuscript is stolen and his life work goes up in smoke do the long-festering wounds afflicting his marriage stand a chance of being healed. Only by wiping away this mythicized past, Condé seems to suggest, can the ancient animosities personified in her protagonists be overcome.

Alas, in this case life seems unlikely to imitate art. The need for remembrance remains strong in postcolonial Jamaica, and the contradictions in question are an indelible part of the nation's history. Consciousness of this troubled past continues to be registered in various ways. To cite but one of many examples, the reviewer of a recent book on Maroons for the *Gleaner* points out, once again, that the Maroons' "history has been flawed by their decision to side with the British colonialists and slave owners against others of African-descent involved in a struggle for freedom and justice." "Regarded by some as an inexcusable misjudgement," he continues, "this fact has clung to their history like a shroud."[50] The ideological problem posed by this aspect of the Maroon past has

Figure 9.8. "A Rebel
Negroe Arm'd and on
his guard" (eighteenth-
century maroon warrior
in Suriname). Engraving
by Francesco Bartolozzi.
From Stedman (1796).

continued to intrigue historians such as Joy Lumsden (2001: 468), who notes
that "the Maroons' almost totally consistent fulfilment of their treaty obligations
has made it difficult, if not impossible, for advocates of a freedom fighter hypoth-
esis to explain and justify Maroon actions during the greater part of their history.
No events have been more unpalatable than the Maroon refusal in 1865 to support the rebels in St. Thomas, their enthusiastic cooperation with government
forces in the suppression of the 'Rebellion' and their capture of the leader, Paul
Bogle." However, as Werner Zips has suggested, the Maroons have their own
perspective on this question, and it cannot be denied that this viewpoint also has
some validity. "Had the Maroons suddenly been transformed from the epitomes
of black resistance fighters to traitors and collaborators with the slaveowning
regime?" he asks. "This question can be answered with a counter-question:
Shouldn't the Maroons themselves have felt abandoned, when after 85 years of
armed combat they were still only a small minority, which was often fought and
betrayed even by fellow blacks?" (Zips 1999: 66–67).[51]

Figure 9.9. "A Coromantyn Free Negroe or Ranger Armed" (eighteenth-century antimaroon soldier in Suriname). Engraving by William Blake. From Stedman (1796). In the Dutch colony of Suriname, as in Jamaica, slaves and free blacks were employed to track down and capture maroons, before the Dutch colonial government concluded peace treaties with the Ndyuka and Saramaka Maroons in the 1760s.

It is important to remember that the widespread resentment that coexists with heroic images of Maroons is a product not only of recent intellectual debates and "official" discourses (such as government-sponsored media representations of the Maroon Wars and of Bogle's rebellion), but also of stories about the past transmitted across the generations within rural communities, particularly in areas close to the Maroon towns. During the 1970s, I repeatedly encountered historically based hostility toward Maroons when traveling around the rural parishes of Portland and St. Thomas (Bilby 1979: 65–67, 126–31). And it is clear that popular sentiment on this question remains ambivalent.

On occasion, these continuing animosities impinge even on the idylls of tourists. In a recent travelogue a visitor from the United States is taken aback by the comments of a young Jamaican tour bus guide near Port Antonio: "When I told her we were going back to Moore Town," notes the American tourist, "she said that there was a lot of anger toward the Maroons for turning in the escaped slaves" (Roskind 2001: 227). These unexpected hard feelings become a recurring theme in the following pages. Later in the book, the same American woman recounts the incident to a Maroon in Moore Town: "I met a young Jamaican tour guide on the beach the other day . . . She considers Maroons bad people because they captured runaway slaves." Recognizing that she has touched a tender spot on both sides of a kind of family feud, she and her traveling companions decide to do what they can to improve the situation. "These angry stories continue to weaken everyone, even today," she tells her Maroon friend (256). The solution offered by these well-meaning New Age seekers from the north is a major "Healing of the Nations" ceremony (parts of which are to be held in Moore Town and Charles Town), a rite of forgiveness during which the descendants of Maroons and the descendants of those who remained on the plantations will join the white descendants of slave holders in exorcising the residue of hatred left by wrongs committed in the distant past. Covered by world media, this symbolic gesture will send healing waves of "One Love" rippling across the planet.[52]

Thus has the private quarrel between "two sister pikni" that is still embodied in Kromanti Play and the narratives of the *fete-man* filtered, however dilutedly, into the globalizing New Age imaginary—which itself has crossed with internationalizing ideas about the possibility of redressing past injustices (especially slavery) through public commemorations, apologies, and reparations (Oostindie 2001). One can be forgiven, in any case, for harboring doubts about the efficacy of imported solutions such as the one proposed above. But the architects of this planned reconciliation might take consolation in knowing that the children of Grandy Nanny and Grandy Sekesu have long been mediating, and symbolically healing, the primordial breach that separates them, in ceremonies of their own (Bilby 1984b: 18–22). Whether a more permanent resolution might be possible, not to mention desirable, is probably something only they and *their* children can determine.

10

Ever Indomitable

All the regular troops in Europe, could not have conquered the wild Negroes, by force of arms.
—**Lieutenant Philip Thicknesse** (1788: 91)

A small body of negroes defied the choicest troops of one of the greatest nations in the world . . .
—**Robert Charles Dallas** (1803a: 123)

[The Maroons'] numbers were few, but their power was great; they say the island, of right, belongs to them.
—**Nancy Prince** (1853: 60)

Once a year, the Maroons of Accompong and Moore Town host major celebrations of their glorious past, to which they invite the general public. During these annual displays of Maroon identity they live up to their reputation as "a proud people." The cliché has a tourist-brochure ring, but it points to an ensemble of ideas, an ethos, that is a crucial part of what it means to be a "true-born" Maroon. Even today Maroons are sometimes said to be "hot headed," "fiery," "fierce," "haughty." Such stereotypical labels may border on caricature, yet they hint at an experiential reality. At the very least, they tell us something about the important role played by affect in the construction and transmission of Maroon identity.

As a neophyte ethnographer, I was struck time and again by the affective basis of "Maroonness." During my first few weeks in Moore Town in 1977, I was puzzled by what appeared to me then as a paradox. On the surface, my new neighbors had little to show for their unique status as Maroons, harboring what at times seemed like little more than a ghostly image of a former identity; but underneath lay powerful emotions that could well up when least expected, catching the unwary ethnographer off guard. As I began to work in private with a number of *fete-man*—Kromanti experts who viewed themselves, and to some extent were viewed by others, as models of "Maroonness"—I came face to face with this emotionally charged sense of self. Away from the crowd, free to act the role of man or woman of knowledge, the ritual specialists of Moore Town performed their identity openly and with striking force. As strong emotions were laid bare before me, I was made to know, in no uncertain terms, that understanding and empathy were inseparable. The Jamaican expression "who feels it knows it" took on new meaning in this Maroon setting.

A month and a half into my stay, I recorded in my journal one such encounter, with a *fete-man* I shall call Ba Will. His words as they appear on the page—I can clearly remember (and feel) them more than two decades later—scarcely hint at the emotional intensity with which they were delivered. As he hammered away at me with his questions, he locked onto my eyes with a deeply penetrating glare I will never forget.

> The amazing thing about [Ba Will] is his extreme pride in being Maroon.
> . . . How many times have I heard it?—"*I* [am] a *Maroon*. I [AM] A MA-
> ROON. Do you believe that? Do you feel that? Or do you *know* that? Look
> in my face, very close. Me seh, look *very* careful, man. You see a Maroon?"

In their own element, these Kromanti specialists were more demonstrative than most Maroons. Yet I was repeatedly surprised when individuals who had not previously shown that side of themselves suddenly erupted into similar displays of deep feeling. Often the catalyst was rum.[1]

Some months later, I commented on one such incident in my journal. The reason it seemed noteworthy was that the individual concerned, a middle-aged Maroon named Ren, had never evidenced such a strong sense of Maroon identity in my presence before, although I had seen him almost daily for the last six months. On the face of it, he was hardly a diehard "traditionalist." As a young man he had emigrated to England, where he had spent several years toiling as a wage laborer on various urban construction projects; upon returning to Moore Town, he had settled back into a life of farming and joined an evangelical church. Like most others belonging to local churches, he claimed to have "given up" attending Play (Kromanti ceremonies)—in which, in any case, he had never been more than an occasional participant.

> Ren entered [a rum shop in Moore Town]. He was obviously feeling his
> spirits and so was more gregarious than usual. He insisted on buying me a
> few pints and having me lend an ear to his commentary, which was spiced
> with bits of Maroon Language— quite deep, even though he had told me
> several times before that he knew hardly any of the Language. Then, as
> Dick [a Maroon in his early twenties who had always professed a total
> disinterest in things Maroon] edged up to us and listened in, Ren began to
> exclaim that he is a Maroon, a definite Maroon, and nobody can ever take
> that from him . . . *never!* They could hold him fast, ten of them at once, and
> put a knife to his throat, but still he would never say that he is not a
> Maroon. They could do anything they want, but they would never ever be
> able to make him say anything other than that he is a full, definite Maroon.

The embattled tone of this proclamation of identity is easily understood in the Jamaican context. In the 1970s, as now, the Maroon communities hung in a delicate state of suspension, poised between a local discourse of Maroon autonomy and a state policy of cooptation and gradual assimilation. It was usually when the Jamaican government had something at stake—when disagreements over electoral politics, jurisdiction and police powers, land rights, and other such matters raised the specter of genuine Maroon autonomy—that the authenticity of claims to a distinct Maroon identity was thrown into question. When it served the ideological needs of the Jamaican state, Maroons could publicly revel in the symbolism of their past. But when "serious" issues such as land valuation, taxation, and clashing notions of "sovereignty" periodically forced the national government to acknowledge the unresolved status of the treaties of 1739, the Maroons were expected to fall into line and relinquish any surviving vestiges of legal or political autonomy.[2] Maroons who vocally pressed their claims were typically met with paternalistic skepticism. Why did they "stubbornly" continue to invoke an anachronistic treaty? Hadn't they been bringing internal disputes to outside courts for years? Were they really different enough from other Jamaicans to merit special treatment under the law? If their communal lands were divided and privately sold to individuals, as was advocated by some, wouldn't the inhabitants of Maroon communities, for all intents and purposes, be indistinguishable from other Jamaicans?

It is precisely when challenged on such points that Maroon emotions are most likely to flare up—whether material resources or more abstract notions of cultural integrity and identity are at issue. The Maroon ethos, evinced in narratives like those that follow, rules out yielding to the conflicting claims of outsiders, unless it is on one's own terms. Any statement or action by an outsider that is perceived as threatening, any affront to the Maroon ideology of proud self-rule, is likely to be met with a swift and firm response. Should a dispute between Maroons and outsiders escalate to the point where aggressive action of any kind, symbolic or real, is taken against a Maroon community, rapid mobilization for defense is a virtual certainty.

Underlying this combative stance is the lingering imprint of a militant past, a history of threatened survival and defiant resistance that is kept alive in Maroon enclaves through daily telling and retelling. Accounts stressing the unconquerability of the ancestors not only instill a defiant sense of pride, but they also serve to remind younger generations that the dangers of the past have not been laid entirely to rest. Many still believe that powerful agents such as those that attempted to destroy the Maroons in pre-treaty times will one day try again.[3] In their view, the only insurance against reenslavement or annihilation is an unyielding stance toward any infringement of the principle of Maroon autonomy. In fact, stories of Maroon indomitability are not limited to the time of war, when collective survival was most severely threatened. Many of the minor skirmishes and altercations between Maroons and outsiders that have taken place since then have made their way into the corpus of Maroon oral traditions; a few are presented later in this chapter.

As recently as 1946, a land dispute in the Moore Town area led to a serious confrontation when Jamaican colonial police entered that community and attempted to arrest a man without first consulting the Maroon colonel and his council. Anticipating trouble, the police command sent well over a hundred men from Port Antonio—an unnecessarily heavy-handed gesture that no one with a knowledge of the Maroon propensity to rise to a challenge would likely have sanctioned. An account of the tense encounter that ensued, written by Colonel C.L.G. Harris some twenty years after the fact, gives an idea of how the narrative past (invoked here by elliptical references to Nanny, the abeng, and the Kromanti drums) is often used to frame more recent events in Maroon discourse:

> The sight of so many armed men storming their gates wrought immediate transformation on the now peaceful Maroons—their cohesion and discipline reached new heights of perfection; the spirit of Nanny lived again. Shattering the morning calm the abeng flung its urgent message across the hills; the drums beat their imperative commands;[4] and the answering echoes brought the kinsmen from Cornwall Barracks, Kent, Ginger House and Comfort Castle with uncanny speed to the scene of potential danger . . . But adopting certain methods which this writer is not at present free to reveal, the Maroons thwarted every design. And as the evening shadows began to lengthen and the clansmen repaired to their O'sofu[5] House, their common meeting place, and the subdued roll of the drums became more and more haunting, more and more enchanting, more and more unnerving, one hundred and twenty-five uniformed men [colonial police officers]—their duty unaccomplished through no fault of theirs—returned to their headquarters with deathless memories of what they had heard and seen.[6]

Colonel Harris's ornate prose clearly sets this passage off from the narratives told by most Maroons, but the message is the same. Oral accounts of such clashes with outside authority, whether these belong to recent times or the more distant past, are usually equally rich in the rhetoric of defiance.

The narratives selected for this chapter illustrate this theme with particular clarity. Each set of texts presented below contains an archetypal image of Maroon indomitability: Maroon warriors bravely standing up to the "tests" of the distrustful British governor during Paul Bogle's rebellion, even as they reaffirm their loyalty to the British crown[7] [1–4]; defiant men and women taking action against government surveyors or other intruders [5–10]; and outraged "older heads" ready to repel anyone with the audacity to try and collect taxes on Maroon lands [11–13]. Emotionally potent images such as these continue to inhabit the consciousness of the "true-born" Chankofi, lying in wait for the first suggestion of a challenge or threat.

This consciousness and the associated emotions remain close to the surface in all of the Maroon communities. I was reminded of just how close in January 2000, while canvassing opinions in Accompong on a proposal by the Jamaican government to establish a nature park or biodiversity reserve in an area of the Cockpit Country overlapping with Maroon communal lands. Despite the repeated gestures by representatives of the Jamaican government to show good intentions, most in the community feared that the proposed project was a trick designed to rob the Maroons of their treaty lands and bring about their demise as a people. Emotions ran high, and I heard so many defiant oaths of resistance that I was unable to keep track of them all. One, uttered by a young man surrounded by an admiring group of teenagers, stands out in my memory: "Me ready fe kill people fe dis likkle piece a land weh Kojo shed blood fa!" (I'm ready to kill people for this little piece of land that Kojo shed blood for!) To this I would add my own admonition: doubt not that this young Maroon meant what he said.

Standing Up to Tests

The following narratives [1–4] focus on a legendary public performance of collective Maroon power—both military and spiritual—in the distant past, during a period when the British colonial government urgently needed proof that the Maroons were still dependable allies and had lost none of the fighting skills for which they were renowned.

Standing Up to Tests: The Maroons Prove Themselves on the Eve of Bogle's War

Despite the statement by one of the narrators to the contrary, the oral tradition referenced by the next four texts [1–4], recounting a tense encounter in Port Antonio between "Governor Eerie" (i.e., Governor Eyre), Colonel Fyfe, and the Maroons during a period of "martial law," is most certainly related to the rebellion led by Paul Bogle in St. Thomas parish in 1865. Indeed, archival evidence confirms that an emergency meeting between the parties mentioned in these narratives actually did take place in Port Antonio shortly after the Morant Bay rebellion began.

As Gad Heuman (1994: 131) points out, the Jamaican government at first doubted the Maroons' loyalty, partly because of a rumor that they had decided to back Bogle.[8] The Maroons' military competence was also in question, since they had not served on a regular basis as a tracking force since emancipation became final in 1838.

Governor Eyre needed reassurance. "When he traveled to Morant Bay two days after the outbreak," Heuman writes, "the Governor took along the former commander of the Maroons, Colonel Alexander Fyfe." Heuman (1994: 131) goes on to tell us that "Fyfe met about 200 Maroons assembled at Port Antonio when he arrived there on 15 October [1865] with Governor Eyre."[9] The details of what transpired during this encounter, however, apparently went unrecorded. If, as the present-day Maroon oral tradition maintains, Governor Eyre and Colonel Fyfe made a bet regarding the Maroons' loyalty and courage, it is not surprising that this detail never made its way into the official records. Such a wager would have remained a private affair between two gentlemen. To the Maroons themselves, however, Colonel Fyfe's dramatic display of confidence in them—his willingness to stake a great deal (his "life") on their loyalty and military skill— would have spoken volumes, and would most likely have impressed them as one of the most memorable things about the encounter.[10]

Heuman (1994: 131) notes that Fyfe, who had commanded some of the Maroon troops sent out more than thirty years earlier to suppress the 1831–32 slave rebellion, "was a highly respected figure among them."[11] At the very least, the historical tradition narrated below, along with the associated praise song to Colonel Fyfe ("Colonel fight fe come, fe honor Maroon"), would seem to bear this out.

In effect, the story casts the Maroons as both loyal and defiant at the same time—loyal toward Colonel Fyfe, whom they knew and trusted, and defiant toward the tyrannical governor, who needed to be humbled with a frightening demonstration of the Maroons' courage and—should it come to that—their indomitability, even in the face of a vengeful tyrant such as the infamous "Governor Eerie."

[1]

> Kanal [Colonel] fight fe come-oo
> fe honor Maroon-ee
> ee—, ee-de-ee—
> me never fail me color, mam[12]
> me never fail-ee
> we cyaan fail we color
> me cyaan fail-oo
> but since me dasha mek we[13]
> we benta war-ee[14]
> we wi benta war-oo
> we wi benta-ee
> mek wi benta war-oo
> we a benta-ee
> mek we benta war-ee
> we a benta-oo
> but since me dasha mek me-oo
> mek we benta war-ee
> me no fraid fe bullet neither, mumma-oo
> me no fraid fe lion, me da tiger, mama

(James Downer, William Watson, and Richard Deans, December 23, 1977)

[2]

One was a man by de name of Isaac Ellis. And one name Briscoe. Those were the leaders in Blaka River [Moore Town] then. Well, they play a good part, for in going out to battle they were the man who really go and raise their men to fight out there, without losing any.

So they went to Port Antonio to meet the colonel. At those days he was a white man, Colonel Fyfe. At the day when them went there, it was Governor Eerie days. He and Fyfe come to Port Antonio on de ship. So when Governor Eerie see de Maroons, him say they were de rebels. Fyfe say no, is the Maroon. Governor say no, is the rebels.

Fyfe say, "no. Well, I will bet you so many thousands, if you throw a bomb at the Maroons, they will out it."

Well, dem mek dem bet, and dem come off along shore, and Governor Eerie put out his soldiers, and Fyfe put out his Maroons, and they order: "fire!"

Well, when it follow de fire now, there were not a Maroon hurt.

So Governor Eerie get frighten now. So him took de Maroons, and him went round to Town Hall—we call it now Port Antonio courthouse—and him give dem rum and gun and thing, and tell dem now fe go and go kill people. It was a *terrible* thing, though!

(Johnny Minott, September 10, 1978)

In the town [Port Antonio] a large number of special and rural constables had been collected by the authorities, and some of the Maroons had come down from Moore Town to assist, but all were without arms or ammunition, beyond a few old guns or swords, that were of little value for any purpose. . . . I personally inspected the Maroons, a fine body of about 150 men, who, in the most loyal spirit, had come down on the day preceding our arrival, ill-armed as they were, determined to protect Port Antonio. They were unbounded in their devotion and loyalty, and were beyond measure delighted to see again their former captain, the Honourable A. G. Fyfe, whom I had brought with me in the Wolverene, and under whose orders they at once placed themselves. (dispatch from Governor Eyre, October 20, 1865, printed in the Supplement to the *London Gazette*, November 17–18, 1865; from clipping in West India Reference Library, National Library of Jamaica)

[3]

Governor Eerie's time. It was at those time that de slaves, or otherwise we would call it "negroes," a who raise a rebellion. Not Bogle's time.

At those time, de Maroon colonel was of de name of Colonel Fyfe. And he sent and him invite de Maroons to Port Antonio. [The Maroons] of Moore Town [were] de Maroon who went.

Well, he comes with de governor to Port Antonio, but it was a rebellion time. That mean man a chop up man—white men, and all those—me no mean a chop up negro, you know. Because, it was a rebellions time.

And when dem reach in Port Antonio, Colonel Fyfe him look over and him saw de Maroon. Him know dem, for him was de colonel, so him must know dem.

De governor say, "a de rebellion that, doing dem rebellious thing."

But Colonel Fyfe say, "no. These are Maroons. And if you throw any bombs out there, de Maroon will out it."

Him say, "no." De governor say, "no, they are rebellious."

And Colonel Fyfe say, "well now, I bet you so many thousand pounds against me life that they are Maroons and if you fling anything out there that burns, de Maroon will out it."

And dem sign papers on de ship.

And de Colonel Fyfe step out.

You hear de Maroon have a sing that sing like this: "Colonel a go come fe honor Maroon . . ." Is de tune. That was Colonel Fyfe dem talking about.

So when him come off, him put his Maroon in line—because de Maroon know him and him know dem—in a ways like a man putting out a army.

And de governor pull out his soldiers, and him say to de governor, him say, "well, fire."

And when de soldiers fire there was no Maroon hurt.

But de Maroon have never hurt a soldier, because it was only just to pass a little test.

Well, at that time Colonel Fyfe tek de Maroon now.

De governor, him say, "go a Port Antoni, de courthouse"—dem call it "Towns Hall" at those days—"and give dem rum and meat and food, and give dem *gun* too!"

At those days gun use with powder, you wad it and . . . (makes a motion as if loading a barrel) . . . to fire. It was not like how we use cartridge these days.

And him tell dem fe come down, go kill people, man. And dem kill people *dread*, you know, man. Dem kill people dead fe true. Because de governor was frightened fe what happen. It was a different time from Bogle's rebellion.

(Johnny Minott, June 4, 1978)

[4]

You have Colonel Fyfe. Maroon colonel. But Maroon no say "colonel," dem say "kanal." So Kanal Fyfe a white man like you. White man. So a fe-dem kanal that.

So Kanal Fyfe *bet* Governor Eerie. Him say if him shoot *one* of de Maroon, him fe tek fe-him life. Governor Eerie a white man too. But a him min deh a Jamaica, so him bet against him. Him [Kanal Fyfe] say if him shoot one of de Maroon, him fe tek him life.

Dem sign for it fe true. Governor Eerie sign fe money, fifty thousand, sixty thousand, fe shoot Maroon fe true.

And when de day . . .

Look ya. Look ya, boy! Ship draw alongside so, "wap!" Soldier pon it. *Soldier*. All Maroon ina line. And when de officer say, "shoot!," all gun go off one time, "di-di-di-di-dim!"

When dem look, dem see smoke, *bare* smoke. So dem *feel* say dem got Maroon. And when de smoke wear off, when de smoke wear off, a so dem see Maroon got him afana [machete] ina dem face. *All* de Maroon put afana a dem face, and dem no shoot one.

A bet him bet. Just a bet. A Kanal Fyfe tell him so, tell Governor Eerie say if him shoot one of de Maroon, him fe tek fe-him, Kanal Fyfe, life. Just a bet. Him say *one*, you know, him no say de whole of dem, him say *one*. If him shoot *one*, him fe tek him life. And when him look fe true, and see, well then, one of de Maroon, not even a chip, not even a *chip* what wrong with Maroon, him have fe draw man so, draw man, draw man, draw man, give Kanal Fyfe.

When [the Maroons] hear Kanal Fyfe [was coming] up a Moore Town, dem say, "Kanal a go come"—that a fe honor Maroon, but dem a true blue forever. That mean say dem naa fail. Dem naa fail. That's right.

> hamba dasha, me lean but me naa fall
> when me go fe lean, me lean right and left side
> me a hamba dasha, but me lean, but me naa fall

(James Downer, September 27, 1978)

Protecting Maroon Lands

With the possible exception of taxation (discussed in the next section), no question has caused more contention between the Maroons and the Jamaican government than that of land rights. From the government's point of view, it has always been apparent that the Maroons' existence as peoples apart rested in large part on their possession of commonly held territories. Following emancipation, when the colonial government decided it would be in its interest to assimilate the Maroons into the general population, the vehicle chosen was the Maroon Lands Allotment Act. This 1842 legislation aimed to abrogate the treaties of 1739 and absorb the Maroons into the emergent peasantry by dividing the communally owned Maroon lands and parceling them out to individual owners (Kopytoff 1973: 270–83). The Maroons of the two main towns, Accompong and Moore Town, simply ignored the new law and it was never enforced. The smaller Windward villages of Charles Town and Scot's Hall, however, eventually did lose some of their corporate land, partly as a result of later attempts to apply this law.

Maroons in all the present-day communities share the perception that the Jamaican government has always been intent on "robbing" them of their sacred "treaty lands." Viewing their communally held lands not only as a sacred inheritance from their ancestors, but also as a key to their survival as distinct peoples, they have staunchly resisted all efforts—whether by outsiders, or by Maroon defectors—to compromise the integrity of these territories (Besson 1997: 209; 2000: 119; Zips 1998).

Maroon narratives about the defense of their lands usually end with the Maroons as the victors. The Maroons' antagonists vary—in some cases being dishonest government surveyors sent to clarify boundaries or resolve disputes or, in others, neighboring landowners encroaching on their territory—but the common thread running through most of these accounts is the heroic use of Maroon spiritual power to overcome such threats.

In the first group of texts below [5–6], concerning a land dispute in the Charles Town area, a Maroon leader, Colonel Rashworth, defies the Jamaican governor to his face, who responds by sending out colonial troops. When the troops surprise the Maroons and take them into custody, the latter use their "Science" to burst their shackles, causing the Governor's soldiers to flee in terror.

Next, Colonel Harris of Moore Town tells of a well-known confrontation between a government surveyor and the Maroons of that community early in the twentieth century [7]. The Maroons had allowed the surveyor onto their lands to help with the construction of a road. According to the Maroons, this surveyor insisted, despite their objections, that the planned road run right through the sacred place they call the [A]safo Ground. In this narrative, the uncooperative government surveyor soon finds himself contending with Kromanti mediums possessed by the enraged spirit of Grandy Nanny. Unnerved by the threatening gestures and strange expressions of defiance around him, he retreats, and the survey is abandoned.[15] The other narrative by Colonel Harris [8] concerns an earlier attempt by the government to survey Maroon lands so they could be divided up and sold to Maroons individually. Concerted action by the council of Moore Town brings the plan to a halt, and the Maroons vow never again to allow a surveyor onto their lands uninvited. It is interesting to note in this connection Mavis Campbell's observation that "all Maroon communities, at some time or another, were opposed to surveyors; Moore Town, however, seems unique in opposing them in such a sustained manner" (Campbell 1988: 174).

Following this, Colonel E. A. Downer of Moore Town, in a narrative recorded around 1960 [9], tells of how a land dispute in the Seaman's Valley area, on the northern border of the Maroon treaty lands, was resolved through diplomatic means. This conflict had been simmering since the 1930s. (As we shall see, it actually had a much deeper history, being rooted in a specific Maroon land claim going back to the late eighteenth century). A non-Maroon family, the Daures, claimed to have purchased a portion of the Seaman's Valley property abutting Moore Town, which the Maroons insisted had been occupied and cultivated by their ancestors from time immemorial. The dispute flared up into a number of open confrontations, leading in 1946 to government intervention, including the sending of a large police detachment to Moore Town (Harris n.d.: 77–79; Scott 1968: 73–74). (This tense standoff received much coverage in the local press, and is the very event glorified by Colonel C.L.G. Harris in the passage from the *Daily Gleaner* quoted in the introduction to this chapter.) Eventually the dispute was settled through negotiation with the colonial government. Colonel Downer's account of this process, in which he played a central role, is noteworthy for its calm, genteel tone, in contrast to several of the other narratives about land disputes presented here. It projects the kind of cool-headed assurance, and is told in the relatively elevated register of English, that would be expected of a Maroon colonel discussing such matters with respected outsiders. But it is no less passionate for this. And in its emphasis on the mutual respect shown between the Maroon colonel and the Jamaican governor—then the highest British authority in the land—as well as the eventual triumph of the Maroon disputants, it conveys the same sense of indomitability as these other narratives.[16]

The final text in this section [10], from Accompong, explicates an old Kromanti song specifically designed, according to the narrator, to raise the spirit of Kojo and inflict a deadly blow against any government surveyor who comes to the area with the intention of "robbing" Maroon lands.[17]

In all these narratives, the indomitability of the Maroon spirit is a dominant theme. When Colonel Rashworth [5–6] barges in on the governor with muddy bare feet and blurts out the incendiary words, "I hear a challenge; I send none, and I refuse none"—or when the Moore Town Maroons, in one of the other narratives [8], categorically refuse to comply with a government-mandated survey, ominously adding, "we are prepared"—there can be no doubt in the listener's mind that the Maroons remain a people who will do whatever is necessary to defend the lands won with the blood of their ancestors.

Protecting Maroon Lands: The Kildair Conflict

The first two narratives below [5–6], told by a Moore Town Maroon, are clearly related to a series of events that actually did take place, probably during the late eighteenth century, but receive only fragmentary mention in the archives. Barbara Kopytoff (1973: 145) writes that "in 1794 a surveyor found that most of the Charles Town Maroons' provisions were grown on lands belonging to the Kildair estate, but that the Maroons, with their long customary use of the land, were unwilling to give it up." She adds that "the resolution of this dispute is not recorded, if indeed it was resolved at all." Mavis Campbell (1988: 171) also mentions the dispute, stating that "when the 1794 survey of Charles Town was taken, it was discovered that [the Maroons] were occupying 94 acres of land belonging to the Kildair property." She goes on to quote the current Charles Town superintendent, who says that the Maroons were "unwilling to give [it] up, having their provisions chiefly upon that land." The superintendent's report makes it clear that the Maroons felt strongly about the lands in question. He writes that "in order to pacify the Maroons, I was under the necessity of stoping [sic] Mr. Graham, the surveyor, from proceeding upon the lines, till a fair statement of their claims, should be laid before Your Honor" (171). Like Kopytoff, Campbell notes that "it is not clear what became of this dispute," adding her guess that "it was probably "quietened down" through interpersonal persuasions and negotiations" (171). The narratives below, however, would seem to suggest that the dispute continued to heat up for some time before negotiations, if they took place at all, had any success.

It is of course possible that the disagreement over Kildair dragged on over the years, and that the confrontation described in the narratives actually occurred at a later point, perhaps in the nineteenth century.[18] Since Charles Town has a long history of post-treaty land disputes, some leading to potentially violent encounters with Jamaican government forces, the narratives below might represent a cumulative oral tradition incorporating elements from several distinct historical periods and episodes. Although the specific reference to Kildair estate would seem to date the events described in these texts to the 1790s, the story contained in them, in effect, might be made to stand for, or impart moral lessons about, any of a number of more recent confrontations with the government over questions of land. One thinks, for instance, of a well-documented crisis that occurred in the 1890s, when the Charles Town Maroons several times occupied a property called Fyfe's Pen. Barbara Kopytoff states that in 1898 "a large band of [Charles Town] Maroons (one news story estimated 200 men with machetes) marched during the night to several estates, parts of which they claimed as theirs." After an incident in which "a police inspector tried to remove the Maroons' flag and was struck on the head," thirteen of the leaders were arrested, and "the Acting Governor marched two companies of regulars to the area, in addition to the large complement of police" (Kopytoff 1973: 313–17). As late as the 1940s, rumors were circulating that the Charles Town Maroons were planning once again to take over Fyfe's Pen (313–17).

That an oral tradition dealing specifically with long-ago events in Charles Town should have been preserved among Moore Town Maroons who live a considerable distance away should come as no surprise. All three Windward Maroon communities (Moore Town, Charles Town, and Scot's Hall) have maintained close ties since the eighteenth century.[19] The Maroons of Charles Town and those of the Moore Town area, in particular, remain closely connected by a history of intermarriage and frequent visiting.

[5]

[It was] in Charles Town, wherein de governor did want to tek a property from de Maroons at those days. When de governor want to tek that place from de Maroons down there, it was under the leadership of a man—those days de colo-nel [of the Maroons] name Rashworth. Well, Governor Eerie send and tell them that him going to take the property. It name Kildair. Well, Rashworth was a man. In those days, they never frequently used to [wear] boots and shoes, you know?

So him roll up him trousers foot and him walk through Papine and go a Kings House, says to de governor, "Morning, Eerie."

Governor say, "Morning, Rashworth."

Him says, "Eerie, I hear a challenge. I send none, and I refuse none."

Straight back to Charles Town him come, him no listen fe hear what de gov-ernor say, you know.

Well, anyway, about three weeks after, Governor Eerie send down three hun-dred soldier down there. Well, from dem drop in Kildair, dem was sleeping three days.[20] Dem have to go away.

It stay for another time, about six month or a year. One day all de Maroons gone to field, you know, de bigger man dem, to work as dem generally do, co-operation work. Governor Eerie send over some five hundred police in there now. And they arrest every little boy, even like my little son there now, anything name "man." But dem never arrest any woman. None of de tactics-man, nor Rashworth himself, wasn't there. They were at bush.

[The police] start to lead dem out [in handcuffs].

Well, a lady name May stand up and him see these incidents, and she jump ina de house, and go pon de abeng and start to sound it. As soon as de abeng start to sound, the men start to rail, and the handcuff start to burst, that over two hundred of de police get dead!—by dem own weapon, by running, you know?—and pitching over. For they was so frighten. They couldn't know that handcuff could burst that way.

(Johnny Minott, September 10, 1978)

The Maroons remain in possession [of the estate of Fyfe's Pen], and not one of them, if we are to believe what they say, intends to move. And nothing can be more precise and emphatic than their language. Suffice it to say that in my own hearing a Maroon said that if the negro constabulary tried to turn them off the grounds they had seized, they would kill every one of them, or die themselves to the last man. This may, of course, have been mere braggadocio, but it did not sound like it when it was said. (Robinson 1898: 750)

[6]

That was [a woman named] May. It was a property named Kildair. Kildair he was fighting for. A Governor Eerie used to fight dem fe that. Now, it is after war finish, you know. After Grandy [Nanny] war finish. Every governor come a Jamaica always fight de Maroon, you know. *Every* governor come always fight de Maroon. I mean—de crown, they do not know what taking place.

Well, dem want to tek way de spot from de Maroon. [It was during the time of] Colonel Rashworth. And Rashworth walk through Papine bush there and go a town. Dat deh a where you go Buff Bay, through de wood and go up, go a town. Him roll up him trousers foot, man. Roll up dem. Ina mud, you know. De man dem there, in those days, dem deh man, they no wear boots, you know. [Rashworth] no wear boot, no wear no boots, and go all with him foot same way ina mud, and go a Kings House.

Him see de governor, and him say, "morning, Eerie."

Him didn't even said, "morning, His Excellency," or anything. Him say, "morning, Eerie. Eerie, me hear you send you chaniz [challenge, in old Maroon creole]. Me hear you chaniz. Me no send none, and me no refuse none."

Him no stay fe hear what de governor say again, and him turn back through Papine bush back a Charles Town.

Couple of days after that, de governor send three thousand soldier down there. Before dem come down there, dem a sleep three day, can't wake. Dem have fe go way.

One day after that, long after that again, dem gone a bush, gone mek digging. *All* de tactics-man dem gone a bush. And dem send policeman in there fe arrest every Maroon, as long as him name "man." All pon little bit of boy, they handcuff dem. But they no trouble no woman at all. And when dem a go with de man dem—nobody no di-de [was there], de man dem gone a bush, go and work—a one woman jump ina house and pawn [grasp] him akrekre so, *talk* ina de abeng, talk ina de abeng so![21] De Maroon man do so [made some motions invoking spiritual power]—handcuff bust! And de police dem run. Some of dem dead. Bayonet run through some of dem. Bayonet run through some of dem. And when de Maroon man dem do so, de handcuff dem bust.

Rashworth was a powerful man, man, as far as me learn.

(Johnny Minott, February 6, 1991)

[7]

It was right out here, you know. Right out by where you pass the post office here. Now, a little house was up on the hill there that belonged to a woman. But her sister lived there with her. She was an aunt of my mother. And they call her Gallie, or Sister Gallie.

So, a surveyor had prepared to come here, and to make a road through Safo House there to go up to Joe Hill, up in the mountain there.

But since it was going to pass through Safo House—you know, Safo House was regarded as sacred, in those days, and Bump Grave [too]—the Maroons say, "no, no. Nothing . . . no road can be made there."

And they say, "all right."

But the Maroons heard that the man was going to come, even though they protested.

So they said, "all right."

The morning, they saw the buggy—in those days, they didn't have motor cars. The buggy with this man was coming, horse-drawn. And so the abeng was sounded.

In those days, when the abeng is sounded, oh my goodness!—if you are on your meal, if you are hungry, very hungry, and you find this meal was there, it didn't matter to you again. You had to answer.

And people swarmed round. And this woman's sister got up, when the abeng sounded. And she started to dance.

So, this sister—that was the older sister—she called to her [the younger sister], just called her name. You know, in those days, people showed so much respect for elders. Now, she didn't say, "now don't do anything like that." Just called her name.

Suppose her name was Mary. She said, "Mary." And the [younger] sister sat down.

And the abeng sounded again. And this younger one got up. And the elder one there called to her again, called her name. And she sat down.

But a little after that—now there was another house down where the shop was burnt down there—and this older woman, her head turn [i.e., she was possessed by a spirit]. And, oh my, they had to tie her. And they couldn't clear her [of the spirit]. She was like a raging beast. They had to use ropes to tie her. And all the dancer-men [i.e., *fete-man*] came, and couldn't clear her. My goodness, she was like a lioness in her lair, guarding her young. And from early morning until late in the day there, they couldn't clear her. As I say, she was tied there. All [even] some of the things in the house, how she broke up the place.

And then at length, now, they saw [a *fete-man* named Richard Rennock] coming. Now from the time he reach out about a chain from the house, everybody notice how he was walking. Not like himself. He was walking. And as he came, and looked in on her, he said: "u sisa kon fi fete obroni fi Braka Ruba. U te en se fi go sjroom. Arete, arete. Tere tere yu wi a fi yarifo suma."[22]

The voice now was not his voice. It was the voice of Grandy Nanny. Everybody knew right away.

That's what he said: "u sisa kon fi fete obroni fi Braka Ruba. U te en se fi go sjroom. Arete, arete. Tere tere yu wi a fi yarifo suma."

And after he said those words, some of the older relatives came and made an apology for her [the woman who had tried to keep her sister from dancing and becoming possessed]. And they cleared her [her sister].

And then, it was that same day that [a Maroon woman] slapped the surveyor down there. And it was something, that day, man—something, that. She was a

> The Maroons of Scots Hall are protesting the entrance upon their property of Government land valuators who have been carrying out in this parish the new land valuation on the unimproved value basis.
>
> Recently valuators were refused entry into the district when Colonel P. Lattibeaudiere gave orders for the abeng to be blown summoning all Maroons in the area to block the entrance of the valuators.
>
> They are relying upon the Treaty of 1739, which allowed them hundreds of acres free of taxation, to escape the new rates. (Anonymous, "Maroons Bar Land Valuators," *Daily Gleaner*, September 4, 1959)

> Forty or fifty years ago, the Moore Town Maroons were jealous of their tribal land laws, and of any attempt of Government to look too closely at their territory. I knew a man who was imprisoned by them on suspicion of being a Government surveyor. From the Maroon point of view, a survey meant possible lopping off, and tax claims. (Anonymous, "Two Centuries of Maroon Life," *Daily Gleaner*, October 4, 1946)

child, at school, a young lady. She just put down her book. And she slapped the surveyor.

And another woman jumped down in the river there. She took a piece of thing and cut her hand. And the blood flowed, and she jumped down in the river, and ran.

The surveyor was so frightened now. At first, there was a spirit of bravado when he came, you know, because he heard that the Maroons said they couldn't go. He thought this was perhaps nonsense. But now, when he saw that there was only a fine line between him and eternity, he called to the D.C. [District Constable].

I think his [the surveyor's] name was Reed. [The District Constable] was D.C. Bailey. Manny Bailey.

So the surveyor say, "D.C. Bailey, I call upon you to do your duty."

He said, "Sir, today is not my day. Today is Maroon day."

It must have been the Survey Department [that decided to send the surveyor], because, you see, *we* claimed the lands up on the hill there. And now, after Nanny had asked for more lands, and so on, and so on, and so, we had the lands there. Lands that were not ours they spoke of as crown lands. So I am not quite clear on this. But when the surveyor had come to look after the lands for us, there were many cultivations, many fields up there.

Any set of people would want to have good roads leading up into your fields, and so on. But, now, it was when the road was to be actually surveyed, and they found that it is through there—through the Safo House—that they were going to make the road, then they objected. They said no. They couldn't allow it through there. So that was how it go. If the road were to be made somewhere else, it would be all right, but not through Safo House.

(Colonel C.L.G. Harris, January 31, 1991)

[8]

Now, the government made a decree that the land should be given to each Maroon—each Maroon should apply for land, and no more than two acres should be given to those who applied, and, if they have children, so much for each child, perhaps half an acre.[23] I don't remember the exact amount. But they gave the acreage, or the size of the plot that should be given. Well, my grandmother, and those of her family, they actually ran out [part of a survey]. In Moore Town, anytime we say "we are going to run land," they mean that they are going to survey it.

So from up at where you call Old Schoolhouse there, where you see that chicken place there, going above the road too, and coming right down, taking in part of the churchyard, going up on the hill there, and coming down right by here, and going over all where you see that second house over there, and going right around, coming right over, and going back up on the hill: that [surveyed area] is known as the Ellis land. You always hear people talk about "run land."

But immediately after it [the initial survey] was done, a meeting was called. And they all agreed that, after all, that was a wrong thing, for the government to demand that we should survey the land. The land should remain unsurveyed, and be owned communally. And so, then and there, no more piece of the land was surveyed. It was just left like that.

And the government brought three resolutions, at various times in the life of the House of Assembly. And the Maroons of Moore Town decided that they would never comply. They made that decision. And they kept their word. They wouldn't survey, and the government couldn't do anything about it.

They [the government] threatened that if it wasn't done, then what they would do.

And the Maroons said, "well, all right, we are prepared. We'll never do it." And they didn't. And then the government just left it like that.

And so that survey that was actually done became null and void. Of course the land was still known—that piece of land—as Ellis land.

(Colonel C.L.G. Harris, February 6, 1991)

[9]

My principles I adore. They are sacred to me. (Addressing the other Maroons present): And I suppose they are just the same to you. But as far as we are concerned, I never try to make myself to be a subordinate more than to a certain extent. Whether we poor or humble, my name and the place of my birth is my credentials. My God first, the place of my birth, and my family in general.[24]

Up to recently, from since I been appointed colonel of the Maroons, there was one colonel, L. G. Harrison, before me, and next, our own native colonel, MacKenzie. And even then before, we know that we are Maroons. And we were told that we are resting there under treaty.

But what do I get to find? Recently we had an upstirring in the Maroon population here concerning some lands. I was appointed by my people to take up the affair with His Excellency the Governor, Sir John Huggins. And I did so. When I was going, I got credentials from my people, from Moore Town and the adjoining district of Cornwall Barracks. I handed in my papers, accompanied by all my officers that were appointed—Major Harris is standing here—Mr. Harris, the secretary, Captain Smith from Barracks, and two or three others. Before Sir John Huggins at King's House, I handed in my credentials from the people.

He asked me if I was a Maroon.

I say, "yes, I'm a born Maroon."

He asked me if I was elected by the people.

I say, "unanimously."

He took the papers, and he said to me, "Colonel, now that I get to know that you have been appointed by the people, I am not afraid to talk to you in the right and proper way. When I came into the island a couple of years ago, I heard . . . I never know that there were Maroons in the island. At least I never know that there were such distinguished people in Jamaica until recently, when there was some land trouble here. I get to see in The Gleaner that there were Maroons that were standing on their treaty."

Those were words by Sir John Huggins.

"I went down to the museum, [continued the governor], and I borrowed a book. And when I came back after reading the book, I said—I point to my breast, and I said—providing I never know that I had people that was standing behind a treaty in this island, and I have made it my resolved determination that, should in case they have any trouble, and they should approach me decently as how you have done, I shall ever make request to satisfy you people. Anyway, your land trouble, colonel, I have got to dive down way into the bottom of it to get the true sense from it. So, anyway, go home and tell your people, don't be in a haste. I will look after their matter, and I will try to satisfy them."

We left King's House. We came home.

We were called back a second time. At that time, Portland was represented by Sir Harold Allan. He accompanied the deputation. When we went to Kings House, His Excellency the Governor consider it was wise to get a surveyor, a

Partially clothed in foliage and equally peculiar attire, one blowing a horn known as the "abeng" all of them making hideous sounds, and beating drums, a crowd of Maroons (about one hundred in number) from Moore Town, 9½miles from this town [of Port Antonio], startled the residents of Seaman's Valley, one mile from Moore Town, at mid-night last Tuesday. . . . The mob marched past [the] home [of Mr. Sylvian Daure, owner of Seaman's Valley Estate] that night to where his deceased relatives have been buried, and there they burned duck-ants' nests and spoke in peculiar languages. (Anonymous, "Maroons Attack the Owner of Seaman's Valley Estate and Make the Night Hideous," *Daily Gleaner*, May 17, 1933)

government surveyor, and survey right around the Maroon lands, in order to find out the trouble. Because the trouble was between the Maroon main lands and the property of Seaman's Valley that was owned by the Daures.

He got the surveyor. And the surveyor came here. And all the Maroons devoted the time. Some was working, they got paid. But I individually as the leader, in order for the protection of the survey . . . if I absent one day, I would never absent two days. And whenever I was absent, my second, our secretary Mr. Harris, was there, to protect the interests of the Maroons, until the whole land was surveyed right through.

The surveyor was Mr. McClure, L. Van McClure. And, after he had left, I got notice from the governor that we were to meet him at King's House for a decision. Sir Harold Allan was there. And if I am saying anything that is false, there is Major Harris standing there, he can bear testimony to what I am saying, because he was one of those that was on the deputation from the starting to the finish. And all the time that we did go in deputation, the funds was subscribed by the Maroon population around here. Every night we had meeting, and they sacrificed themselves of their pennies and truppence in order to take us to Kingston, and be back. Because the land that we were fighting for was for each and every Maroon.

Anyway, that had lasted a couple of months, and the job was through. When we got notice that I should meet Sir John Huggins and his staff at King's House . . . because I got a tip from some source that in the survey finding, the land was only forty acres short [rather than the two hundred plus acres the Maroons were claiming]. But I was satisfied to myself, where the lands that we had been fighting for, we had due claim to the land. You see? So, I wrote back to His Excellency the Governor, and asked him to get out the old original plan of 1782, the work of Dougald McPherson, the surveyor that surveyed the Maroon grant lands. That was in the year 1782.[25]

And I said to His Excellency, "please get a copy of that said same title—diagram—Dougald McPherson's work of 1782, and put it on the table for me."

We went to King's House. And there were all sort of officials around the table. And His Excellency the Governor opened the speech.

He said, "Colonel, I am very glad that you have come. But the only one thing—I have tried my utmost endeavor to satisfy your people. You see the pain that I have taken. But it is much regrettable that according to the surveyor's report, it is just that your land is only forty acres short."

When he said so, the surveyor-general said, "I will take care of that, sir, just leave that to me."

And the surveyor-general got up, and he said, "you see, Colonel, the work that was done by government surveying is quite a different principle today. First-time they go down into the ditches, but now they stretch across the ditch. So that forty acres short is done owing to the modern surveyor, to what is going on."

I said, "yes, Your Excellency, I thank you very much for the pain and trouble that you have taken to settle this matter. And I do hope, sir, that the surveyor Mr. McClure has given a good account of how we tried to protect him and help him to go through his work."

I say, "well, sir, I'm very sorry, but anyway, I can't state about the surveying, because the surveyor has got a plan, and he is supposed to work by his plan. So as far as surveying is concerned, I am perfectly satisfied. But I am asking you, sir, have you got that old original plan of 1782?"

He said, "yes."

I suppose every one of the gentlemen around the table was clapping.

I said, "anyone that is around the table, please read the inscription that is written to the bottom of that plan."

Because *we* had seen the plan before! And we knew exactly what was written there. I may not have seen it, but older people hinted me what was written there.[26] And we were still hunting for that plan. And that was one of the exact plan that was given to us.

And then they started to read, they say, "I, Dougald McPherson"—that is the inscription that is written like a title deed at the bottom of the plan—"I duly surveyed one thousand acres of land known as Moore Town. But in reaching the border line between the patent of Charles Knight and Barbara Stevenson, I have found where the Maroons had penetrated over on these two patents. I communicated with the imperial government, because I was afraid that the Maroons might make trouble if I destroyed their fields. And they said to me that I must circle around the fields. Don't destroy it, just circle around the fields. When I circled around it, I found where the Maroons had penetrated 276 acres on those two patents—patents of Barbara Stevenson and Charles Knight. Therefore the Moore Town lot was increased from 1,000 acres to 1,276 acres. So help me God."[27]

And when the matter was clarified before His Excellency the Governor, he simply stretched across the table, and he shook me hand.

His Excellency the Governor Sir John Huggins, K.C.M.G., M.C., was in conference for over one hour yesterday at King's House with a deputation, led by the Hon. Sir Harold Allan, Kt., O.B.E. representing the Maroons of Moore Town, Portland.

The Hon. J. Leslie Cundall, acting Attorney General, and Mr. H. Lindo, of the Secretariat, Major F. J. Quinton, Director of Surveyors, and Mr. L. Van McClure, Government Surveyor were also present.

Members of the deputation were: Colonel E. A. Downer, Mr. J. T. Harris, M.P.B., Secretary of the Moore Town Maroons, Captain Leonard Smith and Major James M. Harris.

Object of the deputation centred on lands in Portland that the Maroons claim they had occupied for over 150 years and that they are now being molested by the owners of Seaman's Valley Estate. . . .

The Governor, according to the deputation, said that as the Maroons have been on the lands so long and had cultivated them, he would suggest that if the Maroons were satisfied, Government would endeavour to procure the lands from the owners for the use of the Maroons. ("Maroons See Governor on Land Claims," Daily Gleaner, April 8, 1949)

And he says, "Colonel, you have honorably won. 1782!"

I says, "Your Excellency, if there is a British law, and if the British law stands for truth and justice, after a person is in charge of land for over 160 years, if he is not entitled to the land as a owner, he is entitled to a squatter's right."

He says, "you are perfectly in honor, you are well honorable."

He turned to me, he says, "Colonel, do you know the owners of the property that you could go? We will back you up with the money to buy those."

I say, "Your Excellency, I wouldn't do it, because I am fighting for justly what I know that I have claim. The people that are claiming the lands have no more right to it more than I do. And I would not be manly to go to work, and then fighting for justly what I know was mine, and then to go offer a bribery of money after. I wouldn't undertake to do that, sir."

He says, "well, all right. Sir Harold, will you communicate with the owners of this property?"

Sir Harold Allan was a Member of Parliament for the parish, and a sincere friend of the Maroons.

He said, "yes, Your Excellency, I'll take care of that."

They bought out 276 acres from the then owners—because they were paying taxes for the land—and they handed it over to me, as a supervisor for those lands, for the Maroon population in general.

So Sir John Huggins has done a remarkable work for we the Maroons.

(Colonel Ernest Downer, December/January, 1960/61)[28]

From the time the Maroons were established as a free body, no dispute had arisen with them till the year 1773, when, some surveyors being employed to mark the lines of the adjoining patents, or grants of crown-lands, for the purpose of determining the boundaries of their 1500 acres conceded by treaty to them, they took alarm, supposing an encroachment to be made on their territory, and threatening the surveyors. (Dallas 1803a: 128)

---

[10]

There was one surveyor [named McPherson] that was cutting the lands again, right around [where] we call Thatch Bottom, and he never fall down, or get any bruise pon any stones or anything, but he start to bleed, bleed blood, that you had was to tie up the foot, right across here, and right down to the ankle. And him bleed, that McPherson.[29] And he get dead, superstitiously. It was ghost that kill him. And . . . (laughs slightly under his breath) . . . so many various things happen.

Kojo says . . . they going to rob the lands. But anytime [surveyors] start to rob the lands, [one] must sing this song (speaking the words): "sáli kóta mónde, sáli kóta mónde, den wai shála dóndi, sáli kóta mónde, den wai shála dóndi, a-ya, a-ya, sáli kóta mónde, den wai shála dóndi." And it will give him [Kojo] power to raise up. (sings):

> sáli kóta mónde
> sáli kóta mónde
> sáli kóta mónde
> de wai shádo dóndi
> ay-ah
> ay-ah
> sáli kóta mónde
> de wai sháda dóndi

And it will give him, Kojo, power to raise up, to raise up from the grave—anytime they coming to rob the land.

(Mann Rowe, December 4, 1999)

Flogging Tax Collectors

"That [i.e., a proposal by the Jamaican government to tax the Maroons] we will not tolerate!" declared Joshua Anderson, 52. "I myself would go back to the bush to fight the Jamaicans, like we fought the white man!"
—Dan Perry, "Past Glories Still Drive Independence-Minded Maroons" (1999)[30]

It might interest you to know that for some time past the descendants of Maroons at Accompong Town have been offering up sacrifices of pigs goats & fowls—blood-offerings in fact—at the spot which is supposed to mark the cite [*sic*] of the grave of old Accompong, one of the parties mentioned in the old "Treaty" of 1738, after whom the Town was named. It is situated on the land where the Town was originally build [*sic*], & which is . . . now known as the old Town & the spot is marked by a large tree, of a kind unknown to me. The ceremonies have been taking place at dead of night accompanied by beating of the "Goombay" & the discharge of firearms, & their object is to invoke the spirit of old Johnny Accompong to prevent the Government from levying taxes on the Maroons. (confidential report from Inspector Herbert T. Thomas to the Inspector General, Black River, October 24, 1904; Maroon Manuscripts from Mahogany Hall, West India Reference Library, National Library of Jamaica)

For Maroons, the idea of taxation has a symbolic weight entirely different from the literal, material burden that taxes represent for other Jamaicans (Harris n.d.: 216–17; Martin 1973: 115–18). Closely tied to the sanctity of Maroon "treaty lands" is the notion that these must forever remain tax-free—a fundamental stipulation, Maroons today argue, of the sacred oath made by their ancestors with the British in 1739. To Maroons, freedom from taxation means freedom from rule by others; it signifies the inviolate principle of Maroon autonomy. Any suggestion that those occupying Maroon lands should be subjected to the same forms of revenue collection imposed on the rest of the country is greeted by most Maroons with indignant disbelief.

Not surprisingly, this has led to many misunderstandings over the years. While the Jamaican state has continued to push for payment of taxes on Maroon lands, claiming that the Maroons enjoy the same government services as other Jamaicans, the Maroons remain adamant on the inviolability of their tax-free status. Every time a government official publicly proclaims that the time has come for Maroons to become full, tax-paying Jamaican citizens, the Maroon leaders and their councils perceive the idea as a grave affront. The impasse over this emotionally charged issue is further complicated by the fact that over the years the original "treaty lands"—with boundaries still in dispute—have been supplemented by additional lands, some granted to Maroon communities as a whole, others paid for by individual Maroons. Whether these too should be considered tax-exempt remains a point of contention.

The ambiguous status of Maroon lands acquired after the treaties is reflected in the following group of narratives [11–13]. At the center of these texts is a nineteenth-century Maroon originally from Charles Town, still remembered by the several names he carried (James Minott, Tom Prince, Jack MacFarlane). A tough, old-time Maroon "fighter" known for his ability to swallow entire eggs raw in the shell, Minott was among the original settlers of Brownsfield, a Maroon branch settlement founded in the 1800s on a newly acquired piece of land in the Rio Grande Valley, a few miles away from Moore Town.

When an employee of the tax office in Port Antonio (in some versions a policeman sent by that office) comes to see him about unpaid taxes on the Brownsfield land, Minott receives him in a friendly manner. "You're not the one who has done this," he says, "it's the *bakra* [white man] who sent you." Before sending him away, he even shares some of the jerk pork and roast yam he had been preparing before the uninvited visitor interrupted him. When the man is gone, Minott goes to the bush to cut a switch, which he tucks under the saddle of his horse (or mule). After riding the eleven or so miles to Port Antonio, he bursts into the government tax office and seizes the tax collector by the arm, pulling him outdoors, so that he can punish him in public. As he whips him with the branch, he castigates him with mocking words: "what do I owe you? . . . why did you send someone to come and corner me?!" Having thus humiliated the offending tax collector for all to see, James Minott—alias Tom Prince, Jack MacFarlane, Wandering Darling— jumps back on the saddle and rides home to Bruk Heart Hill, never again to be bothered by such violations of Maroon autonomy.

Such "great" and "wonderful" men of old, to quote the descendant of James Minott who narrates the second to last text below [12], live on as exemplars of the Maroon indomitability that has helped protect the de facto tax-free status that residents of Moore Town and Accompong enjoy to this day.

[11]

Yes, talking about Tom Prince, Jack MacFarlane, Wandering Darling: cover ina fowl basket, so him nyam fowl egg. Him name Tom Prince. Wandering Darling. Him come from Bangor Ridge.[31] That man now a fe-Johnny Minott [a nineteenth-century Maroon with the same name as one of the narrators in this book] father, same Manku-Hole Jinal father. Him min a *old* fighter way back, him min a old fighter. Jack MacFarlane, Wandering Darling, cover ina fowl basket, and him nyam fowl egg. That mean say him would tek it and put it ina him mouth and nyam go a him belly. That mean say him sabi.[32] Raw egg.

All those man a man who beat collector who collect taxes, like how you woulda got you land. [He was] a Maroon. And dem beat collector, you know. [He] just draw him supple-jack [a whip made from a particular shrub], and just shove it ina him horse—sabi-so [understanding, wisdom]—and just go down, and just draw collector out of de office, and just wap him [struck him with heavy blows], wap him, wap him! . . . [with his] switch. Just wap him: "wap, wap, wap!"

(James Downer, August 23, 1978)

[12]

[James Minott] is a man who plant nuff yam. And de year when him yam bear plenty, him say him a Jack MacFarlane. And de year when it don't bear, him say, well, him a Wandering Darling. That's why they call him so. That mean him do not have plenty yam that year.

In those days, when he have de property [of Brownsfield], he have de property and him owe taxes for everything. But him did not pay taxes. And dem send a policeman to him for it. [It was] before my father time, before Thomas [the narrator's grandfather] time. Is not a simple time. And when de policeman coming, him stay down a Bruk Heart Hill, and call to him. Round de road down so, man. Is a place at de road, dem call it Bruk Heart Hill.

Well, de policeman call to him. But then him say, "me can't look after you today. Go and come back tomorrow."

Well, de policeman go back and come back. And when him come, him carry de paper come give him. Remember, dem roast yam and jerk pork those days, because dem a hunter. And him give him roast yam and jerk pork, and de man gone.

And him go a bush and cut him some jack [the plant used to make the supple-jack whip], and mount him mule and go a Portie—Port Antonio—and get de collector, fe catch him and wap him skin good, ask him what him owe him: "What me owe you? Wha' you send fe me come corner me for? Wha' me owe you?!"

And him jump back pon him mule, come straight a Brownsfield. Him was a very wonderful man that. Him was a Maroon. Him jump back pon him mule and come back a Brownsfield. Those men were great, man.

(Johnny Minott, February 6, 1991)

[13]

A man name Tom Prince, Jack MacFarlane, James Minott. Wandering Jack MacFarlane. You can see how that man is such a *large* man, because him have so much name.

That mean say, him a come from Bangor Ridge—Charles Town, Bangor Ridge. Some [possessing] ghost[s] would call it Kushu Ridge, or Bangor Ridge. [When possessing a *fete-man* in Moore Town], de ghost [of a Charles Town Maroon] himself woulda say him a come from "Bangor Ridge."

So de man name MacFarlane. Him name James Minott. Same man! So you can see what sort of man.

That man, him live at Brownsfield, but him come from Bangor Ridge. So when you go up a Brownsfield, him min live way up pon de hill there. You must see a road turn gone pon de hill up there. A up there de *olden* time people min live.

So, him know about taxes fe de land. So bakra send collector. Maroon people call it "collector." So when dem go fe go call him, him [the collector] have fe

---

> The Maroons of Moore Town were in uproar here recently when they were served with notices to pay taxes for Moore Town, which they claim is their free Treaty Land, given to them for over 100 years.
>
> They were also served rates to pay individual taxes for Kent instead of a rate in the usual way—as a property. No prior notice had been given to the Maroons that they would be required to pay taxes.
>
> They view this matter with great alarm claiming that all the Maroons' possessions are undivided and that the tax papers have been surcharged. (Anonymous, "Maroons to Pay Taxes," *Daily Gleaner*, June 28, 1957)

---

stay down a one place dem call name Bruk [Broke] Heart Hill. That mean to say, if you heart is like a stone, any time you reach a Bruk Heart Hill, you heart come down. That time, that power wha' you go with, it have fe cool. Any time you stay down, call him up a top yard, if him answer say you fe come, you can go. But if him say no, you naa go.

So, dem have a man, and dem send him fe come collect taxes—that mean say a money him a go collect.

Him [Jack MacFarlane] is a man who hunt wild hog. A Maroon man, you know. Jack MacFarlane. Him a man who hunt wild hog and roast him yam, roast afu [a variety of hard yellow yam]. Him roast afu, and him jerk him meat. *Jerk meat.* That's right.

And him call [to the collector]. Him say, "boy! . . ."

That time bakra go up to him.

[He then said to the collector, realizing that it was a black man rather than a white man]: "A so bakra send collector come in." Him say, "boy, a no you do, a bakra send you."

So when him come, him scrape him yam, scrape him yam.

(The narrator's glass of rum suddenly falls off the railing next to him onto the ground.)

You see a truth me a tell you?[33] Sinti come from sali-water come lick me lasi, "plom!"[34]

[Back to the narrative]:

Him scrape him yam, him give you piece, him nyam de yam, *nyam* de yam. Him give him de wild hog meat, and de fat and everything. And him nyam done. Him give de collector. And him done.

Listen wha' me a say good.

Him have him supple-jack. *Nice* supple-jack. Him got him horse, you know—him opongko [horse, in Kromanti language], then, him opongko. Him put it pon him opongko good, de supple-jack. Him push it ina de saddle. Him jump pon it. Dem deh Maroon man wear leggings. Him jump pon him horse back.

Figure 10.1. Annual Maroon celebration, Accompong, January 2002. In center is abeng blower Ralston Reid, and on the right, leading the procession, Colonel Sydney Peddie. Photo: K. Bilby.

When him go down a Port Antonio, him get ina collector office. Him draw collector, catch him hand. Him draw collector from out there, draw out there, whip him out there (claps his hands twice). Flog him. *Flog* collector! Flog him, ina de collector backside.

Him come up, go up pon him horse, and him go back a him yard.

Him no pay no money.

(James Downer, September 24, 1978)

11

Never to Forget

Secrecy, Trust, and Betrayal

Only your friend know your secret,
so only he could reveal it.
—**Bob Marley, "Who the Cap Fit" (1976)**

Yai [eye] see, mouth shut.
He that keepeth his mouth, keepeth his life.
You chat too much, you see you father dead [or, in some versions, you see
your father's debt].
A no everything good fe eat good fe talk (not everything that is good to eat
is good to talk).[1]
Ef fish min shut him mouth, hook kudn catch him (if the fish had shut his
mouth, the hook wouldn't have been able to catch him).
—**Jamaican Maroon proverbs**

[A] part of the frustration in dealing with certain aspects of Maroon affairs
arises from the imperative of secrecy. Secrecy was a pivotal part of their
strategy. This secrecy also precluded any intimate knowledge of their
communities.
—**Mavis Campbell (1988: 5)**

"Trust no shadow after dark," cautions a well-known Jamaican maxim. A Maroon version might well read: "trust no one, ever." Words to live, or die, by.

Secrecy, trust, and betrayal are themes that permeate Maroon consciousness—ideological linchpins that remain at the center of the Maroon ethos. While these ethical abstractions may well represent human universals (taking on different forms when filtered through the prism of a particular culture), they have unusual salience in the Maroon context. For Maroons, secrecy, trust, and the ever-present danger of betrayal are fundamental principles, defining elements of the Maroon condition.[2]

Birth into a Maroon community constitutes a kind of initiation into a secret society. Elsewhere—among many West African peoples, for instance, or in North America, with its fraternal orders and college initiations—secret societies are but parts of a larger social fabric, and their memberships cut across other institutions and social segments. Jamaican Maroons, in contrast, belong to a "secret society" that, at least in theory, encompasses an entire ethnic group; every "true-born"

Maroon, every one of Nanny's *yoyo*, is—or should be—a member.[3] Socialization into this closed society, this ethnic community of both shared "blood" and shared secrets, begins early and continues throughout one's life in a variety of contexts both formal and informal, ranging from Kromanti Play and Maroon council meetings to rum shop gatherings and chance encounters between fellow Maroons and non-Maroon visitors.

Among the most important members of this closed society are the spirits of ancestors; it is they who are the ultimate enforcers of secrecy. One who speaks too freely of "Maroon things" in the presence of "Strangers" (outsiders) runs the risk of incurring the wrath of the *bigi pripri* (Maroon ancestors). One who consciously gives away—or, worse yet, sells—Maroon secrets to a non-Maroon invites disaster: illness, misfortune, and very possibly, death, inflicted by the ever-watchful ancestors. As one Maroon informant told an anthropologist, "'plenty people in Moore Town dead, and plenty sick and can't cure,' because they talked to outsiders about Maroon things—a betrayal of the group that is severely sanctioned by the spirits" (Martin 1973: 72). Although ultimate judgment on such matters rests with the ancestors, friends and family also exert subtle pressures in daily life, reminding fellow Maroons suspected of speaking too openly with outsiders not to overstep the bounds of proper behavior.

The boundaries between what is restricted "inside knowledge" and what can be openly discussed with outsiders are not entirely clear; this renders the whole question of secrecy that much more complex and compelling. Everyone knows that certain areas are off-limits. Almost anything to do with Kromanti Play, for example, should not be discussed in any detail with *obroni*, nor esoteric historical knowledge of the kind preserved in certain old Maroon songs. But even when it comes to less sensitive topics, such as Maroon hunting techniques or culinary practices, just how much can be revealed to non-Maroons remains unclear. In the absence of precise guidelines, it is best to play it safe and restrict conversations with outsiders, particularly when these touch on "Maroon things," to the most superficial level of knowledge. This cautious front merely serves to strengthen the impression among outsiders living in neighboring areas that Maroons are by nature a "secretive people."

When confronted with more persistent outsiders—those unwilling to drop their probing questions—Maroons throw up a seemingly impenetrable wall of secrecy. To fend off meddlesome queries, they have developed and honed a complex set of strategies of evasion, and mastering these is part of the socialization of every "good Maroon." Leann Martin, an anthropologist who came up against such defensive tactics repeatedly while questioning informants in Moore Town, provides us with an accurate description of some of the techniques regularly employed to keep the overly curious at bay. "Strangers," she writes, "are kept friendly by such tactful methods as placing the responsibility for exclusion on the natural or supernatural forces determining one's parentage rather than on human choice, by 'misunderstanding' visitors' questions instead of refusing to answer them, or by explaining restrictions on the outsiders' knowledge and behavior in terms of its necessity for the protection of the outsider himself, or for the safety of his Maroon friends" (Martin 1973: 178).

This kind of institutionalized evasive maneuvering is known to Maroons as "dodging." The term refers not just to skillful avoidance of invasive questions, but to any kind of calculated evasion or trickery, any act of "hiding," whether for self- defense or for personal gain.[4] The concept of dodging is integral to Maroon understandings of their identity. It is seen as a quintessentially Maroon behavior, part of the cultural inheritance that binds present-day Maroons to their ancestors. It is no accident that the English/Jamaican Creole verb *to dodge*, used to express this cardinal Maroon cultural concept, continues to have an equivalent in the esoteric Kromanti language preserved by Maroon *fete-man*: the Akan-derived word, *jijifo*.[5] Just as Kromanti warriors in the ancient days used to *jijifo* the *obroni* enemy, employing evasion and other guerrilla tactics to mislead and trap British troops, their descendants rely on artful "dodging" to hide and protect sensitive Maroon knowledge from outsiders, who continue to be seen as potential enemies that might one day attempt to use such knowledge to destroy them.

As part of this ensemble of ideas surrounding the fundamental concept of "dodging," the Maroon preoccupation with secrecy reflects the historically conditioned imperative of self-preservation, both individual and collective. For secrets shared can easily become secrets betrayed.[6] Very much as among the Saramaka Maroons of Suriname, "the fear of group betrayal, forged in slavery and the decades of war, remains a cornerstone" of the Jamaican Maroon moral system (Price 1983: 12). In the days of war, collective survival was threatened by Maroon "traitors" who, finding the hardships of life in the forest unbearable, defected to the *bakra* enemy and "sold" strategic secrets to them in exchange for promises of freedom and other rewards (Kopytoff 1978: 294) (see chapter 6). Because of such defectors, some of whom operated as spies, the whites were able to discover and target a number of the Maroons' hidden refuges, resulting in critical setbacks for the latter. The risk of betrayal also exists at the individual level. Today, as in the past, the survival of the individual *fete-man* is thought to depend on a secret arsenal of spiritual techniques, a personal "key" that he keeps to himself as a last defense in the event of an overpowering challenge. The *fete-man* must never reveal these ultimate personal secrets, even to those with whom he is most intimate, for one never knows when a trusted colleague (or a lover) may turn against one. Betrayal is a constant possibility, and one might end up defeated by a former (or false) friend who uses one's own secrets, or reveals them to one's enemies, for this very purpose. For this reason, every *fete-man* resolves to go to the grave with his most highly valued secrets intact.

The rationale behind this precaution, in fact, is shared by the entire Maroon community, though it is expressed most clearly by those who deal directly with the powers of Kromanti. Every Maroon is taught from a young age that knowledge is to be dispensed in increments; one must prove himself worthy before being granted access to knowledge of certain kinds. Even relatively common knowledge may be shielded from those considered untrustworthy or irresponsible. For those who wish to know more, particularly of sensitive domains such as Kromanti Play, learning is a rigorous process entailing numerous hurdles and tests, and success depends on a gradual accumulation of trust. But all Maroons recognize that trust, as crucial as it is, is fragile. Early on, through observation and deduction, they learn to hedge their bets. Like Kromanti specialists, most Maroons recognize that one must never reveal all of what one knows, for to do so is to become vulnerable to betrayal. This protective principle—the idea that one most always guard a portion of one's knowledge as a last defense—represents a primary Maroon value, a fundamental tenet that runs as a recurrent theme through many of the narratives in this book. Like Saramaka Maroons in Suriname, Jamaican Maroons continue to teach their children, "never tell another more than half of what you know" (Price 1983: 17).[7]

Keeping and Revealing Secrets

It may be difficult for persons not familiar with Jamaica to accept the fact that in an island of 4,511 square miles the beliefs and practices of groups and individuals have been kept secret for centuries.
—Janet Bedasse and Nella Stewart (1996: 63)

Presented below are a number of direct statements about Maroon secrecy [1–7], followed by two versions of an archetypal story of betrayal [8–9]. In this cautionary story, a powerful *fete-man*, John Swipple-Man (sometimes called by the name of a great wartime leader, Swiplomento, in recognition of his great power), loses his life when he places too much trust in his wife, Aflinting (known to some as Ayinting), revealing to her the secret of his last defense (as well as the one weak point that can be used to overcome it).[8] Closing the section is a "deep" Kromanti song, a powerful Country chant, that warns against placing too much trust in friends: you can "walk with them, talk with them," even "sleep with them," cautions the song, but you must never let down your guard [10].

[1]

You cut him futu, him waka better [if you cut off his leg, he will walk better]. Any damn thing wha' you do with de Maroon, him [continue to] exist. Because Maroon got a book, a secret book wha' hand down from generation to generation, which is a secret.
(Noel Lewis, February 2, 1991)

[2]

You want to hear something about de Maroons? Now, de white people, Maroon call dem "bábasí o wénkeni." White people—like you, and your wife. And we de Maroon do not quickly to taking people in, without we have you test. So we de Maroon, we have to try you people in and out, with our herb, which is our Grandy Nanny weed—bush, rum, water, and so forth. And we have a personal person [who] know you people, what you come about. If you mean for war, peace, or what it may be, we already know. So, as you people come around and trying to hear something, we all are timid to hear you, and to let [you] in our private prerogatives—for we are true blue Maroon who never fail. We never fail, nor we never fall. We can fight the Battle of Waterloo and Trafalgar, and never lose. So we the Maroon, we can never be backgrounded, in anywhere.

(Mother "F," 1952)[9]

[3]

There was a man who come to understand our things. And when we fix our things and tell dem, they go and declare war on us.

And we cannot explain ourself, for if I explain myself, later or sooner you hear that I am a dead woman.

I had to keep *my* secret. *My* grandmother secret made for me to keep. And no one coming here can tell you anything far toward de secret. If you tell as far [as] de secret, de Maroon town will spoil. And if you go and come back, you will never see us again. So is a secret that we have to keep.

Do not step too far to understand de Maroon traditional. It will hurt you, or your wife.

(Mother "F," 1952)[10]

[4]

Me naa give you more [knowledge] than you fe get. But mark you, before you journey complete, you know, de hardest thing wha' you woulda want—Grandy [Nanny] have a certain secret there wha' me can't tell you—Grandy secret. Like you have a secret wha' you didn't tell you mumma.

(Sydney McDonald, September 4, 1978)

[5]

May I tell you this. You would like to get de details of everything. You wouldn't get de details of everything, because a part of a key is there, wherein if you fe know de key, you a go spend months, and you have fe go through de tradition, find out from de people [i.e., the ancestors] if we can tell you de key. That key is a very ridiculous key ["ridiculous" because it is so awesome]. That a fe-me key. [It] keep everything steady. You see, every nation supposed to have a secret. Most have a secret. My secret I can't let out—de whole of de tune—out of de box.

(Sydney McDonald, September 9, 1978)

[6]

De older head man die. Nuff of those men don't reveal nothing, keep all thing as secret to fe-dem self. So nuff of those men now know some of de facts dem that dem don't talk. So after dem don't talk it now, it hard fe de yoyo down here fe catch up on it.

Maroon is a funny type of people. Some of dem say, "wha' you no know, you no going know it." Because there is a secret ina it.

(Noel Lewis, February 4, 1991)

[7]

You see Maroon? Maroon a deep thing. Maroon people, you fe catch wha' you see dem a do. And if you no catch it, you lost out of it. You see? Dem a pick up nothing and show you say that something here can do this or do that. You have fe see dem. And when dem just do a thing, you catch it and hold it ina you head, and just know say, well, after dem, a you going come. A so Maroon people grow, especially first-time. So you have fe catch.

(Ferdinand Bennett, January 26, 1991)

[8]

There was a man living in Moore Town. And de man was so witty that *no gun* couldn't shoot him.

And him wife call to de enemy, and say him know de way fe shoot de man, and dem give him certain amount of money.

And him say, "all right. Go a shop, buy one pipe, chalk pipe. And when you come with de chalk pipe, broke de chalk pipe, and tek off de shank of de chalk pipe, and tek that chalk pipe, and load de gun. And look fe him. No lick him pon him body. Anytime you see him a go up one little hill, as you hear say him lift de foot, as him lift de foot bottom so, knock him right under here so (he pats the sole of his foot). And anytime you knock him under here so him *dead.*"

So that's de only way dem coulda shoot him, is to shoot him under him foot bottom and kill him, load de gun with a chalk pipe.

But de man was so witty that nobody can't shoot him, you can't do him nothing. And de wife call back to de enemy [that] a fight against him, and say, "anytime him a go up a hill . . ."

Dem time those man no min wear boot. A dem naked foot. So same as him deh go up de hill now and put him foot so now fe go go up de hill so now, dem must lick him right under here so with de gun and kill him (pats the sole of his foot). And so said, so done.

And when de man deh go up de hill, same as him deh go up de hill and do him foot bottom so—"ram!"—dem shoot him right under here so and kill him. Dem couldn't knock him nowhere pon him body again to hurt him but right underneath here so.

You know, woman and man, a no all time dem will [get along with each other]. So, through de mix-up come in now, de man deh go fe-him way now, and de woman deh go fe-him way now.

A sell de wife sell him husband. Because dem give him certain amount of money fe find out de man secret. And de wife now tell it to de enemy.

(Hardie Stanford, February 27, 1982)

[9]

We have a man. We call de man Swiplomento. And *nobody* can't shoot de man. *Nobody* can't shoot de man. Nobody can't fling no shot pon de man and affect de man.

You see you wife wha' you have there? Be careful of her. She's a dangerous woman. Fe-me wife wha' me have, me be careful of her. She's a dangerous woman. And de next man wife also dangerous.

We have a man. We call him Swiplomento. No fling no shot out a de man. You can't catch him. Lick him up here so—de shot 'bup, bup'—it gone like breeze.

And him have him wife.

And dem *pay* de woman, say, "a you husband. And we shot after him, we lick him with gun shot, and we can't catch him. Now, a you husband. You *must* know him secret."

And dem pay de woman certain amount of thousand dollars fe expose him husband to dem, fe kill him husband. Fart a raas![11] And de woman tek dem money.

De woman say, "well, you see me husband? Dem call him Swiplomento. And no bother lick him nowhere here so, and nowhere here so, him head, or him chest, or no spot pon him body. You can't kill him. But me going tell you fe mind me husband. Get you bridgeloader—gun. Pipe shank."

Him say, "trim you gun. And load de gun with de pipe shank. And watch me husband *damn* well."

Lawd! Woman! Woe be unto woman. Christ say, "woe be unto woman." Woman is no *damn* good. And a woman mek me and you a suffer ina God world today.

Him say, "no lick me husband nowhere about here so. No knock him no-where about a him body here so. You can't manage him. Him swipple more than you. Him Swiplomento. Dem call him Swiplomento. But notice him damn good. No tek no cartridge. Tek chalk pipe."

Him say, "tek de chalk pipe, broke de chalk, and tek off de part there, put ina you mouth. And tek it and load de gun. And *watch* me husband damn careful. When you see him deh walk here so a hill, notice him damn good. Anytime you see him do so—going up de hill—lick him there under de foot bottom! Lick him there under de foot bottom, and you conquer him."

And de enemy watch him husband damn good. Lawd God! And same as de man deh go up de hill and do so, here so (indicates the sole of his foot) expose.
"Ya-boom!" Dem kill him to fart! One damn lick.
Dem kill him. Because him tell him wife de last secret of him.
Aflinting *pay* fe kill him husband, John Swipple-Man. Grandy Aflinting *pay* de nation fe kill him husband, Swiplomento, with de pipe shank load ina de gun, and lick him, when him deh climb de hill.
(Hardie Stanford, February 7, 1991)

[10]

> talk wid dem-oo
> seh sleep wid dem-oo
> but mind anabeti
> seh yo-ee
> nyaba-ee, yo-ee
> o kumfu nyaba-ee, yo-ee
> poor nanabeti, yo-ee
> kumfu nyaba-ee, yo-ee
> bin a nyaba-ee, yo-ee
> poor nanabeti, yo-ee

Walk with dem, talk with dem, sleep with dem, but mind anabeti.[12] A Country. Mind youself. Mind how you talk with de man. Listen me: walk with dem, and talk with dem, sleep with dem, but mind you friend. Because you a poor anabeti. Mind you friend, or mind *anybody*, when you a talk with dem.
(James Downer, October 4, 1978)

Dodging

The following texts [11–16], all centering on "dodging," include a number of narratives about a very special and much-coveted *pakit* (personal spirit controlled by a *fete-man*). The story of this spirit entity, known as a *dodge-him-oo pakit*, has been preserved in a Kromanti song. In this story, some brothers (the number varies) go together to a Kromanti specialist (or in one case, to a cemetery) to acquire pakits so that they might learn how to tap the powers of Kromanti. When they leave, one of the brothers tricks the others, claiming to have forgotten something at the yard of the *fete-man*; this ruse allows him to return to the specialist alone so that he can secretly obtain another pakit that none of the others will know he possesses. This clever act of "dodging" wins the man a particularly powerful *dodge-him-oo pakit*—a personal spirit specialized in powers of deception and evasion. He now has greater power than all his brothers, and should they ever turn against him, he will have the advantage (knowing all about their pakits, while they know nothing about his own secret *dodge-him-oo pakit*).

Every time the Kromanti song associated with this story is performed, it summons up images of this spiritual coup, suggesting both the benefits of skillful dodging, and the importance of always keeping at least a portion of one's secret knowledge entirely to oneself.

[11]

[Three men once went to a Maroon Science man to get pakits. All of them learned the same things from him, and then they started on their way back home.]

And when dem go a pass, one say him forgot something. And him turn back. And when him go, de Maroon man learn him plenty more. And when him go down, him throw him sing, say: "dodge him-oo, kumfu, me wi dodge you, kumfu, me dodge you, kumfu, me wi dodge you."

Him [the Maroon Science man] give [pakits to] three of dem, but a de [same] one something min hold de three of dem. That mean to say, is only what one can manage. De other two can't manage it. De one wha' left and go back, now, him learn plenty more [than the other two].

(Mansel Sutherland, August 5, 1978)

[12]

Dem got one something a bush wha' dem call name *pakit*. Dem got one something a bush wha' dem call name *pakit*. Listen me. A four of dem. De four pakit wha' deh a bush [were] Dodge-him-oo, Kumujin, Konkonsa . . .

[He refuses to name the fourth one.]

(Leonard Whyte, August 17, 1978)

[13]

It was five brother.[13] The five of them left fe go a burying ground, fe go tek pakit. And when dem go, all dem tek one-one [one for each]. A four pakit di-de [were there].

One [brother] no get none. So when dem come a road, when dem tek four, none no left fe [that brother]. Him say him no want none. Is a good thing none no left, because him no want none.

When dem come a road, him say [to the others], "mm-mm . . . my God, me left me chalk, you know. Me chalk left same place where me min sit down. Me a go back fe me chalk."

When him go back fe him chalk, him a go tek one of wha' de other brother tek, same way: that a "Dodge-him-oo."

"Dodge-him-oo" mean to say, wha' me show you say a this bottle, a no it; a de mug [what I've shown you and said is this bottle, is not; it's the mug] (referring to a bottle and mug sitting on the table before him).

So when him come a road, him say, "dodge-oo, dodge-oo, dodge-him-oo pensa, dodge-oo, dodge-oo, kumfu, you dodge him-ee, dodge-ee, dodge him-ee, dodge-ee, you can dodge him-ee, one time, dodge him-ee, one time, you can dodge him-ee, two time, dodge-oo, dodge-oo, dodge him-oo pensa pra me-oo, dodge-oo, dodge-oo, kumfu, you dodge him-ee, dodge-ee."

A Dodge-him-oo pakit mean that, wha' you show de person, a no it you deh do [what you show the person, it isn't that that you're doing]—everything—the pakit, and your future. That is a man or a woman that dodge you ina everything wha' him going tell you or do fe you—de pakit, and de action.

So, one of de five get a Dodge-him-oo pakit, and that a de same one wha' one of de four tek. But him no know say a it him tek. So every dodge him try fe dodge him in, him find out. Two of dem share de same pakit, but de other one, de first brother, no know say a him tek it too. So every work him work fe dodge him-oo, dat deh one, de last one, find out too. Him look pon him [and] laugh.

(Leonard Whyte, September 6, 1978)

[14]

There were two men, two Maroon men. And when them go to buy their pakit, at most times, two of dem go, and dem buy dem pakit wha' dem have fe work with. When dem come a road, one say, "brother, me left something."

Him say, "brother, wha' you left?"

Him wouldn't tell him.

Him say, "tan here so till me come back."

De other one go, and him go back.

And when him come back, him say, "you jet [get] what you go for?"

And him say, "yes."

You know wha' him go buy? Dodge-him-oo key—Dodge-him-oo pakit.[14]

That Dodge-him-oo pakit, when me going do de something, me dodge you, you no know wha' me deh do. A wha' de man go back go buy.

So [dodge-him-oo pakit] a de key. Until today, Maroon got dem use. (sings)
    when time again
    dodge him-oo kumfu du mi

(Richard Barnes, September 6, 1978)

[15]

Me will give dem [those who come for teaching] little something, but me can't give dem everything, man. Me no have fe dodge meself, man? Me can't let go everything. (laughs) "Dodge him-oo pensa." A so me say. "Dodge him-oo, kumfu, dodge him-oo pensa, dodge him-oo pensa, dodge him-oo, kumfu." A so you have fe do it, man. You can't let go everything. A so me say, man. Him can't let go everything so. Because sometime man tek you own stick and broke fe-you head, you know. Sometime you, [the] same teacher, him hurt you [with what you've taught him].

(Kenneth Harris, July 21, 1978)

[16]

I want to tell you something. When a man sick, I have a key, and I can't give me good friend de key.

We, de Maroon, dodge from one another. And I want to tell you why we dodge. You want to know more than I. And I want to know more, just as you.

(Sydney McDonald, September 9, 1978)

The Treacherous Feast

> The Maroons were betrayed; and as we trace them through to Nova Scotia and Sierra Leone, we find that the generation of the 1795 War never allowed themselves to forget it.
> —Mavis Campbell (1988: 259)

> Even today, two hundred years after it happened, many Maroons at both Scott's Hall and Moore Town can retell it in vivid detail as though it happened yesterday.
> —Bev Carey (1997: 491)

This last section [17–40] is devoted to one of the most widely known Maroon oral traditions. The story of the "treacherous feast," which in the Windward communities continues to be associated with a well-known Kromanti song, contains one of the most poignant and effective representations of the interlinked themes of trust and betrayal.[15] The traitors here are those in whom the Maroons were asked to place their trust following the treaties of 1739: their former enemies, the British. In making peace, the Maroons and the British had sealed their new friendship and heralded this new era of mutual trust with a sacred blood oath. The violation of this sacred trust by the deceitful British colonial governor, who intends to entrap the Maroons by luring them under false pretenses to a feast of reconciliation, stands out as a particularly egregious example of betrayal. At the same time, the story demonstrates the situational nature of trust and distrust, and the need to balance these opposing principles according to the circumstances of the moment. In the end, it is the trust placed by the Maroons in a sympathetic slave (in some versions, a Maroon living in town)—a blacksmith who hammers out a warning—that allows the more fortunate among them to "dodge" the plans of the perfidious governor and return to the safety of their villages unharmed.

As I have shown elsewhere (Bilby 1984a), this Maroon oral tradition is clearly related to events that occurred during and after the Second Maroon War of 1795. In that year, a local dispute between a few Maroons and a white planter in the western part of the island escalated into a full-blown war, largely because of the bad faith and bellicosity of the recently installed Jamaican governor, Alexander Lindsay, Earl of Balcarres. The Maroon perspective on this important episode in British colonial history lends strong support to the view that the war "was pro-

Figure 11.1. "Trelawney Town, the Chief Residence of the Maroons." An engraving produced around the time of the Second Maroon War. From Edwards (1801a).

voked above all by the arrogance and insensitivity of Lord Balcarres" (Ward 1990: 402).

The only Maroons to engage the British directly in battle during this conflict were those of Trelawny Town in the parish of St. James—the community in the Cockpit Country originally founded by the Leeward Maroon leader Kojo (Cudjoe). For reasons that are not entirely clear, the other Leeward Maroon community, Accompong Town in St. Elizabeth—though it had been founded by Kojo's "brother" Accompong and was closely connected to Trelawny Town by ties of kinship and marriage—sided with the British (Campbell 1988: 219–20, 251–52).[16] For their part, the Windward Maroons of Charles Town and Moore Town stayed in the background, preparing—after more than five decades of peace—to go back to war against the whites if necessary.

The governor was taken aback by the determination and military skill of the Trelawny Maroons. In response to his demands for a full surrender, they had burned down their town and retreated deep into the Cockpit Country, where they could fight on their own guerrilla terms. What Balcarres had thought would be over after a few minor skirmishes had grown into a protracted, bloody war. "Tying down numerous troops and militia," writes David Geggus (1987: 379), "the Trelawny Maroons inflicted humiliating losses and were defeated only by a combination of artillery, hunting dogs, loyal slave rangers, and the neighboring Maroons of Accompong Town, able guerrilla fighters like themselves, who knew their home terrain." In fact, the Trelawnys were "defeated" more by the duplicity

Figure 11.2. "The Maroons in Ambush on the Dromilly Estate," 1796. A scene from the Second Maroon War. Painting by François Jules Bourgoin. National Library of Jamaica.

of their adversary, Balcarres, than by any of the other factors. Finding that his troops were suffering heavy casualties and unable to dislodge the enemy, the governor eventually realized that brute force would not bring the desired results. The only option was to negotiate with the Maroons. This he did with unusual deceit.

That Balcarres broke numerous promises to his opponents from Trelawny Town is painfully evident in the written record (Bilby 1984a: 9–21). The final and most flagrant breach of trust came with the governor's decision to disregard his earlier promise to the Trelawny Town Maroons, communicated through his commanding field officer, Major-General George Walpole, that they would not be deported from Jamaica if they abided by the proposed terms of peace. With this understanding, the Trelawnys put down their arms and presented themselves, a few at a time, to the governor. However, as his correspondence clearly shows, Balcarres "considered the treaty a meaningless ploy" (Lockett 1999: 9–10). Once his Maroon enemies were safely in his hands, the governor invoked a spurious technicality to achieve his ends, claiming that they had violated the treaty negotiated by Walpole by coming in after the deadline and could therefore be shipped off the island en masse.[17] Consequently, virtually the entire population of Trelawny Town—nearly 600 Maroons—was deported to Halifax, Nova Scotia, in

1796 and, a few years later, carried to Sierra Leone on the coast of West Africa (Campbell 1990, 1993; Lockett 1999; Hinds 2001; Grant 2002).

The sad fate of these Trelawny Maroons, and the British deception that made it possible, is recorded in the first group of narratives presented below—those given by Accompong Maroons, whose ancestors had once considered themselves and the Trelawny (Kojo's Town) Maroons a single people. Most of these Leeward Maroon versions of the tradition of the "treacherous feast" involve a ship docked in the northern port of Montego Bay (or sometimes, the nearby port of Falmouth).[18] The Trelawny captives are invited to a "feast" on board this vessel, which then sails away with them.[19] This duplicitous act has come to represent the long trail of deceitful maneuvers that characterized the British performance during the Second Maroon War.[20]

The lesser-known part of this story concerns the Windward Maroons in the Blue Mountains on the opposite side of the island. Fearing that the Maroons of Charles Town and Moore Town might join the fight to the west, Balcarres ordered them to the capital to swear an oath of obeisance. The Windwards, however, wisely chose to keep their distance from the conflict; they would throw their weight on neither side, preferring to wait and see how things unfolded. The governor was infuriated by their failure to appear before him.

If Balcarres doubted the Windwards' loyalty to the crown, the Maroons had every reason to suspect the governor of treachery. They had no doubt heard of the mistreatment—the shackling and incarceration—of the two delegations of Leeward Maroons that had come to Montego Bay to discuss the escalating tensions in good faith, before the war had fully erupted.

While the war raged in the Cockpit Country, Balcarres continued his attempts to coax the Maroons of Charles Town and Moore Town to the capital with blandishments and gifts. Hiding out in the Blue Mountains, these Maroons would have none of it. According to the white superintendent in Moore Town, Charles Douglas, they believed that the governor's real intention was to entrap them and deport them from Jamaica. Balcarres' correspondence shows unequivocally that they were right. The governor had in fact devised a scheme to guarantee that "the Maroon Power [would be] assuredly at an end" in Jamaica: he was planning to lure "the Nanny Town People" to Kingston under false pretenses, where they would "fall into the snare," and like the Trelawny Maroons, be "sent out of the Island" (Bilby 1984a: 16). Present-day oral traditions strongly suggest that the Windward Maroons received intelligence that confirmed their suspicions about the governor's intentions and, before it was too late, pulled back and cut off further negotiations.[21] In the Moore Town narratives that follow, the blacksmith who uses a secret "language" to warn the arriving Maroons to turn back effectively embodies the system of intelligence that saved them from extinction.[22]

Balcarres' letters do not reveal specifically whether a duplicitous feast of reconciliation was to be part of his plan.[23] But the treacherous feast at the center of

Windward Maroon oral traditions about these events points accurately enough to the deceitful designs of the villainous Balcarres.[24] Only by relying on their intelligence network and heeding the lessons of their ancestors—who had always taught them to remain on guard, lest their former enemy try to reenslave or annihilate them—did Nanny's people manage to foil Balcarres's plot against them.

By March 1796, Kojo's people had fallen victim to Balcarres's ploy. In a letter of March 26, Balcarres was able to gloat, "thus has ended the Nation of Trelawny Maroons, a People, which Historians assert, were not to be overcome, but would ultimately acquire the Dominion of this Island" (PRO: CO 137/96, 117). Had the corrupt governor's plans for disposing of Nanny's descendants met with similar success, the Windward Maroon communities, like the Leeward Maroon capital of Trelawny Town, would most likely have disappeared long ago from the face of the earth—a fate that the Katawud people of today, partly because of narratives such as those that follow, continue to fear and guard against.

As we enter the twenty-first century, this story of misplaced trust and inhuman treachery speaks to Maroons as powerfully as ever—particularly Windward Maroons, who know that they are here today only because their ancestors, many generations ago, made the right choice when a deceitful governor abused a sacred trust and brought them to the brink of annihilation. It is, to those who continue to recite it, a sort of passion play, connecting past and future. In a time of great uncertainty, a time when threats to their collective survival hover once again over the horizon, a key question for Jamaica's Maroons remains where to place their trust in the years ahead.

I. Leeward Maroon Voices

> To the ordinary observer there is little or nothing to differentiate the Maroons from the ordinary "bush-negroes," although they seem to possess more than an ordinary share of suspiciousness—a suspiciousness which was engendered by the treatment which their brothers of Trelawny Town received from Balcarres, and has been kept alive at odd times by subsequent actions.
> —Frank Cundall (1915: 336)

[17]

It was a trick dem ben have. And dem [the whites] call dem [the Maroons of Kojo's Town] go to Montego Bay on a met [public gathering]. A feast dem min got down there. But dem ben deh pon de beach. De ship was there, ready fe dem. For that time, is a mek-up business fe tek dem away. And then while dem was there, dem call dem on de ship. And all of dem go up pon de ship. And dem tek dem—all of dem.

(Alfred Rowe, January 9, 1991)

[18]

Dem [the whites] have ship. Dem [the Maroons] ben deh come a de feast. Dem fe go eat ina de ship. Everybody eat together. But one man was there now, him never go on ina de ship. Him deh pon de top [deck]. And meanwhile everybody gone in now, de massa fe de ship draw de anchor. Him draw de anchor, and de ship start out, and de man him jump off. So is it mek dem Maroon deh over Halifax.

A only that one man ben save. Dem say him must come now. Him never go in. So is it mek him save. But de other rest wha' ben go a Montego Bay, everybody gone. For de ship gone with dem, and dem can't come out now, you know. So me hear.

Dem [the whites] want carry dem way. You know? Dem ben want carry dem way to fe-dem country. Then dem say now dem fe mek dem mek a feast, and dem will catch dem. For after when dem gone in, gone dine now, de man him will sail way with dem.

But one man wha' save, me hear say him name Missa Fowler. Fowler. One of de Maroon man name Fowler. Him name Fowler. And some of fe-him relation, dem still alive here [in Accompong] now. De older one dem dead off, but some of dem still leave back.

Fe-we old people, [my] old grandmother—him tell we all dem deh.

(Magdalene Reid, January 9, 1991)

[19]

The Maroon town in St. James [i.e., Trelawny Town] was a fort of the Maroons, where the Maroons lived. And the purpose for the Maroons being there was to protect their territory, like Accompong, so that invaders do not come in, or come behind them, so to speak. So, what I discovered, and what I understand, is that the Maroons there were fooled somehow. Because a portion of the Maroon from here [in Accompong] went to live there, to build up that fort. And they were actually fooled by the British that they were going to have a party for them in Montego Bay, and they were to come to Montego Bay. They went there. And they put them on board a ship, nearby the sea. And one man on board discovered that the ship was moving out into deep waters with them while they were there having a nice time and eating. And he jumped out and swam to shore, and came back. And he came back, and he did not stay at Maroon Town down there, but he came back to Accompong here, and he lived. And some years ago, I understand that [this] Fowler—his name was Fowler—had a son. A gentleman was living here in Accompong, that I knew, who was Mr. Fowler. And I heard he was the grandson of the man who came off that ship and came back to live in Accompong, some years ago.

(Colonel Harris Cawley, November 15, 1999)

[20]

It was a place down in St. James. Yes, it was down in St. James, at a place called Vaughansfield [near Trelawny Town]. Well, I understand that it was two Maroons who catch a pig. And dem kill de pig. And this white man now claim that it was his. You no know? And dem tek action.

And dem [the whites] brought a ship to Falmouth. And dem call those Maroons down there. Those Maroon down there [in Kojo's Town, i.e., Trelawny Town] were different from we up here [in Accompong Town], you know. Yes, there is a old Maroon settlement over there at a place dem call Flagstaff. Dem did have a battlefield up there, with dem big guns and such.

So after when dem call those people now to Falmouth, and put dem on de ship, and when everybody was seated, dem sail away de ship. And dem carry dem away to Sierra Leone. Dem remove dem to Halifax, and some other places.

You see, dem [the Maroons] didn't have de knowledge [that] that is what dem was about to do. Dem [the whites] just invite dem to a feast. It was a feast dem plan. So dem get de Maroons. If you come here now, and you say you going have a feast, you going find people from all about gathering, you know, not having de idea to say is trickery you a play pon dem.

I don't remember how many Maroon from Accompong here dem find [mistakenly captured on the ship, along with those from Kojo's Town]. And dem release dem, and send dem home back.

(Thomas Rowe, January 7, 1991)

[21]

When Kojo was going to St. James, him says to his brother, "Accompong, you stay here in de east. I'll go down de west to prevent bad weather from get behind us."

And when one [Maroon] dies up here [in Accompong Town, St. Elizabeth], they [the Maroons of Kojo's Town in St. James] will come up and bury that dead. And when one dead down there, dem will go back down there. Dem will come down there and bury that dead. And each burial was cost sixty pounds. That was plenty money to bury a dead in those days.

All right.

They was going on to a considerable time. There was a Maroon died up inside here. And they [some Maroons from Trelawny Town] came up here [to Accompong], and bury that dead [i.e., they helped out with burial rites]. And after they have bury de dead, they was walking around de district. And when dem reach over yonder there, right in front of where you came and saw me a while ago, there was an old lady dem call Na Austin got de first treaty book.

So one of dem say to de old lady, "Na Austin, what sort of book this?"

She say, "no we treaty book?"

And one of de visiting team [from Kojo's Town] say, "treaty book?"

Him [Na Austin] say, "yes."

[A Maroon settlement] in St. James was broken up after the 1795 Maroon Rebellion and the people shipped to Nova Scotia, some of them later on to Sierra Leone in Africa—or so I was told. . . . The Accompong Maroons speak of this, as of other events in their history, as though they happened but yesterday. (F. Seal Coon, "A Day with the Maroons," *Daily Gleaner*, May 25, 1955)

Na Austin say then, "unu no got one too?"

Him say, "no."

And dem go away indignant. Although they [the Kojo's Town Maroons] was de smallest portion of Maroons, dem believe that since Kojo down at Vaughansfield in St. James, *they* should got de treaty. And dem setting to fight this [Accompong Town] Maroon fe their treaty.

Colonel Accompong, him says, "before Maroon and Maroon should go to war, then mek we deliver de treaty book to dem, and mek peace really"—him mean peace continually.

De very morning that de St. James Maroon was coming to fight this town fe this treaty, this treaty book, Accompong send a man on mule back with de treaty to go and deliver to dem.

All right.

Dem could receive it and go way in peace.

Three weeks time, there was an elderly woman in Vaughansfield caught myalism [was possessed by the spirit of an ancestor]. And him was sounding de alarm that dem must bring back Anferi Town[25] treaty book, otherwise various things going to happen in this place.[26]

Dem never tek heed.

And there is a fellow by de name of Montague. He was haunted and taunted. And him went and stole a pig from a white gentleman, one Jack Vance. And dem call him and court-martial him, and put on de cat-o-nine upon him. And him start to put fire to houses and cane field, and everything, and fe burn it up.

All right.

I hold the Treaty signed by Major General Walpole on the one part, Col. Montague James, the Chief of the Maroons on the other part & ratified by me absolutely as nothing. (undated letter of January 1796 from Governor Balcarres to the Duke of Portland: P.R.O.: CO 137/96:112)

I must . . . secure the Persons of the Rebels by any Means that may present themselves. If I neglect this opportunity, it may not recur.— Under such Idea, I have resolv'd to accede to the Terms, but I can only look upon them, when carried into Effect as Preliminary; because I feel, that if I stop there, I shall not have done the Business either to my own satisfaction, or that of the Country in General. (letter of December 26, 1795, from Governor Balcarres to the attorney general of Jamaica: PRO/CO 137/96: 67–68)

Then now, Montague say, "what?! A white man come flog we for we own right, and we a Maroon?"

A so he start to put fire and destroy everything. Then de Kojo's Town Maroons first treaty book was burned up in 1795. Kojo died in 1792.

It was Accompong from here, and de second man, George Fowler, went down to St. James at Kojo's Town [Trelawny Town], at Flagstaff, and suppressed de rebellion.

And, all right, in spite of that, dem [the whites] say dem going to keep feasting down there. And dem [the Kojo's Town Maroons] went down there. Meanwhile dem went down there, dem [the whites] say dem going to have de feast in Mo Bay. Dem [the Kojo's Town Maroons] went down, and dem [the whites] call dem up here into a barricade house, barricade up de house, into a upstairs house. And there was a ship alongside de harbor. And [it] tek dem. Dem couldn't escape, because if dem jump out de harbor, dem would jump in right down in de seas.

And dem took dem right on. And from there to Cuba. And from thence, from Cuba now, to Halifax. And if you go down to Freetown in Africa now, you see plenty of de Maroons down there.

(Mann Rowe, January 7, 1991)

[22]

Those Maroons [who were deported from Jamaica], it was a war break out in St. James. And when de war break out down there, is Colonel Accompong that send his men there and go pacify de war down there. What de war come for, there was a fellow by de name of Montague that catch a pig for a white man. De white man was one Jack Vance. And dem call Montague and him wife, and dem put on de cat-o-nine deh pon him.

And him say, "what?! De white man come cat me?! All right!"

And him start to put fire to houses and cane field, and all of that.

And a so dem [the British] come up with soldiers from Sav-la-Mar, right up. And when de first pair [of Maroons] reach Flamstead, de last pair just coming out, and they took dem. All right. And that wasn't satisfied. They say dem going to keep feasting fe de Maroons. And dem took de Maroons dem from Vaughansfield right down to Mo Bay. And dem say, when dem go down there, [they] says dem going get dance [i.e., an entertainment] there pon de sea, pon de ship, on de ship, in de sea—de waters.

And thus dem tek dem from there to Cuba, and from Cuba to Halifax, and from Halifax to Nigeria in Africa. And some of de Maroon is still there. A Africa they go back to, though, to Africa, to their father's lands.

They want to destroy dem, de Maroons dem, want to destroy de Maroons. That's why they say they going to tek dem, and tek dem from Montego Bay, dem put dem into upstairs house that dem couldn't jump out. If dem jump out, they would be jumping in the sea. And dem tek it from there now, and say dem going keep dance pon ship pon sea. Dem tek dem, dem sail dem right away, to Cuba, and from Cuba to Halifax, and after Halifax right down to Sierra Leone, and from Sierra Leone right into Africa.

George Fowler and James Bryan, de two of dem, dem was from here. And when dem [the whites] discover that those two was from [Accompong Town]— a two peacemaker—dem tek dem right back from Halifax and come land them back right in Accompong here. James Fowler and George Bryan.[27] That time it was Accompong that send dem down there fe go mek peace, fe go mek peace with these rebels, with de fighting that was going on down there.

(Mann Rowe, December 4, 1999)

[23]

After the treaty was signed, then Generalissimo Kojo said to his brother [Accompong], "you stay here in the eastern part of the island. You stay here in the east. Right here. And I will go down to the west"—that is St. James, that is Flagstaff [the location of Trelawny Town] in St. James—"to prevent abrono [the white man] from get behind us."

Because dem did got no confident in British governor Edward Trelawny.

De quarrel [between the Accompong Town Maroons and Trelawny Town Maroons] was that a dem must got de treaty. Although they [the Trelawny Town Maroons] was the smallest portion of de Maroon, but yet since Kojo him live down there, then a dem must got it. And dem *threaten* to fight this town for de treaty. Then my grandfather tell, before Maroon and Maroon shoulda go to war fe de treaty, deliver de treaty to dem. De very time that dem coming up to this town fe de treaty, then my grandfather send de treaty, me grandfather [send] a man on a horse to go down and deliver de treaty to him down there [at Trelawny Town], that dem never go to war again. Dem never go to war again.

But they was haunted and taunted. One old lady caught myalism, and tell dem that dem must bring back Anferi Town treaty book, otherwise bad things going to happen in St. James. Well, that was it, that was it.

And de thing happen so. A so did cause Montague haunt and taunt so, and stole de pig. And that start a rebellion down at St. James.

There was a fellow by de name of Montague. But he was a Maroon. And he took a pig that belonging to one Jack Vance. Jack Vance was a white man. And him tek that pig to send it up here fe de six of January celebration. And then so dem lay hold on him, and dem put on de cat-o-nine upon him. And him get indignant, say a white man come cat him. And him start to put fire to houses, and cane field, and all dem thing there. And dem [the British] come up with soldiers from Savana-la-Mar right down to Flagstaff in St. James.

Then it was Colonel Rowe. Colonel H. O. [Henry Octavius] Rowe [of Accompong] sent down one James Bryan, and George Fowler, go down there to help stop de rebellion.

All right. Then now, they says that dem going to take feasting for de Maroons down there. And when dem go down there, dem already secure a place, a upstairs house in Montego Bay, and put de Maroon dem up there, say dem going to keep de dance pon sea, on de sea, on a ship. And dem take dem up into a two-story house. And if dem try to escape, if dem drop out of it, dem would be dropping in de sea.

So dem tek dem from there now to Cuba, and from Cuba to Halifax, and from Halifax—where they call that again?—to Nigeria in Africa. [They] took plenty of de Maroon. And they freeze out plenty of dem to death [in Halifax]. Dem freeze out plenty of dem to death.

So, a so dem carry some of de Maroon dem right back to Africa, to Nigeria, to Nigeria in Africa. Nigeria is de place dem call Gold Coast.

(Mann Rowe, December 20, 1999)

[24]

Those Maroons in St. James were deported. I'll tell you how that happen.

Before de Maroons in St. James were deported, they always attend one another celebrations. De Maroons here would go down and attend their celebration, and they in turn would come up and attend de Maroon celebration [in Accompong Town]. Well, on one occasion they came up, and they saw de treaty. So they claim that, being Maroon Town [i.e., Trelawny Town, in St. James] was Kojo's domain, they should have de treaty down there. So they plan to come and fight these Maroons [of Accompong] to claim de treaty.

Well, de plan didn't work. You know? They forfeit it [the treaty]. Well, having that idea, there was a animosity between de two Maroon settlements. So they didn't attend one another celebration anymore.

Well, in those days, in those former days, all de Maroons run animals together. They wouldn't have identical marks to prove that this pig was mine, or that cow was yours. Because all de animals run together. Well, de Maroons in Maroon Town [i.e., Kojo's Town, Trelawny Town] were celebrating. And they run short of meat. Well, in their haste now they catch two pigs, not even stopping to realize that de pigs were not de Maroon pig, but were Englishmen's pigs. Because Englishman live there, and Maroon live there also. So they catch those two pig, and dress dem in their feasting.

Well, de Englishmen, they discovered that de two pigs were missing. What they should have done, they should have report to Kojo, according to de treaty that was signed. If de Maroons do de English any hurt, they should report back to de chief. Or if de English did de Maroons anything, de Maroons should report back their chief. But contrary [to this], they catch these two Maroons, and inflict punishment upon dem. And that start another rebellion, with de St. James Maroons. None of de Accompong Maroons were involved.

So, they went to war, and both sides lose men—valuable men too.

Well, in de final analysis, they ask that de Maroons should surrender, should stop hostility, and everybody come peaceable. Well, a that de Maroon did.

Well, not long after they come to this agreement, they invite de Maroons to Montego Bay, to celebrate. You know? And when de Maroons were gathered, a long house was by de seaside. And when de Maroons were gathered in, they lock de doors on dem, and push dem on board a ship at gunpoint. And they took dem to Kingston Harbor. When they go way to Kingston Harbor, they scrutinize and found that two Maroons from this village [Accompong Town] was on de ship. Those two they send back to Accompong.

Well, they took de rest to Halifax in Canada. And, you know, coming from a warm country, and going to such a cold country, they didn't fare well. Moreover, they did have some hard work that they were not accustom. So plenty of dem die out. They report back to de Jamaica House of Assembly to send dem back to Jamaica. Instead of doing that, they send dem further up, Nova Scotia. Still a colder region. They appeal to Jamaica House of Assemble again. They send dem right back to Sierra Leone in Africa.

That is what happen to de St. James Maroons.

(Colonel Martin-Luther Wright, January 8, 1991)

[25]

[The place called Flagstaff, in the parish of St. James] was once a Maroon community. But Flagstaff is no more. Because Flagstaff was the Maroon village [formerly known as Kojo's Town, or Trelawny Town] that was overthrown by the British in the Second Maroon War. Those were the Maroons now that are living in Sierra Leone. You see? These Maroon that was living in Flagstaff, they are the ones now that was transported from here. Even a man from this community [Accompong] by the name of Fowler. He was taken from here, went over to there to help them to solve the problem of the war between them. And he was taken on the ship too.

It was the Second Maroon War. It causes from some problem with some pig, and the superintendent. I don't know too much about that, because it was over in that side [i.e., in St. James, among the Trelawny Town Maroons]. But anyhow, what I heard, it was that war, and then the authorities in St. James did ask the Maroons authorities here to help them to solve that problem. And they sent down some of their officers from the Maroon community here to Montego Bay to negotiate with the leaders there at the time, about the second war that break out. And while they were on the ship—they were taken to a ship, and there they were discussing—and when they realized, they were on sea.

The Maroon leadership from here make a report about it, and call back the two men from here to return. And they did return. They bring them, after a period of time they brought them back. One of them was [known] by the name of Fowler. And his relatives are here [in Accompong] up to now.

(Melville Curry, November 14, 1999)

Figure 11.3. Edwin Peddie playing gumbay drum at January 6 Maroon celebration, Accompong, 1991. Photo: K. Bilby.

Figure 11.4. Arthur Pinkney playing goombay (gumbay) drum, Freetown, Sierra Leone, 1977. Photo: K. Bilby.

Figure 11.5. Colonel Martin-Luther Wright with gumbay drum, Accompong, 1978. Photo: K. Bilby.

Figure 11.6. Morlai Kamara with goombay (gumbay) drum. Freetown, Sierra Leone, 1977. Photo: K. Bilby.

Figure 11.7. St. John's Maroon Church, Freetown, Sierra Leone, 1977. Photo: Sheila P. Kelley.

Una adu o! Wi na denh Marun wey dey na Salown na Afrika wey denh bin bring wi ansestoz denh, (denh) ol kam dong. Wi dey na wan pat na Fritaun wey denh kol Marun Taun en wi na denh Hamiltin so ef eni Hamiltin denh dey dey so i sey una na wi fambul so dat wi sen adu foh wi, en wi go lek foh no au una (dey) geton dey, bikos wi don setul naya so nau so wi don rigad wi sef az Afrikanz heh heh. Una– una kin sen meseyj kam to wi, wi dey Pasival Strit nomba twenti-eyt, na Fritaun.

Hello you all! We are the Maroons who are in Sierra Leone in Africa where they brought our ancestors, they all came down. We're in a part of Freetown that they call Maroon Town, and we're the Hamiltons, so if there are any Hamiltons over there [among the Maroons in Jamaica], he [Bilby] said you're our family, so that we send our greetings, and we would like to know how you all are getting on there, because we've settled over here now, so we regard ourselves as Africans. You all, you can send a message to us, we're at Percival Street number 28, in Freetown. (tape-recorded message from Mrs. Hamilton of Maroon Town, Sierra Leone to the Maroons of Jamaica; recorded by the author in Freetown, Sierra Leone, in August 1977, and played back for the Maroon councils of Moore Town, Accompong, and Scot's Hall a few months later; Krio transcription by Ian Hancock)

Figure 11.8. Plaque inside St. John's Maroon Church, Freetown, Sierra Leone, 1977. Photo: K. Bilby.

Wel, mi na bon Marun pikin, from di bakbown. So, a dey na Marun
Choch ya, dey wok; a don prich ya, a don du evritin, bot nau, a don
so tayad a dey wok az ey kea-teyka. En, a dey kari on di wok naisli.
En a owp God go gi mi de peyshent foh kari on naisli az a dey du so.
Am Jeymz Magnos Nikul, en a gladi foh wey God inh sef put mi foh
du soch kain ov wok. Bikos, bai dat, wen a dey ya, a kip mi sef
kwayat from evri ivul weyz. A rimemba sey, a dey in di aus ov God.
So am veri veri glad foh dat. A sidom wan dey na inh mi fren kam
mit mi, i sey, ef a kin laik foh sey somting to ram. Na (da) meyk mi
sef a dey tok di wod. So, na di wod dat. A dey tok am na Krio as ey
Marun bon pikin.

Well, I'm a born Maroon descendant, from the backbone. So, I'm in
the Maroon Church here, working. I've preached here, I've done
everything, but now, I've become so tired I'm working as a caretaker. And I'm carrying on the work nicely. And I hope God will give
me the patience to carry on nicely as I'm doing so. I'm James
Magnus Nicol, and I'm glad being where God himself put me to do
this kind of work. Because, by that, when I'm here, I keep myself
quiet from all evil ways. I remember that I'm in the house of God. So
I'm very very glad for that. I was sitting down one day, it was him, my
friend [Bilby] who came to meet me, he asked if I would like to say
something to him. That's why I'm speaking the words myself. So,
those are the words. I'm saying it in Krio as a born Maroon descendant. (tape-recorded message from James Magnus Nicol, caretaker
of St. John's Maroon Church; recorded by the author in Freetown,
Sierra Leone, in August 1977, and played back for the Maroon councils of Moore Town, Accompong, and Scot's Hall a few months later;
Krio transcription by Ian Hancock)

Figure 11.9. James Magnus Nicol, Jamaican Maroon descendant, caretaker of St. John's Maroon Church, Freetown, Sierra Leone, 1977. Photo: K. Bilby.

Claims of the Jamaica Maroons settled at Sierra Leone.

The questions which are raised by the Letter of Major General Walpole are.−

1st. Whether faith was broken with the Maroons when they were removed from Jamaica contrary to the Treaty of Peace which the Major General concluded with them in December 1795.

2dly. Whether, if faith was broken with them in the circumstance of their removal, any claim can be founded thereupon by them or their descendants now resident at Sierra Leone. . . .

For myself as far as I can form a judgement, looking to the whole course of proceeding in respect to the Maroons,−the seizure of the six Chiefs,−the imprisonment of the 31 on the 11th of August and the final deportation of the entire Tribe,−I confess I can think nothing else of it than that it began continued and ended in treachery. (W. Taylor, "Claims of the Jamaica Maroons settled at Sierra Leone to be sent back to Jamaica, on questions raised by M. Gen'l Walpole," c. 1835; PRO/CO 142/33)

In June, 1841, a number of people arrived from Sierra Leone at Jamaica; these were Maroons who were banished from the island. They were some of the original natives who inhabited the mountains, and were determined to destroy the whites. . . . the English, finding themselves defeated in all their plans to subdue them, proposed to take them by craft. They made a feast in a large tavern in Kingston, and invited them to come. After they had eaten, they were invited on board three ships of war that were all ready to set sail for Sierra Leone; many of them were infants in their mother's arms, they were well taken care of by the English and instructed; they were removed about the year 1796—they are bright and intelligent; I saw and conversed with them; when they heard of the abolition of slavery, they sent a petition to Queen Victoria that they might return to Jamaica, which was granted. Several of them were very old when they returned; they were men and women when they left the island, they had not forgot the injuries they had received from the hands of man, nor the mercies of God to them, nor his judgments to their enemies. (nineteenth-century author Nancy Prince, relating oral testimony heard from Kojo's Town [Trelawny Town] Maroons who had returned to Jamaica from Sierra Leone more than 40 years after their deportation; in Prince [1853: 59–60])

II. Windward Maroon Voices

[26]

gone-oo, Maroon gone-ee
gone-oo, Maroon gone-ee
Ma, me yeri war a Cholan [Trelawny][28]
me cry out hooray
Maroon deh ya
we no gone home-ee

wish you well-oo, Maroon, wish you well-ee
wish you well-oo, Maroon, wish you well-ee
Ma, me yeri war a Cholan
me cry out hooray
Maroon deh ya
we no gone home-ee

fare thee well-oo, Maroon, fare thee well-oo

fare thee well-oo, Maroon, fare thee well-ee
dem raise war a St. James
fe cry out hooray
but Maroon deh ya
we no gone home yet-ee[29]

(James Downer, William Watson, and Richard Deans, December 23, 1977)

[27]

We got some people, you know, at a place dem call San Blas.[30] All dem people there a Maroon, you know. All de people wha' you see in San Blas a we.
    All right.
    Dem come here, catch we, carry go way ina sea belly. We no min know say ship woulda move with we. Meanwhile, dem tek we, carry go way. You understand wha' me say?
    [They] catch all of we, carry go a San Blas. They will know. [They] catch we, carry go way, put de ship ina de water there. A wha' dem do in there, say dem mek feast, we will eat. Meanwhile, we in there e eat, de ship gone way. So, a so de business go, long time aback. But all de long time back, we must [still] look out for it. Wha' done one time will done another time again. So, me deh look out fe that.

(John Harris, December 7, 1958)[31]

[28]

Dem mek de feast and call you. And you don't know nothing. You go fe go eat. And dem lay hold on you, and capture you, and get you fe do what dem want you to do. Right? Yeah.
    When dem go, dem [the whites] kind of mek feast fe de people dem, and tell dem say dem going feast fe dem. So dem must come to de feast. And when dem go there now, dem capture dem, and get dem to do what dem want to do.

(Adolphus Whyte, February 3, 1991)

[29]

Dem goes on to mek a feast there, and invite dem to come. But while they were going on now, there was *one* that they capture ina their lot, one Maroon one dem capture ina fe-dem lot. And him see dem coming. Is a blacksmith man. And him start to play on his anvil, you know? (makes as if beating on an anvil, making a rhythmic noise) (sings)
    hanamo moko braiam
    It mean say you hand going go a konso-konso, you hand going go a prison, handcuff going go a you hand.[32] Because anytime you get underneath de place,

and dem lock de door, no mercy fe you again. You can't come out, you have fe subdue.

And dem couldn't catch dem.

(Uriah McLean, June 23, 1978)

[30]

De one who a carry on de handcuff, a same African. But him couldn't talk out plain, you know. Because probably him give de man, dem [the whites] tek it.

It stand fe prison, man: "onamo o moki braiam, konson-konso, yu ki brabo, yu kil self." That mean say a same nation. So if him sell nation, him sell himself. So him give dem that, and dem tek it.

But if a now[adays], dem couldn't tek it, because dem no reach here so with knowledge. Young people wouldn't know, man. [The older people] lock up de whole of dem and go way. But de older set, dem tek it.

Listen to de word, you know: "onamo moki braiam, konson-konso-oy, yu kil brabo, yu kil yuself." That mean say, a him own. So him can't sell nation, be-cause if him sell nation, him sell himself.

(Kenneth Harris, July 21, 1978)

[31]

They have a gate where de government form. And they kill a cow, and they mek ready. Well, Grandy Nanny was coming, and when dem coming, dem met de people dem. Dem deh cooking, and dem [the Maroons] improvise to dem, say, "let me eat."

Well, one go and eat. But dem [the whites] no want catch [only] one. One more go and eat. And they go until they eat off de food—and without any resis-tance.

Well, after they eat off de food, they have a man out there making shackle—wha' we call handcuff. When him pick up de anvil, lick de hammer, "bam!," him say: "o si o dábra, hanamo o moko braiam, dami konsem-konsem, dami yedeng." That meaning to say, him making shackle fe de people dem.

Well, through de half of kin wha' come from abroad know de language, they never come in de trap. They never come in de trap! Through de man dem learn de history, and know it, when dem say, "o siyumandi, siyumande piti, you siyumande titi," de people dem escape way. Because dem deh kin.

So when de man making de shackle now, him say, "o si o dábra, si o dábra, hanamo moko braiam, dami konsem-konsem, dami yedeng."

De people dem know direct say a shackle him a mek fe handcuff dem.

(David Phillips, July 17, 1978)

[32]

When dem did want to catch de Maroon dem at Rockfort, dem mek a hutch [temporary structure], and mek a peace, and call dem fe come—de bakra, white man, white people [invite them]. Dem [the whites] want dem fe come, catch dem, fe mek slave.

But that man now was a old Maroon slavery man. So him sit down now and a beat him iron, a beat him iron, and a sing, a sing: (sings)

    hanamo moko braiam
    hanamo moko braiam
    a mi kil konson-konso
    hanamo o moko braiam

That mean to say, *when* him sing now, de rest of people dem hear de sing now, and dem no come. Because if dem come now, dem catch dem and mek slave. But him beat de iron now, and call dem, and tell dem say, don't come near, because de white man want to catch dem and mek slave. And dem turn back. A de full source of it that.

Dem catch that man deh. That Maroon man now, dem pen him up into a place there now, and that one Maroon man pen up there. And dem want fe catch de rest now fe come and mek slave. But that one Maroon man now, him was a blacksmith. And him was there beating de iron.

And *one* of dem into de lot now hear, when him beat de iron, what him say. And when him throw him sing and say "hanamo moko braiam, konson-konso," that mean to say now de bakra going catch dem, carry go put a prison, mek slave. So dem not to come near.

He was singing. He was singing and beating de handcuffs, you see. So him was singing, and tell dem say, "hanamo moko braiam." "Konson-konso" mean handcuff, you know. He was knocking de iron and singing, and tell dem that if dem come near, de white man going catch dem. He was knocking de two piece of iron, two piece of iron—blacksmith iron—two piece. He was a blacksmith, you know. So him was knocking de two piece of iron and singing de Country, into de iron, (sings)

    hanamo moko braiam
    hanamo moko braiam
    a mi kil konson-konso
    hanamo moko braiam . . .

. . . that if dem come near now, de bakra going catch dem, carry go mek slave.

So when one of dem hear de singing now, dem tek time. Dem tek time, and back [out], so till all of dem gone, and no go into de hutch. And all of dem reach Blaka River [Moore Town].

(Margaret Harris, June 1, 1978)

[33]

Dem took away a part of Kojo people to Nova Scotia. And then now, they was trying to tek fe-Nanny's people. They *invited* dem, de English invited de Maroons of Nanny Town to a fort, near on Kingston. So when they went there, they didn't know what was going on. They invited dem to a feast. But when they went there, they heard this Bongo man. I mean, de Bongo man *know* what was de problem. He was there making de handcuffs. It was in slavery, but I mean, it was after de peace treaty. You understand. And then it was he who signal de Maroons, and let de Maroons know that it was bad for dem. And then dem never enter. They retreat.

He play de iron [metallic percussion instrument] in his own Country. It was both in his Country and de Maroon Country, because de Maroon know. Maroon min able to know about de song, and de meaning.

He was singing: "o enamo moko braiam, o enamo moko braiam, ki konson-konson, ki bobo sef, anyu ani-oo, yoyani-ee, yoyandi kofi-oo, yoyani-oo, o tikyánde kofi, ki kwako debra, ani-oo, yoyani-ee."

So dem a realize. You understand. Because de Maroon know *all* about it. And they retreat. They turn back. They scatter in de woods.

(Charles Aarons, June 26, 1978)

[34]

That time me no deh a this world. But dem say when dem set fe Maroon, and dem want fe catch dem up a Rockfort, government— white people—invite [them].

A that mek dem can't manage Maroon people.

White people send say dem going have feast, and invite dem. And dem come a Rockfort. Dem got man in there a work. So dem going lock up de place now. And de Maroon dem, anywhere dem run go, dem must drop ina hole, up a de Rockfort, fe catch dem fe kill dem.

So dem send fe peace, send say fe come. And Kojo and him people dem go. And I think a few big man go from Charles Town. But none from Moore Town didn't go.

So when dem was there, dem waiting fe de Moore Town Maroon dem fe come. So dem no ready. Dem di-de.

So one man a mek de handcuff. Dem say that man a Maroon, and dem [the whites] don't know. So when de few man dem come, dem say dem must stay there now fe walk up and down till when everybody come. But when him mek de handcuff, him beat it so. (taps out a rhythm, and sings)

    anamo-oo
    a kumfu du mi
    anamo-oo
    a kumfu du mi

So one of de man from Charles Town catch de abrebu [indirect expression, or coded words], and him go up to de man. And him say to him say wha' him say.

Him [the blacksmith] say, "me glad you catch me at wha' me deh say.

Abrebu mi e throw give. A catch dem want catch unu. But a wait dem will wait fe de balance."

(she whispers) Him say, "all right, bakra." Him say, "all right, all right."

And de man di-de [was there]. And de man go up to de other one. Dem talk. Him say, "we a go way. But mek we go one-one [one at a time]."

And till dem fe come fe de other balance, every Maroon gone way, one-one—sake of that man. A that me hear.

But meanwhile dem gone, Maroon e *tear* drum a Moore Town now [i.e., the Maroons were holding a very serious Kromanti Play in their own town]. Down here [in Moore Town], Maroon man and Nanny know say a trap dem e set fe dem. Dem know, and dem no go nowhere.

So in *all* de time, de bakra dem no fraid *no* Maroon like up here [in Moore Town].

[They sent a message to the governor, saying] "when lion a sleep, you mustn't trouble him tail. When lion a sleep, you no fe play with him hair. No play with him, because if him wake up, a hell."[33]

A me tell you that. A wha' me know.

So dem [the whites] can't manage dem. [But] dem manage Kojo. Dem min tek way land from dem [Maroons of Kojo Town], a fight dem down there fe land.

Dem have fe send come here, come invite we down there. But not a *bakra* naa tek no land from we. If we tell you say bakra trouble we, we will lie. Bakra naa trouble we [nowadays]. Bakra naa trouble Maroon.

(Ruth Lindsay, February 1, 1991)

[35]

De white man call to de Maroons dem, say dem must come to Kingston. Is there him going to mek a feast.

There was a Bongo man who was slave there, [who] de white man have there all de time.[34] When de people dem coming in, de Bongo man a sing. Him can't talk in de crowd. De Bongo man say: (sings)

    o enamo o moko braiam

    o enamo o moko braiam

    so konson-konso

    me say o man bunta we

    o enamo o moko braiam

De Bongo man say, de people dem come fe *food*, but de white man going hold dem, put on handcuff a dem *hand*.

You, or me, who understand de language, who know de language, you come to de other man, you say, "man! You no hear wha' de Bongo man say? Bongo man say de white man going handcuff you *now*. So mek we left food and go home back."

De Bongo man see dem, and him deh play, and de nyuman [young man] come and listen: "teng, teng-teng-teng, ki-teng-ken-teng, ki-teng-ken-teng, ti-ka teng-ken-teng, ki-teng-ken-ten." (sings)

> o enamo o moko braiam
> o enamo o moko braiam (laughs)
> o enamo o moko braiam . . .

. . . a Bongo man tune . . .

> o enamo o moko braiam . . .

. . . "teng, ki-ting-ken-teng, ki-ting-ken-teng, ki-ta teng-ken-teng."

Maroon man turn him ears and him hear wha' him deh say.

Him say to him people dem, him say, "unu no *hear*? Unu tan there deh mind food, unu no hear? De Bongo man say white man going defeat we now sake of food. Well, mek we go *home*!"

And those who understand de language back [out] and back [out] till dem come outside. And when de crowd lessen, de white man come out.

And him say to de Bongo man say, "but me no see de place full of people a while ago? A *who* send dem home?"

De Bongo man say, "bakra, me no know, because me deh ya long time, long fe see me people dem, and me deh play me drum, me tune, fe enjoy with dem."

De white man say to Bongo man, "is so you tell dem so!! Come out! Go, and go along with dem too!"

And de white man turn out de whole of dem, turn out de whole of de people now, inside de place, who left, because dem was very few, through de tune that de Bongo man sing.

Bongo man sing him tune there, Bongo man say, "o nyam o, moko braiam"—mean say white man a go handcuff dem. And de people dem know de language, de black people, and a come out.

So de white man never get to defeat de people dem. And de white man get vex, and send dem, send home de few wha' left. Him send home everybody.

(Richard Barnes, September 12, 1978)

[36]

Bakra [nearly] defeat Maroon two time, you know. Him nearly defeat dem when de food short. And him defeat dem again when bakra call fe come mek peace with Maroon. Him defeat dem to de final.

Now, bakra call Maroon fe come mek peace. And bakra set up every instrument fe kill Maroon that deh day, fe catch dem, tek dem, mek slave, ill treat dem. Because him going tek dem fe true. And de big house where me hear say him a mek de feast and sign dem treaty ina, me hear say one little old man di-de [was there]—but a Bongo man. And de Bongo man di-de deh mek him handcuff and shackle (laughs), deh mek him handcuff and shackle, wha' bakra pay him fe mek, handcuff and shackle, fe when de Maroon dem come there now, dem going *lock* dem up ina de house, and handcuff and shackle dem.

All right.

But in everything, you know, some of we gluttonous more than some, and man will tek food, catch some man, but no all man.

When dem go, and hear about de feast now, and de treaty wha' deh go sign, dem feel good. Everybody set go down, "blup, blup," gone in. But at all time, you got one cunny [cunning, shrewd] more than monkey, deh a corner.

When one of dem deh go up, one of dem call to de other one, "tell me something. A so unu deh run deh go? Unu listen wha' de Bongo man iron deh say."

Hm! One of dem stand up. When de Bongo man see say one stand up, de Bongo man tek him two piece of iron, "ping-ping-ping-ping-ping-ping-ping-ping . . . ping-ping-ping-ping-ping-ping . . ." (sings)

> o dina mo-oo
> o moko braiam
> o dina mo-oo
> o moko braiam
> o kil wi konson-konson
> o kil babina sem
> o dena mo-oo
> o moko braiam

One of dem look pon one.

"Come here, man! Come here, man, come here, man, come here, man! Listen de Bongo, listen de tune wha' de man sing!"

De Bongo man knock again, "ping-ping-ping-ping-ping-ping-ping . . . ping-ping-ping-ping-ping-ping . . ." (sings)

> o dena mo-oo
> o moko braiam
> o dena mo-oo
> o moko braiam
> o kil wi konson-konson
> kil babina sem-ee

Hm! De other one deh look now. Some of dem gone chock ina de building [all the way into the building]. Dem cotch [rest temporarily], dem tek time, call dem out, call out everybody, call out everybody.

When dem come, dem say, "unu listen wha' de iron deh say."

That time poor thing bakra no know wha' deh go on. Because de man n'e talk [with his mouth, in a language the whites could understand] to none of dem. De man deh pon him iron, "ti-tíng, ti-tíng, ti-tíng . . ." (sings)

> o dena mo-oo
> o moko braiam
> o dena mo-oo
> o moko braiam
> o kil wi konson-konson
> kil babina sem-ee

Well, dem say, "all right, hear wha' de Bongo man [say]. De Bongo man say how much in year bakra got him here fe mek handcuff and shackle fe come shackle we."

That a wah de Bongo man play de iron mek dem know.

This other one call de other one: "you no hear de tune de Bongo man deh play?"

And everybody step out of de place. And from dem step out of de place, a that mek you got plenty Maroon area all St. Elizabeth, all about dem place there. Because some of de Maroon dem, from dem turn, dem no come back this way. Dem go that way. And dem scatter. Because bakra decide fe catch dem. So de whole of dem no tek de one way. Some come back a Moore Town here. And some go that way there. And some go Hayfield. Some go Trelawny, some go Westmoreland, all over. So a that mek Maroon scatter up and down, up and down, way to St. Elizabeth.

Me know that teachment, man. Me hear it, man. Me learn it, man. Me old people, man. Me older head, man. A no me mek it, man, a me older head tell me, man.

(Hardie Stanford, February 1, 1991)

[37]

Bakra say, well, all right, him a go mek Maroon get de feast, get something to eat. That mean to say, everybody coming one time. Dem [the whites] a mek apologize.

So when dem min in de ship, one of de one say him want tobacco. So when him go round, [he] hear de blacksmith him knock pon him iron. Him a listen. And when him a listen, him no know wha' de blacksmith a knock say. Him turn back, and him come.

Him say, "honku . . ." Him say, "when me go over, me hear de man knock."

So when him min hear de man knock that something so, him no know wha' de man a say.

So him say [to his uncle], "it better you go, go listen."

Him say, "yes."

And when him go and him hear de something knock too, him stand up.

And when him [the blacksmith] knock it, him a tell him say bakra a go carry dem way. A carry bakra a go carry dem way. *Bakra* a carry dem way.

When him come back, him couldn't talk to dem, tell dem say, "you know say a so bakra a go carry we way?"—everybody a grumble, everybody a grumble [i.e., everybody was talking and making noise during the feast].

And when dem look, dem see man a come fe true. Some of dem come and swap, some of dem come and swap.

That mean say, Moore Town Maroon pull back, Charles Town Maroon turn back, Accompong Town Maroon turn back.

But Kojo Town *like food*—licky-licky [greedy for food]—you know, Maroon

---

The Moore-town Maroons have deserved and obtained my thanks for their quiet and orderly behaviour.—How is it possible that they can believe that I am their enemy, when I have declared myself their Friend?—When I speak, they hear the speech of the King. If they are afraid, let them stay where they are, until their Fears are past, and then come to me; but if they come now, I shall be very happy to see them. (letter of September 30, 1795, from Governor Balcarres to the Maroons of Moore Town, to be read to them by Charles Douglas, the superintendent of that community [Crawford 1840: 78])

---

dem licky. Dem want de food fe eat, a de food dem want. [They] too craven [greedy], dem like to eat. So Kojo Town broke! So no Maroon live there.

When Thomas Osbourne reach a Moore Town, him send go to governor, him say, "when lion a sleep, you no fe play with him tail, because him got *one* gray hair ina him head tell him something, and if you mek him wake, and you mek him gray hair raise up, fe you that go."

(James Downer, June 6, 1978)

[38]

When dem mek de peace with de governor, that was Governor Eerie.[35] That was Governor Eerie, after he has cause Kojo's Town Maroon to go away. That meaning, they contact Moore Town. And de governor send [to] dem and tell dem that he's going to have a feast, for since de war all over, dem never have no eating and drinking, you know?

Well, de Maroons was a people at those times [who] like rum and meat very much. And they all went to Kingston. Well, when dem went, de governor put dem in a space—come like a pen, you know? But there was plenty place around in there. So dem inside there.

Tomorrow going to be de feast. That time de governor plan de ship—de feast was to mek *on* de ship. In de meantime, [while they were] eating and drinking, de ship pull out.

That's how dem lose Kojo's Town too, you know. In de middle of eating and drinking, de mind becomes stiff, so you are drunk. De ship sail off. They do it same way, in Kingston. That's how dem lose Kojo's Town. Those type of Maroon is right in Sierra Leone now. They were there now, and de Englishman carry dem so, somewhere down in Halifax. And dem start to multiply so much that de Canadian government call de English government to move dem, and dem move dem back to Sierra Leone.

———— ❧ ————

> Supposing the surrender of the Trelawny Maroons compleated, I mean to act in this Way.... to re-embark the Dogs in Mr. Atkinson's Vessel, & to send her up to Anotto Bay. To summon the Charles-town Maroons to come in a Body to Kingston, in compliance with my former order, which must be obeyed. Mr. Shirley to give them private assurances, as if from himself, that they may depend upon not being touch'd; that he is certain I will only speak to them & send them home; but that he knows I am as obstinate as a Mule, & that altho' he has great Weight with me, he is afraid that I will let loose the Dogs upon them; but that he also knows I have a great deal of mildness, provided I am not cross'd; & that he further knows my wish is to make Friends of them, & not to make War upon them.... That altho' he answers for all this, yet as I am very proud & will give no assurances, they must rely only upon him. There is the strongest Presumption to suppose that all this will go well.—After this Body is dismissed, the Nanny Town people will fall into the snare—they will come down in Full Expectation that they are complying with an obstinate Whim of the Commander in Chief.—I will secure them, & they shall share exactly the fate of the Trelawny Maroons. . . . By effecting this, the Maroon Power is assuredly at an end, whether they are sent out of the Island, or established in it, under certain Regulations. (letter of December 26, 1795, from Governor Balcarres to the attorney general of Ja-maica, outlining his plans to lure the Moore Town Maroons into a "snare" and deport them, following the surrender of the Trelawny Town Maroons: PRO/CO, 137/96: 67–68)

I want tell you something. I learn a lots from my uncles, and even older head than my uncles, who tell me a lots about de Maroon histories. Nuff of de time, when I meet my colleagues—when I say "my colleagues," I mean me and my Maroon friends—and I hear dem talk certain things, I have to ask dem question, and say, "no, man, it can't be so, it must be *so*." Because they are talking about what they see in books, or what they hear. You see what I mean? [My knowl-edge is coming] directly [from] de older heads.

So when these men went, it was under my great grandfather days, as major. Those days de Maroon never have a Maroon man as a colonel. Those days [it] was a white man be de colonel. But he [my great grandfather] was de major. He was de highest position of de Maroon in those days, de major.

And when dem went to Kingston, dem send out a young man to go buy tobacco for de man who smoke. So when de young man went, going down de street, him hear this man, de blacksmith, a play his iron, play his iron, play his iron, play his iron. But is his hammer him beating still. But him was playing on his iron.

Now that is another tactics. He was a blacksmith. *But*, he was a Maroon. He was a Maroon. But he have got de instance, knowing what was going to tek place. Him get some sound, knowing that is what going to tek place.

Good.

De Maroons of Moore Town at those days, through de government got dem, dem never look into techniques to find out what it was going to be like. Dem just tek de message [of invitation].

All right.

When dem was there, and that fellow go out, and him hear de man play him iron, him go to buy tobacco, and him stand up and him listen. But him feel say how de man play de iron, knocking de hammer pon de iron, it must be something.

So when him buy him tobacco and him go round back, him say to him uncle—him uncle a bigger man—him say, "uncle, I go round de street and I hear a man a play iron there, and how I hear de man a play iron there never good."

De uncle say, "all right, boy."

And de uncle tek him tobacco and him go outside. And him [the young man] direct de uncle where [to go].

So when de uncle going down, and this fellow a play iron still, him see say this man is a big man, who shoulda understand de Maroon traditions.

He play his iron now, because him know that him [the uncle] would understand what he is saying pon him iron playing. And when him play his iron, when him see de man coming down now, him say, "well—hear . . ."

Him [the uncle] saw him man know how to play iron.

And when him play iron, him play iron, and when him play iron, him play iron, him play iron, de man understand what he's saying. De man understand wha' him saying. And right there, *him don't talking* [with his mouth]. But he play his iron, and him tell him what going to happen, and what is going to tek place, and what is de plan of de governor.

De man say, "all right."

And him come in back. And when him come in, him climb a tree, and him sung a tune. Him couldn't really go and tell everybody say, well, is what is going to happen, for it was plenty of dem. Him just climb a tree, and him sing a tune, and from de tune sing, everybody realize and know what is going to tek place, and everybody move out.

Moore Town dem come. Dem come, come in Moore Town. So when de governor look fe dem, fe de feast [that] plan tomorrow, all of dem deh back a Moore Town.

And that man name was Robert Osbourne—de major wha' I was telling you, fe de Maroons. His name was Robert Osbourne.

(Johnny Minott, June 4, 1978)

[39]

Well, Moore Town was there, and Governor Eerie sought plans to carry dem away, as how he do Kojo's town. At those days it was under de leadership of a man name Robert Osbourne. That is my great-grandfather. He was de major at those days, for at those time it was de white man being de colonel.

He [Governor Eerie] invite dem now to a feast, saying that from war over, dem never have a feast, so dem must come to Kingston and mek dem have a feast.

Well, dem all went. When they went, they were put in a place like a pen, you know? But, you know, generally man smoke. So, dem send out a young chap to go and buy tobacco. So when he went down de street, there was a man there, a blacksmith. He wasn't from Moore Town, but he was a Maroon. He sabi what was going to happen—that mean he *know* what was going to happen. So he start beating his iron—but he was playing a tune! You understand, when I say playing a tune, he is talking something on his iron. For de Maroon have plenty of tactics when it come to de iron-playing. And de other Maroon man know what de other Maroon man says.

Well, this chap going down to buy his tobacco, he hear this man start to play his iron, play his iron.

Him says, "it look funny."

But him never quite understood as far, because he was a young chap.

Anyway, when him went back in camp, he says to his uncle, "uncle, this thing looks funny. I go down de street and I saw a man, a blacksmith man, a play, and I know I hear that man knock that iron. Looks something funny."

Uncle says, "all right, boy, mek I go."

Well, him carry de uncle direct to de spot. Well, when de fellow [the black-smith] see de uncle, now—you know, him was a elder man with more under-standing—he start to play his iron. And de uncle realize what was happening.

Him turn back into de camp, and him climb a tree, and he sang a song. And all Maroons there, from he sang de song, know what he meant. And everybody leave there to Moore Town.

So, when de governor realize, de morning, there were not even one Maroon in Kingston. Every bit in Moore Town.

Well, when he [Major Osbourne] reach Moore Town, he send back and tele-gram Eerie, and says, "when lion a sleep, you musn't play with him tail, for ev-ery gray hair ina him head tell him something."

And dem never trouble Moore Town again, up till today.

[The song the uncle sang from the tree was]:

    o siyumande—
    o siyumande
    gyat kóduma-oo
    say yáriko péisa-ee
    werewu ketu nanti-oo
    say we no siyumande

[The song that the blacksmith was playing on his anvil and singing was]:
   hanamo o moko braiam

(Johnny Minott, September 10, 1978)

[40]

Now, there was a time when de Maroons fought strenuously with their leader
Nanny. And after de Maroons has become victorious, then they got their free-
doms. But it was *not* satisfactory to their opposers. And so their opposers
thought within themselves that they could go around and work in some envious
direction to entrap de Maroons again. And so they plan that—making a feast—
and call de Maroon to de feast [so that] they would be able to entrap de Maroons again.

So, they plan that feast in Kingston. And de Maroons have to walk all de way
through de bushes to go to Kingston, to be entertained in that feast.

At de planning of that feast, de people who plan de feast got a man to build
handcuff. They got a man there building handcuffs. That man was a man of
what is called de Bongo race. And that Bongo man talk Bongo language. And
Bongo know Maroon language. And Maroon know Bongo language. You understand.

So de Maroons took their lamp and journey from here. Dem was going to
Kingston.

Now, when they got to this place right up at de east point of Kingston here,
first part of Kingston, there is a point there right where they has build a cement
factory. That place was called Rockfort. I have been there in de twenties [i.e.,
the 1920s]. Yes! I have been there in de twenties, to pass through de arch that
was across de road. And so they fix de arch of that point, and de Maroon was
coming from de east point to enter into Kingston.

So when they got to de arch, there was de Bongo man [with] his little place
there where he operates. And, you know, these iron business, they use it with
blacksmith business—coal, anvil, and bellows. Bellows blows de fire. So this man
was there now, making these handcuffs. He knew what it was all about.

De first Maroon appear to de entrance there. De Bongo man saw him coming. De Bongo man speak in *his* language, when he was hitting de hammer:
"hanamo moko braiam, hanamo moko braiam, konson-konso, konson-konso."

Maroon him listen carefully. And de Bongo man was telling dem that he was
making de handcuff to handcuff dem, when they gets into de place there, for de
feast.

Maroon man stand up and listen. Him says, "all right."

De company of dem that was coming run back to de back of de line, and tell
de others that it was a dangerous situation. It was not so much a feast, it was
something to entrap dem.

So well, de first one now, he goes in, and he went to where they were having
de feast. And he help himself quite all right, out of de feast.

He says to dem [the whites], "give me some. Let me get back to de others, because we are from a far journey, we are tired."

That one get something. And he went back. Another one came in, him says de same thing: "we are from a far journey."

And they [the whites] knew that they were from a far journey, of course. And it is a big amount of dem. Some *tired* on de way.

That one help himself, and he took something. He gone back to give de others. And so they went in, pair by pair, one by one, and enjoy de feast there, and went back home. No entrap!

They [the whites] found out that they couldn't entrap dem, they were so wise.

It was from de Bongo man language that de Maroon understand: "hanamo moko braiam, konson-konso!" He was telling de Maroons that dem going to put dem into prison. "Konson-konso" mean prison!—handcuff. Yes.

[The Bongo man told them in his language]: "I am making handcuff for dem to handcuff you, to put you into prison!"

(George Sterling, April 4, 1978)

[In Moore Town] we were accompanied to the House of Mr. Forbes by the Maroon Colonel McKenzie; who told us, that when the Society's Missionaries first came to the Town & erected the Schoolhouse, the Maroons were very suspicious of their intentions; & would never assemble in the building for Public worship at night without placing Scouts in the skirts of the town to guard against surprise: for they were apprehensive that it was a trick of the white people to get them together in one house, in order that they might surround it, while the Maroons were engaged in prayer, take them prisoners & ship them off the Island: as had been done in the case of the Trelawney Maroons, who surrendered on the pledge that they would be allowed to remain in the Island! (letter of June 5, 1837, from Reverends Panton and Griffith to Lay Secretary in London: Archives of the Church Missionary Society, London, M4/13)

The Maroons have a strong aversion to be employed with Troops. After the perfidy of the island to those who capitulated at the last Maroon war [of 1795–96] they have an inherent dread of remaining long in positions in which they know they are powerless to frustrate treachery. (letter from Colonel Alexander Fyfe, commander of Maroon troops during the Morant Bay Rebellion, to Governor Eyre, October 31, 1865; cited in Lumsden [2001: 479])

12

Coda

The Right to Persist

Is the Maroon bloodline being gradually phased out in the Jamaican society accounting for the National Motto "Out of Many, One People"? [Colonel Harris of Moore Town] was asked.
"I do not not think so," he replied.
—Wilbert Hemming (1984)[1]

"Out of many people, one nation," the Jamaican national motto, is but one example of the rising pressure for assimilation [of the Maroons] into the general population.
—Werner Zips (1999b: 90)

"We want to remain as the Maroons forever. We don't want to be integrated (into Jamaica) at all, and we want to bring back some of the old traditions," said [Accompong Maroon Colonel Sydney] Peddie, 65.
—Dan Perry, "Past Glories Still Drive Independence-Minded Maroons" (1999)[2]

Jamaican Maroons, like those they have traditionally viewed as outsiders, cannot escape from a globalizing world of ideas. In the new intellectual space opened up by "the postmodern condition," the very terms upon which cherished concepts of ethnic identity such as their own are predicated can appear suspect, if not vacuous. "Inside" versus "outside," *Yenkunkun* versus *obroni*—such clear-cut dichotomies, based on essentialized notions of bounded Selves and Others, do not always find favor these days, particularly among social scientists and other students of culture who have gradually awakened to the contingent nature of all social formations. It has been noted from time to time that the recent shifts in thought that allow contemporary theorists of culture and society to cope with increasingly fluid and unbounded social terrains may at the same time pose a potential "crisis of authenticity" for submerged or otherwise unassimilated peoples (whether "tribes," "ethnic groups," "minorities," or "stateless nations") who are struggling in the face of encroaching state power to maintain control over their collective, as well as individual, lives. The very concept of "identity" that forms part of the arsenal of threatened peoples (along with related concepts such as "tradition" and "boundaries") is increasingly problematized (Handler 1994; Brubaker and Cooper 2000; Yelvington 2002: 240–43). It is now widely acknowledged, after all, that "traditions" are (to a greater or lesser extent) invented or reinvented rather than just received; that communities and groups long imagined (and analyzed) as clearly bounded units have always been parts of larger social fields and processes; that ethnic and other essentialized "identities" are not only socially/culturally constructed, but precipitates of ever-shifting political and economic relations and forces. This general reorientation of social theory would seem to throw into question the very idea of meaningful social and cultural continuity. As Rosalind Shaw (2002: 9) has pointed out, "given that disjuncture, rupture, and instability currently enjoy analytic privilege, a focus on memory as reproduction raises problematic issues of the historical continuity of social and cultural forms." By bringing debates about the nature of social reality back to fundamental questions of materiality and power, from which they ought never to become detached, these current intellectual trends expose some of the bases of the various advancing forms of domination that have become so conspicuous of late—most of them related to a reinvigorated, continually globalizing capitalism—to needed critical scrutiny. In doing so, they perhaps provide a theoretically informed starting point for resistance to these large-scale forms of domination.

But the starting point for peoples such as the Jamaican Maroons is a different one. Their ongoing resistance to domination remains rooted in the historical moment of their birth as a people. The identity they claim is *both* essentialized *and* the product of an actual, specifiable history of military, political, and economic struggle of which they remain acutely conscious. That much is clear. Nonetheless, a "crisis of authenticity" increasingly looms over them, and it is exacerbated by the extent to which the cultural identity that they feel is indisputably theirs is lodged in mind (and in "spirit") rather than embodied in matter—the degree to which it remains invisible and intangible to those on the "outside." In contrast, in Suriname and French Guiana, where other Maroon peoples such as the Saramaka, Ndyuka, and Aluku are engaged in ongoing struggles to hold on to their lands and their right to a separate existence (Lenoir 1975; Bilby 1989a, 1990; Price 1995, 1998b; Price and Price 2002), these Maroon ethnic groups at least have the benefit of a cultural distinctness that no one seriously questions, since so much of it remains on the surface. As Richard Price (2002: xiii) notes, the Guianese Maroons have always been, and to a large extent still are, recognized for their "radical difference from the other peoples of Suriname and French Guiana," reflected in "such exotic practices as polygyny, oracular divination, spirit possession, body scarification, and ancestor worship, as well as distinctive styles of music, dance, plastic arts and countless other aspects of daily life" (and I would add to this list, very importantly, native language). Such "radical," readily observable cultural difference between Maroons and non-Maroons has not existed in Jamaica for many decades—perhaps for well over a century.

In dwelling in this book on the distinctive "intimate culture" that Jamaican Maroons have maintained beneath the surface, I may be indulging in what David Scott (1991: 263) has criticized (in his reading of the work of Melville Herskovits and Richard Price on the Saramaka Maroons of Suriname) as an "attempt to place the "cultures" of the ex-African/ex-slave in relation to what we might call an authentic past, that is, an anthropologically identifiable, ethnologically recoverable, and textually re-presentable past." If so, I do so without apology. (I would point out, however, that the trope of the "ex-African/ex-slave" discussed by Scott—a sort of generalized and largely decontextualized "anthropological object" forming part of a "metonymic narrative" that Scott seeks to problematize as a theoretical product of the political and ideological preoccupations of intellectuals in the United States during the early twentieth century—is here replaced with the historically specific, materially grounded "Maroon communities of Jamaica"). At a more general level, Scott (1991: 266–67) disputes the kind of "anthropological problematic that sees its task as one of representing authentic pasts," going so far as to question the conceptual premise "that pasts are preservable and representable."[3]

In my view, the connection that Maroons themselves assert between their cultural present and an authentic past—one that may not, after all, be beyond identification, recovery, and re-presentation, both through their own words and the words of others—*must* be given serious consideration. To do otherwise would be to arrogate a fundamental existential right: the right to define oneself (whether individually or collectively). It would be not only to deny the historical agency of these Maroons, but, in effect, to deprive them of their right to continuing self-knowledge. It would also be to take a side—the wrong side, I believe—in the ongoing controversy over whether the present-day Maroon communities have a legitimate claim to the lands they have held in common for well over two centuries, and whether they are entitled to some measure of continuing legal and political autonomy. It should be clear enough that representations of pasts as "authentic" or "inauthentic" may have very real and serious consequences for those whose pasts are in question. (And, if pasts are neither "preservable" nor "representable," as Scott seems to suggest, then how can one know whether or not they are "authentic"?)

One is reminded here of that now famous trial in Massachusetts more than two decades ago, when it was determined through legal argumentation and adjudication that a particular people who had always known themselves to be Indians were not, in fact, an Indian people (Clifford 1988: 277–346) (one can't help but recall, with some irony, Carey Robinson's assertion in an earlier chapter that, in contrast to Jamaican Maroons, "North American Indians at least have a grasp of their history"). Like Jamaican Maroons, the Mashpee (Wampanoag) Indians of Cape Cod no longer spoke the language of their ancestors (which appears to have died out in the eighteenth century), they were on the surface culturally difficult to tell apart from their neighbors, and the range of phenotypes represented among them made their "racial" categorization problematic; nonetheless, there was abundant evidence that the Mashpees had maintained a distinct, historically continuous ethnic identity over some three centuries, and that (in addition to commonly held lands) they also possessed "private" cultural traditions, some of them of considerable historical depth, that distinguished them from their non-Indian neighbors (Weinstein 1986; Campisi 1991: 67–150). Despite a legion of anthropological experts who testified to that effect, and an eminent attorney who "urged the jury not to rob them of their identity" (Campisi 1991: 53), judge and jury concluded that the Mashpees were neither an Indian people nor an Indian "tribe," and that their attempt to regain lands acquired from them in contravention of federal law was therefore not valid.

The intangibility of the distinct identity claimed by the Mashpees—its invisibility to most outsiders—was a recurring theme during the trial. The attorneys opposing the Mashpees' claim argued that "to be a tribe the community must be visibly Indian. It must have a language, dress, songs, and ceremonies" (Campisi 1991: 30). One of the lawyers asserted that the racial ambiguity of the Mashpees "gave them a questionable claim to being Indian"; furthermore, "their cultural identity, he scornfully argued, was restricted to a few recipes" (53). As the judge himself put it, "if you are going to make that kind of distinction [between the Mashpees and other citizens, in terms of their rights over disputed lands] as a constitutional question, you have to show that there is a real honest-to-God difference between that group and everybody else" (58). In the end it mattered little that, according to those ethnographers who knew them, the Mashpees had maintained "aspects of their aboriginal cultural values and beliefs to the present"; or that "the tribal core remains the closeness of family ties, the sense of a common history and heritage, the attachment to ancestral land, even though it is no longer theirs to control, the closed nature of tribal membership, the intimacy of social relations, the differential treatment accorded to members and non-members, and, above all, the sense of themselves as a unique social and political entity" (158). Regardless of what they knew about themselves, the Mashpees lost the case, and the view that (in the words of an assistant district attorney) "they are not a tribe, they are individuals who are assimilated into American society and culture" now had the force of law (157). After all was said and done, the Mashpee plaintiffs, not surprisingly, "could not fathom the justice of a system that said, in effect, you may have a legitimate claim to the land, but you can't bring it because we don't believe you are who you say you are" (151). In the face of this assault on their ability (not to mention their right) to know who they are (and to attempt to determine their future accordingly), the Mashpees have been no quicker to relinquish an identity that is historically deep, and deeply felt, than have the Jamaican Maroons, who also continue to be denied a "real," legal existence in the present. On the contrary, says Campisi (158), "the efforts of the town's leaders and lawyers over the past ten years to deny the existence of the tribe have only reinforced their sense of solidarity."

The Mashpee case is but one among a number of recent examples of repressed peoplehood in which cultural ambiguity or invisibility has become, or promises to become, a pivotal theme. Spread across the eastern and midwestern United

States, for instance, are a large number of culturally or racially ambiguous "Indian" or "mixed" communities who seem, despite surface appearances, to have resisted assimilation and retained a distinct sense of identity; in the southeastern states alone, one still finds "a variety of lesser-known tribal remnants and "composite" groups," as well as "the better-documented groups such as Catawba, Lumbee, and Tunica" (Paredes 1992: 4; see also Porter 1979, 1986; Blu 1980; Campisi 1990; Cleland 2001). Some of these, "such as the Poarch Creeks, have retained very little of native language and culture but have maintained a solid identity as Indian throughout history even though they have mixed considerably with non-Indians, especially in recent decades. Yet others are of uncertain tribal origins and their claim to an Indian identity is a matter of continuing debate" (Paredes 1992: 5). Some have successfully negotiated state or federal recognition of ethnic identities previously held in doubt, and a few have asserted previously "hidden" identities by publishing or actively contributing to local histories of their own (e.g., Waugaman and Moretti-Langholtz 2000; Nemattanew 2002). Are the identity claims of such culturally invisible "remnant" peoples necessarily any less compelling than those of similarly small but better established (and ethnically less ambiguous) American Indian peoples who, in their struggles for collective survival, have been somewhat more successful in maintaining visibly distinct cultures and languages, along with separate political institutions? (One thinks of the Iroquois nations of New York State and Canada, with their long tradition of resistance to assimilation alongside varying degrees of ongoing culture loss [Hauptman 1986].) On what basis do we—"we" meaning anyone looking on from the outside—give greater credence to the identity claims of one submerged (yet ostensibly unassimilated) people over another?

These are, admittedly, difficult questions. Precisely because claims to identity in such cases may be so hard for outsiders to "verify," one must accept that among the claimants may be "fake Indians" (Paredes 1992: 6)—much like the "impostors" who have emerged to claim Maroon identity in Jamaica from time to time. In the United States, the recent proliferation of Indian casinos, some of which have already generated untold wealth, has raised the stakes so high that the picture can only become yet more clouded as increasing numbers of "wannabe" contenders attempt to cash in. The shallower varieties of identity politics to which so many in the *fin de siècle* United States (and other parts of the world) have become accustomed, based on relatively transparent forms of "ethnic" mobilization for instrumental purposes, will likely make it more and more difficult to argue for the authenticity of submerged identities—even those most clearly continuous with real and meaningful pasts.

In contrast to the more fleeting manifestations of ethnicity sometimes associated with contemporary identity politics, the Jamaican Maroon case points to an existential, affective dimension of identity with surprising staying power, a collective sense of self that is clearly a product of long historical experience. The persistence into the 21st century of "hidden Others" such as these Maroons should wean us of any reductionist impulse to locate "history" exclusively in material conditions, or to recognize authentic identities only in the more tangible remains of the past. Now that all but a few traces of the material world from which their ancestors emerged as a people are forever gone, along with most of the outward trappings that once distinguished them from the surrounding population, who can say with authority whether the inhabitants of the present-day Maroon communities are, or are not, who they say they are? To pose such questions is to engage, as they say, in an argument with history. And in this argument, the voices presented in this book cannot be ignored. Their side of the argument carries the assertion—and it is a persuasive one—that the Maroons of today have not only the right to exist, but the right to *persist*, as they have done to the present, against all odds. Because their story resonates with so many people around the world, it is an argument that is not likely to go away.

Epilogue

Ethnographic Presents and Future Pasts

The "presents" out of which this book emerged are now past. No one—including this author—can say how many Kromanti specialists remain in the Maroon communities of Jamaica. Most of the Kromanti practitioners who speak in this book are no longer here "in the flesh." Already, by the late 1970s, there were clear indications that very few among the younger generation were receiving serious training in the Kromanti tradition. At that time, what remained of Kromanti Play was clearly in decline in all the Maroon towns—even in the Moore Town area, where the tradition had arguably been best preserved.

The apparent waning of the Maroons' ancestral religion evidences the same kinds of damaging cultural contradictions, bred by colonialism, that linger on in other parts of Jamaica. Some say that the old Maroon religion received a "death blow" from Colonel C.L.G. Harris of Moore Town himself—the most influential Maroon leader of the twentieth century, and one of the staunchest and most eloquent defenders of the Maroons' right to maintain their unique heritage. As a young man, shortly after returning to his community in the 1950s to become a school teacher, Colonel Harris decided to put a stop to the open practice of Kromanti Play in Moore Town. Looking through the lens of the "proper" British education he had received in Kingston, he had come to believe that the compelling power of Kromanti ceremonies, which at the time were held in the center of the community virtually every night, would distract young Maroons and have an adverse effect on their educational advancement, limiting their opportunities in the *obroni* world (Scott 1968: 38; Harris n.d.: 137–39; Roskind 2001: 244–45). This policy did not put an end to Kromanti ceremonies, but forced them underground. Although Colonel Harris later had a change of heart and reversed his position on this question, the religion of his ancestors, according to some, never fully recovered.

A few decades earlier, in the 1930s, a somewhat similar scenario had unfolded on the other side of the island in Accompong. There, a young Maroon named Thomas "Jim-Jim" Cawley, who was later to become colonel of that community, converted to Christianity and directly challenged the old Kromanti religion by burning down the sacred house where the spirits of Kojo and the other early Maroon ancestors were regularly consulted through *myal*, or spirit possession

(Kopytoff 1987). Although remnants of the old religion were retained and continued to surface briefly every year during the January 6 Maroon celebrations, most residents of Accompong no longer consulted their ancestors in times of need. Gradually, the Kromanti language of Accompong faded away, along with much of the other knowledge tied to the Kromanti religious tradition.

It would be unwise, however, to draw firm conclusions about the future from this. Only the Maroons themselves can know how much of the spirit of their past remains with them. It is significant, perhaps, that Colonel Harris Cawley, who led Accompong during the 1980s as one of the most uncompromising advocates of Maroon "sovereignty" to date, is the son of the same Christian convert who successfully challenged the power of that community's Kromanti practitioners in the 1930s. While in office, Colonel Cawley (the son) helped to maintain the annual traditional rites to the first-time ancestors, despite strong objections from some of Accompong's churchgoers.

Over the years, with each repeated visit to Accompong, I have been impressed with the apparent growth of revitalistic feeling among Maroons both young and old. Jean Besson goes so far as to speak of the reemergence of the traditional Maroon religion in Accompong; while carrying out fieldwork there during the late 1980s and 1990s she "found a renewed Myal ritual focusing on Cudjoe" (Besson 2001: 96).

Moore Town, for its part, gives the impression of quiescence. Nanny's children, according to some of the elders, continue to drift away from their ancestral moorings. Like other Jamaicans, Maroons in Moore Town have long been vulnerable to missionaries who bring the promise of educational and economic "betterment" along with the gospel of personal salvation. Over the last century and a half, Grandy Nanny's stronghold has gradually lowered its defenses and opened its arms to several competing Christian churches. First to arrive, in the mid-nineteenth century, was the Anglican Church; next, in the 1930s and 40s, came the Baptists, Jehovah's Witnesses, and Seventh Day Adventists; a few years later, these were joined by the A.M.E. Zion Church and the Church of God. These new presences have never been kindly disposed toward the older ancestral presence that lies at the heart of this book; the present generation continues to pay for the spiritual alternatives offered by these newcomers with an ongoing loss of knowledge about the Maroon past.

The newest contender in this field is by far the most successful. In 1990, a charismatic female leader split off from Moore Town's A.M.E. Zion Church to found a new Revivalist church of her own. Throughout the 1990s and into the new millennium, Miss Mack (known more formally as Mother Roberts) has been the dominant spiritual presence in Moore Town. People come from across Jamaica—indeed, many travel from other countries—to be healed by her ministrations, which center on the shamanistic extraction of spiritually harmful objects from the afflicted body. On some days, the road leading into the center of Moore Town becomes clogged with parked cars, as dozens of visiting passengers wait

Epilogue.1. A
Maroon *fete-man*
with Bible, Moore
Town, 1978.
Photo: K. Bilby.

patiently in line to be treated by the renowned healer. Mother Roberts's techniques closely resemble performances by "myalists"—Afro-Christian spiritual
healers—described by disapproving missionaries in nineteenth-century Jamaica;
indeed, they have a thing or two in common with the Maroon Kromanti tradition
itself.

Most of those who flock to Moore Town for healing see the wonders performed in this new temple as an extension of the Maroons' legendary spiritual
power, passed down from the ancestors. Few miss the significance of the fact that,
in this Maroon town founded by the great Nanny herself, the leading healer is a
woman. Mother Roberts insists that her powers come from the Holy Spirit. But
many Moore Town Maroons (including some in her church) will tell you there is
nothing new about this; for centuries, those who work in the Kromanti tradition
have recognized *Yankipong*, the Supreme Being, as the source of all life and
therefore the ultimate source of all spiritual power. And some of Mother
Roberts's followers have no doubt that she owes more to the *bigi pripri*—the
spirits of the Maroon ancestors—than she is ready to acknowledge in public.

After all, they point out, her own father was not just a *fete-man*, but also one of the most notable Kromanti specialists of the second half of the twentieth century.

His is among the voices featured in this book. Shortly before the last time I left his yard, he predicted—accurately—that I would never again see him "in the flesh." (His time to join the ancestors came barely a year after this.) As I walked off, he consoled me with an old-time Maroon proverb, reminding me that "foul futu n'e kil in pikin, konjo siid neva laas" (a hen does not kill her young when she steps on them, nor is the seed of a yam ever lost). Like young chicks that survive the hazards and difficult lessons of youth to produce new generations, the seeds of the hardier species of yams that can sometimes be found growing in the wild in Jamaica contain the potential to reproduce forever. One such seed is all it takes to grow a new crop. As we ponder the uncertain times ahead, it is well to remember, along with the keepers of the Kromanti tradition, that it took no more than a small bundle of spiritually charged "seeds," carefully concealed and smuggled across the ocean by Grandy Nanny, to enable those of her generation to survive the extraordinary challenges they faced more than two and a half centuries ago. In such deathless "memories," perhaps, lie the seeds of a still promising future.

"And are the maroons still free?" asked Ken.

"Yes, their descendants still have the lands that were given to them and their independent government, just as if they were not in the middle of a British island" . . .

"Are they still afraid that someone will try to make slaves of them again?" asked Ken.

"They haven't been disturbed for two hundred years and they do not intend to be" . . . (Owen 1949: 192–93)

Appendix

List of Narrators and Locations of Interviews/Conversations

Moore Town Maroons

Charles Aarons, Moore Town (1978; 1991)

Caleb Anderson, Comfort Castle, Portland (1991)

Richard Barnes, Comfort Castle, Portland (1978; 1982; 1991)

Ferdinand Bennett, Hayfield, St. Thomas (1991)

Charles Bernard, Comfort Castle, Portland (1978; 1982)

George Bernard, Cornwall Barracks, Portland (1978)

Elizabeth Brown, Moore Town (1977)

Major John Crawford, Moore Town (1958) (interviewed by David DeCamp)

Richard Deans, Moore Town (1977; 1978)

Robert Dennis, Moore Town (1978)

Colonel E. A. Downer, Moore Town (1960/61) (interviewed by Laura B. Murray)

James Downer, Seaman's Valley, Portland (1977; 1978; 1991)

David Gray, Comfort Castle, Portland (1978)

Colonel C.L.G. Harris, Moore Town (1978; 1982; 1991)

J. T. Harris, Moore Town (1960/61) (interviewed by Laura B. Murray)

John Harris, Moore Town (1958) (interviewed by David DeCamp)

Kenneth Harris, Soho, St. Thomas (1978)

Margaret Harris, Kent, Portland (1978; 1991)

William Harris, Moore Town (1978)

Dungu Johnson, Dumfries, St. Thomas (1978)

Nehemiah Johnson, Hall Head, St. Thomas (1978)

Noel Lewis, Comfort Castle, Portland (1991)

Ruth Lindsay, Moore Town (1991)

Sydney McDonald, Rivers View, Portland (1978)

Uriah McLean, Kent, Portland (1978)

Johnny Minott, Brownsfield, Portland (1978; 1991)

George Osbourne, Kent, Portland (1978)

Emmanuel Palmer, Moore Town (1978)

David Phillips, Soho, St. Thomas (1978)

Emmanuel Salvin, Seaman's Valley, Portland (1978)
Henry Shepherd, Stony Hill, Portland (1978; 1991)
Hardie Stanford, Moore Town (1977; 1978; 1982; 1991)
George Sterling, Moore Town (1978)
Mansel Sutherland, Seaforth, St. Thomas (1978)
C. U. Walters, Johns Town, St. Thomas (1950) (interviewed by Joseph G. Moore)
William Watson, Seaman's Valley, Portland (1977; 1978)
Adolphus Whyte, Comfort Castle, Portland (1978; 1982; 1991)
Leonard Whyte, Cornwall Barracks, Portland (1978)

Charles Town Maroons

William Shackleford, Charles Town (1978)

Scot's Hall Maroons

Abraham Goodwin, Scot's Hall (1978)

Accompong Maroons

Colonel Harris Cawley, Accompong (1999)
Johnny Chambers, Accompong (1978; 1991)
Melville Curry, Accompong (1999)
Geretius McKenzie, Accompong (1991)
Magdalene Reid, Accompong (1991)
Alfred Rowe, Accompong (1991)
Emmanuel Rowe, Accompong (1959) (interviewed by David DeCamp)
Colonel H. A. Rowe, Accompong (1937) (correspondence with Joseph J. Williams)
Mann Rowe, Accompong (1978; 1991; 1999)
Thomas Rowe, Accompong (1991)
Colonel Martin-Luther Wright, Accompong (1978; 1991)

Kumina Practitioners

Rolland Bailey, Spring Garden, St. Thomas (1978)
Arthur McNaughton, Port Antonio, Portland (1978)
Eric Minott, Prospect, St. Thomas (1978)

Notes

Chapter 1. Living Maroon Knowledge

1. The Kromanti practitioners with whom I worked refused direct payment for their help in acquiring knowledge. However, they expected me to "rub their eyes" with token gifts of rum, tobacco, food, and other items, as well as small gifts of cash, with amounts left up to me. (In Maroon parlance, such token gifts, as well as other kinds of "ritual payment"—for instance, the small donations that coffin builders and grave diggers expect from the community—are known as "eyesight" [Harris n.d.: 109].) In fact, this was the only kind of remuneration that was possible for me, for the modest grant from the Organization of American States that supported my work was barely enough to cover my own upkeep and travel expenses. I am convinced that if I had been able to afford more substantial amounts and had approached my teachers as paid "informants," I would have failed to gain access to most of what I eventually learned; it would have looked too much like I was attempting to "buy" this sensitive knowledge in order to avoid the rigorous process normally required to acquire it. There is a strong ethic among Kromanti practitioners (and among Maroons more generally) against the "selling" of knowledge—seen as a form of "selling out" one's people—and any indication that an individual is prepared to sell (or buy) knowledge of this kind is taken as a sign that he is unworthy of it. Beyond this, there are strong spiritual sanctions against "selling" Maroon knowledge, enforced by the ancestors (discussed in detail in chapter 1).

2. This particular ceremony, like most of the Kromanti dances I attended, was a private healing ceremony to which only a select few from the Moore Town community were invited.

3. Throughout this book, for the sake of economy, I use the male form, *fete-man*, unless the reference is specifically to a female practitioner, when I use the female form (*fete-woman*, or *fete-uman*). This should not be taken to suggest that women play a role of lesser value in the Kromanti tradition. It is a remarkable fact that women take part in this warrior tradition on an equal footing with men and are equally respected as Kromanti "fighters" (spiritual combatants). Indeed, as we shall see, the most famous historical Kromanti practitioner of them all, Grandy Nanny, was a woman. Furthermore, a number of the Kromanti specialists who worked with me and contributed narratives to this book were women. Nonetheless, during the period of my fieldwork, a large majority of practicing specialists were men, and this is another reason the male form of the term appears more often in this book than the female one.

4. "Scott's Hall" is the spelling most commonly encountered in recent sources (as well as on maps and road signs in Jamaica). However, Colonel Prehay, the leader of that community, informed me that he and others in his community prefer to spell the name as it

sometimes appears in older documents: "Scot's Hall." Deferring to their wishes, I use the latter spelling throughout this book.

5. In a few instances, I *was* told explicitly that I must not make public a particular name or detail that had been disclosed to me; in these exceptional cases, I have honored my commitment not to reveal the information in question.

6. Wilbert Hemming, "An In-Depth Study of the Maroons of Jamaica," *Star*, October 23, 1984. As indicated in this article, Colonel Harris has himself produced a number of book-length manuscripts about the cultural heritage of the Moore Town Maroons (most notably, Harris n.d.); unfortunately, these remain unpublished.

7. For a detailed description and analysis of this distinctive "Maroon spirit language," known only to Windward Maroons, see Bilby (1983).

8. Mashazal is the name for Comfort Castle in the old Maroon creole ("Maroon spirit language") spoken by Windward Maroons during Kromanti ceremonies. It is derived from Marshall's Hall, the name of a now-abandoned settlement near Comfort Castle; it was here that a group of Maroons from Moore Town settled in the late eighteenth or early nineteenth century (Agorsah 1994a: 168), before moving to the latter location, where their present-day descendants live.

9. This is the album that was eventually released as *Survival* (Island Records, ILPS 9542, 1979). It is not entirely clear why the title was changed before the album's release. Kwame Dawes (2002: 44–45, 267) discusses the importance of Marley's original title of *Black Survival*.

10. The insights of Sidney Mintz (1961; 1969; 1974: 75–81) on the question of "resistance" versus "accommodation"—and his call for greater subtlety in approaching this problem—represent an important turning point in scholarly attempts to grapple with the ways in which the enslaved in the Americas responded to their enslavement.

Chapter 2. Imagining Jamaica's Maroons

1. As Kofi Agorsah (1994a: 187) notes, the expedition that visited Nanny Town in July 1967 would not have been able to locate this sacred site without the help of Maroon guides from Moore Town. In fact, it was a Moore Town Maroon, Leopold Shelton, who discovered the inscribed stone referred to here, on a return trip to the area seven months after the expedition. Before his discovery, the leaders of the expedition had felt they had "no absolute proof" that the place they had visited was actually the site of Nanny Town, despite the assurances of the Maroon guides that this was the correct location (Tuelon 1968: 308–9). See also Hart (1985: 78, 82n11).

2. This is true whether Jamaican national identity is imagined in terms of the "creole nationalism" that was promoted by the "brown" middle class, which became dominant after independence, or the forms of "black nationalism" that continue to coexist uneasily with this middle-class ideology (Thomas 2000; Bogues 2002). Even the contrasting identity suggested by the condition of "modern blackness" with which many younger Jamaicans, according to Thomas (2000), now identify implicates the Maroons—not only because many young Maroons themselves identify with this condition, but also, as we shall see, because the imagery and symbolic power of the Maroon mythos (if not the actual "folk culture" maintained by present-day Maroons) continues to resonate for many who share in the condition of "modern blackness," both in Jamaica and abroad.

3. For background on the large and growing body of fiction and literary criticism treating the "maroon" theme in various parts of the Caribbean, see Silenieks (1984), Phaf

(1990), Bansart (1993), Fleischmann (1993), Lalla (1996), Rochmann (2000), and James (2002).

4. Among the prominent urban Jamaicans who have told me in conversations that they are Maroons (meaning literal descendants) are a television producer, a university professor, and a founding member of Jamaica's most famous reggae band, The Wailers.

5. A typical newspaper story about the dancehall star states that "Mama Dottie (Buju's mother) is a direct descendant of the Maroons and he proudly affirms that he gets his rebellious streak from his mother" (Andrea HooFung, "Buju Banton: 'Dus Off and Start from Scratch Again!'" *Weekend Star*, August 28, 1993).

6. The concept of "intimate culture," as used here, draws on the work of A. L. Epstein (1978).

7. The idea that Maroons are distinguishable from other Jamaicans of African descent solely on the basis of phenotype goes back at least to the late eighteenth century. See, for instance, Dallas (1803a: 88) and Stewart (1808: 295). By the end of the nineteenth century, many writers had begun to sound less certain on this question (e.g., Robinson 1898: 797; Pullen-Burry 1903: 157). A physical anthropological study on "race crossing" in Jamaica, done in the 1920s, says simply that the Maroons "have had little contact with the Whites for four or five generations, and constitute a nearly 'pure stock' of Negroes" (Davenport and Steggerda 1929: 6). Writing in the 1950s, Anton Long (1956: 12, 104), after summarizing accounts from previous centuries portraying the Maroons as physically distinctive, states that "no such distinctive appearance is evident today." Banks (1980: 91) notes the continuing popular perception that "these people were supposed to look different from the ordinary Jamaica countryman—taller, straighter, more muscular, and with a slight reddish tint to their skin." My own observations in areas surrounding the Maroon communities, made over many years, have shown that, when put to an empirical test, claims about being able consistently to distinguish Maroons from other Jamaicans solely by physical appearance (height, skin color, facial structure, hair texture, or other features) invariably prove false. On the basis of her fieldwork among Scot's Hall Maroons, anthropologist Victoria Durant-Gonzalez (1976: 20) similarly concluded that "identity cannot be established through physical characteristics, for Maroons, 'full' or otherwise, look like the majority of Jamaicans who are classified in the population as 'Africans and Afro-Europeans.'" Based on her more recent fieldwork with Maroons on the other side of the island, Grace Jennings (1999: 20) writes that "the Accompong Maroons are no different in appearance from other Jamaicans."

8. In view of this potential for maintaining ethnic anonymity, it is interesting that ethnic stereotypes of Maroons continue to flourish in some parts of Jamaica. During the 1970s, many Maroons in Moore Town told me that until relatively recently, people in neighboring communities often insulted them by claiming that under their clothing, Maroons, like monkeys, had tails—one among several stereotypes of "primitiveness" applied to them. (Similarly, Saramaka Maroons state that in the past some coastal Afro-Surinamers would refer to them derisively as "monkeys" [Price 1983: 12].) The same negative imagery was encountered by Jennings (1999: 20), who was moved to remark that "contrary to a number of misinformed reports and stereotypes, [Jamaican Maroons] do not have tails, neither are their eyes red."

9. Anonymous, "The Maroons," *Daily Gleaner*, June 20, 1939.

10. From an interview recorded by Laura B. Murray in Moore Town in 1960 or 1961.

The original tape on which the interview is preserved is archived at the Indiana University Archives of Traditional Music (accession no. 61-020-F; OT 269).

11. At another point, Robinson (1969: 155) becomes somewhat less abstract in his claims, citing "blood" as the primary vehicle of transmission of what he calls "the ancient warrior strain." Here Robinson is exemplifying a very common theme in discussions of "indomitability" as a fundamental aspect of the "Jamaican personality"; such mythic representations, attributing the ostensible aggressiveness of the "Jamaican character" to some Maroon (sometimes glossed as "Ashanti") essence that is supposed to have diffused into the population at large, recur frequently in present-day writings about Jamaican popular culture (especially treatments of reggae and Rastafari as forms of resistance). This mythic Maroon imagery has also been invoked to explain the violence of the international Jamaican drug posses of the 1980s and 1990s (e.g., Small 1995: 150–54, 355–56).

12. The same tendency can be seen in James (2002)—a more recent book-length treatment of the "maroon" theme in English-language Caribbean literature. A welcome exception is Angelita Reyes's (2002: 78–112) recent discussion connecting "Maroon Nanny" with a number of literary themes or tropes (e.g., the spiritually empowered "rebel woman"). Almost alone among scholars working on "maroon" themes in the field of literary criticism, Reyes attempted to enrich her understandings by conducting interviews with actual, living Maroons in a present-day Maroon community (in this case, Moore Town). Another literary figure (in this case, one not from the Caribbean) who spent a considerable amount of time with actual Maroons before writing about them (very productively, I might add) is Russell Banks (1980; 1995).

13. Anonymous, *Daily News*, October 12, 1975.

14. Anonymous, "Cockpit Tour—Back to 'Roots' Experience," *Daily Gleaner*, August 24, 1977.

15. Paul Robertson, "Speech by Hon. Dr. Paul Robertson, Minister of Information and Culture at Opening of 'The Maroons' Exhibition, Institute of Jamaica, Tuesday, October 24, 1989," manuscript, Institute of Jamaica, Kingston.

16. Ulrich D. Simmonds, "Land of 'Go and Come Back,'" *Daily Gleaner*, July 22, 1954.

17. Mavis Campbell, "The Maroons of Jamaica," *Sunday Gleaner*, May 27, 1973. See also Campbell (1973: 54).

18. Sharon Morgan, "Out of Many, One People: The Mystical Maroons," *Sunday Gleaner*, May 8, 1988.

19. William Strong, "Maroons and Myth," *Daily Gleaner*, January 25, 1974.

20. Lumsden (2001: 486) is among a number of recent writers who have recognized the pitfalls of judging the actions of Maroons in previous centuries in terms of present-day understandings and values. "The combination of sincere loyalty to sworn allegiances [e.g., the Maroons' post-treaty allegiance to the British] with the pursuit of narrow group self-interest," she reminds us, "is foreign to twentieth-century ideological interpretations and sensibilities, but it is the key to the actions of the Maroons and others like them." Referring specifically to the Morant Bay Rebellion, Lumsden calls into question the "ideological" supposition that the Maroons "ought not to have joined with the White colonial regime to suppress their fellow Blacks," arguing that "this is an attempt to force nineteenth-century Maroons into a twentieth-century model of Black solidarity, which it is clear was not a part of their *Weltanschauung*" (472).

21. Some scholars have retroactively passed judgment on the Maroons by attempting to

place themselves in the minds of those who remained enslaved on plantations after 1739. Orlando Patterson, for instance, asserts that the slave population "could only interpret" the Maroons' acceptance of the controversial clauses of the treaties requiring them to capture runaways as "a completely unnecessary sellout" (Patterson 1970: 312). Writers of fiction, including Patterson (inhabiting his novelist persona), have also stereotypically imagined the post-treaty Maroons in a highly negative light, sometimes depicting them (as opposed to their heroic pre-treaty forerunners) as wantonly cruel, indeed "savage," as well as bitter and broken in spirit. Examples of such representations are found in Patterson's *Die the Long Day* (1972: 47, 235) and Maryse Condé's *The Children of Segu* (1990: 284, 286, 294). Such images square neither with written descriptions from the time nor with present-day Maroons' visions of their post-treaty ancestors, which are filled with the same unambiguous sense of pride in being Maroon that the present generation continues to feel. Zips (1999b: 230) has made much the same point, criticizing writers such as Patterson and Mavis Campbell for coming "to a conclusion that interpreted the Maroons as a cadre of colonial-dependent 'mimic men' who had lost their self-confidence, inculcated a feeling of helplessness, and negated their own cultural values."

22. Such treaties—which typically included clauses requiring maroon groups to hunt down and return future runaways—were made in Brazil, Cuba, Colombia, Ecuador, Hispaniola, Mexico, and Suriname, among other places. Detractors of the Jamaican Maroons rarely take this broader picture into account, tending to view the Maroons' self-interested collaboration with the colonial government after the treaties as if this were a singular act of "betrayal" unique to Jamaica.

23. In a recent, carefully researched reexamination of the role of the Maroons in the Morant Bay Rebellion, Joy Lumsden (2002: 485–86) concludes that the atrocities and cruelties for which the Maroons continue to be blamed were greatly exaggerated during the official investigation by the Royal Commission in 1866, for a number of reasons, ranging from frequent misidentifications of perpetrators as Maroons to the uncritical acceptance of second-hand reports based on hearsay by detractors of the Maroons.

24. For more on the Abeng group and the periodical of the same name founded by them, see Nettleford (1972: 113–70) and Lewis (1997). The failure of this group to recognize the continuing power of distinctive local histories caused them certain problems. According to Lewis (1997: 7), "distributors of the paper were chased out of parts of St. Thomas and Portland because of the people's memory of the negative role that the Maroons had played alongside the British in the repression of the 1865 rebellion." Had the newspaper been distributed in the Maroon communities themselves, the response to this symbolic use of the abeng would likely have been critical in an entirely different way; the Maroons remain highly sensitive to the appropriation of such symbols by non-Maroons.

25. For an illuminating discussion of the complex cultural politics of which this ideological shift was a part, see Thomas (2000), who examines how the relationship between "Africanness" and "Blackness" has varied in representations of the Jamaican cultural heritage. The symbolism of the heroic Maroons has significance for constructions of both "Africanness" and "Blackness" in Jamaica, and therefore has played some part in almost all such representations (including the "creole nationalist" ones to which she gives special attention).

26. Interestingly enough, in the considerably revised edition of his history that came out nearly two decades after Nanny was proclaimed a National Hero, Robinson (1993: 102) excised this passage and replaced it with a rather elaborate and confident-sounding

description of the figure whose existence he had once questioned. Robinson does not explain how he arrived at this new certitude, nor does he indicate how he was able to enhance his knowledge of Nanny's personal characteristics.

27. Both Brathwaite and Mathurin depended on original research by Bev Carey, a Windward Maroon descendant who had begun collecting oral traditions in Moore Town and the surrounding area several years earlier (see Carey n.d., 1997). In several publications, Brathwaite has called for a greater and more critical use of oral traditions in Caribbean historiography. As he points out in a number of more recent writings (Brathwaite 1989, 1994), his 1970s research on Nanny and the Maroon perspective it attempts to incorporate have been unjustly ignored by professional historians since then.

28. Some two decades later, the Jamaica National Heritage Trust placed another monument to "The Rt. Excellent Nanny of the Windward Maroons" in Heroes Park in Kingston. Incorporating an innovative "kinetic sculpture" intended to emulate the sound of the abeng, it was officially dedicated on October 14, 1999.

29. This ceremony took place a week after I arrived in Moore Town for my first field trip. I am somewhat embarrassed to admit that I slept through the first part of it, having stayed up the night before till dawn to observe (from a distance) a ceremony held by the Maroons for themselves. To prepare for the momentous event the following day, the Maroons had organized an all-night Kromanti Play on the site of Bump Grave (an ancient Maroon burial mound near the center of Moore Town), during which they consulted with their ancestors through possessed spirit mediums.

30. By 2003, the Accompong celebration, which had previously lasted only one day, had been expanded to cover two days; in that year, according to the local press, more than 25,000 visitors attended. Dennise Williams, "25,000 Came to Accompong," *Jamaica Observer*, January 12, 2003.

31. Interview conducted by the author in Accompong on January 8, 1991. In mentioning the "Peace Cave," Colonel Wright is alluding to a major battle against the British won by the Leeward Maroons shortly before the treaty of 1738/9. (The Leeward treaty was signed on the 1st of March, which would put it in 1738 going by the Julian calendar, but in 1739 according to the Gregorian calendar.) A well-known oral tradition about this battle is presented and discussed in chapter 5.

32. Anonymous, "Thompson in Senate: Maroons Have No Special Rights under Jamaican Laws," *Daily Gleaner*, February 10, 1973; Anonymous, "Manley Seeks Closer Links with Maroons," *Daily Gleaner*, June 4, 1972.

33. Dan Perry, "Past Glories Still Drive Independence-Minded Maroons," *Daily Ardmoreite* (Ardmore, Oklahoma), April 24, 1999.

34. Fittingly, the epilogue of Colonel Harris's unpublished manuscript, *The Maroons of Moore Town (A Colonel Speaks)*, completed in 1977, consists of disapproving reflections on the increasingly frequent attempts by non-Maroons to appropriate symbols of the Maroon heritage for nationalist or other purposes (Harris n.d.: 227–28).

35. Anthropologist Chris de Beet, who was in Accompong carrying out fieldwork during this period, has written about the common view among Maroons in that community that they form "een staat binnen een staat" (a state within a state) (de Beet 1992: 186). In the 1990s, according to Zips (1999b: 231), the Accompong government went so far as to begin the practice of "boldly stamping tourists' passports with the Accompong Military State imprint."

36. The idea that British authorities might be persuaded to take some interest in the

plight of the Maroons in the postindependence era is hardly far-fetched. As Zips (1996: 287–89) discovered, the Maroon case was raised with some concern in the British House of Commons by Labour MP Tom Driberg on the eve of Jamaican independence in 1962.

37. For instance, in 1980, Governor-General Florizel Glasspole publicly "reminded the Maroons that they are not isolated from the rest of Jamaica neither are they a nation within a nation as is often rumoured" (Anonymous, "Maroons not a Nation within a Nation," *Daily Gleaner*, October 1, 1980).

38. "The Public Says," *Star*, May 25, 1985.

39. Dionne Jackson Miller, "Beauty Queens and the Real Jamaica," *Daily Gleaner*, September 21, 2000.

40. Although some Maroons in the Windward communities reject the term *Maroon* as a "real" name, stating that it was given to them by the English (in contrast to their "private" names for themselves, such as Katawud, Yenkunkun, or Chankofi), virtually all present-day Maroons recognize this "English name" as an ethnically specific label that should be used in the present, whether by themselves or outsiders, only to refer to those who can legitimately claim descent from the first-time fighters who made the treaty of 1739.

41. The quoted phrase is from Mavis Campbell (1988: 260), who ends her formidable study of the Jamaican Maroons with an assertion that raises more questions than it answers: "That some of the Maroon communities exist today," she asserts, "is due to atavistic stubbornness."

42. The Windward Maroon community of Moore Town was accessible by wheeled vehicles as early as 1886 (Barker and Spence 1988: 200). By the 1960s, it could be said that "an outstanding characteristic today is that virtually every family in Moore Town has lost immediate members to migration" (Scott 1968: 41). Many of the Maroons I knew in Moore Town, Scot's Hall, and Accompong in the 1970s had spent years living in England or the United States before returning to settle down in their own communities. Others continued to travel back and forth. Major U.S. cities such as New York, Philadelphia, and Boston have small, but significant, permanent Jamaican Maroon populations. Accompong Maroons living in Brooklyn have even played an important role in the election of Maroon officials back in Jamaica (Zips 1999b: 208). Other enclaves of Accompong Maroons can be found in London and Bradford, England (Besson 1998: 150). Despite continuing media representations of Accompong as a remote backwater essentially cut off from the rest of the world, this community has, since the late 1990s, boasted dozens of cell phones (the village's high elevation helps to ensure good reception most of the time).

43. Nonetheless, probably based on Martha Beckwith's earlier reports on the Windward Maroons, as well as his student Katherine Dunham's later success in ferreting out certain clear "Africanisms" in Accompong (Dunham 1946), Herskovits rated the Jamaican Maroons quite high on his famous "Scale of Intensity of New World Africanisms" (originally formulated in the early 1940s), classifying them as "very African" in their magic, folklore, and music (Herskovits 1966: 43).

44. Anonymous, *Jamaica* (Lausanne: Editions Berlitz, 1981), p. 33.

45. Christopher Baker, *Jamaica* (Melbourne: Lonely Planet Publications, 1996), p. 77.

46. Christopher Baker, *Passport's Illustrated Travel Guide to Jamaica* (Chicago: Passport Books, 1995), p. 75.

47. Polly Thomas and Adam Vaitilingam, *The Rough Guide to Jamaica* (London, Penguin Books, 1997), pp. 140–41, 143. *The Rough Guide* has similar things to say about the

Accompong Maroons. For instance, "though older residents claim direct descendancy from fearsome Maroon leaders Nanny and Cudjoe, there are relatively few 'real' Maroons left in the town" (p. 236). As for the sacred site known to Accompong Maroons as the Peace Cave (see chapter 5 of this book), "it's so small and insignificant-looking that it's hard to imagine that history was made here" (p. 237).

48. For example, during the 1990s, young Maroons in Moore Town began to market T-shirts on which they printed words and phrases from the esoteric (and secret) Maroon language known as Kromanti, along with English translations. And in both Moore Town and Accompong, craftsmen have begun to produce simplified versions of Maroon drums for sale to visitors.

49. A journalist who visited Accompong in the early 1990s noted that Jamaican entrepreneurs were showing increasing interest in that community. "At least one Jamaican developer," he wrote, "sees great potential for the Maroon lands as an attraction, especially for black Americans, and is studying the creation of a theme park, animated by Maroons wearing period costumes and bearing replicas of old muskets. 'We are looking at building a typical African-style village,' said Kamau Kambui, the developer" (Howard W. French, "Accompong Journal: British Repulsed, But Tourists Are Another Story," *New York Times*, December 21, 1992). Within the last few years, a Jamaican government agency, the Tourism Development Project Company (TDPCo), has become directly involved in staging portions of the annual celebration in Accompong. As one commentator in the local press noted, "the TDPCo thinks that Accompong has 'great potential' as a tourist attraction . . . The question which faces the Maroons is, whether the tremendous tourism potential of their tradition should supercede the need to maintain their customs" (Anonymous, "Maroons and Tourism," *Star*, January 8, 2002). In another recent newspaper report, the director of standards at TDPCo—after pointing out that her company had "signed a memorandum of understanding with the community not to change anything that the community doesn't want"—is quoted as saying that "our vision is for Accompong Town to be a walking museum, with a view to keeping everything intact for the next generation. . . . We know that this is a good tourism commercial product. When we first came, we thought that more information about the Maroons and structures in the place were needed. So in addition to infrastructure, we have done some training in hospitality (bed & breakfast), fire safety, conflict resolution, and we also sought to teach the younger children their Maroon history" (Dennise Williams, "25,000 Came to Accompong," *Jamaica Observer*, January 12, 2003).

50. Amy Wilentz, "Beyond the Sun," *Condé Nast Traveler*, February, 1991, p. 88.

51. Plans to promote the Maroon cultural heritage received an important boost in November 2003, when UNESCO officially proclaimed the "Moore Town musical heritage" a "Masterpiece of the Oral and Intangible Heritage of Humanity." This award could have a significant impact on Moore Town, and by extension, the other Maroon communities. It carries with it a substantial grant, a portion of which is to go to the building of a cultural museum in the center of Moore Town. According to one report, as a part of this project, "the Music of Moore Town will be integrated into the Jamaican school curricula through Maroon songs and music" (Institute of Jamaica, "UNESCO to Give Moore Town Maroons US $900,000," June 8, 2004, Go-Local Jamaica web site, <http://www.golocaljamaica.com/readarticle.php?ArticleID=3098>). The report glosses over the disquieting implications of such cultural appropriation.

52. To provide a recent example of this continuing appeal: during a visit to the eastern

Maroon community of Moore Town in 1991, I happened upon the Brooklyn rap group XCLAN, who characterize themselves as ambassadors of the Blackwatch Movement—an African-American organization devoted to "the ideological expansion of Black Nationalism, Afro-centricity, and pan-Africanism" (Zips 1995: 47). XCLAN was in Moore Town to make a music video that might capture something of the Maroon spirit of struggle. A number of Moore Town elders accepted the group's invitation to contribute Maroon dance moves to the video.

53. The power of the Jamaican Maroon epic to inspire is historically deeper than one might think. For instance, Toussaint Louverture, during the struggle for Haitian liberation, made reference to "the past resistance of the Jamaica Maroons as an example of black heroism" (Geggus 1987: 280).

54. In criticizing Afroz's flights of fancy, I do not mean to suggest that there were no African Muslims among the early Maroons, or that such individuals left no traces in Maroon culture. On the contrary, as Dalby (1971: 45–46) shows, the esoteric Kromanti language of the Windward Maroons contains at least a few words or phrases that clearly betray Islamic/Arabic origins. Despite what Afroz would have us believe, though, there is no evidence to suggest that Islam ever exerted a strong, not to mention dominant, influence among the Maroons. Perhaps most tellingly, it is clear that the ancestor-focused Kromanti religious tradition of the present-day Windward Maroons owes no more to Islam than it does to Christianity (which is to say, little if anything).

55. Anonymous, "Maroons Seek Control of Cultural Heritage," *Daily Gleaner*, August 10, 1994.

56. Maroon delegations from Moore Town and Accompong, including leaders from both communities, had previously received some direct and intense exposure to such questions of politicized cultural representation when they participated in a special "Maroon Program" (co-curated by folklorist Diana Baird N'Diaye and the author of this book) at the Smithsonian Institution's Festival of American Folklife in Washington, D.C. in 1992 (see Bilby and N'Diaye 1992; Price and Price 1994; Kurin 1997: 131–37).

57. Viviene Evans, "Maroons Attack 'Rape' of Their Heritage," *Jamaica Observer*, July 22–24, 1994. Since 1962, the various Maroon communities have repeatedly lobbied the Jamaican government for some sort of constitutional recognition of their special status, so far to no avail (Zips 1996). In a 1991 article, for example, it is reported that "the Maroons, the island's first free Black people are upset that discussions are taking place about Constitutional Reform and they are not a part of it; and they intend to do something about it. . . . The Maroons feel that they were cheated out of their rights by not being recognised in the 1962 Constitution and are now seeking to correct that" ("Maroons on the 'Warpath' over Constitution," *Boulevard News* [St. Andrew, Jamaica], May 2–15, 1991).

58. John Horner, "The Great Maroon Treaty Myth," *Daily Gleaner*, October 4, 1946.

59. As Jean Besson (2002: 160) suggests, "oral tradition, even when historically inaccurate, may have a symbolic role that is valuable to both the narrator in portraying the past and the ethnographer in interpreting the present."

60. The power of oral narrative in the construction of forms of collective knowledge has been given too little attention in the literature on Jamaican culture. One outstanding exception is the ethnographic work of John Homiak (1985) on oral culture among Rastafari elders. See also Homiak (1995) on what he calls "dub history," and the uses of oral testimony in creating knowledge of the Rasta past.

61. "Veracity" is treated here, in a somewhat flexible way, as a genuine, recoverable relationship, on any of various levels, between present text and actual past events or circumstances.

62. In *To Slay the Hydra* (Price 1983b), as opposed to *First-Time*, the focus is on the version of history recorded in Dutch archival documents, though the excerpts from these documents included in the book are annotated and enriched with references to related Saramaka oral traditions. Taken together, these complementary volumes provide a particularly well-balanced and nuanced view of the Saramakas' formative years.

63. My archival research in England included work at the Public Record Office (1982, 1985), the British Museum (1985), the House of Commons (Parliamentary Papers) (1985), and the School of Oriental and African Studies (Methodist Missionary Society Archives) (1985). In Jamaica I consulted documents at the National Archives, Spanish Town; the National Library (formerly West India Reference Library), Kingston; the University of the West Indies (West India Collection), Mona; and the parish libraries of Portland (Port Antonio), St. Thomas (Morant Bay), and St. Mary (Port Maria). My work in the Jamaican repositories occurred sporadically between 1978 and 2002. I have also drawn on unpublished research done by the late Barbara Kopytoff at the West India Reference Library in Kingston and the Church Missionary Society Archives in London.

64. Another reviewer of Campbell's history registered a similar complaint, pointing out that although "she has undertaken field work among contemporary Jamaican Maroon settlements," the "results do not seem to have been very enlightening" (Ward 1990: 399).

65. A notable exception is the archaeologist Kofi Agorsah, who went out of his way to invite Maroon leaders and delegations to the Symposium on Maroon Heritage that he organized at the University of the West Indies in Kingston in November 1991. Not only did Colonel Harris (of Moore Town) and Colonel Wright (of Accompong) participate, but both also presented very interesting papers, which were published in the resulting volume (see Agorsah 1994; Harris 1994; Wright 1994).

66. Among the earlier works that might be positioned in this stream—and all have contributed to my thinking about Jamaican Maroon narratives and their relationship to the past—are Cohen (1977), Rosaldo (1980), Price (1983a), and Sahlins (1985). Other works I have found stimulating in this connection are Borofsky (1987), Dening (1988), Portelli (1991), Tonkin (1992), and Price (1998a). Also of interest are a number of case studies by folklorists and anthropologists treating the relationship between narrative (both oral and written), historical representation, and identity among certain small, marginalized (and often ethnically ambiguous) rural communities in the United States; see especially Montell (1970), Cohen (1974), and Blu (1979). Notable recent attempts to investigate varying manifestations of historical consciousness among particular non-Western peoples (often in relation to Western historical representations of these same peoples) include Abercrombie (1998), Lambek (1998), Carey (2001), Dinwoodie (2002), Emoff (2002), and Whitehead (2003). See also Ballinger (2002) on historical consciousness and cultural identity in the Balkans and the ways these have been shaped by historical displacement and the transformation of state borders. A very useful recent overview of the crosscultural study of relations between history, memory, and identity is Yelvington (2002).

67. This is not to suggest that those who concern themselves most directly with "history"—professional historians—continue to cling any more than other scholars to the naive forms of positivism in vogue in the nineteenth century. Social historians, for instance,

have long been sensitive to the fundamental importance of perspective in interpreting the past. Antihegemonic hermeneutics crowd the pages of academic publications by historians, historically minded social scientists, and literary scholars interested in the past, who remind us of the importance of "subject position." Nor is the concept of oral history a new one. But one might still ask whether writers of history in general, including those intent on accessing "subaltern" pasts, have gone far enough in exploring forms of "evidence" not owing their existence to the written word—the dominance of which appears to remain secure, as evidenced by the supremacy of the "text" (whether literal or metaphorical) in Western academic analyses (or "deconstructions") of the past.

68. A noteworthy recent example of such use of encoded oral data from another part of the Caribbean is McDaniel (1998), which analyzes songs from the Big Drum ritual in Carriacou as a form of what the author calls "rememory." See also Erim (1990) on the use of songs as historical documents in West Africa.

69. For an example of a recent attempt to employ such present-day oral data to gain access to the experience of the enslaved (in this case, a portion of the previously inaccessible religious meanings of the Jonkonnu festival in Jamaica during the slavery era), see Bilby (1999a). See also Robertson (2000) on oral historical traditions in Saint Lucia. It should be noted that much of the better documented work on oral history among rural African descendants in the Caribbean has centered on traditions that reflect the experiences of postemancipation indentured African laborers who arrived after 1840 (e.g., Schuler 1980, 2002; Bilby and Fu-Kiau 1983; Warner-Lewis 1991), or the experiences of freed people shortly after the abolition of slavery (e.g., Smith and Smith 1986; Smith and Smith 2003). Just how much, and what kinds of, orally transmitted knowledge of life during the slavery era survive (perhaps under the surface) in rural Caribbean communities is a question that has yet to be investigated in a sustained, systematic manner. Answering this question will most likely require long-term ethnography designed specifically for this purpose, carried out in particular Caribbean settings. Brodber's and Besson's studies represent some of the first steps in this direction.

70. Among the few works of scholarship making substantial use of Jamaican Maroon oral historical traditions are Brathwaite (1977), Bilby (1984a; 1984b; 1995; 1997), Hart (1950; 1985), Kopytoff (1987), Carey (1997), Zips (1999a), and Besson (2001). Also deserving mention are two valuable works by authors who are Moore Town Maroons themselves. The first, by Milton McFarlane (1977), consists of a narrative about the Maroon past that is highly idiosyncratic, not only in that it focuses almost exclusively on the Leeward Maroon hero Cudjoe (rather than Nanny or other important Moore Town ancestors, as would be expected of Windward Maroon oral traditions), but also in that it is based on stories related by a single individual, the author's grandfather, "Grandpa Wallen." There is much to suggest that McFarlane's narrative is highly embellished; for instance, several of the names he gives for prominent historical Maroons (e.g., Naquan, Belembo, Kishee, and Sefu) do not appear in any of the narratives I recorded, and were not recognized by any of the Kromanti practitioners with whom I worked. In contrast, the second work by a Moore Town author, a book-length manuscript by Colonel C.L.G. Harris (n.d.), does overlap to a considerable extent with the narratives featured in the present book. The large variety of Moore Town oral traditions contained in Colonel Harris's manuscript agree in many details with those I encountered among Kromanti practitioners. Unfortunately, this important work remains unpublished as of this writing. Maroons in other parts of the Americas also maintain oral traditions that can be of much

value to historians (as the Prices' work on Surinamese Maroons clearly shows). For a recent treatment of oral historical traditions among a Maroon people in the Bahamas, the Black Seminoles of Andros Island, see Howard (2002). See also Palacio (1998) on oral history among the Garifuna, an Afro-Amerindian Maroon people living on the Atlantic coast of Central America.

71. The literature on this question is voluminous, if somewhat contentious; see Vansina (1965) for a classic discussion of the problem. For a specific case study of the ways in which oral historical traditions may be altered by "feedback" from written and other sources, see Henige (1973).

72. Nor was it a coincidence that in 1991, when a major symposium on Maroon heritage was held at the University of the West Indies (with Maroon participation), the opening address was given by the High Commissioner of the Federal Republic of Nigeria, E. N. Ugochukwu (see Ugochukwu 1994).

73. During his visit on August 2, 1997, Flight Lieutenant Rawlings presented the Accompong Maroons with a plaque to commemorate the occasion, along with a carved wooden stool; both are now on display in that community's cultural center/museum.

74. On the epistemological difficulties of the general question of the relationship between "truthfulness, history and identity," see Tonkin (1992: 113–36).

Chapter 3. Leaving and Recalling Africa

1. Readers familiar with Richard Price's study of Saramaka Maroon historical consciousness in Suriname, *First-Time* (Price 1983), will notice that the same expression, "first-time," is occasionally used in this book with reference to Jamaican Maroons. This is because Maroons in Jamaica themselves use it to express concepts very similar to those denoted by the Saramaka term that Price translates into English as "first-time." In Jamaican Creole, the compound word *first-time* simply means "formerly, in the past" (Cassidy and Le Page 1980: 180). But Jamaican Maroons also use the term more specifically, as do Saramakas and other Guianese Maroons, to reference the early part of their history—the time of their liberation struggles and their birth as a people.

2. During the eighteenth and early nineteenth centuries, *Guinea bird* was a common term in Jamaica for people born in Africa. Cassidy and Le Page (1980: 213) define it as "a negro imported from Africa (in contrast to a CREOLE)."

3. It is difficult to know with any certainty what location in Africa Anabo refers to. One very plausible possibility is the town of Anomabo (variously spelled Anamabo, Anomabu, or Annamaboe) on the coast of Ghana (formerly known as the Gold Coast). Located in the Fanti region, Anomabo played a significant role in the slave trade. Another possible derivation—though a much less likely one—is Annobón, the name of an island off the coast of West Africa, near Cameroon.

4. "She dumb herself" meaning that she ingested a magical substance that temporarily rendered her mute, so that even if the whites were to try to force her to talk, she wouldn't be able to.

5. Bongo here refers to those Jamaicans descended from slaves who remained on plantations (as opposed to Maroons), and more specifically, to the people in St. Thomas parish who practice the Kumina religion.

6. Despite this assertion that Bongo people (i.e., those belonging to the "nation" that practices Kumina) cannot fly, Kumina devotees in St. Thomas parish themselves have many oral traditions about ancestors attempting to fly back to Africa. According to these

traditions, some of them succeeded. See Schuler (1980: 93–96) and Bilby and Fu-Kiau (1983: 21–25) for examples.

7. *Numa* is a Maroon Kromanti term meaning "bird"; from Twi *anomáa* ("bird, fowl") (Christaller 1933: 351), or a related Akan language.

8. For another version of this song, see Dalby (1971: 49–50). Variants of the same song are also sung by Kumina practitioners in St. Thomas parish (Bilby and Fu-Kiau 1983: 23–25). Three versions, one sung by a St. Thomas Kumina devotee and the other two performed by Moore Town Maroons (one with full drum ensemble), can be heard on Bilby (1985).

9. *Koko* (or *okoko*) is a Maroon Kromanti term meaning "chicken." The Kromanti quote here is referencing the plight of the brother who ate salt; like a chicken, he is unable to fly more than a very short distance.

10. Variants of this Maroon oral tradition may be found in Harris (n.d.: 34–35) and Carey (1997: 154–55).

11. In the community of Scot's Hall, there is a tendency to use the name *Ashanti* (rather than *Kromanti*) to refer to the overarching "tribe" under which all the others are subsumed. But the term *Kromanti* (or *Karamanti*) is sometimes used there as well. See Schafer (1973: 240) for a discussion of the linkage between remembered "tribes" and notions of descent in that community.

12. Among Maroons today, this ostensible linkage between named ancestral African "tribes" and British surnames appears to be unique to the Windward communities on the eastern side of the island. There is strong evidence, however, that a comparable pattern of perceived linkages existed in the western Leeward community of Accompong until fairly recently, although it appears now to be all but forgotten there. Our evidence comes from the anthropologist Archibald Cooper and his wife, Elizabeth Marriott Cooper, who spent approximately one year together in Accompong during the 1930s. In a letter written roughly halfway into their field trip, Elizabeth notes a new and exciting "discovery": "You know the . . . people here all came from Africa to begin with. Now they didn't come from just one tribe but from many different ones. The founders of the Town came from a certain number of these tribes. Well, do you know that today the descendents [sic] of these founders have kept track of which particular tribe they are descended from! For instance, the Fosters here belong to the old Ebo nation; the Reids, to the Mundengo; the Rowes to the Fanti" (letter from Elizabeth Cooper to her mother, May 22, 1939, Cooper MSS). Another piece of evidence consists of a fragmentary jotting among their field notes, where we find prominent Accompong family names systematically matched with names of African "nations" as follows: "Foster-Ebo; Rowe-Fanti; Reid-Mandinga; White-Congo; Miles-Apunga." Finally, a journal entry written not long before their departure suggests that the Coopers were beginning to learn that this system of correspondences existed (as it does today in the Windward communities) more as a mythological construct than an on-the-ground reality: "I asked her [a knowledgeable elder known as Mama Rachel] who was Ebo. She said she didn't know. I said, 'it isn't Foster is it?' Rachel: 'It's according to the breed.' I felt that she really didn't know who belonged to what nation, and that she wasn't just trying to avoid telling me" (Cooper MSS, field journal, entry of October 6, 1939). As late as 1950, some in Accompong still claimed to be descended primarily from one or another early Maroon leader. The colonel at that time was quoted as saying: "I belong to the line of Quaco. Captain Rowe is descended from Johnny, and Major Foster traces his ancestry to Cuffee. The truth is that there is hardly a Maroon who in some degree is not

related to the treaty captains" (Basso 1960: 84–85). Even at present, traces of an ideology of "tribal descent" still exist in Accompong. As Besson (1997: 314) states, "today there are attenuated 'Coromantee' and 'Congo' ethnicities among some Creole maroons in Accompong, expressed in terms of stereotypes of phenotype and speech."

13. There seems to be some consensus in the case of the Papa tribe, which is fairly consistently identified with the "Osbourne tribe"; but the specific African tribes said to correspond to the Ellis and Harris family lines vary considerably.

14. There is not sufficient space here to discuss these Jamaican Maroon ideas about "tribal" descent from a comparative perspective. But one finds very interesting parallels in a number of other parts of the African diaspora. See, for instance, Hill (1977: 304–16) for a discussion of a similar set of ideas about "tribal" descent from African "nations" linked with patrilineally transmitted English surnames (and, in this case, actual agnatic lineages) in Carriacou, Grenada; as among Jamaican Maroons, this descent ideology is closely tied to ceremonial structure and musical practice (Hill 1977: 342–67; McDaniel 1998). Also worth noting is a strong similarity with certain beliefs among Guianese Maroons concerning the transmission of food prohibitions and other ritual proscriptions along descent lines. Like the English patronyms linked in theory with African "tribes" and associated ritual food prohibitions among Jamaican Maroons, the alimentary "taboos" known as *táta-tjína* or *tata-kina* among the Saramaka and Aluku Maroons of Suriname and French Guiana are inherited from one's father (Price 1975: 52; Hurault 1961: 32–33). These parallels among widely separated peoples of African descent represent strong evidence of important shared African cultural continuities at the level of ideas, and ought to be explored further.

15. This linkage between "weeds" and "tribes" has been noted in passing by a number of other ethnographers. Among the 82 medicinal herbs listed in Milton Cohen's study of medical beliefs and practices in Moore Town is one called "Mandingo-weed" (Cohen 1973: 107). Writing about Scot's Hall, Schafer (1973: 229) mentions an herb used for spiritual purposes in Kromanti ceremonies called "Mandingo prapra weed" (here he is in fact fusing two distinct herbs, Mandinga weed and Prapra [or Papa] weed).

16. From tape recording of interview conducted by Laura B. Murray in Moore Town in 1960 or 1961. J. T. Harris was secretary of the Moore Town Maroons at the time. The tape has been preserved as part of the Laura B. Murray collection at the Indiana University Archives of Traditional Music (accession no. 61-020-F; OT 269).

17. The term *Chankofi* has multiple meanings among Windward Maroons. At times it is used to refer to a specific "tribe" (alongside others such as Papa, Mandinga, or Ibo) from which certain Maroon family lines are thought to be descended. Sometimes, as in this passage, it is singled out and distinguished from other tribes whose names are remembered, being characterized as the "highest" or "most powerful" of all the tribes among the Maroons. On other occasions it is used as an ethnonym that covers the entire Windward Maroon population, much like the terms *Katawud*, *Yenkunkun*, or *Yoyo*. An example of the latter usage is provided by Kofi Agorsah (1992: 2, 9), who states that the Moore Town Maroons refer to themselves as "True blu chankofi piti bo." According to him, "this is a Maroon expression roughly meaning 'I am a full-blooded descendant (son/daughter) of a Maroon.' It is an expression of identity and reaffirmation of solidarity and loyalty, usually called into play when two or more Maroons meet and exchange greetings. It clears the way for the discussion of matters that should remain within Maroon circles." Carey (1997: 225, 406) renders the word as "Champkofi" or "Champkuffee," and concludes that it refers to "a clan of Eastern Maroons under Cudjoe." However, I have never heard the term

used in this way among Windward Maroons; the many Moore Town Maroons with whom I discussed the word always used it as a self-identifying term, and claimed that it referred specifically to the eastern Maroons under Grandy Nanny, not a group of Maroons under Cudjoe, whether in the western or eastern part of the island. Carey's interpretation appears to be based on a well-known passage from R. C. Dallas's history rather than on oral traditions. Dallas (1803a: 30–31) writes that some time before 1730 a group of Windward Maroons who identified themselves as "Cottawoods" or "Cattawoods" separated from a larger body and migrated to the west, where they joined the Leeward Maroons under the leadership of Cudjoe. Even at the time of his writing (some sixty years after the treaties), the "Cottawoods," according to Dallas, continued to use this name to distinguish themselves from the older Leeward group they had joined, who were known as "Kencuffees." The resemblance between "Chankofi" and "Kencuffee" may indeed indicate some historical relationship. However, unlike Dallas, who represents "Cottawoods" and "Kencuffees" as distinct groups, Maroons in present-day Moore Town view the terms *Katawud* and *Chankofi* as near-synonyms, and in fact sometimes use them interchangeably. To add to the confusion, an archival document of 1734 states that a group of eastern Maroons were attempting a "March to John Cuffees Town, somewhere to Leeward, which they could not Do from their Weakness thro Hunger and fluxes without some releif [sic] of provisions in particular" (PRO/CO 137/21, 207). And another document of 1735 mentions that after the fall of Nanny Town, the Maroons of that community separated "into several bodies, one of which consisting of about 140 men, women and children—now making way to St. Elizabeth to find some remote places to settle, or to join one John Cuffee, Captain of another Gang of Rebells, that way" (Campbell 1988: 92).

The term *Chankofi* (which is also sometimes pronounced /jánkofi/ in Moore Town) may well be derived from the name John Cuffee. Perhaps John Cuffee's people were not originally Leeward Maroons in St. Elizabeth, but rather members of the Windward Maroon federation who had preceded the others on the trek to the west (or whose original town was located somewhat west of Nanny Town, but not all the way over in St. Elizabeth on the other side of the island); or perhaps John Cuffee's group had indeed been located in St. Elizabeth previously, but decided to join the Nanny Town visitors when they returned to live in the eastern part of the island, thus becoming a recognized (indeed, prominent) "tribe" among the Windward Maroons.

18. This oral tradition demonstrates with perfect clarity that, as Jean Besson points out, "this fruitful mango tree, with its sign proclaiming common kinship, is a powerful incorporating symbol of the creole maroon community" (Besson 1997: 217). According to her, "it is said to be the place where the two rebel 'tribes' of Congos and Coromantees met to forge an alliance, through inter-marriage, in opposition to the plantation-military regime" (Besson 2000: 120).

Chapter 4. Captivity and Marronage

1. Burning Spear (Winston Rodney), "Slavery Days" (45 rpm record, Fox: Jamaica, Jack Ruby 6123 P, 1975); also on the album *Marcus Garvey* (Island Records: Los Angeles, ILPS 9377, 1975).

2. Burning Spear's song "Queen of the Mountain" appears on the album *Resistance* (Heartbeat Records: Cambridge, MA, HB CD 33, 1986). The title of this reggae song refers to Nanny of the Maroons.

3. Windsor Estate, which for a time was under the control of the United Fruit Company,

was one of the more important employers of Indian indentured workers in Portland parish. Other estates near Moore Town that employed substantial numbers of indentured Indians were Golden Vale and Fellowship (Mansingh and Mansingh 1999: 171). Such laborers continued to be recruited for work on Jamaican estates until 1917.

4. Mansingh and Mansingh (1999: 75–82) describe the common mistreatment of Indian indentured workers in Jamaica, which sometimes included whipping, along with other forms of physical torture and abuse.

5. See Carey (1997: 137) for a very similar Maroon oral tradition.

6. See Lewin (2000: 86) for a similar song (given by a non-Maroon woman) about slaves being disciplined on the treadmill, handed down, she said, by her "slave grandfather."

7. The earliest known Jamaican reference to this theme of calculated premature burial of slaves occurs in a work published anonymously by Robert Charles Dallas in London in 1790, titled *A Short Journey in the West Indies in Which are Interspersed Curious Anecdotes and Characters* (Anonymous 1790). See Ashcroft (1980: 95).

8. According to Lewis (1834: 203–4), the events alluded to in the song occurred around 1788 on an estate called Spring Garden, with a sadistic owner named Bedward.

9. See Jacobs (1972) for a detailed analysis of this oral tradition.

10. This song is widely known in the Moore Town area, where it is often sung in the style known as *jawbone* at Kromanti ceremonies. It is clearly related to an old song known elsewhere on the island, still remembered in the 1970s by one of the oldest living descendants (then age 100) of the slaves attached to the Worthy Park plantation in what is today St. Catherine parish (Craton and Greenland 1978: 378–79). The mention (in some versions of the song) of "seven years" spent working for the white man/overseer apparently represents an allusion to the biblical idea of jubilee, as this had been subversively reinterpreted by slaves in Jamaica during the nineteenth century. In a letter written to his Jamaican Maroon half-sister in 1817, radical thinker Robert Wedderburn states that "the slaves begin to talk that if their masters were Christians they would not hold them in slavery any longer than seven years, for that is the extent of the law of Moses" (Linebaugh and Rediker 2000: 312).

11. This song belongs to a tradition of celebrating the abolition of slavery that goes back to the mid-nineteenth century in Jamaica. Since then, in some parts of the island, Emancipation Day has been celebrated every August 1 with song and dance. See Lewin (2000: 87, 113–18) on the performances known as "Bruckins," still practiced in some communities to commemorate Emancipation. A related Bruckins tradition was once practiced by Maroons in Moore Town (Harris n.d.: 108), where, according to Colonel C.L.G. Harris (1994: 59–60), it "enjoyed phenomenal popularity up to the first quarter of the twentieth century."

12. Archaeologists have concluded that this structure was built by British forces during the military occupation of Nanny Town in the early 1730s (Agorsah 1994a: 176–77, 182). Present-day Maroons, however, are virtually unanimous in insisting that it was constructed by their ancestors and used by Nanny for special purposes of her own.

13. This song is often performed as a *jawbone* song in Kromanti Play.

14. This oral tradition accurately reflects the fact that many of the enslaved in Jamaica were severely overworked, being forced at times to continue their labor in the fields, mills, and boiling houses through the night. Dallas (1803b: 339) observed that "during crop, a great number of the plantation negroes, by spells, is kept at work the whole night. . . . The

languor with which work is undertaken after a sleepless night is evident to the eye, and in its effects: the exertions of the fresh sink to the level of those made by the wearied and sleepy whom they join, and whose labours through a long, dark night, give a dulness to those of the day."

15. According to the narrator, Ashanti was the name given by a portion of the early Windward Maroons to their new territory in the interior of Jamaica, alluding to the African ethnic origins of Nanny and some of the other Maroon leaders.

16. John Thomas is the name in the old Maroon creole for St. Thomas parish.

17. Meaning that the spirits possessing them guided their footsteps.

18. *Seke* (or *sheke*) is an archaic Maroon pronunciation of *jege*.

19. Meaning that it stings him to be giving away such knowledge to an outsider.

20. Henry Shepherd is referring here to an oral tradition I heard from several other Maroons as well: during the time of war, Nanny planted a spiritually empowered tree (according to some, a "lime" tree, known as *obosu* in Kromanti language) at the doorway to the "stone wall," near the center of Nanny Town. The tree served as a kind of test for her soldiers. Before entering, a warrior would have to "greet" the tree with a particular Kromanti phrase meaning "I am a man," and then would have to rub up against the long thorns protruding from it, to show that his body was properly protected against sharp objects, and to prove that he was worthy of the name "Maroon."

21. The Jamaican feminist writer and poet Michelle Cliff is probably the first to explore the literary possibilities offered by the mythic tradition of the two sister pikni, in her novel *Abeng*, apparently after encountering the story in Bilby and Steady (1981: 457–58). See Cliff (1984; 1986: 8–9). For earlier mentions of this oral tradition in scholarly literature, see Dalby (1971: 49–50n20) and Martin (1973: 156).

22. Other interpretations are of course possible, and to focus on the mythic dimension of this oral tradition is in no way to deny that the historical person named Nanny might actually have had a sister known by one or more of the names ascribed to her in these texts, or that these texts might in certain other respects depict this sister accurately. For another oral tradition concerning "Grandy Secesu," see Carey (1997: 387, 412, 447).

23. Similar oral traditions using kinship metaphors to represent elements of the social landscape are found elsewhere in Jamaica. See, for example, Besson (2001: 96).

24. Despite this image, some present-day Maroon healers do combine "foreign" oils and powders with traditional Kromanti herbal treatments (Bilby 1981: 80–81); to my knowledge, however, few if any Maroon Kromanti specialists have abandoned herbs and replaced them entirely with imported materials.

25. Interactions between Maroons and Kumina practitioners in ritual contexts, and the role played by the tradition of "two sister pikni" in such settings, are described at length in Bilby (1979: 124–203).

26. David Dalby also heard the names Shanti Rose and Fanti Rose in Moore Town in 1970, in connection with the story of the two sister pikni. See Dalby (1971: 49–50) for his differing interpretation of this oral tradition.

27. *Battle* is here pronounced /bakl/. This is a play on words, since *battle* and *bottle* are homophonous (*bakl*) in Jamaican Creole. The narrator is saying that we all know that no glass bottle has ever rotted (just as the battles fought by Nanny could never become "rotten" enough to make her give up).

28. This is an alternate pronunciation of Blemandora, a Maroon word meaning a distant, vague place or country.

29. This might relate to a dance Nanny did while singing her song. Cf. Jamaican Creole *calembe, kelembi*: "a dance of African origin, and the music and song that went with it. It is now less practised than formerly, and is falling into disrepute" (Cassidy and Le Page 1980: 89).

30. *Tambu*, as used here, is an alternate name for the music of Kumina, and the drums on which it is played; it is also the name of a distinctive style of Maroon music influenced by Kumina drumming.

31. This is a reference to the two drums used in Kumina, the *bandu* and the *kyas*, which are turned on their sides and mounted by the players.

32. Oral traditions around the theme of fleeing with children are also found among Guianese Maroons. See Bilby (1995) for a detailed comparison of the "abandoned child" narratives of Jamaican Maroons with those told by the Aluku Maroons of French Guiana and Suriname. There are also non-Maroon oral traditions, in Jamaica and other parts of Afro-America, that display certain parallels with this "abandoned child" motif. See, for example, Schuler (1980: 108–9). Also worth noting here is the North American "abandoned child" story told so poignantly by Toni Morrison in her novel *Beloved* (1987). Based on an actual occurrence in 1856, when a fleeing slave named Margaret Garner killed her young daughter and attempted suicide to prevent pursuing marshals from capturing and returning them to slavery (Reyes 2002: 56–77), Morrison's moving homage to the many forgotten ancestors sacrificed to the slave trade has much in common with these Maroon narratives. A crucial difference, however, from the Maroon perspective, is that the Maroon mother sacrifices her child to ensure her own survival, as well as the collective survival of the group. In the Maroon scenario, suicide is not an option, for the basic premise is the determination to survive at all costs; nor does infanticide occur for the purpose of sparing the young victim from a life of suffering. The notion of employing infanticide (and/or suicide) as an ultimate act of defiance against the enslavers, explored very productively by Reyes (2002: 33–77), would appear to be alien to Maroon understandings of their "abandoned child" narratives.

33. This old Maroon creole phrase, "popo Keto, a wi ar," may be glossed as: "poor Keto, it is all of us" [who are suffering the hardships of war].

34. *Dákuma* (also sometimes pronounced *dakú*, or *dakó*) is a word in the Maroon Kromanti language meaning "child" (Bilby 1983: 74).

35. A version of this song recorded in Moore Town in 1978, backed by a full Kromanti drum ensemble, may be heard on Bilby (1992).

36. The narrator later explained that Shedo was the name of the mother whose child was lost in the woods. (Other narrators, however, claim that Shedo was the name of the child itself).

37. In certain variants of this oral tradition, such as the one here, the lost child, Shedo, builds a drum and uses it to reveal his whereabouts so that the other Maroons can find him. This version serves as a kind of "origin myth" for the *printing* (Kromanti drum), explaining how the first-time Maroons learned to make and communicate with this instrument. Another example of this variant can be found in Harris (n.d.: 31–33).

38. Meaning that, having heard this much of the story, I (the listener) have gotten into an area of "deep" Maroon knowledge.

39. That events of the kind described in this narrative did in fact occur is corroborated by archival records. Campbell (1988: 68), for instance, cites a document from 1732 that tells of a child who had been abducted, along with eight women, by a group of Maroons

during a raid on a plantation; the child was "dashed against a rock and left for dead" as the Maroons were retreating, and was "later found barely alive." In the same vein, Angelita Reyes (2002: 80), who has spent time in Moore Town gathering Maroon oral traditions, writes that "children who were in the Maroon camps were also at risk. For example, any baby who cried could be smothered if his crying risked the group's safety and hiding." Unfortunately, she does not indicate what her source is for this information.

40. This was later glossed by the narrator as follows: "me get old and weak, me back turn, me no man again."

41. Apparently a variant pronunciation of *légonanan/légonan*, a term in old Maroon creole, meaning "distant place, far" (Bilby 1983: 75).

42. Harris (n.d.: 55–56) records what appears to be a related oral tradition about a non-Maroon female spirit worker named Congoyerrie.

43. The expression *Jack Mandora* is the first part of a formula traditionally used to end an Anansi story (Cassidy and Le Page 1980: 239). Here there would seem to be some connection with the Maroon term *Blemandora*, meaning "a distant, vague place or country." In the previous narrative about a woman fleeing with her baby down a precipitous ravine, Hardie Stanford referred to the name of the associated spring as Lagunanan, a Maroon term (sometimes pronounced *legonanan* or *legonan*) that is synonymous with Blemandora. Cf. Jackmandoore: "a spring which flows into the Dry River" (near the present-day Windward Maroon town of Comfort Castle) (Agorsah 1994: 168).

44. Another name for the hill more commonly known as Watch Hill.

Chapter 5. Living by One's Wits

1. Kenneth Pringle (1938: 29–51) explored sections of the Blue Mountains and Johncrow Mountains on foot with Maroon guides in the 1930s. His evocative descriptions provide some idea of the difficulty of moving through this rugged wilderness, to which the earliest Maroon ancestors had to adapt.

2. C.L.G. Harris (1994: 57) discusses the importance of cacoon and thatch-head for Moore Town Maroons.

3. When interviewed for an oral history project in Kingston during the 1970s, an elderly Trench Town resident recalled the importance of Maroon herbal healers even for urban dwellers (Anonymous 1976: 30). Scott (1968: 55–56) indicates that the belief in Maroons as superior herbalists and healers was still found across the island in the 1960s. Interactions between Maroon healers and the non-Maroon patients who come to them for help are described in some detail in Bilby (1979: 73–92).

4. It should be noted that all of the narratives in this section are from Windward Maroon communities. The only reason for this is that I spent more time in these communities (especially Moore Town) than in the Leeward community of Accompong, and therefore had the opportunity to learn more about the uses of plants from Windward Maroons. Very similar narratives are found in Accompong. See, for instance, Besson (2001: 95) and Zips (1999: 76–84).

5. *Indi* is a Maroon Kromanti term that has a number of different meanings, including "belly," "hand," and "ear." In this passage, it is used at one point to mean "belly," and at another to mean "ear."

6. The forest vine known as cacoon stores significant amounts of water. When it is cut in the proper manner, water seeps out and can be caught in the mouth. Maroon woodsmen still depend on this source of refreshment when making extended hunting trips into the

forest. The plant is also used for camouflage (as discussed later in this chapter). Wild pine was also an important source of fresh water for the early Maroons. The strategic value of this plant eventually became known to the British as well, as in the following description from the late eighteenth century: "All the water . . . was exhausted, and the enemy's only resource was in the leaves of the *wild-pine* . . . By the conformation of its leaves, it catches and retains water from every shower. Each leaf resembles a spout, and forms at its base a natural bucket or reservoir" (Edwards 1801b: 347). For more on the survival uses of wild pine, see Pringle (1938: 49) and Zips (1999: 77).

7. From a tape recording of an interview conducted by Frederic G. Cassidy in Moore Town in 1952.

8. Here the narrator is spontaneously "cutting" Kromanti language and quoting a number of old Maroon Country songs, drawing on the power of the Maroon ancestors.

9. In Jamaican Creole, *trash* refers to parts of any crop plant or vegetable product removed while it is growing, or left over after processing or use (Cassidy and Le Page 1980: 449). Among Maroons, however, the term is often used in a more specific sense to refer to plants used for medicinal or spiritual purposes. The common Maroon expression, to *rub trash*, means "to use herbs for medicinal/spiritual reasons" and, by extension, "to do Maroon spiritual work." The word has purely positive connotations and is never used by Maroons in the standard English sense of "refuse" or "garbage."

10. See Robinson (1969: 120–25) on the use of dogs during the Second Maroon War in Jamaica.

11. The variants of the song found in Moore Town, Scot's Hall, and Charles Town are different enough to suggest that it was a very long time ago that they branched off from a common ancestral version.

12. Schafer (1973: 229) was told of this song while in Scot's Hall. He renders the words as follows: "Joa fa river Joa day." He was told, as was I, that it is one of the first three or four—and one of the most important—of the opening songs used to begin a Kromanti Play in Scot's Hall.

13. From a tape recording of a Kromanti Play made by the author in Charles Town. Part of this recording can be heard on Bilby (1992).

14. For background on the historical development and functions of the asafo military societies in the area known today as Ghana, see Datta and Porter (1971). There has been some debate over whether the Akan asafo system developed relatively recently, perhaps during the nineteenth century, as a result of European influences, or whether it is much older and represents, in part, an extension of an indigenous form of military organization. After reviewing the historical literature, Datta and Porter (1971: 293) argue that "there is evidence to suggest strongly that it was in existence by at least the middle of the seventeenth century." These authors do not consider evidence from the Americas; but the fact that Jamaican Maroons have retained the term *Asafo*, and that it refers among them to a sacred space linked with Kromanti religious and military practices that go back at least to the early eighteenth century (pre-treaty times), may be seen as some of the strongest existing evidence in support of their argument.

15. I have found one archival reference to a "Captain Phillip" in connection with the military campaigns against the Windward Maroons. In a listing of "the Negroes [i.e., slaves or free blacks serving as soldiers] that were Shott" during a military expedition against the Maroons in 1731 appears the following: "Capt. Phillip shot thro' his right thigh" ("Copy of Christopher Allen's Journall," entry of March 16, 1731, PRO/CO 137/

54, 56). This individual was apparently an officer with the black troops who fought against the Maroons along with the British. Whether or not he later defected to the Maroons and lent his military skills to them is not known. It is also possible that he was originally with the Maroons, and later changed sides to fight with the British. Richard Hart (1950: 58) cites another document from 1732 that tells of an apparent Maroon defector named Philip who offered to guide a party against the Windward Maroons.

16. The area near Moore Town called Sanda remains a sacred place for Maroons. The Kromanti powers that were tapped by the ancestors while preparing for war (as described in the above narratives) are said to linger in the area, and there are also widely known oral traditions about miracles that have occurred there in the more recent past. See Harris (n.d.: 35–36) and Carey (1997: 183).

17. For Hart's summary of this oral tradition, based on the testimony of a number of Moore Town Maroons in 1944, see Hart (1985: 84–85). See also Hart (1950: 64) and Harris (n.d.: 14–17).

18. The opinion of one British officer who fought against the Windward Maroons in the period immediately before the treaty lends credence to the Maroon perspective: "such who are unacquainted with [Jamaica] will be surprised when they are told, that all the regular troops in Europe, could not have conquered the wild Negroes [i.e., Maroons], by force of arms; and if Mr. Trelawney [the Jamaican governor who authorized the treaty] had not wisely given them, what they contended for, LIBERTY, they would, in all probability have been, at this day, masters of the whole country" (Thicknesse 1788: 91). The same officer goes on to state that "I never heard of any Party, whether of Militia, or Regulars, that could stand against the ambushes of those People" (106).

19. Maroons also explicitly credit various other strategic resources discussed in this chapter, such as the abeng language, for the ultimate "victory" of their ancestors. As a Scot's Hall Maroon told Victoria Durant-Gonzalez (1976: 15), "the abeng is blown in the language of the Maroons, that is how the Maroons licked [beat] the British."

20. From a tape recording made by David DeCamp in Moore Town on December 8, 1958. The narrator was major of the Moore Town Maroons at the time.

21. Similar oral traditions encountered by Jean Besson (2001: 87) among the Leeward Maroons point to the importance of ongoing ties between Maroons and plantation slaves in the planning of raids. According to Accompong Maroons today, the plantation slaves "distracted the plantocracy with cane-field fires so that the Maroons could raid plantations for cattle" (Besson 1995: 311).

22. This narrative apparently represents a fusion of what the narrator learned from his "grand-uncle" and what he later read in the children's book *Queen of the Mountain*, where the main character, Nanny, devises a plan that involves having one of her fictional lieutenants "creep stealthily to the well at the English plantation and poison the drinking water" (Cousins 1967: 35–36).

23. *Bráye* is a Maroon Kromanti word meaning to wrap oneself in something. It also refers to a type of wraparound garment, similar to a loincloth, which, according to some ritual specialists, was traditionally placed on the body of a deceased Maroon before burial for religious reasons.

24. There is evidence that similar strategies were employed by the Leeward Maroons. According to Dallas (1803a: 49–50), the British emissaries who marched into the Cockpit Country to make peace with Kojo's people in 1739 eventually became aware of a protected

"dell," in which "were secured the Maroon women and children, and all their valuable things deposited."

25. Oral traditions regarding Woman Town are discussed in Harris (n.d.: 70), Brathwaite (1977: 12), Bilby and Steady (1981: 454–55), Campbell (1988: 179), Bilby (1995: 171–73), and Carey (1997), among other sources. The existence of such a settlement among the Windward Maroons is also documented in contemporary written sources. In one letter written by a British officer in 1731, there is mention of a "Town and Great Cave where they send their Women and Children to, when any Party comes upon them; The Cave is very large with two great Troughts to hold Watter" (PRO/CO 137/53, 303). Another archival document, from January 1732, states that a guide working for British anti-Maroon troops "believes he knows the town where the rebels hide their women and children, and can show a party the way thither" (Hart 1950: 58). See Hoogbergen (1990: 92–93, 97, 200–201), Bilby (1989b: 160), and Bilby (1995: 173, 178) for very similar oral traditions among the Aluku Maroons of French Guiana and Suriname, which are also supported by eighteenth-century documents found in Dutch archives.

26. Readers unfamiliar with Jamaican Creole need to be cautioned against interpreting this phrase to mean that the women at Woman Town were naked. It means, rather, that there were *only* women there.

27. As a verb, *bari* means to bundle palm fronds for easy transportation, using a technique that involves folding and crisscrossing the leaves. (The term is apparently used only by Maroons; in any case, it does not appear in the *Dictionary of Jamaican English*.) In writing the name of the historic site above Moore Town, I use the spelling Barry Hill because that is how most literate Maroons render it. I have chosen, however, to spell the associated verb phonemically, since there is no evidence that it is derived from the name Barry or any other English word. Carey (1997: 618), in contrast, chooses to use the English spelling even for the verb, when she writes of "barrying up thatch as Nanny did."

28. This place name is full of special significance in this context. Cassidy and Le Page (1980: 265) define *krakasa* as the palm *Thrinax rex*, adding that "the only place where this palm grows is on the steep escarpments and limestone rocks of the John Crow Mountains" (that is, in the heart of the Windward Maroon territory). They further note that "it is known locally as Cracasa and the leaves are used for thatching."

29. This is a technique with a long history in various parts of Africa. For a documented example from Sierra Leone in the early seventeenth century, see Shaw (2002: 57).

30. For a description of the Maroon tinderbox and its importance to Windward Maroon hunters and farmers in the past, see Harris (1994: 51).

31. Among Windward Maroons there is a general rule against eating goat (although this prohibition is increasingly ignored), and goats are never sacrificed at Kromanti Play. As Joseph Moore (1953: 66) noted, "because goat meat is tabu for Maroons, they use the pig as a sacrificial animal in their ceremonies, while in [Kumina] the goat is always used." Hurston (1938: 70) attended a joint Maroon-Kumina ceremony in 1936, during which the Maroons separately prepared a pig off to the side (because the goat being prepared nearby by the Kumina devotees was prohibited for them).

32. In some written sources, rendered as Chatter River.

33. The very same military technique was used by the ancestors of the Saramaka Maroons in their battles against Dutch troops in eighteenth-century Suriname. Like Jamaican Maroons, present-day Saramaka historians continue to recite oral accounts of these events (Price 1983b: 20–21).

34. This oral tradition about rolling stones or boulders onto the approaching enemy is also mentioned in Carey (1997: 254).

35. Like many other important Maroon sites mentioned in archival documents, the exact location of Carrion Crow Hill (in some sources, called Carrion Crow Mountain)—mentioned in one of the eighteenth-century documents quoted below as a site where Maroons rolled boulders onto their enemies—has not yet been firmly established (Agorsah 1994: 169). Both Alan Tuelon (1968: 306) and Bev Carey (1997: 249, 279) believe that it is the same mountain known to Maroons as Old Abraham.

36. "Econ. Ms. Accom. Seminar," p. 3, Cooper MSS.

37. Told to Hart by Charles Reid (commonly known as "Commander Reid," a famous Accompong Kromanti specialist during the first part of the twentieth century) and a number of other Maroons in Accompong in 1943 (Hart 1985: 116; see also Hart 1950: 69). Jean Besson (1997: 220) and Olive Lewin (2002: 168) also mention this oral tradition.

38. "Econ. Ms. Accom. Seminar," p. 3. Cooper MSS.

39. This theme of sparing a lone British soldier or two to return and "tell the tale" occurs in Moore Town not only in connection with narratives about what I have called "fighting fire with fire," but also in a number of other oral traditions. See, for instance, Colonel Harris's narrative about Nanny's pot in Tanna (1984: 20).

40. Meaning that while she was possessed by a spirit, it was revealed to her that the British were about to attack.

41. According to Colonel Wright (1994: 66) of Accompong Town, this name—which is one of the names by which Maroons know the original site of Accompong (now popularly known as Old Town)—is derived from "Humphrey Town." Other Maroons, however, have told me that it is an "African name." Although Colonel Wright writes it "Amphrey Town," I have chosen to spell it in a way that reflects the pronunciation of it I have always heard: /ámféri/ or /ánféri/. Laura Tanna similarly spells it Anferry Town; and her Accompong informant, Mann Rowe, even spelled it out for her as "A-N-F-E-R-R-Y T-O-W-N" (Tanna 1984: 19).

42. Barbara Kopytoff (1977: 141–42) discusses the Maroon origins of jerk pork and provides a recipe from Accompong.

43. In 1971, when David Locke carried out ethnographic research on the production of jerk pork in Boston Bay (by then already locally famous for this product), he was repeatedly told that "Boston Bay is the only town in Jamaica which specializes in making 'jerk pork'" (Locke 1972: ii). According to oral traditions in that community, the Maroons were the first in the island to use this method of preparation, and the Boston Bay tradition of jerking had been learned from them. Locke found, as did I when I arrived six years later, that the only non-Maroon place other than Boston Bay where jerk pork was regularly available was next to the public market in Port Antonio; and all the sellers there were from Boston Bay (123–33). Locke makes no mention of other kinds of jerk dishes, such as chicken or fish, and I do not recall any being available in the late 1970s. Because of its jerk tradition (which now includes chicken and fish in addition to pork), Boston Bay is today an important tourist attraction.

44. One of the complaints of the Trelawny Town Maroons who were deported to Nova Scotia after the Second Maroon War of 1795 centered on "the absence of wild hogs to hunt" in that part of the world (Hinds 2001: 221); this perhaps gives some indication of the importance of this practice in Maroon culture.

45. The value of jerk pork as a survival food rests partly on its shelf life; the process of

jerking, as well as the spices used, serve to preserve the meat so that it can be stored for emergencies. Depending on various factors in the preparation process, it can be made to last anywhere from days to weeks without refrigeration (Locke 1972: 105–6).

46. See Campbell (1978: 67) for an interesting description of some of the "rules" and rituals accompanying hog hunting.

47. When adventurer Kenneth Pringle hiked past Nanny Town in the 1930s, his Maroon guides told him that their revered ancestress "was a huntress of the wild hog" (Pringle 1938: 36).

48. See Zora Neale Hurston's marvelous recounting of an Accompong Maroon hunting expedition in which she participated in 1936 (Hurston 1938: 30–37) and described with much the same sense of excitement as the narratives reproduced here. In a letter written in 1937, Hurston called hunting the wild hog "one of the most exciting things in the western world" (Kaplan 2002: 389).

49. Cassidy and Le Page (1980: 87) define *caban* as "a platform of green sticks on which pork is jerked." One nineteenth-century writer observed that "this is called about the Blue Mountain Valley a 'patta,' while among the Maroons, and in the Cuna-Cuna district it is known as a 'caban'" (Thomas 1890: 87).

50. From a tape recording made by Frederic G. Cassidy in Moore Town in 1952.

51. Esau Rowe was the brother of both Colonel H. A. Rowe and the narrator, Emmanuel "Baba" Rowe. Some two decades earlier, he had also participated in the hunt for wild hog described by Zora Neale Hurston (1938: 31–37).

52. From a tape recording made by David DeCamp in Accompong on June 5, 1959. The narrator, known more commonly as Baba Rowe, was a well-known storyteller and the brother of the former colonel of the Accompong Maroons, Henry Augustus Rowe. See Le Page and DeCamp (1960: 127–79). When visiting travel writer Patrick Leigh Fermor asked Baba Rowe what jerk pork tasted like, the latter "joined his hands in prayer, and turned his eyes to heaven" (Fermor 1950: 368–69).

Chapter 6. Prominent Presences: Memorable Persons, Places, and Deeds

1. Pérez (1995) discusses the important role played by landscape in the continuing consciousness of the past among a "maroon descendant community" in Venezuela. It is interesting that in this community, Aripao, even though historical traditions concerning the maroon past are not nearly as well preserved or elaborate as among the Jamaican Maroons, knowledge of this past continues to be encoded in the physical landscape explored and occupied by the ancestors. See also Medina (2003), Santos-Granero (1998), Vidal (2003), and Whitehead (2003) for recent discussions of the ways in which history is inscribed in local landscapes among a number of Amazonian peoples.

2. Writing in the 1960s, for instance, Carey Robinson (1969: 54) expressed uncertainty as to whether "Nanny did in fact exist," going on to argue that although "latter-day Windward Maroons treasure the legends of Nanny and acclaim her as their greatest leader . . . the only real leader of the Windward Maroons who is mentioned with authenticity during the period is Quao."

3. See Brathwaite (1977; 1994). By the 1980s, even the most cautious historians, such as Mavis Campbell, could agree that "we can feel confident that there existed a historical personage called Nanny" (Campbell 1988: 177).

4. Anonymous, "Remarkable Nanny," *Jamaica Observer*, November 2, 2001. Nowadays such recognition of Nanny as a major historical figure is not limited to the Jamaican

popular press. The prestigious Gilder Lehrman Center for the Study of Slavery, Resistance, and Abolition at Yale University, founded by historian David Brion Davis, has chosen to use as its logo the imaginary "portrait" of Nanny created for the Jamaican five-hundred dollar bill—an ironic choice, given that many Maroon elders in Moore Town feel that its portrayal of their founding ancestress is inaccurate. The logo can be viewed at the center's Web site at www.yale.edu/glc/info/nanny.html.

5. As should be apparent from previous chapters, this Kromanti phrase, almost always attributed to Nanny, can be heard in many different narrative contexts, varying slightly in pronunciation. Explanations of its specific meaning vary from individual to individual, but most who know the phrase agree that it contains a larger message of defiance. One Windward Maroon informant glossed the term *Asante kotoko* for Beverley Hall-Alleyne (1982: 37) as "the *Asante* (Maroons) will never die." Colonel Harris of Moore Town states that the expression "had its roots in the long war with the British [when] every Maroon would stoutly declare that if the foe should succeed in killing a thousand of them, then a thousand more would rise up [like the quills of a porcupine] to defend and preserve their freedom" (Harris 1994: 42). The phrase is no doubt derived from Asante-Twi; in the latter language, Ashanti Kotoko (or Asante Kotoko) refers to the supreme council under the Asante king. According to Ellis (1887: 276–77), a literal translation of this epithet would be "Ashanti Porcupine," meaning that, like a porcupine, the king's council "cannot be molested without injury." Asante Kotoko is also the name of one of Ghana's best-known football (soccer) clubs today; founded in 1935 in the Asante capital of Kumasi, the team's official symbol is the porcupine, its nickname the Porcupine Warriors, and its motto *wo kum apem a, apem beba* (if you kill a thousand, another thousand, and tens of thousands more, will emerge to conquer you).

6. The same could once be said of the western Maroon community of Accompong and the spirits of its ancestors, especially before the late 1930s, when the original Kromanti religion of this community received a dramatic challenge from Maroon Christian converts that led to its near total demise (Kopytoff 1987). Writing of the Accompong Town he knew in 1939, Archibald Cooper could still say: "One of the leaders of the rebels, named Accompong, was the founder of this particular village. Today, two hundred years later he is just as much a part of the village as if he were alive. He is the community's super-sacred ghost & as such is called the 'Town Master.' Everybody knows what the Town Master looks like—he rides a big white horse, wears a black military uniform, with shiny gold buttons, & a gleaming white pith helmet. He rides through the village on inspection trips, maybe every month or so . . . The reality of Accompong's, Nanny's, and Quaco's existence is affirmed by the fact that they are on the scene, in the same company with spirits of recently deceased ancestors. Thus the continuity of the present day community with the Old Time Maroons of the war days is affirmed" (Cooper MSS, "Indianapolis on Obeah," and "Historical Summary of the Maroons Past and Present").

7. In Windward Maroon tradition, a returning spirit is said to *baan* (born) or, less commonly, to *namesake* the child in whom it is reincarnating. Such spirits typically reveal themselves through dreams shortly before a child is born. In some cases, however, it later becomes evident, after the child becomes ill and fails to respond to treatment, that a false identification has been made, in which case corrective measures must be taken. Once the correct spirit is revealed, libations or other offerings may be made in apology, and from then on the child will have to be called by the newly revealed name. See Harris (n.d.: 37–38; 1994: 43–44) for further background on this system of reincarnation. A similar pattern

was common among the Leeward Maroons of Accompong until at least the 1940s. Archibald Cooper, for example, was told that constant crying, spasms, and a swollen belly were typical symptoms in a baby not given the name of the proper returning spirit (Cooper MSS, note dated September 22 [1939], "Duppies" folder). Related systems of reincarnation can be found in other parts of Afro-America, such as Brazil and Cuba (Bastide 1965: 14–27), but the clearest parallels are from the Guianas. See, for instance, Hurault (1961: 221) for a description of the very similar reincarnating spirits known as *nenseki* (derived from English, *namesake*) among the Aluku Maroons of French Guiana and Suriname. See also Price (1975: 51–52) on Saramaka *nêséki*.

8. For example, in a "Return of the Number of Maroons belonging to the different Maroon Towns" compiled by the superintendents of the various communities in July and August of 1824, eight Moore Town Maroon women with estimated ages 28–77 are listed as having the name Nanny. Interestingly enough, in the other Windward Maroon communities, the numbers were much smaller. Charles Town had only two, and Scot's Hall none. Accompong also had none (Papers Relating to Slaves in the West Indies 1825: 21–33). Among the Trelawny Town Maroons brought to Sierra Leone in 1800, there was at least one Nanny—Nanny Baily (Campbell 1993: 48).

9. The Ellis family line (often spoken of as "the Ellis tribe") is reputed to be one of the most knowledgeable and powerful in the recent history of Moore Town. Because of its preeminence in the domain of what Maroons today call Science (control over spirits), this "tribe" has also become known as "the Pingwing tribe"—in reference to its members' ability to inflict rapid and severe damage on enemies. (The plant known as *pingwing* [*Bromelia pinguin*], often used in Jamaica and other parts of the Caribbean to make hedges, must be handled with caution because of its treacherous, extremely prickly leaves [Cassidy and Le Page 1980: 351].) Nanny Ellis is but one of a long line of outstanding dancers and healers from the "Pingwing tribe" to have achieved fame. She is remembered not only as a medium of Grandy Nanny, but also as the person responsible for making Brownsfield (a Maroon branch settlement founded by a man who left Moore Town with his family in the nineteenth century) a center of spiritual power. Up until the 1980s, Brownsfield was one of the few locations in the Moore Town area where public Kromanti ceremonies (open to any Maroon, not just those specially invited) were still regularly held.

10. Colonel C.L.G. Harris, "Nanny at Last!" *Daily Gleaner*, July 2, 1994.

11. When possessing spirits in Kromanti Play come to stay for any length of time, their mediums always have their heads tied with a specially prepared cloth known as a *sagl* (saddle), without which the spirit is unable properly to "mount" its *haas* ("horse"—i.e., medium). See Bilby (1981: 62–67).

12. From a field recording made by the author in Scot's Hall. A version of the song, performed by Scot's Hall Maroons with full drum ensemble, can be heard on Bilby (1992).

13. The narrator glossed these words, spoken by Nanny, as "my children are before me, and my children are behind me."

14. This passage clearly illustrates the occasional mingling in Windward Maroon narratives of descriptions and images from written sources with those passed on exclusively through oral channels. In this case, the narrator has read a widely circulated children's booklet published in 1967 by the Jamaican ministry of education, *Queen of the Mountain*, a fictionalized account that has been one of the main sources of information about the Maroons for Jamaican schoolchildren. Consider the following passage: "at a signal from Nanny's hands, the drummers stopped playing . . . the gathering turned to hear what the

leader had to say . . . her extended hand was held not in blessing, but to command the obedience of her subjects" (Cousins 1967: 22). On the same page and on the cover as well is a dramatic drawing of an imaginary Nanny standing before her assembled troops with arms raised. Unlike the oral account presented here, however, the booklet makes no reference to the Maroons (in this context or any other) calling Nanny "mother," nor does it portray Nanny putting her hand on the head of the drum to interrupt a song and demand the attention of all those present, a gesture often used by possessed mediums in Kromanti Play today.

15. Johnny Chambers, the Accompong Maroon singer who learned this song from his grandmother, explained that it was originally sung by Grandy Nanny shortly after the conclusion of the peace treaties in 1739 to urge all the different groups of Maroons to come together in unity, put down their arms, and obey the terms of the pact. (A version of the song can be heard on Bilby [1992].) After listening to the song, the Congolese scholar Fu-Kiau kia Bunseki concluded that the words are partly of Kikongo origin (Bilby 1981b: 11). Such evidence of Central African linguistic influence points to the inadequacy of the common view that Jamaican Maroons are almost exclusively of Akan (Ashanti/Fanti) origin. There is a good deal of evidence, both historical and contemporary, suggesting that the early Maroons were more ethnically diverse than generally thought (see Kopytoff 1976). Such evidence can be found today not only in the esoteric Maroon Kromanti language (Dalby 1971) and in Kromanti song texts, but in other cultural domains as well (as we saw in the discussion of Maroon oral traditions referring to multiple "tribal" origins in chapter 3). Another example, noted by Jean Besson and other authors, is the existence of "ethnic burial grounds" in Accompong. "Oral history states that these burial grounds represent the Congo and Coromantee origins of the First-Time Maroons and their immediate descendants, who founded the Accompong community" (Besson 1997: 216).

16. Meaning that, when possessing a medium today, her spirit doesn't stay long enough to perform any spiritual work.

17. In my own research among the Aluku Maroons, I found that Aluku *bwi* (spiritually empowered protective bracelets) are still routinely prepared by being placed for a time in special pots containing certain herbs; although these pots are never exposed to fire, this process is known as *boli a bwi* ("cooking" or "boiling" the bracelet). Interestingly, Carey (1997: 352) explicitly characterizes Nanny's pot as a container holding herbs: "Nanny is reported to have used another type of science, to have *placed a pot of herbs which boiled without fire*, along a narrow path to a precipice *creating noxious fumes* to stupefy the soldiers and cause them to stumble, to fall over the precipice to their death on the stones in the Stony and Macungo (Nanny) Rivers below" (italics in original).

18. The difficulty that some Jamaican intellectuals have in accepting this oral tradition on the Maroons' own terms is exemplified in Vic Reid's novel *Nanny-Town*. Here, the tradition of Nanny as bullet catcher is "fictionalized" out of existence. Nanny is portrayed not as an actual bullet catcher, but rather as a clever purveyor of disinformation who purposefully fabricates such stories (which her own people are not supposed to believe) in order to strike fear in the Englishman's heart (Reid 1983: 46–47).

19. In fact, Thomas never made explicit mention of any of Nanny's body parts; all he said was that "she never went into battle armed like the rest, but received the bullets of the enemy that were aimed at her, and returned them with fatal effect, in a manner of which decency forbids a nearer description" (Thomas 1890: 36).

20. It is interesting to note that Carey, whose research on Maroon oral traditions was

used by Brathwaite during the 1970s to argue for official recognition of Nanny as a National Hero, has not changed her position on this question for more than two decades, despite Brathwaite's (1977: 33) disapproving comment that "even Beverley Carey, herself a Maroon and one of the finest indigenous reconstructors of Maroon history, has been forced into the repetition of this ridiculous story, although she does her best to make it more 'reasonable.'"

21. Gottlieb (2000: 52–53) falls victim to just this kind of "cleaning up" of oral traditions by "educated" Maroons who wish not to offend squeamish outsiders. Drawing examples from a dissertation on the Moore Town Maroons by anthropologist Leann Martin (1973), Gottlieb treats a written account of Nanny's bullet catching authored by the highly literate Maroon leader C.L.G. Harris for the *Daily Gleaner*—a version Harris "edited" for similarly "educated" readers—as the authentic oral tradition; at the same time Gottlieb discounts an "orally" performed version reported by Martin (replete with elaborate gestures miming the use of Nanny's buttocks) as a "deteriorated" facsimile. Gottlieb fails to recognize that, despite his "cleaning up" of the story for newsprint, Colonel Harris himself considers the supposedly "deteriorated" version to be the authentic one. For instance, when telling the story to a trained folklorist who would presumably be less easily offended than the average reader of the *Gleaner*, Colonel Harris reinserted (though in a typically delicate manner) the reference to Nanny's "privates" (see Tanna 1984: 20).

22. In a recent book, Angelita Reyes (2002: 82), who during the 1980s collected oral traditions from Maroons in Moore Town, also concurs: "they said that [Nanny] could shoot bullets at the British from her behind."

23. This is a Kromanti code word used to alert fellow Maroons to the presence (usually unwelcome in Maroon communities) of a member of the Jamaican police force.

24. There is overwhelming evidence that the Jamaican Maroon ideas about spiritually induced bodily invulnerability that survive in the context of Kromanti Play (and in stories about Nanny)—including the idea of bullet catching—have African origins. Similar spiritual traditions are well attested among the Akan-speaking peoples who contributed many members to the early Maroon groups. Ellis (1887: 138–39), for example, describes a ritual in which Ashanti "priests" and "priestesses" demonstrate their powers by stepping into a series of blazing fires; those who are properly prepared "will receive no injury and suffer no pain from the fire." There is no reason, however, to believe that such traditions among the Jamaican Maroons were derived exclusively from Akan-speaking peoples; similar rites are found across West and Central Africa. Among the Temne of Sierra Leone, for instance, certain spiritual techniques are used to create a state of "ritual impenetrability" that "has a great deal in common with other techniques of ritual bulletproofing and invisibility in different parts of Africa" (Shaw 2002: 56, 60). The Temne Poro cult, in particular, makes use of certain "medicines" that give members "miraculous capacities such as being unharmed when cut by weapons (an ability that they demonstrate in public performances by cutting themselves with knives)" (60). Similar techniques used in Senegal and Guinea-Conakry are described in detail in an experiential account by Green (2001). Such African-derived spiritual traditions of bodily protection have survived not only in Jamaica, but in several other parts of the Americas as well. In Cuba, for example, *rumba de cuchillo*, an esoteric variety of rumba performed by *abakuá* initiates, involves "dancing while rapidly passing sharp knives over one's body and face" (Moore 1997: 185). And in the Guianas, the Kumanti (Kromanti) traditions of Maroon peoples such as the Aluku and Ndyuka make use of techniques for inducing bodily invulnerability very similar to those used by

Jamaican Maroons (Hurault 1961: 249–51; Bilby 1995: 174–77; Herskovits and Herskovits 1934: 17). According to Melville and Frances Herskovits (1934: 350), Saramaka Kromanti (Komantí) "includes powers which endow the members with resistance to bullets, and to all things that cut or lacerate, like knives and thorns and glass." In a number of recent wars in both Africa and the Americas, similar ideas about spiritual protection have been applied (and at times, some would argue, distorted and abused). During the civil war in Suriname in the 1980s, for instance, the predominantly Ndyuka Maroon 'Jungle Commando' routinely resorted to Kumanti war *obia* [obeah] passed down from the Maroon ancestors to neutralize enemy bullets (Bilby 1990: 511–16; Polimé and Thoden van Velzen 1988: 99, 107–8, 115; Thoden van Velzen 1990). In the Liberian wars of the 1990s, on the other side of the ocean, "almost all the fighters believed that it was possible to obtain spiritual medicine which would make them invulnerable to bullets and successful in battle" (Ellis 1999: 261). Similarly, "in the rebel war that has been waged in Sierra Leone since 1991, techniques for the protection of the body have taken on a new and horrific relevance . . . [as] soldiers, rebels, civil militia fighters, and many civilians . . . wear medicines that either repel bullets or produce a Darkness that enables wearers to see enemies before they themselves are seen" (Shaw 2002: 62). (For more on Jamaican Maroon spiritual traditions related to bodily protection, see chapter 9.)

25. Brathwaite (1977: 34) himself recognizes the symbolic potency of Nanny's body language, admitting that "she probably made a gesture of contempt and derision at or towards the British, using that part of her body that black women have traditionally used to convey that meaning. Or rather, since she was a symbol of our defiance, the folk imagination probably froze her in that symbolic gesture of defiance."

26. Another important message carried by the image of Nanny catching bullets—as understood by the feminist writers cited above, and others (e.g., Mathurin 1975; Ellis 1986: 27; Bush 1990; Davies and Fido 1990; Johnson 1990; James 2002: 105–9; Reyes 2002)—is that of female power. This aspect of the legend has contributed to the spread of Nanny's fame beyond Jamaica and the Caribbean.

27. From a handwritten field notebook kept by Helen Roberts in 1921, p. 4. The notebook is labeled "Jamaica. Jan.–Mar. 1921. Expressions, Language, Names, etc." Roberts MSS/AFC.

28. It is possible that in paraphrasing this oral tradition some time after it was related to her, Roberts added the detail about Nanny having caught bullets "in her hands." In Roberts's raw field notes (from which the narrative presented before this one was extracted), Nanny "turn herself and catch balls," implying that she turned her back to the gunfire and used a different part of her body. However, Roberts's colleague Martha Beckwith paraphrased the same oral tradition (which she probably heard narrated by Colonel Rowe on the very same occasion that Roberts did, while the two were carrying out fieldwork together in 1921) as follows: "Rowe said that no bullets could touch their men during the conflict because old Nanny stood with her back to the enemy and, attracting all the balls to herself, caught them between her thighs just as boys sometimes catch a ball" (Beckwith 1929: 192). It seems likely that Beckwith, like Roberts, added the oblique reference to using the hands ("just as boys sometimes catch a ball"). But it is also quite possible that Colonel Rowe himself added this element so as not to offend the sensibilities of his visitors, two genteel white ladies from the United States.

29. Helen H. Roberts, *Song Hunting in Jamaica*, p. 47. Unpublished ms., Roberts MSS/YU, group 1410.

30. Cooper MSS, "Historical Summary of the Maroons Past and Present," pp. 4–5.

31. From a tape-recorded interview with C. U. Walters, an herbalist of partial Maroon descent, conducted by Joseph G. Moore in Morant Bay in 1950.

32. Meaning that when Nanny was done, she turned her back and shook the bottom of her dress at the British soldiers. This is understood by Maroons (and other Jamaicans) as a taunting gesture of defiance.

33. *Laas* is an older Maroon pronunciation of *raas* (a vulgar Jamaican Creole term for buttocks). In the oldest form of Maroon creole it is pronounced *lási* (Bilby 1983: 44, 75).

34. Meaning that he is beginning to feel the powerful spirits invoked by the song; he feels himself heating up as they approach.

35. *Tándabásokom* is an expression in old Maroon creole meaning literally "to stand up" (it can be analyzed as "stand-up-so-come"). Its most common use, however, is a ritual one. It is believed that if one loses one's footing and is about to slip, one can utter this phrase, invoking spiritual powers that will prevent a fall. Since the very steep terrain farmed by Maroons in the Moore Town area can be treacherous, with foot paths that are dangerously slick after heavy rains, the expression is heard quite often in that community. By extension, the phrase is also used more generally to express one's determination to stand up to a challenge or difficult situation, much like the Rastafarian expression "stand firm" (as in "stand firm, or you a go feed worm" [be strong, or your corpse will feed the worms]).

36. Meaning, Nanny took her bottom and turned it into a gun.

37. Here the narrator states clearly the meaning of the formulaic Kromanti words Nanny uttered every time the whites fired a shot: "kill it, kill de shot" (i.e., "render the bullets ineffective"). This Maroon ritual expression (*o jéeku[m]*) is very likely derived from Twi or a related Akan language; it is possible that it fuses two distinct Akan words, *gyè* + *kù(m)*. The Twi verb *gyè* means "to take (especially what is offered or given), to accept, receive." Common constructions using this verb, according to Christaller's Twi dictionary, include *gye bó* ("to receive a stone, be hit by a stone"), and *gyè . . . só* ("to take up, i.e., answer, return an answer, respond, reply; *to return the firing of the enemy*" [italics mine]). The second part of the Maroon phrase may be from Twi or Fanti *kùm*, *kūm* ("to kill, slay, put to death; to defeat, overcome, vanquish, destroy"); cf. *kùm* "to prevent the effect or efficiency of, to render ineffective, inefficient") (Christaller 1933: 156, 266, 269–70). The semantic associations of these Akan terms resonate quite strikingly with the central components of most narratives about Nanny's bullet catching—that is, receiving and returning enemy fire and defeating the enemy by rendering his bullets ineffective.

38. A rough translation of what the narrator says to Nanny would be: "All right, Nanny. I shouldn't have told that young man that thing, but that's how it is. You see it's no lie I'm telling. He wants to know what used to happen in the time of old, and [how] you all fought the war and those things. That's what used to happen. He wants to know about the time of old, what used to happen. So I have to tell him about what you had and what you did with it in the past."

39. Dalby (1971: 49) points out that the name represented in the Windward treaty as "Apong" is probably derived from an Akan personal name, Opong.

40. Referring to his linguistic research among the Windward Maroons, David Dalby (1971: 48) suggests that "it is perhaps significant that Colonel Latibaudiere [of Scot's Hall], while making reference to Nanny and to the leaders of the Leeward Maroons, made no reference to Quao." When I worked in Scot's Hall some years later, I also found that

Quao was rarely, if ever, mentioned in that community; and the same was true in Moore Town and Charles Town.

41. See the section of chapter 5 titled "Staying to the River."

42. I am most grateful to the late Barbara Kopytoff for originally pointing me to this written reference to Captain Welcome, which persuaded me of the likely value of carrying out further archival research.

43. Although Captain Welcome appears to have died during the 1760s, his name continued to be passed on as a family name among Windward Maroons into the nineteenth century. In a census of 1824, for instance, a 38-year-old woman named Diana Welcome is among those listed for Moore Town (Papers Relating to Slaves in the West Indies 1825: 31).

44. One possible explanation is that those British military personnel involved in the drafting of the treaty, given their very limited understanding of the dynamics of leadership among the Windward Maroons, misjudged—perhaps were even *led* by certain interested Maroon parties to overestimate—the relative importance of some of the leaders whose names they recorded in the treaty in the overall scheme of Windward politics. (This lack of understanding might also help to explain the omission of Nanny from the treaty; see Zips [1999b: 217–19] for some plausible speculations on why Nanny receives no mention in that document.) Another possible explanation is that "Welcome" might simply have been one of several names for one of the captains mentioned in the treaty—perhaps a name by which he was, or later became, more commonly known. Most Maroons today continue to be known by several names, in addition to the "official" names that appear on legal or church documents. Although there is a tendency in Maroon communities, as elsewhere in Jamaica, particularly in formal contexts, to discount such alternate names as "mere" nicknames or "pet names," these informal names are often more widely known to other members of one's community, and certainly more frequently used, than the "official" names.

45. The wording of a number of other oral accounts (not included here) suggests that the first-time ancestor remembered as Granfa Parro may have become fused over time with the person called Swiplomento; perhaps "Parro" was simply another of Swiplomento's names. A few Maroon elders, for instance, claim that Nanny's husband was known as Granfara Pa Rose, Granfara Rose, or, simply, Pa Rose, while others (usually those with no knowledge of Granfa Swiplomento) state that it was Granfara *Parro* who was her husband. Yet others (such as one of the narrators above) state that Nanny's "husband" had both a "Maroon name" (Mento, or Swiplomento) and an "English name" (Rose Harris). The frequent occurrence of the name "Rose" in connection with an ancestor specifically said to have been Nanny's "husband" or "man" gains in significance when we recall the alternate names by which Nanny and her sister Sekesu are said to have been known: Shanti *Rose* and Fanti *Rose* (or vice versa). (Also of interest is the fact that there exists an oral tradition in Accompong that holds that Nanny's "English name" was Matilda Rowe [Campbell 1988: v; Besson 1997: 226; Barbara Kopytoff, field notes, 1960s; Kenneth Bilby, field notes, 1991]; it is possible that in this case, what was originally *Ro'*—an abbreviation of "rose," as in Granfara Pa Ro'—was over time assimilated to "Rowe," a prominent family name in Accompong.) Although we have no conclusive evidence, all of this would seem to suggest that [Granfa] "Parro" may simply be a contraction of [Granfa] "Pa Rose"—i.e., "Pa Ro'." The name "Parro" may also be related to "Apollo," another prominent Maroon among Nanny's people, according to the same document of 1734 cited below. (The English name *Apollo* is phonologically relatively close to *Parro*, and the latter might actually be derived

from the former [/l/ and /r/ sometimes being interchangeable in older forms of Maroon creole (Bilby 1983: 43–45)]; another possibility is that the British individual responsible for the first version of this written document heard a name that Maroons pronounced /paro/, /palo/, /aparo/ or /apalo/ as "Apollo.") In any case, it is interesting to note that Apollo and Scipio (a Maroon leader discussed below in connection with Swiplomento) apparently escaped from the same plantation; according to this document, they both once belonged to one Samuel Orgill. In fact, it is not implausible that Apollo and Scipio are the same person, just as Parro and Swiplomento (from the oral tradition) may be.

46. As we have seen, the pronunciation of Swiplomento's name varies considerably. (I have chosen here to use "Swiplomento" as a standard spelling only because it seems the most common pronunciation.) Of the various forms, /síplioménto/, /sípriomento/, and /sífioménto/ (none of which appear in the above texts) would seem to come closest to Scipio (which was almost certainly pronounced /sípio/). (In an unpublished manuscript, Colonel Harris of Moore Town spells the name of this early leader Cipri O'mente [Harris n.d.: 15].) The fact that the name is often abbreviated to "Mento" in narratives suggests either that it was once a two-part name, or that it was originally two separate names that over time became one. If detached from its ending—/ménto/—then the name would become /síplio/, /síprio/, /swíplo/, /sífio/, or /swífio/—all reasonably close to /sípio/. Also supporting this interpretation is the fact that two of the more common versions of the name—Swiplomento and Swifomento—are consciously associated with Jamaican Creole terms seen as descriptive of this outstanding ancestor's character and abilities. Some narrators say (as in one of the above texts) that Granfa Swiplomento is known by this name because his highly developed Kromanti powers made him extraordinarily *swipple* (meaning slippery, tricky, clever); in contrast, those who call him Swifomento point out that as a fighter and *fete-man* he was exceptionally *swif* (i.e., swift). Given the well-known Jamaican penchant for word play and other forms of linguistic inventiveness (of which "Rasta talk" is but the best known example), it is reasonable to surmise that the more richly evocative variants such as Swiplomento (i.e., Swipple-o-Mento) and Swifomento (Swif-o-Mento) are the more recent ones and that they evolved out of forms such as Sipliomento and Sifiomento that show no such evidence of semantic extension.

47. Scipio was a common name among Jamaican slaves during the eighteenth and nineteenth centuries, reflecting the practice then in vogue of naming slaves after "classical" figures ("Scipio" being the name of a famous Roman general) (Campbell 1988: 74). It is not clear, however, whether this Maroon leader's name, if acquired on a plantation before his escape, was actually derived from that of the Roman general or simply rendered by British scribes from another similar-sounding name—perhaps one of non-European origin—in a form that matched their expectations. (In a discussion of naming practices among slaves in South Carolina, Charles Joyner [1985: 218–19] points out that in some cases slave names assumed to refer to European "classical" figures such as Scipio might actually represent African names misunderstood by European listeners: "if a slave couple informed their master that they had named their son *Keta*, a common name among the Yoruba, Hausa, and Bambara, the master might have understood the child's name to be *Cato*.") We do know that Scipio probably escaped from plantation slavery rather than having been born in the forest, since he is referred to in one of the documents above as "Mr. Orgills Scipio." In any case, we can savor the irony of the situation: a slave who might have mockingly been named by his owner after a great Roman general in fact rose to *become* a great general—one whom the British were unable to defeat. It is also possible—indeed,

quite likely—that this Maroon leader was known by several names; after escaping into the forest he may have kept his plantation name (if that is what it was), while adding to it, or alternating it with, another name or names (such as Mento).

48. The last section of this Kromanti oration consists of a string of old-time Maroon proverbs.

49. See, for a very revealing comparison, the Saramaka Maroon story of "Kwasímu-kámba's gambit" (Price 1979; 1983: 153–59). This oral historical tradition, about a slave who fled to the Saramaka, only to return to the coast and betray the location and strategic secrets of his former "friends" to the whites, seems to Richard Price (1983: 159) "to encapsulate principles that stand at the very heart of Saramaka life."

50. In a recent conversation with George Sterling of Moore Town (one of the contributors to the present book), Robert Roskind (2001: 254–56) was told of a "white woman" named "Missy Blay Washee" (no doubt the same Missy Be Kwashi mentioned here) who befriended the Maroons during the war with the British, only to sell them out at a later point. First taking ritual precautions by offering rum to the ancestors, Sterling then pointed out to Roskind that the story of this woman and other such first-time accounts belonged to a realm of Maroon knowledge that was rarely shared with non-Maroons. "She was a friend of Nanny," he explained, "but really a spy for the English and she betrayed us" (254). The story might be connected with the narratives about the white traitor Dunbar and his Maroon friend Kwashi told later in this chapter [67–68].

51. From a tape recording of an interview by David DeCamp in Moore Town in 1958. The narrator is speaking here to some young Maroon bystanders who are suggesting that he should be more open with DeCamp, whose questions about Maroon life the narrator has been "dodging." (DeCamp had just asked a sensitive question, wanting to know how many Maroons lived in Moore Town; population counts by outsiders have never been allowed in this community.) The narrator complains that as soon as these younger Maroons learn something, they are ready to go out and give the knowledge away, just as a trusted individual, Missy Be Kwashi, once sold Maroon secrets to the whites. DeCamp is purposefully kept in the dark about the meaning of the entire conversation.

52. This early Maroon leader's name might have a special meaning in the context of these stories of shifting loyalty and betrayal. Writing of Jamaican oral narrative traditions, Jacobs (1945: 97) states that "malicious cunning in a slave led to representing him as Anancy; but if more sympathy was felt with his subtle[t]y, *Puss* seems to have been preferred. Indeed, Puss appears as the one person whom Anancy cannot deceive."

53. Meaning, "when you go to that place, take this thing and rub it on your body like this" (to make yourself invisible).

54. *Opéte bíu sáka*: a common Maroon curse in the Kromanti language, meaning "may the johncrow (vulture) eat you."

55. Colonel C.L.G. Harris (1994: 48) of Moore Town briefly discusses this song, although he gives it a different interpretation, stating that it describes events among the Leeward Maroons during the Second Maroon War of 1795 (a connection he might have made through having read well-known published accounts of that war [e.g., Dallas 1803], in which a Trelawny Town Maroon named Dunbar plays an important role).

56. Also compare the name of another "white" traitor and spy remembered in Moore Town oral traditions: Missy Be *Kwashi* (see text no. 60 in this chapter).

57. *Backra* (not to be confused with *bakra*, meaning "white person") refers to a type of

plant, "a species of the genus *Phytolacca* [which is one type of calalu]" (Cassidy and Le Page 1980: 18).

Chapter 7. The Chosen People

1. Earlier references to the Maroons' perception of themselves as a "chosen people" include Cohen (1973: 172), Bilby (1979: 61), and Campbell (1984: 52).

2. Referring to the very oral tradition that forms the subject of this chapter, Bev Carey (1997: 304), herself a Maroon descendant, also explicitly draws a parallel between the early Maroons and the ancient Israelites.

3. Parts of this oral tradition have appeared in a few written sources over the last few decades, including Carey (n.d.: 26, 98); Harris (n.d.: 3); Mathurin (1975: 37), and Bilby and Steady (1981: 458–59). See also C.L.G. Harris, "The 'Spirit of Nanny,'" *Daily Gleaner*, August 6, 1967; and Carey (1997: 288).

4. Do-an-Consider is one of the several names by which Maroons remember the wartime leader more commonly known as Mento or Swiplomento.

5. The implication being that he summoned the other Maroon leaders to a meeting, either with the abeng or with drum language.

6. Meaning, "I don't consider that there is a God."

7. Meaning that they had to hold on to their children to protect them from being hurt by the oracular object wildly thrashing about with such force that it was destroying the plate.

8. Accompong Maroons use the phrase "skin of the island" to express their belief that Maroons are the oldest continuous inhabitants of Jamaica and thus entitled to special rights (an idea that rests, in part, on claims of partial Arawak [Taino] Indian ancestry). (The Jamaican Creole *skin*, or *kin*—as well as its cognates in several other creole languages—is sometimes used to refer to the entire human body, rather than just its external covering [Cassidy and Le Page 1980: 411]; "skin of the island," therefore, might best be rendered in standard English as "body of the island.") As the original "body of the island," some Accompong Maroons distinguish themselves from other Jamaicans of African descent; they believe the ancestors of these "sons of slaves," or, in Kromanti language, *abrono*, arrived on the island at a later point; their descendants are therefore not entitled to the same special consideration. The expression is also sometimes used to convey the idea that the Maroons have served as the protective "skin" of the island, guarding it against penetration by foreign invaders (as they were bound by their treaties to do). This expression ("skin of the island") has been used in Accompong since at least the 1930s, as documented by anthropologist Archibald Cooper in his field notes ("Historical Summary of the Maroons Past and Present," Cooper MSS).

9. As Martin (1973: 98) found, Moore Town oral traditions also state that Watch Hill "burns for no verifiable reason almost every year, 'according to the hours when Nanny was fighting.'" Many Maroons say that this is why the peak remains bald: its upper section spontaneously catches fire every few years (a phenomenon thought to be caused by the Maroon ancestors).

10. By going beyond a literal interpretation of this oral tradition, I do not mean to challenge the Maroons' insistence that it describes an event that actually occurred. As I have argued elsewhere (Bilby 1995: 173–74), the "miracle food" theme probably stems in part from African-derived ritual or spiritual techniques tied to horticultural practices, some intended to increase crop yields. Similar "miracle food" stories are found in other

parts of Afro-America. One example occurs in Eric Roach's poem "The Ballad of Canga" (1955), about a renegade slave in Tobago with very powerful obeah—so powerful, in fact, that he is able to plant a banana shoot and reap fruit from it only an hour later. As Albert Helman (1956: 177) notes, parallel oral traditions are also found in Suriname and other parts of the Caribbean.

Chapter 8. Underwritten with Blood

1. Although the first British envoys appear to have been sent in the mid-1730s, Campbell (1988: 58, 66) points out that the idea of suing the Maroons for peace was actually conceived by Governor Robert Hunter at the beginning of that decade, nearly ten years before treaties were successfully concluded.

2. There are grounds for believing that Nanny's people knew of Kojo's treaty with the British almost as soon as it was concluded. Alan Tuelon (1968: 308) cites an archival document indicating that the signing of that treaty was actually witnessed by one of Nanny's officers—"the captain of the Windward gang who had not long before joined [the Leeward Maroons] with 100 shott."

3. Richard Hart (1985: 126) states that "not all the Maroons, neither those to windward nor those to leeward, approved of the treaties that had been concluded." Among the evidence he cites is a 1740 document in which the Jamaican governor confirms that the Windward Maroons had agreed to the peace, "a few skulkers excepted." The Windward treaty itself, as Hart points out, suggests that the peacemakers anticipated trouble from these "skulkers": it envisaged (in the ninth clause) that the main Maroon signatory, Quao, might need assistance from his new British allies should he "be disturbed by a greater number of rebels than he is able to fight." See also Campbell (1988: 178–79).

4. Occasionally, Granfa Mento is cast in this role as well. In some variants of this oral tradition, all four (or five) of the original "top generals" refuse the peace, leaving Nanny alone to pursue this path of reconciliation.

5. For discussions of this land grant, a copy of which remains in the Jamaican National Archives in Spanish Town, see Kopytoff (1973: 138–39), Campbell (1988: 174–81), and Harris (1994: 37).

6. For instance, the preamble to the act ratifying the 1739 Leeward Maroon treaty refers to "the late *submission* of Cudjoe, and all the *rebels* under his command, to His Majesty's government" (Kopytoff 1973: 280; underlining in original).

7. See chapter 4, text no. 37.

8. In Jamaican Creole, the terms for "battle" and "bottle" are pronounced the same way: /bakl/.

9. Here the narrator is making reference to the sacred oath that would have to be sworn by the Maroons and the whites in order to bring about a lasting peace. Ojedu finds repugnant the idea of mixing and drinking his blood with that of the whites.

10. The narrator is referring to an archaeological expedition to Nanny Town led by an English soldier, Lt. Harley Nott, in 1973, for which he served as a guide. Bev Carey (1997: 290), who participated in the same expedition, has her own interpretation of the night noises that unnerved some of the outsiders who dared remain in the Nanny Town area after dark: "The author heard the large landslide at night off the nearby mountain—a landslide occurring in the driest weather in months, in much the same manner as the boulders had been thrown off Abraham's Mountain to chase away attacking militia men" (a Maroon military stratagem discussed in chapter 5).

11. *Kremu nanti* is a Maroon Kromanti expression meaning "to die."

12. Baka River and Blaka River: two common Maroon pronunciations of "Back River," a tributary of the Rio Grande that joins Stony River and eventually leads to Nanny Town.

13. These are two commonly heard Jamaican proverbs.

14. *Dodge-him-oo pensa* is a fragment of Kromanti language referring to the traditional Maroon practice of "dodging" the queries of outsiders, which, as the narrator affirms here, remains in force until today. This Kromanti phrase is also the name of a particular type of Maroon *pakit*, or personal spirit, and occurs in at least one well-known Maroon song, discussed in chapter 11.

15. *Congo-worm* is a worm "that supposedly eats the body after burial" (Cassidy and Le Page 1980: 118). In the song, Ojedu sarcastically refers to the British officer as a "dandy man," and threatens him with a defiant insult: "the congo-worm will eat your corpse!"

16. "Lion and tiger" here referring to Nanny's British enemies.

17. A recent example of the public invocation of the symbolism of the treaties occurred in 2000, when Colonel Wallace Sterling of Moore Town joined with the Earl of Portland, who happened to be on a visit from England, in an event widely covered by the media—"a re-enactment of the signing of the Peace Treaty at the Court House square in Port Antonio" (Anonymous, "Earl of Portland, Maroon Colonel Reenact Peace Treaty," *Jamaica Observer*, October 28, 2000). (The Earl is a descendant of the Duke of Portland, who established the eastern parish of Portland in 1723, while he was Governor of Jamaica; up until the treaty of 1739, most of what was to become Portland parish was in reality ruled by the Windward Maroons.)

18. Bilby (1997) provides a detailed discussion of the evidence supporting this conclusion, comparing Jamaican Maroon oral traditions such as those featured in this chapter with Guianese Maroon oral traditions concerning the blood treaties made by their own ancestors and both the French and Dutch during the eighteenth century. Unlike British sources, both French and Dutch colonial documents corroborate the Guianese Maroon versions, clearly describing the blood oaths the European negotiators were required to take in order to conclude peace with the ancestors of the Aluku, Ndyuka, and Saramaka Maroons.

19. Excerpt from a letter written by Colonel Rowe to Father Joseph J. Williams, dated July 13, 1937. Published in McLaughlin (2000: 69).

20. In Jamaican Creole, *mash* means "to destroy, spoil" (Cassidy and Le Page 1980: 295); so the meaning of this sentence is "a blood treaty can never be destroyed."

21. From a tape recording of an interview conducted by Frederic G. Cassidy in Moore Town in 1952.

22. Meaning a drink of water from the spiritually powerful Back River will do one good.

23. See chapter 11 for a detailed discussion of the song and related oral tradition to which this is an elliptical reference.

24. Here the narrator uses a Maroon Kromanti phrase to refer to the sacred oath that was sworn by the Maroons and the whites to bring about a lasting peace. As we have seen, the oath required the former enemies to mix and drink each other's blood. The Kromanti phrase *cut bujufra* is clearly derived from an Akan expression, *abogyafrá*. The entry on this term in Christaller's (1933: 35–36) Twi dictionary includes the following example of usage: "me nè no di abogyafrá . . . *we have mixed our blood; we both are of the same blood.*"

(*Bógyá* is defined by Christaller [35–36] as "blood; a person related by blood, kinsman, kinswoman.")

25. A rough translation of this aside to Nanny would be: "An outsider is here in my home, and he is a young man. He wants to know about how things went, how you fought the war, and all like that. So, you mustn't be angry. But what I've seen, that's what I'm telling. Don't be angry."

26. A Maroon Kromanti phrase that the narrator refused to explain.

27. Here the narrator is addressing the Maroon ancestors, apologizing for revealing too much to an *obroni*. He says: "[Maroon] children, an outsider is in my home. I'm not the one who wants it so. The outsider wants it so."

28. The narrator later explained that this was a different man from the Kojo who led the Leeward Maroons and signed their treaty in the western part of the island. Rather, this man was a Windward Maroon who fought with Nanny's people.

Chapter 9. Maroons and the "Other Side of People"

1. Some Kromanti ceremonies are held to propitiate a Maroon ancestor who has punished a living Maroon for a transgression; in such cases, the disgruntled ancestor is "begged" to stop afflicting the patient with misfortune or illness. The majority of Kromanti ceremonies, however, involve the kind of spiritual combat between opposed forces discussed here.

2. The central area at Kromanti dances, where drummers and dancers interact, is spoken of as a "ring." Colonel Harris of Moore Town describes the *ring* as "a circular opening formed by the drummers, ordinary dancers, singers and spectators" at Kromanti Play (Harris n.d.: 28).

3. See Neil Whitehead's recent ethnography (2002) of spiritual warfare in the shamanic practices of the Patamuna and other Guianese Amerindian peoples for some striking parallels with (as well as critical differences from) the Jamaican Maroon spiritual battles discussed in this chapter.

4. Wishing not to offend contemporary sensibilities, some Maroons publicly deny that their post-treaty ancestors ever captured runaway slaves; others admit but downplay the role of Maroons in such actions (e.g., Harris n.d.: 48–49; Harris 1995: 94–96; Martin 1973: 162–63). But there is ample evidence, both written and oral, that tracking of runaway slaves played an important part in post-treaty Maroon life until 1834 (Jacobs 1945: 74–75; Kopytoff 1973: 168–70; Hart 1985: 124–28; Campbell 1988: 152–53). As "private" Maroon narratives such as those that follow reveal, there remains considerable consciousness of this aspect of the Maroon past in present-day Maroon communities.

5. It should be pointed out that the fates awaiting escaped slaves returned by Maroons varied; not all of those captured received harsh punishment. Barry Higman (1976: 181) tells of a man named Dublin, for instance, who "ran away first in August 1829, but was brought in two months later by the Maroons; in February 1830 he left the plantation for four months and on his return was forgiven; less than a month later he ran away for another six weeks, being brought out of the Mandeville workhouse and forgiven."

6. Writing of the Leeward Maroons, Mavis Campbell conjectures, quite reasonably, that the tracking down of runaways might have had an importance to the Maroons beyond the economic returns it provided. "It also appears to have served, equally, a strategic purpose—strategic in the sense that Cudjoe may well have been delighted to see some of the great warriors among his men occupied in a manner befitting their training and incli-

nation ... Cudjoes' warriors, with no engagement to occupy them, might have turned their frustrations inward on their own communities" (Campbell 1988: 152–53).

7. Even in comparing the hunted slave to a "wild pig," the intention of the narrator is not to dehumanize him, but to emphasize his fierceness (a quality that, in this society of former warriors, is respected and admired).

8. Carl Campbell (1984: 51) reminds us of the need for greater subtlety in thinking about this historical relationship. "While the theme of hatred between Maroons and slaves can generally be documented," he writes, "it would be a gross oversimplification to believe that the relations were not more complex. Clearly Maroons in many cases had intimate ties with slaves on nearby estates which might have dampened their enthusiasm to hunt for runaway slaves from these estates. But other Maroons, not so connected would be willing to hunt for them." Similarly, Brymner (1895: 86) states that the post-treaty Maroons "kept up a constant intercourse with the plantation slaves, forming temporary marriages with them, for the marriage tie sat lightly on them, the children of these marriages becoming slaves, following the condition of the mother."

9. This is a Country song often performed in Kromanti Play; it is considered one of the more powerful songs in the Moore Town Kromanti repertoire. A version of the song performed with full drum ensemble can be heard on Bilby (1992).

10. The "two side" refers to Maroons (on one side) versus those Jamaicans who remained in slavery and their descendants (on the other side).

11. This song is often heard at Kromanti Play, sometimes performed in the style known as Mindanga, at other times in the John Thomas style.

12. Another Country song sometimes performed at Kromanti Play in the Moore Town area.

13. The narrator later explained that to "cross a tune" means to respond to a person's song by "throwing" a more powerful song of one's own. If done quickly enough, this will cancel out the powers invoked by your opponent's song.

14. Meaning that the boy died. ("Come to yonder" is a Maroon expression meaning to die.)

15. Meaning that before he went deep into the forest, the Kongo boy's father put a spiritually potent substance on him so that the Guinea man wouldn't be able to kill him. But when the boy got into the forest, he found that what he had gotten from his father wasn't of any help in fighting the Guinea man, since his mother had spoiled its power by quarreling with his father.

16. Meaning, "I'm not going to let him know how things are. Since he says he knows things, let him go ahead and show what he knows."

17. Meaning, "your mother said you could work for more money. So, you see a bigger man there now. Kill him."

18. Meaning, "your mother said you could work for more money. So now, here's the bigger amount of money now. You said you could kill him. So don't you see that he's killed you now [instead]?"

19. Writing before Bob Marley burst onto the world scene, Clinton Black (1966: 111), following Frank Cundall (1930: 9), asserted that "with the probable exception of Columbus, no other person connected with Jamaica has been the subject of as many publications as Jack Mansong."

20. Among the early nineteenth-century fictionalizations of Three Finger Jack are Burdett (1800), Earle (1800), and Fawcett [Murray] (1800). A near-exhaustive bibliogra-

phy of nineteenth-century publications on this legendary figure may be found in Cundall (1930). The legend of Three Finger Jack, revised to suit changing sensibilities, was revived for a series of influential theatrical performances in both London and New York during the early 1820s. Among the performers of this role was the eminent African-American actor Ira Aldridge. "It was Aldridge's portrayal of Jack Mansong," writes Mellin (2000: 45), "that influenced not only his fast-rising acting career but also the passage of the English Abolition Bill of 1833." For further background on the performances of "Obi; or Three-Finger'd Jack" that were staged at the African Theater in Manhattan during the early 1820s, see Warner (2001).

21. According to one definition, Nago, in Jamaican Creole, is "a term of contempt originally applied by Creole blacks to African-born slaves; now signifying a very black, ugly, or stupid negro" (from Ewe *anago*, "a Yoruba negro") (Cassidy and Le Page 1980: 314–15). Among Maroons, the term denotes African origins and blackness, but lacks the negative connotations.

22. The written record confirms that at least one *kumfu joni* opponent—a non-Maroon obeah man—was among the persons pursued and killed by Maroon trackers during the Morant Bay rebellion. This man, named James Williams, was shot by a Maroon party led by Joseph Briscoe—the famous Moore Town *fete-man* who appears in several narratives in this chapter. According to Lumsden (2001: 485), "Briscoe claimed that the African [i.e., James Williams], whom he identified as the obeah man, was working for the 'rebels.'"

23. The "three days of darkness" mentioned in this narrative may reflect actual weather conditions at the time. According to the report of Colonel Fyfe, the British officer responsible for leading the Maroon detachments during Bogle's rebellion, "the march from Moore Town [to St. Thomas, to suppress the rebellion] took place in the 'heaviest rain' Fyfe had ever seen, raising the problems of crossing rivers, exposure for the men and wet percussion caps" (Lumsden 2001: 475). The heavy rains continued for several days, hindering Fyfe and the Maroon troops as they continued their campaign through St. Thomas.

24. Stating a view shared by many other Maroons, Colonel C.L.G. Harris of Moore Town has characterized Bogle's rebellion as a "foolhardy scheme" and "a plan that, barring a succession of miracles, was doomed to failure" (Harris 1995: 96). After reviewing a substantial portion of the written record of the Morant Bay Rebellion, Joy Lumsden (2001: 486) came to similar conclusions.

25. Colonel Fyfe's written correspondence from 1865 agrees with the present-day Maroon oral accounts on this point; according to Fyfe, Bogle was surprised and captured by the Maroons while "coming out of the bush with a sugar cane in his hand" (Lumsden 2001: 476).

26. In his recent history of the Bogle rebellion, Gad Heuman (1994: 87–91) provides archival evidence showing that "Paul Bogle clearly wanted the Maroons on his side." According to the testimonies of several Maroons after the rebellion, Bogle and a number of his followers actually visited the village of Hayfield (a branch settlement founded by Moore Town Maroons) before the outbreak to get a sense of whether he could depend on the support of the Maroons. According to one of these deponents, "Bogle discussed going to Moore Town," where he intended to ask them "not to interfere with what he wanted to do." The Hayfield Maroons "prayed with their visitors but offered them no encouragement." While inconclusive on this point, archival documents do suggest that at least a portion of the Hayfield Maroons may have cooperated for a time with Bogle. Shortly after the eruption in Morant Bay, Bogle and others "reportedly signed a call to arms, which

included the claim that the Maroons had sent a proclamation to them to 'meet them at Hayfield at once without delay, that they will put us in the way how to act'" (Lumsden 2001: 471). Apparently, Bogle did not reach Moore Town before the rebellion broke out, and therefore did not have the chance to present his request directly to Maroon leaders in that town. (See also Carey 1997: 571–73.)

27. According to James Walters, a Maroon interviewed shortly after the rebellion, one of Bogle's followers who visited Hayfield stated that "we want to beat all the brown and white off the island" (Heuman 1994: 88).

28. In an article published in 1967, Colonel Harris of Moore Town also invoked the name of "Joseph Briscoe" in connection with Maroon oral traditions about the pursuit of Bogle, stating that "it would be more true to say that Bogle surrendered to Briscoe than that he was captured." (C.L.G. Harris, "The Maroons Praised and Condemned," *Daily Gleaner*, July 23, 1967. See also Harris [n.d.: 52].)

29. Captain Joseph Briscoe is also mentioned in a number of eyewitness reports on the suppression of the rebellion cited by Heuman (1994: 132–33). See also Carey (1997: 583, 596) and Lumsden (2001: 483–85).

30. Bev Carey's archival research also confirms that it was Briscoe and the detachment under his command that apprehended Bogle (Carey 1997: 605). According to Lumsden (2001: 476), Colonel Fyfe was also with the Maroon party that "took Bogle unawares."

31. The comment about Bogle being a "foreigner" could, however, be read as a rhetorical statement, meant to suggest that he was an "African" (i.e., a member or sympathizer of the "Bongo nation" that practices Kumina)—as some Maroons, as well as some Kumina practitioners in St. Thomas parish, assert—rather than a "Jamaica creole" (Bilby and Fu-Kiau 1983: 28–29, 104). This interpretation seems all the more likely when it is realized that the narrator, like virtually every other Jamaican, is well aware that Paul Bogle is an officially recognized National Hero and therefore must be a Jamaican, not a "foreigner."

32. Oral traditions about Briscoe's role in capturing Bogle survived into the twentieth century even in the Leeward community of Accompong, on the other side of the island. There, a Maroon told Beckwith (1929: 186) that "Moore Town Maroons, they [are] harsh, especially one named Old Brisco—that was the baddest of all. First they killed Bogle—shove the bayonet right through him!" (This last embellishment—Briscoe killing Bogle with a bayonet—is not found in Windward Maroon accounts.)

33. This song, as the narrator later pointed out, is sung by Maroons as a digging song—a work song used in cultivating fields—and is not normally used in Kromanti Play.

34. Bev Carey also encountered a variant of this oral tradition, which has Bogle and/or his followers dressing as women so as to escape their pursuers (Carey 1997: 592). As recently as 1946, a similar technique was used by the Maroons of Moore Town in helping a wanted man with whom they sympathized escape the notice of British colonial police; the man was "dressed in the manner of a woman with ample breasts" (Harris n.d.: 79).

35. The narrator has turned around the name of this Jamaican National Hero, which was actually George William Gordon.

36. Bogle's chapel was in fact burned down by soldiers, nearly a week before he was captured (Holt 1992: 302).

37. A mixture of old Maroon creole and Kromanti language, meaning "Young man! What did you do? What did you do?! Today we're going to kill you all."

38. In attempting to explain an uncharacteristic killing spree by the Maroons in Torrington—a community not far from the specific spot mentioned by Ruth Lindsay in her

narrative below as the place where the unfortunate Maroon fighter lost his eye—Lumsden (2001: 484–85) points out that "the Maroons were angered at being fired at, and having one of their number wounded in the eye, and probably did fire at stragglers trying to get out of the village."

39. This oral tradition concerning Bangula and the Maroons who challenged him is also discussed in Harris (n.d.: 53–54).

40. *Maloon*: according to Maroon narrators, this is the way old-time "Bongo men" or Africans used to pronounce "Maroon."

41. According to the narrator, this refers not to Trelawny parish, also called Cholan by old-time Maroons, but to an unknown place near Manchioneal in Portland parish.

42. *Mawoon*: an old-time pronunciation of "Maroon" (cf. *Maloon* above).

43. Meaning, "your asshole [literally, 'your shit'] heats up before you fart."

44. By "babies," the narrator means dolls resembling babies, used in some forms of obeah.

45. E. D. Hastings, "Another View of Maroons," *Daily Gleaner*, January 15, 2001.

46. Lloyd Jeffrey, "Support the Maroons," *Jamaica Observer*, May 5, 2001. The "talk back" comment quoted here was taken from: http://www.jamaicaobserver.com/talkback/readpost.asp?artid=7825&item=6098.

47. Aduku Addae, "'Black-Out' as Dangerous as 'White-Out'!," *Jamaica Observer*, September 4, 2002.

48. Condé appears to have taken the title of her novella, as well as some of her understandings of the Jamaican social landscape, from a 1980 play called *Nana Yah*, by the Jamaican dramatist Jean Small. During the 1980s, this piece, about "the attributes of the Jamaican Heroine NANNY," was performed in Jamaica and other parts of the Caribbean by the Sistren Theatre Collective (Small 1987: 10). Some of the themes explored in *Nanna-ya* are also addressed in Condé's epic novel from around the same period, *The Children of Segu* (1990 [1985]); the work includes many interesting representations of Jamaican Maroons through the eyes of one of her protagonists, a returning descendant of a Trelawny Town Maroon who had been deported to Sierra Leone following the Second Maroon War of 1795 (Condé 1990: 207–99). (For a detailed discussion of this critical episode in Maroon history, see chapter 11.)

49. We know that Tacky relied on spiritual powers much like those used by Maroon *fete-man*. He used these for protection against both his Maroon opponents and his *bakra* (white) foes. The outcome of this famous contest between non-Maroon *kumfu joni* and Maroon *fete-man* is well known: the power of Tacky's Maroon opponents proved to be the greater. Edward Long (1774: 451–52) tells of how Tacky and his followers were prepared by one of his ritual specialists, "an old Coromantin who, with others of his profession, had been a chief in counseling and instigating the credulous herd, to whom these priests administered a powder, which, being rubbed on their bodies, was to make them invulnerable: they persuaded them into a belief, that Tacky, their generalissimo in the woods, could not possibly be hurt by the white men, for that he caught all the bullets fired at him in his hand, and hurled them back with destruction to his foes. This old impostor was caught whilst he was tricked up with all his feathers, teeth, and other implements of magic, and in this attire suffered military execution by hanging."

50. Balford Henry, "Mixed-Up Messages" (review of *Black Rebels: African Caribbean Freedom Fighters*, by Werner Zips), *Sunday Gleaner*, January 2, 2000.

51. Colonel Harris of Moore Town himself has written that "it must be remembered

that other blacks were often used to varying extents in the campaigns against the Maroons. . . . In fact," he adds, "there were those [non-Maroon blacks] who looked forward to such engagements in joyful anticipation" (Harris n.d.: 48). Citing Michael Craton, David Geggus (1987: 293) writes of "the ease with which slaves were recruited in the [British] colonies to fight black rebels."

52. Further background on this vision of a ceremony of forgiveness can be found in Roskind (2001), and on the author's web site at <www.rastaheart.com>.

Chapter 10. Ever Indomitable

1. Rum (*insa* in Kromanti language) is important in such contexts not only because it loosens inhibitions and stimulates free expression of emotions, but also because it is an important ingredient in Kromanti ceremonies; among its uses, it is offered to ancestors (in the form of libations) and employed in controlling spirits.

2. This pattern emerged long before Jamaica achieved political independence in 1962. A close observer of both the Maroons and the colonial government during the period just prior to independence succinctly described the government's tendency to dismiss Maroon claims to a special status: "It must be emphasised that true [Maroon] autonomy does not exist: the Government is quick to dwell upon its catholicity in things political if the Maroons attempt to demand any privileges to which they imagine themselves entitled" (Russell 1960: 209).

3. There is a strong parallel here with present-day Surinamese Maroons. See Richard Price's discussion titled "Those Times Shall Come Again" (Price 1983: 11–14).

4. The reference here is to the "drum language" preserved by Windward Maroons, which remains closely linked to the abeng language. The eighteenth-century Maroons of Nanny Town used drums, like the abeng, to communicate strategic messages, as indicated by the testimony of a captured Maroon in 1733 that a "gang of 100 was to lay on Carion Crow Hill, & 100 More Hobbys [plantation] Way, that a Drum was to be placed on the Ridge over the Town to View the Partys & the women in the town to burn the houses in case the Party should be too strong, if not the three Gangs to surround them on the beat of Drum, all under the Command of Scipio" ("Copy of the confession made by Seyrus a negro belonging to Mr. Geo. Taylor," 1733, PRO/CO 137/20, 179). Drum language is still used in Moore Town to announce the beginning of a Kromanti Play or to send various other messages, as well as to communicate with spirits. Examples of Moore Town drum language (known as Country) can be heard on Bilby (1992).

5. Common spelling used by some literate Maroons for what I render as Asafo House.

6. Colonel C.L.G. Harris, "The Treaty Is Not Abolished!" *Daily Gleaner*, July 30, 1967, p. 11.

7. In the Maroon view, this loyalty involved no subordination to the British government, for it was given of the Maroons' own will and was based on a treaty between equals.

8. For further evidence of the government's doubts about the loyalty of the Maroons at the beginning of the rebellion, see Carey (1997: 591–92) and Lumsden (2001: 471).

9. Carey (1997: 583) provides additional details on the preparations made by the Maroons for their eventual encounter with Governor Eyre (accompanied by Colonel Fyfe) in Port Antonio. See also Lumsden (2001: 474–75).

10. According to Lumsden (2001: 479), "it is clear that Fyfe distinguished the Maroons sharply from the rest of the Black population for whom he had none of the affection and respect which he had for the Maroons. One of the sources of Fyfe's feelings for the Ma-

roons becomes clear when he noted Eyre's intention of making him officially their Colonel, and added: 'in my formal Commission I should like to be also termed "& Chief" as I wish to consider them Jamaica Highlanders'"—a reference to the original highlanders in Scotland. See also Carey (1997: 603) for evidence of Fyfe's confidence in the Maroons.

11. As Carey (1997: 527, 602) and Lumsden (2001: 469) note, Fyfe (whose name was sometimes spelled "Fyffe") was also for a time the superintendent of the Windward Maroon community of Charles Town.

12. The "color" referred to here is "true-blue" (as in "true-blue Maroon").

13. Cassidy and Le Page (1980: 143), citing H.P. Jacobs, state that *dasha* or *dasher* is "a word meaning a lover, but the M[oore] T[own] Maroons call the Governor their 'dasha.'" Depending on the circumstances, the term can be honorific or sarcastic.

14. *Benta* is a Jamaican Creole term meaning "to venture; to undertake something hazardous" (Cassidy and Le Page 1980: 39).

15. A version of this oral tradition is also found in Harris (n.d.: 119–21). See also Martin (1973: 171–72).

16. Scott (1968: 70–77) provides a detailed discussion of this protracted dispute over land in Seaman's Valley, which includes not only the Maroon perspective, but also the rather different view of the colonial government (as reported in the Jamaican press). See also Harris (n.d.: 58–59, 77–79).

17. One related oral tradition that remains well known in Accompong tells of how a Maroon officer who allegedly helped a government surveyor in 1938 to cheat that community out of a portion of its communal land was attacked by the spirit of Kojo, which killed him before the survey was completed by "shooting" his heart, causing it to burst.

18. It should be mentioned that the appearance in these texts of a figure named "Governor Eerie" cannot be used to help locate the events they describe in time—despite the fact that "Eerie" is how Maroons pronounce the name of John Edward Eyre, governor of Jamaica from 1862 to 1865 and responsible for the enormous loss of life in the wake of the Morant Bay rebellion. Among the Maroons, the name "Governor Eerie" has come to symbolize tyranny and injustice in general, and has been transferred in this capacity to a number of oral traditions relating to other periods. For instance, as we shall see, in narratives connected with the Second Maroon War of 1795–96, the actual "villain" of that time, Governor Balcarres, is often replaced by "Governor Eerie."

19. In 1824, for instance, eight Charles Town Maroons (six adult women and two children) were listed as residing in Moore Town (Papers Relating to Slaves in the West Indies 1825: 33). And a missionary living in Moore Town in 1838 noted that "it has been the universal custom among the Maroons, although these Towns [Moore Town and Charles Town] are thirty miles apart, to flock in crowds to each others funerals; & to omit to send to call them is an affront, not to be overlooked" (Report of Moore Town, Pollitt Journal, entry of June 10, 1838, Archives of the Church Missionary Society, London, M5/326).

20. The implication being that the Maroons' Science put them to sleep for three days straight.

21. *Akrekre* is an esoteric name for the abeng (Maroon signaling horn) in Maroon Kromanti language (Bilby 1983: 73).

22. This quote is in the old Maroon creole and means, "your sister has come to fight the whites for Back River [i.e., New Nanny Town/Moore Town]. You tell her to go sit down. All right, all right. Today you will have to kill someone."

23. This appears to be a reference to the Maroon Lands Allotment Act of 1842, which specified that "each adult Maroon was to receive two acres for himself, and one acre for each dependent child, unless the total amount of land in the Maroon grant required that smaller allotments be made" (Kopytoff 1973: 275).

24. "My family in general": likely a reference to the entire Moore Town Maroon community, which is often spoken of as a single "family."

25. For a detailed discussion of the original land dispute that led to this survey in the early 1780s, see Campbell (1988: 172–74).

26. This statement by Colonel Downer is significant in a number of ways. For one thing, it shows that Maroon notions of their history, despite the assumptions of many outsiders to the contrary, are not based entirely in orality; since the time of the treaties, Maroon leaders, many of them literate in recent times, have been exposed to, and to some extent been involved in the production of, colonial documents concerning them. Moreover, it suggests that understandings of such documents have long been mediated through oral traditions into which they have been incorporated (see, for instance, Harris [1994: 37–39]). Whereas the various Maroon councils have inherited, and remain in possession of, a number of actual historical documents of this kind, knowledge of others—including, in some communities, the peace treaties themselves—has apparently been passed on exclusively, or primarily, through oral channels. When Colonel Downer says of this survey of 1782, "I may not have seen it, but older people hinted me what was written there," this is what he appears to be suggesting with regard to this particular document. The same is suggested by Barbara Kopytoff: "the surveyor in this important matter [of 1782] was a Mr. Dugald McPherson; his name is still remembered in Moore Town, and was frequently cited in later land disputes" (Kopytoff 1973: 140). People in Moore Town told Clarissa Scott that the community had once possessed the original copy of the 1782 survey, but had made the mistake of lending it to the colonial government in the early 1930s in an attempt to resolve this same land dispute; the government had never returned it, despite the Maroons' repeated entreaties (Scott 1968: 75–76). According to Colonel Harris (n.d.: 58–59), this occurred in 1933. The Maroons took the diagram to a court hearing in Port Antonio, leaving it in the care of the authorities there. In what the Colonel calls "an amazing piece of chicanery in high places," the court apparently misplaced it. "The Maroons have never forgotten this piece of injustice rendered them at the very seat of justice," remarks the Colonel, "and today they regard it as the ancient forerunner of others of later years." The relationship between literacy, orality, archival record keeping, and power in Jamaica—and the particular shape this has taken in Maroon communities—is an area ripe for further research along the lines carried out by Rappaport (1994) and Wogan (2004) in Andean communities.

27. A copy of this document, a survey of "Muretown" dated July 31, 1782, is still held by the Jamaica Survey Department. (See Harris [1994: 38] for a redrawn version.) The notes that the surveyor, Dougald (or Dugall) McPherson, included on his diagram actually read as follows: the "above Platt contains 1270 Acres of Land, more than was granted by the Honourable House of Assembly for the use of the Maroons but as the present Survey cut off great part of their Provision Grounds it was out of my Powers and out of the Power of the Superintendents to [convince?] them to narrow their bounds without raising disputes of the most disagreeable Nature and it has been in their possession forty years and the survey now legally compleated without injuring any of the Neighouring Settlers. I made my

returns and hopes his Honour will take matters into his Considerations" (Campbell 1988: 173–74).

28. This narrative was recorded by the Jamaican musicologist Laura B. Murray in Moore Town, while she was carrying out a field study of Jamaican folk music in 1960–61. Colonel Downer addresses her much as Maroon colonels would be expected to address any government official or other respected visitor from Kingston. The original tape is archived at the Indiana University Archives of Traditional Music (accession no. 61-020-F; OT 269).

29. It is not known whether this is the same person as the surveyor named Dougald McPherson, mentioned in the previous narrative from Moore Town. If so, it would help to place the event described in this oral tradition in the late eighteenth or early nineteenth century.

30. *Daily Ardmoreite* (Ardmore, Oklahoma), April 24, 1999.

31. Bangor Ridge is an old name for Charles Town among contemporary Maroons. The related name Bangor Wood is also sometimes used to refer to Charles Town.

32. *Sabi* means "know, understand" in old Maroon creole (Bilby 1983: 77). The meaning here is that Jack MacFarlane was very wise.

33. When he asks this rhetorical question—"you see a truth me a tell you?" (do you see that I'm telling you the truth?)—he is referring to the glass of rum that just fell to the ground for no apparent reason. The implication, as he later told me, was that the spirits of his "older heads" had knocked the glass off the railing to send a signal, because they were concerned about his revealing too much Maroon knowledge to a non-Maroon. (If he had not been revealing the truth, then the spirits would not have cared.)

34. This formulaic Maroon expression—which means "something has come from across the sea and beat my ass, 'plom!'"—incorporates elements of the old form of Maroon creole (e.g., *sali-water*, meaning "salt water" or "the ocean," and *lasi*, meaning "arse"). It may be uttered, for example, when one feels that one has received a "blow" from a spirit.

Chapter 11. Never to Forget: Secrecy, Trust, and Betrayal

1. Although this proverb has a special resonance among the Maroons, it is widely known in Jamaica. Chevannes (1995: 111) cites the same proverb to illustrate "the notion of public and private domains" and "the importance of guarding domestic privacy" throughout Jamaica.

2. Olive Lewin (2000: 119) has written of "the tendency towards the secrecy that characterizes so many Jamaican mento, work and other traditional songs." Laura Tanna (1984: 6) similarly remarks on the secrecy she has often encountered in working as a folklorist in rural Jamaica. Although I would not deny that this holds true for much of Jamaica, in my experience (which includes fieldwork in non-Maroon areas in Portland, St. Thomas, St. Mary, and St. Elizabeth parishes, as well as other parts of rural Jamaica), the secrecy encountered in Moore Town and other Windward Maroon communities (and to a much lesser extent in Accompong) is of an entirely different order. It is central to the Maroon value system and strategically applied (through the systematic behavior known as "dodging") with a protective care and determination that I have not encountered in any other Jamaican communities.

3. Martha Beckwith, who briefly visited a number of Maroon settlements in the open-

ing decades of the twentieth century, understood this, explicitly characterizing the Maroons as "a kind of secret society" (Beckwith 1929: 191).

4. In Jamaica more generally, it should be noted, the verb "dodge" has similar meanings not found in standard British or American English; according to Cassidy and Le Page (1980: 153), the term means: "to hide or secrete oneself, esp[ecially] so as to watch somebody else while being unseen oneself; to hide from (someone) so as to observe his actions." This shares with the Maroon usage the connotation of clever evasion.

5. The Maroon Kromanti term *jijifo* is very likely derived from Twi, *gyigyé* ("to lead astray; to entice, decoy, cheat, deceive, delude"); cf. *gyigyéfó* ("a person who engages in such behavior; a deceiver") (Christaller 1933: 160–61).

6. A Maroon from the community of Scot's Hall explained the rationale behind the Maroons' legendary secrecy particularly clearly to visiting anthropologist Victoria Durant-Gonzalez: "When I attempted to discuss Coromantee [i.e., Kromanti] with Mass Bongo, one of the oldest men in the district, he refused, saying, 'The dance is Maroon secret. This is the only protection that we have. It is through the dance that we beat the British and if I tell it to you then we can be conquered by any enemy'" (Durant-Gonzalez 1976: 11).

7. Elsewhere, Price (1983: 14) notes that "the heart of Saramaka morality . . . is that knowledge is power, and that one must never reveal all of what one knows."

8. This story is seen as an account of an event that actually occurred among the Windward Maroons in Jamaica. It is interesting how close the story is, structurally and thematically, to folktales and oral historical traditions used by Saramakas (and other Maroons) in Suriname to embody fundamental moral precepts regarding protection of knowledge and the danger of betrayal (Price 1979; Price 1983: 13–14, 159). For other Jamaican Maroon stories incorporating this theme of betrayal through exposure of secrets, see chapter 9.

9. From a tape-recorded interview conducted by Frederic G. Cassidy in Moore Town in 1952.

10. From a tape-recorded interview conducted by Frederic G. Cassidy in Moore Town in 1952.

11. A strong curse; he is expressing his anger and contempt for the treacherous wife in the story.

12. *Anabeti* is a Maroon Kromanti term that the narrator refused to discuss further.

13. The narrator later named the five brothers as Bruza, Isaac Whyte, Joe Myer, Joe Whyte, and Zachie Whyte. All five were Maroons from the community of Marshall's Hall (whose descendants now live in nearby Comfort Castle).

14. The narrator later explained that the pakit's full name is "Dodge-him-oo-kumfu-du-mi," and that it is the spirit of a man, not an animal. Its primary use is to help its owner hide things (including the truth) from others.

15. A more detailed discussion of the oral tradition on which this section focuses can be found in Bilby (1984a), including extensive passages from British archival documents that relate to the same events. See also Harris (n.d.: 70–74), Carey (1997: 490–93), and Lewin (2000: 163–64). Colonel Harris (n.d.: 73) refers to the story as "the tale of the promised feast."

16. According to some Accompong residents today (and as indicated in some of the narratives that follow), the refusal of the Accompong Maroons to come to the aid of their relatives in Trelawny Town during the Second Maroon War can be explained by a grudge that had long been festering between the two communities. The Accompong Maroons had

several years before come into possession of the Maroons' only copy of the Treaty of 1739. Shortly before the war of 1795, they had "lent" the treaty to the Trelawny Maroons with the understanding that it would soon be returned. The latter, however, refused to return it. The tensions over this question remained unresolved when war broke out in 1795. In any case, there is evidence that the warriors from Accompong fought only half-heartedly against their Trelawny Town relatives; they tried their best to distance themselves from the conflict (Stewart 1808: 283).

17. As Furness (1965: 46) notes, "even though the Maroons had not strictly observed the treaty by surrendering on 1st January, [Walpole] had let them understand that they would lose none of the treaty's benefits by surrendering afterwards."

18. This Leeward Maroon oral tradition is briefly mentioned in Lewin (2000: 163). Barbara Kopytoff also heard multiple versions of the story while conducting fieldwork in Accompong during the 1960s (personal communication, 1982).

19. Archival documents show that the Trelawny Maroons were in fact detained on ships for a significant period of time before they were carried off to Nova Scotia. While awaiting finalization of the arrangements that would allow the deportation of the Maroons to Halifax, Balcarres kept "the Maroons on board the transports but at anchor" (Kup 1975: 344). According to one report, the Maroons were detained during this period on three separate ships anchored in Port Royal Bay (Hinds 2001: 208). Eventually, they "were put on board the ship (the Dover) that transported them to Nova Scotia in April 1796, although they did not set sail until May 8 of the same year" (Lockett 1999: 10–11).

20. This element of the Accompong oral tradition of the treacherous feast—the ship used to entrap the Maroons and carry them away—clearly resonates with stories told in various parts of the African diaspora about the initial capture and enslavement of Africans. Michael Gomez (1998: 199–208) offers some insightful reflections on what he calls the "red cloth stories" of the African-American oral tradition—accounts that state that some of the African ancestors were lured onto European ships by displays of scarce and attractive commodities (especially red cloth); once the inquisitive Africans were on board, the ships would sail off, trapping them forever. (In one of the stories mentioned by Gomez, the victims are lured by the sounds of a "whistle.") These stories, as Gomez notes, represent to their tellers "essential truths" about the experience of enslavement; at their core lies "the notion of deception," a fundamental recognition of the duplicity of the enslavers (1998: 199). Aluku Maroons in French Guiana and Suriname recite very similar oral traditions about their ancestors' initial capture, as I found when carrying out fieldwork among them during the 1980s. According to them, the Africans were lured into European encampments, and eventually onto their ships, by the sounds of festive music. More recent research by Anne Bailey (2005) on oral traditions among the Anlo Ewe of present-day Ghana reveals that strikingly similar stories exist in Africa. These African accounts offer clear corroboration of the red cloth stories (and related oral traditions) told on the other side of the ocean; as Bailey (38–43) found, they are also supported by a handful of contemporaneous written sources. See Bailey (27–56, 108–13) for a detailed discussion of these Ewe oral traditions; of particular interest are her interpretive comments on the metaphorical meanings of these stories (49–53) and their significance as "cautionary tales" (53–56).

21. Citing a piece of the governor's correspondence archived at the Public Record Office in London, Michael Mullin (1992: 184) provides a tantalizing bit of evidence regarding some of the intelligence on which the Maroons might have relied. According to this document, Balcarres had invoked the treaty and summoned the Windward Maroons

to wait on him in Kingston; however, "sensing a trap, the Mooretown Maroons refused to move until they had consulted a nearby plantation obeahman."

22. This element of the Windward Maroon story of the treacherous feast was heard by the folklorist Martha Beckwith when she visited Moore Town in the early 1920s: "the story runs that a captive Maroon working at a blacksmith's anvil saw some of his fellows landing from a boat and hammered out a warning" (Beckwith 1929: 193). She provides no further context for the story, simply citing it as an example of the Maroons' ability to send paralinguistic messages using a variety of instruments. It should be noted, in any case, that this part of the oral tradition is entirely plausible. Anvils are among the wide variety of "instruments" traditionally used for "speaking" in various parts of West Africa. For instance, in the early 1960s, the ethnomusicologist Gerhard Kubik recorded a Yoruba blacksmith in Oshogbo, Nigeria. While working in the forge, the blacksmith "spoke" in rhythmic patterns on his anvil, beating out a variety of salutations and proverbs. This recording can be heard on a tape titled "Yoruba Talking Instruments," archived at the Schomburg Center for Research in Black Culture in New York (illustrated talk by Gerhard Kubik, London, Transcription Feature Service, 1962: Sc Audio C-21).

23. There can be no doubt, in any case, that Balcarres did attempt to mollify the Moore Town Maroons by offering them a feast (paid for by the Jamaican Assembly), in response to their expressions of distrust and their refusal to appear before him in Kingston. A government document dated but a few days before the letter in which Balcarres reveals his plans to ensnare the Moore Town Maroons states that "the committee are of opinion the account of captain Douglas [superintendent of the Moore Town Maroons], for supplying the maroon negroes at Moore-Town with fresh beef and rum, amounting to the sum of 108l. 3s. 4d. ought to be referred to the committee for examining and settling the accounts arising in consequence of martial law" (*Journals of the Assembly of Jamaica* [volume 9, December 20, 1795, p. 429]). Apparently the Maroons in Moore Town spurned the governor's offering of food and rum, for in the letter of December 26 in which he unveils his treacherous scheme, Balcarres complains that "the Nanny-Town-Maroons . . . sullenly rejected the bounty of the Assembly" (PRO/CO 137/96, 68).

24. Of those Maroons who were sent to Nova Scotia and then Sierra Leone, Campbell (1988: 257) notes that they "never lost their implacable hatred for Balcarres, who betrayed them. In one of their numerous engaging petitions from Nova Scotia, they begged the British monarch never to send 'any of dem poor cotch [Scottish] Lord for Gubner again.'"

25. An older name for Accompong Town (and more specifically, the section known today as Old Town).

26. This element from oral tradition, regarding the conflict between Accompong Town and Trelawny Town over possession of the treaty on the eve of the war, is corroborated by Dallas (1803a: 146), who similarly cites the resulting tensions as one of the reasons the Accompong Maroons did not join in the rebellion. The Maroon oral tradition gives us an inside perspective on how these tensions were being played out before the war. The seriousness of the breach between the two communities over this question is indicated by the "sounding of an alarm" by a spirit medium, Na Austin, who warns the people in Trelawny Town, while possessed by an ancestor, that if the "treaty book" is not returned to Accompong, bad things will occur. Right after this, war erupts, and the Accompong Maroons side with the whites.

27. Here he has confused the two individuals, switching their last names.

28. *Cholan* is an old Maroon pronunciation for "Trelawny," heard, for instance, in the speech of possessing ancestors in the Moore Town area.

29. This song, often performed in the context of Kromanti Play in Moore Town, belongs to the category known as *jawbone*. Most of those who sing it remain well aware that it alludes to the deportation of their fellow Maroons of Kojo's Town from Jamaica in the distant past. These are the people to whom the song is saying "fare thee well"—the Maroons of Trelawny Town who have "gone" from Jamaica to another land.

30. The narrator may be confusing San Blas, off the coast of Panama, with Sierra Leone.

31. From a tape recording of an interview conducted by David DeCamp in Moore Town in 1958.

32. *Konso-konso* (sometimes pronounced *konson-konso*, or *konson-konson*) is a Maroon Kromanti term usually glossed—as in this case—as "handcuffs" or "shackles" (or, by extension, "prison") (derived from Twi [or related Akan language], *ngkònsongkónsong* "chain, fetters" [Christaller 1933: 253]).

33. This proverbial warning—"when the lion is sleeping, you mustn't play with [or trouble] his tail"—is an integral part of this oral tradition; it occurred in several other versions of the story of the treacherous feast that I collected but was unable to include in this book (as well as a few of those below). When the Maroon protagonists send this defiant message back to the deceitful governor who has tried but failed to entrap them, they are expressing once again—as every Maroon who listens to this story understands—the spirit of indomitability that forms the subject of chapter 10.

34. In this version of the story and several others, the blacksmith is portrayed as a "Bongo man," meaning in this instance not only a non-Maroon African, but also a member of the same "nation" as those people who today practice the Kumina religion. That he was able to communicate with the Maroons in a shared African language is today invoked as "proof" that the Maroon and Kumina (Bongo) "nations" are closely related. (See the section of chapter 4 on the tradition of "Two Sister Pikni.") We see in these variants of the story, once again, how Maroon oral traditions may be reworked and applied toward particular ends in the present. (In other variants, including some presented here, the blacksmith is portrayed as a Maroon living in town, or one held captive in connection with the war on the other side of the island.)

35. Here, and in some of the following texts, another infamous tyrant, Governor Eyre (pronounced "Eerie" by Maroons), who ruled during the 1860s, is confused with his predecessor, Lord Balcarres.

Chapter 12. Coda: The Right to Persist

1. Wilbert Hemming, "An In-Depth Study of the Maroons of Jamaica," *Star*, October 23, 1984.

2. *Daily Ardmoreite* (Ardmore, Oklahoma), April 24, 1999.

3. Scott's aim appears to be to problematize the idea that "anthropologically identifiable, ethnologically recoverable pasts" are the only kind with legitimacy or "truth value" in theorizing identities in the African diaspora (or anywhere else, for that matter). If so, I am in sympathy with that part of his argument. Clearly, such a narrow framing of the relationship between historical consciousness and identity would be misguided; indeed, it would cause one to lose sight of much of what is most important and meaningful about diaspora discourses surrounding questions of identity—for example, the tactical uses of

recently reimagined "pasts" within existing fields of power (Rastafari conceptualizations of identity being a case in point). But the leap Scott makes from this part of the argument to his own conceptual premise that no "pasts" are ever (even partially?) "preservable" or "representable" seems to me unfounded and unnecessary. I would argue that "pasts" (embodied, for instance, in stories) can be *both* strategically useful in the present, and to some extent "verifiable" reflections of actual, specific past events or circumstances, as they seem to be in the Jamaican Maroon case; there is no reason the two cannot co-occur.

Glossary

Abbreviations

AC = term (or special sense) found in all four of the main Maroon communities, but not outside of Maroon areas

JC = Jamaican Creole term, found across the island

MC = term from archaic form of Maroon creole, nowadays heard primarily in speech of mediums possessed by spirits of ancestors

MK = esoteric term from Maroon Kromanti ritual language

WC = found only in Windward Maroon communities

a is, are (JC)

a (preposition) at; in; on; to (JC)

a particle used before a verb to indicate durative aspect or progressive action in present or future (JC)

abeng cow's horn used by Maroons to communicate messages via a secret "abeng language" (from Twi *abeng*; "animal's horn, musical instrument" [Cassidy and Le Page 1980: 2]) (AC)

abebu (also **abrebu, obrobro, obrobo**) indirect reference; coded language; proverb (from Twi *abebu*; "telling proverbs"; or from various Akan cognates) (MK) (WC)

abrono white person; non-Maroon person (of any ethnic group); outsider (found only in Accompong)

afana machete, cutlass (from Akan *afaná, afena, afona*; "sword" [Cassidy and Le Page 1980: 4]) (MK) (WC)

afu a common variety of hard yellow yam (from Twi *afúw*; "plantation, cultivated ground" [Cassidy and Le Page 1980: 5]) (JC)

akrekre (also **akeke, akete, kete**) abeng, signaling horn (probably from Twi *kéte*; "a flute or pipe played before kings" [Christaller 1933: 235]; or Ewe *kete*; "a flute") (MK) (WC)

am him, her, it (MC) (WC)

ambush the act of camouflage, or the materials (vegetation) used in camouflage; to wear this camouflage (this is a special Maroon sense, distinct from the more general standard English sense of "unexpected attack") (AC)

anabo (also **nanabo, ananabo**) type of tree bearing a pretty, licorice-flavored bean (Cassidy and Le Page 1980: 9) (JC)

asasi ground, earth (from Twi *asàsé*, "the earth, the globe that we inhabit" [Christaller 1933: 429–30]) (MK) (WC)

anangka (also **nangka**) snake (from Twi *o-nangká*, "a large horned snake" [Christaller 1933: 329]) (MK) (WC)

Asafo House/Ground see **Safo Ground**

ba brother, male friend (term of address) (MC) (AC)

baan (said of an ancestral spirit) to reincarnate in the body of a living person (from English *born*) (WC)

bakra white person; person of European descent (from Igbo or Efik *mbakará*, "white man" [Cassidy and Le Page 1980: 18]) (JC)

bari to bundle palm fronds for easy transportation, using a technique that involves folding and crisscrossing the leaves (MC) (WC)

bati (or, **batty**) buttock(s) (JC)

ben was, were; verbal auxiliary used to express past time (JC)

bigi big, large (from English *big*) (MC) (WC)

bigi pripri Maroon ancestors; ancestral spirits (from English *big + people*) (MC) (WC)

bing rear end, behind, buttocks (MC) (WC)

bobosi awengkini (also **babasi o wenkeni**) police officer; white person; more generally, any outsider (this is a code term used to alert fellow Maroons to the presence of a member of the Jamaican police force, or any potentially threatening outsider) (MK) (WC)

Bongo of or related to the African "nation" of people who practice the Kumina religion (this specific Maroon and Kumina usage has positive connotations) (in JC more generally, the term refers to anything considered to be African, and usually has pejorative connotations, except among Rastafarians, who have redefined it as a positive term)

bubby female breast(s) (JC)

bujufra (also **bujufwa**) blood (from Twi *bógyá*, "blood"; cf. Twi *me nè no di abogyafrá*, "we have mixed our blood, we are of the same blood" [Christaller 1933: 35–36]) (MK) (WC)

busha overseer; boss; person in position of authority (from English *overseer*) (JC)

business-man Kromanti practitioner; *fete-man* (MC) (WC)

busu small, edible freshwater snail (*Neritina vigrinea*), used to make soup (Cassidy and Le Page 1980: 85); symbolically important to Maroons as a survival food (JC; but found almost exclusively in Portland parish, near Windward Maroon communities)

buta bow (from Kikongo *buta*, "bow") (Cassidy and Le Page 1980: 85) (AC)

bwai boy (JC)

caban a platform of green sticks on which pork or other kinds of meat are jerked (Cassidy and Le Page 1980: 87) (WC)

cabbage skin another name for the cabbage-tree [the *Areca* or some other palm with edible terminal bud], alluding to the broad lower sheath of the bough that has several uses (Cassidy and Le Page 1980: 87) (JC)

cacoon a wild vine (*Entada gigas*) (Cassidy and Le Page 1980: 88) that has special symbolic significance for Maroons as a survival food and a form of camouflage; the plant produces an edible bean that Maroons continue to use as a food supplement (JC)

calalu name given to several plants having edible leaves, eaten as greens, in soups, medicinally; any leaves eaten as greens (from Tupí *caárurú*, "a fat or thick leaf") (Cassidy and Le Page 1980: 89) (JC)

captain Maroon officer, who serves under the **colonel**

chamu chamu code term meaning, "stop talking, you are saying too much" (MK) (WC)

Chankofi name of a dominant "tribe" or "nation" among the early Windward Maroons; more generally, any "true-born Maroon" in the present (possibly from John Cuffee, name of a leader of an early band of Maroons) (MC) (WC)

colonel (or **kanal**) elected leader of a Maroon community (AC)

cotch to support, lean on; stop or rest temporarily; temporary resting place (JC)

Country (capitalized when used in this specific sense) African-derived ritual language; categories of songs sung in such languages (the term is used in this sense by both Maroons and Kumina devotees, though the ritual languages to which the term refers are different in the two cases—i.e., Kromanti in the case of "Maroon Country" versus Kongo in the case of Kumina or "Bongo Country")

cunny cunning, clever, shrewd, tricky (JC)

da is, are (JC)

da (preposition) at; in; on; to (JC)

da particle used before a verb to indicate durative aspect or progressive action in present or future (JC)

dasha dashing person; well-dressed person; dandy; lover; used by Maroons in the past, sometimes sarcastically, to refer to British governors or other whites in positions of authority (MC) (WC)

debekri (also **debrekin, debeklin, debekin**) dawn, daybreak (MC) (WC)

deh to be (in a location); there (JC)

deh particle used before a verb to indicate durative aspect or progressive action in present or future (JC)

diindi limb (hand, arm, foot, leg); clothes (MC) (WC)

dodge to evade and/or hide from (the term refers not just to skillful avoidance of invasive questions, but to any kind of calculated evasion or trickery, any act of "hiding," whether for self-defense or personal gain) (WC)

doti earth, soil; the ground (probably from Twi *dòté*, "soil, earth, clay, mud," influenced by English *dirt, dirty*) (Cassidy and Le Page 1980: 157, 166) (JC)

duppy ghost; spirit of a deceased human being (from Bupe *dupe*, "ghost") (Cassidy and Le Page 1980: 164) (JC)

e particle used before a verb to indicate durative aspect or progressive action in present or future (MC) (WC)

fe for; to (infinitive); must (from English *for*) (JC)

fe-me, fe-you, fe-we, fe-unu, fe-dem possessive forms of personal pronouns: my, mine; your, yours; our, ours; your, yours (plural); their, theirs (JC)

fete to fight; to dance Kromanti as a form of spiritual warfare (from English *fight*) (MC) (WC)

fete-man (feminine form is **fete-woman**, or **fete-uman**) Maroon Kromanti practitioner; Maroon ritual specialist, dancer, and healer (from English *fight* + *man/woman*) (MC) (WC)

futu leg (entire limb); foot (MC) (WC)

gourdy (or **gourdie**) a large gourd or calabash used as a container (most often for carrying water) (JC)

grandy grandmother; more generally, older woman (often used as a respectful term of address) (JC); term of address and/or reference used for a medium (male or female) possessed by the spirit of a female ancestor (MC) (WC)

granfa (also **granfara**) respectful term of address for an older man; also used as a term of address and/or reference for a medium (male or female) possessed by the spirit of a male ancestor (from English *grandfather*) (MC) (WC)

haas medium; person possessed by the spirit of an ancestor (from English *horse*) (MC) (WC)

head turn possession by a spirit; *you head turn* = "you became possessed by a spirit" (WC)

hofa (also **ofa**) how (MC) (WC)

honku (also **onku, honki, onki**) uncle; more generally, older man (often used as a respectful term of address) (from English *uncle*) (MC) (WC)

honti (also **onti**) what, which; where (interrogative) (MC) (WC)

indi hand; belly; ear(s) (MC) (WC)

insa rum (from Twi *nsá*, "strong drink, intoxicating liquor, palm wine" [Christaller 1933: 417]) (MK) (WC)

insho water (from Twi *nsú*, "water" [Christaller 1933: 478]) (MK) (WC)

intete hamper; type of large basket (from Kikongo *ntete*, "hamper" [Cassidy and Le Page 1980: 237]) (JC)

jabin crow (also **jabbering crow**) Jamaican crow (*Corvus jamaicensis*), which flies in flocks and makes noises likened to human speech (Cassidy and Le Page 1980: 238) (JC)

janga river prawn, crayfish (*Macrobrachium jamaicensis*) used locally as an article of food (possibly from Doulla-Bakweri *njanga*, "crayfish") (Cassidy and Le Page 1980: 243) (JC)

jege spiritually empowered object used by Maroon Kromanti practitioners for a variety of purposes (most often for divination) (MC) (WC)

jet to get (MC) (WC)

jija restless, nervous, jittery; impatient (MC) (WC)

jijifo to evade or hide from; *dodge* (from Twi *gyigyé*, "to lead astray; to entice, decoy, cheat, deceive, delude"; cf. Twi *gyigyéfó*, "a person who engages in such behavior; a deceiver" [Christaller 1933: 160–61]) (MK) (WC)

johncrow vulture, buzzard (JC)

jonga Maroon lance or spear (from Kikongo *edionga*, *dyónga*, "spear, harpoon, lance, javelin, pike, blade, sword") (WC)

kaja (also **kandia**) type of tree, with highly flammable wood (WC)

kanda a palm bough, especially the large lower sheath that holds it to the tree (from Kikongo *kánda*, "the lower part of a palm lath") (JC)

Katawud (also **Kyatawud, Cottawood**) Maroon; member of the Maroon "nation" (said to be from English *scatter* + English *wood*) (WC)

kesu to stand up; sit down (can mean either, depending on context) (MC) (WC)

konjo type of wild yam (MC) (WC) (the equivalent in JC is *kronjo* or *krongo* [Cassidy and Le Page 1980: 132])

konso-konso (also **konson-konso, konson-konson**) handcuffs, shackles; (by extension) prison (from Twi *ngkònsongkónsong* "chain, fetters" [Christaller 1933: 253]) (MK) (WC)

kremu nanti to die (some older Maroons gloss the expression in English as "to climb to the stars," or "climb to the sky") (MK) (WC)

Kromanti (also **Koromanti, Kramanti, Karamanti, Karamantic**) form of spiritual practice, and the associated dance, music, and esoteric language; also name of one of the main African "tribes" or "nations" from which Maroons claim to be descended (from *Cormantin*, the name of a fort and village on the coast of what is today Ghana) (AC)

Kromanti Play (also **Kromanti Dance**) Maroon ceremony held to contact ancestors and seek their aid in healing, or in the resolution of other problems

kumfu (also **kumfu-man**) Kromanti practitioner; Maroon ritual specialist (from Twi *o-kòmfó*, "priest, soothsayer, diviner, sorcerer" [Christaller 1933: 248]) (MK) (WC)

kumfu joni non-Maroon obeah man; outside ritual specialist (MK) (WC)

Kumina African-derived religion centered in the eastern part of Jamaica (especially St. Thomas parish), and the associated dance and music; it is clearly related to Central African, and particularly, Kongo, spiritual traditions; its practitioners are ethnically and culturally distinct from Windward Maroons, who live in the same general part of the island

kwatamassa assistant to *fete-man* in Kromanti ceremonies (from English *quartermaster*)

laas an older Maroon pronunciation of *raas* (a vulgar JC term for buttocks, ass) (from English *arse*)

lasi same as *laas* (heard in most archaic forms of MC) (WC)

Leeward Maroons term used by non-Maroons to refer to the Maroons of Accompong (and formerly those of Trelawny Town) in the western part of Jamaica

major Maroon officer, who serves under the **colonel**

makoka any grub or grublike worm (Cassidy and Le Page 1980: 283, 289) (JC)

Maroon escaped slave, or descendant of escaped slaves (lower case, when used in this broad, generic sense); person born of Maroon parents in one of the four major present-day Jamaican Maroon communities, or any other person held by the inhabitants of these communities to be descended in large part from the "first-time" people who founded these communities (capitalized when used in this more specific sense)

mek, mek we to make; let, let's (JC)

min was, were; verbal auxiliary used to express past time (JC)

mumma mama; mother (JC)

myal spirit possession; state of being possessed by an ancestor spirit (MC) (AC) (JC; archaic outside of Maroon communities)

na is, are (MC) (WC)

na (preposition) at; in; on; to (MC) (WC)

naa won't; isn't; doesn't (JC)

n'e won't; isn't; doesn't (MC) (WC)

niega non-Maroon person of African descent (AC); any person of African descent (sometimes derogatory) (JC)

nuff much, a lot, plenty (from English *enough*) (JC)

numa bird (from Twi *anomaá*, "bird, fowl" [Christaller 1933: 351]) (MK) (WC)

nyaba to dance (MK) (WC)

Nyabinghi Rastafarian ceremony of worship, and associated music and dance

nyam to eat (JC)

Nyami (also **Tata Nyami**) God, the Supreme Creator (from Twi *Onyàmé*, "God, the Creator of all things" [Christaller 1933: 356]) (MK) (WC)

nyuman man (especially, young man) (from English *young man*) (MC) (WC)

o he, she, it (MC) (WC)

obeah spiritual power (originally used by Maroons to refer to the ancestral power accessed through the Kromanti tradition; the term is most often avoided today because of its stigmatization in other parts of Jamaica, where it has come to mean "harmful sorcery"; the term most often used by Maroons today, as in other parts of the island, is *Science*) (JC)

obraye (also **braye**) to enwrap; type of loincloth said to have been worn by Maroon ancestors during the time of war, still used sometimes for burials (possibly from Twi *o-barehyía*, "a cartouche, cartridge belt all around the loins" [Christaller 1933: 8]) (MK) (WC)

obroni non-Maroon person; outsider; outside place (from Twi *o-buro-ní*, "European, white man, mulatto" [Christaller 1933: 54]) (MK) (WC)

obwasu (also **obwesu**) calabash bowl (MK) (WC)

obwato child (MK) (WC)

okrema chickenhawk (from Twi *akoromá*, "bird of prey, hawk" [Christaller 1933: 257]) (MK) (WC)

okrema drummer (from Twi *o-kyeremá*, "drummer" [Christaller 1933: 295]) (MK) (WC)

opete vulture, buzzard (from Twi *o-pété*, "vulture" [Christaller 1933: 391]) (MK) (WC)

opongko horse (from Twi *o-pon(g)kó*, "horse" [Christaller 1933: 400]) (MK) (WC)

osunudaja (also **asunudaja**) Maroon lance or spear; *jonga* (probably from Twi *e-sóno*, "elephant" [Cassidy and Le Page 1980: 14] + English *dagger*) (MK) (WC)

otua gun (from Twi *o-túo*, "musket, gun" [Christaller 1933: 543]) (MK) (WC)

paki (or **packy**) the calabash fruit; calabash bowl (from Twi *apákyi*, "a broad calabash with a cover; also the whole calabash" [Cassidy and Le Page 1980: 335]) (JC)

pakit a personal spirit owned and controlled by a Maroon Kromanti practitioner; the material manifestation of such a spirit in the form of an animal such as a snake, bird, or crayfish (MC) (WC)

pakit-man a Kromanti practitioner who possesses and uses one or more *pakit*s (MC) (WC)

pikibo child (MC) (WC)

pikin child (MC) (WC)

pikni (also **pickney**) child (JC)

pinya ideophone representing the cry of a chickenhawk

Play (capitalized when used in this specific sense) shorthand for the Maroon Kromanti ceremony known as Kromanti Play or Kromanti Dance (WC)

prandes house, yard, home (from English *plantation*) (MC) (WC)

pre (also **pres**) place (from English *place*) (MC) (WC)

prem (also **prim**) to prime, prepare (especially for spiritual work) (MC) (WC)

pripri people (from English *people*) (MC) (WC)

puppa papa; father (JC)

puropuro pure (from English *pure*) (MC) (WC)

quatty (also **quattie**) small unit of money (JC)

raas buttocks, ass (vulgar) (from English *arse*) (JC)

raatid! exclamation indicating anger, annoyance, amazement, and the like (JC)

rub trash to use herbs for medicinal and/or spiritual reasons; by extension, to do Maroon spiritual work more generally; the word has purely positive connotations, and is never used by Maroons in the standard English sense of "refuse" or "garbage" (WC)

sa sister, female friend (term of address) (MC) (AC)

sabi to know; knowledge, wisdom (MC) (WC) (archaic in JC)

sabi-man person of knowledge (MC) (WC)

sabreke (also **yebeke, yabeke**) goat (from Twi *asebérekyi-e*, "goat" [Christaller 1933: 435]) (MK) (WC)

Safo Ground (also **Asafo Ground, Asafo House**) structure in which Maroons once regularly held public Kromanti dance ceremonies; area where this structure was once located (from Twi *asàfo*, "company, society, association; community; [religious] congregation; warriors association" [Christaller 1933: 419]) (Maroons also sometimes call this ceremonial area "muster ground")

sagl head-tie worn by *fete-man* in Kromanti ceremonies when possessed by ancestor spirits (from English *saddle*) (MC) (WC)

Science (capitalized when used in this specific sense) spiritual power (JC)

shref, shrelf, shwelf, etc. (also **shref-shref**) self, oneself; same; used to give a positive answer to the question, "Yenkunkun"? (meaning "Are you a Maroon?") (from English *self*) (MC) (WC)

sipple (also **swipple**) slippery; tricky, dangerous (JC)

siton stone (from English *stone*) (MC) (WC)

Stranger (capitalized when used in this specific sense) non-Maroon; outsider; *obroni* (WC)

suma person; somebody (from English *someone*) (MC) (WC)

sumadi person; somebody (from English *somebody*) (JC)

supple jack type of climbing shrub; whip made from this shrub (JC)

swiri to swear; also refers to power acquired by swearing an oath to, or making a pact with, a spirit (from English *swear*) (MC) (WC)

swiri-man (also **swii-swii-man**) ritual specialist (Maroon or other) (MC) (WC)

taki to talk, speak (from English *talk*) (MC) (WC)

takifa money (from Twi *taku-fá*, "a weight of gold equal to about half of sixpence halfpenny" [Christaller 1933: 490]) (MK) (WC)

tan to stay, remain; stand (from English *stand*) (JC)

tandabasokom! stand up!; ritual expression, can be used to invoke spiritual powers that will help regain one's footing when one has begun to slip or trip and is about to fall down (from English *stand-up-so-come*) (MC) (WC)

tata father; also used as a respectful term of address for an older male (JC)

tatu small house or hut, usually with a thatch roof (JC)

tek to take (from English *take*) (JC)

tere today (from English *today*) (MC) (WC)

thatch-head heart of palm (various species), symbolically important to Maroons as a survival food (WC)

three-eye-man (also **triiyaiman**) coconut (MC) (WC)

timbambu fire; also name of an ancestral "tribe" from which some Maroons claim to be descended (MK) (WC)

titei-man (**titai-man**) Maroon Kromanti practitioner; *fete-man* (from English *tie* + *man*) (MC) (WC)

tonbaig to turn back (from English *turn back*) (MC) (WC)

trash plants used for medicinal or spiritual purposes (WC); parts of any crop plant or vegetable product removed while it is growing, or left over after processing or use (JC)

tuakwantan crossroads (from English *two* + Twi *ngkwán-ta*, "cross-road, crossway" [Christaller 1933: 283]) (MK) (WC)

tuajina to have a conversation in private (from Twi *tu agyiná*, "to consult apart; deliberate; take counsel with; give advice" [Christaller 1933: 162]) (MK) (WC)

unu you (plural); you all (from Igbo *unu*, "you" (plural) [Cassidy and Le Page 1980: 457]) (JC)

waitamigl (also **white-a-middle**) person of partial Maroon descent (WC)

waka to walk (from English *walk*) (MC) (WC)

wawatu to honor; welcome, greet warmly; hug, embrace; congratulate; bestow formal recognition on a leader (MC) (WC)

weed term most often used by Maroons to mean "herb" (though it can refer to any wild plant); it has none of the connotations of "harmful plant" or "nuisance" found in its British or American English cognates (WC)

wild pine epiphytic plants of genus *Tillandsia* (Cassidy and Le Page 1980: 477); important as a source of water in the deep forest (JC)

Windward Maroons term used by non-Maroons to refer to Maroons from any of the three major communities in the eastern part of Jamaica (Moore Town, Charles Town, or Scot's Hall)

wudu forest (from English *woods*) (MC) (WC)

wudu bere deep in the forest (from English *woods* + *belly*) (MC) (WC)

ya here (from English *here*) (JC)

yanga to move (in dancing or walking) in a shaking or swaying manner that is "stylish" or provocative (probably derived from Common Bantu *-yáng-*, "dance about in joy") (Cassidy and Le Page 1980: 484) (JC)

Yankipong (also **Yankipong Asasi**) God, the Supreme Creator (from Twi *Onyankopong*, "God the Creator" + Twi *asàsé*, "the earth, the globe that we inhabit; it is also personified and invoked after Onyankopong" [Christaller 1933: 429–30]) (MK) (WC)

yarifo (also **yarefo**) sick (person); dead (person); to injure or kill (from Twi *o-yaréfó*, "sick person, patient" [Christaller 1933: 582]) (MK) (WC)

ye here (from English *here*) (MC)

Yenkunkun Maroon; member of the Maroon "nation"; *Katawud* (probably from Twi *yen(g)ko*, "friend, companion, neighbor, fellow man" [Christaller 1933: 588]) (MK) (WC)

yeri to hear (from English *hear*) (JC)

yoyo child, baby; generation; descendant of Grandy Nanny; by extension, Maroon; member of the Maroon "nation"; *Katawud* (MK) (WC)

References

Abbreviations for Manuscript Sources

BM/Add MSS
Additional Manuscripts, Edward Long Papers, British Museum, London
Cooper MSS
Archibald Cooper Papers, West India Collection, University of the West Indies Library, Mona, Jamaica
PRO/CO
Colonial Office Series, Public Record Office, London
Roberts MSS/AFC
Helen H. Roberts Papers, American Folklife Center, Library of Congress, Washington, D.C.
Roberts MSS/YU
Helen H. Roberts Papers, Manuscripts and Archives, Sterling Memorial Library, Yale University, New Haven, Conn.

Published Works

Abercrombie, Thomas A. 1998. *Pathways of Memory and Power: Ethnography and History Among an Andean People*. Madison: University of Wisconsin Press.
Afroz, Sultana. 1999a. The Manifestation of Tawid: The Muslim Heritage of the Maroons in Jamaica. *Caribbean Quarterly* 45(1): 27–40.
———. 1999b. From Moors to Marronage: The Islamic Heritage of the Maroons in Jamaica. *Journal of Muslim Minority Affairs* 19(2): 161–79.
Agorsah, E. Kofi. 1992. Archaeology and the Maroon Heritage in Jamaica. *Jamaica Journal* 24(2): 2–3, 5–9.
———. 1994a. Archaeology of Maroon Settlements in Jamaica. In *Maroon Heritage: Archaeological, Ethnographic and Historical Perspectives*. E. Kofi Agorsah, ed., 163–87. Kingston: Canoe Press.
Agorsah, E. Kofi, ed. 1994b. *Maroon Heritage: Archaeological, Ethnographic and Historical Perspectives*. Kingston: Canoe Press, University of the West Indies.
Anonymous. 1976. A Chat with Mr. Aston. *Peenie Wallie* 1(2): 29–31.
Anonymous (Robert Charles Dallas). 1790. *A Short Journey in the West Indies, in Which Are Interspersed Curious Anecdotes and Characters*. London: Published by the author.
Ashcroft, Michael. 1980. Robert Charles Dallas Identified as the Author of an Anonymous Book About Jamaica. *Jamaica Journal* 14(44): 94–101.
Atkins, John. 1735. *A Voyage to Guinea, Brasil, and the West-Indies*. London: Caesar Ward and Richard Chandler.

Bailey, Anne C. 2005. *African Voices of the Atlantic Slave Trade.* Boston: Beacon Press.

Bakker, Eveline, Leo Dalhuisen, Maurits Hassankhan, and Frans Steegh. 1993. *Geschiedenis van Suriname: van stam tot staat.* Zutphen, The Netherlands: Walburg Pers.

Ballinger, Pamela. 2002. *History in Exile: Memory and Identity at the Borders of the Balkans.* Princeton: Princeton University Press.

Banks, Russell. 1980. *The Book of Jamaica.* Boston: Houghton Mifflin.

———. 1995. *Rule of the Bone.* New York: HarperCollins.

Bansart, Andrés. 1993. El Cimarrón en la literatura caribeña. *Espace Caraïbe* 1:125–37.

Barker, David, and Balfour Spence. 1988. Afro-Caribbean Agriculture: A Jamaican Maroon Community in Transition. *The Geographical Journal* 154(2): 198–208.

Basso, Hamilton. 1960. *A Quota of Seaweed: Persons and Places in Brazil, Spain, Honduras, Jamaica, Tahiti, and Samoa.* Garden City, N.Y.: Doubleday.

Bastide, Roger. 1965. La théorie de la réincarnation chez les Afro-Américains. In *Réincarnation et vie mystique en Afrique noire,* 9–29. Paris: Presses Universitaires de France.

Beckwith, Martha Warren. 1929. *Black Roadways: A Study of Jamaican Folk Life.* Chapel Hill: University of North Carolina Press.

Bedasse, Janet, and Nella Stewart. 1996. The Maroons of Jamaica: One with Mother Earth. In *Traditional Peoples and Biodiversity Conservation in Large Tropical Landscapes.* Kent H. Redford and Jane A. Mansour, eds., 57–73. Arlington, Va.: The Nature Conservancy.

Beet, Chris de. 1992. Een staat in een staat: een vergelijking tussen de Surinaamse en Jamaicaanse Marrons. *Oso: Tijdschrift Voor Surinaamse Taalkunde, Letterkunde, Cultuur en Geschiedenis* 11(2): 186–93.

Bennett, Louise. 1982. *Selected Poems.* Kingston: Sangster.

———. 1993. *Aunty Roachy Seh.* Kingston: Sangster.

Besson, Jean. 1995. Free Villagers, Rastafarians and Modern Maroons: From Resistance to Identity. In *Born Out of Resistance: On Caribbean Cultural Creativity.* Wim Hoogbergen, ed., 301–14. Utrecht: ISOR.

———. 1997. Caribbean Common Tenures and Capitalism: The Accompong Maroons of Jamaica. *Plantation Society in the Americas* 4(2/3): 201–32.

———. 1998. Changing Perceptions of Gender in the Caribbean Region: The Case of the Jamaican Peasantry. In *Caribbean Portraits: Essays on Gender Ideologies and Identities.* Christine Barrow, ed., 133–55. Kingston: Ian Randle.

———. 2000. The Appropriation of Lands of Law by Lands of Myth in the Caribbean Region. In *Land, Law and Environment: Mythical Land, Legal Boundaries.* Allen Abramson and Dimitrios Theodossopoulos, eds., 116–35. London: Pluto Press.

———. 2001. Empowering and Engendering Hidden Histories in Caribbean Peasant Communities. In *History and Histories in the Caribbean.* Thomas Bremer and Ulrich Fleischmann, eds., 69–113. Madrid: Bibliotheca Iberoamericana.

———. 2002. *Martha Brae's Two Histories: European Expansion and Caribbean Culture-Building in Jamaica.* Chapel Hill: University of North Carolina Press.

Bilby, Kenneth M. 1979. Partisan Spirits: Ritual Interaction and Maroon Identity in Eastern Jamaica. Master's thesis, Wesleyan University, Middletown, Conn.

———. 1981a. The Kromanti Dance of the Windward Maroons of Jamaica. *Nieuwe West-Indische Gids* 55(1/2): 52–101.

————. 1981b. *Music of the Maroons of Jamaica*. New York: Folkways Records and Service Corp.

————. 1983. How the "Older Heads" Talk: A Jamaican Maroon Spirit Possession Language and Its Relationship to the Creoles of Suriname and Sierra Leone. *Nieuwe West-Indische Gids* 57(1/2): 37–88.

————. 1984a. The Treacherous Feast: A Jamaican Maroon Historical Myth. *Bijdragen tot de Taal-, Land- en Volkenkunde* 140:1–31.

————. 1984b. "Two Sister Pikni": A Historical Tradition of Dual Ethnogenesis in Eastern Jamaica. *Caribbean Quarterly* 30(3/4): 10–25.

————. 1985. *Jamaican Ritual Music from the Mountains and the Coast*. New York: Lyrichord.

————. 1989a. The Aluku and the Communes: A Problematic Policy of Assimilation in French Guiana. *Cultural Survival Quarterly* 13(3): 71–75.

————. 1989b. Divided Loyalties: Local Politics and the Play of States among the Aluku. *New West Indian Guide* 63(3/4): 143–73.

————. 1990. The Remaking of the Aluku: Culture, Politics, and Maroon Ethnicity in French South America. Ph.D. dissertation, Johns Hopkins University, Baltimore, Md.

————. 1994a. Maroon Culture as a Distinct Variant of Jamaican Culture. In *Maroon Heritage: Archaeological, Ethnographic and Historical Perspectives*. E. Kofi Agorsah, ed., 72–85. Kingston: Canoe Press.

————. 1994b. Time and History Among a Maroon People: The Aluku. In *Time in the Black Experience*. Joseph K. Adjaye, ed., 141–60. Westport, Conn.: Greenwood Press.

————. 1995. Oral Traditions in Two Maroon Societies: The Windward Maroons of Jamaica and the Aluku Maroons of French Guiana and Suriname. In *Born Out of Resistance: On Caribbean Cultural Creativity*. Wim Hoogbergen, ed., 169–80. Utrecht: ISOR.

————. 1997. Swearing by the Past, Swearing to the Future: Sacred Oaths, Alliances, and Treaties Among the Guianese and Jamaican Maroons. *Ethnohistory* 44(4): 655–89.

————. 1999a. Gumbay, Myal, and the Great House: New Evidence on the Religious Background of Jonkonnu in Jamaica. *ACIJ Research Review* (African-Caribbean Institute of Jamaica) 4:47–70.

————. 1999b. Neither Here Nor There: The Place of "Community" in the Jamaican Religious Imagination. In *Religion, Diaspora, and Cultural Identity: A Reader in the Anglophone Caribbean*. John W. Pulis, ed., 311–35. Amsterdam: Gordon and Breach.

————. 2002. Maroon Autonomy in Jamaica. *Cultural Survival Quarterly* 25(4): 26–31.

Bilby, Kenneth M., ed. 1992. *Drums of Defiance: Maroon Music from the Earliest Free Black Communities of Jamaica*. Washington, D.C.: Smithsonian Folkways.

Bilby, Kenneth M., and Filomina Chioma Steady. 1981. Black Women and Survival: A Maroon Case. In *The Black Woman Cross-Culturally*. Filomina Chioma Steady, ed., 451–67. Cambridge, Mass.: Schenkman.

Bilby, Kenneth M., and Fu-Kiau kia Bunseki. 1983. *Kumina: A Kongo-Based Tradition in the New World*. Cahiers du CEDAF. Brussels: Centre d'Etude et de Documentation Africaines.

Bilby, Kenneth M., and Diana Baird N'Diaye. 1992. Creativity and Resistance: Maroon Culture in the Americas. In *1992 Festival of American Folklife*. Peter Seitel, ed., 54–61. Washington, D.C.: Smithsonian Institution.

Birhan, Farika. 1985. The Maroons: African Freedom Fighters in the Hills of Jamaica. *Reggae and African Beat*, August, 23–25.

Black, Clinton V. 1965. *History of Jamaica*, 3rd ed. London: Collins.

———. 1966. *Tales of Old Jamaica*. London: Collins.

Bleby, Henry. 1868. *The Reign of Terror: A Narrative of Facts Concerning Ex-Governor Eyre, George William Gordon, and the Jamaica Atrocities*. London: William Nichols.

Bloch, Marc. 1953. *The Historian's Craft*. Peter Putnam, trans. New York: Vintage Books.

Blu, Karen. 1979. The Uses of History for Ethnic Identity. In *Currents in Anthropology: Essays in Honor of Sol Tax*. Robert Hinshaw, ed., 271–85. The Hague: Mouton.

Blu, Karen I. 1980. *The Lumbee Problem: The Making of an American Indian People*. Cambridge: Cambridge University Press.

Bogues, Anthony. 2002. Nationalism and Jamaican Political Thought. In *Jamaica in Slavery and Freedom: History, Heritage and Culture*. Kathleen E. A. Monteith and Glen Richards, eds., 363–87. Kingston: University of the West Indies Press.

Bolland, Nigel. 1994. Current Caribbean Research Five Centuries after Columbus. *Latin American Research Review* 29(3): 202–19.

Boots, Francis (Ateronhiatakon). 1989. Iroquoian Use of Wampum. In *New Voices from the Longhouse*. Joseph Bruchac, ed., 34–39. Greenfield Center, N.Y.: Greenfield Review Press.

Borofsky, Robert. 1987. *Making History: Pukapukan and Anthropological Constructions of Knowledge*. Cambridge: Cambridge University Press.

Brathwaite, Edward. 1971. *The Development of Creole Society in Jamaica 1770–1820*. Oxford: Clarendon Press.

Brathwaite, Edward Kamau. 1977. *Wars of Respect: Nanny, Sam Sharpe and the Struggle for People's Liberation*. Kingston: Agency for Public Information.

———. 1989. Maroon and Marooned. *Jamaica Journal* 22(3): 51–56.

———. 1994. Nanny, Palmares and the Caribbean Maroon Connexion. In *Maroon Heritage: Archaeological, Ethnographic and Historical Perspectives*. E. Kofi Agorsah, ed., 119–38. Kingston: Canoe Press.

Breeze, Jean "Binta." 1995. Nanny. In *Sounding Off! Music as Subversion/resistance/revolution*. Ron Sakolsky and Fred Wei-Han Ho, eds., 261. Brooklyn: Autonomedia.

———. 1997. Maroon Song. In *On the Edge of an Island*. Jean "Binta" Breeze. Newcastle upon Tyne: Bloodaxe Books.

Brodber, Erna. 1983. Oral Sources and the Creation of a Social History of the Caribbean. *Jamaica Journal* 16(4): 2–11.

Brown, Stewart, Mervyn Morris, and Gordon Rohlehr, eds. 1989. *Voiceprint: An Anthology of Oral and Related Poetry from the Caribbean*. Essex, U.K.: Longman.

Brubaker, Roger, and Frederick Cooper. 2000. Beyond "Identity." *Theory and Society* 29(1): 1–47.

Brymner, D. 1895. The Jamaica Maroons: How They Came to Nova Scotia—How They Left It. *Transactions of the Royal Society of Canada* 1:81–90.

Burdett, William. 1800. *Life and Exploits of Mansong, Commonly Called Three-Finger'd Jack*. Sommerstown [London]: A. Neil.

Bush, Barbara. 1990. *Slave Women in Caribbean Society, 1650–1838*. Bloomington: Indiana University Press.

Caldecott, A. 1898. *The Church in the West Indies*. London: Society for Promoting Christian Knowledge.

Campbell, Carl. 1984. Missionaries and Maroons: Conflict and Resistance in Accompong,

Charles Town and Moore Town (Jamaica) 1837–1838. *Jamaican Historical Review* 14:42–58.

Campbell, Festus Amtac. 1978. *Echoes of Mount Portland*. Kingston: Crown Press.

Campbell, Mavis. 1973. The Maroons of Jamaica: Imperium in Imperio? *Pan-African Journal* 6(1): 45–55.

———. 1988. *The Maroons of Jamaica 1655–1796: A History of Resistance, Collaboration & Betrayal*. Granby, Mass.: Bergin and Garvey.

———. 1990. *Nova Scotia and the Fighting Maroons: A Documentary History*. Williamsburg, Va.: College of William and Mary.

———. 1993. *Back to Africa: George Ross and the Maroons from Nova Scotia to Sierra Leone*. Trenton, N.J.: Africa World Press.

Campisi, Jack. 1990. The New England Tribes and Their Quest for Justice. In *The Pequots in Southern New England*. Laurence M. Hauptman and James D. Wherry, eds., 179–93. Norman: University of Oklahoma Press.

———. 1991. *The Mashpee Indians: Tribe on Trial*. Syracuse: Syracuse University Press.

Carey, Bev. 1997. *The Maroon Story: The Authentic and Original History of the Maroons in the History of Jamaica, 1490–1880*. Gordon Town, Jamaica: Agouti Press.

———. n.d. A History of the Maroon Peoples of Jamaica, Unpublished ms. at National Library of Jamaica, ms. no. 1937. Kingston.

Carey, David. 2001. *Our Elders Teach Us: Maya-Kaqchikel Historical Perspectives*. Tuscaloosa: University of Alabama Press.

Carley, Mary Manning. 1963. *Jamaica: The Old and the New*. New York: Praeger.

Carnegie, Charles V. 2002. *Postnationalism Prefigured: Caribbean Borderlands*. New Brunswick, N.J.: Rutgers University Press.

Carter, Hazel. 1996. The Language of Kumina and Beele Play. *ACIJ Research Review* (African Caribbean Institute of Jamaica) 3:66–129.

Cassidy, F. G., and R. B. Le Page. 1980. *Dictionary of Jamaican English*, 2nd ed. Cambridge: Cambridge University Press.

Cawley, Harris N. n.d. *The Sound of the Abeng: A Short Synopsis of the Accompong Maroons*. Accompong, Jamaica: H. Cawley.

Chevannes, Barry. 1995. The Phallus and the Outcast: The Symbolism of the Dreadlocks in Jamaica. In *Rastafari and Other African-Caribbean Worldviews*. Barry Chevannes, ed., 97–126. London: Macmillan.

Christaller, Rev. J. G. 1933. *Dictionary of the Asante and Fante Language, Called Tshi (Twi)*, 2nd ed. Basel: Basel Evangelical Missionary Society.

Cleland, Charles E. 2001. *The Place of the Pike: A History of the Bay Mills Indian Community*. Ann Arbor: University of Michigan Press.

Cliff, Michelle. 1984. *Abeng*. Trumansburg, N.Y.: The Crossing Press.

———. 1986. "I Found God in Myself and I Loved Her/ I Loved Her Fiercely": More Thoughts on the Work of Black Women Artists. *Journal of Feminist Studies in Religion* 2(1): 7–39.

Clifford, James. 1988. *The Predicament of Culture*. Cambridge, Mass.: Harvard University Press.

Cobb, Charles E., Jr. 1985. Jamaica: Hard Times, High Hopes. *National Geographic* 167(1): 114–40.

Cohen, David Steven. 1974. *The Ramapo Mountain People*. New Brunswick, N.J.: Rutgers University Press.

Cohen, David William. 1977. *Womunafu's Bunafu: A Study of Authority in a Nineteenth-Century African Community*. Princeton: Princeton University Press.

Cohen, Milton J. 1974. Medical Beliefs and Practices of the Maroons of Moore Town. Ph.D. dissertation, New York University, New York.

Condé, Maryse. 1985. *Pays mêlé suivi de Nanna-Ya*. Paris: Hatier.

———. 1990. *The Children of Segu*. Linda Coverdale, trans. New York: Ballantine.

———. 1999. *Land of Many Colors and Nanna-Ya*. Nicole Ball, trans. Lincoln: University of Nebraska Press.

Connerton, Paul. 1989. *How Societies Remember*. Cambridge: Cambridge University Press.

Cousins, Phyllis M. 1967. *Queen of the Mountain*. Kingston: Ministry of Education.

Craton, Michael. 1977. Perceptions of Slavery: A Preliminary Excursion Into the Possibilities of Oral History in Rural Jamaica. In *Old Roots in New Lands: Historical and Anthropological Perspectives on Black Experiences in the Americas*. Ann M. Pescatello, ed., 263–83. Westport, Conn.: Greenwood Press.

———. 1982. *Testing the Chains: Resistance to Slavery in the British West Indies*. Ithaca, N.Y.: Cornell University Press.

Craton, Michael, and Garry Greenland. 1978. *Searching for the Invisible Man: Slaves and Plantation Life in Jamaica*. Cambridge, Mass.: Harvard University Press.

Crawford, A.W.C. Lindsay. 1840. *Lives of the Lindsays*, vol. 3. London: Wigan.

Cundall, Frank. 1915. *Historic Jamaica*. London: Institute of Jamaica and West India Committee.

———. 1930. Three-Fingered Jack: The Terror of Jamaica. *West India Committee Circular* 45(816–18): 9–10, 36–37, 55–56.

Dalby, David. 1971. Ashanti Survivals in the Language and Traditions of the Windward Maroons of Jamaica. *African Language Studies* 12:31–51.

Dallas, Robert Charles. 1803a. *The History of the Maroons, from Their Origin to the Establishment of Their Chief Tribe at Sierra Leone*, vol. 1. London: T. N. Longman and O. Rees.

———. 1803b. *The History of the Maroons, from Their Origin to the Establishment of Their Chief Tribe at Sierra Leone*, vol. 2. London: T. N. Longman and O. Rees.

Dance, Daryl C. 1985. *Folklore from Contemporary Jamaicans*. Knoxville: University of Tennessee Press.

Datta, Ansu K., and R. Porter. 1971. The *Asafo* System in Historical Perspective. *Journal of African History* 12(2): 279–97.

Davenport, C. B., and Morris Steggerda. 1929. *Race Crossing in Jamaica*. Washington, D.C.: Carnegie Institution of Washington.

Davies, Carole Boyce, and Elaine Savory Fido. 1990. Talking It Over: Women, Writing and Feminism. In *Out of the Kumbla: Caribbean Women and Literature*. Carole Boyce Davies and Elaine Savory Fido, eds., ix–xx. Trenton, N.J.: Africa World Press.

Dawes, Kwame. 2002. *Bob Marley: Lyrical Genius*. London: Sanctuary.

Dening, Greg. 1988. *History's Anthropology: The Death of William Gooch*. Lanham, Md.: University Press of America.

Dinwoodie, David W. 2002. *Reserve Memories: The Power of the Past in a Chilcotin Community*. Lincoln: University of Nebraska Press.

Dunham, Katherine. 1946. *Journey to Accompong*. New York: Henry Holt.

Durant-Gonzalez, Victoria. 1976. Role and Status of Rural Jamaican Women: Higglering and Mothering. Ph.D. dissertation, University of California, Berkeley.

Earle, William. 1800. *Obi, or the History of Three-Fingered Jack*. London: Earle and Hemet.

Edwards, Bryan. 1796. *The Proceedings of the Governor and Assembly of Jamaica in Regard to the Maroon Negroes*. London: John Stockdale.

————. 1801a. *The History, Civil and Commercial, of the British Colonies in the West Indies*, vol. 1. London: John Stockdale.

————. 1801b. *The History, Civil and Commercial, of the British Colonies in the West Indies*, vol. 3. London: John Stockdale.

Ellis, A. B. 1887. *The Tshi-Speaking Peoples of the Gold Coast of West Africa*. London: Chapman and Hall.

Ellis, Pat, ed. 1986. *Women of the Caribbean*. London: Zed Books.

Ellis, Stephen. 1999. *The Mask of Anarchy: The Destruction of Liberia and the Religious Dimension of an African Civil War*. New York: New York University Press.

Emoff, Ron. 2002. *Recollecting from the Past: Musical Practice and Spirit Possession on the East Coast of Madagascar*. Middletown, Conn.: Wesleyan University Press.

Epstein, A. L. 1978. *Ethos and Identity*. London: Tavistock.

Erim, E. 1990. Songs as Sources of History. *West African Journal of Archaeology* 20:54–62.

Eyre, L. Alan. 1973. Jack Mansong: Bloodshed or Brotherhood. *Jamaica Journal* 7(4): 9–14.

Fawcett [John?]. 1800. *Obi; or, Three Finger'd Jack*. London: William Murray.

Fermor, Patrick Leigh. 1950. *The Traveller's Tree*. New York: Harper and Brothers.

Fleischmann, Ulrich. 1993. Maroons, Writers, and History. In *Slavery in the Americas*. Wolfgang Binder, ed., 565–79. Würzburg, Germany: Königshausen und Neumann.

Ford-Smith, Honor. 1987. Introduction. In *Lionheart Gal: Life Stories of Jamaican Women*. Sistren and Honor Ford-Smith, eds. Toronto: Sister Vision.

Furchgott, Eve, ed. n.d. *Servants of the Dream: Prospectus on Culture, Justice and the Humanities*. San Francisco: Kerista Consciousness Church.

Furness, A. E. 1965. The Maroon War of 1795. *Jamaican Historical Review* 5(2): 30–49.

Geggus, David. 1987. The Enigma of Jamaica in the 1790s: New Light on the Causes of Slave Rebellions. *William and Mary Quarterly* (3rd Series) 44(2): 274–99.

Genovese, Eugene D. 1979. *From Rebellion to Revolution: Afro-American Slave Revolts in the Making of the Modern World*. Baton Rouge: Louisiana State University Press.

Givens, Shelby Matthew. 1984. An Ethnographic Study of Social Control and Dispute Settlement Among the Aluku Maroons of French Guiana and Surinam, South America. Ph.D. dissertation, University of California, Berkeley.

Gomez, Michael A. 1998. *Exchanging Our Country Marks: The Transformation of African Identities in the Colonial and Antebellum South*. Chapel Hill: University of North Carolina Press.

Goodison, Lorna. 1984. Nanny. *Caribbean Quarterly* 30(3&4): 127.

Gottlieb, Karla Lewis. 2000. *"The Mother of Us All": A History of Queen Nanny, Leader of the Windward Jamaican Maroons*. Trenton, N.J.: Africa World Press.

Grant, John N. 2002. *The Maroons in Nova Scotia*. Halifax: Formac.

Green, Toby. 2001. *Meeting the Invisible Man: Secrets and Magic in West Africa*. London: Weidenfeld and Nicolson.

Guss, David M. 2000. *The Festive State: Race, Ethnicity, and Nationalism as Cultural Performance.* Berkeley: University of California Press.

Hall-Alleyne, Beverley. 1982. Asante Kotoko: The Maroons of Jamaica. *African-Caribbean Institute of Jamaica Newsletter* 7:3–40.

Handler, Richard. 1991. Who Owns the Past? History, Cultural Property, and the Logic of Possessive Individualism. In *The Politics of Culture.* Brett Williams, ed., 63–74. Washington, D.C.: Smithsonian Institution Press.

———. 1994. Is "Identity" a Useful Cross-Cultural Concept? In *Commemorations: The Politics of National Identity.* John R. Gillis, ed., 27–40. Princeton: Princeton University Press.

Harris, C.L.G. 1994. The True Traditions of My Ancestors. In *Maroon Heritage: Archaeological, Ethnographic and Historical Perspectives.* E. Kofi Agorsah, ed., 36–63. Kingston: Canoe Press.

———. 1995. *On My Honour (a Tale of the Maroons).* Kingston: Published by the author.

———. n.d. The Maroons of Moore Town (a Colonel Speaks). Unpublished ms.

Hart, Richard. 1950. Cudjoe and the First Maroon War in Jamaica. *Caribbean Historical Review* 1(1): 46–79.

———. 1985. *Slaves Who Abolished Slavery, Vol. 2. Blacks in Rebellion.* Kingston: Institute of Social and Economic Research, University of the West Indies.

Hauptman, Laurence M. 1986. *The Iroquois Struggle for Survival.* Syracuse: Syracuse University Press.

Helman, Albert. 1956. Een West-Indische ballade. *Vox Guyanae* 2(4): 177–79.

Henige, David P. 1973. The Problem of Feedback in Oral Tradition: Four Examples from the Fante Coastlands. *Journal of African History* 14(2): 223–35.

Hernandez, Helen. 1983. *The Maroons—Who Are They?* Kingston: JAMAL Foundation.

Herskovits, Melville J. 1966. *The New World Negro.* Bloomington: Indiana University Press.

Herskovits, Melville J., and Frances S. Herskovits. 1934. *Rebel Destiny: Among the Bush Negroes of Dutch Guiana.* New York: McGraw-Hill.

Heuman, Gad. 1994. *"The Killing Time": The Morant Bay Rebellion in Jamaica.* London: Macmillan.

Higman, B. W. 1976. *Slave Population and Economy in Jamaica, 1807–1834.* Cambridge: Cambridge University Press.

———. 1999. *Writing West Indian Histories.* London: Macmillan.

Hill, Donald R. 1977. *The Impact of Migration on the Metropolitan and Folk Society of Carriacou, Grenada.* New York: American Museum of Natural History.

Hill, Jonathan D., ed. 1988. *Rethinking History and Myth: Indigenous South American Perspectives on the Past.* Urbana: University of Illinois Press.

Hinds, Allister. 2001. "Deportees in Nova Scotia": The Jamaican Maroons, 1796–1800. In *Working Slavery, Pricing Freedom.* Verene Shepherd, ed., 206–22. New York: Palgrave.

Hofmeyr, Isabel. 1993. *"We Spend Our Years as a Tale That is Told": Oral Historical Narrative in a South African Chiefdom.* Portsmouth, N.H.: Heinemann.

Hogg, Donald W. 1960. The Convince Cult in Jamaica. *Yale University Publications in Anthropology* 58. New Haven: Yale University Press.

Holt, Thomas C. 1992. *The Problem of Freedom: Race, Labor, and Politics in Jamaica and Britain, 1832–1938.* Baltimore: Johns Hopkins University Press.

Homiak, John P. 1985. The "Ancients of Days" Seated Black: Eldership, Oral Tradition, and Ritual in Rastafari Culture. Ph.D. dissertation, Brandeis University, Waltham, Mass.

———. 1995. Dub History: Soundings on Rastafari Livity and Language. In *Rastafari and Other African-Caribbean Worldviews*. Barry Chevannes, ed., 127–81. London: Macmillan.

———. 1999. Movements of Jah People: From Soundscapes to Mediascape. In *Religion, Diaspora, and Cultural Identity: A Reader in the Anglophone Caribbean*. John W. Pulis, ed., 87–123. Amsterdam: Gordon and Breach.

Hoogbergen, Wim. 1990. *The Boni Maroon Wars in Suriname*. Leiden: E. J. Brill.

Howard, Rosalyn. 2002. *Black Seminoles in the Bahamas*. Gainesville: University Press of Florida.

Hurault, Jean. 1961. *Les Noirs Réfugiés Boni de la Guyane Française*. Dakar: IFAN.

Hurston, Zora Neale. 1938. *Tell My Horse*. Philadelphia: Lippincott.

Jacobs, H. P. 1945. The Untapped Sources of Jamaican History. *Jamaican Historical Review* 1(1): 92–98.

———. 1972. Old Bedward of Spring Garden. *Jamaica Journal* 6(2): 9–13.

Jacobs, H. P., ed. 1949. Roger Hope Elletson Letter Book, 1766–1768. *Jamaican Historical Review* 2(1): 77–119.

James, Cynthia. 2002. *The Maroon Narrative: Caribbean Literature in English across Boundaries, Ethnicities, and Centuries*. Portsmouth, N.H.: Heinemann.

Jennings, Grace M. A. 1999. Retained Cultural Traditions: A Way of Reforming the Curriculum of the Jamaican Maroons. Ph.D. dissertation, Ohio University, Athens.

Johnson, Anthony. 2001. *Jamaican Leaders*. Kingston: Teejay.

Johnson, Brian D. 1983. The Land of Look Behind. *Equinox* 2(11): 48–65.

Johnson, Lemuel A. 1990. A-Beng: (Re)Calling the Body in(to) Question. In *Out of the Kumbla: Caribbean Women and Literature*. Carole Boyce Davies and Elaine Savory Fido, eds., 111–42. Trenton, N.J.: Africa World Press.

Johnson, Linton Kwesi. 1991. *Tings and Times*. Newcastle upon Tyne: Bloodaxe Books.

Joyner, Charles. 1985. *Down by the Riverside: A South Carolina Slave Community*. Urbana: University of Illinois Press.

Kaplan, Carla, ed. 2002. *Zora Neale Hurston: A Life in Letters*. New York: Doubleday.

Kopytoff, Barbara. 1973. The Maroons of Jamaica: An Ethnohistorical Study of Incomplete Polities, 1655–1905. Ph.D. dissertation, University of Pennsylvania, Philadelphia.

———. 1976. The Development of Jamaican Maroon Ethnicity. *Caribbean Quarterly* 22(2/3): 33–50.

———. 1977. Maroon Jerk Pork and Other Jamaican Cooking. In *The Anthropologists' Cookbook*. Jessica Kuper, ed., 141–46. London: Routledge and Kegan Paul.

———. 1978. The Early Political Development of Jamaican Maroon Societies. *William and Mary Quarterly* (3rd Series) 35:287–307.

———. 1979. Colonial Treaty as Sacred Charter of the Jamaican Maroons. *Ethnohistory* 26(1): 45–64.

———. 1987. Religious Change Among the Jamaican Maroons: The Ascendance of the Christian God Within a Traditional Cosmology. *Journal of Social History* 20:463–84.

Kup, A. P. 1975. Alexander Lindsay, 6th Earl of Balcarres, Lieutenant Governor of Jamaica 1794–1801. *Bulletin of the John Rylands University Library of Manchester* 57(2): 327–65.

Kurin, Richard. 1997. *Reflections of a Culture Broker: A View from the Smithsonian.* Washington, D.C.: Smithsonian Institution Press.

Lalla, Barbara. 1996. *Defining Jamaican Fiction: Maroonage and the Discourse of Survival.* Tuscaloosa: University of Alabama Press.

Lambek, Michael. 1998. The Sakalava Poiesis of History: Realizing the Past through Spirit Possession in Madagascar. *American Ethnologist* 25(2): 106–27.

Lawrence, A. W. 1964. *Trade Castles and Forts of West Africa.* Palo Alto, Calif.: Stanford University Press.

Lenoir, J. D. 1975. Suriname National Development and Maroon Cultural Autonomy. *Social and Economic Studies* 24:308–19.

Le Page, R. B., and David DeCamp. 1960. *Creole Language Studies* I. London: Macmillan.

Lewin, Olive. 2000. *Rock It Come Over: The Folk Music of Jamaica.* Kingston: University of the West Indies Press.

Lewis, Matthew Gregory. 1834. *Journal of a West-India Proprietor.* London: Murray.

Lewis, Rupert. 1997. Learning to Blow the Abeng: A Critical Look at Anti-Establishment Movements of the 1960s and 1970s. *Small Axe* 1(1): 5–17.

Linebaugh, Peter, and Marcus Rediker. 2000. *The Many-Headed Hydra: Sailors, Slaves, Commoners, and the Hidden History of the Revolutionary Atlantic.* Boston: Beacon Press.

Locke, David. 1972. Jerk Pork. B.A. honors thesis, Wesleyan University, Middletown, Conn.

Lockett, James D. 1999. The Deportation of the Maroons of Trelawny Town to Nova Scotia, Then Back to Africa. *Journal of Black Studies* 30(1): 5–14.

Long, Anton V. 1956. *Jamaica and the New Order 1827–1847.* Kingston: Institute of Social and Economic Research, University College of the West Indies.

Long, Edward. 1774. *The History of Jamaica*, vol. 2. London: T. Lowndes.

Lumsden, Joy. 2001. "A Brave and Loyal People": The Role of the Maroons in the Morant Bay Rebellion in 1865. In *Working Slavery, Pricing Freedom.* Verene Shepherd, ed., 467–89. New York: Palgrave.

Mansingh, Laxmi, and Ajai Mansingh. 1999. *Home Away from Home: 150 Years of Indian Presence in Jamaica, 1845–1995.* Kingston: Ian Randle.

Martin, Leann. 1972. Why Maroons? *Current Anthropology* 13(1): 143–44.

———. 1973. Maroon Identity: Processes of Persistence in Moore Town. Ph.D. dissertation, University of California, Riverside.

Mathurin, Lucille. 1975. *The Rebel Woman in the British West Indies During Slavery.* Kingston: Institute of Jamaica.

McDaniel, Lorna. 1990. The Flying Africans: Extent and Strength of the Myth in the Americas. *New West Indian Guide* 64(1/2): 28–40.

———. 1998. *The Big Drum Ritual of Carriacou: Praisesongs in Rememory of Flight.* Gainesville: University Press of Florida.

McFarlane, Milton. 1977. *Cudjoe the Maroon.* London: Allison and Busby.

McLaughlin, Gerard Leo. 2000. *Jesuitana Jamaica: Historical Profiles 1837–1996.* Kingston: Arawak Publications.

Medina, Domingo A. 2003. From Keeping It Oral to Writing to Mapping: The Kuyujani Legacy and the De'kuana Self-Demarcation Project. In *Histories and Historicities in Amazonia.* Neil L. Whitehead, ed., 3–32. Lincoln: University of Nebraska Press.

Mellin, Barbara Rizza. 2000. Acting Out. *The New Crisis* 107(5): 44–46.

Mintz, Sidney W. 1961. Review of Stanley Elkins, *Slavery. American Anthropologist* 63:579–87.

———. 1969. Slavery and the Slaves. *Caribbean Studies* 8:65–70.

———. 1974. *Caribbean Transformations*. Chicago: Aldine.

Montell, William Lynwood. 1970. *The Saga of Coe Ridge: A Study in Oral History*. Knoxville: University of Tennessee Press.

Moore, Joseph G. 1953. Religion of Jamaican Negroes: A Study of Afro-Jamaican Acculturation. Ph.D. dissertation, Northwestern University, Evanston, Ill.

Moore, Robin D. 1997. *Nationalizing Blackness: Afrocubanismo and Artistic Revolution in Havana, 1920–1940*. Pittsburgh: University of Pittsburgh Press.

Morris, Mervyn. 1990. Printing the Performance. *Jamaica Journal* 23(1): 21–24, 26.

Morrison, Toni. 1987. *Beloved*. New York: Penguin.

Mullin, Michael. 1992. *Africa in America*. Urbana: University of Illinois Press.

Nemattanew (Chief Ray Crazy Horse). 2002. *Morrisville: A Native Hidden Community*. Rancocas, N.J.: Powhatan Press.

Nettleford, Rex M. 1972. *Identity, Race and Protest in Jamaica*. New York: William Morrow.

Nicholas, Tracy. 1979. *Rastafari: A Way of Life*. Garden City, N.Y.: Anchor Books.

Olivier, Lord. 1933. *The Myth of Governor Eyre*. London: Leonard and Virginia Woolf.

Oostindie, Gert, ed. 2001. *Facing up to the Past: Perspectives on the Commemoration of Slavery from Africa, the Americas and Europe*. Kingston: Ian Randle.

Owen, Ruth Bryan. 1949. *Caribbean Caravel*. New York: Dodd, Mead.

Palacio, Joseph O. 1998. Reconstructing Garifuna Oral History—Techniques and Methods in the Study of a Caribbean People. *Journal of Eastern Caribbean Studies* 34(1): 1–24.

Papers Relating to Slaves in the West Indies. 1825. *Papers Relating to the Manumission, Government, and Population of Slaves in the West Indies*. London: House of Commons.

Paredes, J. Anthony, ed. 1992. *Indians of the Southeastern United States in the Late 20th Century*. Tuscaloosa: University of Alabama Press.

Patterson, Orlando. 1969. *The Sociology of Slavery*. Rutherford, N.J.: Fairleigh Dickinson University Press.

———. 1970. Slavery and Slave Revolts: A Sociohistorical Analysis of the First Maroon War, 1665–1740. *Social and Economic Studies* 19:289–325.

———. 1972. *Die the Long Day*. New York: William Morrow.

Pérez, Berta E. 1995. Versions and Images of Historical Landscape in Aripao, a Maroon Descendant Community in Southern Venezuela. *América Negra* 10 (December): 129–48.

Phaf, Ineke. 1990. La nación cimarrona en el imaginario del Caribe no-hispánico. *Revista de Crítica Literaria Latinoamericana* 26(31/32): 67–97.

Polimé, T. S., and H.U.E. Thoden van Velzen. 1988. *Vluchtelingen, opstandelingen en andere Bosnegers van Oost-Suriname, 1986–1988*. Utrecht: Instituut voor Culturele Antropologie, Centrum voor Caraïbische Studies.

Portelli, Alessandro. 1991. *The Death of Luigi Trastulli and Other Stories: Form and Meaning in Oral History*. Albany: State University of New York Press.

Porter, Frank W., III. 1979. Strategies for Survival: The Nanticoke Indians in a Hostile World. *Ethnohistory* 26:325–45.

Porter, Frank W., III, ed. 1986. *Strategies for Survival: American Indians in the Eastern United States*. Westport, Conn.: Greenwood Press.

Poyer, Lin. 1993. *The Ngatik Massacre: History and Identity on a Micronesian Atoll*. Washington, D.C.: Smithsonian Institution Press.

Price, Richard. 1975. *Saramaka Social Structure*. Rio Piedras: Institute of Caribbean Studies, University of Puerto Rico.

———. 1979. Kwasímukámba's Gambit. *Bijdragen tot de Taal-, Land- en Volkenkunde* 135:151–69.

———. 1983a. *First-Time: The Historical Vision of an Afro-American People*. Baltimore: Johns Hopkins University Press.

———. 1983b. *To Slay the Hydra: Dutch Colonial Perspectives on the Saramaka Wars*. Ann Arbor: Karoma Publishers.

———. 1990. *Alabi's World*. Baltimore: Johns Hopkins University Press.

———. 1995. Executing Ethnicity: The Killings in Suriname. *Cultural Anthropology* 10:437–71.

———. 1996a. Introduction: Maroons and Their Communities. In *Maroon Societies*. Richard Price, ed., 1–30. Baltimore: Johns Hopkins University Press.

———. 1996b. Preface to the 1996 Edition. In *Maroon Societies*. Richard Price, ed., xi–xl. Baltimore: Johns Hopkins University Press.

———. 1998a. *The Convict and the Colonel*. Boston: Beacon Press.

———. 1998b. Scrapping Maroon History: Brazil's Promise, Suriname's Shame. *New West Indian Guide* 72(3/4): 233–55.

———. 2002. Preface. In *First-Time: The Historical Vision of an African American People*, 2nd ed., xi–xvi. Chicago: University of Chicago Press.

Price, Richard, ed. 1973. *Maroon Societies: Rebel Slave Communities in the Americas*. Garden City, N.Y.: Anchor Books.

Price, Richard, and Sally Price. 1994. *On the Mall: Presenting Maroon Tradition-Bearers at the 1992 Festival of American Folklife*. Bloomington: Folklore Institute, Indiana University.

———. 2002. Maroons Under Assault in Suriname and French Guiana. *Cultural Survival Quarterly* 25(4): 38–45.

Prince, Nancy. 1853. *A Narrative of the Life and Travels of Mrs. Nancy Prince*. 2nd ed. Boston: Published by the author.

Pringle, Kenneth. 1938. *Waters of the West*. London: George Allen and Unwin.

Pullen-Burry, B. 1903. *Jamaica as It is, 1903*. London: T. Fisher Unwin.

Rappaport, Joanne. 1990. *The Politics of Memory: Native Historical Interpretation in the Colombian Andes*. Cambridge: Cambridge University Press.

———. 1994. *Cumbe Reborn: An Andean Ethnography of History*. Chicago: University of Chicago Press.

Redden, J. E., and N. Owusu. 1963. *Twi Basic Course*. Washington, D.C.: Foreign Service Institute, U.S. Department of State.

Reid, Vic. 1983. *Nanny-Town*. Kingston: Jamaica Publishing House.

Reyes, Angelita. 2002. *Mothering Across Cultures: Postcolonial Representations*. Minneapolis: University of Minnesota Press.

Roberts, Walter Adolphe. 1955. *Jamaica: The Portrait of an Island*. New York: Coward-McCann.

Robertson, Claire. 2000. Claiming Freedom: Abolition and Identity in Saint Lucian History. *Journal of Caribbean History* 34(1/2): 89–129.

Robinson, Carey. 1969. *The Fighting Maroons of Jamaica*. Kingston: William Collins and Sangster.

———. 1993. *The Iron Thorn: The Defeat of the British by the Jamaican Maroons*. Kingston: Kingston Publishers.

Robinson, Phil. 1898. A Dress Rehearsal of Rebellion among the Maroons at Annotto Bay. *The Contemporary Review* (London) 74:746–50.

Rochmann, Marie-Christine. 2000. *L'Esclave fugitif dans la littérature antillaise: sur la déclive du morne*. Paris: Karthala.

Rodríguez, Sylvia. 1996. *The Matachines Dance: Ritual Symbolism and Interethnic Relations in the Upper Rio Grande Valley*. Albuquerque: University of New Mexico Press.

Rosaldo, Renato. 1980. *Ilongot Headhunting, 1883–1974: A Study in Society and History*. Stanford: Stanford University Press.

Roskind, Robert. 2001. *Rasta Heart: A Journey into One Love*. Blowing Rock, N.C.: One Love Press.

Russell, Norman. 1960. The Maroons Today. *Jamaican Historical Society Bulletin* 2(13): 209–10.

Sahlins, Marshall. 1985. *Islands of History*. Chicago: University of Chicago Press.

Santos-Granero, Fernando. 1998. Writing History into the Landscape: Space, Myth, and Ritual in Contemporary Amazonia. *American Ethnologist* 25(2): 128–48.

Schafer, Daniel Lee. 1973. The Maroons of Jamaica: African Slave Rebels in the Caribbean. Ph.D. dissertation, University of Minnesota, Minneapolis.

Schuler, Monica. 1970. Ethnic Slave Rebellions in the Caribbean and the Guianas. *Journal of Social History* 3(4): 374–85.

———. 1980. *"Alas, Alas, Kongo": A Social History of Indentured African Immigration Into Jamaica, 1841–1865*. Baltimore: Johns Hopkins University Press.

———. 2002. Liberated Central Africans in Nineteenth-Century Guyana. In *Central Africans and Cultural Transformations in the American Diaspora*. Linda M. Heywood, ed., 319–52. Cambridge: Cambridge University Press.

Scott, Clarissa Stewart. 1968. Cultural Stability in the Maroon Village of Moore Town, Jamaica. Master's thesis, Florida Atlantic University, Boca Raton.

———. 1973. On the Maroons. *Current Anthropology* 14(5): 543–44.

Scott, David. 1991. That Event, This Memory: Notes on the Anthropology of African Diasporas in the New World. *Diaspora* 1(3): 261–84.

Shaw, Rosalind. 2002. *Memories of the Slave Trade: Ritual and the Historical Imagination in Sierra Leone*. Chicago: University of Chicago Press.

Silenieks, Juris. 1984. The Maroon Figure in Caribbean Francophone Prose. In *Voices from Under: Black Narrative in Latin America and the Caribbean*. William Luis, ed., 115–25. Westport, Conn.: Greenwood Press.

Singer, Wendy. 1997. *Creating Histories: Oral Narratives and the Politics of History-Making*. Oxford: Oxford University Press.

Sioui, Georges. 1989. *Pour une autohistoire amérindienne: essai sur les fondements d'une morale sociale*. Quebec City: Les Presses de l'Université Laval.

Small, Geoff. 1995. *Ruthless: The Global Rise of the Yardies*. London: Warner.

Small, Jean. 1987. Ethnodramaturgy: Unconscious Modes of Self-Presentation in the Caribbean and Their Implications for an Indigenous Theatre. *African Caribbean Institute of Jamaica Newsletter* 13:4–10.

Smith, Keithlyn B., and Fernando C. Smith. 1986. *To Shoot Hard Labour: The Life and Times of Samuel Smith, an Antiguan Workingman 1877–1982*. Scarborough, Ontario: Edan's Publishers.

———. 2003. *To Shoot Hard Labour: The Life and Times of Samuel Smith, an Antiguan Workingman 1877–1982*, vol. 2. Toronto, Ontario: Edan's Publishers.

Stedman, John Gabriel. 1796. *Narrative of a Five-Years' Expedition, Against the Revolted Negroes of Surinam*. London: J. Johnson and J. Edwards.

Stewart, John. 1808. *An Account of Jamaica and Its Inhabitants*. London: Longman, Hurst, Rees, and Orme.

Tanna, Laura. 1984. *Jamaican Folk Tales and Oral Histories*. Kingston: Institute of Jamaica.

Thicknesse, Philip. 1788. *Memoirs and Anecdotes of Philip Thicknesse, Late Lieutenant Governor of Land Guard Fort, and Unfortunately Father to George Touchet, Baron Audley*. London: Printed for the Author.

Thoden van Velzen, H.U.E. 1990. The Maroon Insurgency: Anthropological Reflections on the Civil War in Suriname. In *Resistance and Rebellion in Suriname: Old and New*. Gary Brana-Shute, ed., 159–88. Williamsburg, Va.: College of William and Mary.

Thomas, Deborah Ann. 2000. "Tradition's not an Intelligence Thing": Jamaican Cultural Politics and the Ascendence of Modern Blackness. Ph.D. dissertation, New York University, New York.

Thomas, Herbert. 1890. *Untrodden Jamaica*. Kingston: Aston Gardner.

Tonkin, Elizabeth. 1992. *Narrating Our Pasts: The Social Construction of Oral History*. Cambridge: Cambridge University Press.

Trouillot, Michel-Rolph. 1995. *Silencing the Past: Power and the Production of History*. Boston: Beacon Press.

Tuelon, Alan E. 1968. The Windward Maroons. *Jamaican Historical Society Bulletin* 4(16): 304–9.

Ugochukwu, E. N. 1994. The Place of the Maroons in Jamaica. In *Maroon Heritage: Archaeological, Ethnographic and Historical Perspectives*. E. Kofi Agorsah, ed., ix–xi. Kingston: Canoe Press, University of the West Indies.

Urton, Gary. 1990. *The History of a Myth: Pacariqtambo and the Origin of the Inkas*. Austin: University of Texas Press.

Vansina, Jan. 1965. *Oral Tradition: A Study in Historical Methodology*. H. M. Wright, trans. Chicago: Aldine.

Vidal, Silvia M. 2003. The Arawak-Speaking Groups of Northwestern Amazonia: Amerindian Cartography as a Way of Preserving and Interpreting the Past. In *Histories and Historicities in Amazonia*. Neil L. Whitehead, ed., 33–57. Lincoln: University of Nebraska Press.

Walters, Wendy W. 1997. "One of Dese Mornings, Bright and Fair,/ Take My Wings and Cleave de Air": The Legend of the Flying Africans and Diasporic Consciousness— Folklore as a Foundation for Literature. *MELUS* 27:3–29.

Ward, Charles J. 1893. *World's Fair: Jamaica at Chicago*. New York: Wm. J. Pell.

Ward, J. R. 1990. Jamaica's Maroons. *Slavery & Abolition* 11(3): 399–403.

Warner, Michael. 2001. A Soliloquy "Lately Spoken at the African Theatre": Race and the Public Sphere in New York City, 1821. *American Literature* 73(1): 1–46.

Warner-Lewis, Maureen. 1991. *Guinea's Other Suns*. Dover, Mass.: Majority Press.

Watson, G. Llewellyn. 1991. *Jamaican Sayings, with Notes on Folklore, Aesthetics, and Social Control*. Tallahassee: Florida A&M University Press.

Waugaman, Sandra F., and Danielle Moretti-Langholtz. 2000. *We're Still Here: Contemporary Virginia Indians Tell Their Stories*. Richmond, Va.: Palari Publishing.

Weinstein, Laurie. 1986. "We're Still Living on Our Traditional Homeland": The Wampanoag Legacy in New England. In *Strategies for Survival: American Indians in the Eastern United States*. Frank W. Porter, III, ed., 85–112. Westport, Conn.: Greenwood Press.

White, Geoffrey M. 1991. *Identity Through History: Living Stories in a Solomon Islands Society*. Cambridge: Cambridge University Press.

Whitehead, Neil L. 2002. *Dark Shamans: Kanaimà and the Poetics of Violent Death*. Durham, N.C.: Duke University Press.

———. 2003. Three Patamuna Trees: Landscape and History in the Guyana Highlands. In *Histories and Historicities in Amazonia*. Neil L. Whitehead, ed., 59–77. Lincoln: University of Nebraska Press.

Whitehead, Neil L., ed. 2003. *Histories and Historicities in Amazonia*. Lincoln: University of Nebraska Press.

Williams, Joseph J. 1934. *Psychic Phenomena of Jamaica*. New York: Dial Press.

Wilson-Tagoe, Nana. 1998. *Historical Thought and Literary Representation in West Indian Literature*. Gainesville: University Press of Florida.

Wogan, Peter. 2004. *Magical Writing in Salasaca: Literacy and Power in Highland Ecuador*. Boulder, Colo.: Westview.

Wright, Martin-Luther. 1994. The Heritage of Accompong Maroons. In *Maroon Heritage: Archaeological, Ethnographic and Historical Perspectives*. E. Kofi Agorsah, ed., 64–71. Kingston: Canoe Press, University of the West Indies.

Wright, Philip, ed. 1966. *Lady Nugent's Journal of Her Residence in Jamaica from 1801 to 1805*, 4th ed. Kingston: Institute of Jamaica.

Yelvington, Kevin A. 2002. History, Memory and Identity: A Programmatic Prolegomenon. *Critique of Anthropology* 22(3): 227–56.

Yelvington, Kevin A., Neill G. Goslin, and Wendy Arriage. 2002. Whose History? Museum-Making and Struggles Over Ethnicity and Representation in the Sunbelt. *Critique of Anthropology* 22(3): 343–79.

Zips, Werner. 1995. "Let's Talk About the Motherland": Jamaican Influences on the African Discourses in the Diaspora. In *Born Out of Resistance: On Caribbean Cultural Creativity*. Wim Hoogbergen, ed., 46–62. Utrecht: ISOR.

———. 1996. Laws in Competition: Traditional Maroon Authorities within Legal Pluralism in Jamaica. *Journal of Legal Pluralism and Unofficial Law* 37/38:279–305.

———. 1998. "We Are Landowners": Territorial Autonomy and Land Tenure in the Jamaican Maroon Community of Accompong. *Journal of Legal Pluralism and Unofficial Law* 40:89–121.

———. 1999a. *Black Rebels: African Caribbean Freedom Fighters in Jamaica*. Kingston: Ian Randle.

———. 1999b. Obscured by Colonial Stories: An Alternative Historical Outline of Akan-Related Chieftaincy in Jamaican Maroon Societies. In *African Chieftaincy in a New Socio-Political Landscape*. E. Adriaan B. van Rouveroy van Nieuwaal and Rijk Van Dijk, eds., 207–39. Hamburg: Lit Verlag.

Index

Page numbers in italics refer to illustrations.

Kenneth Bilby is a research associate at the Smithsonian Institution. He is the coauthor of *Caribbean Currents: Caribbean Music from Rumba to Reggae*, which received the Caribbean Studies Association's Gordon K. Lewis Award for Caribbean Scholarship in 1996.